The American Political Economy

This volume brings together leading political scientists to explore the distinctive features of the American political economy. The introductory chapter provides a comparatively informed framework for analyzing the interplay of markets and politics in the United States, focusing on three key factors: uniquely fragmented and decentralized political institutions; an interest group landscape characterized by weak labor organizations and powerful, parochial business groups; and an entrenched legacy of ethno-racial divisions embedded in both government and markets. Subsequent chapters look at the fundamental dynamics that result, including the place of the courts in multi-venue politics, the political economy of labor, sectional conflict within and across cities and regions, the consolidation of financial markets and corporate monopoly and monopsony power, and the ongoing rise of the knowledge economy. Together, the chapters provide a revealing new map of the politics of democratic capitalism in the United States.

Jacob S. Hacker is Stanley Resor Professor of Political Science at Yale University. He is the author or coauthor of six books, including, most recently, *Let Them Eat Tweets* and *American Amnesia* (with Paul Pierson) (2020).

Alexander Hertel-Fernandez is Associate Professor at Columbia University. He studies the politics of US public policy with a focus on labor, business, and the workplace. He is the author of *Politics at Work* (2018), which won the 2019 Robert A. Dahl and Gladys Kammerer Awards from the American Political Science Association, and *State Capture*.

Paul Pierson is John Gross Professor of Political Science at University of California, Berkeley. He is the author or coauthor of six books on American and comparative politics, including *Let Them Eat Tweets* and *American Amnesia* (with Hacker) (2020).

Kathleen Thelen is Ford Professor of Political Science at Massachusetts Institute of Technology. Her research examines the origins and impact of political-economic institutions in the rich democracies. Her books include *Varieties of Liberalization and the New Politics of Social Solidarity* (Cambridge, 2014) and *How Institutions Evolve* (Cambridge, 2008), which won the Woodrow Wilson Foundation Award of the American Political Science Association.

The American Political Economy

Politics, Markets, and Power

Edited by

JACOB S. HACKER

Yale University

ALEXANDER HERTEL-FERNANDEZ

Columbia University

PAUL PIERSON

University of California, Berkeley

KATHLEEN THELEN

Massachusetts Institute of Technology

CAMBRIDGE
UNIVERSITY PRESS

CAMBRIDGE
UNIVERSITY PRESS

University Printing House, Cambridge CB2 8BS, United Kingdom

One Liberty Plaza, 20th Floor, New York, NY 10006, USA

477 Williamstown Road, Port Melbourne, VIC 3207, Australia

314–321, 3rd Floor, Plot 3, Splendor Forum, Jasola District Centre, New Delhi – 110025, India

103 Penang Road, #05–06/07, Visioncrest Commercial, Singapore 238467

Cambridge University Press is part of the University of Cambridge.

It furthers the University's mission by disseminating knowledge in the pursuit of education, learning, and research at the highest international levels of excellence.

www.cambridge.org
Information on this title: www.cambridge.org/9781316516362
DOI: 10.1017/9781009029841

© Cambridge University Press 2022

This publication is in copyright. Subject to statutory exception and to the provisions of relevant collective licensing agreements, no reproduction of any part may take place without the written permission of Cambridge University Press.

First published 2022

A catalogue record for this publication is available from the British Library.

Library of Congress Cataloging-in-Publication Data
NAMES: Hacker, Jacob S., editor. | Hertel-Fernandez, Alexander, 1986– editor. | Pierson, Paul, editor. | Thelen, Kathleen Ann, editor.
TITLE: The American political economy : politics, markets, and power / Jacob S. Hacker, Yale University, Connecticut, Alexander Hertel-Fernandez, Columbia University, New York, Paul Pierson, University of California, Berkeley, Kathleen Thelen, Academy of Sciences of the Czech Republic, Prague.
DESCRIPTION: Cambridge, United Kingdom ; New York, NY : Cambridge University Press, 2021. | Includes bibliographical references.
IDENTIFIERS: LCCN 2021017733 (print) | LCCN 2021017734 (ebook) | ISBN 9781316516362 (hardback) | ISBN 9781009014861 (paperback) | ISBN 9781009029841 (ebook)
SUBJECTS: LCSH: Income distribution – Political aspects – United States. | Wealth – Political aspects – United States. | BISAC: POLITICAL SCIENCE / American Government / General | POLITICAL SCIENCE / American Government / General
CLASSIFICATION: LCC HC110.15 A685 2021 (print) | LCC HC110.15 (ebook) | DDC 339.2/20973–dc23
LC record available at https://lccn.loc.gov/2021017733
LC ebook record available at https://lccn.loc.gov/2021017734

ISBN 978-1-316-51636-2 Hardback
ISBN 978-1-009-01486-1 Paperback

Cambridge University Press has no responsibility for the persistence or accuracy of URLs for external or third-party internet websites referred to in this publication and does not guarantee that any content on such websites is, or will remain, accurate or appropriate.

Contents

Figures

Tables

Contributors

Ben Ansell, University of Oxford

Lucy Barnes, University College London

Benjamin Braun, Max Planck Institute for the Study of Societies

Jane Gingrich, University of Oxford

Jacob M. Grumbach, University of Washington

Jacob S. Hacker, Yale University

Alexander Hertel-Fernandez, Columbia University

Nathan J. Kelly, University of Tennessee, Knoxville

Jana Morgan, University of Tennessee, Knoxville

Suresh Naidu, Columbia University

Thomas K. Ogorzalek, Co-director of Chicago Democracy Project

Paul Pierson, University of California, Berkeley

K. Sabeel Rahman, Brooklyn Law School

Herman Mark Schwartz, University of Virginia

David Soskice, London School of Economics

Kathleen Thelen, Massachusetts Institute of Technology

Chloe N. Thurston, Northwestern University

Jessica Trounstine, University of California, Merced

Acknowledgments

In the two years we have been working on this project, we have accumulated many debts, and so it is a pleasure to be able to acknowledge some of the people who have contributed to its successful completion.

We extend thanks, first and foremost, to the William and Flora Hewlett Foundation, which provided the funding for this initiative. We owe a debt of gratitude to Larry Kramer for his vision; we are delighted to be a part of Hewlett's path-breaking efforts to broaden and enhance economic discourse in the United States. We also could not have wished for more enthusiastic support than we received from Jennifer Harris, who has been our project's biggest booster. We are grateful to Raquel Abdala and Gail Claspell for their invaluable support with respect to finances and budgets. We look forward to working with all of them and with Brian Kettenring, as well as with the members of our Advisory Board – Sarah Anzia, Devin Caughey, Peter Hall, Jamila Michener, Jonathan Rodden, Maya Sen, and Leah Stokes – in the next phases of our joint work.

For comments on individual chapters, and in some cases on the entire book, we thank Devin Caughey, Peter Hall, Jonathan Rodden, and the two anonymous reviewers for Cambridge University Press (one of whom provided comments so extensive and helpful that we dearly wish we could extend personalized thanks). We are grateful as well to our contributors, who provided input into each and every one of the other chapters in the volume. We also received critical input on specific aspects of our arguments from Jacco Bomhoff, Yonah Freemark, Kate Krimmel, Nicola Lacey, Wolfgang Seibel, and Kai Wegrich.

We have benefited from superb administrative and logistical support throughout the project. Pam Lamonaca (Yale) and Kate Searle (MIT) both contributed mightily – Pam managing a complex budget spanning four institutions, and Kate organizing two workshops with her characteristic combination of efficiency and good humor.

We thank Sara Doskow of Cambridge University Press for all she has done to encourage and promote this work. Angie Jo and Sam Zacher provided invaluable assistance with pulling the manuscript together in preparation for publication. When the going got tough, Sam kept us going.

Finally, we thank the authors who contributed to this volume, all of whom brought their A-games to a many-round event. This distinguished group has taught us a great deal about the American political economy. Working with them has been not just intellectually exhilarating but also a whole lot of fun. Above all, it has been a deeply inspiring process – and we hope some of the inspiration we felt carries forward to the readers of this volume as well.

INTRODUCTION

The American Political Economy: A Framework and Agenda for Research

Jacob S. Hacker, Alexander Hertel-Fernandez, Paul Pierson, and Kathleen Thelen

The COVID-19 pandemic that struck the United States in early 2020 amplified already-stark economic and political divisions and revealed a nation unprepared to launch an immediate public health and economic response. Whether it was the fragmentation of the American federal system, the glaring racial and class disparities in economic and health outcomes, or the weaknesses of America's tattered safety net, the crisis brought America's distinctive mix of multi-venue governance, limited social protections, weak labor power, and loosely regulated markets prominently – and often tragically – into display.

This book is about that distinctive US political-economic mix: its sources, its dynamics, its consequences, and its contemporary evolution. The contributors work within an emerging field that we call "American Political Economy" (APE). In particular, they seek to understand the interaction of markets and government in America's increasingly unequal and polarized polity. This agenda holds extraordinary promise, both for understanding the dramatic transformation of America's distinctive political economy over recent decades and for reorienting political science in productive directions. As we explore in the Epilogue to this volume, the COVID-19 crisis provides but one window – albeit a particularly revealing one – on features of the US political system that current approaches to studying American politics too often miss.

In recent years, these features have become the focus of a growing number of scholars of American politics, as well as comparative scholars who include the United States in their analyses. Their pioneering work is referenced and showcased throughout this volume. Yet there remains a large gap between what we know and what we need to know about the American political economy. This book seeks to narrow that gap.

In this introductory chapter, we lay out the foundations for our effort. First, we clarify what we mean by "American political economy" – which we see as both an important field of inquiry and a broad approach to understanding how economic and political phenomena are linked in affluent democracies like the United States. To do so, we draw on and extend the vibrant research program in Comparative Political Economy (CPE). The approach we advocate emphasizes that politics is a developmental process in which outcomes, institutions, and power relations are forged through long-term conflicts within and across multiple institutional venues. Crucially, these conflicts have spatial as well as distributional and temporal dimensions – that is, they involve divisions between places and across geographic boundaries as well as among people and groups over time. Though the spatial dimensions of political economy are important everywhere, America's federal structure of governance and territorially based elections foster particularly high-stakes battles over "who gets what, when, how, *where*."

Although our approach is inspired by CPE, our goal is to develop a field of *American* political economy – a field with strong ties to CPE but a disciplinary home in the study of American politics. With some notable exceptions (e.g., Beramendi 2012; Iversen and Soskice 2019; Kenworthy and Pontusson 2005; Martin 1991; Martin 2000; Martin and Swank 2012; Wiedemann 2021), CPE does not focus much on the key features that make the American political economy so distinctive. Far more problematic, many students of American politics pay strikingly little attention to these features. The result is that highly distinctive and hugely consequential aspects of the American political economy are too often neglected or taken for granted by the enormous community of scholars studying the US polity.

In the next section of the chapter, we turn to what we see as the three most important of these distinctive features. First, an unusual "Tudor polity" featuring divided power, an outsized role for the courts, and an emphasis on local self-rule (Huntington 1968) limits many policy capacities of national authorities while encouraging territorially grounded contestation within and among subnational governments. Such contestation hinders the broad provision of public goods and deeply affects the distribution of advantage and disadvantage within the American political economy.

Second, these long-term conflicts feature a distinctive form of interplay among organized interests. The nation's peculiar institutional terrain advantages political actors with the capacity to work across multiple venues, over extended periods, and in a political environment where coordinated government action is difficult and strategies of evasion and exit from regulatory constraints are often successful. These capacities are characteristic of organized groups, not individual voters. Moreover, organized groups not only seek to influence governance directly. They also seek to shape how and whether political parties respond to voters, and they have vital resources that parties and politicians want. Accordingly, despite frequent elections and the valorization of representative government, voter influence in American politics is highly mediated and conditional. When voters matter, how they are mobilized, and what they are mobilized for – all are powerfully shaped by the long-term strategies of organized economic interests. Of particular importance, we argue, is the "issue bundling" (Rodden 2018) that parties engage in within America's two-party system – the appeals, policies, and identities they highlight and those they do not – as they try to balance their need to attract voters with their desire to maintain support among key organized interests.

Third, centuries of racial oppression and division have deeply shaped the contours of the American political economy. Long-established structures of public policy and social organization both reflect and reinforce those embedded racial inequalities. In turn, this entrenched order has profound effects not just on voter attitudes, but on the basic structure of the economy, on contending interests and their policy preferences and strategies, on the formation and goals of party-group coalitions, and on the ways in which these coalitions are advantaged or disadvantaged by America's distinctive institutions.

A focus on these three key features of the American political economy – multi-venue governance, distinctive interest organization, and systemic racial division – can be used to address questions at the heart of contemporary politics and governance. Indeed, a crucial goal of this volume is to show that fundamental questions about politics in the United States – fundamental in that they concern dynamics that profoundly affect citizens, durably impact society, and powerfully illuminate how democratic institutions work in market societies – cannot be answered convincingly without attention to the core topics and interactions just discussed.

Thus, in the latter part of the chapter, we take up three such questions that our framework helps answer, drawing on the other chapters in the volume as we do so. First, why has the organized business community in the United States simultaneously narrowed its goals and increased its power over the past generation? Second, why has the mainstream conservative party in the United States – to a degree unrivaled within the world of advanced democracies – embraced a program of ethno-nationalist politics, antidemocratic measures, inegalitarian priorities, and state dismantling? Third, why does America's early lead in the development of a postindustrial knowledge economy based on urban density and digital technology appear to be increasingly threatened? In answering these questions, we highlight the analytic benefits of our framework for the study of American politics as well as for CPE, especially when compared with bodies of research that focus largely or exclusively on voter opinion and electoral behavior.

Finally, we close the chapter by briefly drawing out what we see as the most important payoffs of a new field committed to the study of American political economy. These payoffs include a greatly improved understanding of the relationship between economic and political inequality, a deeper appreciation of how multi-venue institutional dynamics shape the distribution of political power, and a more sophisticated conception of the key role of geography in political-economic conflict. Above all, we argue that a field of APE can foster a stronger social scientific approach to vital substantive topics, from America's halting efforts to tackle climate change to the US response to a global pandemic – topics of deep concern not just to students of American politics, but to citizens and policymakers as well.

WHY A FIELD OF "AMERICAN POLITICAL ECONOMY"?

Political economy has multiple meanings in the social sciences. For our purposes, the term refers to *the study of how economic and political systems are linked.* As a field of inquiry, political economy is premised on the idea – amply borne out by research in the field – that these linkages are very strong and very important. Political interventions deeply influence the shape of the economy. In turn, the distribution of economic resources, patterns of economic activity, and the incentives that those distributions and patterns create profoundly influence the shape of politics. The field of political economy investigates these linkages to strengthen our understanding of processes of political and economic development that have far-reaching effects on people's lives.

THE GAINS FROM COMPARATIVE POLITICAL ECONOMY

The study of political economy within political science has been markedly uneven.[1] The main places where research on contemporary political

[1] By contrast, the related field of sociology features a strong strand of scholarship in economic sociology (including important work by Frank Dobbin, Neil Fligstein, Greta

economies has flourished are in the subfields of international relations (which has a longstanding and vibrant research program in International Political Economy—IPE), and in the subfield of comparative politics, where it operates under the banner of Comparative Political Economy. The IPE and CPE research communities both have much to offer students of American politics. IPE, for instance, has produced a rich literature on how American political dynamics and economic development are linked to the United States' status as a global hegemon, and we take on board IPE's basic insight that the American political economy is distinctive because of its central role in the global economy. Nonetheless, it is the latter research community, CPE, that provides the primary intellectual inspiration for this project.

CPE grew out of a fundamental realization: national variants of capitalist democracies, even those with similar levels of income and productivity, exhibit striking variation along important dimensions, from inequality to unionization to corporate organization to women's economic empowerment. Despite competition and cooperation among these national systems, these differences have been very durable (Hall and Soskice 2001). National systems change over time, often dramatically. But their distinctiveness on fundamental dimensions remains apparent.

Crucial to progress in CPE has been the recognition that politics is a central source of these durable differences. In contrast to dominant perspectives that emphasize the naturalness and homogeneity of what we casually call "markets," CPE has emphasized that markets inevitably involve substantial governance (Vogel 2018). All modern economies provide a range of public goods (e.g., infrastructure, research and development, public health, and education). To different degrees, they also all protect against damaging externalities (e.g., pollution, congestion, consumer injury, and systemic financial crises). All provide citizens with at least some basic safeguards against economic risks (e.g., poverty, old age, unemployment, and disability). And all shape the organization and strategies of key market actors (e.g., through regulations governing union formation, capital markets, and the internal governance of corporations).

The question, CPE has shown, is not *whether* governments become deeply involved in the economy. Rather, it is the *form* of that involvement.

Krippner, and Monica Prasad, among many others). Likewise, an emerging field of "law and political economy" is making signal contributions in this area (e.g., work by David Grewal, Sabeel Rahman, Brishen Rogers, and others).

The deployment of public authority is universal within modern market economies, affecting both the structure of the "private" economy and the organization and behavior of those within it. But sustained variation in national economies indicates that there are many ways to construct markets and that different systems have very different consequences for the lives of citizens and for the particular kinds of economic activity that will flourish (Hall and Soskice 2001).

The field of comparative political economy arose to understand the political roots and effects of these enduring differences – hence, *political* economy. Since the 1970s, CPE has developed into a vibrant research program carried out by an intellectually pluralistic community of scholars. This program has produced large cumulative gains in knowledge drawing on diverse theoretical perspectives and using multiple research methods – from quantitative and qualitative analyses; to small-*n* and large-*n* cross-national comparisons; to behaviorally and institutionally focused inquiries. No academic community has contributed more to our understanding of how democracies and markets coevolve over extended periods of time.

In the process, CPE has not just highlighted enduring differences across national systems; it has also contributed to a broader understanding of politics. Because of its comparative vantage point, CPE has yielded crucial insights into how state structures, electoral and party systems, and societal cleavages are shaped by the interaction of markets and democracy. Even more important, CPE has expanded our field of vision. This literature insists that we should focus our attention "where the action is," even if scholarly convention might direct them elsewhere. Rather than assuming that political power rests in, say, legislatures, analysts should turn their gaze toward the diverse and often understudied arenas (from courts to regulatory agencies to local administration to private coordinating institutions like firms, banks, and trade associations) where resourceful actors are actually trying to advance their interests.

The recognition that governance generates distinctive outcomes across a broad range of venues and over extended periods of time has brought to light features of politics that other analytic approaches often neglected – including, crucially, the role of organized actors with strong incentives to mobilize in ways that allow them to use or shape political and market institutions. Precisely because these patterns of governance are so consequential, powerful actors devote extensive resources to shaping them. Often, these actors, alone and in coalition, will be aligned with and operate through particular political parties.

What CPE provides, in short, is a capacious view of politics that extends the conventional focus on voters and elections to include features of the institutional terrain that produce durable patterns of economic governance – patterns that often give enduring advantages to some actors over others.

FOUNDATIONS OF OUR APPROACH

These insights animate our approach to the American political economy. Drawing on CPE, we argue that a field of APE should be centrally concerned with the ways in which *institutional configurations* shape *coalitional politics* to produce long-term *developmental processes*. Let us unpack each of these elements in turn.

The first insight that guides our approach is that political economies comprise *institutional configurations*. Political institutions – including electoral rules, the number and nature of veto points, and the allocation of authority between national and more localized government – have profound effects on the preferences, political capabilities, and strategies of relevant political actors. Analyses that take these institutional features for granted, or focus on single institutions at a time, are unlikely to capture these effects.

The second insight is that political-economic outcomes are forged within these institutions through *coalitional politics*. The realm of durable, consequential policy often privileges organized interests. While mass politics can influence what goes on in this realm, building and transforming large-scale policies requires sustained efforts by well-resourced and highly motivated organized actors, operating in interaction (and often in partnership) with other similarly institutionalized actors, especially political parties.

The third insight that animates our vision of American political economy is that coalitional politics plays out within institutional configurations through extended *developmental processes*. Policy regimes are formed and reformed through multiple rounds of contestation across multiple sites of political activity. Critical actions rarely occur simultaneously or instantaneously, and most of them have long legacies. Political economies carry their histories with them – their economic organizations, industrial structures, and social and political cleavages are all deeply influenced by previous political contestation and its consequences. In a perspective focused on *developmental processes*, then, *institutional configurations* and *coalitional politics* are mutually constitutive of each other. Institutional configurations shape coalitional dynamics, and in turn are shaped by them.

This perspective also carries with it a central message about political and economic power: it may be most consequential where it is least visible. Resourceful and long-lasting political actors prefer not to have to fight constantly for their interests; far better to embed imbalances of power in durable arrangements within the political economy, whether those be private market institutions, rules of the political game, or entrenched public policies. Powerful actors and coalitions often seek to organize governance in ways that effectively remove important issues from direct political contestation, or ensure that any consideration occurs within arenas and under constraints that favor their interests. Indeed, this kind of agenda control may well be the most significant product of sustained, effective political pressure. As E. E. Schattschneider famously put it, "Some issues are organized into politics while others are organized out" (Schattschneider 1960: 71). The fact that some matters receive limited or highly constrained attention in national legislatures or in election contests, for example, should not be taken as a sign that the matter is of marginal importance or removed from politics. It may mean quite the opposite: that powerful interests have successfully insulated preferred practices from popular or legislative challenge.

This insight is an organizing principle of this volume, and it should be an animating principle of the field we hope to foster. Many of the contributors to this volume investigate arenas and policies that are outside the field of vision of conventional studies of American politics, such as antitrust, intellectual property, the regulation of credit, and the power of employers in labor markets. They do so not because they deem these matters vital (though they often do) but because some of the most powerful interests in the United States deem them vital, investing enormous resources, time, and organization into influencing their constitution and evolution. By looking beyond one narrow set of formal political institutions (such as legislatures) or one particular set of political actors (such as voters), these CPE-inspired scholars avoid taking the scope of economic governance as given and thus missing the power relations embedded in taken-for-granted features of markets and politics. Unfortunately, this sort of political economy has largely failed to develop as a distinct area of research within the study of American politics.

WHY POLITICAL ECONOMY IS NEGLECTED IN AMERICAN POLITICS RESEARCH

The lack of a vibrant field of APE is puzzling. Not only is the American political economy highly unusual and highly important in the world economy, but the American politics subfield itself is vast. Never in history have so many political scientists studied a single polity. Yet most "Americanists" have defined their subject matter in relatively narrow and formalistic terms. Indeed, when students of American politics speak of "political economy," they usually mean the use of formal modeling or economics-style research to understand politics, rather than the study of how US economic and political systems are linked. Work focusing on political economy as a vital substantive area of American political life, though growing in scope and influence, remains on the periphery of the subfield.[2] Instead, much of the energy of Americanists has been directed toward the study of individual political behavior: elections, public opinion, political participation, and so on. This work may concern economic sources of political behavior, but it often misses organized political action or how political behavior is shaped by America's distinctive political and market institutions.

In part, this restricted focus reflects the odd division of labor within political science. Because Americanists almost always study American politics in isolation, they have limited incentive or leverage to examine the striking differences among rich democracies. As a result, they often take for granted highly consequential structural features of the United States, whether these are institutional peculiarities (such as first-past-the-post electoral rules, presidentialism, the distinctive role of the courts, and a highly decentralized form of federalism) or unusual characteristics of the American economy (such as low rates of unionization, a large and loosely regulated financial sector, and the weakness of encompassing employer associations).

To be sure, there is a rich tradition of research on American political institutions. Yet this work has a cabined quality that undercuts its capacity to speak to issues of political economy. When Americanists study governing institutions, they typically focus on a handful of specific formal political institutions (especially Congress) and not the many economic institutions that make up the political economy as a whole (such as firms, banks, business associations, and labor organizations). Just as significant, Americanists often study institutions in isolation from one another, rarely considering the multi-venue contestation so characteristic of the American political economy. Indeed,

[2] Though for important new complementary efforts, see, for instance, the new *Journal of Political Institutions and Political Economy* and recent efforts investigating local and urban political economy (Anzia forthcoming; Trounstine 2020).

even institutionally minded work is often grounded in the assumption that voters and elections are where the action really is. As a result, institutions are often cast narrowly as rules that structure dyadic relationships of representation, relationships in which electoral competition is the crucial backdrop for the actions of elected officials.

This is not to say that students of American politics have ignored issues of political economy altogether. An interest in these questions, in part motivated by cross-national observations about America's unusual trajectory, was integral to a previous generation of work in American political development (APD). Distinguished political scientists including Richard Bensel, David Greenstone, Ira Katznelson, Elizabeth Sanders, Martin Shefter, Theda Skocpol, and Stephen Skowronek sought to understand the distinctive aspects of the American state, the character of contestation over government authority, and the development of organized groups and movements. Not all this work centered on political economy. But compared with research on American politics more broadly, pioneering APD work was unusually attentive to the relationship between capitalism and democracy and the coevolution of the American economy and the American polity. Yet this strand of scholarship has become increasingly cut off from the rest of the American politics subfield. More important, APD is increasingly understood as the study of the past, and often the distant past. As valuable as such work can be, the ability to explore and explain recent wrenching shifts in the American political economy cannot rest on historical analogizing alone.

In recent years, one of these wrenching shifts has become so dramatic and undeniable that students of American politics have found it impossible to ignore: the stark and growing economic divide in the United States. Prominent political scientists outside the APD tradition including Larry Bartels, Martin Gilens, and Nolan McCarty have helped spark a flurry of pathbreaking research on inequality and American politics. But despite the evident value of this new work, the boundaries of the American politics mainstream have often constrained it. Mirroring the larger subfield's focus on what David Mayhew described as the "electoral connection," inquiries into political inequality are typically framed around the question of whether elected officials are responsive to the concerns of nonaffluent voters or not. When, as is often the case, the conclusion is essentially "no," analysts often pivot, seeking better ways to measure or conceptualize the dependent and independent variables. Important as this work is, therefore, it typically leaves unaddressed other features of the American political economy – beyond the electoral connection – that might explain skyrocketing inequality and corresponding gaps in political representation.

In short, central features of the study of American politics today have hindered the development of a vibrant field of APE. Despite the enormous intellectual energy devoted to understanding the American polity, some of the most fundamental trends in contemporary American politics receive too limited attention. These include the massive economic dislocations wrought by the knowledge economy, the stark imbalances of power between business and labor, and the acute mismatch between sclerotic political institutions and turbo-charged markets that have marked recent decades. These are not just issues of utmost importance to policymakers and citizens; they are central to understanding how American politics works. The lack of a field of American political economy carries a heavy price.

THE BENEFITS TO COMPARATIVE POLITICAL ECONOMY

Applying these insights to the study of the American political economy will not only deepen our understanding of American politics; it will also enrich and inform our understanding of advanced capitalism more broadly. For all the contributions that CPE has made, it has, as noted, paid relatively little attention to the American political economy. There are many reasons for this, including the fact that American politics has been carved out as a stand-alone subfield. Whatever the reason, the integration of the United States into cross-national frameworks has been halting and limited.

Instead, much of the comparative research focuses on Europe's so-called coordinated market economies (CMEs). In these studies – many inspired by the influential "Varieties of Capitalism" perspective (Hall and Soskice 2001) – the United States often appears as little more than a foil, the archetypal example of the alternative "liberal" market economy (LME) model, in which economic relationships tend to be mediated through the market, rather than the state or corporatist institutions. The CME/LME dichotomy has had the salutary effect of opening up cross-Atlantic comparisons (see also Kenworthy 2004; Pontusson 2005). But it has had the negative effect of blurring the distinctions among LMEs; and it may also have discouraged CPE scholars from digging more deeply into the particularities of the American case (with some important exceptions, including, among others, Martin 1991, 2000; and Prasad 2006, 2012).

Of course, such blurring really matters only if these particularities are highly consequential. With respect to the American political economy, they are. As work in International Political Economy has emphasized, the United States is the world's most important economy, is home to many of the world's most dominant companies, and possesses outsized influence over international institutions, rule-making, and standard-setting, as well as the privileges of a dominant currency. At the same time, the United States is the largest example of a consumer-driven economy (rather than investment- or export-driven economy) based on high levels of household debt encouraged by financial deregulation (a classification suggested by recent CPE work in the vein of Baccaro and Pontusson 2016). More important for present purposes, it is also an outlier – in many respects, a stark outlier, even among LMEs – along dimensions fundamental to the politics of postindustrial democracies. We will discuss these dimensions at greater length in the next section. For now, we highlight three of the most significant:

- *A Fragmented and "Territorialized" State.* The United States has a uniquely fragmented political system. This has had a profound impact on the evolution of the American political economy, including structures of public policy, the organization of economic interests, and the nature of basic cleavages and coalitions. Distributional and power conflicts play out among *places* as well as *people,* and among *jurisdictions* as well as *organizations.* Contestation over economic governance is situated within an extremely complex, spatially dispersed, and decentralized multi-tiered, multi-venue space. Importantly and unusually, courts play a central role in making policy and in governing the relationships across these venues.
- *Fragmented Economic Organizations.* By comparative standards, both employer associations and labor unions have limited capacity to solve economic collective action and commitment problems. This fragmentation and the weakness of labor and state institutions reduce the incentives for individual firms to moderate their demands, accept regulatory restraints, or adopt a longer-term perspective. Partisan polarization, and especially the rightward tilt of the GOP, along with changes in capital markets, have further exacerbated the incentives of businesses to "go it alone." While the "LME" label calls attention to several of these features (especially atomized interest organizations), the United States is

distinctive even relative to other LMEs on these dimensions. Other LMEs share one or more of these characteristics. The United States is an outlier with regard to *all of them.*

- *Deep Racial Cleavages.* Racial divisions are constitutive of the American political economy. They have often undercut support for systems of compensation, redistribution, and public goods provision, as well as for the mass organizations, such as unions, that play a central role in representing citizens in the market and politics. Coupled with federalism, racial divisions have also played a profound role in shaping the spatial development of the American political economy. Key features of the American polity have encouraged the growth of racially and economically exclusive social enclaves. Intense segregation along class and racial lines not only discourages the provision of inclusively provided public goods, such as high-quality public education; it has also fostered the spatial concentration of disadvantage, with profound consequences for ethnic and racial minorities, but also for coalition formation and policy contestation. The racial divide also feeds back into mass politics by encouraging a reservoir of resentment that can be politically exploited.

Although we stress the distinctive nature of US economic and political arrangements, we are not arguing for a return to exceptionalist conceptions of the United States. Instead, we believe focusing on the unusual features of the American political economy will both enrich the work of American-focused scholars and contribute to the understanding of other advanced democracies. As we describe in more detail at the end of the chapter, embracing an APE approach points to new substantive outcomes and political-economic features for comparativists to study.

No less important, exploration of the American political economy can better integrate CPE and the study of American politics – and do so on more productive common foundations than the relatively narrow focus on elections, voter opinion, and representation that often characterizes mainstream American politics work. There are surely features of advanced political economies that are explained well by focusing on variations in voter opinion or electoral dynamics. However, we believe the greatest insights will come from integrating such analyses into a framework that continues to place a heavy focus on organized contestation over substantive issues and the institutions that mediate that contestation.

Fulfilling all of the goals we have identified is too big a task for a single volume, even one combining the research efforts of many scholars. Our aim instead is to map the distinctive terrain of the American political economy and begin filling in the ground-level details for a few of the most important places on this map. In the remainder of this chapter, we seek to situate the American case more accurately within the broader world of advanced capitalism, identify some central questions about the American political economy that warrant extensive investigation, and highlight promising initial work on some of these questions. In doing so, we hope to advance a vibrant research program on this vital subject – one that simultaneously broadens American politics research and enriches the comparative study of advanced political economies.

TOWARD A FIELD OF AMERICAN POLITICAL ECONOMY

A good map provides two forms of guidance: it highlights the most important features of the landscape, and it organizes them in ways essential for navigation. Similarly, our approach identifies fundamental features of the American political economy and explains how they should guide our understanding. We focus on three such linked observations and claims. First, because American political institutions are so fragmented, the study of APE must grapple with how conflicts are waged within and across multiple venues. Second, in the context of such multi-venue conflict, analysts need to foreground and conceptualize the distinctive challenges of coalition-building among organized interests, within and beyond parties. Third, the imprint of race is everywhere, and many of the most intense ways in which racial divisions manifest themselves emerge more clearly in a framework that emphasizes group contestation over extended periods of time within an institutionally fragmented polity.

AN EXCEPTIONALLY FRAGMENTED INSTITUTIONAL LANDSCAPE

The American political system splinters public authority both horizontally and vertically. This fragmentation at once encourages gridlock and offers an unusually wide variety of venues for actors to pursue their objectives. Horizontally, American political institutions disperse power across different branches, incorporating a large number of entry and veto points for policymaking. Vertically, the United States delegates substantial governing authority to subnational units (states, but also cities and localities) – authority that in many other countries rests with national governments. Relative to other federal countries, the United States also does far less to standardize, subsidize, or coordinate the decision-making of subnational governments (e.g., OECD 2016b). Four specific features of this distinctive landscape stand out: an extreme separation of powers, an often weak and fragmented bureaucracy, an unusually powerful legal system, and a particularly stark form of decentralization.

An Extreme Separation of Powers. All rich democracies contain electorally generated veto points, but as Table I.1 documents, the United States is an extreme case (Stepan and Linz 2011). American national institutions erect substantial barriers to new legislation, requiring bills to clear two separate legislative chambers and (typically) gain the assent of the president. In effect, the executive and each chamber of the legislature hold a veto. Over the past four decades, the Senate filibuster – an entrenched rule of Senate procedure rather than a constitutional feature – has become an additional formidable point of blockage in the system. The filibuster allows 41 of the Senate's 100 members – who, given malapportionment, could represent as little as a tenth of the US population – to block most types of legislation from becoming law. At the same time, barriers to US constitutional reform are unusually high. Not included in Table I.1 but no less significant is the power of the American courts, which can also exercise a veto over legislation and shape the way in which laws are interpreted and enforced.

The effects of this institutional obstacle course are not neutral. As Kelly and Morgan emphasize in their contribution to this volume, America's extreme separation of powers creates the greatest hurdles for those who seek to use active national policies to shape the economy or to adapt such policies to changing circumstances over time. By contrast, defending existing arrangements and policies – and the power imbalances they embody – is much easier. Not only do American political institutions generally favor those who back the status quo, they also generally favor those equipped to operate flexibly and durably across the nation's extraordinarily complex institutional space – a key reason why organized actors enjoy important advantages.

A Fragmented – and Often Weak – State Bureaucracy. On top of this institutional splintering, the United States features an unusually weak and fragmented state bureaucracy (cf. Carpenter 2001; King and Lieberman 2009). Regulatory power and prerogatives are distributed across parallel but distinct agencies, across different regulatory regimes at the state level, and across different venues, with a large role for the courts. This fragmented

TABLE 1.1 *Number of Electorally generated veto players in rich democracies*

Number of veto players: one N = 12.5	*Unitary state; parliamentary, unicameral* Finland, Greece, Luxembourg, Portugal, New Zealand, Sweden, Denmark, Iceland, Norway	*Unitary state; parliamentary, bicameral but upper chamber lacks veto* UK, Ireland	*Federal; parliamentary, bicameral but the upper chamber and the member states lack a veto* Austria	*Unitary state; bicameral, but upper chamber has weak veto, semi-presidential system* France (non-cohabitation)
Number of veto players: two N = 7.5	*Unitary state; parliamentary, bicameral where upper chamber has some veto power* Italy, Japan, Netherlands	*Federal; parliamentary, bicameral, with upper chamber veto, and the member states exercise veto power only through the upper chamber* Germany	*Asymmetrically federal; parliamentary, bicameral with weak upper chamber veto power, but regions have some constitutionally embedded veto powers on some, not all, issues* Belgium, Spain, Canada	*Unitary state; bicameral but upper chamber has weak veto, semi-presidential system* France (cohabitation)
Number of veto players: three N=2	*Federal, parliamentary. Upper chamber has veto. Frequent referendums in which a law passed by both houses can be vetoed unless a "double majority" approve the law* Switzerland and Australia			
Number of veto players: four N=1	*Federal, bicameral with both houses having absolute veto. President has veto that can only be overridden by a two-thirds vote in both houses. Standard process for amending the Constitution requires that three-fourths of states ratify an amendment proposed by both houses of Congress.* United States			

Source: Stepan and Linz 2011: 845.

system provides uncommonly fertile terrain for powerful economic actors to pursue aggressive strategies of regulatory arbitrage, exploiting wide gaps between the jurisdictions, powers, and attentions of American agencies. To take but one example of significance for contemporary economic dynamics, the Department of Justice and the Federal Trade Commission – one part of the executive branch, the other an independent agency – share responsibility for antitrust enforcement. Not only are the lines between these two federal entities blurry, so too are the respective roles of the federal government and the states, which have their own antitrust statutes and thus their own powers to investigate and sanction companies for anticompetitive practices.

The American bureaucracy is also less professionalized and more politicized than is the norm in other rich democracies. Incoming presidents make over 4,000 political appointments within the executive branch. Many of these individuals occupy critical nodes in the policy process (Piaker 2016). By contrast, European Prime Ministers appoint the top cabinet officials who can each bring in a few policy advisors, but a permanent professional civil service largely staffs the ministries.[3] Unlike European civil servants, who generally undergo specialized bureaucratic training, agency personnel in the United States mostly share a common educational and social background with economic elites, leading them to lean more favorably toward those elites (Kwak 2014). And even where regulators operate in good faith, their sheer lack of independent research and analytical capacity often renders them dependent on private actors for data, information, and the expertise needed to grasp the complexities of modern corporate arrangements (Awrey 2012; Baxter 2011; Wagner 2010).

An Outsized Role for the Courts. Another distinctive feature of the American institutional environment is the highly influential role of the courts. Indeed, in describing the persistence of premodern "Tudor" arrangements in the United States, Samuel Huntington (1968: 134) famously drew attention to the peculiar strength of judicial review. Most European states, Huntington noted, separated the legislative and judicial functions of the courts in the process of state-building, while the two

[3] Cabinet officials are often allowed to bring a few political advisors with them into the executive branch, but here too the numbers are limited – sometimes by law (e.g., in Denmark, where each minster is allowed but one political advisor appointee) or by convention. Either way, the numbers of political appointees to European bureaucracies are far lower than in the United States – at the high end numbering in the dozens (OECD 2007).

remained fused in the United States. As a result, American judges possess "immense political influence" to dictate to legislatures what the law should be. According to the typology of judicial review assembled by Arend Lijphart (2012), only Germany's Federal Constitutional Court approaches the US Supreme Court in its power.

A Particular Kind of Decentralization. Finally, political authority in the United States is unusually decentralized. The United States is hardly the only federal system. Yet other federalized democracies either delegate more limited powers to state governments or include coordination and leveling mechanisms, including extensive revenue sharing, that inhibit the kinds of regime-shopping and fiscal competition that are commonplace in the American context. Indeed, the United States is the only rich federal system that has neither general revenue sharing nor explicit equalization policies to reduce inequalities in spending capacity across subnational governments (e.g., OECD 2016). Thus, not only do state and local decision-makers play an unusually prominent role in policy formation in the United States, that role is unusually shaped by the inequality of resources on which those decision-makers can draw (see also Kelly and Witko 2012).

Table I.2 provides a summary of cross-national differences in decentralization, identifying the level of government primarily responsible for setting policy with regard to criminal justice, zoning, and education in the United States, with comparisons to England/Wales, France, and the federal states of Canada and Germany. While this table necessarily simplifies complex details within each country, one pattern stands out: control over important public responsibilities in the United States is much more decentralized than in other countries – even other federal countries like Canada and Germany. In areas of policy that are particularly critical in the knowledge economy – including education, zoning, transportation, and taxation – states and localities loom large.

This extreme form of decentralization is an often-underappreciated aspect of the American political economy (Lacey and Soskice 2015; Soskice 2010), and it has profound effects. The high degree of state and local autonomy "denationalizes" important areas of public policy, exacerbating spatial inequalities by inhibiting the sharing of resources and the pooling of risk. It also opens possibilities for mobile actors to venue shop, maneuvering across states and localities to find the most favorable structures of political authority, often putting downward pressure on regulations and taxes. Highly fateful as well, the extensive powers delegated to local governments in the United States have long been a cornerstone of durable racial inequalities. These decentralized

TABLE 1.2 *Principal locus of authority for key policies*[4]

	Criminal Justice				
	Police	Prosecutors	Judges	Zoning	Education
National	UK	UK	UK	UK	UK
	France	France	France	France	France
State/	Canada	Canada	Canada	Canada	Canada
Province	Germany	Germany	Germany		Germany
Local				Germany	
	USA	USA	USA	USA	USA

powers have been instrumental to the sustained use of government coercion against racial and ethnic minorities, first in the form of Jim Crow and later with the growth of mass incarceration, punitive policing, and stricter rules for the receipt of public assistance (Gibson 2013; Mickey 2015; Soss and Weaver 2017). In an era of deep racial inequities, they are also heavily implicated in what is often called "opportunity hoarding," in which privileged communities use jurisdictional boundaries to limit redistribution, in-migration, and the provision of public goods to less affluent (and almost always more diverse) neighboring places (Freemark et al. 2020; Trounstine 2018).

COMBAT AND COALITION-BUILDING WITHIN A FRAGMENTED POLITY

We come to the second central element of our approach: the distinctive character of coalition-building among organized interests within a multi-venue, multi-tiered political economy. As we have emphasized, CPE has

[4] This table is modeled on table 0.1 in Nicola Lacey and David Soskice (2015: 458). We adopt the OECD convention, defining "local" to include "counties, cities, districts, municipalities, councils or shires" (see, e.g., OECD 2019: 6 under definitions). Assignment of levels for the United States, the United Kingdom, and Canada are based on Lacey and Soskice. For Germany, we consulted country experts, in particular Wolfgang Seibel and Kai Wegrich; see also Kersten (2018); Schoch (2018); and Seibel (2017). For France, we consulted country experts, in particular Jacco Bomhoff and Yonah Freemark; see also Freemark et al. (2020); Le Galès and Pierson (2019); for judicial appointments: www.conseil-superieur-magistrature.fr/le-csm/nos-missions.

shown that conflict among organized interests is central to explaining the enormous cross-national and longitudinal variation in political and policy outcomes. However, scholars working in the Varieties of Capitalism tradition have often downplayed the role of organized interests in LMEs (where firms are seen to coordinate through the market). In fact, these interests loom especially large in the United States, though not, of course, in the way that they do in more coordinated market economies. The same institutional fragmentation that discourages private coordination creates distinct opportunities for public influence. American political institutions have always privileged organized actors capable of effectively navigating its multiple sites of power. Recent developments in the broader social and economic context have reinforced this bias, tilting outcomes further toward economic elites.

For organized interests, political fragmentation has three major effects: it generates veto points, it encourages heterogeneity of preferences, and it facilitates venue arbitrage. These effects in turn discourage certain kinds of group strategies, particularly those that rest on the creation of encompassing economic organizations or long-run credible commitments or that require the ongoing coordination and updating of policy. Instead, organized interests are drawn toward strategies, coalitions, and policy agendas that exploit veto points and the decentralization of public authority – including those that rest on the "structural" power that comes from policymakers' sensitivity to capital flight in the context of decentralized fiscal competition (Hacker and Pierson 2002; Robertson 2018). In sum, the diversity and multiplicity of venues in America's fragmented system profoundly alters the terrain of political contestation, advantaging organized actors with the resources and reach to venue shop, while creating powerful incentives for individuals and organizations to hoard resources and free-ride on public goods provision.

The difficulty of constructing broad organizations and coordinating policy is, of course, central to the idea of LMEs – they are, after all, being contrasted with "coordinated" market economies. Yet within the family of LMEs, the United States is at a distant remove from its siblings as a result of its fragmented political institutions (see, especially, Martin and Swank 2012). Moreover, it is at a growing remove. In recent decades, rising elite polarization has interacted with longstanding institutional fragmentation to raise the barriers to national policy change ever higher (Binder 2003; but see Curry and Lee 2019). Gridlock not only means new challenges go unaddressed; it also encourages policy drift (Hacker 2004) – the growing mismatch between stalemated policies and changing social circumstances – as well as subnational policy action (Grumbach 2018). The ongoing erosion of national administrative capacity has only reinforced the incentives for powerful economic actors to work to block government action and go it alone. It has also enhanced the role of alternative sites of policymaking, especially the courts and state governments – which has further increased the political advantages of well-resourced groups.

The Power of Repeat, Multi-Venue Players. These political advantages reflect a basic feature of contemporary American politics that the mainstream focus on voters and elections too often obscures. The same trends that complicate coordinated national action make it harder for disorganized and diffuse interests to get what they want. Organized interests of the sort just discussed thrive because they have long time horizons and the resources to navigate a complex institutional landscape. Disorganized interests suffer because they do not.

Among these disorganized interests is the broad electorate. Though voters hold the disciplining power of the ballot, they nonetheless face a civic landscape of daunting complexity and clouded accountability. Moreover, policy is increasingly made in venues that are more complex and more insulated from direct electoral oversight than are Congress or the presidency. Elections are fundamental in all representative governments, and party coalitions necessarily rest on the development of relatively stable alliances with voters. But the same forces that give organized interests a stronger hand in shaping the substantive products of governance – even if only by holding public authority at bay – limit and make more fragile the opportunities for voters to do the same (Arnold 1990). Recall Schattschneider's focus on the power of agenda control: as the relative sway of the well-organized and highly resourceful grows, their ability to shape the alternatives – to block those they disfavor and move those they favor further from the reach of regular contestation – also grows.

All of these tendencies are on vivid display in the American legal system. In no other rich democracy is the judiciary or professional legal expertise so privileged in policymaking, and this is especially true in domains that affect business (Kagan 2019; Pistor 2019; see also Bonica and Sen 2021). Exercising influence within the legal system requires superior resources, specialized expertise, and the ability to stay in the game for the duration, making it an ideal setting for organized interests with all three attributes to spare. The courts provide a low-profile arena in which well-resourced interests are able to pursue their policy aims, strengthen their allies and weaken their opponents, and even effectively nullify legislation or administrative interventions they oppose, regardless of whether voters are favorable toward those policies (Culpepper 2010; Rahman and Thelen, this volume). It is an arena for the organized and resourceful, and for repeat (rather than one-shot) players.

In a fragmented system, organization confers power, and durable organization confers greater power. This not only privileges organized interests within US policymaking, but also gives organized economic interests a distinctive and important role within US party coalitions. This is the central insight of recent revisionist work on the role and nature of parties in American politics (Bawn et al. 2012). CPE has always seen organized groups and political parties as closely linked. Indeed, a major payoff of applying insights from CPE to the study of the American political economy is the ability to draw on both classic and recent scholarship on the linkages between parties, electoral rules, and the representation of societal interests. For example, scholars working in the CPE tradition have increasingly explored the sort of spatial skews in representation and intensified urban/rural cleavages that are central to the American electoral system (Rodden 2019).

The innovation of the new revisionist scholarship on American parties is that such links take a specific and no less important form in the United States, where parties and organized groups represent two of the most durable and consequential vehicles for coordination in a highly fragmented system. In part, this is a function of America's entrenched two-partyism, which reflects both federal electoral rules and the centripetal pressures of a single, separately elected national executive (Drutman 2020). Two-partyism increases the need and incentives for parties to coordinate broad and durable coalitions based on policy bundles that contain items attractive both to resourceful repeat players and to ordinary voters. Especially in the current era of nationalized party politics (Pierson and Schickler 2020), in which regionally distinct factions within national parties are vanishing, such coordination is no small challenge. As we have argued, however, organized interests have gained relative advantage over this same period, making them a more promising source of coordinating power for parties with few other such sources.

In the revisionist scholarship on parties, these interests are cast as "intense policy demanders" – organized groups that seek "to capture and use government for their particular goals" and which in return can offer money, expertise, personnel, and other valuable resources to those parties and the elected and appointed officials aligned with them (Bawn et al. 2012, 571; Krimmel 2017; Schlozman 2015). These intense demanders are so valuable to parties precisely because coordination is so hard in the American system. Especially in recent decades, organized groups have enjoyed marked advantages over individual voters in bending parties toward their priorities, particularly when those voters are not affluent (Gilens 2012; Gilens and Page 2014). They are well informed, while many voters are either loyal partisans or do not have enough information to adequately distinguish party positions on complex issues (Converse 1964; Delli Carpini and Keeter 1997; Zaller 1992). They are able to work across multiple sites of public authority, while voters have difficulty holding politicians accountable when policy is being made in obscure venues or through deliberate drift (Rogers 2017). And they are in it for the long term, while voters who can be plausibly swayed from one party to the other are typically focused on shorter-term dynamics (Achen and Bartels 2016).

The field of American political economy that we advocate offers an excellent opportunity to extend and refine this line of analysis. The fundamental insight is that the agendas of parties – indeed, the full range of actions by partisan officials, especially those that implicate government authority – reflect not just voter preferences, but also clashes among organized groups. Intense policy demanders seek to influence parties precisely because they see parties as decisive instruments for using the coercive power of government to impose policies that have large enduring effects on a range of important outcomes. The considerable role of organized groups in party politics should thus be seen as one important dimension of the broader role of organized interests in shaping the political economy. At the same time, situating partisan contestation within the broader context of the American political economy brings into clearer view another fundamental feature of American politics – one that has been tied up with party competition since the birth of the republic: the enduring and evolving cleavage between those privileged by the US racial order and those subjugated by it.

RACE AND THE AMERICAN POLITICAL ECONOMY

No other rich democracy's political economy has been more defined by racial hierarchy than the United States' (King and Smith 2005;

Lieberman 2011). The distinctive demands of a Southern economy built on slavery shaped the Constitution's framing. Divisions around race have reverberated through American politics ever since. Racial exclusion and violence have so profoundly disadvantaged minority groups in substantial part because they have become so deeply embedded in the structure of the American political economy.

Seeing race as a constitutive feature of the American political economy increases our appreciation of the multiple ways in which racial division has influenced American politics. We think it only strengthens our understanding of how race has shaped citizens' political beliefs and behaviors – a principal focus of research on "race, ethnicity, and politics" (REP) within the American politics subfield. Yet we also think it opens up new opportunities to build on pioneering REP work that has gone beyond this behavioral focus (Michener 2019; Soss and Weaver 2017). Understanding the ways in which race has shaped the American political economy helps us better grasp the entrenchment of racially discriminatory economic structures, the place of race and ethnicity in group and party coalitions, and the ways in which America's distinctive institutions – including its distinctive welfare state – have placed significant bounds on the scope and character of American racial progress.

The Racialization of US Policy. A principal reason that American racial divisions run so deep is because of the ways they are reinforced through institutions and policies developed over generations. In critical ways, these discriminatory structures were built on regional divides, resulting in sectional divisions in both political representation and economic interests (Bensel 1984). After the abandonment of post–Civil War Reconstruction, political elites in former slave states built a "Southern cage" to contain and channel the growth of the American state so it did not challenge the economic and political hierarchies that characterized their "authoritarian enclaves" within a putatively democratic polity (Gibson 2013; Katznelson 2013; Mickey 2015).

With segregationists holding disproportionate power over national policy, the American regulatory and welfare state developed within that Southern cage. The result was a bifurcated system of social provision that separated a largely white core of social insurance from a disproportionately minority periphery of limited and decentralized means-tested benefits (Lieberman 1998). The same separation emerged in the nation's unusual and extensive publicly subsidized "private welfare regime" (Hacker 2002), including its decentralized but highly subsidized system for encouraging home ownership and higher education. As Thurston documents in her chapter, tax-subsidized private provision in housing and education, intersecting with differential access to credit, largely bypassed Black Americans even as it fostered greater economic security and the accumulation of assets among working- and middle-class whites. Meanwhile, the United States' heavy reliance on ostensibly private employment-based health and retirement benefits – benefits that in fact owed much to favorable tax policies and federal rules governing collective bargaining – also divided the workforce into "insiders" and "outsiders" based on access to private benefits, with Blacks and other minorities much more likely to be outsiders. Because this "submerged state" both provided and hid extensive subsidies for whites, it undermined economic solidarity and encouraged white resentment of the considerably smaller but much more visible support available to the minority poor (e.g., King 1995; Mettler 2011, 2018).

Racial divisions have intensified, and in turn been intensified by, the territorially structured elements of American governance. Physical segregation is a hallmark of racial division, and, in the American context, its consequences have proved especially profound. Recall that the United States is a huge outlier in the extent to which it gives local authorities latitude over such critical aspects of governance as education, zoning, and criminal justice. These policies and institutions greatly increase both the motivation for segregation and its consequences. In her contribution to this volume, Jessica Trounstine shows how powerful incentives for spatial segregation stemmed from and then exacerbated differences in policy packages, and hence preferences, among communities (Trounstine 2018 and in this volume). Backed by influential political actors, public authorities explicitly deployed racial criteria in constructing the urban and suburban contours of modern America (Weir 2005; Rothstein 2017). These spatial divisions within an increasingly unequal political economy strengthened the motives and the means for powerful groups to cling tenaciously to "local control" as a way to maintain their separateness and guard their privilege.

Just as opportunity is hoarded in the American political economy, disadvantage is concentrated and institutionalized. Privileged enclaves are mirrored in the development of what Soss and Weaver (2017) call "race-class subjugated communities." These communities are on the receiving end of America's intense isolation and stigmatization of neighborhoods with large populations of low-income minorities. Institutional incentives to sort and hoard, along with the decline of industrial cities in the Northeast and Midwest, have created large and durable disadvantages that cannot be understood without seeing the development of the American political economy as racially constituted (Wilson 1987, 1996).

A crucial dimension of this spatially structured concentration of disadvantage is an extraordinarily expansive carceral state that disproportionately ensnares minority Americans (e.g., Forman 2017; Gottschalk 2006; Hinton 2016). Recent estimates put the total number of incarcerated individuals at a staggering 2.3 million – a more than four-fold increase since 1980 (Prison Policy Initiative n.d.; Sawyer and Wagner 2020) and more than six times the level of the typical OECD nation on a per capita basis (Hamilton Project 2014). These burdens are disproportionately borne by minorities and in particular Black men, who face lifetime risks of incarceration roughly six times those of their white counterparts (Hinton et al. 2018). While the drivers of mass incarceration are numerous, the unusually decentralized system of US criminal prosecution plays a central role (Pfaff 2017). Unlike in most other countries, these prosecutors are typically locally elected officers with immense discretion. Often running in low-turnout elections dominated by white homeowners concerned about maintaining property values, these prosecutors have strong incentives to be seen as tough on crime – and thus charge a greater number of arrestees with heavier offenses (see also Lacey and Soskice 2015).

Among the many profound ways that the carceral state shapes the everyday lives of minority Americans are its deep effects on American labor markets (Western and Beckett 1999). On a basic level, the US system of mass incarceration pulls a significant swath of men, disproportionally Black men without high school degrees, out of continued schooling or the labor market. These effects persist beyond time in prison or jail because employment options for those with criminal records are so limited (Pager 2003; Western and Pettit 2010). While cross-national typologies often describe the United States as having relatively unregulated labor markets, mass incarceration is in effect a nationwide labor-market policy that weakens the employment opportunities of some of America's most vulnerable workers, while contributing to the already-difficult challenge of fostering robust collective organizations representing workers without a college degree who have lost out in the knowledge economy (Reich and Prins 2020; Western and Beckett 1999).

Indeed, once we see race as constitutive of the American political economy, we see too that the fundamental cleavages that have long run through the American working class are not only ideational but also deeply economic. Institutionalized racial biases now manifest themselves as stark economic divisions between, as well as within, racial and ethnic groups. One such division, highlighted in the chapter by Ansell and Gingrich, is related to "positional competition" (Hirsch 1976). Goods that involve social or spatial crowding create a dynamic of musical chairs, where limited supply creates bidding wars. Intense, costly positional competition is manifest in two cornerstones of the knowledge economy: housing in the country's most dynamic urban areas (Le Galès and Pierson 2019) and the advanced educational opportunities that provide access to high status jobs (Grusky et al. 2019).

Because of these self-reinforcing sources of positional advantage, outright discrimination (though still tragically common) is no longer necessary to preserve profound inequalities of opportunity. Increased competition over key positional goods means that inherited assets create *durable* advantages. With more and more resources required to compete in these markets, those without such assets are shunted to less-favorable niches. This is the context in which to understand America's huge racial wealth gap – typical Black households have one-tenth the wealth of typical white ones, and this is true across similarly educated households (Hanks et al. 2018; McIntosh et al. 2020). Segregation in housing and employment and differential access to credit also leave Black and Hispanic families uniquely vulnerable to recessions and financial crises (Lowery 2013).

In sum, race is deeply embedded in structures of public and private governance that define the United States' distinctive political economy. American capitalism is, and has always been, tied up with "racial capitalism" (e.g., Darity, Hamilton, and Stewart 2015; Dawson and Francis 2016; and Harris and Lieberman 2013; see also Baradaran 2019; Rothstein 2017; Taylor 2019). These structures, imbued with and defining of racial divisions, have profound effects on how economic, social, and political life are experienced and interpreted in the United States. Equally important, they have profound effects on the nature of divisions among groups, and on the prospects of either addressing or exacerbating those divisions through political action, as we discuss in the next section.

PUTTING THE PIECES TOGETHER

The three features of the American political economy that we have emphasized – the extreme fragmentation of political authority, the role of organized interests within this fragmented system, and the centrality of racial (and associated spatial) inequalities – are both descriptive and conceptual. That is, they both highlight some of the defining characteristics of the American political economy and provide a framework for understanding some of the most consequential ongoing developments in the American political economy.

To illustrate that potential, we now turn to three questions of immense contemporary importance: (1) why organized business in the United States has simultaneously narrowed its goals and increased its power, especially relative to organized labor; (2) why the Republican Party in the United States has diverged from mainstream conservatism abroad to embrace an increasingly extreme form of ethno-nationalism, even while intensifying its insistence on inegalitarian policies and antidemocratic measures; and (3) why the nation's dominant role in the transition to the knowledge economy seems increasingly precarious as it fails to reproduce the necessary political supports. In each case, we seek to show that our approach highlights neglected questions and offers persuasive explanations.

THE GROWING POWER OF BUSINESS AND ECONOMIC ELITES

In recent decades, American political science has had strikingly little to say about the growing organization and influence of the United States' increasingly consolidated and politically muscular business community. When scholars have tackled the topic, their approach has generally reflected the constraining divisions of the subfield, focusing on business's role in a single domain (such as Congress) or particular expressions of corporate power (for example, the donations or lobbying of individual firms).

Although this work deserves applause, it also suggests the limits of viewing the role of economic interests through the subfield's restricted lens. Large-scale interests whose wealth and power are grounded in economic production have a unique potential to influence governance not just because of their massive resources but also because of their central structural role in the economy. Over the last forty years, corporations have aggressively deployed these strengths, augmenting their activities and organization to prosper in a political economy displaying weakening national policy capacity and an increasing role for multi-venue policymaking. No less important, the same trends that give business interests increasing leverage have systematically weakened a key source of countervailing power: organized labor.

How a Multi-venue Polity Favors Business. Our approach to understanding organized interests starts with a simple premise: economic interests try to achieve their goals using the specific tools and venues at their disposal. Like journalists urged to "follow the money," those who study the political economy gain clarity by seeking to understand what is at stake. This, in turn, means thinking about policy substance. In most conflicts that bridge the economy and polity, the critical prize is the ability to shape the terms, distribution, and boundaries of economic governance, and the contest for this prize is waged over an extended period and on multiple fronts.

What makes this general proposition so crucial for understanding the *American* political economy is that US business interests have become increasingly well-resourced repeat players capable of operating in multiple venues simultaneously (Hertel-Fernandez 2019). In pursuit of the prize of policy control, organized interests have effectively run roughshod over distinctions central to the American politics subfield, from the traditional lines between federal, state, and local policymaking to those delimiting the scope and interplay of legislative and judicial politics.

Consider the corporate response to campaigns to raise the minimum wage in US cities (e.g., Rolf 2016). Facing the prospect of higher labor costs, businesses have increasingly taken advantage of the overlapping jurisdictional power that states possess over lower levels of government. As Hertel-Fernandez describes in his chapter, business groups have worked with Republican legislatures to pass laws barring cities from passing higher minimum wages in well over half of states (Hertel-Fernandez 2019). Such patterns are also clearly evident in state-by-state battles over climate policy, as extractive industries mobilize to roll back laws supporting the production of renewable energy (Stokes 2020).

Or consider the role of business in America's distinctive legal system. Rahman and Thelen's contribution to this volume shows how business interests have used their formidable capacities to reshape the courts (see also Ash et al. 2020), with enormous consequences for the political economy. Among many other examples, they have eviscerated the once-common strategy of class-action lawsuits and created the legal basis for sweeping mandatory arbitration and non-compete clauses that have greatly reduced the legal – and thus economic – power of workers (Colvin 2018; Colvin and Shierholz 2019; Staszak 2015).

The Distinctive Sources of Business Power. Another conventional distinction that organized economic interests have exploded is the line between market power and political power. As comparative political economists have prominently argued (Braun 2020; Busemeyer and Thelen 2020; Culpepper 2015; Culpepper and Reinke 2014), the power of economic interests is inherently linked to their dual presence in markets and politics. That is, it is "structural" (Block 1977; Lindblom 1982; Witko et al. 2021) as well as "instrumental." When faced with policies they dislike, corporate managers do not have to run to public officials; they can simply threaten to hold up investment, stop production, fire workers, or relocate. When faced with challenges to their market power, they can act unilaterally to try to quash those challenges by adopting new production strategies, corporate governance structures, or management techniques. In turn, elected officials who recognize these structural advantages may change their behavior to satisfy firm preferences or to accept private exercises of power – even when firms do not use their instrumental power to pressure them to do so. Politicians are especially likely to be sensitive to corporate threats when the mass public is more concerned about the economy, if capital is especially mobile, or if their constituents are more likely to be affected by capital strikes or layoffs.

America's fragmented political system creates ample opportunities for the exercise of structural power. By promoting gridlock, it reduces the chance of authoritative responses to exercises of market clout. By promoting decentralization, it allows mobile firms to pressure local and state governments into adopting favorable regulatory and tax policies (e.g., Hacker and Pierson 2002; although see Ogorzalek in this volume for evidence on how the threat of capital flight might be lower in some urban areas that businesses desire to operate in, opening the door to more redistributive policies and regulations). On top of this, as Naidu's chapter in this volume discusses, the tilt of American labor law toward employers has accentuated these sources of structural power – because they not only reduce the ability of workers to push back in the market but also limit the extent to which unions can reduce business's structural power through negotiation over production, investment, and relocation decisions.

Thus, the weakness and fragmentation of governing power in the United States accentuate the ability of business to achieve many of its key goals unilaterally. They also increase the relative informational advantages of organized interests compared to public officials. The effects are especially notable at the state level: in many states, legislators serve only part-time, with barely any staff to help them with research or drafting legislation. Well-funded business-backed groups gain influence by providing the legislative language, research, and political strategy that lawmakers might otherwise lack (e.g., Hertel-Fernandez 2019). Even at the federal level, inadequate resources and capacity sometimes force Congress and agencies to rely on private-sector actors for information and data, reducing incentives to robustly regulate firms (Carpenter and Moss 2013; Drutman 2010). Together, these institutional conditions amplify the power of firms and economic elites in ways that simply do not register in most research on American politics (e.g., Ansolabehere et al. 2003; Fowler et al. 2020; Smith 2000).

One important example is the growing power of asset-management firms within the American political economy. The last two decades have witnessed the rise of enormous financial entities that combine extreme concentration of stock ownership with high diversification. These powerful new actors exercise what Benjamin Braun, in his chapter, calls "infrastructural power" (another form of structural power) by virtue of their close connections to government entities that oversee transactions in those markets, particularly central banks (see also Braun 2020; on the more general role of financial institutions in the Fed, see e.g., Jacobs and King 2016). Such power was on display recently when the Federal Reserve turned to one such firm, BlackRock, to manage the vast corporate bond purchases it undertook in response to the COVID-19 crisis (Tett 2020). In effect, the priorities of asset managers are now a fundamental influence on the calculus of public officials and the corporations they regulate.

The Narrowing of Business Policy Objectives. It is not just the nature of business power that has evolved; so too have the purposes toward which that power is put. Where capital must contend with a powerful state and strong labor movement, business managers develop very specific expectations about which political demands are realistic and which are not. Over time, firms facing greater countervailing pressures adapt their business models to accommodate these constraints, which further reinforces shifts in their political objectives. In Europe, these constraints have traditionally encouraged employers to adopt a longer-term, more consensual perspective on production and underwritten more equitable economic regimes (Huber and Stephens 2001; Martin and Swank 2012; Streeck 1997).[5]

[5] In the meantime, evidence is accumulating that these "beneficial constraints" have loosened considerably in Europe's coordinated market economies, even if most observers still see significant differences between the American and European varieties of capitalism.

In the United States, by contrast, businesses have far fewer incentives to compromise with the state or other social partners or to adopt longer-term perspectives. American corporations are thus more likely than their counterparts abroad to operate on a model where they "smash and grab" and advance by "moving fast and breaking things." When mechanisms to enforce collective action are weak, free riding is both rational and profitable. Why should corporate executives voluntarily accede to proposals that would raise their taxes or increase wages and labor standards when they know their competitors may evade these constraints and when they have so many strategies and resources to defeat them?

Many of today's most dynamic firms grew precisely by taking advantage of the weak regulatory and enforcement regime in the United States. Amazon, for example, was able to establish its dominance in the online retail sector in part by pressing ahead aggressively before state, local, and federal officials had developed approaches to taxing internet commerce, which gave them a major advantage over brick and mortar stores. Other firms such as Uber have had much more success in the United States than in Europe in pursuing brazen strategies of defying the law altogether, flagrantly ignoring existing transit and taxi regulations and daring cities to confront them (Thelen 2018).

Developments in American capital markets reinforce this pressure for short-term and narrow priorities. Financialization has not just created new actors wielding enhanced powers; it has narrowed the objectives these powerful actors pursue (see, especially, Davis 2009; Krippner 2012). The pressures of capital markets have encouraged a massive concentration of wealth, driven the "fissurization" of work through outsourcing and subcontracting (Lazonick and O'Sullivan 2000; Weil 2014), and pushed firms to focus on short-term returns, rather than on long-term investments (Davies et al. 2014). Companies facing these incentives are encouraged to seek favorable changes in policy or use labor arrangements that yield quick quarterly returns but not necessarily long-term value (Galston 2015; Salter 2012).

Climate policy offers a striking example of corporate short-termism. Despite the massive threats that global climate change poses to the American economy – and despite encouraging if vague statements of support from many business leaders – there is no serious organized business constituency for reform. Instead, it is the business interests that stand to lose the most from regulation of carbon emissions – extractive industries and utilities – that have figured most prominently in recent debates over climate change legislation (Mildenberger 2020). These carbon producers have, in turn, used all the veto points the fragmented US political economy provides to stymie action, bringing federal litigation against new federal climate rules, lobbying administrative agencies to roll back regulations, and erecting roadblocks to state-level action (Skocpol 2013; Stokes 2020).

Labor's Weak and Declining Position. A key contributor to the distinctive orientation of American employers is the relative lack of effective societal checks on concentrated economic power. For many of the same reasons that organized business has gained ground, organized labor has sharply declined. In the United States today, a mere 12 percent of full-time workers (including in the public sector) are covered by union contracts, well below levels in most rich democracies (Visser 2019).

The weak and declining position of labor is one of the clearest and most consequential contemporary examples of policy drift, as Kelly and Morgan argue in their contribution to this volume (see also Galvin and Hacker 2020). Labor laws developed in the mid-twentieth century are completely mismatched to current economic and firm structures (Andrias 2016). Business groups and individual firms have taken advantage of this mismatch to adopt the most aggressive anti-union strategies seen in the advanced industrial world (Logan 2006). In contrast to Europe, where unions often bargain for entire industries, American unions are legally required to organize individual workplaces one at a time (for an extended comparative analysis, see Thelen 2019). This unusual model further increases the incentives for firms to oppose labor representation. Unlike in systems of sectoral bargaining, individual businesses face a stark competitive disadvantage from unionization – including higher private benefit costs – because of competition from nonunion counterparts within their industry.

The decline of American unions weighs heavily on outcomes across the labor market. Given the racial constitution of the American political economy, however, the impact on workers of color has been disproportionately intense. Just as racial minorities were long locked out of credit markets and opportunities for asset accumulation, they were late entrants into the unionized workforce (Rosenfeld 2014). Although the unionization rate of Black Americans (especially Black women) exceeds the rate of their white counterparts, this is mostly because they are more likely to be covered by public sector unions. In the private sector workforce, Black Americans showcase the stark erosion of labor unions and its negative consequences for vulnerable workers outside of declining unionized sectors (Windham 2017).

More recently, public sector labor unions have also come under intense attack, as described in detail in Hertel-Fernandez's chapter. Public employment has been a critical means of advancement for Black workers because private sector opportunities have remained comparatively limited. Ironically, the disproportionate employment of Black Americans in the public sector has allowed business groups and other anti-union forces to tap into a powerful well of white racial resentment, fusing animus toward minorities with perceptions of lazy and undeserving government workers (Cramer 2016). Thus, the highly successful campaign against public sector unions not only threatens the already-tenuous economic gains that minority workers have made, it also points to a second fundamental development our framework helps explain: the rise of a business-backed party coalition allying economic conservatives with racially resentful whites that has gained increasing capacity to reshape the American political economy.

THE TRANSFORMATION OF AMERICAN CONSERVATISM

Even before the election of Donald Trump, the Republican Party stood out among major conservative parties for its extreme positions on a range of issues, including the role of unions and the welfare state, openness to immigration, and concern about climate change (Hacker and Pierson 2020). Since the election, comparativists and Americanists alike have stressed the evident affinities between right-wing populism in Europe and the appeals and electoral base of President Trump and his party. Unlike fringe right-wing parties in other rich nations, however, the Republican Party is both a plurality-seeking conservative party and one closely allied with powerful economic elites. The political economy approach that we have outlined helps explain these unusual features.

The Spatial Political Economy of Grievance. In all rich democracies, right-wing populism has thrived in nonurban regions excluded from the main centers of the knowledge economy and has featured strong elements of nativism, racism, and religious chauvinism (Gidron and Hall 2019). In the United States, however, right-wing backlash has been able to draw on a particularly long, ugly, and intense history of racial division. This deep reservoir of racial resentment has widened the opening for the race-based political appeals that have been central to the polarization of American politics since well before right-wing populism's current rise (Jardina 2019; Mutz 2018; Sides, Tesler, and Vavrick 2018). White Americans' perceptions of social protections – and indeed, the public sector more generally – are highly racialized and have become more so (Filindra and Kaplan 2020; Gilens 1999; Jardina 2019; Tesler 2012). Immigration-stoked demographic change has only heightened and widened these racial perceptions and prejudices, especially in communities that are still overwhelmingly white.

All this has created tremendous opportunities for political strategies that play on racial and cultural divisions. As comparative scholars have emphasized, right-wing populism resonates most in contexts where inequality is rising (Tavits and Potter 2014) and where highly stratified systems of education and social provision do comparatively little for those most threatened by the decline of the industrial economy (Iversen and Soskice 2019). Such highly stratified systems, it should be recalled, are not just arbitrary outputs of American governance. They are, in substantial part, a direct consequence of a polity riven with racial cleavages. Thus, racial divisions embedded in the American political economy exacerbate unequal opportunity, weaken social protections, *and* channel discontent with these realities into racial backlash. These divisions also undercut support for policies that might create common cause between disadvantaged whites and disadvantaged minorities and weaken social organizations like unions that could construct cross-racial coalitions (Frymer and Grumbach 2020). Understanding how race constitutes the American political economy thus helps explain how the economic and sociocultural foundations of America's intense ethnonationalist surge are deeply intertwined (Hacker and Pierson 2020).

Coalition Politics and "Plutocratic Populism." An essential and distinctive feature of American right-wing populism is that it has accompanied, and broadly reinforced, the rising political power of business and the wealthy. Economic elites are central to the backlash coalition organized and mobilized by and through the Republican Party. While forces of right-wing populism have emerged in many countries, the United States is unusual in the extent to which these forces have taken root in the mainstream right, and become allied with the most potent business coalitions and the lion's share of politically active wealth. The result is an American hybrid of ethnonationalist backlash and inegalitarian policymaking that might be called "plutocratic populism" (Hacker and Pierson 2020). The ethnonationalist backlash has gotten most of the attention, but central to this unstable but powerful hybrid is the ability of the Republican Party to attract key business interests with extremely conservative economic policies.

We have already discussed why American business interests are uncommonly narrow and short-term oriented. Although there are pockets of corporate leadership that have invested in alternative outcomes, key features of America's political economy militate against elite collective action on behalf of positive-sum policies. The economy's biggest winners have a strong desire to protect their gains. The pervasive generation of wealth through low taxes and efforts to weaken countervailing institutions offers considerable incentives to support an anti-statist agenda. Meanwhile, the intense commitment and free-rider problems that we have discussed encourage particularism and short-termism and undercut a potential centrist coalition.

Nowhere is this behavior clearer than in the United States' failure to address climate change. The Republican Party stands alone among major parties in advanced democracies, not just rejecting efforts to regulate carbon emissions but denying the very existence of human-caused climate change (e.g., Batstrand 2015). In turn, the GOP's positions reflect a close alliance with powerful libertarian donors and extractive business interests (Hacker and Pierson 2016; Page et al. 2018; Skocpol 2013; Skocpol and Hertel-Fernandez 2016; Stokes 2020).

The Vulnerability of American Institutions. As we have noted, the Republican Party is a traditionally mainstream party that has become a right-wing insurgent force. How can a plurality-seeking party that is capable of capturing Congress and the White House successfully use themes and tactics that are elsewhere the stock-in-trade of right-wing parties largely unable to form governing coalitions? Once again, America's political institutions play a starring role. The same fragmentation that advantages business allows a unified party reliant on elite money and rural support to translate intense minority sentiment into a strong hold on governing power.

American electoral arrangements amplify the influence of rural areas in two distinct but related ways. First, they give the party that dominates rural states a strong edge in the Senate, since even the least populous states get two senators. Indeed, Republicans have held the Senate for over half of the past twenty years, despite not having won a majority of votes cast in Senate elections in all but two of those years (Brownstein 2020). Some of this edge also carries over to the Electoral College – America's atavistic means of electing the president, which gives each state Electoral College representation equal to the combined number of Senators and House members in Congress and which has twice in the past quarter century allowed Republicans to win the presidency while losing the popular vote.

Second, the growing strength of the GOP in non-urban areas makes it easier for Republicans to maximize the translation of votes into federal House and state-legislative seats. Given the contemporary urban-rural divide, when parties are sorted geographically and seats allocated through single-member-district elections, densely populated urban areas inevitably feature large numbers of "wasted votes," enhancing the relative power of rural voters. The unusual decentralization of US electoral administration allows state-level Republicans to magnify this advantage, giving them an edge in drawing districts that concentrate Democratic voters in urban districts (Powell et al. 2020; Rodden 2019). Such partisan gerrymandering has been crucial to recent GOP success at the state and national levels (Hacker and Pierson 2020).

Republicans' plutocratic-populist coalition also benefits from political institutions that allow national minority sentiment to capture a majority party and the presidency. This is a path to power not available in parliamentary democracies using proportional representation, where minority factions may be able to join governing coalitions but lack viable routes to unified power. The unusually large role of the courts comes in here, too, for the party's dominance in specific states and regions has allowed social and economic conservatives to join forces in state judicial elections. At the national level, control of the Senate and presidency has allowed the party to stack a federal bench that has enormous power to block and alter federal policy for decades to come. Since 1988, Republicans have lost the popular vote in every presidential election but one; yet they have appointed six of the nine justices on the Supreme Court. Thus, America's peculiar form of right-wing populism is rooted in, and in turn has reinforced, the unusual structure of the American political economy.

These dynamics also have stark implications for American economic policy. Even if they coexist with ongoing, if imbalanced, democratic contestation, these patterns pose a very specific challenge for the United States as it continues to transition toward an urban-based knowledge economy.

THE SUSTAINABILITY OF THE AMERICAN KNOWLEDGE ECONOMY

The rise of the knowledge economy constitutes a profound economic, social, and political rupture (Boix 2019; Iversen and Soskice 2019). In all rich nations, it has fundamentally altered economic relationships, policy demands, and the political coalitions that underpin them. These effects have been particularly profound in the United States, long on the leading edge of this transformation. As the character of America's right-wing reaction suggests, however, not all of these effects are conducive to the nation's continued leadership in the transition to a knowledge economy.

In his contribution to this volume, David Soskice brings together both traditional and novel explanations for the United States' remarkable early lead. The nation's superpower role and its massive national security apparatus gave it an enormous head start, laying the foundation for spectacular growth in emerging sectors of the knowledge economy (Schwartz 2019). The national security state did not just bankroll key technologies; it also incorporated commercial goals into its contracting to attract private partners and advance innovation (Weiss 2014). Unmatched federal spending provided a huge R&D boost, generated a large pool of workers with advanced skills, and seeded the key technologies that continue to drive private-sector innovation (Lazonick and Mazzucato 2013).

Beyond the United States' superpower status, many of the distinctive features of the American political economy that we have emphasized encouraged the continued rise of the knowledge economy. Emerging powerhouse firms, Soskice notes, clearly benefited from the sheer scale of the American market. But these firms also thrived in a context of flexible (often weak) and decentralized governance, permeable boundaries among professions, a large and very competitive system of higher education, and flexible and ample supplies of financial capital.

Because the United States led the transition to the knowledge economy and continues to dominate its frontier sectors, research on the American political economy can provide substantial insights into the political dynamics associated with this transition. At the same time, the unique features of the United States explored in this chapter appear to have made it increasingly difficult for American policymakers to develop and adapt the appropriate institutions and policies for continued success in the knowledge economy, especially as more and more countries position themselves to compete in the same economic space. Though top American firms seem likely to dominate global commerce for some time, the systemic US advantages that fostered them may not. These challenges, too, carry important implications for CPE as well as for American politics research.

We focus on four strains in particular: the capture of key markets by leading firms, wage stagnation and firm labor market power, the underprovision of public goods, and the intensifying spatial inequalities that have come together with organized business power to propel an intense political backlash.

From Leadership to Capture. As Schwartz notes in his contribution to this volume, one of the key features of the transition away from Fordism is the increasing centrality of employment-poor but intellectual-property-rich firms at the top of deeply fissured value chains. These firms have benefited from several features of the American political economy. They have been able to exploit intense fragmentation and weak state capacity to develop new markets and expand rapidly to achieve dominance within them. They have also been largely unimpeded by organized labor, whose beleaguered representatives present few obstacles to business strategies that have emphasized labor shedding (Davis 2015; Weil 2014). And they have benefited from abundant capital, fed in part by skyrocketing inequality (Braun 2020; Kenney and Zysman 2019). Vast reserves of private capital have allowed prominent companies like Uber to take losses year after year as they scale up and to blow through regulatory barriers and then absorb the resulting fines and legal costs as the price of market dominance (Cremers and Sepe 2018; Frisch 2016; Pollman and Barry 2017: 384; Rahman and Thelen 2019).

These advantages for individual firms, however, may be much less conducive to the continued strength of the knowledge economy overall. Increasingly, the actors who spurred new markets are capturing them. Some of the most dynamic sectors display inherent tendencies toward monopoly; without real pushback, little stands between superstar firms and winner-take-all outcomes. America's fractured regulatory landscape allows companies to exploit jurisdictional competition, while the veto-ridden institutional terrain at the national level provides ample opportunities to engage in blocking strategies to head off regulatory challenges. The fiercely deregulatory turn of the Republican Party, spurred by intense corporate mobilization, has further undercut the prospects for effective regulation, as has the rightward turn of the nation's courts.

All these factors have promoted the uncommonly high level of economic concentration that now characterizes the American political economy (Christophers 2016; Philippon 2019). Consolidation is especially pronounced in the most visible tech firms, but the dominance of corporate giants is becoming pervasive across all types of sectors from retail hardware to amusement parks to meat processing (Leonhardt 2018; Philippon 2019). In turn, rising market power not only increases the political influence of these corporate players and their ability to quash potential upstarts; it is also a key factor in the mixed fortunes of American workers (Marinescu and Hovenkamp 2019; Autor et al. 2017).

Wage Stagnation and Employer Power. Growing concentrations of wealth and corporate power are implicated in two of the more puzzling dynamics of the US labor market: wage stagnation despite years of employment growth, and declining labor force participation relative to the recent past as well as to contemporary trends in other rich democracies. Even before the COVID crisis, real wages for the average American worker had risen a mere 3 percent since the 1970s (and declined for the bottom 20 percent). A key reason, as Naidu argues in his chapter, is employer power in the US labor market (Naidu et al. 2018; see also Azar et al. 2020; Nunn et al. 2018), with estimates suggesting that labor's share of economic output would have been 10 to 23 percent higher if US labor markets were competitive (Naidu et al. 2018).

One important factor in the rise in employer labor market power is the decline of countervailing pressures on business, like vigorous workplace standards enforcement and a vibrant labor movement. Another factor, especially pronounced in less urban areas and therefore critical in the politically fraught geographic polarization of the US economy, is employment concentration (Marinescu and Hovenkamp 2019; see also Benmelech et al. 2018; Bivens et al. 2018). As corporate consolidation has shifted firm headquarters and operations into dense urban areas (Manduca 2019; see also Nunn et al. 2018), smaller cities and towns suffer reduced employment opportunities for workers and therefore less worker bargaining power, dampened local spending, declining civic and charitable involvement of local corporations, and the continued exodus of educated and younger residents.

Under-Provision of Key Collective Goods. We have already stressed that racial cleavages in the American political economy undercut the political capacity to supply public goods. We have also emphasized that the institutional terrain of the American political economy actively encourages negative or blocking power, and tends to discourage long-term collective action to support broadly distributed opportunities and public goods. Pressures on firms to generate short-term returns for their shareholders reinforce these tendencies. Instead of investing in future innovations, firms sitting on huge piles of cash have strong incentives and few countervailing disincentives to direct those resources to shareholders. Once virtually nonexistent, stock buybacks have soared. The pharmaceutical industry offers one striking example: from 2006 to 2015, eighteen of the largest publicly traded drug companies spent more on stock buybacks and dividends than they did on research and development (Lazonick et al. 2017).

The problem is not limited to corporate investment. Public R&D spending has taken an even more significant hit. As Barnes points out in her contribution to this volume, fragmented political institutions and intense economic inequality in the United States have interfered not only with redistribution but also with knowledge investments that yield broad aggregate benefits. Over the last half century, R&D spending by the federal government has plummeted as a share of the economy, falling from a peak of nearly 2 percent of GDP in the mid-1960s to around 0.7 percent in the late 1990s, before rebounding slightly in recent years. The United States, once the biggest public spender by far, now ranks ninth in the world on government R&D expenditures as a share of GDP. Excluding defense, the United States ranks thirty-ninth (Hacker and Pierson 2016).

The United States is also losing its leading position in education. Success in knowledge economies depends crucially on broad access to high-quality education and training at all levels. Yet, as we have seen, local control and segregation produce vast disparities in the quality and outcomes of K–12 education across the country (see also Ansell and Gingrich, this volume). The United States also continues to lag behind Europe in offering early childhood education and high-quality vocational education and training, as well as in providing retraining for adults through active labor market policies. With regard to higher education, where the United States was once the clear leader, many European countries have now surpassed American outcomes (Barnes, this volume). The costs and financing of college have turned high-quality education into a rationed, positional good that preserves the best opportunities for the most privileged segments of society (Mettler 2014). Corporations may be able to find qualified workers – at times by importing them from abroad – but future innovations and opportunities may be lost because of the erosion of public goods that built America's knowledge economy.

Spatial Inequality. As we have emphasized, the field of American political economy must rest on a deeper understanding of the spatial dimensions of politics and economics. The knowledge economy encourages and thrives within urban agglomeration economies, generating and reinforcing urban-rural cleavages as it develops. In the United States, these trends have intersected with longstanding patterns of resource hoarding and free riding to undercut the public policies and political coalitions necessary for both broad access to economic opportunity and long-term public investments in infrastructure, housing, and education.

Spatial divides are felt most acutely in the growing rural-urban cleavage in American politics. Yet they also run straight though some of the country's most dynamic urban centers. Exorbitant housing costs – driven in large part by the exclusionary zoning policies described in Trounstine's and Ogorzalek's chapters – force the lower-income (disproportionately minority) workers who service knowledge economy professionals further to the geographic periphery. These emerging divisions have transformed long-standing relationships among distinctive regional economies and between states and cities within those regions, as well as patterns of national political contestation. In short, they have reshaped the spatial political economy – in ways that have sparked intense backlash against the knowledge economy itself.

The United States continues to drive innovation across the globe. Yet the dynamics we have outlined underscore the ways in which the fragmentation of American public governance has actively promoted intense concentrations of private wealth and deep geographic and racial divisions. As the chapter by Grumbach, Hacker, and Pierson outlines, the major party coalitions today build on these concentrations and divisions at both the state and national levels. New economic realities may advantage urban "blue" places, but longstanding institutions and policies advantage non-urban "red" places. In these politically pivotal areas, a combination of corporate power and racial resentment feeds backlash against the knowledge economy and limits the development of a positive-sum model for encouraging its continued growth.

THE PAYOFFS TO DEVELOPING A FIELD OF AMERICAN POLITICAL ECONOMY

The premise of this volume is that a better picture of the American political economy will offer new perspectives and opportunities for both students of American politics and students of comparative political economy. We have discussed these payoffs throughout this chapter. To close, however, we want to highlight three that are showcased in the chapters to come: a stronger grasp of the links between economic and political inequality, a deeper understanding of the spatial dimensions of political economies, and a sharper focus on the central importance of governance, especially on issues like climate change and health care where the stakes are enormously high.

UNDERSTANDING THE LINK BETWEEN ECONOMIC AND POLITICAL INEQUALITY

As we have noted, scholars have amply documented the ways in which government decisions tend to favor the wealthy in an era of rising inequality. Useful as this work has been, however, much of it has focused on the question of whether public policies or elected officials are responsive to affluent versus lower-income Americans. This is an important question. But it is not the only way to think about how economic advantage translates into political power.

A focus on the American political economy as a whole shifts our gaze. As we have seen, there are many, many ways that advantaged actors can bring about favored outcomes without directly affecting public opinion or election results. Perhaps the most important – and hardest to see – are the ways in which they can change and exploit institutional rules so that the decision-making processes are stacked in their favor. Under these circumstances, economically powerful groups tilt the entire terrain of policymaking toward their preferences, well beyond any single election or legislative debate. Even better from their standpoint, they make such outcomes look like "natural" products of the market or inadvertent consequences of policy inaction, when both the market and the inaction are, in major part, engineered.

Furthermore, a political economy perspective draws attention to some of the most important yet least examined actors in the US policymaking process: businesses and the coalitions that represent them. It is these well-resourced organizations that are often most invested and best positioned to compete in long-run "organized combat" over policy across multiple institutional venues (Hacker and Pierson 2010). In addition to their control over resources that elected officials value, businesses are constituent parts of, and key players within, the market economy. (The same is true of labor, though it is in a much weaker position in the United States.) By virtue of their role as employers and investors, businesses possess structural power they can leverage in ways unavailable to most other political groups (for a new examination of elite structural power in Congress, see Witko et al. 2021).

We have emphasized that the power of economic elites also stems from their greater ability (in general and relative to other organized interests) to move effectively across sites of political contestation. Students of American politics tend to study political institutions one at a time, but the most influential political actors often operate across all of these venues more or less simultaneously. Indeed, the influence of these actors rests in significant part on their capacity to work across venues to constrain, redirect, or evade exercises of political authority. A multi-venue perspective makes this clearer and, in doing so, provides a more accurate picture of key actors' relative power, as well as the purposes to which that power is put.

Comparativists have typically been more mindful of organized interests and their influence. But besides bringing this important focus to the American political economy, our perspective highlights some aspects of group and power dynamics that are generally neglected in CPE as well as American politics research. In particular, our framework underscores the tendencies toward monopoly and monopsony in the knowledge economy, the heightened role of financial asset managers, and the special role of the courts and regulatory structures in policing (or not) these developments. These emergent sources of structural and instrumental power may translate into influence over economic governance, depending on countries' existing political and economic regimes. Such influence can be heightened by venue-based competition in decentralized political settings – a dynamic prominent within the American political economy, but also of great, and perhaps increasing, importance in other countries and supranational institutions (such as the European Union), too.

EMPHASIZING THE SPATIAL DIMENSIONS OF POLITICAL ECONOMY

Political economies operate across geographic space, and different political institutions distribute power and resources across that space in different ways. In the United States, these spatial dynamics are unusual. They also have profound effects.

The highly decentralized form that federalism takes in the United States is a fundamental feature of the American political economy. In the US federal system, not only does very broad state and local autonomy overlap with, and often supersede, federal authority; this extreme fragmentation is coupled with very modest transfers to reduce fiscal inequalities and, in many cases, with relatively limited national (or state) standards. This distinctive combination is critical to the evolution of policy structures and political cleavages within the United States.

Nowhere is this clearer than with regard to America's deep urban-rural and intra-urban conflicts over public goods, with their heavy overlay of racial division. Students of American politics and scholars of CPE alike can benefit from a heightened recognition that structures of strong local autonomy offer a critical institutional means through which racial cleavages can be stoked, built into policy and institutions, and insulated from challenge. These spatial divisions shape and reinforce stark inequalities in structures of opportunity. In turn, these inequalities can become fundamental contributors to party strategies and coalition formation.

The spatial aspects of the American political economy take on even greater prominence because of the constitution's territorially based structures of representation. Winner-take-all single-member districts, the US Senate, and the Electoral College all overrepresent rural areas at the expense of urban ones. Cities are economically advantaged in the knowledge economy, but politically disadvantaged in American politics (Rodden 2019). As a result, the policies preferred by the most economically dynamic places tend to be underprovided at both the state and federal levels.

Both these points are clearly relevant for comparative political economists and Americanists alike. And both are likely to become increasingly important with the transition to an innovation-oriented economy grounded in urban agglomerations. If cities are the engines of growth for knowledge-oriented industries, then the success of a country's transition to, and maintenance of, a strong knowledge economy will depend on the degree to which its political institutions – and the party coalitions that form within them – give voice to the priorities of urban areas, mitigate inequalities within these areas, and dampen spatial cleavages between them and rural areas. The chapter by Ansell and Gingrich illustrates the potential payoffs to a comparative perspective on these questions, showing how electoral arrangements powerfully mediate political conflicts across places. Such work will be important to illuminating not just the sustainability of knowledge economies, but the concord and governability of diverse societies – and even the fate of the planet itself.

CLIMATE CHANGE AND OTHER SUBSTANTIVE STAKES OF GOVERNANCE

Ultimately, the field of American political economy demands that we care about what government does. Not only is policy the main prize of organized interests; it is also a powerful influence on the terrain of political conflict itself. Students of American politics often approach their work starting from either voter behavior or formal institutions. Drawing from CPE, we have argued instead for starting with the ways in which public authority is exercised to shape the interaction of markets and government. The advantages of this approach are clearest when we look at the most consequential conflicts shaping modern political economies. We have touched on many such battles; we close by emphasizing what may be the most fateful.

Climate change poses an existential choice: either current growth models built on fossil fuel extraction will end, or life as we know it will. A rich and growing body of scholarship examines the political dynamics shaping national responses to this crisis (see Bernauer 2013; Mildenberger 2020; and Stokes 2020 for good reviews of the comparative and US-focused literatures). Yet much of this work is centered either on the general collective-action problem posed by climate change (at both the national and international levels) or on the general features of public opinion and individual psychology that make a response to this problem so difficult. Despite these general challenges, there is enormous variation in how and to what extent countries have responded (Mildenberger 2020). In other words, some countries have tackled the collective-action problem better than others. Moreover, these differences seem to reflect variations in institutions and organized interests more than the specifics of public opinion. Indeed, even within the United States, public opinion is a poor guide for explaining state-level ambition in climate initiatives (e.g., Borick et al. 2015; Stokes 2020).

The hostility of the American political economy to bold climate policies highlights some of the biggest institutional and organizational barriers to action. Although the federal structure of American government has facilitated subnational breakthroughs in some states (e.g., Rabe 1999), these steps have generally proved fragile and nowhere near what is necessary to avert warming trends (Stokes 2020). Meanwhile, the national response has been slow and erratic. Our approach helps explain why. The central insight is that tackling climate change involves imposing losses on a highly resourceful sector of the business community that profits from its ability to offload huge external costs on society and stands to see untransferable assets extinguished if these costs must be internalized (e.g., Farrell 2016; Kim et al. 2016; Mildenberger 2020; Stokes 2020). The problem of tackling climate change thus hinges on how the organization of interests, the character of party competition, and the structure of political institutions weakens or empowers these sectors (Skocpol 2013; Stokes 2020).

For all the reasons we have elaborated, the American political economy is highly favorable to such interests. The US response to climate change is thus a revealing example of the kinds of power imbalances and policy challenges that our approach helps identify and explain. The COVID-19 crisis – examined in the Epilogue to this volume – provides another example. Early in the crisis, even as ordinary Americans and small businesses faced risks and losses of unprecedented proportions, large corporations and their representatives were able to get privileged treatment from the federal government in a range of areas. For those not able to receive such favorable treatment, the crisis cast fresh light on the degree to which personal debt and highly uneven housing assets have substituted for a stronger set of social protections or a more aggressive national export or investment strategy (Ansell 2014; Bacarro and Pontusson 2016; Prasad 2006).

The COVID crisis also cast a bright light on what may be the highest-salience policy domain shaped by the power of private interests – namely, America's enormously fragmented and costly health system. There is no way to understand why the United States spends so much more per capita on health care than any other rich democracy, or why this costly system is so much less risk-protecting in so many key respects, without delving deeply into institutional configurations, coalitional politics, and development processes that bear the heavy imprint of America's powerful medical-industrial complex.

On these and other high-stakes issues, the ability of the American political economy to produce positive-sum outcomes seems increasingly in doubt. This is a problem for the United States and, indeed, because of the United States' special role in the world economy, for all nations. It is also an opportunity for learning. The lessons it provides about how institutions and organizations shape national responses to crucial challenges can guide both comparative and US-focused scholarship. Above all, they can help to reorient disciplinary concerns toward features of the political economy with broad, deep, and enduring impacts – features that may make the difference between prosperity and poverty, power and powerlessness, and even life and death.

These are just a few of the ways that an APE perspective can illuminate new areas of research and enrich existing debates in both the American and comparative subfields. At a moment when the relationship between capitalism and democracy cries out for attention, the task of building a true field of American political economy could not be more urgent.

I

POLITICAL ARENAS AND ACTORS

1

Hurdles to Shared Prosperity: Congress, Parties, and the National Policy Process in an Era of Inequality

Nathan J. Kelly and Jana Morgan

Since the 1980s, income concentration has increased dramatically, with the top 1 percent increasing their share from 10.7 percent in 1980 to 20.2 percent in 2014 (an 89 percent increase), and the top 0.01 percent income share increasing even more – by approximately 230 percent.[1] Before the turn of the twenty-first century, scholars seeking to explain rising inequality emphasized structural economic change and demographics, focusing on factors such as deindustrialization, globalization, aging, union decline, and skill-biased technological change (Alderson and Nielsen 2002; Berman et al. 1998; Bound and Johnson 1992; Danziger and Gottschalk 1995; Goldin and Katz 2008). In this work, politics and policy played, at most, a peripheral role in explaining the ebb and flow of American inequality. But newer scholarship has given politics a more central place in our understanding of income disparity.

This scholarship collectively argues that policy outcomes produced at the intersection of political behavior and political institutions are essential for understanding changes in economic inequality and the decline of shared prosperity. Democratic victories in presidential elections (Bartels 2008; Campbell 2011; Kelly 2009; Kenworthy 2010), congressional races (Volscho and Kelly 2012), and state-level contests (Franko and Witko 2017; Hatch and Rigby 2014; Kelly and Witko 2012) translate into more economic equality when compared to the alternative of greater Republican power. However, the choices voters make at the polls are motivated by concerns about economic inequality only in the rare

[1] Top income share data are from the World Inequality Database (https://wid.world/country/usa/, accessed 3/28/2019). Income concept is pretax national income.

circumstance when politicians make explicit linkages between policy proposals and inequality (Achen and Bartels 2016; Bartels 2005; Franko et al. 2013). Additionally, when the preferences of the rich and the poor diverge, the rich are often more likely to get what they want (Enns 2015; Gilens 2012; Gilens and Page 2014; Page et al. 2018; Soroka and Wlezien 2008). The interest system overrepresents the voices of economic elites (Schlozman et al. 2012).[2] And a wide variety of policies have worsened inequality (Bucci 2018; Feigenbaum et al. 2019; Hacker and Pierson 2010; Volscho and Kelly 2012).

At the same time, a growing body of research has analyzed how economic inequality affects the American political system. Work on policy feedback finds that the design of tax policy, welfare, and a variety of other social policies can shape support for redistributive programs (Faricy 2015; Howard 1993; Mettler 2011; 2005; Mettler and SoRelle 2014). Scholars of public opinion have found that inequality tends to undermine public demand for redistribution, although centering distributional issues in the political debate can help strengthen support for redistribution as inequality increases (Franko et al. 2013; Kelly and Enns 2010; Luttig 2013).

The resurgence of scholarly interest in economic inequality is a welcome development. Indeed, the core questions motivating this line of research are essential for understanding the US political economy and answering them enables us to make sense of many puzzling dimensions of American politics and policymaking. But to this point, the distribution of economic resources, the stratification of power structures, and the links between economic power and political influence – that is, issues at the substantive core of the American political economy – remain at the periphery of research on America's national political institutions.

In this chapter, we seek to bring a substantive political economy perspective to US legislative institutions. We present two key theoretical insights. First, that the design of American political institutions is biased toward economic elites because it contributes to policy inaction in a context where the status quo favors economic elites. Second, that the limited policy action that does occur in a time of polarization tends to exacerbate economic inequality. Using several decades of data on economic inequality and policy production, we identify several aggregate

[2] We use the term economic elite as a shorthand way of referring to actors at the very top of the economic ladder – those occupying the top 1 percent (or less) of the income or wealth distribution, though empirically we typically focus on the income distribution.

patterns consistent with our theoretical argument. Income inequality and policy stagnation are strongly associated over time, and the effect of policy stagnation on income inequality becomes increasingly inegalitarian as the existing gap between the rich and the poor grows. Additionally, as income inequality has increased in the United States, policy action in the realm of domestic economic policy (the domain in which redistributive policies are categorized) has declined while activity in other domains such as immigration and crime has increased. Beyond these aggregate patterns we discuss how financial deregulation, a policy with dramatic benefits for economic elites, found sufficient bipartisan support to overcome gridlock while labor law (which has the potential to empower middle- and lower-income workers) has suffered from policy stagnation in the face of rising inequality.

AMERICAN INEQUALITY AND INSTITUTIONAL DESIGN IN COMPARATIVE PERSPECTIVE

Compared to other rich democracies, the US income distribution is distinct. Figure 1.1 plots top 1 percent income shares from 1980 to the present in the United States, Australia, Canada, France, Germany, and Italy.[3] These data show that income concentration in the United States stands out both in its level and its path over time. The left-hand panels plot concentration of pretax income[4] – panel A plots raw values while panel C adjusts the series by zeroing out each country at 1980 in order to focus on change. These panels demonstrate that pretax income is more concentrated in the United States than in any of the comparison countries. The United States was slightly more unequal than other countries in 1980, and the gap between the United States and others has grown. By the mid-2000s, the top 1 percent share of pretax income in the United States was more than double that of the most equal countries examined here (Australia and Italy). Every country saw at least some increase in income concentration since 1980, but the United States is a clear outlier, with top 1 percent income share roughly doubling from around 10 percent to just over 20 percent by 2014.

Turning to the right side of the figure, panels B and D plot income concentration based on post-transfer rather than pretax income.

[3] Data from the World Inequality Database (http://wid.world).

[4] For all countries but Australia, the unit of analysis is split-share adults, in which tax unit income is divided equally across adults in the tax unit. For Australia, the unit of analysis is individuals.

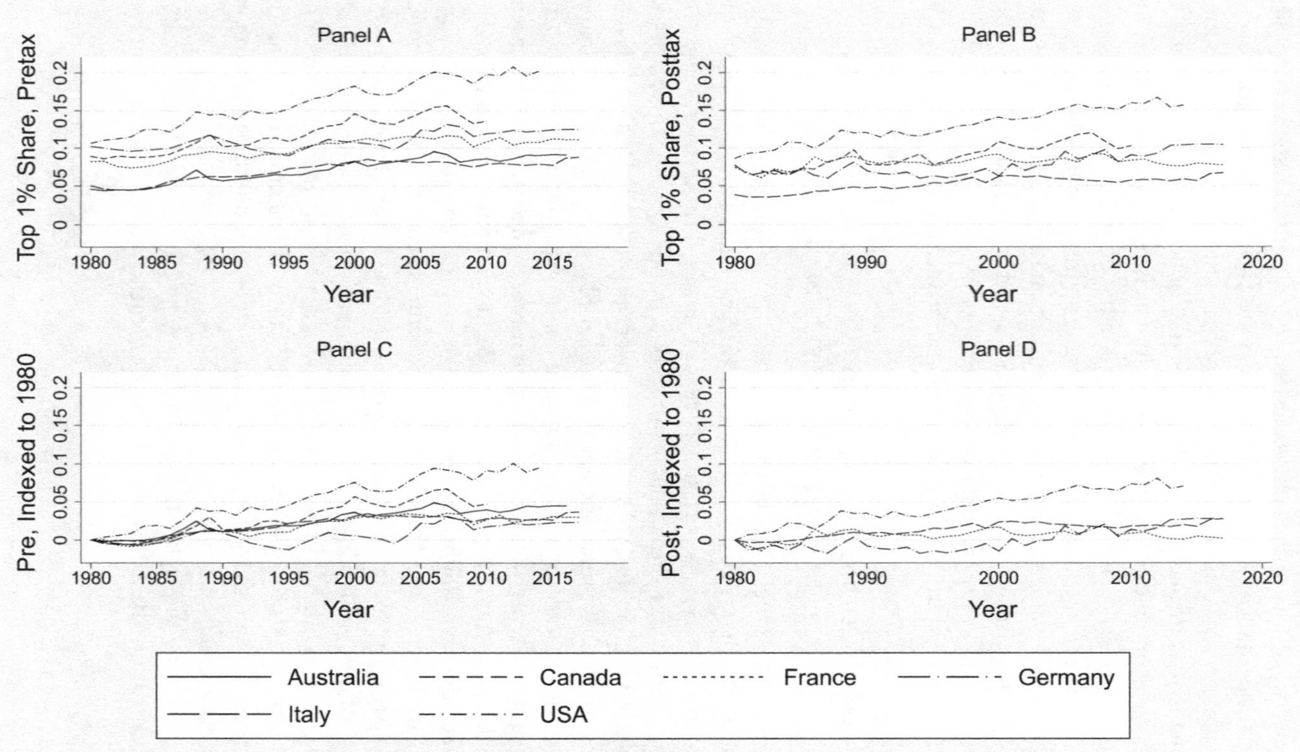

FIGURE 1.1 Top 1% income share in the United States and five other rich democracies

Unsurprisingly, taxes reduce income concentration in every country. In fact, for countries other than the United States, accounting for the effects of transfers renders their level of income concentration relatively flat since 1980. Not so for the United States, where income inequality expanded consequentially whether transfers are accounted for or not. The evidence here is clear: inequality is higher in the United States than the comparison countries – it started higher and evolved in a more unequal direction. And this widening divide between the United States and other countries is the result of greater increases in American market inequality as well as comparatively little policy effort to counter inegalitarian market forces.

Why has inequality been allowed to escalate largely unchecked in the United States even as other countries have acted more aggressively to limit rising posttax inequality? Answering this question requires understanding distinctive features of the United States political economy. One such aspect of the US system, which has received attention in both comparative and American politics scholarship, is the proliferation of veto points throughout the American policy process. The separation of powers in the presidential system as well as the bicameral legislature contribute to unusually high bars for policy action in the United States. Although American presidents have gained more ability to act unitarily, the constitutional structure of separate powers remains intact. Additionally, not only does the US legislative structure require policies to navigate two chambers, but legislators elected to the House and Senate follow different sets of rules and norms and serve different constituencies, with Senators being elected statewide and most of the House elected in substate districts. As a result, the division of legislative power frequently adds significant complications to the policymaking process and makes disagreement across the two chambers more likely.

This proliferation of veto points produces bias toward the status quo, and status quo bias is often tantamount to elite bias. Those who controlled or limited policymaking options in the past have created the status quo of the present. Thus, maintaining the status quo preserves the preferences of those who constructed existing institutions and policy legacies. While there is some churning in precisely who occupies the upper echelon of the American economy, the status quo favors those with power and resources, as they are the people and organizations for whom the current system is working. In the United States, the present system has enabled considerable inequality between the rich and the rest, and this pattern is likely to perpetuate unless policy interventions can somehow disrupt the policy-scape in which this economic status quo was developed.[5]

Considerable cross-national evidence supports the idea that status quo bias induced by veto points limits redistribution, undermines welfare-state generosity, and exacerbates inequality (Stepan and Linz 2011). Studies focused on postindustrial democracies find a negative relationship between the number of veto points and a country's redistributive effort, social spending, and income equality (Birchfield and Crepaz 1998; Crepaz and Moser 2004; Huber and Stephens 2001; Swank 2002). These are some of the most robust findings in comparative political economy research, and the US case typifies these patterns with its proliferation of veto points and its weak redistributive effort, low social spending, and high inequality.

This comparative political economy perspective helps foreground the significance of institutional design for understanding America's political economy and its implications for distributional outcomes. But focusing on cross-national variation necessarily involves painting with a broad brush. To understand precisely how the status quo bias of American institutions has increasingly reproduced and reinforced inegalitarian outcomes over time, we need to consider the operation of specific political institutions. We must analyze how both the institutions themselves and the social and economic conditions with which they interact have changed in ways that have contributed to deepening rather than alleviating inequality.

Toward that goal, we turn our focus to Congress. As the national legislative body, Congress is situated at the center of policy processes with potential to shape distributional outcomes, but its two chambers also comprise the system's most significant veto points. We analyze how this institutional logic has intersected with changing economic and social realities in ways that have allowed status quo bias to work in favor of economic elites. Congress is particularly well-positioned to shape economic outcomes, through action as well as inaction. Existing congressional politics scholarship has tended either

[5] Other major dislocations could serve a similar role in disrupting the status quo. For instance, evidence suggests the Great Depression contributed to the end of the Gilded Age, the last cycle of accelerating economic inequality. However, the more recent financial crisis, which precipitated the onset of the aptly named "Great Recession" of 2007–9, produced a slight blip in rising inequality, but failed to generate a major disjuncture. The perpetuation of the inequality, despite the potentially disruptive Great Recession, only serves to further emphasize the centrality of *policy* interventions for altering existing economic structures and raises serious doubts about whether the shock of COVID-19 will fundamentally disrupt existing economic and racial disparities.

to emphasize gridlock or to advance claims that policy change still happens despite institutional constraints. In contrast, the political economy lens we employ helps illuminate both outcomes. Our evidence demonstrates how both policy stasis and policy change have worked to intensify existing advantage, limiting egalitarian policies while simultaneously making way for inegalitarian ones, ultimately exacerbating disparities in the American system.

STATUS QUO BIAS AND BIPARTISANSHIP IN CONGRESS

American institutional design has been largely static for several decades, yet static institutions interact with other societal conditions in ways that can contribute to important dynamics. The number of veto points in a single country rarely changes, but the degree of status quo bias these veto points impose varies depending on other facets of the policy environment. One application of this logic is incorporated into the comparative political economy literature through its distinction between veto *points* and veto *players*, which are essentially veto points that become activated when actors within one veto point substantively disagree with those in another (Tsebelis 1999).

In this vein, scholars of congressional politics have focused on the causes and consequences of substantive (dis)agreement within and across actors and institutions in the legislative branch. Institutional theories have argued that gridlock and policy inaction are the norm in Congress (Binder 2003; Brady and Volden 2005; Koger 2010), and have emphasized that even when new policies *are* enacted, they are often not substantially different from the original status quo (Clinton 2012). Krehbiel's pivotal politics model incorporates partisan dynamics into these general arguments concerning stasis in congressional policymaking by emphasizing how the tendency toward gridlock is heightened as the parties move apart ideologically (Krehbiel 1998). Inertia and inaction dominate the narrative in this line of work.

But a second strand of literature emphasizes the ability of parties to overcome legislative gridlock in a polarized environment. Several varieties of partisan theories of congressional policymaking, including conditional party government, strategic party government, and cartel theory, all emphasize how majority parties dominate the policymaking process and realize legislative objectives that advance the party's ideological preferences (Aldrich and Rohde 2000; Cox and McCubbins 2005; Finocchiaro and Rohde 2008; Koger and Lebo 2017).

Both institutional and partisan theories of Congress point toward the central importance of party polarization for understanding policymaking, but they view the implications of polarization quite differently. Under the conditions of party polarization that have become one of the most notable features of contemporary American politics, party-centric views of legislative politics see parties as better able to control the legislative process and advance their goals. But institutional theories argue that this polarization makes lawmaking more challenging in the context of a bicameral legislature in which a super-majority is required to pass laws. Thus, party polarization can be a double-edged sword for legislative effectiveness, perhaps making it easier for majority parties to control the agenda but more difficult to realize policy change.

Other scholars, however, argue that legislative actors have essentially adapted to an institutional setting where policymaking is difficult, devising skills and procedures to facilitate compromise and accomplish consequential policy change. Parties are not irrelevant for these theories of lawmaking, but because a substantial amount of consensus across party lines must be reached before Congress can formally act, parties are not central. Views of policymaking that emphasize action rather than stasis argue that policy is made even in challenging institutional and political contexts. David Mayhew exemplifies this perspective in *Divided We Govern*, which makes the well-known argument that Congress is quite capable of enacting important legislation in the context of divided government, with landmark laws typically generating broad bipartisan support (Mayhew 2005).

James Curry and Frances Lee (2019) have expanded this argument in what they refer to as "non-party government." Instead of centering the role of parties in the legislative process or emphasizing congressional inaction, Curry and Lee see bipartisan compromise as the hallmark of congressional activity. Analyzing decades of lawmaking, they find that bipartisan coalitions are essentially no less common during the current era of high party polarization than they were in less polarized times past. One potential implication is that the institutional design of Congress dominates other factors, requiring bipartisan negotiation and compromise irrespective of variations in partisan power and polarization.

How might we reconcile these competing perspectives on the legislative process and the role of partisan competition in Congress? Each offers useful insights, but none fully explains the precise patterns of action and inaction that characterize congressional policymaking. In a sense, both "non-partisan" and "partisan" models of policymaking provide a one-size-fits all theoretical framework for understanding policymaking. To develop a broadly generalizable model of the legislative process, existing perspectives downplay the possibility that different processes are at work for different types of policy, rendering them less useful as standalone frameworks for understanding connections between polarization, policymaking, and distributional outcomes. We argue that a political economy approach, which has been largely overlooked in studies of US parties and Congress, helps make sense of these patterns by illuminating how institutional design and partisan dynamics interact with economic structures to facilitate action on a small set of substantive policy goals and inaction or busywork elsewhere.

THE DISTRIBUTIONAL POLITICAL ECONOMY OF PARTIES, POLARIZATION, AND POLICY (IN)ACTION

It might seem odd to characterize prior research on political parties and the US Congress as paying insufficient attention to political economy. In some sense, research on legislative institutions is the subfield of American politics most attentive to political economy. Public choice perspectives rooted in economic theory are common in congressional research, and arguments about rent-seeking behavior by corporations and other particularized interests in the legislative process appear frequently in work on legislative institutions, policymaking, and voting behavior in Congress (Arnold 1990; Cox and Magar 1999; Diermeier et al. 2005; Kau et al. 1982; Mayhew 1974). Research on parties and Congress has no shortage of microeconomic theoretical foundations.

What is uncommon, however, is a *substantive* political economy perspective. By substantive political economy, we mean a theoretical framework that places economic hierarchies and stratification as central, focusing on how political decision-making shapes and is shaped by macroeconomic outcomes, particularly those that are distributional and class or race correlated. Understanding how macroeconomic structures and associated social hierarchies interact with politics offers considerable insight into the workings of partisan competition and congressional policymaking, well beyond the ideas existing studies have gleaned from microeconomic logics of congressional behavior.

A substantive political economy perspective on parties, polarization, and lawmaking shifts the analytical focus from how much policy is made to what the content of policy is and who wins or loses when policy changes or remains stagnant.[6] Previously, we identified three seemingly contradictory findings from prior work: (1) the general tendency of status quo maintenance in the legislative arena, (2) the role of parties in shaping legislative agendas and policy, and (3) the ongoing prevalence of bipartisan compromise in successful attempts at policy change. To reconcile these patterns, we turn toward an account that draws on structural power theory, which enables us to make sense of policy action as well as inaction and connects these policymaking patterns to the economic hierarchies that enable and reinforce them.

Our argument is that America's institutional design is biased toward elites, and this elite bias has only intensified as economic disparities have widened. Under current conditions, this bias manifests in both a tendency to protect the status quo and a related tendency for bipartisan coalitions to produce substantive policy changes *of a particular sort*, namely those advancing the goals of economic elites. Policy inaction is beneficial to elite actors in part because those at the pinnacle of the current economic and political power structure benefit disproportionately from maintaining a status quo that enabled their position at the top of the hierarchy. But occasionally elites seek policy change to further their interests, and we argue that as inequality has risen, increasing ideological polarization – along with changes in the internal dynamics of both the Democratic and Republican parties – has made it increasingly likely that the sorts of substantive policies able to generate sufficient bipartisan support are those that sustain or even exacerbate existing economic hierarchies that benefit the elite.

These dynamics reflect structural power at work – individuals, corporations, and groups situated in privileged economic positions exert considerable leverage over policy processes by virtue of their (perceived) role in fostering prosperity for all.[7] Detailed discussions of structural power and its consequences for the policy process can be found in the introductory chapter of this volume as well as our other work on the topic (Witko et al. 2021). For our purposes here, it is sufficient to emphasize that structural power theory expects almost all politicians – regardless of their partisan affiliation – to want to make sure these economic influencers remain invested in sustaining the economy (Swank 1992). In essence, structural

[6] Some studies, of course, pay a great deal of attention to these issues. A sampling includes Bartels 2016; Erikson et al. 2003; Hacker and Pierson 2010; and McCarty et al. 2006.

[7] For discussions on the material and ideational foundations of structural power, see Bell 2012; Block 1977; Culpepper 2015; and Fairfield 2015.

power exists when certain actors have power simply due to the position that they occupy in a stratified economy. As result, policies that advance wealthy interests manage to attract bipartisan support, allowing them to advance successfully through the circuitous legislative process while policy efforts they oppose tend to fall short. The discussion that follows provides support for these expectations, demonstrating how a political economy approach generally, and structural power theory specifically, help illuminate the peculiar patterns of congressional action and inaction that are unexplained by other approaches.

THE INEGALITARIAN CONSEQUENCES OF POLICY STAGNATION

There are at least three scenarios in which policy stagnation may have distributional effects. The first and most overt is *policy sclerosis*, which happens when problems emerge but policies to address them cannot gain traction. Rising inequality has been a defining characteristic of the US economy for forty years, yet there is still contention over whether this constitutes a "problem" and even greater disagreement over what should be done. Those who profit from ignoring the problem, of course, are situated at the top of the economic hierarchy and possess considerable structural power, while the beneficiaries of such policy change lack any such leverage. Second, *policy drift* occurs when shifting economic or societal conditions change the effects of the existing policy structure in ways that increasingly align with (or drift toward) the interests of actors who then intentionally block action in in these domains (Hacker 2004, 2005; Hacker et al. 2015; Mettler 2016). In such cases, simply blocking policy reform works to benefit that actor. The minimum wage is one of many examples of policy drift, as inflation erodes the real value of a constant nominal minimum wage level over time (Bartels 2016; Galvin 2016).[8] Although policy drift and policy sclerosis both result from inaction, they differ in two important ways: (1) unlike drift, sclerosis does not require the meaning or impact of existing policy to change, rather sclerosis results any time a new or potential problem arises and policymakers do not act to address it, and (2) sclerosis may occur without intent on the part of political actors. Third, policy

[8] Other examples of policy drift come from the domains of public insurance provision, social welfare, labor law and enforcement, infrastructure, and education. See Beland 2007; Galvin and Hacker 2020; Mettler 2016; and Rocco 2017.

stagnation can work to reinforce existing hierarchies through *policy stretching*. Stretching happens when existing policies are applied in domains or to problems they were never intended to address. Policy stretching typically occurs outside Congress, in regulatory or legal contexts where bureaucrats and judges make choices about how to apply, extend, or interpret statutory guidance. For example, in the throes of the Great Recession, regulators stretched the existing policy framework of federal deposit insurance to provide government guarantees backstopping the debts of FDIC banks as well as their bank holding companies and commercial subsidiaries (Funk and Hirschman 2014; Geithner 2014; Katz 2015; Rahman and Thelen, this volume).

Policy stagnation does not always and in every case benefit economic elites. Sometimes an inability to enact policy reforms has led to de facto expansions of the welfare state as societal conditions have changed, such as the extensions of disability benefits and healthcare (Galvin and Hacker 2020). And regulators occasionally stretch existing policy to benefit ordinary Americans, as when the 1963 Clean Air Act has been used to impose limits on greenhouse gases not stipulated in the statute itself. But these are exceptions. Absent some exogenous egalitarian change in the economy, congressional action is needed to counter the dynamics producing rising levels of inequality. Policy sclerosis does nothing to address these inegalitarian processes, and policy drift and policy stretching most often work to reproduce and deepen inequality, not counteract it. Status quo bias in the contemporary United States, then, is elite bias.

Status quo bias makes successful policy change more challenging. Yet in the current context of deep inequality, the weak and marginalized typically need policy *change* to accomplish their goals. In contrast, because elites benefit from the existing power hierarchy, accomplishing their goals often requires less direct policy action – drift, stretching, and sclerosis often suit their aims perfectly. Moreover, elite interests possess greater structural power and more resources, which they can leverage to prevent threatening policy change. Thus, the tendency toward stagnation often aligns with elite interests. And as inequality deepens, power advantages for economic elites are likely to increase as well, making it easier for established elites to block equality-promoting policy change. As a result, the distributional consequences of policy inaction are likely to become even more inegalitarian when existing levels of inequality are high. That is, inaction is most likely to reproduce and exacerbate inequalities when disparities are already extreme.

PARTY DYNAMICS, POLARIZATION, AND INEGALITARIAN POLICY ACTION

The second part of our argument relates to policy *action*. Even in the current context of hyper-polarization, legislative policymaking occurs. Government programs are funded (even if by continuing resolutions rather than the regular appropriations process). Some new issues are addressed, and outdated policies are updated. In line with this perspective, Curry and Lee (2019) have argued that bipartisan compromise remains the norm. Unlike work emphasizing congressional polarization and stalemate, they emphasize how party leaders manage to negotiate and build consensus. In their view, leaders prove their mettle not by holding their caucuses together to win ideological battles, but by generating bipartisan policy agreements.

Juxtaposed against the focus on partisan conflict, this "bipartisan lawmaking" argument disrupts the received wisdom. But in many ways, "bipartisan lawmaking" repackages and repurposes Mayhew's familiar arguments about legislating under divided government, which expects compromise. Viewed through Mayhew's lens, it is much less surprising that institutional imperatives continue to incentivize majority parties to compromise, negotiate, and co-opt members of the minority despite rising polarization. Absent major institutional reform, which has not been forthcoming, the institutional requirements of congressional policymaking continue to demand legislative processes that produce some bipartisan compromise.

While the process of bipartisan lawmaking is superficially the same, this approach stops short of considering how policy outcomes might vary depending on the policymaking environment as a political economy approach would do. To understand the implications of bipartisan lawmaking for the *substance* of policy outcomes, we must ask how this policymaking environment may shape the kinds of policy that can (and cannot) generate consensus. A political economy approach to understanding policymaking allows us to specify the kinds of action that are most and least likely given the dimensions of the contemporary policymaking context.

To begin, while legislators have incentives to legislate effectively, the difficulty of consensus-building around substantively significant policy is challenging in the current context. When obstacles to accomplishing meaningful policy change are steep, legislators may resort to generating identifiable outputs however they can. As a result, they are likely to turn their energy toward less controversial and less meaningful policy actions, such as basic institutional maintenance or bureaucratic housekeeping, rather than attempting significant policy change on controversial economic issues (Morgan 2011). Thus, while the overall quantity of policymaking may appear similar, a polarized context is likely to result in policymaking focused on essential tasks and maintenance, not reimagining entire policy frameworks. Although such minimalist policy action is not precisely stagnation, it cannot accomplish the sort of change necessary to disrupt entrenched systems of inequality that privilege wealthy elites.

In addition to the tendency toward policy action that does not rock the boat, the current policymaking environment is likely to intersect with incentives for bipartisan compromise in ways that bias meaningful policy changes toward the interests of economic elites. Several features of the environment contribute to this pattern. First, polarization has been *asymmetric*, with Republicans shifting to the right rather than Democrats shifting left. While legislators may manage to sustain respectable levels of legislative output despite polarization, substantive policy outcomes that can generate bipartisan support are likely to be more ideologically conservative under the contemporary dynamic of asymmetric polarization. Because conservative policies tend to favor the interests of economic elites (Kelly 2009), a combination of asymmetric polarization and bipartisan lawmaking are likely to produce outcomes that favor wealthy interests.

Relatedly, internal party dynamics are likely to interact with institutional incentives toward cooperation in ways that shape policy content. Republicans are more ideologically organized than Democrats, who pursue a coalitional strategy bringing together numerous groups under a more diverse ideological umbrella (Grossman and Hopkins 2016). If policy action requires co-opting members of the opposing party, this difference in organizational strategy places Democrats at a competitive disadvantage and is therefore consequential for the content of policy. Since Democrats are a diverse coalition, using group-focused concessions to peel off parts of that coalition is an effective way to build bipartisan support. In contrast, the ideological cohesiveness of Republicans makes co-opting them more challenging. As a result, the sorts of policies around which coalitions can be built are again likely to be more conservative and in line with elite interests.

In addition, the structure of the interest system is likely to shape the substantive outcomes produced in a status quo biased system that requires bipartisan compromise. Two contemporary dynamics are particularly relevant. First, as economic inequality has risen, those at the top have disproportionate access to financial resources that facilitate political influence. Second, labor unions, which once provided some counterbalance to wealthy interests, have declined. Although corporations and other elite interests have always had substantial resources to intervene in policy processes, their influence has expanded at the same time that union decline has undermined an important organizational presence for middle- and lower-class interests (Witko et al. 2021). Because of these processes, Democrats have relied increasingly on support from high-income elites. This makes them easier targets for Republican co-optation, particularly on economic issues.

To recap, US institutions create status quo bias and require bipartisan lawmaking. When these institutions operate alongside deep economic inequalities, asymmetric polarization, and diffuse and declining lower-class power resources, both policy action and inaction tend to favor economic elites. Status quo bias benefits elite interests who are already situated at the top of the hierarchy and are often well served by policy inaction. Moreover, this elite tilt to the status quo is only exacerbated as economic inequality rises. At the same time, the nature of party polarization and internal party dynamics, particularly as inequality has grown and lower-class power resources have declined, have made it increasingly likely that the areas where bipartisan compromise flourish lack substance or favor the interests of economic elites.

EVIDENCE OF ELITE ADVANTAGES IN LEGISLATIVE POLICY (IN)ACTION

Although it is beyond the scope of this chapter to evaluate all the expectations that flow from this argument, in the space that remains we present some evidence of the theorized patterns. In addition, our prior work (with colleagues) has provided considerable insight into the ways policy (in) action shapes income concentration and has different trajectories and substantive outcomes depending on the distribution of economic resources (Enns et al. 2014; Kelly 2020; Witko et al. forthcoming). Here, we start with some aggregate evidence of linkages between policy stagnation, bipartisan lawmaking, and rising inequality in the United States. We then discuss patterns in specific domains, which illustrate how processes producing both policy successes and failures have aligned with the interests of economic elites.

REPRODUCING HIERARCHY THROUGH STAGNATION

In general, we expect a connection between the policy stasis generated by status quo bias, with the inegalitarian effects of status quo bias becoming more prevalent as inequality rises. To measure policy stasis, we use an index of policy stagnation that incorporates the overall volume of national legislative policymaking weighted for the importance of the policies produced and coded so that higher values indicate *less* policy output.[9] To capture income concentration, we use the share of market income received by the top 1 percent of tax units inclusive of capital gains.[10] Figure 1.2 examines the relationship between the standardized versions of these measures in the United States over time.

The association between the two variables is strong (r = 0.61). While the two series occasionally diverge, overall when inequality increases, so does

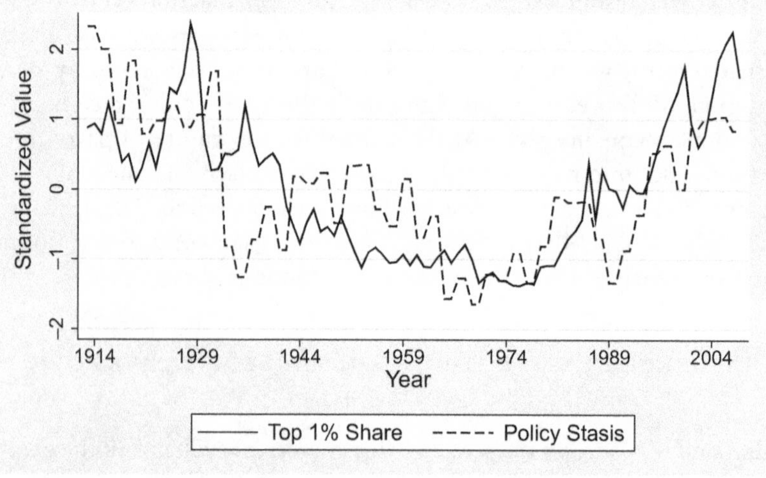

FIGURE 1.2 Policy stasis and income concentration, 1913–2007

[9] See Grant and Kelly 2008. The measure is similar to a factor score based on the number of public laws passed in each Congress as well as several additional measures that capture important lawmaking. In essence, multiple measures of legislative productivity are combined into a summary index of legislative output. The constituent measures include counts of landmark laws from historians and political scientists, as well as counts of total laws passed. The simplest way to think about this measure is that it captures the amount of legislation approved, weighted for importance. This is why the measure we use here has a U-shape while some other measures show a steady decline in productivity from the New Deal onward.

[10] Data from the World Inequality Database (https://wid.world/).

policy stasis. Conversely, when inequality declines, policy stasis does as well. And this positive relationship between inequality and stasis manifests in both the pre- and post-1960 periods. A natural next question is whether this association represents a causal relationship and, if so, which direction causation flows. A simple Granger causality test offers some leverage on these issues. This test starts with the logic that the best way to predict a future value of a variable is to look at the recent past. If additional explanatory power is produced by including past values of other variables in addition to the outcome of interest, then Granger causality is present. We find Granger causality running in both directions, from policy stasis to income concentration and from income concentration to policy stasis. That is, there is a statistically significant effect of lagged policy stasis on income concentration while controlling for past values of income concentration as well as a statistically significant effect of lagged income concentration on policy stasis while controlling for lagged values of policy stasis. This provides evidence in line with our expectation that policy inaction generally contributes to inequality, and also that inaction increases as inequality rises.

Next, we consider whether policy stagnation is always associated with rising income concentration or whether the distributional effects of stagnation differ depending on the current level of inequality. Our argument suggests that the level of inequality in the policy environment conditions the degree to which policy inaction benefits the rich: as inequality rises, we expect wealthy interests to capitalize even more on status quo bias. To evaluate this expectation, we conduct a time-series regression analysis in the form of an error correction model (ECM) with top income shares (TIS) as the outcome and policy stagnation (PS) as the explanatory variable, using annual data from the Great Depression to the Great Recession (1939–2006):[11]

$$\Delta TIS_t = \alpha_0 + \alpha_1 TIS_{t-1} + \beta_1 \Delta PS_t + \beta_2 PS_{t-1} + \beta_3 (PS_{t-1} * TIS_{t-1}) + e_t.$$

This analysis estimates a short-term effect (β_1) for policy stagnation on inequality as well as a long-term effect spread out over time (β_2). We also include a multiplicative interaction between the lagged level of stagnation

[11] An ECM is appropriate here because these two variables are co-integrated. In the previous VAR analysis, we saw evidence of two-way causation between income concentration and policy stagnation, which raises potential concern about the exogeneity of policy stagnation in the ECM we estimate. However, when we estimate an ECM with policy stagnation as the outcome and income concentration as the explanatory variable, we find that the exogeneity assumption of the ECM is satisfied.

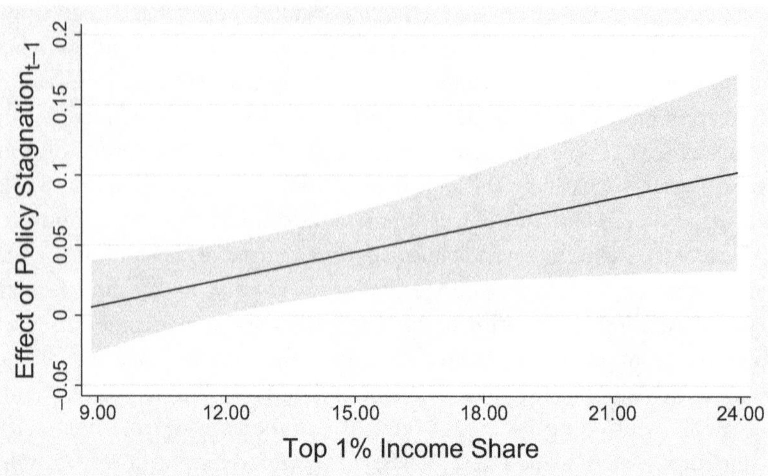

FIGURE 1.3 Inegalitarian effects of policy stagnation increase as income concentration rises, 1939–2006

and the lagged level of inequality. The coefficient for this interaction term (β_3) allows us to assess whether the effect of stagnation increases as inequality rises.

We use the estimates from this ECM to create Figure 1.3, which depicts the long-run coefficient for policy stagnation at observed levels of top shares. The results show that the effect of policy stagnation on inequality varies depending on the existing level of income concentration. On the left side of the chart, when inequality is at its lowest levels, the effect of policy stagnation is indistinguishable from zero. However, as inequality rises, the inegalitarian effects emerge and increase. This is evidence that the economic implications of stagnation are shaped by the existing distribution of economic resources. As we have theorized, when income is concentrated, inaction serves to further entrench the existing economic hierarchy, while policy action is essential for disrupting inequality. But when inequality is already low, policy stagnation is not a relevant factor in shaping distributional outcomes.

POLICY ACTION PROTECTS THE STATUS QUO IN TIMES OF INEQUALITY

The aforementioned analysis demonstrates that policy stagnation exacerbates inequality, especially when income concentration is already high.

However, even when status quo bias predominates and policy is relatively stagnant, bipartisan lawmaking continues, at least to some extent. But we have argued that the substance of policy that garners bipartisan support varies depending on the policy environment. In the current context of high inequality and its associated complex of asymmetric polarization and declining lower-class power resources, we expect policy activity to be both less substantive and more favorable to elite interests.

To begin considering these expectations, we examine how income concentration is correlated with policymaking in three broad domains: domestic economic policy (including tax rates and fiscal policy more generally), government operations, and immigration and crime.[12] In broad strokes, substantive economic policymaking, which would presumably modify the economic status quo, is likely to decline under conditions of greater inequality, while legislators instead devote attention to housekeeping and diversionary (i.e., noneconomic) issues. Figure 1.4 charts the proportion of public laws addressing each topic from 1949 to 2008 (standardized to aid comparison) along with the top 1 percent income share.

Several notable patterns emerge. First, income concentration has a sizable negative correlation with domestic economic policymaking (r = –0.80). As inequality increases, legislators enact less policy directly connected to economic outcomes and distributional decisions about resource allocation. Second, policy action in the domain of government operations is strongly positively correlated with inequality (r = 0.87). Government operations policymaking can be thought of as basic housekeeping – budgetary requests, civil service, appointments, procurement, etc. And as inequality rises, a greater proportion of lawmaking deals with matters that are essential but mundane. Finally, income inequality is positively correlated with policy production concerning crime and immigration.

These patterns suggest policymakers are less likely to enact policies that might disrupt the economic status quo under conditions of high inequality. Instead, they focus lawmaking on essential but economically inconsequential government operations or on substantive issues like crime and

[12] Data from Policy Agendas Project US public laws dataset (www.comparativeagendas.net/, accessed 5/2/2020). Categories are based on major topic codes. Government operations is topic code 20. Domestic economic policy includes macroeconomic (code 1), agriculture (4), labor (5), transportation (10), housing (14), and banking and commerce (15). Immigration (9) and crime (12) comprise our third category. We calculate the proportion of all public laws (including those not included in our three categories) that fall within each domain.

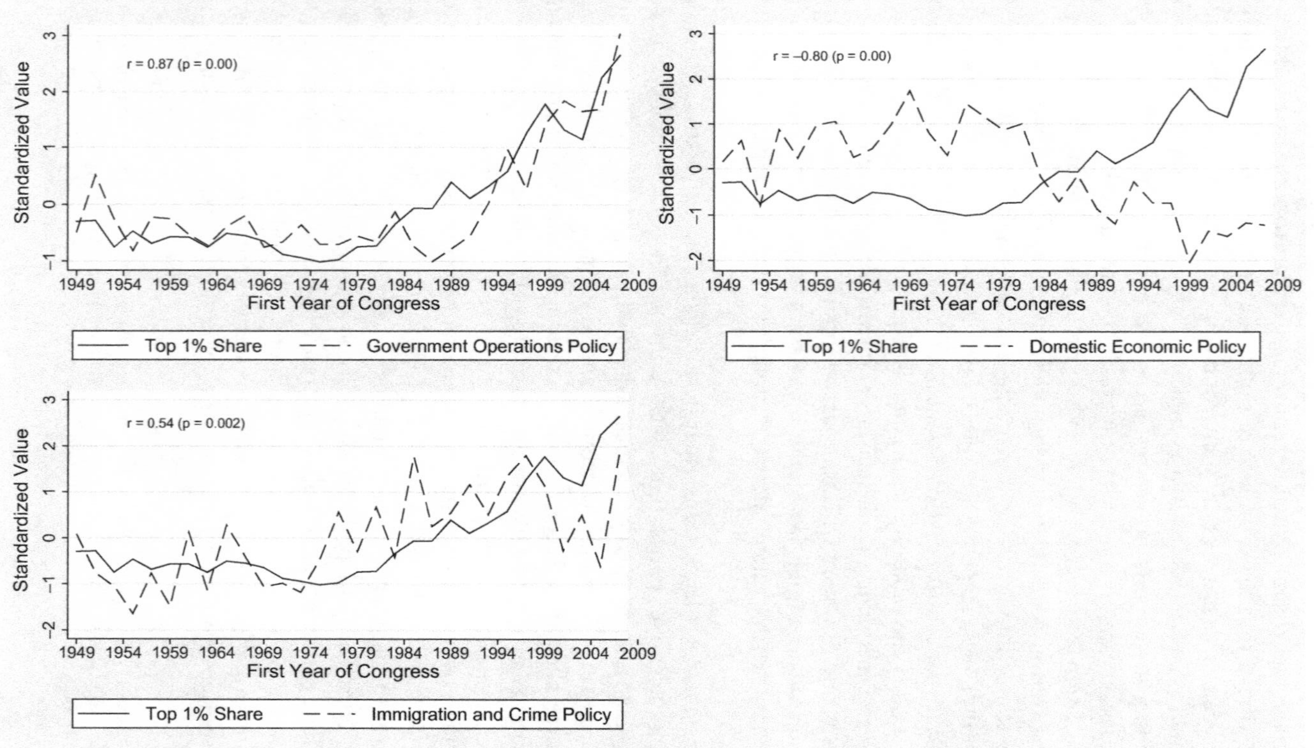

FIGURE 1.4 Income concentration and the topics of public laws

immigration, which may divert attention away from inequality and other economic concerns. Analyzing the substance of policy in this way indicates that even though bipartisan policy production may continue under conditions of rising inequality and asymmetric polarization, the issues that gain bipartisan support vary considerably. While policy activity has continued, its content has become less focused on changes that might alter the economic status quo.

POLICY ACTION FOR THE RICH, POLICY STAGNATION FOR THE REST

Economic policymaking declines significantly as inequality rises, although even in this domain some activity occurs. However, our political economy model of policymaking suggests that when economic lawmaking does happen in the current American policy environment, it is likely to reinforce existing hierarchies that favor elite interests. To illustrate this process, we consider policymaking in two specific economic domains – financial deregulation and labor law. The dynamics of financial deregulation demonstrate how the cross-pressures facing the Democratic party occasionally enable bipartisan economic policy action that favors elite interests, while patterns of policy stagnation and drift in labor law emphasize how status quo bias works against the interests of ordinary Americans.

In the realm of financial deregulation, significant policy changes, as well as policy stretching, have advanced the interests of economic elites, with deregulation being one of the key policy actions contributing to rising inequality (Hacker and Pierson 2010; Volscho and Kelly 2012). As wages stagnated and inequality escalated in the 1980s and 1990s, Congress largely ignored these issues and instead focused considerable attention on deregulating finance – a policy goal prioritized by the wealthiest and most structurally powerful sector in the American economy as they aimed to expand their already-escalating profits. By our count, Congress debated dozens of financial deregulation bills and passed at least ten different laws on behalf of various financial sector interests during this period. Ultimately, in the late 1990s, when all major financial sector interests finally converged around the goal of completely deconstructing Depression-era regulatory restrictions, policymakers obliged (Suárez and Kolodny 2011). The resulting Gramm-Leach-Bliley legislation eliminated the existing regulatory framework and deepened the dramatic concentration of wealth in the financial sector.

The structural power of a united financial sector along with well-targeted outreach to cross-pressured Democrats enabled these wealthy interests to quickly overcome status quo bias and accomplish major deregulatory reform in the space of a single congressional term despite divided government. Throughout the Gramm-Leach-Bliley policy process, finance exploited its structural power advantage and convinced policymakers on both sides of the aisle that financial deregulation was essential to American prosperity. Republican and Democratic members of Congress frequently pointed to the structural significance of finance as a central rationale motivating their commitment to financial deregulation, calling finance "the irrigation system for our economy" and lauding deregulation as "vital for the future of our country."[13] Democratic support for deregulation may seem particularly surprising given the party's typical ideological orientation, but by the 1990s campaign support for Democrats from the financial sector had increased substantially (Witko et al. 2021) and the Democratic position on this issue became quite similar to that of Republicans, despite polarization in other domains (Kelly 2020). Individual Democrats who were particularly receptive to the idea of finance as structurally significant or especially reliant on financial sector contributions played key roles at critical points in the policy process enabling deregulation to advance.[14]

Despite some efforts to reinvigorate financial sector oversight in the aftermath of the Great Recession (2007–9), the most advantaged financial interests managed to preserve their basic business models and shield their profits first by convincing bureaucrats to protect many financial companies from losses and then by minimizing postcrisis re-regulatory policy efforts, as epitomized in the 2010 Dodd-Frank policy process. In more recent years, financial interests have regained the upper hand in shaping policy outcomes toward greater deregulation. They have accomplished their goals not only though through policy stretching, which has successfully undermined the resources and regulatory will for oversight (Ziegler and Wooley 2016), but also through additional bipartisan lawmaking, which has resulted in new statutory reductions in regulation (e.g., 2018 Economic Growth, Regulatory Relief and Consumer Protection Act). When wealthy interests have sought policy action to accomplish financial deregulation, they have been able to exercise considerable influence over

[13] Quotes from congressional floor speeches in the debate surrounding Gramm-Leach-Bliley, 106th Congress.

[14] For more details on the way the economic power of affluent financial sector interests facilitated this dramatic reform and thereby increased their profits and intensified inequality, see Keller and Kelly (2015) and Witko et al. (2021).

Republicans as well as cross-pressured Democrats to build the necessary bipartisan consensus. In other moments, they have used the tendency toward policy stagnation, namely blocking maneuvers and policy stretching, to limit regulatory reach.

In contrast, policymaking on behalf of lower- and middle-class Americans in the arena of labor law has been plagued by sclerosis and drift. Legislation that would facilitate union certification through "card check" – a process by which unions gain recognition when a majority of workers sign union cards rather than the more onerous procedure of requiring a vote – has been at the top of organized labor's list of employment law priorities for decades. But structurally powerful interests maintain staunch opposition to card check legislation and have mobilized their enormous resource advantage to block policy change. As a result, even when Democrats controlled both chambers of Congress during the Obama administration, union efforts to advance card check legislation stalled because they could not construct the necessary bipartisan coalition in the Senate (Francia 2013). Status quo bias and the resulting policy sclerosis in this case clearly favored wealthy interests.

The main area of labor law where organized labor has made modest headway in Congress has been with regard to the minimum wage, with the most recent statutory increases in the federal minimum coming in 1996 and 2007. But these occasional bursts of legislative action conceal a policy arena dominated by inaction and drift. The logic of federal minimum wage policy requires congressional action just to allow wages to keep pace with inflation. In practice, this has meant that as inequality has increased and pro-elite status quo bias has intensified over the past thirty years, minimum wage workers have suffered increasingly long periods in which the real value of their wages have declined and their families have fallen into poverty. Despite being an issue with widespread public support and minimal economic cost (Bartels 2008), accomplishing even small minimum wage increases has required herculean effort by organized labor and their pro-worker allies in order to overcome modest business opposition and build sufficient consensus to change the law. Indeed, the minimum wage has most often appeared on the congressional agenda as a way to provide political cover for the simultaneous passage of other far less popular provisions benefitting business or other wealthy interests.

Thus, actors in the finance sector have frequently been able to leverage their structural position and economic resources to win support from cross-pressured Democrats to overcome status quo bias and accomplish policy change. On the other hand, policy stagnation in pro-worker employment law illustrates the fundamental disadvantages lower- and middle-class interests face in accomplishing policy action that might disrupt conditions of deep economic inequality. Here wealthy interests prefer inaction, and their structural power and resource advantage easily keeps union initiatives sidelined. Overcoming this opposition in the current policy environment is nearly impossible: even small adjustments in the most basic employment protection, the minimum wage, have required extraordinary leveraging of organizational resources on behalf of lower-class interests.

CONCLUSION

The focus of this chapter has been on legislative policymaking institutions and how they fit into the broader American political economy. National policy institutions are biased toward the status quo, yet bipartisan compromise still enables certain policy changes to occur. We have argued that the general systemic bias toward the status quo tends to benefit economic elites and impede the policy changes needed to undermine economic disparities. At the same time, rising inequality and asymmetric polarization have made it more likely that the policy proposals capable of gaining sufficient bipartisan support to overcome status quo bias are policies that further exacerbate existing inequalities.

Our analysis also coincides with arguments made elsewhere in the volume. Exploring how institutional design interacts with social conditions is an ongoing theme. Our chapter also points to the importance of understanding how fundamental economic change and firm reorganization shapes political power, which is explored more deeply in Ben Ansell and Jane Gingrich's excellent chapter. As well, Alex Hertel-Fernandez takes a much deeper dive into the history of the American labor movement, which expands on our brief discussion of stagnation in the domain of labor law. Our chapter has also only scratched the surface with regard to the central role of federalism in America's political economy, which is a theme that is much more fully addressed in Jacob Grumbach, Jacob Hacker, and Paul Pierson's incisive analysis.

Our goal has been to place the US Congress squarely into a substantive political economy perspective. While existing institutional perspectives on Congress are useful, work that links the arrangement of legislative institutions and the behavior of actors within those institutions to stratified economic structures and outcomes is too rare. The political economy perspective on congressional policymaking that we have developed here points to the important ways that political conditions, legislative institutions, and class-based disparities are linked. We have only scratched the surface with the analysis conducted here, and we look hopefully toward future efforts to more fully theorize and empirically assess how economic power relations are reflected in legislative institutions and behavior, and how these institutions can serve to reinforce or undermine existing disparities.

2

The Role of the Law in the American Political Economy

K. Sabeel Rahman and Kathleen Thelen

On the same day that the White House announced the nomination of Brett Kavanaugh to the US Supreme Court, it turned to business groups to aid in the public relations campaign to secure his confirmation (Goldstein 2018). Once seated, Kavanaugh solidified a strong pro-business orientation on the nation's highest court, an orientation further consolidated with the eleventh-hour appointment of Amy Coney Barrett in the run-up to the November 2020 election. Meanwhile, the entire federal bench was also being transformed through the confirmations – at an unprecedented pace – of a string of young conservative jurists in the Trump administration (Ruiz et al. 2020). Most of the newest additions are drawn from the membership lists of the Federalist Society, a powerful organization composed of lawyers and legal scholars committed to an originalist reading of the American constitution and a radical free market economic ideology.

This chapter examines the role of the judiciary in the American political economy, tracing the impact of the law and the courts on political-economic institutions and outcomes, with an emphasis on developments since the 1970s. There is no dearth of literature on the courts in political science. Indeed, an entire subfield of public law is devoted to the American legal system (see, among many others, Barnes and Burke 2015; Epp 1998, 2009; Melnick 1983, 1994; Rosenberg 1991), and the literature on American political development has long emphasized the role of the courts in the origins of the country's distinctive institutional arrangements (e.g.,

We are grateful for valuable input on this chapter from the other authors in this volume. We extend thanks as well to the participants in the MPIfG workshop in January 2020, especially Martin Höpner and Fritz Scharpf.

Gilman 1993; Skowronek 1982). There exists as well a small but important group of studies that compare the role of the courts in the United States to that in other rich democracies (see, especially, Kagan 2001, 2019; also Kelemen 2011). Beyond political science, historians and legal scholars have revisited important instances in which business interests have engaged the judiciary to shape the political economy (e.g., Forbath 1991; Maclean 2017; Winkler 2018). So far, however, there is no overarching analysis that situates the United States in a comparative frame to illuminate the role the judiciary has been playing in shaping important political-economic institutions and outcomes in the current period.

This is a huge gap because there is ample reason to think that the impact of the courts on the American political economy, already significant, is growing. In a sweeping analysis of several decades of Supreme Court rulings, Epstein, Landes, and Posner (2013) find that the Roberts court has delivered more business-friendly decisions than any other court in the postwar period. While some decisions mark major, highly visible departures from precedent (as, for example, in the *Janus* decision discussed in the following), many others – not just at the Supreme Court but also in lower-level courts – turn on seemingly smaller, often technical matters. The cumulative effect, however, has been to tilt outcomes in a decidedly business-friendly direction.

Organized business interests do not always get their way, but we argue that they enjoy distinctive advantages in the United States. Business interests thrive in the "quiet politics" venue of the courts (Culpepper 2010). And within this setting, they also enjoy all the advantages Marc Galanter attributes to "repeat players" over "one shotters" (Galanter 1974). While "one shotters" can score victory in particular cases, repeat players are able to build up extensive legal expertise, cultivate close relationships with institutional incumbents, and play a long-term strategy. Crucially, Galanter emphasizes that these advantages *cumulate over time,* resulting in a gradual shift of law in favor of repeat players.

In this chapter, we argue that within the American legal system, organized business interests are examples of Galanter's repeat players *par excellence.* Their presence is pervasive at all levels, their influence is targeted at achieving specific legal and policy outcomes, and they are in it for the long run. Unlike legislative and presidential politics, where the clash of interests is played out more openly, the strategic exercise of influence through the judiciary operates more subtly, beneath the veneer of neutral, objective doctrines of law and the formalism of legal reasoning. Yet beneath this veneer, the courts have served as a critical arena in which business interests have secured key victories that have shaped the trajectory of American capitalism. Within the literature on the political economy of the rich democracies, the judiciary is a crucial, understudied, alternative avenue through which business interests have been able not just to nudge outcomes, but to tilt the playing field as a whole, to their advantage.

This chapter proceeds in six steps. We begin by comparing the United States to other countries in order to highlight the distinctive role of the courts in the American political economy. The second section then sketches, in broad strokes, the historical trajectory through which the courts have shaped the contours of the political-economic landscape in the United States. The third section traces business strategies on the terrain of the law since the 1970s, highlighting the interconnections across several distinct arenas of influence: in the legal academy through donations supporting the cultivation of a cadre of conservative jurists, in the political realm through growing involvement in judicial elections and appointments to the bench, and in the courts themselves through litigation on behalf of business interests at all levels. The fourth section then documents the use of the law by business interests to achieve lasting institutional changes across three broad realms: (a) measures aimed at enhancing corporate power vis-à-vis the state and other organized groups, (b) attacks on potential countervailing forces (particularly labor unions), and (c) efforts to hobble the regulatory capacities of the state itself. The fifth section considers how the courts fit into the rest of the political-economic landscape, linking the present analysis to other contributions in this volume by drawing out the ways in which the courts operate as a strategic field of action separate from but in close interaction with business interests in other arenas. Echoing Galanter, this section emphasizes how the legal landscape in the United States privileges business interests that command the kinds of resources that allow them to achieve durable gains and to accomplish some of their most cherished aims outside the glare of democratic politics. A final section concludes.

THE ROLE OF THE COURTS: THE AMERICAN POLITICAL ECONOMY IN COMPARATIVE PERSPECTIVE

Compared to other rich democracies, the American judiciary is more powerful, more politicized, and more directly involved in shaping outcomes in the political economy. The power of the judiciary is largely a matter of constitutional design and long-standing historical practice.

In Europe, the principle of parliamentary supremacy prevailed, fusing executive and legislative powers and assigning the courts a clearly subordinate position. This is a feature that distinguishes the United States not just from Europe's "coordinated" market economies, but also from other "liberal" market economies such as Britain, which lacked any form of judicial review of legislative action until very recently (2005), and then with a much narrower charge.[1]

The US judiciary is also uncommonly politicized, and the composition of the courts itself is contested in ways that are highly unusual among the rich democracies. Appointments to the Supreme Court are now intense partisan battles, increasingly accompanied by campaigning by outside interest groups (Cameron et al. 2018; Sessa-Hawkins and Perez 2017).[2] These features are unheard of in Europe, where high court appointments typically require strong bipartisan agreement (via supermajority rules, for example). More generally, and beyond the high courts, seats on the bench in Europe are a matter of rigorous civil service education and testing, internal promotion and/or appointment by special neutral judicial bodies (Kagan 2001). In the United States, by contrast, partisanship and ideology play significant roles in shaping the selection of all federal judicial nominees, particularly for the higher-level courts (Federal Appeals Courts), whose impact on political outcomes resonates most widely (Bonica and Sen 2017).

Selection procedures for seats on lower courts in the United States are, if anything, more unusual in comparative perspective. A very large majority of state judges face some kind of popular election: fully 90 percent are elected or confirmed by voters, and in thirty-eight states all judges are popularly elected (Shugerman 2012: 3). Judicial races at these levels are tantalizing targets for interest-group influence. Election to lower-level courts are low-salience events in which uninformed voters are at a distinct disadvantage relative to interest groups with high levels of information and intense interest in the outcome. Campaign spending and "dark money" contributions from outside groups play a significant and growing role in state Supreme Court elections in the United States (Keith et al. 2019; Sessa-Hawkins and Perez 2017).

[1] Many other countries have constitutional courts that have authority to interpret the constitution, but in other advanced democracies these courts are either less powerful, or less politicized, or (usually) both.

[2] Hasen (2013: 244–50), for example, documents increasing partisan polarization around Supreme Court nominees, with a growing number of no votes even for successful candidates.

Finally, the courts are themselves a critical arena of political contestation. As pointed out in the introduction to this volume, the American judiciary performs many of the administrative functions that in European countries are managed by an elite and professionalized bureaucracy. Robert Kagan's seminal analysis of "adversarial legalism" underscores the stark difference between the United States and its advanced democratic peers on this dimension. While other rich democracies rely on administration and policy implementation through professional bureaucracies, corporatist negotiation, or government-appointed expert bodies, the United States "more often relies on courts, lawyers, legal threats, and legal contestation in making and implementing public policies" (Kagan 2019: 3). Courts are thus central actors shaping key aspects of the American political economy – among other ways, through their interpretation of common law disputes over property, contract, and tort law, and through their judicial oversight of states' "police power" to legislate in the name of public welfare.

Current partisan polarization has only heightened the importance of the courts in shaping policy outcomes (Hasen 2013; McCubbins et al. 1995). The Supreme Court has always had the final say on matters of constitutional interpretation. However, as Hasen (2013) points out, political gridlock magnifies the role of the Court on matters of statutory interpretation as well. In principle, Congress always has the power to revise the Court's interpretation of a federal statute by amending it or by passing a new law. However, it is increasingly difficult to assemble the supermajorities needed to "correct" the Court's interpretation of important legislation. Political stalemate thus drives an increase in the power of the Court "whether or not the Justices affirmatively seek that additional power" (Hasen 2013: 208). Hasen documents a dramatic drop in congressional overrides of the Supreme Court's statutory interpretations since 1991 and shows that bipartisan override activity "essentially halted" in 2009. He concludes that under current conditions of gridlock and polarization, "the Court's word on the meaning of statutes is now final almost as often as its word on constitutional interpretation" (209).

In sum, compared to other rich democracies, the courts play an outsized role in the American political economy. This impact, however, is mostly invisible to the average citizen because political contestation within the judiciary plays out quite differently from more visible and conventional forms of political warfare. Courts operate on the basis of legal doctrine, precedent, and professional norms, but behind the putatively neutral rulings, there are always normative and political judgment calls being made in interpreting and applying statutes and Constitutional provisions. Thus, the most successful repeat players are those who are able to operate across multiple venues, to influence not just the outcome of individual cases, or the composition of specific courts, but also the evolution of legal reasoning and the conventional wisdom on which the legal community draws. Within the United States, organized business interests are uniquely well-placed to exercise this broad influence.

ORIGINS AND EVOLUTION: THE ROLE OF THE LAW IN THE AMERICAN POLITICAL ECONOMY

The role of the courts in shaping the architecture of the political economy has been a central theme in American political development. The administrative state in the United States grew up in the shadow of a powerful judiciary that shaped both the character of internal government relations and the relationship between state and market (see, especially, Skowronek 1982). The unabashedly pro-business orientation of the courts at the turn of the century was a major flashpoint of political conflict. The infamous 1905 *Lochner* v. *New York* case, in which the Supreme Court struck down a state law providing for minimum working-time protections for bakers, became a symbol for the court's radical laissez faire orientation. Similar counter-majoritarian decisions on a range of issues from private property rights to takings to worker protections formed the basis of a pro-business judiciary and set the stage for the political clashes over the law in the early twentieth century (Shugerman 2012).

Progressive Era reformers ultimately succeeded in building administrative capacities at the federal level. However, reformist success typically turned either on limiting the influence of courts, or on winning judicial decisions validating these new forms of state power. The result was what Gary Gerstle (2017) has called an "improvisational" approach to state formation, a fractured landscape in which the courts continued to be an important arena of conflict in which well-resourced, sophisticated business actors could still exercise influence. The nascent administrative apparatus in the United States did not displace the courts, but instead was layered on top of and around the preexisting court-based policymaking regime, which continued to operate in parallel with it.

The political crisis of the Great Depression and the state-building mission of the New Deal ultimately neutralized longstanding judicial hostility to administrative power, and even the Supreme Court made its peace with the rising federal administrative state (Tushnet 2011). However, business interests did not give up the fight. Leading industrialists led by the Du Pont brothers founded and generously funded the American Liberty League as a vehicle through which to mount litigation and court-based challenges to New Deal regulations. Focusing heavily on individual liberty and freedom of contract claims, the League's legal strategy strongly foreshadowed today's resurgent civil-libertarian challenges to the regulation of economic activity (see, especially, Kessler 2016 on this "First Amendment Lochnerism"). While the League itself failed in the face of Roosevelt's overwhelming Democratic majorities in Congress, the legal arguments developed during this period would provide the repertoire for later normative and political claims that would gain more traction as the political environment shifted from the New Deal consensus to an increasingly anti-government and pro-business political context in the late twentieth century (Metzger 2017).

Some of the foundations of the current attack on the regulatory state were laid already in the 1950s and 1960s, when an emerging crop of conservative legal scholars mounted an intellectual assault on the prevailing New Deal order in an "effort to reconstitute liberalism as a bulwark against collectivist challenges and increasing government regulation of business" (van Horn 2011: 1528). These ideas took root in the "Chicago School" of law and economics, which drew on philosophical and organizational foundations laid in the immediate postwar years by Friedrich Hayek to confront what he and others considered the twin dangers of totalitarianism and communism. Central to the Chicago School approach was an unshakable belief in the value of free markets. The economist Ronald Coase exercised enormous influence in the School's early years; his institution-building efforts included the founding of a new journal (*The Journal of Law and Economics*, 1958) and the establishment of a center staffed by libertarian scholars (the "Committee on a Free Society").

The emergence of this powerful intellectual movement resonated deeply with business interests whose long-simmering discontent with the New Deal settlement grew increasingly intense in the years of the Warren Court, when judicial power was brought to bear to extend the power and regulatory reach of the federal government in society and economy. Congress had relied on private litigation to enforce federal statutes since the late nineteenth century. But legislative changes in the 1960s expanded access to the courts through changes in standing to sue, the inclusion in some laws of "citizen-suit" provisions that allowed private parties to initiate cases, "fee shifting" arrangements in which defendants would be responsible for all legal costs if the plaintiff prevailed, and – perhaps most importantly – an amendment to the Federal Rules of Civil Procedure Act that made it easier for parties to bring class action suits (Burbank and Farhang 2017: ch. 3; Kagan 2019: 57; see also Decker 2016: 32–34).

These changes fueled the rise of the liberal legal movement, giving a host of new actors – including civil rights groups and proponents of environmental and consumer protection – tools to bring recalcitrant states and business interests to heel through litigation. Indeed, as David Vogel noted, in the 1970s "the public interest movement replaced organized labor as the central countervailing force to the power and values of American business" (Vogel 1989: 293). This was quite a reversal from jurisprudence in the late nineteenth century, when business interests were the ones to turn to the courts, mostly to contest government regulation as a violation of their individual or property rights (Kagan 2019: ch. 11). It was not long, though, before these developments provoked an intense conservative "counterrevolution" (Burbank and Farhang 2017: 3).

BUSINESS STRATEGY AND CONSERVATIVE JURISPRUDENCE IN THE MODERN ERA

Concerted pushback on the part of business is often seen to have begun with a 1971 memorandum written by future Supreme Court Justice Lewis F. Powell addressed to the US Chamber of Commerce. Powell excoriated the American business community for its complacency in the face of what he considered the dire threat to free enterprise posed by the expansion of the regulatory state. He pointed out that defenders of the free market had not recognized the "neglected opportunity" the courts offered, which the public interest legal movement had cleverly exploited. And he famously argued that the judiciary could be an important instrument for social, economic, and political change for business as well (Hacker and Pierson 2010: 117–19).

In fact, the roots of the business countermobilization were multiple, and many of them predate Powell's call to action. Yet the memo was revealing, and the Chamber did become a crucial hub in the business pushback, not just against public interest law but against the regulatory state as such. Then-president Richard Lesher began the effort in 1975 by founding a National Legal Center for the Public Interest, essentially picking up where the Liberty League had left off. Conservatives who had earlier railed against the growing influence of the judiciary came "to embrace legal activism," arguing that federal bureaucracies had exceeded their authority by violating the rights of property owners and businesspeople. The lawsuits they brought "spoke the language of individual constitutionally based rights – as secured by the Bill of Rights and extended by the Fourteenth Amendment" (Decker 2016: 71).

Today's business counteroffensive is more sophisticated and multidimensional than its predecessors, developing over decades and operating across several interrelated arenas. This section explores three areas of strategic focus: cultivating the conservative legal movement in the academy, forging a robust political coalition through strategic litigation, and shaping the composition of the judiciary itself through intense involvement in judicial elections and appointments to the bench. Narrow perspectives that focus on one or the other of these arenas inevitably produce a highly incomplete picture. It is only when we zoom out and look to the larger landscape of parallel and complementary initiatives in which business interests have been involved that we can begin to see the interconnections and synergies among them. A wide-angle view also reveals a diverse set of allies – conservative philanthropists, lobbyists, party officials, conservative legal advocacy organizations, and think tanks – operating across these multiple sites of influence.

Cultivating the Conservative Legal Movement

Steven Teles tells the story of the rise of the conservative legal movement as the triumph of powerful intellectual minds and skilled scholarly entrepreneurs who were driven by shared ideological convictions rather than material motives. Indeed, Teles argues that the success of the conservative legal movement came only after it had distanced itself from business actors. In his account, earlier conservative efforts had been "hampered by their alliance with the business community" (Teles 2008: 88). He argues that the movement took off only after power shifted "from the movement's material [corporate] base to those with primarily cultural and intellectual motivations" (2008: 59).

But Teles's otherwise masterful study understates the role of business interests in actively supporting these early intellectual endeavors and in cultivating the subsequent evolution of the conservative legal movement. As van Horn (2018: 478) documents, "from the time of the birth of Chicago law and economics in 1946, there has been an active corporate presence." Large companies facilitated the growth of the movement, bankrolling fellowships in the 1950s and 1960s, financing conferences and other initiatives that were aimed at "reshap[ing] the views of faculty and students so that they would be more sympathetic toward corporations" (van Horn 2018: 486–87). Corporate support was critical, for example, in underwriting the influential Manne workshops – two- to three-week training courses for law faculty and judges designed to familiarize them with the market-oriented cost-benefit analysis that was central to the law and economics approach to jurisprudence (Ash et al. 2020). Manne himself emphasized the importance of mobilizing business support in his quest to fund a law school specializing in this kind of legal training, a law school "especially designed to serve the needs with which these men are familiar" (qtd. in Teles 2008: 103).

Although this new generation of conservative legal scholars and activists were not acting at the behest of specific corporate interests, the views they articulated clearly resonated with long-standing business grievances against the regulatory state. Valorizing self-correcting markets and critiquing government as prone to special interest capture, their arguments echoed central themes of the laissez-faire conservatism of the pre–New Deal era. So it is not surprising that conservative foundations with close ties to industry such as Olin (chemicals) were deeply involved in these efforts from the start. They were joined by others over time. Charles Koch, for example, was an early supporter – and generous patron – of the Institute for Justice, which Teles (2008: ch. 7) singles out as one of the most important hubs of the conservative public interest law movement.

These new strands of legal thinking found organizational anchoring in the Federalist Society, established in 1982, whose founders focused on further developing conservative legal doctrine and on cultivating a cadre of legal experts steeped in this tradition. Generous funding from corporation-linked philanthropies allowed the Federalist Society to host workshops, debates, and conventions, and to develop beachheads in elite law schools across the United States. Individual companies have contributed to the cause by investing in academic centers such as the Institute for Contemporary Studies in California, which leveraged donations from IBM, Chase, and Texaco, alongside funding from conservative philanthropies like the Olin Foundation, to focus on training a new generation of antitrust lawyers and on reshaping legal pedagogy around pro-business, Chicago School economics (Maclean 2017: 115–26). Similar efforts drove the founding of law and economics centers at George Mason University and elsewhere in the 1980s (Maclean 2017: 115–26).

These business investments have paid off. Ash, Chen, and Naidu (2020) conducted an exhaustive study of the impact on judicial decisions of attendance at the Manne Economic Institute for federal judges. By the early 1990s, more than half of all federal judges had attended this Institute and the question the authors ask is what impact, if any, did this have on their subsequent behavior on the bench. Analyzing hundreds of thousands of votes in Federal Circuit courts through 2013, they found that judges who had participated in the Manne economic training program between 1976 and 1999 rendered more conservative verdicts in economics cases and ruled against regulatory agencies – particularly the Environmental Protection Agency and the National Labor Relations Board – more often than judges who had not attended the program. Text analysis revealed that these judges were also more likely to invoke the specific language and cost-benefit logic of economics in their opinions – language that can then be cited in future decisions (Ash et al. 2020: 3).[3]

Through long-term investment in organizations like the Federalist Society and the seeding of prestigious legal scholarships, chairs, and faculty positions, conservative and corporate donors have successfully created a self-sustaining ecosystem of conservative legal practitioners who share a common worldview. Their funding has allowed these groups to develop compelling intellectual critiques of the New Deal constitutional order, incorporating insights from economics to advocate for the efficiency of free market approaches to public policy. Most importantly, the Federalist Society now provides a pipeline of talent from which future judges, policy-makers, and business officials can be drawn (Teles 2008: 137).

Conservative politicians looking to promote like-minded jurists now know exactly how to find them even within a legal academy that still leans liberal. Bonica and Sen (2017: 559) show that ideology plays an especially prominent role in judicial selection where judges are appointed or elected in partisan elections. Because the pool of conservative candidates coming out of elite law schools is smaller than the pool of liberal candidates, conservative graduates are significantly more likely than their liberal colleagues to be tapped to serve on federal courts of appeals and state high courts – nine times more likely in the case of federal circuit courts, and, narrowing the comparison to graduates of Harvard, Yale, and Chicago, twelve times more likely (2017: 588–89).

The linkages between business and the conservative legal movement have become increasingly dense over time. Key hubs in the conservative academic network such as George Mason University's Economics Department and Law School continue to enjoy generous funding from corporate interests

[3] Besides showing that judicial decision and text outcomes did not diverge prior to program attendance, the authors show that the estimated effects of attending Manne do not change when controlling for partisanship (the party of the nominating president) and for time-specific effects of variables that predict the timing of attendance, lending confidence that selection bias is not driving the results.

(Hartocollis 2018) and the Federalist Society itself is supported in part by funding from these same business interests.[4] Alumni of these programs now occupy key positions not just in the judiciary but in government as well. Paik et al.'s (2011) analysis of networks of lawyers who are active in national policymaking reveals especially dense ties among business (as opposed to religious) conservatives, an outcome they attribute in part to "umbrella groups" such as the Federalist Society, the Heritage Foundation, and the American Enterprise Institute that integrate ideologically aligned lawyers by providing opportunities for interaction and cooperation in public policymaking.

Coalition Building through Strategic Litigation

The maturation of the conservative legal movement coincided with an important leadership change at the Chamber, which, in 1997, came under the more inspired, and more radical, leadership of Tom Donahue. As president, Donahue ramped up the Chamber's activities in direct pro-business litigation and in state judicial elections. A first target was tort reform, strategically chosen for its broad appeal and ability to unify a business community that is otherwise often rent with divisions (Carter 2002: 32). In most other countries, compensation for various injuries is dealt with by bureaucratic agencies or social insurance funds (in corporatist countries, often administered with parity representation of business and labor interests). In the United States, by contrast, harms are litigated in court, and the tort law system notoriously is associated with unpredictable and often very large damages, including in some cases huge pain and suffering compensation. This has been a massive thorn in the side of business, and the Chamber's Institute for Legal Reform spent tens of millions of dollars in the 2000s on tort litigation alone (Hacker and Pierson 2016: 223).

Donahue took up this cause with gusto, placing it at the center of a successful fundraising and membership drive. The attack on the plaintiff's bar not only unified diverse business interests; it also cemented an alliance with the Republican party leadership by taking on the trial lawyers' bench, an important constituency and major source of funding for Democratic

[4] A leaked program from the 2019 annual Federalist Society gala celebrating Brett Kavanaugh's confirmation listed a number of major corporations as sponsors of the event. See www.theguardian.com/technology/2019/nov/14/facebook-federalist-society-brett-kavanaugh-gala.

candidates in key states. Tort reform was also a galvanizing issue for the American Legislative Exchange Council (ALEC), a network linking business interests directly to conservative state legislators. Pivoting from its previous heavy focus on social issues, ALEC developed model state legislation for tort reform and ran a successful lobbying campaign that resulted in twenty-three states introducing caps on tort suit damages, thirty-four states limiting – in some cases, banning – tort suit punitive damages, and thirty-eight states introducing maximum allowable penalties (Hertel-Fernandez 2019: 63). ALEC's strategic reorientation drew in more corporate members, putting the organization on much more stable financial and organizational footing by scoring successes on an issue of central importance to a wide variety of companies.

The impact of the business offensive in this area has been profound. Burbank and Farhang trace the trajectory of the conservative counterrevolution against the private enforcement apparatus that had flourished in the 1960s. They show how business interests increasingly turned to the courts after efforts at outright legislative retrenchment at the national level had failed: "Recognizing the political infeasibility of retrenching substantive rights, the movement's strategy was to undermine the infrastructure for enforcing them" (Burbank and Farhang 2017: 3). Their empirical investigation of private enforcement cases documents a significant uptick in Chamber activity in this area after 1995 (2017: 164–65). Based on exhaustive analysis of Supreme Court decisions over the past several decades that dealt with standing, private rights of action, damages, fees, and arbitration, they show that "business defendants are prevailing at an extraordinary rate" (2017: 130). Plaintiff success has fallen steadily over the last forty years, and by 2014, plaintiffs were losing 90 percent of the time (2017: 22).

The Chamber's National Chamber Litigation Center (NCLC) is engaged in a broad range of business-oriented litigation, extending far beyond the issue of torts. The Center has invested especially heavily in its Supreme Court practice, and has been extremely successful in getting its cases heard. The Court typically agrees to hear about 5 percent of certiorari petitions it receives but cases supported by the Chamber enjoy a significantly higher take-up rate – 25 percent in the 2017–18 term and a whopping 40 percent in the 2018–19 term (Frazelle 2019: 4). Robin Conrad, who led the Chamber's litigation efforts for decades, boasted an especially successful record at that level. In her first year at the helm, the NCLC secured three key victories in a single day, a "high court hat trick" (Winkler 2018: 323). Under her leadership, the Chamber honed its tactics, and Conrad earned high praise for the role she played in "taking a more strategic approach to shaping the law in areas such as punitive damages, class actions, and securities litigation" (US Chamber Litigation Center 2007). Indeed, the Chamber's win rate is enviable. During the Roberts Court, the Chamber's position has prevailed in 70 percent of cases in which it took a stand, up from 56 percent in the Rehnquist era and just 43 percent during the Burger Court (Frazelle 2019: 3).

Shaping the Composition of the Bench

The strategic initiatives outlined above are intimately linked to a third arena of business influence, namely working to shift the personnel who comprise the judiciary writ large. In the context of the anti-tort campaign, business interests were willing to pour large sums of money into efforts to replace state supreme court judges they viewed as biased toward plaintiffs or inclined toward big awards. In one well-known case, they lobbied heavily on a 1986 California ballot measure that resulted in the replacement of liberal state supreme court justice Rose Bird with a more business-friendly conservative (Cairns 2016: 176). The Chamber's Institute for Legal Reform – heavily funded by a handful of anonymous donors – pours enormous resources into financing the campaigns of its preferred candidates in state-level judicial races and state attorneys general elections (Surgey 2020; also Hacker and Pierson 2016: 223–24).

Campaign spending in such races has risen considerably over the last two decades. State judicial elections are no longer the "sleepy affairs" they were before 2000 (Carter 2002; Katz 2018). Katz notes that in 2014, the Institute for Legal Reform raised $45 million in revenue and spent a third of it on political campaigns, including significant contributions to judicial races (Katz 2018: 320). Conference calls identify priority ("Tier 1") targets who are then singled out for special attention and funding (Katz 2018: 325). The 2016 election set a new record for spending on state supreme court elections, as twenty-seven judges were elected in races in which spending reached $1 m or more, with the lion's share of contributions coming from outside groups (*The Economist* 2019). Attorney general races have also become intensely partisan affairs, with business interests (led by the fossil fuel industry) heavily involved in funding their preferred candidates (Savit 2017; Surgey 2020).

The Chamber works closely with Republican party allies in these efforts. Its Institute for Legal Reform is the second-largest source of funding (behind another conservative organization, the Judicial Crisis

Network – which similarly relies on a small number of anonymous contributions) in funding the Republican Attorneys General Association, which spearheads efforts to increase the number of Republican AGs across the country (Bennett 2018; Surgey 2020). The Chamber also works alongside the Judicial Fairness committee, an organization founded in 2014 by the Republican State Leadership Committee that is focused specifically on "elect[ing] down-ballot, state-level conservatives to the judiciary" (Keith et al. 2019: 10).

These efforts, in combination with the now-steady supply of conservative jurists coming out of top law schools, have been crucial in shifting the composition of the courts at all levels, but the alliance with the GOP in transforming the federal bench has been especially effective. Republican allies of business lobbies systematically slow-walked judicial confirmations under the Clinton and Obama presidencies, and then radically ramped up the pace of confirming conservative judges for the resulting vacancies in the Bush II and Trump administrations. Trump alone appointed more than a quarter of all federal appellate court judges (fifty-one total appointments across all thirteen circuits, all but eight with ties to the Federalist Society) (Livni 2020). At the Supreme Court level, conservative groups heavily promoted the appointment of Neil Gorsuch, and the Judicial Crisis Network poured $10 million into the lobbying effort to seat Brett Kavanaugh (Keith et al. 2019: 2; Massoglia 2020).[5]

Changes in the composition of the courts – through election and appointment – now allow business interests to venue shop, strategically targeting their efforts to weaken the regulatory constraints they face. Republican AGs work closely with industry and conservative advocacy groups to mount "coordinated AG-directed litigation" aimed at revising or reversing unwelcome legislation or administrative actions (Savit 2017: 850). States where business influence in politics is especially strong offer a more effective route for business-friendly litigation, for example arising through right-leaning judicial districts in states like Texas, and through conservative circuits like the Fifth Circuit Court of Appeals. From here, otherwise peripheral business-friendly legal theories – like the ones that drove the *Sibelius* case that challenged the Obama administration's signature healthcare policy, the Affordable Care Act – can quickly skyrocket from the status of theory to being heard in the Supreme Court itself

[5] Leonard Leo, co-chair of the Federalist society, lists Kavanagh's appointment (along with that of Gorsuch, Alito, and Roberts) as among his greatest accomplishments (https://fedsoc.org/contributors/leonard-leo).

(Balkin 2012; Tushnet 2013). The Republican Party has leveraged this infrastructure to engage in an increasingly aggressive strategy of what Brian Highsmith (2019) calls "partisan constitutionalism," in which party leaders work with business allies and conservative and libertarian advocacy groups, enlisting partisan judges and making strategic use of the courts in order to "re-litigate" legislative losses "on a more favorable battleground" (Highsmith 2019: 920).

In sum, panning out to take a wide-angle view of business investments across multiple sites, a larger pattern of influence emerges. The interaction of developments across this entire field shapes political outcomes in ways that are difficult to track because the dynamics are so different from raw power politics. Standards of legal argumentation, appeals to prior case law and precedent, and the boundaries of statutory or Constitutional text provide limits, if highly plastic ones, on what kinds of decisions can be reached in the particular factual scenario presented by a lawsuit. But patient investment in academic institutions that have been promoting alternative lines of legal analysis contributed to shifting the terms of scholarly debate and the boundaries of legal conventional wisdom. Judges who come to see themselves as players in a larger partisan or political battle are more willing to push the boundaries of precedent and legal norms. And, through strategic litigation, organized business groups both capitalize on and advance these developments.

Donald McGahn, the former White House Counsel who spearheaded the Trump administration's efforts to place conservative jurists on the federal bench to do battle against the administrative state, was explicit about the strategic connections across these different arenas of influence: "There is a coherent plan here where actually the judicial selection and the deregulatory effort are really the flip side of the same coin" (Barnes and Mufson 2018). Yet these connections are lost on all but the most attentive observers of the judiciary. It is precisely because of how diffuse the court system is that business interests that are able to operate across the entire landscape of law schools, courts, elections, and traditional political influence can enjoy an enormous strategic advantage even if these efforts have taken decades to come together.

COURTS AND THE AMERICAN POLITICAL ECONOMY: THE STRATEGIC USE OF LEGAL DOCTRINE

The developments outlined above set the stage for key legal battles through which business interests have been able to exercise significant influence on the contemporary political economy. This section outlines how business has been able to assert its interests through litigation and legal doctrine in three ways: through measures aimed at enhancing corporate power, weakening countervailing forces (especially labor), and undermining the state's regulatory capacity. These three doctrinal areas come to the forefront because they have been major political economic battlegrounds in which business interests have used the courts to expand the zone of corporate discretion and rewrite the legal capacities and immunities afforded them in ways that enhance and extend corporate power. In most of the following cases, the plaintiffs are firms or business groups with long-standing interests in dismantling New Deal–era economic regulations. As highly resourced, repeat players, these litigants have been successful in part by bringing repeated lawsuits in favorable jurisdictions, and by designing these interventions strategically in order to create vehicles that are most likely to reach the Supreme Court and win the support of an increasingly conservative federal judiciary.

Enhancing Corporate Power and Capacity

First, business interests in the United States have successfully pursued cases that remove regulatory and other constraints on big business itself, enabling corporations to further concentrate their economic and political power. The infamous *Citizens United* v. *FEC* case, which removed limits on corporate campaign contributions, represents one such key shift, expanding the ability of business interests to wield influence in elections. Indeed, the effects of *Citizens United* on state legislatures are already visible: studies have found that increased spending by outside groups bolstered the chances of Republican candidates while also, independently, leading to a rightward shift in the ideology of those who were elected (Abdul-Razzak et al. 2019; Harvey and Mattia 2019).

The *Citizens United* decision built on a longer trajectory of legal doctrine going back to the very start of the modern conservative legal movement and the Chamber's lobbying efforts. Earlier cases, in particular *First National Bank* v. *Belotti* (1978) and *Buckley* v. *Valeo* (1976), set up the doctrinal arguments that corporations possess free-speech rights, and that financial donations constitute speech – two key legal building blocks that made *Citizens United* possible. As Adam Cohen (2021: 149) notes, *Citizens United* was the product of a well-orchestrated campaign. He shows how a network of conservative activists, associated with James Bopp's James Madison Center for Free Speech, served as a "brain trust" for the case. Meanwhile, the well-known repeat litigant and fellow of the

American Enterprise Institute, Ed Blum, tapped into his base of conservative corporate donors to help organize the long-term financing for these litigation efforts.

In another line of cases, courts have found that the First Amendment rights to speech for corporations can be read as providing protection against various state regulations. Perhaps the best known of these is the *Hobby Lobby* case, which found the First Amendment rights of a closely held corporation required a carve-out from complying with civil rights laws where the corporate owner has religious objections. In *Sorell* v. *IMS Health*, data mining and pharmaceutical companies brought a suit to challenge a patient confidentiality law. In its decision, the Court struck down a Vermont law that would have barred the use of patients' private prescription information for marketing purposes as a violation of pharmaceutical firms' First Amendment rights to engage in corporate speech (Purdy 2014). Seizing on these developments, pharmaceutical companies are now pushing to be exempted from FDA disclosure requirements for their drugs, claiming protection for their corporate speech rights (Kapczynski 2018). While these cases involved somewhat different areas of legal doctrine and different political constituencies – civil rights/religious liberties, business regulation – what unites them is a shared attack on government regulation, and an empowerment of corporate interests to resist it.

Another area in which the courts have enhanced the power of business interests is through antitrust rulings that promote economic concentration rather than limit it. In one recent example, the court sided with credit card companies by rejecting an antitrust challenge to the extractive "merchant fees" that companies like Visa and Amex impose on small businesses. In the case, *Ohio* v. *American Express* (2018) the Supreme Court's five-vote conservative majority held that such merchant platforms were "two-sided markets" that did not suffer from conventional problems of market concentration – despite significant evidence that credit card companies were abusing their market power to impose heavy fees on small businesses.

The deregulatory tendencies we have been describing for the United States are certainly in evidence in Europe, though there are some important differences.[6] In general, the European Union tends to enforce antitrust

[6] Space constraints do not allow for an extended treatment of the ways in which the European Court of Justice has promoted deregulation. Suffice it to say that the economic liberties that are instantiated in the EU Treaty, and the Court's interpretation and enforcement of the Treaty's "four freedoms," have given the entire European project a strong neoliberal slant (Scharpf 1999).

more rigorously (Philippon 2019: ch. 6), and in Europe, laws protecting the civil rights of individual citizens (e.g., nondiscrimination as in the *Hobby Lobby* case) would always prevail over the rights of corporations (or firm managers operating in that capacity). Rulings of the European Court of Justice have pushed in a liberalizing direction, but the foundational logic on which many of the US Supreme Court decisions have rested – the extension of First Amendment rights to corporations – has no equivalent in Europe. Thus, EU law does not provide a way for business interests to expropriate and claim for themselves the rights and liberties that we typically attach to individuals in the way that has become common in the United States.

Weakening Countervailing Forces

Second, business interests in the United States have successfully leveraged legal doctrine to shift the balance of power between capital and labor through cases that undercut the countervailing power of workers and other groups to exercise political voice and to contest the political interests of business. In *Janus* v. *AFSCME*, the Court inhibited the ability of public sector unions to charge union dues as a violation of First Amendment protections of freedom of speech. Business has a keen interest in diminishing the power and depleting the financial resources of public sector unions because of the role these unions play in electing Democrats and in lobbying for progressive policies (Hertel-Fernandez, this volume). The *Janus* decision was the result of a protracted back-and-forth between conservative interests and Justice Samuel Alito in particular, who used dissents on earlier cases to invite further challenges by strongly signaling a willingness to overturn a long-standing precedent allowing the collection of agency fees (Cohen 2021).

As noted by Hertel-Fernandez (this volume) business interests including the Koch brothers bankrolled the groups, notably the National Right to Work Legal Defense Foundation, who supplied the arguments deployed in the *Janus* case (see also Cohen 2021: 215; McNicholas and Jones 2018). Republican politicians like Illinois governor Bruce Rauner (himself a businessman) championed the case, while conservative judicial appointments – specifically, the seating of Justice Neil Gorsuch – secured the victory for business. As soon as the decision came down, the Freedom Foundation – a conservative nonprofit funded by the Koch brothers – mobilized a grass roots campaign to encourage public workers to stop contributing to the unions that represent them (Eidelson 2018).

Reducing access to the courts through restrictions on class action suits and the use of mandatory forced arbitration clauses has been another high priority for the Chamber of Commerce, and an area in which it has enjoyed significant success (Public Citizen 2008). As Sarah Staszak (2015) has emphasized, it has become increasingly difficult for disadvantaged groups and individuals to have their day in court. She observes that many of the advances of the rights revolution of the 1960s have been scaled back in a series of subtle and often highly technical changes to the rules and legal procedures associated with bringing class action suits. It is now simply much more difficult than before to form a class – and without a class there is really no way to sue, given the prohibitive costs to individuals to bring separate suits and the meagre damages that could be recovered in this way. As an example, she cites a 2011 class action case brought by the female employees of Wal-Mart for systemic gender discrimination in hiring and promotion (*Wal-Mart Stores, Inc.* v. *Dukes et al.*). The Supreme Court threw the case out without ever addressing the substantive claims because a 5–4 conservative majority decided that the women could not be certified as a class (Staszak 2015: 2; see also Corkery 2017). While the goal of scaling back access to the courts emanated from a variety of sources over time, Staszak argues that since the 1990s it has drawn most of its power from Republican legislators and lobbyists keen to thwart public interest litigation of this sort (2015: 116; see also Burbank and Farhang 2017).

Mandatory arbitration clauses similarly operate to tilt the playing field heavily in favor of business interests. For example, in a series of cases, courts have found that the Federal Arbitration Act, which allows for contractual arbitration clauses to bypass conventional judicial proceedings for dispute resolution, can be interpreted to supplant existing regulatory requirements (see, e.g., Liptak 2018; 2019). Workers whose employment contracts contain arbitration clauses, or consumers using services whose fine print includes an arbitration provision, now find themselves unable to bring claims to court, or even to invoke regulatory protections for labor and consumer rights (see, especially, Colvin 2018). Employers have seized on these legal developments, and now regularly insert mandatory arbitration clauses in employment contracts. Studies show that the share of workers covered by such provisions rose steadily after a key 1991 decision (*Gilmer* v. *Interstate/Johnson Lane*), from about 2 percent of all workers in 1992 to well over half (56.2 percent) of all private sector nonunion employees by 2017. Even in low-pay sectors such as the retail and hospitality industries, large shares of workers are now subject to forced arbitration (Colvin 2018: 2, 8-9). In 2018, the Supreme Court ruled that these clauses could even override the National Labor Relations Act, requiring employees to bring labor disputes through arbitration instead of more worker-friendly administrative or judicial proceedings (Epic Systems 2018; see, especially, Hamaji et al. 2019).[7]

Here again, there are few direct parallels in Europe. With respect to labor representation, *Janus*-like attacks on unions are not as easily mounted because labor's right to collective bargaining is anchored in the constitution in most European countries. These rights are not (as in the United States) an extension of the individual rights of workers (e.g., Forbath 1991), but instead rest on separate bodies of law that expressly recognize the rights of unions as the collective representatives of workers. Employment law in most European countries also explicitly recognizes the power asymmetries involved in employment relationships, and proceeds from the view that the state has an obligation to protect the rights of the weaker party. Among other things, this means that the kinds of mandatory arbitration clauses that are slipped into many individual employment contracts in the United States would be unthinkable in most cases in Europe, where individuals cannot simply sign away their right to collective representation.[8] Finally, the fact that European jurisdictions do not typically provide mechanisms for class action suits[9] means that the labor claims described previously in most cases would either be resolved in political or administrative forums or subject to collective bargaining.

Undermining State Regulatory Capacities

Finally, business interests in the United States have been remarkably successful in winning cases that establish limitations on the very capacities of government itself, effectively precluding more far-reaching regulations or redistributive policies that might arise in the future. Here the overall

[7] A 2015 Report by the Consumer Financial Protection Bureau documents how arbitration agreements have had a similarly chilling effect on the ability of consumers to seek and realize relief in disputes, and how companies use mandatory arbitration to avoid costly class action suits (CFPB 2015).

[8] Organized labor's rights have been more contested at the European level, and here the record is more mixed – with unions suffering some setbacks (regarding the application of collectively bargained standards to posted workers, for example), but also some wins (extending collective agreements to misclassified independent contractors). But generally, the position of unions is far more secure in Europe.

[9] Although the EU is moving closer to allowing class action suits by consumers (Taylor 2019).

story – of a hollowing out of state regulatory capacities – is similar to that in Europe, even if the mechanisms are quite different. In Europe, the shift of regulatory authority over much economic activity to the European level itself compromises national control, and a large literature shows that the overall thrust of ECJ jurisprudence has tilted in a decided deregulatory direction (see, e.g., Grimm 2015; Höpner 2015; Scharpf 1999, 2010, 2017; Schmidt 2018).

In the United States, however, organized business interests have played a more central role. Many of the First Amendment cases expanding corporate power noted previously operate by negating governmental regulatory authority. But there are other, more direct, challenges to federal regulations on business as well. For example, in the 2011 case of *Business Roundtable* v. *SEC*, the Business Roundtable brought a suit challenging the Securities and Exchange Commission's "proxy access" rule, a regulation mandated by the 2010 Dodd-Frank financial reform legislation that aimed to expand shareholders' ability to hold management accountable through shareholder elections. Under the Administrative Procedures Act, regulatory agencies must provide a cost-benefit analysis to show that regulations are not "arbitrary and capricious." In the case, the BRT successfully weaponized procedural claims to argue that the SEC's cost-benefit analysis of the proxy access rule was insufficient. The argument carried the day, despite extensive research and documentation from the SEC assessing the trade-offs and implications of the policy, and despite strong legislative authorization from Congress to pursue the rule.

This strategy of undermining regulation through the imposition of ever-higher barriers to success represents a long-running theme in business-driven litigation. Consider as another example the famous *NFIB* v. *Sibelius* case, brought by the National Federation of Independent Business to challenge the Obama administration's Affordable Care Act. In a textbook case that illustrates the connections across the political, legal, and academic arenas, twenty-six Republican AGs joined the business federation's suit to strike down the legislation. Working together with libertarian think tanks such as the Heritage Foundation, whose legal team helped select the venue and craft the legal arguments, ACA opponents elevated the case politically by framing the issue in terms that resonated with the public while also lending legitimacy to previously marginal constitutional claims (Highsmith 2019).

While the individual mandate requiring individuals to purchase health insurance survived judicial scrutiny, the Supreme Court imposed two potentially severe restraints on future redistributive social welfare policies. First, *Sibelius* now questions whether the Federal government can induce states to join a federal regulatory regime by providing financial incentives. Such incentives had been a mainstay of federal–state cooperative welfare regimes including Medicare and Social Security, but the Court found that federal incentives that are *too* enticing may be deemed unconstitutionally coercive. Second, *Sibelius* also suggested a limit to federal legislative power under the Commerce Clause, limiting it to apply only to "commercial activity," suggesting that Congress could not mandate individuals to act in a particular way by regulating "inactivity" – such as the "inaction" involved in not buying health insurance. While the exact implications of the inactivity requirement are unknown, inserting this additional hurdle for future legislation represents a loaded gun that could come back to undermine federal policymaking going forward.

The battle over the ACA offers another particularly stark example of how the fusion of partisan political activism, a conservative legal ecosystem, and business interests can exercise powerful influence on the political economy through law. When initially proposed, the libertarian argument that the government could not mandate individuals to purchase health insurance or regulate insurance companies was viewed as non-credible, so far out of mainstream legal doctrine as to not be a threat. Yet a combination of intellectual entrepreneurship by leading conservative legal scholars and think tanks, the socialization and popularization of these theories in the media and in Congress, and the uptake of these arguments by the Chamber and the National Federation of Independent Business radically shifted the political context (Highsmith 2019). Legal theories espoused by ACA opponents had entered the mainstream – and with favorable jurists on the Court, a ruling striking it down was suddenly plausible (Tushnet 2013). Political entrepreneurs then drove the case forward: the Republican administration in the State of Florida brought the initial ACA lawsuit, and with a favorable ruling in the conservative Eleventh Circuit of Appeals, the case was on its way to the Supreme Court.

Much of the legal scholarship views the different battles we have outlined as doctrinally unrelated to one another, grounded in different legal frameworks – freedom of contract, rights of corporate personhood, or states' rights. Depending on the issue, the specific doctrines that are invoked are opportunistically different. In some cases, legal strategies involve repurposing old doctrines (e.g., the First Amendment); some rely on originalist thinking, others on the market-efficiency logic of law and economics. However, by putting them in the same political-economic frame we can see them as part of a single political project of defending centers of business and economic power, weakening countervailing forces, and undermining the regulatory powers of the state.

LAW AND DEEP CAPTURE OF POLITICAL ECONOMIC POLICYMAKING

The cumulative result of this conservative judicial activism has been to tilt the playing field in favor of business interests (Purdy 2018). We have highlighted some of the most visible cases, but the reality is that most litigation disputes involve policies that operate in the deep background of the political-economic regime, out of the limelight of mainstream political debates and media attention. As Burbank and Farhang put it: the courts have provided "a pathway to retrenchment that is remote from public view, and this subterranean quality is reinforced by the slow-moving, evolutionary nature of case-by-case policy change" (Burbank and Farhang 2017: 22–23). While business interests do lose some high-profile cases, they have been successful at shifting background procedural rules, step-by-step, to great effect (see Tushnet 2013: 204).

Sophisticated, well-resourced, repeat players like big business are especially well positioned to shape outcomes in these ways. Many of the cases we have discussed were driven by plaintiffs who are themselves corporations or lobbying and advocacy groups that operate on their behalf – the Business Roundtable, the National Right to Work Committee, the National Federation of Independent Business, or the Chamber of Commerce. The financial resources these corporate litigants can bring have vastly outpaced the ability of countervailing actors and public interest groups to keep up. However, as we have emphasized, these victories are not just the product of greater resourcing for businesses to pursue expensive litigation campaigns. They have rested as well on complementary efforts aimed at shaping the ideologies and personnel of the judiciary in a more business-friendly direction. Decisions like *Citizens United*, *Sibelius*, *Hobby Lobby*, and *Sorrell* are thus also the outcomes of a less-visible, longer-running process through which business interests have sought to channel influence on the legal terrain.

Defenders of the Supreme Court insist that the pro-business decisions it has handed down are not the result of systematic bias, but arise from Justices' genuinely held moral and legal beliefs about interpretation and jurisprudence (see, e.g., Adler 2016). Yet the intellectual and ideological orientation of the Court (and of the lower courts) itself reflects the fruits of a more multifaceted long game of influence on legal doctrine and state judicial politics since the 1970s. Indeed, the rapidity with which contentious legal theories from the Right migrated into appellate courts and then to the Supreme Court highlights the power of patient investment and networked movement-building among business interests, conservative politicians, and the conservative legal movement in the academy. Consider, for example, how litigants in the ACA cases worked with partisan state Attorneys General to launch the suits that drove the case. Or how the ideological skew of particular geographic circuit courts – such as the heavily conservative Fifth or Eleventh Circuits – provided a fast track for this and other contentious cases to reach the Supreme Court. By concentrating lobbying and advocacy efforts on a few key nodes in the legal system, particularly ones that are often not as visible to the mass public such as AG offices and lower court appointments, organized interests can exercise outsized influence on the legal system as whole.

The combined result of these efforts has been subtle, long-term, and deeply durable shifts in features of the regulatory environment that are of central interest to business. This is not the kind of pay-to-play or raw lobbying we associate with business power in legislative or electoral contexts. Rather, influence operates through two related mechanisms. First, active support of the conservative legal movement creates an expansive network linking legal scholars, business lawyers, policymakers, and commentators who share a common cultural, sociological, and ideological orientation. This network is porous and overlapping, connecting legal conservatives with corporate interests, political operatives and activists, and GOP party officials. The result is an ecosystem that produces a repertoire of legal and political arguments that help make more plausible claims like those that undermined the ACA or asserted corporate personhood rights – legal theories that without this infrastructure, would not gain visibility or traction.

Second, these networks also shift the occupants of key policymaking and judicial offices. As Nick Carnes has suggested in his work on legislative capture, elite cultural capture operates not just by changing the voices that speak in courtrooms through litigation; it also changes the *listeners* of those arguments (Carnes 2013). As more judges and policymakers are themselves drawn from groups participating in these formative intellectual spaces, novel legal arguments that favor business interests – whether deploying the First Amendment in new ways or applying economic reasoning to legal questions – do not just find more effective articulation in courtrooms and policy debates, but also more receptive audiences for these arguments.

These deep cultural investments are particularly effective in the legal domain, where the resources of ordinary voters are arguably at their weakest. Mass mobilizations with respect to the courts overwhelmingly center on social issues, while citizens remain largely unaware of the ramifications of most of the pro-business decisions we have discussed. Moreover, given law's self-conception as a community of practice insulated from politics and premised on pure legal reasoning, the existence of a community of self-identified legal thinkers who identify with the kinds of legal doctrines that favor business interests represents a fertile substrate upon which to build the kinds of electoral, political, and litigation strategies that have yielded victories like *Janus* and *NFIB*.

CONCLUSION

A comprehensive account of business interests and their strategic actions and investments within in the American judicial and legal system is beyond the scope of one essay. This chapter offers a start by sketching in broad brushstrokes the interplay between business interests and the legal system across key domains, and the effects on public policy and the structure of the American political economy as a whole. Several central themes emerge from this story that are ripe for future scholarship in this area.

First, courts and the law are a terrain of strategic political action – albeit one that operates in a different form than ordinary electoral politics. The success of the late twentieth-century conservative counter-revolution owes much to the ability of the conservative movement and its business allies to operate across different sites of policymaking – elections, legislatures, bureaucracies, courts – and to do so at both the state and federal levels. As such, the courts are deeply imbricated in the multi-level, multi-venue political playing field depicted in the Introduction of this volume. Indeed, the courts form a critical node in that landscape because of the ways in which judicial power can be leveraged to constrain or enable other forms of state power: striking down legislation, creatively interpreting statutes to narrow or expand their scope, and strategically avoiding legal disputes that might challenge background disparities of power and influence in the economy. Furthermore, the fact that the activities of the judiciary, especially of lower and state courts, operate beneath the radar for most voters and even much of the media magnifies the ability of organized interests to build and exercise influence in this domain.

Second, the domain of law and courts as a terrain of political contestation operates on a very different timescale than that in other political arenas, which in turn drives very different strategies for building influence. The power that business interests had secured via the legal system by the late twentieth century did not come easily. In fact, this achievement involved a stunning comeback from the near-total defeat of business interests in the early New Deal era. It stemmed from a decades-long investment in an ideational infrastructure that cultivated members and alliances across the fields of law, business, and politics, which facilitated the very gradual formation and validation of conservative legal concepts that could be weaponized decades later by business litigants. These types of strategies require a heavy investment of resources over long time horizons and significant coordination – precisely the strengths that characterize repeat players like business interests.

3

Collective Action, Law, and the Fragmented Development of the American Labor Movement

Alexander Hertel-Fernandez

The study of American political economy requires focus on a very different set of actors than does the conventional study of American politics as practiced by contemporary scholars. In particular, the core questions surrounding the American political economy call for a deep understanding of the preferences, power, and tactics of organized actors – and the ways that those organized actors both influence, and are influenced by, economic and political institutions. And within the universe of US organized interests, *producer and class interests* are especially relevant, encompassing labor, business, and increasingly, wealthy Americans that are collectively constitutive of the political economy. Such a political economy perspective contrasts with other approaches that either do not center economic interests or treat such interests as relatively interchangeable with one another.

In this chapter, I consider the development of the American labor movement, focusing closely on the intersection between law, collective action, geographic and territorial divisions of political authority, and labor's political and economic power. A central argument of this chapter is how disruptive – and even illegal – collective action by workers can produce changes in public policy that entrench labor's clout in the market and in politics.

Yet US public policies have also increasingly constrained the labor movement, and this chapter discusses the ways that early policy decisions fragmented American unions along both sectoral and geographic lines, with enduring consequences through present day. Indeed, a comparative analysis of labor law across rich democracies reveals that the division of American labor law across both sectors, but especially levels of government, is relatively unique. That fragmentation has weakened labor's capacity to shape national politics and to take advantage of otherwise-favorable political opportunities.

Just as importantly, I consider how polarization, especially among donors, private-sector businesses, and activists on the political right, has fueled a backlash to the public-sector labor movement, aided by labor's sectoral and geographic fragmentation. This backlash fused racial resentment in the mass public together with coordination among elite corporate and individual donors, reflecting a broader strategy within the contemporary GOP coalition (also described in our Introduction). The conservative counteroffensive against labor has also been aided by businesses' advantages in cross-state advocacy, including state lawmakers' fears of capital flight, another distinctive element of US federalism.

Taken together, this chapter underscores several major themes developed in the introduction to this volume, including the effects of territorial and geographic division of US political authority, long-term repercussions of political alliances between private-sector businesses, increasingly conservative activists, and right-leaning donors on US public policies, and the central role of the courts and the law for the nature of the US political economy.

WHAT IS DISTINCTIVE ABOUT THE AMERICAN LABOR MOVEMENT?

Figure 3.1 summarizes the historical development of unions in the United States, focusing on total union membership in the public and private sectors from 1930 through 2019. It illustrates three key facts about the US labor movement: (1) public-sector unions followed a very different trajectory than did private-sector unions, reflecting a separate legal regime and underlying set of political developments; (2) private-sector unions have been in steep decline since their peak in the 1950s so that membership in private-sector unions is now lower than it was before the passage of the 1935 federal law recognizing the right of private-sector workers to organize and bargain collectively; and (3) although membership in public-sector unions is currently substantially higher than in the private sector, government union membership rolls have been steadily declining since the 2000s.

How unusual are these characteristics of the American labor movement? Figures 3.2 and 3.3 lay out the picture of similar trends in other

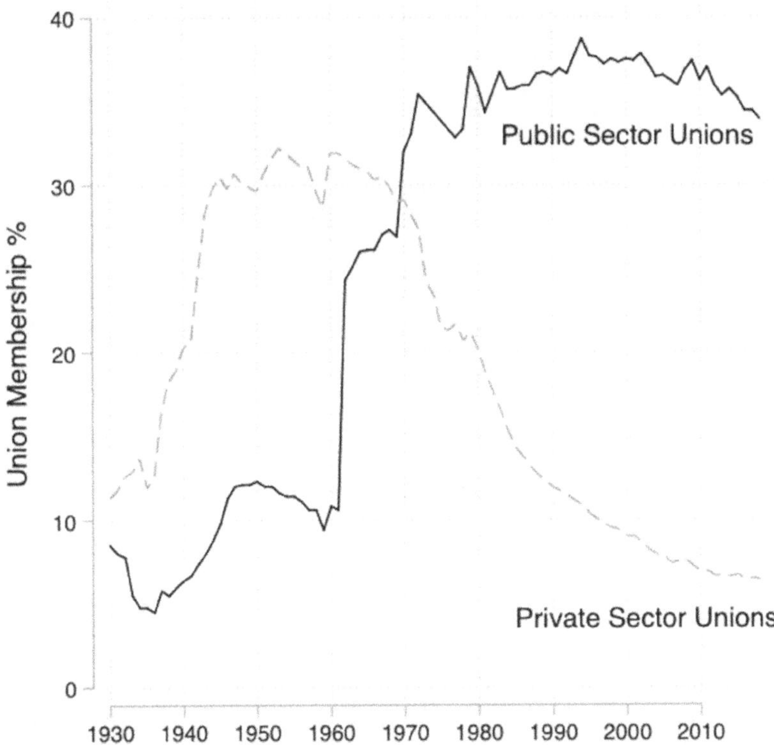

FIGURE 3.1 The historical development of the US labor movement
Notes: Union density before 1972 from the Troy-Sheflin series reported in Eidlin 2018; Bureau of Labor Statistics thereafter.

advanced economies with data from the ICTWSS Database.[1] Figure 3.2 plots trends in union coverage – that is, the proportion of workers covered by collective bargaining agreements – and union membership. Here the United States stands out for two features: not only are its union coverage and membership rates among the lowest of peer rich democracies, but unlike many other countries there is essentially no difference between its coverage and membership rates. That is because American labor law as enshrined in the 1935 National Labor Relations Act built a system of labor organizing and bargaining centered on establishments – individual plants, stores, or factories – rather than on companies as a whole, or even

[1] J. Visser, ICTWSS Database, version 6.1. Amsterdam: Amsterdam Institute for Advanced Labour Studies (AIAS), University of Amsterdam. November 2019.

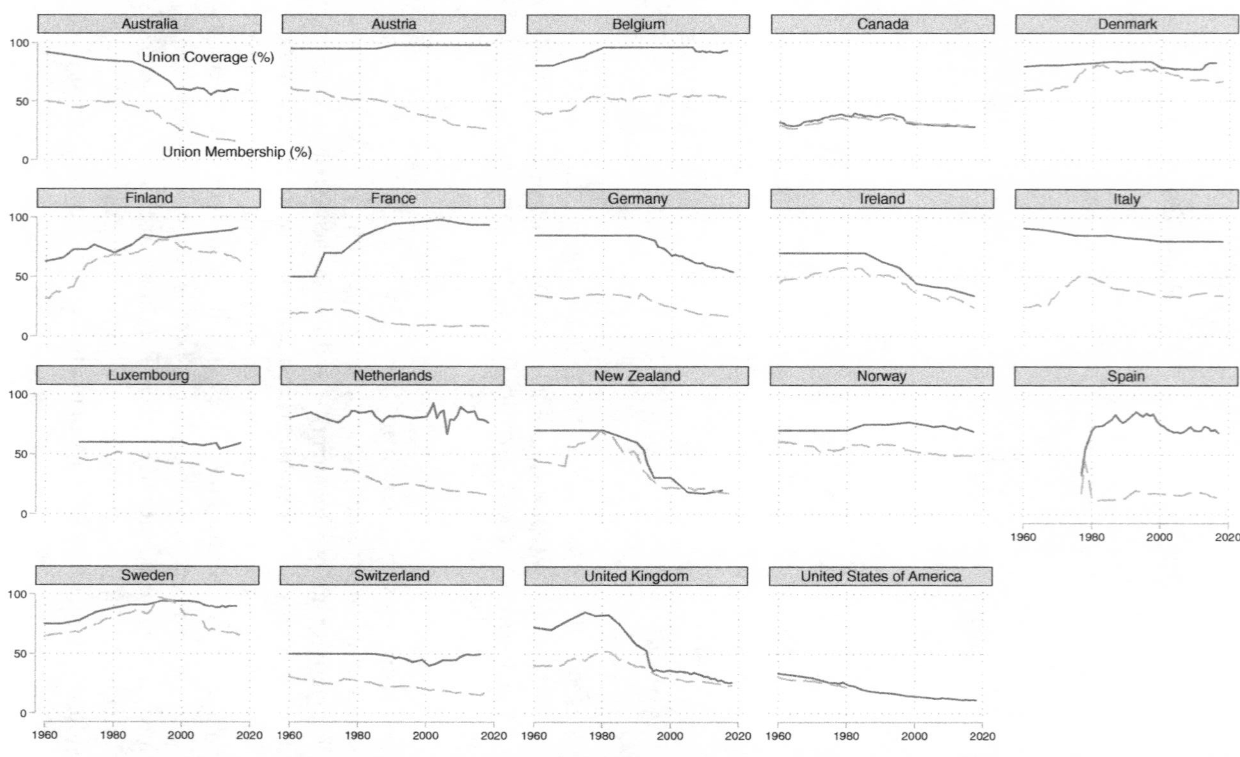

FIGURE 3.2 Union coverage and membership rates in advanced democracies

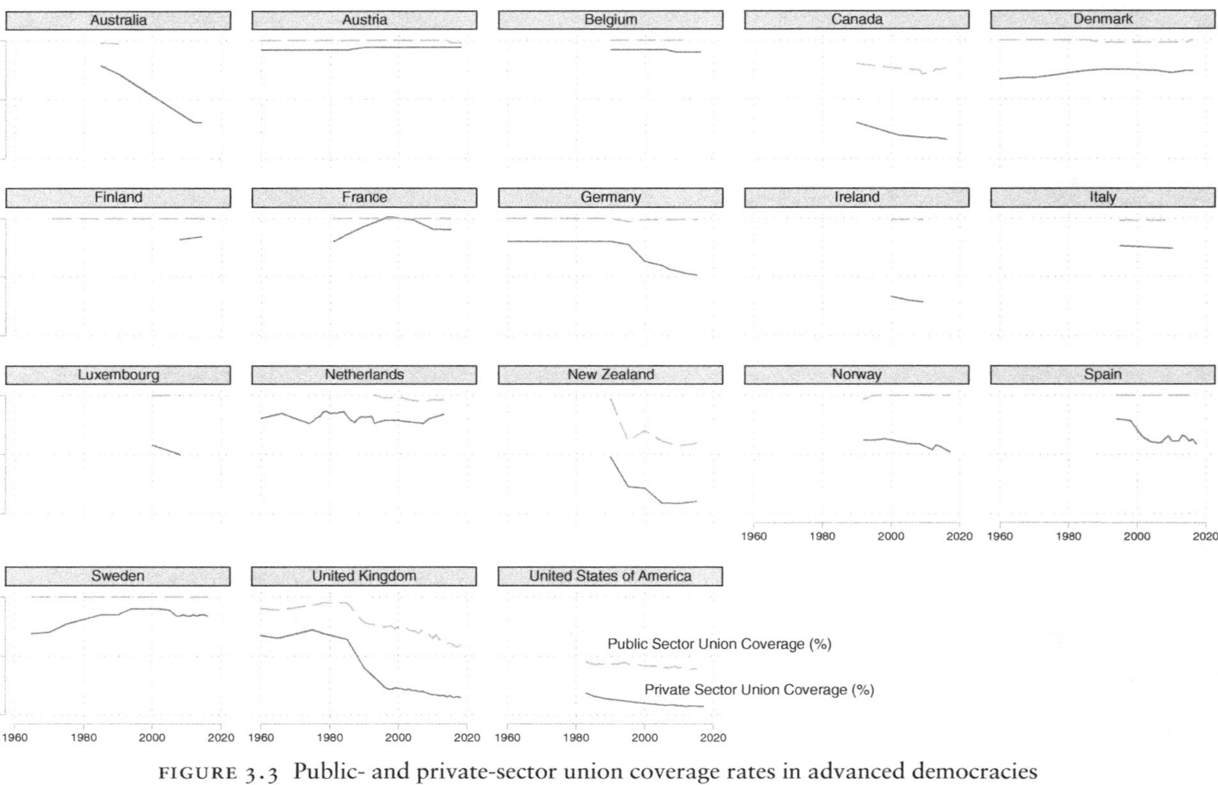

FIGURE 3.3 Public- and private-sector union coverage rates in advanced democracies

regions or sectors as in other countries, like Germany. As many other scholars have noted, this enterprise-based model of unionization has contributed mightily to the woes of the US private-sector labor movement (e.g., Andrias 2016; Naidu, this volume). Figure 3.3 compares union coverage rates in the public and private sectors. Again, the United States stands out as a relative outlier for its relatively low levels of *both* public and private-sector coverage. While other countries have different levels of union strength between the public and private sectors, few other countries have such low and declining levels of labor, particularly in the government sector. Only the United Kingdom and New Zealand exhibited similar drops in public-sector union coverage in recent decades – yet both the British and New Zealand government union coverage rates have stabilized at rates much higher than in the United States.

Why have unionization rates in the United States fallen so sharply, especially in the public sector? To answer that question, we can first look to the comparative data again to see what is different about the structure of American labor laws. What sets the United States apart from other rich democracies is not necessarily that it has separate laws governing public and private unions; many other countries treat government and private-sector workers differently when it comes to union recognition, collective bargaining, and strike rights. Rather, what makes the United States distinct is the low level of rights afforded to *all* workers as well as the institutional fragmentation of public-sector labor rights across subnational units.

Only one other rich democracy – Canada – delegates as much control over union rights to subnational governments as does the United States (OECD 1994). But even in Canada, union rights are more uniform than in the United States. Canadian teachers, for instance, enjoy collective bargaining rights (albeit with variable scope) in all thirteen provinces and territories, and at least some strike rights in eleven provinces and territories (Hanson 2013). By comparison, local governments are only required to bargain with American teachers in thirty-three states and teachers only have strike rights in thirteen states. American labor rights, especially in the public sector, are thus uniquely geographically uneven in comparative perspective.

Comparisons of government union membership across provinces and states tell a similar story (McCartin 2008; Walker 2014). In 2019, US public union membership rates varied from just 7 percent in South Carolina to 66 percent in New York – a 59 percentage point gap. Across the northern border, rates of public union coverage in

Canadian provinces in 2019 ranged from 71 percent in Ontario to 88 percent in Prince Edward Island, a gap of only 17 points. What accounts for that uneven subnational development in the United States? To answer that question, we must return to the New Deal era, when the Franklin Delano Roosevelt administration enacted new legislation guaranteeing workers their first federal rights to organize and collectively bargain with employers in the 1935 National Labor Relations Act (or NLRA).

A STALLED NATIONAL LABOR MOVEMENT IN THE NEW DEAL ERA

The Wagner Act, as the NLRA was dubbed, reflected a series of significant compromises, setting in place a firm-centered organizing and bargaining model for American unions that ultimately restricted their reach and power, especially given recent changes in corporate governance practices (e.g., Andrias 2016; Andrias and Rogers 2018). Not only does the NLRA require unions to organize store by store or factory by factory, greatly increasing the costs of organizing an entire business or sector, but a firm-centered approach also raises employers' incentives for fighting unionization efforts if they must compete against nonunion firms within their region or industry (e.g., Dimick 2014). Yet even in spite of these important limits, the Wagner Act offered what previous state and federal legislation had not: a federally protected national right to form and join a union and bargain collectively with employers.

In a testament to the law's ambition, shortly after the NLRA passed employers began efforts to retrench labor's hard-won rights to restore employer prerogatives in the workplace. In a series of landmark decisions, the Supreme Court began siding with employers to restrict the scope of the NLRA, especially on the issues of strikes and the "right to manage" (Pope 2004). No less important was a turn against labor in the mass public, most pronounced in the South but also present among Northern Democrats as well (Schickler and Caughey 2011). While it is difficult to isolate specific causes for the public's souring on the labor movement, the timing of the shifts corresponded to an upsurge in labor militancy that the public viewed as illegitimate, especially in the run-up to the war. This dynamic points to a tension that the labor movement faced repeatedly throughout history: balancing the need for aggressive workplace actions that can amass political and economic power to secure changes in public policy against the risk of public backlash.

Although the Roosevelt administration and Northern Democratic leaders staved off the most significant efforts to curtail labor rights, Republicans, allied with anti-labor Southern Democrats, continued to use the resources of Congress to campaign against the labor movement and ultimately succeeded in gaining sufficient power in the 80th Congress to pass, over President Harry Truman's veto, the 1947 amendments to the NLRA. Supported by businesses and anti-union conservatives in both parties, the Taft-Hartley Act imposed new federal restrictions on union activities, including strikes and boycotts, granted employers expanded rights to curb unionization drives, and excluded low-level managers and supervisors from the reach of NLRA rights (Lichtenstein 1998). Perhaps most prominently, the law barred closed shops (requiring employers to hire union members) and permitted states to enact their own restrictions on union or agency fee shops – provisions in collectively bargained agreements whereby unions could require workers to either join the union after starting work or to pay fees to the union to cover the costs of collective bargaining and other union services. Perversely, Taft-Hartley meant that state governments could *limit* union rights under the NLRA, but given the statute's otherwise broad preemption language as interpreted by the courts, states could not pass policies *expanding* union rights. As we will see, labor's opponents have taken advantage of this asymmetry to retrench the power of labor (see also Galvin and Hacker 2020).

The passage of Taft-Hartley thus foreclosed a number of union organizing strategies that would have helped the labor movement retain and gain clout against increasingly aggressive employer opposition. But it also had another pernicious consequence for the labor movement that would reverberate over the years: it meant that private-sector unions could never gain a significant presence outside of their Midwestern and Northeastern strongholds during the long New Deal era. The Congress of Industrial Organization launched its ambitious "Operation Dixie" campaign in 1946 to overcome this geographic limitation and build political and economic strength in the solidly anti-union South. But in an irony of poor timing, the CIO's campaign began just months before anti-union capitalists and conservatives gained new tools for opposing unions with the Taft-Hartley Act. Without such support from government, the resistance from the white political and economic leadership of the South "proved overwhelming" (Lichtenstein 1989, 136).

The lost possibility of a truly national private-sector labor movement matters because of the territoriality and federalism present in American political institutions: without uniform power established across the states, the labor movement could not make a sustained bid for influence either at the state level (with control of state legislatures, courts, and governorships) *or* in Congress and the White House (through labor's relationship to local and state political parties electing candidates to federal office) outside of the states in which they gained an initial industrial foothold in the New Deal. Those curbs on national power have also limited unions' ability to pass labor law reforms that might have created new political opportunities. Quite strikingly, the only labor legislation passed since the New Deal has generally involved further restrictions on union activities – a powerful example of Congressional policy drift (explored in more detail in the Kelly and Morgan chapter of this volume; see also Galvin and Hacker 2020).

The fragmentation of the labor movement along geographic lines was joined by fragmentation along sectoral lines, as public sector workers were excluded from the rights afforded by the National Labor Relations Act. By 1935, government employees were a substantial – and growing – part of the US workforce. According to Department of Labor estimates, in the year that the NLRA passed there were just over 2.7 million state and local government employees, including over 1 million teachers and other educators, and another 820,000 federal employees. Yet as political scientist Alexis Walker (2014) has uncovered, barely any mention was made of these public employees (or their unions) in the drafting of the NLRA's text. And perhaps even more surprisingly, the major public-sector unions at the time (including the American Federation of State, County, and Municipal Employee's founding local in Wisconsin) were largely positive about the Wagner Act, encouraging their Members of Congress to support the bill in spite of the absence of any recognition of union rights for public-sector employees.

Congressional drafters of labor relations bills were well aware of the exclusion and thought that it was necessary to avoid a heated confrontation over an already-complex set of proposals. There was simply no consensus over the extension of labor rights to government employees at the time, and public-sector unions were pessimistic about their chances of gaining legal recognition even in local and state government. Indeed, among Roosevelt's prolabor allies there was a shared sense that government employees were different from private-sector workers and the nature of their relationship to the state meant that it was not possible to collectively bargain with public-sector unions. Roosevelt himself had explained that he felt the "very nature and purposes" of government work implied that it was "impossible for administrative officials to represent fully or to bind the employer in mutual discussions with Government employee organizations" (qtd. in Cornell 1958: 48). As a result, government employee unions would need to wait for several more decades to gain the same degree of legal recognition of their rights to organize and collectively bargain – and even then, those rights would be granted at the local and state level, not from the federal government. In this way, sectoral exclusions drove further geographic fragmentation.

STRIKE WAVES PAVE THE WAY FOR RECOGNITION OF PUBLIC-SECTOR UNIONS OUTSIDE OF NATIONAL LAW

By the 1950s, many city and municipal public workers had begun forming and joining unions, even though they had no widely recognized legal protections or rights to bargain collectively with their employers (Cornell 1958). Mounting pressure led several large cities, including Philadelphia, to develop bargaining and negotiation procedures for some of these unions. In an important burst of activity in the late 1950s and early 1960s, Wisconsin passed a law recognizing bargaining rights for its municipal employees (1959), New York City established bargaining procedures for its teachers after educators, represented by the newly formed United Federation of Teachers, went on a massive day-long strike (1961), and President John F. Kennedy promulgated an Executive Order recognizing the right of federal employees to join unions of their choosing (1962).

The New York City teachers offered the playbook for how other government employees would eventually gain and expand their bargaining rights: sustained, high-profile, and very much illegal strikes (Shelton 2017). Indeed, what made public union – and especially teacher union – mobilization in the 1960s and 1970s notable was the fact that so many states and localities imposed stiff penalties on striking public-sector workers, motivated by the belief that public-sector work was not comparable to the private sector and should not be disrupted with strikes (Burns 2014). In fact, in passing initial legislation to recognize the bargaining rights of public-sector employees, many states added or bolstered bans on strikes to ensure labor peace (Anzia and Moe 2016; Paglayan 2019); in 1955, only seven states imposed legal bans on teacher strikes, but by 1975 that figure had grown to thirty-one states.[2] In all, a total of nineteen of the

[2] National Bureau of Economic Research Public Sector Collective Bargaining Law Data Set, with updates from Kim Rueben and Leslie Finger.

thirty-three mandatory collective bargaining laws introduced over this period included bolstered bans on strikes (Paglayan 2019).

Thus, in order to further expand their union rights and push for higher salaries and benefits, many public-sector workers (and especially teachers) broke the law through their strikes and other collective actions. As the head of the UFT argued, even if state law said otherwise, teachers "have the right to strike [as an] ultimate weapon."[3] More recent quantitative analysis examining the passage of teacher collective bargaining rights across the states reveals the critical importance of strikes for teacher pay and classroom conditions: the expansion of collective bargaining rights *only* increased school spending and teacher pay – reflections of the material gains of labor's demands – where teachers possessed a credible strike threat (Paglayan 2019).

The geographic and numerical reach of these public-sector strikes, especially among teachers, cannot be overstated and headlines from the *New York Times* during this period offer a flavor of its massive scope: "Michigan Teacher Strikes Delay School for 500,000" (1967); "Three-Week Strike by Florida Public School Teachers Appeared at an End Today" (1968); "Teachers Vote to Strike Today: A Million Pupils Here Affected [in New York City] (1975); and "Ohio Teachers Adopt New 'Reverse Strike' Shock Tactic to Gain Tax Money for Schools and Substantial Raises" (1968). The country went from seeing an average of three teacher strikes per year in the 1950s to *300* teacher strikes in the 1960s, and over *100* in 1967 (Shelton 2017). At their peak, the teacher strikes involved over 324,000 educators in 1975.

It is not surprising that teachers were at the vanguard of the new public-sector activism. Teachers accounted for one of the largest occupations within the growing government employee workforce. Out of the 8.5 million public-sector workers employed in 1950, 2.3 million worked for local public schools – roughly the same number of workers as were employed by the entire federal government. Unlike other government workers who might be concentrated in a few large cities, moreover, teachers were employed in nearly every city or town, giving their movement broad and deep reach across the country. And perhaps most important, teachers held highly visible and respected roles in their communities, with social ties to students and families – ties cutting across class and party, if not race. All of those features gave teachers powerful leverage that they could use in their collective action.

[3] "Teachers Group Firm on Strikes." 1961. *New York Times*: November 27.

Together, the large-scale collective action by teachers and other public-sector employees transformed the landscape of labor law and the labor movement more generally. While "only a small fraction of schoolteachers" had bargaining rights before 1961, by the end of the 1970s, 72 percent of all public school teachers were members of a union with legally recognized bargaining rights (Shelton 2017).

The reverberations of the massive public-sector strike waves from the 1960s and 1970s continue to present day, captured in the legislation recognizing the collective bargaining rights of teachers and, through it, in the organizational clout of public-sector labor unions (Anzia and Moe 2016; Flavin and Hartney 2015; Hartney 2014). This is a clear example of how large-scale labor collective action can feed back into public policy – with implications for political and economic organization decades later. Figure 3.4 summarizes the relationship between the historical intensity of teacher strikes in the 1960s and 1970s and present-day public policy and political resources available to teachers unions across the states.

The left-hand plot indicates the scope of collective bargaining rights enjoyed by teachers unions in 2018, averaging together a 0–3 scale for collective bargaining coverage on a variety of issues, where 0 indicates the absence of collective bargaining altogether, 1 indicates that unions are prohibited from bargaining on an issue, 2 indicates that unions and employers are permitted to negotiate over an issue but are not required to do so, and 3 indicates that the issue is mandatory for the parties to cover. As Figure 3.4 makes clear, states like Pennsylvania, Illinois, and Alaska that had greater strike activity during the critical 1960s and 1970s period continue to possess broader collective bargaining rights today. But it is not just a friendlier legal regime. Teachers unions enjoy greater organizational clout, too, as captured in the right-hand plot that examines the revenue collected by state education associations in 2018 (or the latest available year reported to the IRS), scaled by the size of a state's public-sector workforce. States with more historical strike activity tend to have teacher unions with greater resources to invest in continued labor and political mobilization in present day (for additional quantitative analysis of this relationship, see Anzia and Moe 2016).

FRAGMENTATION OF THE PUBLIC-SECTOR LABOR MOVEMENT – AND COUNTERMOBILIZATION ON THE RIGHT

Returning to Figure 3.1, we can see that the rise of the public-sector labor movement occurred just as private-sector unions were steadily losing

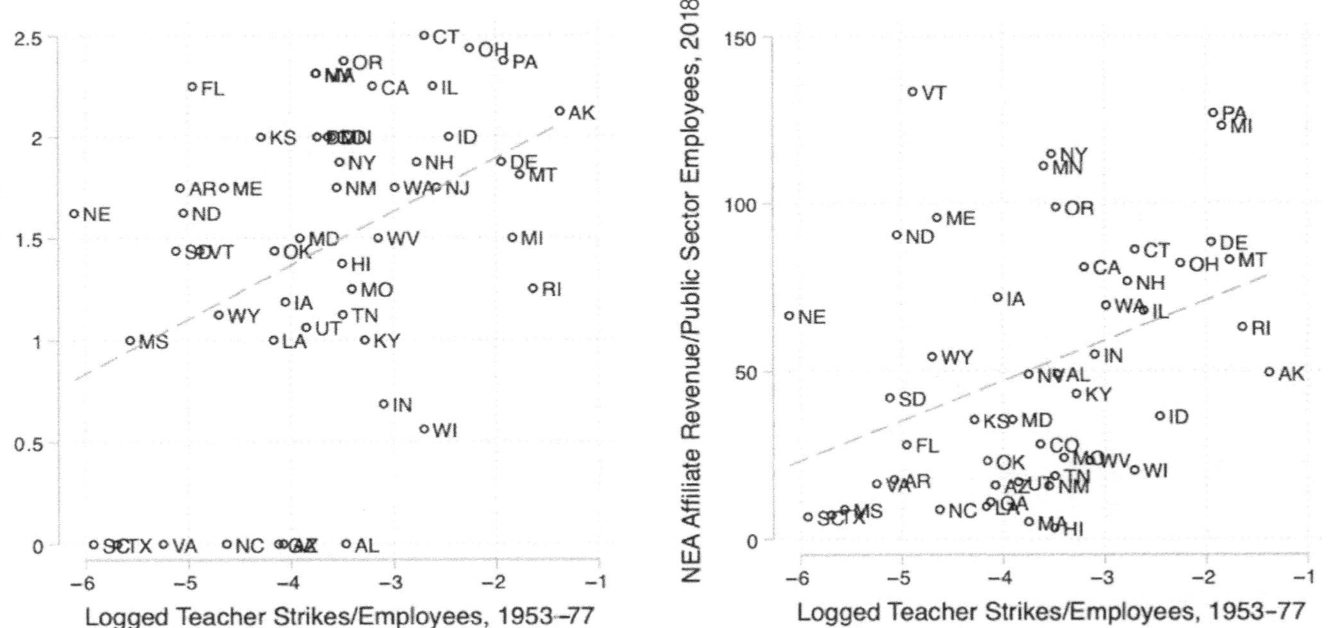

FIGURE 3.4 The long-run political consequences of 1960s and 1970s teacher strikes

Note: Teacher collective bargaining rights data from author's review of state law. NEA revenue from IRS 990 filings. Public-sector workforce, teacher strikes, and state employment from Bureau of Labor Statistics.

members in the face of major shifts in the economy alongside intensified employer opposition (Farber and Western 2001; Lichtenstein 2002; Logan 2006). The newly militant public-sector unions might have shored up the national labor movement as a whole. And they might have also provided a crucial linkage for the labor movement across the states, given that private-sector unions had historically struggled to connect intermediary linkages between their organization at the local, shop-floor level and at the national or international union level (Weir 2009; Hertel-Fernandez 2019b: ch. 7). By comparison, public-sector unions depended on state government for their recognition and bargaining, and therefore had good reason to establish a strong state-level presence (Skocpol et al. 2000).

Crucial to that vision of a more unified labor movement was the passage of federal legislation that would have enshrined the collective bargaining rights of public-sector employees into national law, ensuring that government workers across all states would have the same rights to form and join unions. But such a vision of unified labor was not to be. Division in the labor movement, an emboldened conservative opposition, and especially a public turn against government-sector strikes scuttled a National Public Employment Relations bill in the mid-1970s – the closest that public sector workers have come to such legislation (McCartin 2008; Walker 2014). Like the backlash against labor during the late New Deal era, the public's growing scorn for government employee activism in the 1970s again illustrates the delicate balance workers face between engaging in disruptive activism needed to secure legislative gains while also preventing backlash when their demands are seen as illegitimate by the mass public. While earlier mobilizations by government employees were supported by broad segments of the population, the public turned against later wildcat strikes and protests seen as a power-hungry grab by government workers during hard economic times (McCartin 2008, 139). No less important, as we will see, was the growing ability of opponents of public sector unions to cast their appeals in racialized terms given the demographics of government employees and the clients they served.

As a result of the failure to expand the reach of government-sector unions, public-sector unions remained similarly geographically constrained as their private-sector counterparts. Instead of corresponding to the concentration of industrial activity across space, however, public-sector unions were concentrated in states according to the favorability of their state laws governing organizing and collective bargaining rights – which in turn reflected strike activity in the 1960s and 1970s. It is only really in the Mid-Atlantic, Northeast, and Pacific coast areas that states continue to have especially strong public-sector unions. In broad swaths of the South and West there is very minimal public union membership – a crucial element to the distinctive political economies in those "red states" documented in the chapter by Grumbach, Hacker, and Pierson in this volume.

Just as with the private-sector labor movement, then, public-sector unions' scope to influence our highly territorialized and federalized political institutions was constrained given their geographic concentration. And even in the states in which public-sector unions retain significant membership, their integration into the broader labor movement remains highly variegated across states. While public-sector unions are working closely with private-sector unions in some states, in others they are much less coordinated with one another, especially when it comes to state politics (Hertel-Fernandez 2019b: ch. 7).

Why does public-sector union integration with the rest of the labor movement matter? To the extent that public-sector unions are not united with private-sector unions, it will be harder for the labor movement to work together and to speak with one political voice. And under those circumstances, labor unions ought to have weaker political clout in state-level politics (see also Ahlquist 2012; Hurd and Lee 2014). That is consistent with arguments advanced by Christina Kinane and Rob Mickey (2018), who make the case that union fragmentation results in reduced union political power.

Weaker incorporation of public- and private-sector unions can even lead private-sector unions to support candidates and policies that run against the interests of their government employee counterparts. For instance, in Wisconsin, the building and construction trades unions supported hard-right GOP Governor Scott Walker – even as Walker pushed for unprecedented cutbacks to public-sector bargaining rights that would devastate government employee unions, and especially those representing teachers (Kaufman 2018). In fact, several building trades unions made hefty campaign contributions to reelect Walker in 2014, well after the effects of public union retrenchment had been felt across the state.[4]

The bifurcation of the public- and private-sector labor movements has implications for mass political behavior, too. The demographic profile of the typical public-sector worker in the United States – and by extension,

[4] See www.wisdc.org/news/press-releases/76-press-release-2015/4888-unions-contributed-more-than-83k-to-help-reelect-walker.

the typical public-sector *union* member – is very different from the private-sector workforce. Public-sector union members are much more likely to be female and to be highly educated (especially with a college degree or more) compared to private-sector workers (Wolfe and Schmitt 2018). Men represent a little over half of the private-sector workforce, but only 42 percent of state and local employee unions. Similarly, only about a third of private-sector workers hold a college degree, compared to over 62 percent of state and local union members. And while the public-sector workforce tilts whiter than the private-sector workforce, Black women in particular are over-represented in state and local government unions compared to white women and men of any race (McNicholas and Jones 2018).

These demographic differences have created potent possibilities for anti-union activists to mobilize gender, class, and racial resentment among private-sector workers against public-sector employees and their unions (Ratliff et al. 2019; Tesler 2016) and are part of the more general racialization of government and public services (e.g., Filindra and Kaplan 2020). As Katherine Cramer has documented persuasively in Wisconsin, prodded on by conservative politicians, media, and activists, private-sector workers in the state – even current and former union members – blamed government employees (and by extension, public-sector unions) for their economic woes (Cramer 2014; 2016). The main complaint of these private-sector workers was a sense that state employees were lazy, out-of-touch professional workers paid exorbitant wages and benefits from taxpayer money. In turn, public-sector largess was the reason why those private-sector workers felt they had not seen wage gains or adequate pension and health benefits (see also Kane and Newman 2019). Wisconsinites holding these feelings about teachers and other public-sector employees then became an important constituency for conservative Republican Governor Scott Walker and his campaign to retrench public-sector union rights after his successful 2010 election and part of the broader Tea Party movement (Skocpol and Williamson 2012).

As the example of the politics of resentment in Wisconsin makes clear, mass opposition to government unions has an elite basis. That elite backlash against public-sector unions, in turn, has its roots in the public-employee strike wave in the 1960s and the 1970s, which spurred an intense countermobilization of businesses and conservative activists that sought to retrench the legal rights that public-sector workers had fought to gain, including in states like Wisconsin that had long supported government employee unions (see also McCartin 2008).

Looking across the states in the 1970s, leading conservative activists were concerned about the rise of the public-sector labor movement, especially teachers, as a formidable presence in state government that were part of a broader national federation. That meant that public-sector unions, like AFSCME (representing federal, state, and local agency workers) and the AFT and NEA (representing teachers), could redistribute financial resources across their affiliates. But it also meant that they could quickly disseminate policy ideas across the states in which they had amassed substantial memberships, pushing for the same policies across many states at the same time.

Crucially, conservatives noted, public-sector unions did not restrict themselves to lobbying on issues narrowly related to their occupations, but rather were involved in a range of other policy areas (Hertel-Fernandez 2019b: ch. 7). One conservative leader noted that at the time, the "most effective lobby in the state legislatures" was the "National Education Association." She continued:

> Many people are deceived by believing that the National Education Association lobbies only for education-related legislation, but they don't. They oppose right to work laws, they oppose balanced budget resolutions, they support comparable work bills, they get involved in just about every piece of major legislation in the state legislature. They are very well organized, extremely well-funded. (qtd. in Hertel-Fernandez 2019b: ch. 1)

Summing up, another conservative leader explained that groups like the newly enlarged teachers unions

> came up with model legislation, which [they] would push in several states at the same time ... [and then they] would use the argument, "Well, if so-and-so passed it, it must be okay." And so the bill would go forward, sometimes in 30 states and more. Usually, the liberal bill moved from committee to floor vote before you [the conservative activists] got prepared and marshaled your arguments, if then. The local [conservative activists] were on their own in each state – and they were overwhelmed. (qtd. in Hertel-Fernandez 2019b: ch. 1)

In response, a small group of right-leaning politicians, aided by several conservative institution-builders and donors, formed the "Conservative Caucus of State Legislators," intended to provide a forum and support network for state elected officials who wanted to promote a more conservative agenda. Later rebranded as the American Legislative Exchange Council (ALEC), this organization would go on to bring together private-sector businesses, conservative activists and donors, and state legislators to craft "model bill" proposals for state governments.

While the issues that ALEC has pursued have changed over time, reflecting the changing composition of its membership, one common through line across its history of bill proposals has been the promotion of bills attacking labor unions – above all unions in the public sector. These include proposals for right-to-work laws banning agency fees, cutbacks to collective bargaining rights, measures to make it more challenging for unions to collect dues, obstacles to union political mobilization, and onerous requirements for regular recertification.

ALEC has never seen these anti-labor bills as ends in themselves. Rather, ALEC has helped its members, especially its corporate members, to understand that passing bills cutting back public union labor rights would weaken liberal political power and make it harder for Democrats to win elections. That, in turn, would pave the way for ALEC to pass legislation favored by its private-sector businesses, libertarian activists, and social conservative advocacy groups.

ALEC's pitch about retrenching public-sector union rights was innovative because there is no reason why all of its members, especially many of its corporate members, would necessarily be invested in battling teachers or other government employees. While school choice reformers and other small-government libertarians had a clear reason to go up against teachers, ALEC's private-sector businesses did not have a direct motive to get behind the drive as opposed to ALEC's other efforts related to tax cuts, regulatory rollbacks, or business-friendly subsidies. Instead, it was a testament to ALEC's coordination as an association that it helped its corporate constituents see the value of using policy not just as a means of achieving specific technical objectives (like promoting school choice or pursuing tax cuts) but rather a way to reshape political power – by defanging their opponents (Feigenbaum et al. 2019; Hertel-Fernandez 2019a). Here we can clearly see the crucial role of business associations (led by political activists and entrepreneurs) in promoting collective action of firms against public unions in contrast to unions in the private sector (see also Martin 2000; Martin and Swank 2012). In this way, ALEC's conservative leaders helped to steer private-sector firms toward the conservative, anti-government agendas documented both in the Introduction and in the chapter by Rahman and Thelen in this volume.

Over time, ALEC's efforts were buttressed by two other cross-state networks also focused on defeating the labor movement: the State Policy Network (SPN; founded in 1986) and Americans for Prosperity (AFP; launched in 2004). While the SPN focused on assembling a network of conservative, business friendly think tanks in each state, AFP built a federated advocacy group of grassroots volunteers and paid staff that could intervene in school board, city council, state, and federal elections and policy debates. But despite representing different constituencies and engaging in different activities, all three organizations promote similar policy priorities, especially when it comes to defeating public-sector labor unions.

These three organizations have championed a number of state-level cutbacks in union rights that have weakened unions and Democratic electoral odds in states like Indiana, Michigan, Wisconsin, Iowa, Kentucky, and West Virginia (Feigenbaum et al. 2019). But importantly, the three conservative networks have not restricted themselves to fighting in the state legislative arena. They have also sought measures to stymie government employee unions through the courts, and SPN think tank affiliates have supported several of the recent federal court decisions that make it harder for public-sector unions to attract and retain members and raise revenue (Hertel-Fernandez 2019b: ch. 7; see also Rahman and Thelen's chapter in this volume).

Most significantly, SPN affiliates helped to provide the intellectual case for the *Janus* v. *AFSCME* decision (and its precursor in *Friedrichs* v. *California Teachers Association*), which ruled that no public-sector union can charge fees to non-members, even if the non-members benefit from union-bargained contracts and grievance procedures. That decision effectively applied right-to-work to all government employees, even in previously non-right-to-work states, like New York, California, and Illinois, greatly hindering the ability of public-sector unions to attract members and sustain revenue. The courts thus helped conservative activists to achieve retrenchment of public-sector union power even in states where those activists could not have hoped to pass new state legislation. In a good illustration of how American political institutions favor organized groups that can move seamlessly between venues, as soon as the decision passed, SPN affiliates worked with AFP's grassroots chapters to contact government employee union members and inform them of their newly gained rights to leave their union without having to pay agency fees, further weakening labor power.

In sum, the wave of public-sector strikes that rolled across the country throughout the 1960s and 1970s deeply reshaped American political terrain. Through these strikes, government employees convinced the public – and ultimately elected officials – of the worthiness of their demands for higher wages, benefits, and collective bargaining. Where public-sector workers organized and engaged in more extensive labor action, they were more likely to see state laws entrench their rights to form unions, collectively bargain, and collect dues. And through those laws, unions were able to organize more members and raise more revenue. Yet the strike wave was incomplete, missing many parts of the country that would never expand bargaining rights or did so only partially, leaving public-sector unions fragmented geographically and sectorally within states. The strike wave also prompted an extensive countermobilization from the right that would come to represent one of the most significant threats to the labor movement in recent decades.

Beyond these obstacles to a truly national public-sector labor movement, there are other reasons to be skeptical of further large-scale government union expansion in the United States. The growth of the public-sector workforce has slowed considerably since the 2000s, limiting the pool of potentially eligible workers to join government employee unions. More generally, there remains deep skepticism among many politicians about increasing the size of the public sector, even on the left (Hacker and Pierson 2016). In recent decades, Democrats, fearful of provoking backlash, have instead relied on subsidized or regulated private alternatives to expand public programs (Howard 1997; Mettler 2011). Not only do such "submerged" or "hidden" policies limit the direct employment of government workers, but they also obscure the role of the state, making it harder to build support for expansions of public authority in the future (Mettler 2011). While some Democrats have moved away from this more modest vision of government – for instance, with proposals for the Green New Deal or Medicare for All as well as the emergency relief program enacted by President Joseph R. Biden in early 2021 – plans to durably expand the size of the state face long odds even with full Democratic control of the White House and Congress.

Instead, future public-sector union activism seems most likely to be successful around policies that raise labor standards but do not necessarily increase the size of government, and focused on states that have been cutting essential public services to the point where even conservative citizens are willing to support boosts in public spending. We now turn to two examples of these campaigns in the "Fight for Fifteen" and the "Red for Ed" movements.

THE NEW LABOR LAW TO THE RESCUE?

Assessing recent developments in labor politics, Kate Andrias (2016) has argued that we are seeing the emergence of a "new labor law" that views unions as political actors and seeks to raise working standards across entire sectors and regions, rather than simply at the level of the individual firm. Chief among these examples of new organizing is the Fight for Fifteen movement. Launched in 2012 among low-wage service and retail workers, the campaign is calling for employers and local, state, and federal officials to raise the minimum wage to $15 an hour and to recognize workers' right to form a union.

Although the movement did not directly involve public-sector employees, there are strong parallels between these protests and the strike waves of the 1960s and 1970s in that both the low-wage workers in recent years and the public-sector workers in earlier decades were seeking to raise their labor standards through state legislation. Moreover, both sets of labor actions were conducted outside of traditional labor law: for the low-wage service workers because they lacked a union and for the public-sector employees because they either did not yet have formal bargaining rights or lacked strike rights. And lastly, the biggest backer of the Fight for Fifteen movement is the Service Employees International Union (SEIU), which is by now the second-largest public-sector union in the country, representing more than a million local and state government workers, public school employees, bus drivers, and childcare providers.[5]

Initially, the Fight for Fifteen movement took the form of walk-outs and strikes among fast-food workers at large chains (like McDonalds, Burger King, KFC, and Papa John), but eventually the protests expanded beyond the restaurant sector to include low-wage workers in other industries, culminating in wide-spread demonstrations in some 340 cities. As the direct action continued, community advocacy groups began pushing for legislative and ballot initiatives to raise minimum wages and create other labor market standards – like paid sick and family leave – in a number of cities and states across the country. The campaign boasts that some 10 million workers are on track to receive a $15 an hour minimum wage, and that 19 million workers have received minimum wage boosts since the movement launched (figures from Ashby 2017). And in major symbolic victories, the Democratic Party adopted the target of a $15 an hour minimum wage in its official platform going into the 2016 election and plans for a federal wage hike to that level were initially included in President Biden's rescue plan in 2021.

These are enormous gains that have directly improved the lives of millions of low-wage American workers and undoubtedly shifted the

[5] www.seiu.org/cards/these-fast-facts-will-tell-you-how-were-organized/.

consensus around labor market standards within the Democratic Party (Greenhouse 2016). But without changing the distribution of political power at the state level, the Fight for Fifteen movement cannot truly reach across the whole country, especially in states controlled by Republicans given the federated structure of American government. Republican-controlled states can simply pass "preemption" laws that squelch the ability of their cities to enact labor market standards exceeding the state level (Hertel-Fernandez 2019b: ch. 7). That means that a city in a preempted state cannot increase its minimum wage beyond the level set by the state's legislature. And that is exactly what Republican governments have done, aided by the conservative cross-state networks I described earlier, above all ALEC. By 2016, nearly six of ten Americans lived in a state that preempted local minimum wage increases and nearly four of ten lived in a state preempting local paid sick or family leave. (Hertel-Fernandez 2019b: ch. 7; Bottari and Fischer 2013). Thus, the full impact of the Fight for Fifteen movement will only be felt in states where Democrats and progressives *already* had a substantial degree of political power. The Fight for Fifteen has no purchase in red state economies.

Beyond the limits of its geographic reach, the Fight for Fifteen movement also faces challenges of sustainability. The initiative was originally launched by the Service Employees International Union in an effort to seed a bold "game changer" that could generate the same sort of energy as the vibrant 1930s organizing efforts of the Congress of Industrial Organizations (Ashby 2017; Rolf 2016). But while the effort undoubtedly met its first goal of changing the national discourse around low-wage work, it fell short on its second goal to organize low-wage workers participating in the campaign into "durable worker organizations" that could "build working-class power" (Rosenblum 2017). And without generating substantial numbers of new, dues-paying union members, it is unclear how much Fight for Fifteen contributes to the organizational strength and long-run revival of the labor movement. In part as a result of these difficult considerations, SEIU looked to be winding down its direct commitment to the movement in 2018 (Jamieson 2018).

If the Fight for Fifteen campaign is to have lasting consequences beyond the minimum wage laws it has succeeded in passing outside of red states, it will likely be through the activists and leaders it has helped to train and by the shifts in public opinion it has led. The question is whether future labor efforts can successfully mobilize those grassroots leaders and the mass public to change legislation in ways that would facilitate greater unionization of the low-wage workforce that Fight for Fifteen failed to accomplish. What made the 1960s and 1970s public strike waves so effective was the way that government workers channeled their energy and mass support into changing laws that not only raised wage and benefit standards for their particular occupations but that also bolstered their *collective* rights to organize and bargain, thereby helping to generate policy feedback effects that empowered public-sector labor unions for decades to come.

A very similar question hangs over the recent teacher strikes, also dubbed the "Red for Ed" movement. In February 2018, a group of activist West Virginian teachers convinced their state's teachers unions to go on strike in response to complaints about persistently low wages and the mounting cost of their health insurance plans (Hampson 2019; Hauser 2018). The strike took many by surprise, especially since it unfolded in a very conservative state with weak public-sector labor unions where teacher strikes are illegal. Even more surprising was the response of the state government: after a two week-long strike that left more than 250,000 children out of school and included marches on the state capitol, the legislature promised teachers and other school employees a 5 percent raise and the creation of a task force to address the issue of health insurance costs (Bidgood 2018).

Inspired by the West Virginia teacher's mobilization – and success – similar walkouts and strikes spread to Oklahoma, Kentucky, Colorado, Arizona, and North Carolina. In all, the strikes included over 350,000 teachers and millions of students, and achieved gains in many of the states. Oklahoma secured salary raises for teachers and support staff, plus a boost in public school funding; Colorado gained a salary increase and a restoration of pre-recession education spending; and Arizona obtained big increases in teacher and staff salaries.

Like the Fight for Fifteen, the 2018 teacher strikes bear a strong resemblance to the "New Labor Law" Andrias describes, as well as the older wave of teachers strikes in the 1960s and 1970s. Like the older teacher strikes, workers were engaging in labor actions outside of traditional labor law (often illegally) in order to raise working standards for an entire sector through the state legislative process rather than through traditional collective bargaining with individual employers or school districts. State governments in these red states were acting like the high turnover, monopsonistic employers documented in the Naidu chapter, this volume, using their labor market power to suppress teacher pay. And much like the Fight for Fifteen movement, the 2018 teacher strikes have secured important wage and benefit gains that were previously unthinkable before large-scale collective action.

But the Fight for Fifteen movement also shares another similarity with the 2018 teacher strikes that conveys the limits of both approaches and sets them apart from the 1960s and 1970s public-sector strike waves: in neither case did the movements secure changes in policy that would grant greater institutional and organizational rights for the workers in the form of new union representation, expanded collective bargaining rights, or strike rights. As a result, it is an open question whether the teacher mobilizations from 2018 can have the same entrenching effects that the 1960s and 1970s teacher strikes did in establishing the enduring organizational and political clout of teachers unions and remaking the map of state union power.

Instead, like Fight for Fifteen, the most significant consequences of the teacher strikes may be their effects on public opinion, as they persuade members of the public of the worthiness of teachers' demands for higher working standards and also provide lessons to others (including teachers, but also workers in other occupations) about what labor collective action can accomplish (Biggs 2005; Soule 1997; Wang and Soule 2012). Qualitatively, there is good reason to think that the teacher strikes have had such effects, as the leaders in later states cited the earlier strikes (and especially the West Virginian strikes) as inspiring them to take action. One of the activists in Arizona who spearheaded that state's strikes said that he believed West Virginia's strike was "inspirational" for Arizona teachers, and that it "woke up a sleeping giant" in classrooms across the country (Arria 2018). Polling I have conducted with Suresh Naidu and Adam Reich backs up the intuition that the 2018 teacher strikes changed how the public thinks about teacher collective action – and about the labor movement more generally (Hertel-Fernandez, Naidu, and Reich forthcoming).

Looking forward then, the 2018 strikes may have not only contributed to a reservoir of public support for legal change and greater labor organization, but also helped to develop a smaller cadre of labor activists who may go on to participate in the costly work of future labor organizing and action (Uetricht and Eidlin 2019). There is early evidence for that theory in how teachers have used the structures and networks constructed during the 2018–19 mass mobilizations to protest unsafe school reopening plans during the COVID-19 pandemic.

It will be up to labor union leaders to take advantage of that supportive public climate and "militant minority" within their ranks in the months and years to come. To the extent that labor unrest in the public sector continues, these conclusions suggest that government employee mobilization is likely to be most successful at making new gains in state revenue and spending, as well as in building union strength, in contexts where politicians have been starving communities of highly valued public services – likely to be made all the more acute given cuts to state and local spending forced by the pandemic downturn. Under those conditions, even conservative voters can be persuaded of the worthiness of public employees' demands for greater resources for important government spending. Those include many states under full or partial Republican control, but also Democratic states like Colorado or California, that have imposed sharp limits on the revenue they can raise on public services like education.

LESSONS FOR UNDERSTANDING THE US LABOR MOVEMENT AND THE AMERICAN POLITICAL ECONOMY

In this chapter, I have sketched out how a political economy perspective on the development of the American labor movement illuminates important themes that might not otherwise emerge with a conventional treatment of unions. Beyond inviting further comparative research on the interaction between public and private-sector labor unions, this chapter also carries several broader insights about the American political economy, relating to geographic and territorial fragmentation, distinctive alliances between private-sector businesses and right-wing political activists and donors, and the role of the law and courts.

Geographic Fragmentation in American Politics. In our Introduction for this volume, we underscored the unique power that states have in the American federal system, and that means actors organized *at the state level* in *multiple states* can exercise considerable influence over policymaking within states (through state legislatures and governors) and at the national level (through the territorially represented Congress and Electoral College). This cross-state clout – or the lack thereof – forms a critical part of the explanation for the relative political weakness of the American labor movement, as well as its brief moments of strength. As the brief comparative analysis illustrated, the decentralization and unevenness of public-sector labor policy is also one of the most unique aspects of the American labor-policy regime looking at other rich democracies. The decentralization of public-sector labor policy also affords disproportionate influence to the business and conservative political coalitions that have emerged in recent decades to challenge union power. This is because decentralization grants businesses greater structural influence over policymaking (Culpepper and Reinke 2014; Hacker and Pierson 2002) and because weakly professionalized state legislatures are more dependent on outside interest groups for legislatives resources and ideas (cf. Hertel-Fernandez 2019a).

Business Alliances against Public-Sector Labor. Large segments of American business have long opposed the expansion of private-sector union power – both on the shop floor and in government (Lichtenstein 2002; cf. Swenson 2002). That is also true of labor unions in other countries (e.g., Korpi 1983). More unusual is the fierce resistance of American firms to government employee unions since the 1970s. Their opposition to public-sector unions is puzzling given that public-sector unions do not directly threaten the prerogatives of most private-sector managers. Why are these businesses committing economic and political resources to weakening the clout of public-sector unions? The answer lies with coalitions of conservative activists, politicians, and donors that successfully convinced corporate executives of the political dividends available from defeating public-sector unions. This reflects a more general long-term alliance between American businesses and conservative politics, alluded to in our Introduction, which has had profound implications for a variety of policy debates, including labor politics. Aligned with conservative movement groups, US businesses have adopted increasingly far-right positions out of step with historical positions and indeed with positions of their counterparts in other countries (e.g., Hacker and Pierson 2016; Martin and Swank 2012). Although this alliance has elite roots, it has also found mass support. Conservative political leaders have tied racial grievances among white voters to resentment of government – and of government employees and their unions. It was possible for entrepreneurial conservative leaders to make this connection using existing racial stereotypes and the overrepresentation of minority Americans, especially Black Americans, in public-sector jobs. This potent combination reflects a more general fusion of ethnonational appeals together with elite business and donor economic interests in the contemporary Republican party (Introduction, this volume; Hacker and Pierson 2020).

The Role of the Law in Constructing the US Political Economy. This chapter lastly joins a long line of scholars in underscoring the importance of the law as an explanation for the development of the American labor movement in mediating political and economic power (e.g., Forbath 1991; Hattam 1993; Orren 1991). But rather than simply reiterating that the law, and its interpretation by an employer-friendly judiciary, structures the opportunities available for unions, this chapter focuses attention on the feedback loops present between collective action and policy. As the enduring example of the 1960s and 1970s strike wave illustrates so vividly, mass labor collective action can change the law, entrenching new rights and resources for workers and therefore strengthening the political position of their unions for years to come. But the reverse is also true: as conservative opponents to unions have long recognized, cutbacks to union rights yield mounting political dividends. If unions are to reverse their decades-long decline, let alone make new gains, they would be wise to draw on large-scale collective action that can imbed new rights into American law once again.

II

RACE, SPACE, AND GOVERNANCE

4

Racial Inequality, Market Inequality, and the American Political Economy

Chloe Thurston

INTRODUCTION

A study of Boston's racial wealth gap made headlines in late 2017 when it revealed that the median net worth of the city's Black households was only $8, compared to $247,000 among white households (Hill 2017; Johnson 2017; Muñoz et al. 2015). The gap in Boston may have been starker than in the nation as a whole, but the latter was also striking. In 2016, the median net worth of Black and Hispanic households nationwide was $17,000 and $20,700, respectively, compared to $171,000 for whites (Dettling et al. 2017). The disparities among households with children were even more pronounced. In 2016, Black households with children held 1 percent of the wealth of non-Hispanic white households with children (Percheski and Gibson-Davis 2020: 1). And though the full impact of the COVID-19 pandemic may not be known for some time, the effect of the Great Recession on the racial wealth gap is instructive. Households of all races experienced declines in net worth, but the decline was sharper for nonwhite families and their recovery slower (Thompson and Suarez 2019).

The persistence of material racial inequality, including the racial wealth gap, has animated much social science scholarship in the past few decades. Scholars have identified a number of contributing factors, including housing, credit, consumer, and labor market discrimination (Pager and Shepherd 2008); historical policy inheritances of the New Deal coalition (Katznelson 2005); familial wealth and the dynamics of intergenerational

I thank Warren Snead and Zach Colton-Max for their helpful research assistance as well as participants from the 2019 and 2020 APE workshops, the 2020 meeting of the American Political Science Association, and Kumar Ramanathan, for feedback on earlier versions.

transfer (Conley 2010; Oliver and Shapiro 1995); misperceptions among whites about the scale of material racial inequality (Kraus et al. 2017); the failure of the federal government to commit its full authority to civil rights enforcement in a sustained manner (King 2017); and the role of predatory business practices in siphoning wealth away from race-class subjugated (RCS) communities (Seamster and Charron-Chénier 2017; Soss and Weaver 2017; Taylor 2019). Underlying many (though not all) of these perspectives is the observation that racism is constitutive of the American political economy (Darity et al. 2015; Dawson and Francis 2016; Harris and Lieberman 2013).

This chapter explores the political economy of racial inequality in the United States, with a focus on its reliance on public-private social policies, a catch-all term I use to encompass indirect policy mechanisms such as third-party delegation, employers, the tax code, and credit supports. At their core, these policies enlist market mechanisms to fulfill the goals of social policy, including protection against risk, meeting basic needs, and securing opportunities for mobility.

The argument is twofold. First, by virtue of their reliance on market mechanisms to deliver basic needs, access to opportunities, and protection against risk, public-private social policies can harden and even amplify existing racial inequalities. This is because the effective value of many public-private social policy benefits is tied to factors such as employment conditions, geography, and familial wealth, which are themselves highly unequal across racial lines. Moreover, beyond amplifying these disparities, public-private social policies may operate in ways that may increase some citizens' exposure to risk.

Second, the policy arrangements underlying these outcomes have proven politically difficult to dislodge for reasons tied to their submerged design and distributional effects. Collective action barriers abound in policies that rely on indirect mechanisms to channel social benefits to citizens. Low visibility compromises citizens' ability to accurately attribute outcomes to the government and hold policymakers accountable. The complex combination of factors contributing to broader racial disparities in economic well-being, moreover, means that even when visibility and attribution challenges are surmounted, advocates struggle with the need to define their demands narrowly in a context that demands a further-reaching set of reforms, as well as committed enforcement. In contrast, private providers benefit from these informational asymmetries. Acutely aware of the role of law and policy in shaping their profitability, they can redeploy those profits into narrowly targeted policy and regulatory demands. In some instances, private providers may threaten to exit a market altogether if regulation becomes too onerous. These dynamics are related to several of the features of the APE highlighted elsewhere in this volume, including the hoarding of opportunities within jurisdictions (Trounstine, this volume), the competition over positional goods such as housing and higher education (Ansell and Gingrich, this volume), and the rise in business concentration and business power (Braun, this volume).

PUBLIC-PRIVATE SOCIAL POLICIES IN THE UNITED STATES

Welfare states are a critical nexus between households and markets in advanced economies. From education, to healthcare, to unemployment insurance, family and sick leave, and child care, various policies and institutions help households, employers, and state actors navigate questions about who bears the costs and risks of training workers, adapting to economic downturns and transformations, as well as to unexpected emergencies, and caring for dependents. How these questions become settled is vastly consequential for households, firms, and governments. The variation in arrangements to address these questions, across time and political borders, and within populations speaks to their fundamentally political nature.

The United States' heavy reliance on market channels and private actors to provide benefits that are directly administered or (in the case of insurance or tort law) redundant in more comprehensive safety nets sets it apart from most other OECD countries, as Figure 4.1 depicts and many have written about (Hacker 2002; Howard 2007; Mettler 2010; Morgan and Campbell 2011; Prasad 2012). On public spending as a percent of GDP alone, the United States at 19 percent is just under the OECD average of 20 percent. The United States is near the top of the pack when it comes to private social spending (12 percent), only below the Netherlands in percentage of GDP (13 percent).

The OECD measure of private social spending is narrowly defined to encompass benefits that are provided through the private sector and have either an element of compulsion or interpersonal risk redistribution and in the United States predominantly capture pension and health insurance. Using a broader definition, Table 4.1 illustrates a range of ways that American social policies used public-private policy channels to secure core goals of the welfare state, including meeting basic needs, protecting against risk, and promoting opportunity (Michener et al. 2020). This

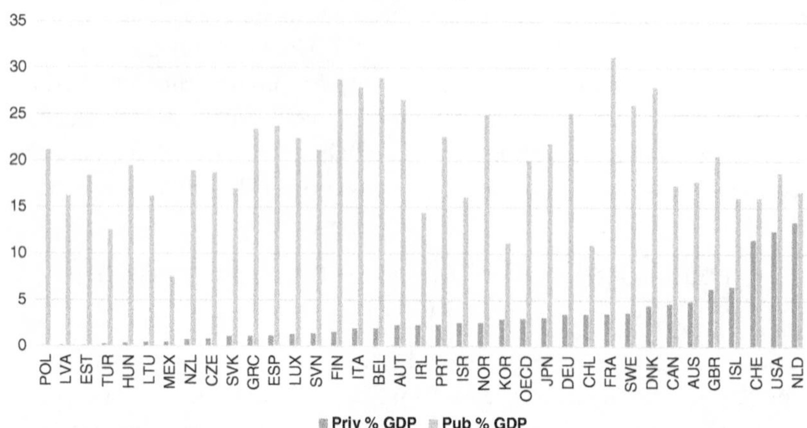

FIGURE 4.1 Public and private social spending in the OECD
Source: OECD

accounting of the public-private welfare state includes, as with the OECD measures, incentives for employers to provide health and retirement benefits, but also extends to regulatory floors like the Americans with Disabilities Act (Howard 2007) or state auto insurance requirements (Fergus 2013), institutions that enable widespread access to credit like Fannie Mae and the Federal Housing Administration (Quinn 2019; Thurston 2018), subsidies for childcare and housing that are publicly financed but distributed through the private sector, and a wide range of tax write-offs and credits. While not a full accounting, a broader perspective on the multiple ways that policies, law, and regulation can fulfill social policy goals through tapping into market mechanisms is important for when we think about the ways that these mechanisms intersect with existing racial inequalities and lines of disadvantage, as discussed in the next section.

STRATIFYING FEATURES OF PUBLIC-PRIVATE SOCIAL POLICIES

A long-recognized feature of public-private social policies is their propensity for stratifying citizens on the basis of their existing market positions, whether employment status, income, or wealth. The ability of citizens to enjoy employer-provided benefits, for example, is tied to whether their employer offers such benefits in the first place. Moreover, as Table 4.2

TABLE 4.1 *Varieties of private, semi-private, or delegated provision*

		Policy Goals		
		Basic Needs	Risk Protection	Social Mobility
Policy Mechanism	Employer-Based	Retirement accounts (ex: 401 (k)s) (ERISA); Dependent care FSA's; Tax-free commuter benefits	Health insurance (tax deductibility of fringe benefits, ACA employer mandate); Health FSA's; Life insurance; Accident/disability insurance; Parental/sick leave	Tuition benefits
	Regulatory Floors/ Minimum Standards	Minimum wage; Americans with Disabilities Act	OSHA; ACA Essential Health Benefits; Auto insurance requirements; Tort law; Family and Medical Leave Act	Gainful employment rule (repealed in 2019)
	Credit Programs	Regulation of credit and fringe banking (e.g. payday loans, check cashing, bail bonds); Home loan programs: FHA, VA; Fannie Mae/Freddie Mac	Consumer Financial Protections; Bankruptcy law	Federal student loans, parent (PLUS) loans, consolidation loans for higher education; Small business loans

(continued)

TABLE 4.1 *(continued)*

	Policy Goals		
	Basic Needs	**Risk Protection**	**Social Mobility**
Grants/Subsidies	Childcare subsidies; Low income home energy assistance program (LIHEAP); Food stamps (SNAP); Rental programs (HOPE VI, Section 8); Pell Grants	National Flood Insurance Program	Pell grants
Individual Tax Write-Offs, Credit	Individual retirement accounts; Dependent care FSA's; Tax free commuter benefits; Earned Income Tax Credit	Health saving account/ Health FSA; Health Insurance Marketplace Premium Tax Credits	529 Coverdells; Deferral of capital gains on sale of principal residence

TABLE 4.2 *Employment benefits offered to workers (by employment status)*

	Full Time	Part Time	Contractor	All Workers
Health insurance	89	35	20	77
Retirement benefits	78	31	16	77
Paid sick leave	77	32	15	67
Life insurance	75	22	11	63
Maternity or paternity leave	63	22	11	54
Tuition assistance	44	17	6	38

Note: Among adults employed for someone else or who work as a contractor in their main job.
Source: Federal Reserve Board of Governors 2018 Survey of Housing Economic Decisionmaking.

shows, workers whose statuses fall short of the standard employment model (full-time, on-site, non-contractor), are less likely to have access to employer-sponsored benefits. Even those who have formal access to employer benefits may find that their income or existing wealth influence their ability to participate fully.

Existing market positions also shape the availability and potential value of tax expenditures. Many expenditures apply only to those who itemize their taxes rather than taking the standard deduction (in the years since the 2017 Tax Cuts and Jobs Act, only 14 percent of households have chosen to itemize). Moreover, their effective value can rise as household incomes rise into higher tax brackets, as well as with the amount households spend on a tax-advantaged good. For these reasons, many public-private social policies are considered to be broadly upwardly redistributive (Faricy 2015; Howard 1997; Mettler 2010).

Public-private social policies may also produce uneven investment returns for their purported beneficiaries. Some types of programs, such as retirement accounts, are explicitly designed as investments to earn future returns for their participants. But even policies not structured as literal investment accounts can serve investment purposes, enabling citizens to access higher education or homeownership. This investment quality of some public-private social programs means we should pay particular attention to factors that may correlate to returns on investment, and how those returns are distributed. To some extent, the value of the investment will vary by broad market conditions (for example, the timing of when one buys a house can matter a lot to future returns, or the state of the stock market when one is about to retire), helping to stratify returns by cohorts. Beyond generational issues, returns can be shaped by factors including household resources, which may enable the user to invest in ways that generate higher returns and also to avoid some forms of riskier debt; the quality and availability of information about different types of investment opportunities; and what types of opportunities one has access to.

Related to each of these is also the role of private providers and marketing. Public-private social policies often rely on the use of incentives to encourage voluntary participation. Social policy marketplaces, which come about as a way to encourage private providers to expand their activities beyond what they would already do voluntarily, may leave discretion for firms and other providers to determine what is marketable and how to market to various segments (Gingrich 2011; Thurston 2018). Because this can affect the pricing and quality of the good provided, how firms understand (and consequently, act on) the different markets in which they operate can also matter for individual outcomes (Fourcade and Healy 2017).

In sum, while public-private social policies serve welfare functions, helping to protect against risk, meet basic needs, or provide access to key opportunities, they can also stratify populations. The question of whether one can access these programs at all, as well as the terms on which one can access these programs is structured by a host of factors, including one's existing social and economic status, the types of opportunities and information available, the quality of the investments pursued, and luck. Moreover, relying on third-party providers for access to social benefits also provides opportunities for differential marketing and pricing that can shape the value of benefits and even turn some forms of benefit into sources of risk. As the next few sections show, these sources of stratification interact with America's racial divides to shape both material racial inequality and the politics of responding to it.

A "RACE-LADEN INSTITUTIONAL ARENA"

The United States' market economy is, to use Frederick Harris and Robert Lieberman's description, a "race-laden institutional arena." Unsurprisingly, the aforementioned lines of stratification are hardly race-neutral, constituting some of the "interconnected forces [that] tend to systematically exclude people of color from the high end of successful, dynamic markets and connect them instead to broken or dysfunctional markets" (Harris and

Lieberman 2013: 24). Public-private social policies produce racial disparities because their delegated design creates opportunities for discrimination and because of their interaction with labor market inequalities, residential segregation, and wealth inequalities.

The delegated structure of many public-private social policies is one source of racial inequality in outcomes. Within more traditional welfare-state programs, it is well established that decentralization and local delegation can enable facially race-neutral policies to exhibit racially disparate outcomes (Lieberman 1998). In public-private social policies, the delegation of policy responsibility to third-party actors, including lenders, employers, real estate agents, college recruiters, and insurers, can similarly create openings for individual-level discrimination. Racial discrimination remains prevalent in labor and housing markets, with the potential to generate disparities in how citizens access and experience (in terms of benefits and risk exposure) public-private social policies. Individual decisions and actions based on stereotypes and discrimination can also accumulate over the course of an exchange or transaction, widening racial disparities (Korver-Glenn 2018; Massey et al. 2016).

Public-private social policies may also interact with preexisting lines of social and economic inequality in ways that amplify inequality. In a polity "pervasively constituted by systems of racial hierarchy since its inception," public policy inputs and their outputs are "profoundly racialized" (Michener 2019: 423; see also King and Smith 2005). For example, the receipt of employer-provided benefits, a cornerstone of the public-private welfare state, is conditioned on access to a labor market marked by racial (and gender) disparities in occupations, hiring, wages, and working conditions (Hamilton et al. 2011; Pager and Shepherd 2008; Shapiro 2017; Warren 2013; Weeden 2019). Even as employer-provided health and pension coverage has mostly been a story of overall decline since the 1980s (Figures 4.2 and 4.3) white workers have throughout this period been more often covered under such arrangements than Hispanic or Black workers. As work by historian Jennifer Klein shows, occupational segregation has historically operated to the exclusion of nonwhite workers from the employer-based welfare state (Klein 2006). Black and Hispanic workers who do have access to employer retirement programs tend to participate at lower rates, make smaller contributions, and are more likely to make early withdrawals than their white counterparts (Rhee 2013; Shapiro et al. 2013). Beyond their link to employer-provided benefits, wage inequalities can also

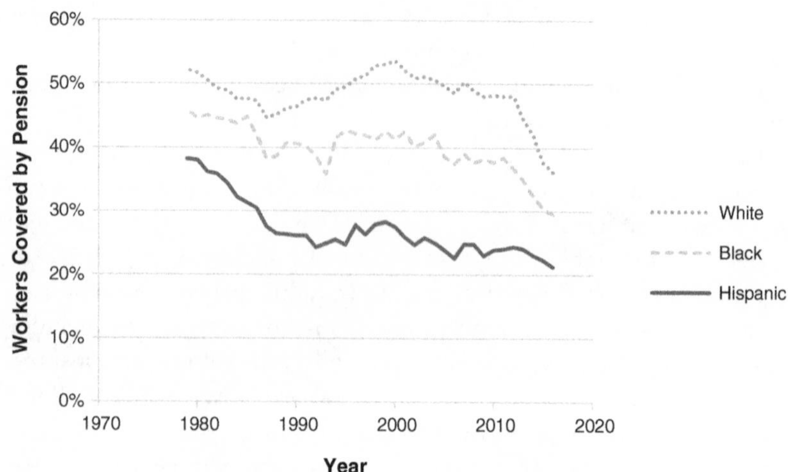

FIGURE 4.2 Employer pension coverage by race
Source: Economic Policy Institute, State of Working America Data Library, "Pension Coverage" 2019. www.epi.org/data/#?subject=pensioncov&r=*

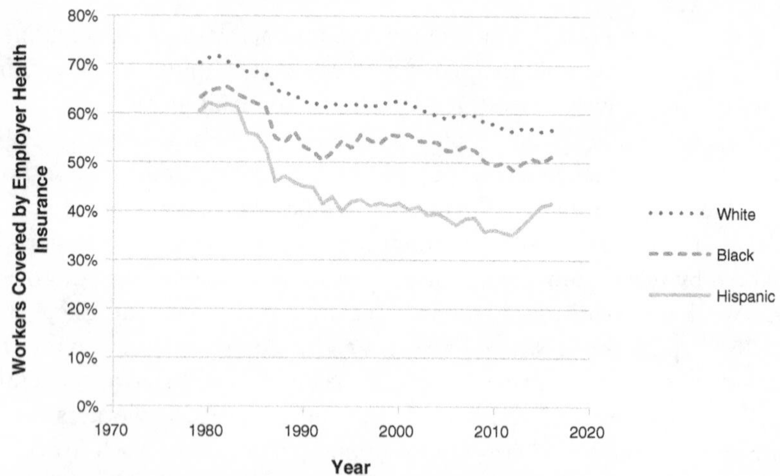

FIGURE 4.3 Employer health insurance coverage by race
Source: Economic Policy Institute, State of Working America Data Library, "Health Insurance" 2019. www.epi.org/data/#?subject=healthcov&r=*

structure whether and the extent to which other public-private social-policy arrangements provide protection against risk and promote opportunity, by influencing the resources available for citizens and households to contribute to tax-advantaged accounts or purchase tax-advantaged goods, as well as the need to take on debt.[1]

The degree and durability of residential segregation in the United States presents another means by which public-private social policies may contribute to racial inequality (Sampson et al. 2002). Neighborhoods contribute to a variety of outcomes, including information about opportunities, the chances of social mobility, the prices one pays for goods like insurance, and the returns to investment in housing. Racial segregation can exacerbate these inequalities (Massey 2007; Perry 2020; Perry et al. 2018; Trounstine 2018).[2]

The costs of residential segregation for members of minority groups, particularly those living in race-class subjugated communities (Soss and Weaver 2017), are multiple. Drivers in majority-minority neighborhoods pay more for auto insurance than drivers with similar backgrounds but living in all-white neighborhoods, effectively distributing wealth from minority to white areas (Fergus 2013). Studies of returns on homeownership find that across US metropolitan areas, homes in majority-Black neighborhoods are valued at roughly half the price as homes in neighborhoods that have no Black residents. Houses of similar quality with similar amenities are worth 23 percent less in majority-Black neighborhoods compared with those that have no Black residents (Perry 2020; Perry et al. 2018). In short, neighborhood racial composition continues to be a strong and powerful predictor of the value of owner-occupied homes, and it is not fully explained by differences in home and neighborhood quality, influencing the relative value of government homeownership policies across racial divides.

Race-class subjugated communities are also frequent targets for predation through public-private social policies. Fringe financial institutions, including payday lenders, check-cashing stores, and loan title companies have a disproportionate presence in marginalized neighborhoods underserved by mainstream financial institutions and with large unbanked populations (Cover et al. 2011). Users pay a premium that may contribute

[1] For example, Hamilton, Austin, and Darity (2011, 3) find that roughly 87 percent of occupations "can be classified as segregated for black men" in the United States. This translates into a wage gap between racialized occupations: the average annual wage of occupations overrepresented by Black men was just over $37,000, versus about $50,500 in occupations where Blacks were unrepresented.

[2] Racial segregation is highest between Blacks and non-Hispanic whites and continues to be more pronounced than economic segregation, even as the latter has risen over time (Jargowsky 2014; Quick and Kahlenberg 2019).

to overall patterns of economic inequality; nevertheless, these institutions exist to fulfill an otherwise unmet demand (Charron-Chénier 2020; Posey 2019; Servon 2017). Similarly, for-profit higher education companies, house sellers, and mortgage lenders often market risky products in RCS neighborhoods. As with fringe banking, these products, though risky, usually fill the genuine needs of residents for credentials and shelter. Students living in racially segregated and RCS communities are more likely to be targeted to for-profit colleges and certificate programs.[3] Such programs fill a demand by young people in low-opportunity neighborhoods for a relatively fast credential with a tie to concrete job opportunities at the end (versus a four-year liberal arts degree) (Holland and DeLuca 2016). But they also are associated with higher debt loads and rates of default, greater rates of non-completion, and lower employment returns than traditional community colleges and four-year nonprofits (Cellini and Turner 2019; Cottom 2017). It is difficult to separate private providers' profit-making strategies and marketing practices from the reality of segregation, which allows for the efficient targeting of RCS communities for higher cost and predatory forms of provision (Taylor 2019).

Finally, and related to each of these, is the role of unequal household wealth and inheritance in how households use and experience public-private social policies. As the introduction to this chapter described, household wealth tracks highly along racial lines. This gap has mostly become more pronounced in recent decades (Figure 4.4), despite the policy gains of the civil rights movement (King 2017). Public-private social policies both contribute to this trend, by tying access to preexisting economic resources, and reflect it, by amplifying differences in participation in such valuable public-private social policies as employer-provided benefits and tax sheltered accounts and by generating differential returns to investments like housing and education (Addo et al. 2016; Klein 2006; Perry et al. 2018; Rhee 2013; Seamster and Charron-Chénier 2017). Higher wealth (or access to parental resources/wealth) enables citizens to take on lower levels of housing and student loan debt, or to buy housing

[3] A 2011 Senate report on the for-profit college industry notes, for example, that at its height the University of Phoenix was spending nearly $400,000 a day on advertising, much of it concentrated in low-income and minority communities. For-profit higher education advertising strategies included putting ads at bus and subway stops in areas of concentrated minority populations, as well as working through public figures popular among African Americans, including Steve Harvey and Al Sharpton (Huelsman 2015). In other instances, for-profit higher educational institutions have been found almost exclusively at college fairs in disadvantaged areas, and not in college fairs with wealthier suburban clienteles.

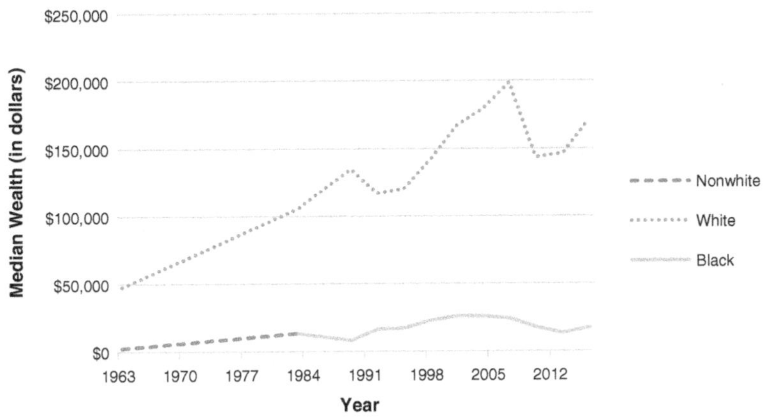

FIGURE 4.4 Median family wealth by race
Source: Urban Institute calculations from Survey of Financial Characteristics of Consumers 1962 (December 31), Survey of Changes in Family Finances 1963, and Survey of Consumer Finances 1983–2016. https://apps.urban.org/features/wealth-inequalit-charts/

in more expensive, higher-opportunity areas, and shapes the types of higher education that young people pursue (Seamster and Charron-Chénier 2017). Having more resources from the outset can also make workers more likely to contribute to tax-advantaged accounts and less likely to have to withdraw from them early (Rhee 2013). Lower (or zero) wealth maps onto a different set of options for citizens, shaping not only the demand for debt but also the types of goods marketed to households (particularly through the mechanism of residential segregation) (Addo et al. 2016; Conley 2010; Flynn et al. 2017; Shapiro 2017; Shapiro et al. 2013; Taylor 2019).

THE ENDURANCE OF MATERIAL RACIAL INEQUALITY THROUGH AN APE LENS

What explains the endurance of public policies that are implicated in racial inequality, and at worst in shaping the conditions for private predation? To be sure, there have been important policy revisions since the civil rights revolution of the 1960s and 1970s, such as the 1988 Fair Housing Act reforms. But alongside civil rights gains have been the further deregulation of some areas of the public-private welfare state – whether directly or through drift. The failure of governments to respond robustly to inequality-generating policy is not for a lack of recognition of the continuing racial disparities in material well-being, or of the role that public policies have played in shaping those disparities (Sullivan et al. 2015). It is also not for a lack of potential responses. On the contrary, a number of creative solutions have been proposed to counter these problems, including getting rid of the most regressive tax expenditures, tightening regulations of predatory lenders and schools, expanding homeownership opportunities, creating a system of baby bonds (Hamilton and Darity 2010), job guarantees programs (Cottom 2017), greater support for families, creative use of financial technology (Foohey and Martin 2021), and proposals for reparations that encompass many of these solutions (Darity and Mullen 2020).

One explanation may be that even if public-private social policies contribute to racial disparities in wealth and well-being, their consequences are simply too narrowly experienced to generate the widespread support needed for reform. On its face, this seems an inadequate explanation given the many ways that political mobilization advantages narrower, concentrated interests. Another possible explanation is that white voters view these outcomes as "minority issues," undermining the prospects for mass electoral reform pressure. And yet, dissatisfaction with some of the basic contours of the public-private welfare state is widespread, suggesting that there is common cause to be made across racial lines. Majorities (sometimes large ones) of Americans are concerned with rising medical costs, the possibility of an unexpected health emergency putting them at financial risk, inadequate retirement savings, the responsibility of making investment decisions, and the costs of higher education (Board of Governors of the Federal Reserve System 2019). Theoretically, the broad concern about these programs could allow for mass pressure for their reform.

An APE framework is helpful for understanding why reform movements have had difficulty forming and then mounting successful challenges to the status quo. Inequalities of power, the concentration of market gains, and the fragmentation of political institutions have generally advantaged well-resourced constituencies over those with fewer resources and organizational power. The following discussion stresses three reasons for the continuation of public-private social policies promoting racial disparities: (1) the demobilizing role of mass policy feedback in privatized policy realms; (2) the particular challenges of contesting outcomes that are structured across multiple, loosely connected realms of policy and private action; and (3) the disproportionate power of private actors and organizations, that flows partially from (1) and (2) but also carries its own dynamics.

THE DIMINISHED ROLE OF POLICY FEEDBACK IN PRIVATIZED POLICY REALMS

In a review of recent efforts to organize a constituency around the racial wealth gap, Kijakazi (2016) noted that one of the basic challenges to policy change was a "lack of a substantial presence of organizations of color in the growing savings and asset building field," as well as the absence of racial minority representation "at the decision-making table" (Kijakazi 2016: 136). Some of the reasons for this may be rooted in well-known tendencies for public-private social policies to be viewed in individual terms, rather than as natural targets for collective and political action.

The difficulties of organizing around public-private social policy arrangements are well established. First, citizens tend to view their access to public-private social benefits in personal terms rather than collective ones, seeing their receipt of goods like employer-provided benefits or a new home as speaking to their individual grit or thrift. The tendency to see benefits as "privately owned and privately earned" undermines the collective ground for grievances (Clemens 2006). This may be becoming even more difficult with the advance of new technologies for managing and pricing risk. For example, while the government mortgage programs of the 1930s through the mid-1960s were "hidden" by virtue of citizens needing to interface directly with private lenders, and only indirectly with the government, private lenders still needed to conform to standardized underwriting criteria, rendering the experience of exclusion a more collective one than in the 1990s and 2000s, when the proliferation of individualized credit scoring and pricing made the experience more difficult to collectivize. The stigma associated with some types of negative outcomes (for example, bankruptcy, excessive debt, foreclosure) may also undermine collective action.

Second, beyond encouraging citizens to view their benefits in individualized terms, the low visibility of the government also matters in shaping citizens' political responses. Public-private social policies operate indirectly – in some cases the government plays only the lightest role in shaping outcomes, for example, by securitizing mortgages made by private lenders (Quinn 2019) or by allowing fringe financial institutions to operate with limited regulation (Posey 2019). Unsatisfactory outcomes are often attributed to the market or specific market providers rather than to policymakers or regulators (SoRelle 2020). If citizens are unable to attribute their receipt of benefits, or their problems with these benefits, to public policies, regulations, and implementation, then they cannot effectively hold governments accountable.

Finally, these challenges may be further exacerbated by the problem of racialized dualisms in feedback effects (Michener 2019; Rosenthal 2020a, 2020b; Thurston 2018). As political scientist Jamila Michener (2019: 425) writes: "Policies often channel resources unevenly and inequitable across racial groups; racial stratification is a key determinant of the advent, alignment, and power of interest groups; and race is a fundamental prism through which experiences of policy are understood and interpreted." Some of these dual interpretive effects may be heightened in public-private social policies, especially those with disparate racial effects in access and returns. This potential has been noted in studies of homeownership. Where white homeowners have historically been inclined to overlook the role of government policy in generating affordable mortgages and affordable suburbs, in favor of viewing their achievement in individualistic and meritocratic terms, civil rights organizations were keenly aware of the role that federal government policies and practices played in excluding Black citizens from the same opportunities (Freund 2010; Thurston 2018). While the latter process of recognition and attribution was central to collective action among excluded groups, bigger disparities in visibility helped to limit the possibilities of such movements and also to subject previously excluded groups to harsh backlash politics.

Beyond the role that dual interpretive effects can play in constraining the opportunities for collective action is the possibility that racialized disparities in the operation and outcomes of these policies can create dual resource effects that enable political participation for some groups and impede it for others. Here, the evidence is mixed. In the realm of fringe financial institutions, political scientist Patricia Posey finds that despite their higher costs and risks, the presence of these institutions does provide crucial resources for neighborhood residents that contribute to the ability to participate politically. However, these resource effects are generally offset by the interpretive effects of their presence in RCS neighborhoods, which signal to many residents political abandonment by their elected representatives (Posey 2019). An additional problem pertains to the resources themselves, which may disappear, lose value, or become new sources of risk for their holder. Studying the relationship of homeownership to democracy, sociologist Jacob Rugh finds that the decline in Black

Americans' homeownership rates since 2004 has reduced their voting turnout, leading him to conclude that the color line in homeownership "undermines the social mobility and electoral representation of Black Americans" (Rugh 2020: 1).

In sum, in policy areas that channel benefits to citizens through indirect mechanisms, features of the policies themselves often impede the generation of mass political support for reform. Part of this is due to their low visibility and traceability, making it difficult for even the beneficiaries of such policies to recognize themselves as beneficiaries of government social programs (Mettler 2011). A related aspect of this is the tendency for citizens with grievances pertaining to public-private social policies to blame market providers or their own personal actions or background, rather than policymakers and regulators (SoRelle 2020). These tendencies are further complicated by the racial disparities in outcomes across many of these policy realms (Rosenthal 2020b). On the one hand, some evidence points to the potential for broader awareness of even less visible public-private policies. But the record is mixed on whether this provides a sufficient basis for collective action. The ability of marginalized groups to more clearly see the role of the government in their marginalization can be offset by the tendency for in-groups to view out-group appeals as demands for special treatment rather than fair or safer access. This counternarrative was prevalent in the wake of the foreclosure crisis that helped to trigger the Great Recession. Moreover, while unequally distributed resources can still have positive effects on political participation, those effects may be offset by the negative messages they send to marginalized groups about the responsiveness of their elected officials (Posey 2019).

ORGANIZATIONAL CHALLENGES FOR ADVOCACY GROUPS

To be sure, these barriers to collective action have been overcome in the past to produce organized efforts to reform public-private social policies, for example, against government-sponsored mortgage redlining; disparities in health, life, and auto insurance pricing and coverage; and consumer credit (Fergus 2013; Thurston 2018). More recently there have been a handful of organized efforts to address mounting student loan debt. And though more often associated with police violence, "A Vision for Black Lives," a platform signed on to by fifty Black Lives Matter–affiliated organizations, was explicit in drawing attention to the ways that public-private social policies have historically contributed to white wealth and mobility, with demands to enable Black communities and citizens to access the same types of opportunities (Cottom 2017).

Such organized pressure, however, is rare. While more work remains to be done to understand the conditions under which organizations and movements of this sort may form, the research that has been done suggests that existing advocacy organizations – rather than ones emerging out of specific grievances about public-private social policies – may be more likely to take up issues surrounding public-private social provision, though there are some exceptions. One reason that existing advocacy organizations have an advantage in mobilizing around issues of exclusion in public-private policies is through their ability to overcome the challenges of individualization and attribution described previously. Organizations with broad constituencies may help to redefine individual grievances toward market actors into collective grievances about public policies. This is how collective action formed around various forms of mortgage exclusion, as organizations, initially writing off observations by their constituents as either individualized instances of discrimination, but eventually coming to view these issues as widespread, linked to policy, and amendable to political change (Thurston 2015, 2018).

But where existing organizations may have informational advantages, responding to the inequalities produced by public-private policies requires resources. These include resources spent researching the scope and causes of racial and other forms of inequality in these programs, the resources spent bringing the causes of exclusion to light and advocating for changes in public policy and business practices, and the resources for monitoring the implementation of laws and regulations after seeming policy successes. Organizations that have prioritized these issues have at times faced objections from within their ranks from those who believe they are focusing on the problems of more privileged members (a development predicted by Strolovitch 2007). The National Organization for Women, for example, decided in the 1970s to take on the issue of sex discrimination in lending, unleashing discontent within the organization about its focus on what was seen as an upper-middle-class (and largely white) issue and threatening to splinter the organization altogether (Thurston 2018). Moreover, even when advocacy organizations have succeeded in bringing about policy changes, they have not always had the resources to expend on the next step of monitoring agencies for implementation and compliance with the new rules. Finally, many organizations rely on philanthropic donations and may not be able to count on sustained support for a focus on public-private social policies when many other priority areas remain (Francis 2019).

Moreover, these problems of continuing inequality, even if shaped by policy, are multifaceted and success in one realm does not necessarily, or usually, generate the scale of change desired in economic outcomes. Again, this is partly because successful change needs to go beyond policy enactment, to monitor (a) whether agencies are actually implementing the policies as desired, and (b) if (and if so how) discriminatory practices are moving to less regulated areas following policy change (Thurston 2018). Another reason is that the outcomes in one area – say, housing – are also loosely related to policies, enforcement, and developments in other areas. This is a point that Tressie McMillan Cottom (2017) makes in relation to for-profit higher educational programs, which are riskier for students than their nonprofit counterparts but also popular due to their convenience and accessibility. Cottom is skeptical that solutions to these problems coming solely from the field of education policy can ever address the underlying structural problem, which is in the labor market. As she points out, the American labor market evolved to demand constant updating of credentials, while placing the cost of updating on individuals rather than firms or society. Looking at the racialized structure of labor market opportunities and returns in the United States, one begins to see why it is not merely enough to change regulations around for-profit educational institutions if one wants to address insecurity, debt, risk, and differential abilities to accumulate wealth.

Cottom's observation about higher education speaks to a challenge faced by many organizations trying to address disparities in economic outcomes: an advocacy strategy aimed at targeting multiple loosely connected policy areas that produce structural inequalities is a risky one even if it more accurately maps the scope of the problem and its possible solutions. As we will see, this constraint is not necessarily faced by private providers. While they may, too, see their fates tied to developments across many loosely connected policy areas, they are advantaged by the incentive and ability to dominate within their narrower policy and regulatory arenas.

PRIVATE PROVIDERS: POWER AND INFORMATION ASYMMETRIES

In contrast to the barriers that mass public and advocacy groups face to successful organizing around these issues, private providers encounter three key advantages. First, while public-private social policies are often less visible to the public and thereby less politicized, the private providers who are incentivized by such policies are keenly aware of them, mirroring the "quiet politics" that have also been recognized in studies of policies surrounding corporate control (Culpepper 2010). Precisely because their business models are shaped by government policies and regulations, they have a strong incentive to pay attention to the existing landscape as well as potential future changes. In the case of publicly-traded companies with a foot in public-private social policy provision, the incentive to closely follow the role of the government in their industry is not merely a suggestion; rather, it is a legal requirement that companies disclose the possible risks to their businesses as part of their SEC 10K filings. Second, this awareness can (and often does) feed back into politics as the winners from these arrangements reinvest their profits in order to maintain or expand their policy-generated advantages (Mettler 2011, 2014; Pusser and Wolcott 2006). Finally, in some instances, private providers may be able to credibly threaten to exit some markets altogether if regulations become too onerous, as scholars of structural business power have noted in other contexts (Culpepper 2015; Lindblom 1977). This exit threat comes up frequently in discussions about regulating some of the more predatory aspects of public-private social policies, including subprime lending and fringe banking regulation, nondiscrimination in insurance coverage and pricing, and for-profit higher education.

The case of for-profit higher education illuminates each of these various sources of business political advantage. The industry, which has roots in the 1944 GI Bill's provisions for supporting education at trade schools, shifted in the 1990s and 2000s, moving from a mom-and-pop model to a much more concentrated model dominated by a few large companies with tens (or hundreds) of thousands of students each. This transformation was aided by the rise of the Internet, which enabled programs to scale in terms of students, less hindered by geography or campus restrictions. Regulatory changes, including the relaxation of an earlier rule requiring that 50 percent of classes needed to be held on a physical campus for an institution to qualify for federal student aid, and the loosening of rules about the overall percentage of revenue that could from federal aid, from 85 percent to 90 percent, were also crucial to the transformation of for-profit higher education (Mettler 2014; Pusser and Wolcott 2006).

While students may not have spent much time considering the role of public policy in shaping how they were able to access higher education, for-profit colleges recognized government's role in shaping their fortunes. In fall 2016, the top eleven for-profit colleges and universities with the highest enrollment were all owned by publicly traded companies, providing a window into the extent that they viewed government policy as related to their business fortunes, through their SEC 10K filings.[4] Across these filings, 42 percent of the risks enumerated in Section 1A explicitly mentioned Title IV and 26 percent made some mention of state-level policies or regulations.[5] Potential loss of eligibility for student aid through Title IV was tied to a range of issues, including rules limiting the compensation of recruiters, continued institutional accreditation, and financial responsibility standards issued by the Department of Education. State-level risks included issues like changes to state licensing or regulatory requirements that might shape their ability to operate or the costs of operation and breaches of state-level privacy laws. To summarize, even if citizens are less aware of the role of the government in shaping their access to some types of goods, the logic clearly did not extend to providers.

In addition to recognizing the stakes of the government's role in their industry, for-profit higher educational institutions were well organized and willing to mobilize politically. The consolidation of the industry beginning in the 1990s went along with changes in its political organization. In 1991, the two major trade associations of proprietary programs merged to form the Career College Association (since 2010, the Association of Private Sector Colleges and Universities), starting its own PAC and hiring lobbyists to work with both parties (Mettler 2014: 88–100).

Figures 4.5 and 4.6 depict the long-term trends in political contributions for the for-profit education sector as a whole. While higher education as a sector has been increasingly active at both state and federal levels of government, one thing that sets for-profits apart from their nonprofit counterparts is the former's ability to donate directly to candidates and parties. For-profit higher educational institutions are also notable for their

[4] The rankings in enrollments come from the *Chronicle of Higher Education* (www.chronicle.com/article/For-Profit-Companies-With-the/244041). The parent companies were Apollo Education Group, Grand Canyon Education, Education Management Corporation, DeVry Education Group, Laureate Education, American Public Education, Career Education Corporation, Strayer Education, Kaplan Higher Education Corporation, Bridgepoint Education, and Capella Education Company.

[5] Author's calculations based on analysis of SEC filings. While there is slight variation in how companies prepare the report, for Section 1A most include a bold header summarizing a particular risk followed by one or more paragraphs with further explanation about that risk. Each of those was considered a unit for the purpose of analysis.

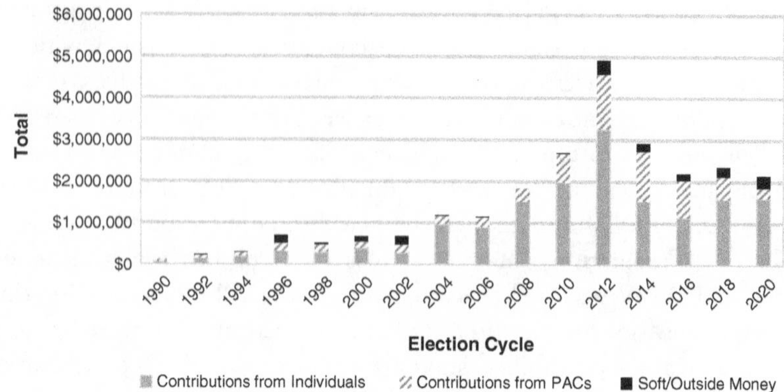

FIGURE 4.5 For-profit education: Contributors
Source: Center for Responsive Politics. www.opensecrets.org/industries/totals.php?cycle=2020&ind=H5300

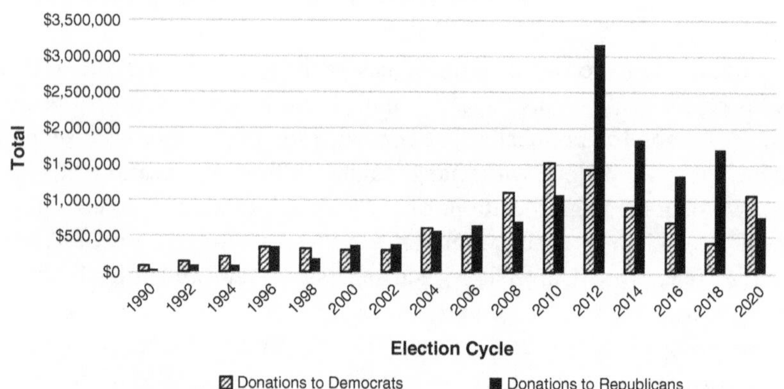

FIGURE 4.6 For-profit education: Party donations
Source: Center for Responsive Politics. www.opensecrets.org/industries/totals.php?cycle=2020&ind=H5300

tendency to pursue "direct benefits such as favorable tax laws, reduced regulatory oversight, and policies that increase profits, or in the case of publicly-traded proprietary institutions, that maximize shareholder interests" (Pusser and Wolcott 2006: 174).

The political mobilization of for-profit higher education companies largely paid off in the 1990s and into the 2000s. While the decades following the GI Bill's passage saw continued bi-partisan efforts to regulate for-profit trade schools when abuses of the program became known, by the late 1990s those regulations began to relax. One example can be seen in the negotiations over the Higher Education Act reauthorization in 1998. Despite a GAO report at the time that found that for-profits were heavily reliant on federal aid and "compared to other schools, had worse outcomes among their students-lower degree completion and job placement rates, and higher loan default rates," Congress ultimately relaxed the 85/15 principle to the 90/10 principle, allowing such institutions to rely even further on revenues from the federal government (Mettler 2014: 104). Rules put in place by Congress in 1992 to restrict for-profit colleges' recruitment practices were watered down by the Department of Education during the George W. Bush administration, allowing for the rise of more aggressive recruitment practices, including the use of call centers (Mettler 2014: 104–5). The next few years saw the further loosening of regulations: in 2006, Congress weakened rules about the percentage of classes that needed to be held on-campus, further expanding for-profits' ability to grow their operations while still using federal aid.

Finally, in building the case for government support and limited regulations, for-profits found a powerful tool in their role as providers of social goods; namely, that tightening regulations or reducing funding could drive them to stop serving the students most in need of credentials. Concerns about access and exit helped to generate common cause between Republicans, who were becoming increasingly supportive of the market-based solution of for-profits, and some Congressional Democrats. While some members of the Congressional Black Caucus were concerned about the negative impact of for-profits on minority students, they also worried about being overly aggressive with the schools, since they were largely filling demands for higher education of minority and low-income populations (Mettler 2014: 95, 103). In the battle over relaxing the 85/15 principle to its current 90/10, John Boehner found common ground with Democrats by arguing that the former "creates an incentive for proprietary schools to raise tuition or move away from urban areas where students are more likely to depend on federal aid" (Mettler 2014: 104). The restriction was ultimately loosened with little controversy.

Is it easier to maintain racial inequality through the submerged policy designs enjoyed by many public-private social policies than in their more visible counterparts? While few scholars of the public-private social policies have tackled the question directly, the lower visibility of such areas may make it more likely that racial inequalities evade detection (or are attributed to non-policy causes), reducing demands for reform. Considering that ignorance of these submerged programs is especially pronounced among white

Americans, it may be difficult to build cross racial coalitions aimed at addressing racial inequalities (Freund 2010; Rosenthal 2020b, 12). Moreover, the accentuated power of organized interests who do benefit from the status quo highlights another potential mechanism making it possible to maintain racial inequality in these programs (Howard 1997; Mettler 2010). Finally, even when influential political actors have detected suboptimal outcomes in the distribution of submerged state benefits, it has been difficult to dislodge racial inequities. Efforts to reform submerged policies may face additional obstacles among the large share of Americans who say they prefer tax breaks to direct social provision, a phenomenon especially pronounced among conservatives (though the effect remains for liberals too) (Haselswerdt and Bartels 2015).

CONCLUSION

The United States' reliance on public-private social policy arrangements to secure goals that might otherwise be designated to more direct forms of taxation and transfer – from protecting against risks to promoting opportunity – contributes to longstanding patterns of material racial inequality. But racial inequality is not just an outcome of American politics. It feeds back into politics by shaping the terrain on which profits are made (and defended) and policies are contested. This makes grappling with the role of race central to understanding the American political economy.

Scholars of American political development have not shied away from explaining the ways in which conflicts over race have come to shape political institutions and behavior, from struggles with taxation, slavery, and state capacity in the early American republic, to the rise of local taxation for schools following the Civil War, to race, immigration, and labor movement formation, to the way that preferences to maintain the Jim Crow social order – including the low-wage workforce – constrained the scope of the New Deal (Dawson and Francis 2016; Einhorn 2006; HoSang and Lowndes 2019; Katznelson 2005; King and Smith 2005). Yet if conflicts involving race have been a core component of how the American political economy has evolved over time, this observation has also tended to contribute to the United States' marginalization in studies of comparative political economy. Many studies fail to mention race at all; others do discuss race, but as an explanation for American exceptionalism (Alesina and Glaeser 2004). By deeming race an exceptional feature of the US case, it may also remove an opportunity to consider the extent to which divides about race which may be more pronounced historically in the

United States also shape the politics of knowledge-economy transition across other countries, especially in the face of demographic change, economic dislocation, and populist backlash – all issues that also structure politics outside of the United States (e.g., Harell et al. 2016; Soroka et al. 2017; Wright and Reeskens 2013).[6]

Finally, while often placed in comparison with Western European countries, the United States' settler colonial past, its constitution as a large multiracial democracy, and its heavy reliance on public-private (or otherwise marketized) forms of social provision, make it well-suited to comparisons with other countries that share some of these underlying social features while varying on other dimensions. Scholars of racial and ethnic politics have done more to consider whether national histories and conceptions of race ought to be used when structuring comparisons (Lieberman 2006; Marx 1998; Thompson 2016). To better understand the relationship between race, political economy, and market-based social provision, it may make more sense to place the United States in comparison with cases like South Africa, where the #FeesMustFall student movements emerging in 2015 were a response to discontent about neoliberal higher education funding and staffing policies, rising student debt at a time of few labor market opportunities, and the lack of progress towards material racial equality (Booysen 2016; Chikane 2018). Or, future comparisons might look toward places with a similar reliance on public-private mechanisms for social benefits, including, for example, Chile or Brazil. In short, thinking more about the role of the American political economy presents an opportunity for deepening and broadening our understanding about the variety of ways that racial divides may manifest themselves in comparative capitalism.

[6] A footnote in a recent comparative treatment qualifies this move: "There is no room to discuss 'American exceptionalism' here. The extreme narrowness and progressiveness of the American welfare state, together with sharply rising inequality and concentration of labor market risks in the poorest strata, are most likely responsible for the stability and polarization of the established parties ... Add to this that in the fragmented, decentralized American parties grid/group themes, particularly that of race, have always been incorporated and do not have to be grated onto a primarily distribution-centered party system" (Kitschelt and Rehm 2015).

5

The Production of Local Inequality: Race, Class, and Land Use in American Cities

Jessica Trounstine

The themes animating this volume are on stark display at the local level in American politics. A great deal of scholarship focused on who governs cities explores how authority is exercised to allocate resources, and how markets, economic power, politics, and policy interrelate (Dahl 1961). The evidence suggests that high-resource actors utilize local political institutions to maintain their economic and social dominance. Local business communities have an outsized influence in local policymaking, because local economies are reliant on their fiscal and leadership investments (Fischel 2001; Foglesong 2001; Logan and Molotch 1986; Peterson 1981; Stone 1989; Tiebout 1956). Homeowners and the wealthy are overrepresented in city political participation as well as in government decision-making (Einstein et al. 2019; Kogan et al. 2018; Oliver and Ha 2007; Trounstine 2018). At the same time, race and racial cleavages are frequently highlighted as dominant drivers of local political outcomes, with white residents overrepresented in electoral and policy outcomes (Browning et al. 1984; Gosnell 1935; Hajnal 2010; Jones-Correa 1998; Kaufmann 2004; Owens 2007; Pinder hughes 1987; Spence 2015). Less often have scholars combined these explanatory strands. Although there are many ways in which institutionalized racism, economic markets, politics, and policy intersect, in this chapter, I focus on the relationship between race, class, land use regulation, and housing markets. I argue that the fragmented structure of governance and public goods provision in the United States has allowed for the institutionalization of inequality. The result is that high-status (wealthy, white) residents have ensconced their opportunity, creating cyclic patterns of advantage and disadvantage.

In the United States (unlike the situation in most developed nations), most public goods are funded and delivered by local governments. There is no comprehensive count of local governments, but the best available evidence suggests that there are more than 90,000 independent substate governmental entities. About 40,000 of these are general-purpose governments like counties, cities, and towns, while the remainder are special districts that handle a specific function like education or mosquito abatement.[1] This means that governance in the United States is significantly divided along both geographic and functional lines.

In the decades since World War II, high socioeconomic status, predominantly white, residents have used this fragmented system to insulate their privilege, forming local (suburban) governments with separate taxing and spending authority and using their land use powers to prohibit the development of housing that would allow lower status individuals to move into the community (Burns 1994; Connolly 2014; Danielson 1976; Hayward 2013; Rothstein 2017; Thurston 2018; Trounstine 2018). In other words, they have generated segregation along race and class lines.

As described by Ansell and Gingrich (this volume), the rise of the knowledge economy and the intensification of competition over housing and schools has meant that this insulation of privilege has become ever more important, widening the gulf between the haves and the have-nots. With patterns of inequality embedded in the geographic fragmentation of local governments, high-resource communities must simply block change in order to maintain their advantage. The insulation of privilege and the fragmentation of local governance has resulted in profound inequalities in access to public goods and enormous barriers to correcting them.

Local suburban governments have played a fundamental role in generating inequality in access to basic public goods like clean water, operational sewers, functional garbage service, effective public safety, and high-quality education by generating race and class segregation through their control over land use. First, I offer a historical overview of how and why segregation patterns have changed over time. Then, I show that metropolitan areas with strict land use control in the suburbs witness a higher level of segregation between cities. I explore the extent to which state governments mitigate these patterns and find that they largely do not. In the final section of the chapter, I show that communities with more high-socioeconomic-status residents receive

[1] www.governing.com/gov-data/number-of-governments-by-state.html

a disproportionate share of municipal spending, allowing them to have higher quality public services.

HISTORICAL DEVELOPMENT OF SEGREGATION

Often, when people think of cities, they have in mind whole metropolitan areas – the urban center and surrounding suburban communities. Or they have in mind only large, densely populated settlements. In this chapter, I use the term city more precisely to mean any legally incorporated entity with its own governing body that has the power to tax and raise revenue, the power to regulate land uses, and the power to enforce the law. In the United States, cities come in a range of sizes, from hundreds of residents to millions, and they go by different names in different states (cities, boroughs, towns, villages). My analysis is focused on cities that are located within metropolitan areas as defined by the Census. I refer to the largest city in the metro area as the central city and all other incorporated communities as suburbs. Unincorporated communities are not included in my analysis.[2] As a federal system, the Constitution divides the authority to govern between the federal government and fifty state governments. Cities are political creations of the states. The extent to which the state devolves authority to localities varies, but all local governments possess some degree of autonomy.

Up through the early 1800s, the United States was a rural nation. Most Americans lived on farms or in small, agricultural communities. Although nascent cities existed, they featured weak governments and a jumble of residential, commercial, and public spaces. In these places, neighborhoods were integrated, with people of different ethnic and racial backgrounds living relatively near each other and the poor living close to the rich. The Civil War and industrial revolution at the end of the nineteenth century brought enormous numbers of migrants and immigrants to urban cores, and Black, Latino, and foreign residents threatened to spill into previously all-white neighborhoods.

[2] According to the Census, an urban place is any area with a population of 2,500 or more; it is a spatial concentration of a large number of people. A metropolitan area is a geographic location that contains at least one large population center, along with adjacent communities that have a high degree of economic and social integration. Cities are a subset of urban places and may or may not be located in metro areas. Cities (and their associated special districts) – not urban places or metropolitan areas – are the predominant providers of local public goods in the United States. In this chapter, my analyses focus on cities and suburbs within metropolitan areas.

Throughout the 1920s and 30s, white homeowning residents sought to bar minorities and poor residents from moving to their neighborhoods.[3] A real-estate guide published by the National Association of Real Estate Boards in 1923 asserted "property values have been sadly depreciated by having a single colored family settle down on a street occupied exclusively by white residents." The guide goes on to prescribe "segregation of the Negro population," as the only "reasonable solution of the problem, no matter how unpleasant or objectionable the thought may be to colored residents" (McMichael and Bingham 1923: 181). Even though the United States population was about 90 percent white, by 1940, all large cities had clearly defined neighborhoods inhabited by people of color (Massey and Denton 1993).[4] Unsurprisingly, cities tended to provide worse public services (e.g. waste removal, street paving, water treatment, schooling) to these neighborhoods (Myrdal 1944; Trounstine 2018).

As a result of the economic collapse during the Great Depression and then material scarcity during the war, the nation faced a severe housing shortage during the 1940s. When increasing numbers of Blacks and Latinos moved from rural areas into cities and to the North and West during the Great Migration, the boundaries of existing neighborhoods of color were pushed to their limits.[5] The massive influx of wartime workers dramatically changed the racial and socioeconomic makeup of many large cities and resulted in explosive social and policy conflicts along racial lines.[6]

In response to these transformations of the 1940s, white homeowners sought to protect their neighborhoods (which they considered to be the reward for their hard work and frugality) from disruption and disorder. As in earlier decades, many whites believed that the pursuit of these goals required racial exclusivity. Sugrue reports that in Detroit, as elsewhere, "a majority of whites looked to increased segregation as the solution to [the] 'colored problem'" (Sugrue 1996: 215). Whites, particularly those who owned their homes, believed that they had a right to certain neighborhoods and the public benefits (e.g., schools, safety) associated with those spaces.

3 Nightingale (2006); Shertzer et al. (2016, 2018)

4 About 10% of the population was Black, about 1.7% of the population could be considered Hispanic/Latino, and about 0.1% Asian. www.latinamericanstudies.org/immigration/Hispanics-US-1850-1990.pdf; www.census.gov/population/www/documentation/twps0076/twps0076.pdf

5 www-bcf.usc.edu/~philipje/Segregation/Haynes_Reports/Contours_PRR_2001-04e.pdf. Hundreds of thousands of Mexican descendants were deported during the Great Depression, so the overall Latino share of the population changed little.

6 Bayer et al. 2007; Bobo et al. 1997; Connolly 2014; Ellen 2000; Emerson et al. 2001; Krysan 2002; Krysan et al. 2008.

Above all else, whites feared that integration would jeopardize their single largest investment – the value of their home (Helper 1969), as well as the quality of their neighborhood (Kruse 2005). Blacks were seen as undesirable *neighbors*, in part, because the features of their *neighborhoods* became associated with individual members of the racial group. Whites came to similar conclusions about Chinese residents in San Francisco (McWilliams 1964; Shah 2001) and Latinos throughout the Southwest (Abrams 1955; McWilliams 1964; Torres-Rouff 2013). This was the case even though people of color and lower-income residents experienced poor neighborhood quality due to a lack of affordable housing options, paltry municipal services, and neglectful landlords, not by their own accord. Thus, the tight coupling between property values, public goods, and racial exclusivity was inexorably tied to the racism embedded in the real estate market (Hayward 2013) and the poor public goods that cities had provided to neighborhoods of color in decades past (Myrdal 1944; Torres-Rouff 2013).

In the 1950s and 60s, Black and Latino Americans' sustained battle for civil, economic, and political rights gained ground. As racial minorities began to contest and even win political representation, the open housing movement brought the possibility of neighborhood integration, and the federal court ordered desegregation of public schools. Whites understood minority demands for integration and court-ordered desegregation plans as undermining their entitlement (Kruse 2005: 126). This period became fraught with uncertainty and fear for many whites as they increasingly joined the ranks of homeowners.

Although many whites agreed on the desirability of residential segregation,[7] they were stymied by various hurdles. The Supreme Court had ruled racial zoning (the designation of certain neighborhoods as being inhabitable only by whites) unconstitutional in 1917, so a perfectly direct policy approach to residential segregation was not an option.[8] Instead, the preservation of white communities required collective action to prevent individual homeowners from selling or leasing to minority residents. As minority populations expanded and white homeownership rates skyrocketed, hundreds of white homeowners' organizations arose in

[7] In 1964 only 27% of white Americans supported general integration (Schuman et al. 1985).

[8] Many white neighborhoods also utilized violence to defend their borders (Hirsch 1983; Meyer 2000). Although tolerated (even encouraged) by the police and political establishment of some cities, murders and arson were technically illegal as well.

the 1940s, 50s, and 60s (Kruse 2005; Sugrue 1996).[9] Such organizations were often created by real estate developers to protect the value of their investment. These (typically all white) "civic associations, productive associations, improvement associations, and homeowners' associations" (Sugrue 1996: 211) fought to maintain the color line and their neighborhoods' exclusivity. They worked to cultivate racial restrictions in housing deeds (even though restrictive covenants had been ruled unenforceable by the Supreme Court in 1948), and pressured real estate agencies and lenders to refuse to sell to Black buyers. They set fire to homes on the Black real estate market and raised funds to repurchase homes that had been sold to Black families (Kruse 2005; Sugrue 1996).[10] In addition to these efforts in the private market, white homeowners and their neighborhood organizations turned to their city governments for protection – to institutionalize their exclusivity. They fought the building of public and multifamily housing in their neighborhoods, sought representation on planning boards, and battled open housing laws (Self 2003). They urged city governments to invoke eminent domain, raze some Black neighborhoods, and run highways through others. But these efforts required sustained political attention and sometimes even failed in the face of the rising Civil Rights Movement. In the end, many of these pro-segregation residents would leave the city altogether – moving to the suburbs where they had much greater political control over community boundaries (Boustan 2010; Nall 2018).

The history of suburban development – that is, the generation of separate governments, outside of the central city, that pool tax dollars and provide public goods – reveals that many suburbs were incorporated in order to ensure the economic and racial homogeneity of residents (Burns 1994; Danielson 1976; Miller 1981). What this means is that the very fragmentation that defines the United States political system was undergirded by a desire for race and class exclusivity. Starting in the 1950s and then, increasingly in the 1960s and 70s, suburban populations boomed (Jackson 1985). Through a combination of federal programs encouraging homeownership, the expansion of the federal highway system, and technological changes in the building of housing and service delivery, suburbs, which were previously small residential communities

[9] In some cases, the link between segregationists and homeowners' groups was direct. For example, the head of Atlanta's West End Cooperative Corporation had his start in community organizing as the head of Klavern No 297's Housing Kommittee (Kruse 2005: 54).

[10] They also served as social organizations welcoming new neighbors and organizing block parties (Sugrue 1996).

near larger population centers, grew exponentially (Rappaport 2005). By 1970, more than half of all metropolitan area populations lived outside of the central city; a figure that would grow to two-thirds over the next thirty years. In general, the people who moved to these new places had higher incomes and more wealth than those who stayed behind. And they were overwhelming white. This racial cast was purposeful.

In the years following the Great Depression and World War II, the federal government promoted white exclusivity in suburban communities through a series of mortgage programs reliant on maps created by the Home Owners Loan Corporation. These color-coded maps graded neighborhoods based on their credit risk, and the race and income of the residents were primary considerations in the rating. Neighborhoods with high concentrations of people of color and/or poor residents were granted the lowest rating – red (the genesis of the term redlining). Areas with racially restrictive covenants were given the highest grade (green). In justifying the high rating of a neighborhood called Arlington Heights in North Berkeley, HOLC wrote, "A great amount of Federal Housing money has been used in financing homes in this area. A long time loan plan, at small monthly payments attracts buyers at prices high in proportion to rental values. Zoned first residential, single family, deed restrictions prohibit Asiatics and Negroes." Similarly, extolling the virtues of West Twin Peaks in San Francisco, HOLC detailed, "Property is protected by single-family deed restrictions and 'first-residential' zoning. There are no racial threats, and maintenance is of a high order."

Prospective buyers seeking mortgages through federal programs were much more likely to be qualified if they were purchasing houses in HOLC's highly rated neighborhoods. Evidence indicates that private lenders also looked to HOLC's guidelines to determine credit worthiness (Rothstein 2017). Developers soon learned that touting racial exclusivity and inserting restrictive covenants into the deeds of their new developments was a sure way to increase property values (Hayward 2013). These practices were officially discontinued by the government after 1968, but by then segregation was already deeply entrenched in metropolitan America. The growth of suburbs has only served to increase divisions between cities and their surrounding communities along both class and race lines.

The demographic makeup of the suburbs in the 1950s and 60s meant that going forward, maintaining segregation simply meant preventing people of color and those with lower socioeconomic status from moving in; a task that was accomplished through land use regulation. As independent municipalities, suburbs have the power to regulate land use for all parcels within their borders. They can enact minimum lot sizes so that all development must be located on a certain acreage of land, preserve open spaces and historic districts, determine the (low) number of multifamily units that will be allowed within city limits, require developers to pay a large share of infrastructure improvements associated with new development, offer long review periods for zoning changes and building permits, and even ban renting altogether.

These kinds of restrictive land use policies became much more common and widespread starting in the 1970s (Been 2018; Elmendorf 2019; Nichols et al. 2013). There is no direct evidence of this proliferation, rather scholars have shown that since the 1970s, as housing prices have risen, housing supply has not kept pace (Glaeser and Gyourko 2018; Glaeser et al. 2005; Glaeser and Ward 2009). Unlike in decades past, today housing prices are decoupled from the cost of construction. Another piece of circumstantial evidence of increased land use regulation is that housing development has lagged behind population and job growth by a considerable amount in the last several decades (Been 2018). The conclusion that researchers have drawn is that this market distortion reflects a constraint on housing supply. After ruling out other alternative explanations like topographical restriction, scholars have largely concluded that land use regulations, along with more active opposition to development from residents in desirable areas, are the most likely culprits. Within metropolitan areas, regulatory stringency across cities is correlated, suggesting that cities learn from each other in the enactment of growth controls (Brueckner 1998).

Who are the residents driving these policies and what are their goals? In the most comprehensive political study of local housing policies to date, Anzia (forthcoming) lays out a framework for thinking about who might participate in the politics of housing and what their interests look like. On the one hand, chambers of commerce, speaking for business interests like developers, are likely to support increased growth and development. Because of their locational ties, Chambers are generally willing and able to focus time and attention on shaping city institutions like the zoning code to promote their goals. On the other hand, homeowners and their associated neighborhood organizations, who are both powerful actors in local politics (Fischel 2001; Hall and Yoder 2019), are generally opposed to new residential development (Einstein et al. 2019; Logan and Rabrenovic 1990; Nall and Marble 2020). Anzia finds that cities with more politically active chambers of commerce and developers tend to have less restrictive housing policies and build more housing units. On the flip side, she finds that cities with more politically active neighborhood associations and higher shares of homeowners are significantly more likely to have restrictive housing policies and build less multifamily housing. Trounstine (2020) shows that neighborhoods with larger shares of homeowners are more likely to vote in favor of development restriction.

There is, and always has been, a large racial gap in homeownership. In 2019, 73 percent of white households owned their homes compared to only 47 percent of Latinos and 41 percent of Black households.[11] And whites continue to express a preference for same-race neighbors (Charles 2003). White homebuyers are willing to pay a housing price premium for homogenous communities (Boustan 2010; Cutler et al. 1999) and white neighborhoods are significantly more supportive of restricting development than neighborhoods of color (Trounstine 2020). A growing Black population leads whites to leave neighborhoods and/or be unwilling to enter them. The size of the minority population that affects white population flows (the tipping point) ranges from about 5 percent to 20 percent (Card et al. 2008). Once a neighborhood reaches the tipping point, it quickly becomes predominantly inhabited by racial and ethnic minorities. White preferences for homogeneity are undoubtedly enhanced by persistent discrimination in the real estate and mortgage industries which limit minority access to some neighborhoods (Bobo 2001; Bobo and Zubrinski 1996; Farley et al. 1994; Galster and Godfrey 2005; Pager and Shepherd 2008). What this means is that a largely white homeowner community is the driving force behind the institutionalization of land use regulations that generate segregation; and their goal has been to maintain the race and class exclusivity of their communities.

SEGREGATION PATTERNS OVER TIME

To show how suburban segregation patterns have changed over time, I calculated a measure of segregation called Thiel's *H* Index, which captures the evenness of the dispersal of groups across geographic units and can be decomposed into intercity segregation and intracity segregation.[12] The measure tells us how diverse each city is relative to the diversity of the

[11] https://libertystreeteconomics.newyorkfed.org/2020/07/inequality-in-us-homeownership-rates-by-race-and-ethnicity.html

[12] Reardon and Firebaugh 2002, Fischer et al. 2004

metropolitan area as a whole while accounting for the degree of segregation within each city. In some metropolitan areas, whites and homeowners tend to be mostly segregated from nonwhites and renters in different neighborhoods within cities (indicating intercity segregation). In other metro areas, race and class divides are more prevalent across city lines (indicating higher intracity segregation). In the extreme, a metropolitan area could be very diverse (say 50 percent white and 50 percent people of color), but each city is comprised solely of one group. This is a very segregated metropolitan area. The measure I use captures the share of total segregation within a metro area that is accounted for across cities, because this reflects the degree to which suburbs differ from the central city (and from each other). It ranges from 0 to 1, with higher values indicating more intracity segregation. Additional details about the *H* Index are provided in Trounstine (2018).

I measured several different demographic characteristics capturing potential race and class segregation. Each measure evaluates the degree of division of members of one group from people who are not members of the group. The groups include whites/people of color, residents under the poverty line/over the poverty line, residents above 90th percentile for income/below the 90th percentile for income, those who are unemployed/employed, renters/homeowners, and college degree/no college degree. The measures are built from Census of Population and Housing data gathered at the Census tract level between 1970 and 2010. I have one observation for each metro area for each year. The results are shown in Table 5.1.

For each of the measures, the share of total segregation across cities has increased over time along both race and class lines. It is notable that the

TABLE 5.1 *Segregation across cities has increased over time*

	Whites/ People of Color	Poor/ Non-Poor	Wealthy/ Non-Wealthy	Unemployed/ Employed	Renters/ Homeowners	College/ Non-College
1970	23%	21%	22%	18%	26%	26%
1980	30%	26%	22%	23%	33%	29%
1990	35%	30%	25%	25%	36%	30%
2000	41%	34%	27%	26%	38%	30%
2010	44%	33%	30%	25%	34%	35%

share of racial segregation across city lines has increased more rapidly than *all* of the measures of class segregation. However, class segregation has also increased. It is likely that as income inequality rises, separation by income across city lines will be exacerbated.

LAND USE REGULATION AND SUBURBAN SEGREGATION

If, as I argued previously, land use regulation has played a role in these changing patterns of segregation, then metropolitan areas with more intense land use regulation in the suburbs should have greater race and class segregation across cities. Because every incorporated city in the United States has a distinct set of policies governing land use, studying the topic is a difficult task. Four broad-scale scholarly attempts have been made to collect data on land use policy[13] and I rely on the most recent survey for my analyses: the Wharton Residential Land Use Regulatory Index (WRLURI) developed by (2008). The index is built from a 2006 survey of local governments and measures characteristics of the regulatory process, rules of local residential land use regulation, and regulatory outcomes. These data were combined to measure the, "stringency of the local regulatory environment in each community" (Gyourko et al. 2008: 3). The survey contains data for more than 2,700 municipalities. I merged these data with the segregation measures described in the last section.

My primary independent variable is drawn from the WRLURI data. For each metropolitan area, I determined the average WRLURI for all suburban communities.[14] I then calculated the difference between the center city's WRLURI and suburban WRLURIs. This difference measure provides an estimate of the degree to which suburban municipalities have more stringent land use regulations than the central city for each metro area. I combined these data with one component of my segregation measure – the level of segregation

[13] Linneman et al. 1990; Glickfield and Levine 1992; Pendall et al. 2006; Gyourko et al. 2008.

[14] The WRLURI is comprised of eleven subindices, all designed so that low scores represent less restrictive land use policy. The WRLURI is centered at zero and has a standard deviation of 1. It ranges from about −2 to +5. Because cities compete for residents and businesses within metropolitan regions, land use stringency levels are metro area specific (Pendall et al. 2006). To account for this, my dependent variable is measured as each city's difference from the minimum regulatory score in the metropolitan area. This variable ranges from 0 to 4.2 with a mean of 0.93 and a standard deviation of 0.77.

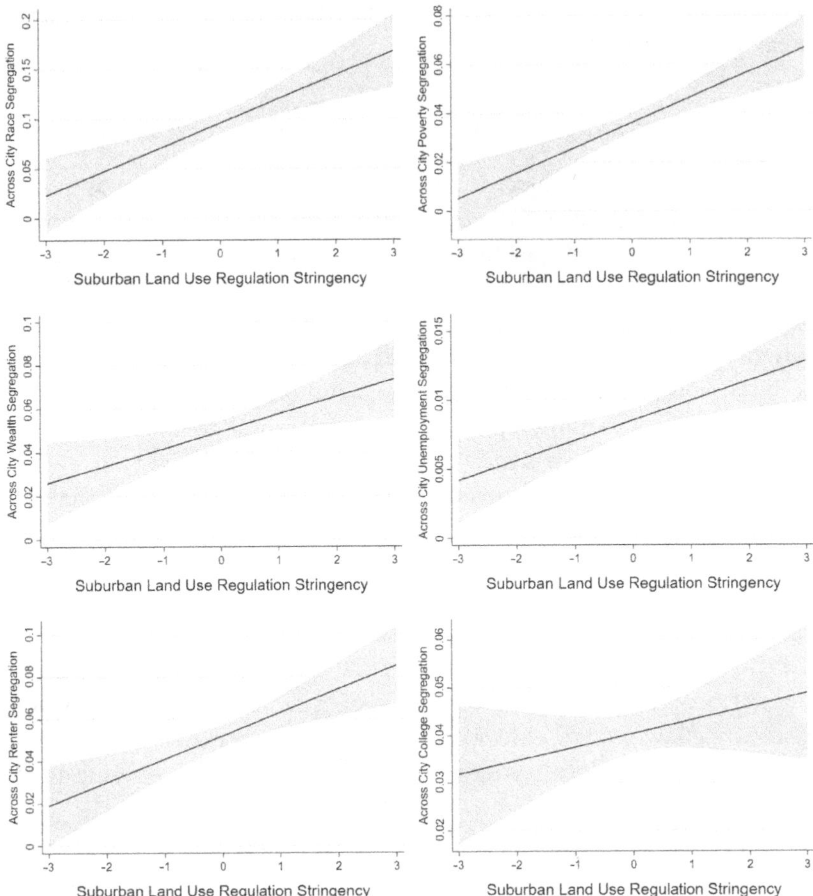

FIGURE 5.1 Land use regulation correlation with race and class segregation

across cities in each metropolitan area as of 2010. I analyzed the correlation between each region's *Across City Segregation* and the *WRLURI Difference* using OLS regression. Figure 5.1 displays the marginal effect of suburban land use regulation stringency on race and class segregation across cities

The figure makes clear that suburban land use controls are significantly related to the extent of intracity segregation in metropolitan areas along both race and class lines. The effect is most powerful with regard to racial segregation. When suburbs have more stringent land use policies, metro areas are more segregated.

CAN STATE GOVERNMENTS MITIGATE SEGREGATION?

Given that cities are subject to dictates from state legislatures and state courts, next, I investigate whether segregation across cities can be mitigated with restrictions on local autonomy. There is a high degree of variation in the degree of local control states offer to substate governments.[15] Since the late 1800s, all states have granted cities the power to raise and spend revenue, decide how and where to provide services, and to police their populations and land within their borders. But different states allow different amounts of local government discretion with regard to structural and functional responsibility (e.g., the power to create new local governments, freedom from state interference in policymaking, judicial protection of local control, and municipal responsibility for key services), and fiscal discretion (e.g., freedom from tax, debt, and expenditure limits). Using several sources, Wolman et al. (2008) construct factor scores on these dimensions. Comparing each state's rank on these two scales reveals that there is very little correlation (−0.13) between them. This suggests that it is *not* the case that states *generally* allow or restrict local autonomy, but rather offer a mixture of policies restricting local governments in some areas but offering them freedom in others.

Regressing my measure of segregation across cities in metro areas on these measures of state control reveals no significant effects. Offering local governments more or less autonomy does not appear to change patterns of segregation between cities and suburbs. This is likely because even the most restrictive states grant local governments substantial authority to regulate land use – a long-range consequence of the overwhelming power of property owners in the generation of local policy and legal doctrine at

[15] There is debate in the literature regarding the definition of local control. For instance, some scholars argue that even if a city has the authority under state law to accomplish some goal (like providing waste disposal services), if the city does not have the economic capacity and management competence to provide such a service, we cannot say that it truly has the authority to do so. Wolman et al. (2008) generate a broad, local autonomy index which captures variation across states along three dimensions: the importance of local government to the intergovernmental system, local government discretion, and local government capacity.

the turn of the twentieth century. The grant to regulate land uses is generally broad and unencumbered.[16] Local governments determine (for example) the density of development, the comingling of residential and business properties, the establishment of building codes, the use of eminent domain for public purposes, and assessment of property. Many state legislatures have engaged in statewide efforts to shape planning and land use regulation. But typically, these efforts have been intended to restrict development overall or require land use plans rather than to limit autonomy of local governments.[17] Although state courts have been somewhat more active in seeking to curb autonomy (by promoting fair share housing requirements or overturning specific zoning decisions, for example), rulings have overwhelmingly tended toward local deference.[18]

Local zoning boards play a particularly powerful role in shaping development. Although most zoning boards are officially advisory, their decisions are typically given a great deal of weight by lawmakers.[19] In several states, zoning board recommendations become law without specific action taken by the city council to overrule them (Anderson, Brees, and Reninger 2008). We know little about the types of people who populate zoning boards. But what we do know indicates an extremely high rate of self-selection among local residents with monetary stake in zoning decisions (Holman forthcoming).

Similarly, although states have different methods and requirements for municipal incorporation and annexation, these are generally highly local decisions and also frequently driven by those with a monetary stake in the outcome. That is, if a group of residents who live outside of a city wants to become an incorporated municipality – state law largely allows them to do so (Briffault 1990). The current legal procedures for incorporation (and their interpretation by state courts) were largely enshrined in state law in the first half of the twentieth century – when white, rural and suburban representatives had outsized influence in state legislatures due to malapportionment. The power of central cities to annex outlying land and populations persisted somewhat longer in Southern and Western states than in the

[16] See Briffault (1990) for an overview of state/local land use law.

[17] In fact, I find that states with more limitations and active courts tend to have significantly *more* suburban land use exclusivity (perhaps indicating that the causal direction is reversed). See Foster and Summers (2005) for state-by-state summaries of state land use law.

[18] See Foster and Summers (2005) for summaries of state court decisions on land use.

[19] See Holman (forthcoming) for an overview of local boards and commissions.

Northeast and Midwest, which is why cities like Los Angeles, Phoenix, and San Jose have such large geographic footprints. But eventually all states came to offer suburbs control over their physical destiny. As a result, the number of incorporated municipalities in metropolitan areas grew throughout the postwar period in all regions, and suburbs gained population, economic activity, and political power (Burns 1994; Danielson 1976; Miller 1981).

SUBURBAN INEQUALITY

Cities are responsible for delivering many functions in the United States including public safety, public goods (like sewers, parks, utilities, garbage), social welfare, and infrastructure (like roads and ports). Most cities do not provide educational services (the vast majority of public schools are handled by school districts, a special-purpose government). Table 5.2 presents the average share of total expenditures going to different services for 2012 in all US cities.

Table 5.2 reveals that basic services – roads, public safety, garbage, and water – comprise the bulk of city expenditures. But, as a result of preference, capacity, and state law, not all cities handle all these functions. The fragmentation of local governance in America means that from city-to-city, packages of public goods and services look very different. According to Freemark, Steil, and Thelen (2020) this situation is unique among developed nations. Canada and European countries either limit local control and/or provide more centralized funding,

TABLE 5.2 *Local expenditures*

Function	Share of Total Expenditure in All Cities
Health, welfare, housing	3%
Education/Libraries	2%
Roads/Highways	30%
Public safety	16%
Parks	3%
Sewerage/Waste/Water	12%
Government admin	17%
Debt interest	2%

thereby reducing inequalities across jurisdictions. In the United States, patterns of expenditure are closely related to economic vitality – some cities have the wealth needed to provide a broad menu of services, others do not. These inequalities are the result of high-resource residents using land use regulation to protect and enhance those resources through residential segregation, a situation that has worsened over time.

As early as the mid-1800s, upper-middle-class residents sought their own local communities (Teaford 1979). This desire for separation led to the explosion of newly incorporated municipalities – the nation's earliest suburbs. But, over the course of the next fifty years, many of these tiny new cities consolidated and/or were annexed into larger central cities for one primary reason: the provision of city services. Prior to 1900, suburban governments were simply unable to provide the quality of sewers, clean water, paved streets, uniformed police forces, and firefighting that was available in the central city. As a result, as cities became more diverse, the forces of separation pulled people into different neighborhoods, but not into different cities.

So, while high socioeconomic status (white, wealthy) residents have always sought to live apart from the unwashed masses, in previous decades, consolidation between cities and annexation of outlying areas made city boundaries malleable so that even those moving to the periphery would have resided within city limits (Teaford 1979). When city boundaries can expand to capture populations that have moved to the outer edges of town, they are able to keep higher resource residents and businesses within the city limits. This means that tax dollars and votes do not escape to the suburbs, and redistribution is possible. But, when high-resource residents can move away from the city *and* are able to establish their own jurisdiction with land use control, taxing, and spending authority, they can prevent city residents from accessing their wealth. Moving outside of city boundaries allowed suburbs to provide high levels of public goods for their residents without having to pay for services for nonresidents.

As Hayward has argued, suburbs offered the opportunity to, "engage in exclusionary zoning practices ... to opt out of supporting public housing ... and even opt out of supporting public transportation within the boundaries of their municipalities," all while allowing suburbanites to "pool their tax monies ... to provide schooling and other public services" (Hayward 2009: 149). Because cities are the predominant providers of local public goods in America, segregation between cities has also meant segregation in access to government benefits. This generation of governmental fragmentation has been both purposeful and effective.

As race and class segregation across city lines has increased, low socioeconomic status residents have less ability to use politics to address inequality. The inverse is also true, in metro areas that are more integrated, the poor and people of color are better able to use politics to generate policy outcomes that are more favorable to them. To analyze the share of resources different cities garner, I used data on inflation-adjusted *Direct General Expenditure Per Capita* from the Census of Governments State and Local Government Finance files from 1977 to 2012.[20] I aggregated all inflation-adjusted expenditures per capita by metropolitan area, for each year. This variable, total expenditures per capita, represents the collective dollars spent by municipal governments in a metropolitan area. I divided each municipality's expenditure by this total to generate the share of metropolitan spending accounted for by each city. I calculated a similar measure for population, generating the share of metropolitan population accounted for by each city. The ratio of these two quantities, the *Spending Equity Ratio*, is my outcome of interest.[21]

This ratio measures the disparity between the percentage of the population represented by a city and the percentage of total resources received by that population. If resources are distributed exactly equally across the population, the ratio takes a value of 1; values less than 1 indicate that the community receives fewer resources than its population size would predict, and values greater than 1 indicate an abundance of resources. Between 1972 and 2012, this measure averaged 0.4 for central cities and 2.5 for suburbs; and the discrepancy has gotten worse over time.[22] Suburban residents receive *two and a half times* the resources that their population share justifies, while central city residents receive less than half the resources that their population share justifies. This is despite the fact that central cities spend more, on average, per resident than do suburbs.

Unsurprisingly, communities with larger populations of racial and ethnic minorities and more lower-class residents have a lower *Spending Equity Ratio*. Table 5.3 shows how the demographics of

[20] The data are collected in years that end with 2 and 7 and I used linear interpolation to generate estimates of city expenditures in 1980, 1990, 2000, and 2011 to match the Census population data. www2.census.gov/pub/outgoing/govs/special60/. Filename is _IndFin_1967-2012.zip.

[21] *Spending Equity Ratio*$_i = \frac{E_i/E}{P_i}$.

[22] Calculated for all cities with more than 1,000 residents and all metropolitan areas in which I have data on more than one city.

TABLE 5.3 *Demographic differences between suburbs and cities, 1927–2012*

	1927		1987		1992		1997		2002		2007		2012	
	Suburbs	Central City	Suburbs	Central City	Suburbs	Central City	Suburbs	Central City	Suburbs	Central City	Suburbs	Central City	Suburbs	Central City
% Non-white	10%	15%	14%	24%	12%	25%	14%	28%	16%	31%	17%	33%	19%	34%
% Renters	61%	58%	36%	43%	27%	42%	26%	42%	26%	42%	27%	43%	27%	43%
Med. Inc			29,858	20,558	27,578	24,582	33,606	29,223	39,111	33,402	43,533	36,804	47,082	39,412
% Poverty			10%	17%	15%	18%	13%	17%	13%	18%	15%	20%	16%	22%
% College			13%	11%	9%	12%	10%	12%	11%	13%	12%	14%	13%	14%
% Unempl	55%	55%			3%	3%	3%	3%	3%	4%	4%	4%	4%	5%

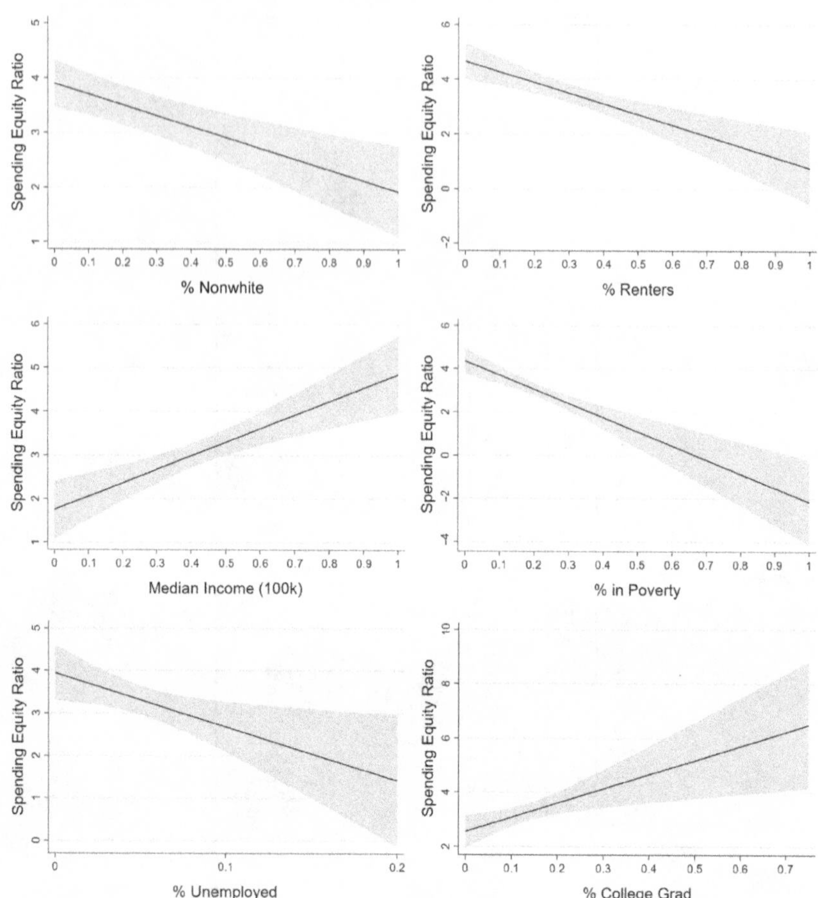

FIGURE 5.2 Effect of race and class city makeup on spending equity

cities and suburbs have diverged over time. Figure 5.2 shows the marginal effect of each demographic measure on spending equity as of 2012.[23]

Aggregating to the metropolitan area level, I found that more segregated metro areas also have more variation in spending from city to city.[24]

[23] The figure presents marginal effects of regressing the *Spending Equity Ratio* each demographic measure, with errors clustered by metropolitan area.

[24] My dependent variable in this analysis is a measure developed by Rhode and Strumpf (2003) called the coefficient of variation (CV). The CV captures the degree of

The data revealed that in metropolitan areas with more segregation across cities – that is, where privileged residents tend to live in different municipalities from non-privileged residents – we see more heterogeneity in municipal budgets.

Combined with the results presented in Figure 5.2, we can see that in segregated metropolitan areas, it is those communities with larger populations of renters, unemployed, non–college educated, people in poverty, and racial minorities that have access to a much smaller share of the total dollars spent by local governments. They have worse service, worse schools, and worse opportunities. Segregation produces inequality. However, this is the one area where state intervention seems to have important consequences. Where state courts have imposed fair-share housing requirements, cities within metropolitan areas witness less variation in spending.

THE GREAT INVERSION

Thus far, the analysis has been predicated on the assumption that privilege exists predominantly in the suburbs. But, in some metro areas, the reality is more complicated. While suburbs were once nearly exclusively populated by white and wealthy homeowners, today many (inner-ring) suburbs have significant concentrations of lower-socioeconomic status, minority residents (Frasure-Yokely 2015). There are some metro areas, like San Francisco, in which the highest resourced individuals live in the central city and the less affluent live outside of it. Ehrenhalt (2013) refers to this pattern as the Great Inversion. In this volume, the chapter by Tom Ogorzalek studies this phenomenon. Ogorzalek finds that land has become much more valuable in some central cities – particularly several that are central to the knowledge economy. He also shows that cities with

heterogeneity in spending for a metropolitan area. It is calculated as the ratio of the standard deviation of spending to the mean of spending.

$$CV_{msa} = \frac{\sqrt{\sum_j P_j(E_j - M)^2}}{M},$$

where E_j is the per capita expenditure of city j, M is the mean per capita expenditure for all cities in the metropolitan area, and P_j is the share of the total metro area population in city j. I regress the CV on racial, renter, and wealth segregation across cities (H_{m_c}). I add fixed effects for year to account for the declining time trend.

steeper land value gradients raise more revenue. Ogorzalek concludes that knowledge economy central cities may have more leverage than they had in the past to engage in serious redistribution because they may no longer fear losing business and wealthy residents to other jurisdictions.

Other research has demonstrated that one of the best predictors of redistributive expenditure is the wealth of the city (Hajnal and Trounstine 2014). That is, cities that can afford to spend money on housing, health, and welfare are more likely to do it. If knowledge economy cities are keeping wealthy residents and businesses within their borders, and engaging in redistributive spending, they may be uniquely poised to address inequality. But this presumes that the process of gentrification has not displaced the residents who need redistributive programs. If rising housing costs mean that the area's neediest residents have been pushed outside of the central city's borders, inequality is unlikely to be lessened. Thus, it is crucial that going forward we gain a clear view of where high versus low socioeconomic status residents live, and what their governments are willing and able to provide. As a first approximation in analyzing this, we can see whether segregation across city lines is lower in metro areas that are heavily invested in the knowledge economy. If this is the case, then the rise of the knowledge economy could help address inequality through local policies.

To identify knowledge economy metro areas, I draw on the research conducted by Ogorzalek in this volume. Ogorzalek analyzes land gradients in forty-two metro areas. To Ogorzalek's list I added two metro areas, San Jose, California, and Hartford, Connecticut, that were highlighted by a Brookings Foundation report, *Redefining Global Cities*, that lists highly productive innovation centers in the United States. Table 5.4 shows that knowledge economy metro areas are even more segregated across jurisdictional lines than other US metro areas.

Although much more research needs to be conducted in order to understand the relationship between the transformation of the economy, redistribution, and population sorting, this initial evidence indicates that knowledge economy employment clustering likely induces and reinforces sorting among residents, increasing gentrification in the central city, and ultimately generating less opportunity for redistribution, rather than

TABLE 5.4 *Segregation across cities among knowledge economy leaders in 2010*

	Whites/ People of Color	Poor/ Non-Poor	Wealthy/ Non-Wealthy	Unemployed/ Employed	Renters/ Home-owners	College/ Non-College
Knowledge Economy Metros	0.124	0.046	0.068	0.010	0.060	0.052
Other Metros	0.082	0.034	0.039	0.008	0.050	0.032

more. That said, many large knowledge economy cities do have significant pockets of poverty and redistributive programs will undoubtedly assist residents who find a way to live or work within the boundaries of the central city. But the rapid increase in housing prices in the *most* productive cities suggests both that housing regulations are being used to restrict supply, and that access to the wealth of these places is likely to become ever more limited over time, increasing inequality and decreasing mobility (Ganong and Shoag 2017).

CONCLUSION

Even after decades of progressive change in racial attitudes and growing concern over income inequality, America remains a segregated nation. Increasingly, segregation has occurred across cities rather than within them. City politics has played a role in this change. As the federal government and developers invested in making suburban places livable, white property owners abandoned exclusivity in the cities and focused their attention on maintaining exclusivity in suburban communities, where politics and policy was easier for them to dominate. And this is where they have stayed. These patterns became fixed by local land use policies: the result has been an increasing degree of separation between cities in metropolitan areas.

Today, the politics of suburban American is quiet and consensual – largely because conflict has been zoned out. Residents of central cities and poorer suburbs cannot affect the politics of exclusive suburbs as a result of fragmentation. The result is dramatic inequalities across places. Suburban communities garner a vastly disproportionate share of resources and guard their advantage using land use regulations to shape the character and structure of their communities. As the knowledge economy continues to transform our nation's metropolitan areas, the solution will be to limit local autonomy or fund public goods at the state or national level. It will require those with access to power and resources to work on behalf of those less privileged and an intense will to overcome deep race and class divisions.

6

The City Re-centered? Local Inequality Mitigation in the 21st Century

Thomas K. Ogorzalek

In the winter of 2019, four surprising pieces of news emerged from New York City in quick succession. First, in mid-January, Mayor Bill de Blasio announced a new program that would provide free healthcare to undocumented immigrants and other uninsured New Yorkers, at an expected cost of $100 million (Goodman 2019b). Across the river in Queens a month later, local activists protested and ultimately defeated the arrival of the Amazon HQ2 corporate campus, which would have employed tens of thousands and generated millions in revenues for city and state coffers (Goodman 2019a). Each of these outcomes runs contrary to long-held expectations about how American cities govern themselves in an era of inequality, mobile wealth, and porous municipal borders: public and private elites partner to court outside investment as a top priority, override grassroots protests, and avoid redistributive programs that might push the wealthy out and draw the poor in. But here was a city, famously bankrupt four decades ago and perennially cash-strapped, declining an influx of high taxpayers and development while simultaneously pledging massive new expenditures.

The third and fourth items help explain this puzzling pattern. Between de Blasio's announcement and Amazon's departure, a financier purchased the world's most expensive apartment in midtown Manhattan (Stewart and Gelles 2019). The NYC Comptroller responded by announcing a proposal for a new luxury real estate tax estimated to generate between $380 and $650 million annually, ostensibly offsetting *both* the healthcare program and the Amazon deal's breakdown. About a year later, Amazon announced it would still expand its presence in New York, despite the loss of the subsidy plan tied to HQ2. Along with Amazon's decision to open a similar site near Washington, DC, the sequence of events in New York reinforced the realization that the world's largest company's location decisions were based more on the special features of these places as the world's economic, political, and military capitals than on the subsidy packages offered by many cities in Amazon's very public competition for the siting of HQ2. They also dramatically demonstrate an emergent feature of American political economy in the postindustrial age: a new irreplaceability of particular sites where democratic processes might modestly check the most powerful private actors in the global economy.

The contributions to this volume answer an important call to examine the political economy of the United States in the current age. Most chapters examine national trends and policies, but a subnational motif runs throughout, and with good reason. As inequality increases not only among people but across places, government responses may intensify or mitigate this tendency toward commodification. In an era of national gridlock, the federal system might provide venues in which to enact policies to respond to new challenges and opportunities presented by the knowledge economy (KE). The contribution to this volume by Hacker, Pierson, and Grumbach illustrates the patterns of dysfunctional governance in some very Republican states at the periphery of the KE; what happens in the very Democratic cities at its heart? Most analyses suggest that local government tends to exacerbate rather than mitigate inequality and citizens' exposure to the market. The framework for local government in the United States intensifies commodification, especially since the federal government drastically cut intergovernmental aid to cities since the 1970s, by not only exposing Americans to market forces but creating a new "marketplace of places" in which many life outcomes are tied to one's place of origin (Caraley 1992; Sampson 2011).

In this chapter, I assess distinctive elements of American big-city political economy that affect decommodification even in the most progressive political communities in the nation. First, I summarize the formidable political, legal, and economic barriers to local policies that might mitigate the inequalities generated by the KE (and modern capitalism broadly).[1]

[1] In this chapter, I follow refer to policies as "inequality mitigating" and "decommodifying" policies interchangeably for the sake of legibility. Most broadly, I mean public policy measures taken to insulate persons from the vicissitudes of cyclical scarcity and encourage the development of their persons and membership in common life in ways not directly connected to their purchasing power, income, or labor force status. This may entail traditional redistributive programs, regulations including "predistributive" efforts to shape market outcomes rather than correct after the fact, public goods provision, and

Second, I identify how one of those barriers, the relative importance of central places, has changed, potentially enabling policy change in places where the KE is strongest. Finally, I assess cross-city patterns in decommodifying policymaking based on this observation, and consider how local policies might help decommodify some aspects of American life.

Overall, passage and serious implementation of such policies are highly contingent, and the use of city policy alone to mitigate overall inequality in the United States is insufficient in any case. In the context of national inaction, however, such action is preferable to nothing at all, and may help provide models that can be adopted elsewhere and help shift ideas about the relationship between community self-government and powerful economic actors.

INEQUALITY MITIGATION IN AMERICAN CITIES?

Problems of inequality in capitalism often hit earlier and more intensely in cities. This was true in the era of industrialization and urbanization and in the "urban crisis" period of deindustrialization and sprawl. Many of the policies the United States has used to ease inequality or provide security from the market originated in or responded to crises in cities and were promoted most forcefully by city leaders (Buenker 1973; Ogorzalek 2018). In today's increasingly globalized, interconnected world, the cities that serve as headquarter sites of the global economy are often characterized by extreme wealth in close proximity with dire poverty, and are again a major site and cause of increased inequality and other associated challenges.

These challenges are present in cities around the world, but US federalism makes local governance more important relative to its wealthy and/or Western peer democracies. Significant substantive policy devolution ostensibly brings some governing decisions closer to the governed and allows for a variety of locally tailored policies. Many have long hoped that cities might be "the hope of democracy" because they are "both the appropriate size for democratic participation and the relevant site for negotiating the relationship between polity and economy" (Howe 1905: 72, qtd. in Schragger 2009). In principle and under the right circumstances, federalism might create "laboratories of democracy" responsive to grassroots organization and working-class interests that could effectively implement decommodifying policies.

other equity-enhancing reforms that mitigate categorical harms that produce, reproduce, or aggravate the material stratification order.

Especially in a moment in which polarization and gridlock have made national institutions unresponsive to emerging challenges, some hopeful analysts have identified a "rebirth of urban democracy" and a "New Localist" perspective suggesting that pragmatic, problem-solving local governments may be more disposed to address major social problems responsively and collaboratively (Barber 2013; Berry et al. 1993; Katz and Nowak 2018; Schragger 2016).

Some factors do suggest that big cities are a good forum for decommodifying policies. These include relatively streamlined constitutions and shared Democratic partisan affiliation of public officials, which help coordinate action; local grassroots traditions, which provide models of past efforts; progressive public opinion, which can reinforce policy demands; and existing inequality in these cities itself, which makes the direness of the challenge more immediate for reluctant leaders. In many cases, municipalities have indeed become "fertile sites for labor and employment policy" that would likely be nonstarters at the federal level (Schragger 2009: 514). Dozens of American states and localities have increased the local minimum wage well above the national floor, and a few (notably San Francisco and the New York plan described previously) have established more robust local health insurance programs, among others.

It is certainly plausible that these "superstar" cities where wealth and connection to the KE are concentrated might serve as class mobility "escalators." These escalators may indeed provide access for a lucky few into the top floors of an unequal society; an even tougher question is whether city policies might be able to leverage that wealth concentration to soften the winner-take-all dynamics of the knowledge economy. Alternatively, without significant governance effort and skill it is just as likely that these places might *only* generate and intensify inequality, while largely excluding many both inside and outside their city limits from the benefits of the KE (Le Galès and Pierson 2019). Especially in the United States, the will and ability of city government to autonomously slow or mitigate rising inequality have been limited, and working-class cityzens remain highly exposed to market forces. This is the paradox of urban governance in the United States: big cities face a high demand for state interventions in markets, but are often constrained (Ogorzalek 2018).

The classic schools of US local politics suggest that the potential for meaningful decommodification through local action is profoundly limited, emphasizing the power of well-resourced actors (especially businesses and homeowners) in determining local outcomes.[2] These barriers to such policymaking can be categorized as related to pluralist politics, constitutional-legal rules, and economic forces. First, as in national politics, business and elite interests tend to enjoy relatively more resources – including money, access to elected officials, free time, and relevant skills – to win overt "pluralist" policy and political fights, including elections, especially when they have significant material interests at stake. Unlike in national politics, the importance of local property taxes for funding local government gives local leaders a strong incentive to coordinate with "growth machine" interests – especially those who own the physical land within the city – to increase (or at least maintain) the exchange value of land, explicitly commodifying communities in the process.

Second, local governments in the United States are the legal creations of their state governments. While many states have "home rule" provisions that delegate a range of internal decisions to cities, these (or any other local policy) can be preempted, negated, limited, or required at any time by their state legislature. While a city may get more policy latitude based on a political relationship between state and city, the constitutional requirement of at least tacit consent to any local policy by state government formally limits the menu of policy options, especially when local and state leaders are not from the same political coalition (Weir et al. 2005). Cities abroad often have more robust legal status alongside (rather than below) states or provinces, eliminating at least one check on their actions.

American local governments do typically functionally control some areas that structure the average person's experiences and security. These include land regulation, which shapes the housing market; education, which shapes most individuals' future earning potential and identity, especially in the knowledge economy; and policing/criminal justice policy, which is particularly important and varied in a nation as punitive as the United States. Policies in these areas might go a significant way in both providing access to the KE and insulating persons from capitalism generally, but more often this devolved structure for policymaking exacerbates rather than eases inequality, in part by bringing market forces into more

[2] The key questions are about whether outcomes derive from unbalanced resources and incentives to compete in a pluralist framework (Dahl 1961 and critics); from elites' imperative to increase rents in the growth machine (Logan and Molotch 1986); from the dependence of local officials on private-sector participation in informal regime coalitions (Stone 1989); or from the fiscal discipline supplied by bond rating agencies and mobile taxpayers (Hackworth 2007; Peterson 1981).

areas of life and making access to some social rights (and sometimes civil and political rights) depend as much on one's address as on membership in the nation.

Elsewhere in this volume, Jessica Trounstine chronicles how local elites have used limited local redistribution while retaining high-quality public goods for themselves. That narrative involves the aforementioned political and legal constraints: elites winning pluralist fights within large cities; and later creating legally insulated enclaves (i.e., suburbs) at the urban periphery but still proximate to the wealth generation of the city itself. Those suburbs powerfully (though plausibly invisibly, for their beneficiaries) shape Americans' lives, but they are also predicated on the insight that at a certain point those elites could not reliably win local political battles: the use of exit by the relatively affluent shows that the inclusion of both rich and poor city dwellers in a large resource pool is a possible tool for redistribution and shared public goods, even if it was never truly equitable.

For central cities, political and legal hurdles can *possibly* be overcome with effective local organizing and state-level coalition building, though this is both rare and difficult. The third category of local redistributive constraint entails economic disciplining action by market actors well beyond the influence of any regular democratic process. One of these is interjurisdictional competition, in which cities must conduct themselves not only as local democracies, but as firms in a competitive "marketplace of places" (Peterson 1981; Tiebout 1956). According to this logic, there are powerful incentives for place-bound cities to satisfy the demands of mobile businesses and taxpayers. The predicted result is a metropolitan "race to the bottom" on most public provision and regulation. Interjurisdictional competition and chronic fiscal precarity present a major challenge for even the most committed would-be decommodifier.

Competition in this marketplace of places is a fundamental feature of American city politics. With no precapitalist past, American cities were nearly all founded as nodes in extractive-industrial-commercial networks, and from their start were in direct competition with each other (Monkkonen 2018). The early pattern of local political economy, in which city boosters sought to enrich themselves by attracting capital and population from elsewhere, still basically describes much of municipal politics today; success in that marketplace is seen as a precondition for other policy projects. This competition exists both within and across metropolitan areas and has changed over time. The nineteenth century was an era of central-city expansion, in which large municipalities frequently annexed surrounding areas, often coercively. In this environment, cities competed by *providing* services and infrastructure, not by limiting their spending, and intrametropolitan competition was far less important for city policy (Monkkonen 2018; Schragger 2009; Smith 2013). New technology and institutional changes around the turn of the twentieth century shifted the parameters of incorporation and annexation, creating fragmented patchworks of local governments in American metropolitan areas. By the late twentieth century, many (perhaps *most)* new municipalities were formed expressly to subsidize real estate developers and/or limit residents' contribution to the central city's common resource pool (Burns 1994; Miller 1981; Trounstine 2018). While the KE is characterized by a "great divergence" in fortunes *between* metropolitan areas, the action was *within* metro areas in the twentieth century, as American cities were surrounded by hundreds of neighboring suburbs, all open for business and wooing the city's tax base in one way or another.

We have long known that such intrametropolitan fractionalization contributes to inefficient and inegalitarian outcomes, and this is particularly true in the United States.[3] American city-regions are more decentralized in their policymaking, more vulnerable to market forces, and more oriented toward business in their policy formation (Savitch and Kantor 2002: 166). Our distinctive pattern of metropolitan governance affects even understandings of the word "city." While Americans usually use this term to invoke the municipality, in comparative urbanist studies of global cities, the appropriate unit of analysis is usually the broad metropolitan region, because this is the place-based web of connections that constitutes social and economic life. In most other nations, it is also a meaningful unit of political life, with a local government vested with significant powers that creates and executes regional plans, distributes resources, and coordinates political action. Metropolitan governments abroad are often created or expanded when cities sprawl beyond their borders. For instance, London has twice expanded to incorporate surrounding boroughs, and the new Grand Paris plan creates a new authority that incorporates most of the Parisian suburbs. Canadian and Australian cities have similar institutions, in federal nations historically and culturally comparable to the United States. These governments have real powers, and their leaders are among the most visible political figures in the nation. Such strong metropolitan-area governments reduce competition within a metro area and can reduce inequality of both provision regimes and social outcomes in a region (Kübler and Rochat 2019). As

[3] For one example and a historiography of this "regionalist" perspective, see (Dreier et al. 2004: ch. 6).

Freemark, Steil, and Thelen note, "Major metropolitan areas throughout the rich democracies exhibit patterns of spatial inequality, but the politics of metropolitan fragmentation and the extent to which they entrench or mitigate these inequalities vary widely" (Freemark et al. 2020: 236). When combined with the national state's weak and decentralized social provision regime, the fact that American metropolitan regional governments are politically obscure, anemic in authority, and narrow and technical in activity means that local governmental fractionalization in the United States is both more intense and more important for policy than it is elsewhere (Freemark et al. 2020). As a result, while "regional efforts attacking problems of social equity [are] feeble and uncommon" (Kantor 2011: 25) in major cities around the world, they are particularly so in American metropolitan regions, in which leaders are forced to be much more solicitous of and dependent on business investment to function well (Savitch and Kantor 2002: 150).

These political, legal, and economic forces work independently and cumulatively to tilt the playing field against the successful implementation of decommodifying policies at the local level. Given these patterns of local political outcomes and constraints on even sympathetic local policymakers, the optimists of the "new localist" school have some explaining to do: What, if anything, has changed about local politics such that we should expect cities to effectively provide inequality-mitigating policies in the twenty-first century? In the next section, I explore one answer with an examination of how the KE has restructured the importance of central places in the American metropolis.

An important caveat must be made explicit before presenting an analysis of one potentially promising shift in the economic forces described in this section: even if the fifty largest American cities each successfully implemented a full suite of policies to ameliorate the rough edges of capitalism and promote the human flourishing of their residents (an unlikely development considering the aforementioned constraints and actual historical outcomes), it would not much affect the inequality or commodification of life for most Americans or the nation as a whole. This is partially because access to most of those policies' benefits would be limited to these cities' residents, who make up about 15 percent of the national population. Moreover, the balance of contemporary fiscal power is overwhelmingly centered in the national government. While most elected officials and domestic government employees are local, about two-thirds of all US government revenues flow to or through Washington, DC; only about 15 percent are collected locally (Brookings/Urban Tax Policy

Center[4]). While the federal government spends about $4 trillion annually, the total expenditures of the fifty largest cities sum to less than 10 percent of that.[5] Local capacity, at least under current arrangements and in historical experience, is simply insufficient to meet the needs of even their own constituents, especially when need is great. This is one of the reasons it was the federal government in partnership with state and local governments that eventually marshalled the robust response to the Great Depression and created the modern American welfare and regulatory states, such as they are (Ogorzalek 2018: ch. 2). Local governments had tried to stave off disaster alone, but were overwhelmed by the constraints described previously. The COVID-19 pandemic has made it plain that local action still works best when supported and complemented by national resources and coordination, even for those principally concerned with outcomes within cities. In a suburban nation, policies must go well beyond local borders in order to include most of the population. Nonetheless, under the right conditions, local governments can use policy to help provide life security and opportunity for their members, and some of their inherent and conditional attributes – size, density, political affinity, progressive ideology – may allow cities to fulfill their functions as democracies as well as firms.

URBAN LAND GRADIENTS AND MARKETPLACES OF PLACES

Public choice accounts of the relationship between mobile taxpayers' power and public policy have an air of durable timelessness to them, but some important parameters in these models entail historically varying features of the urban landscape. For instance, the ease of movement between jurisdictions is a function of technology and the availability of alternative jurisdictions, neither of which is constant across nations, city-regions, or time. Similarly, most models of interjurisdictional competition rely on a relative parity of the spatial benefits across locations. Each of these features of Tiebout's (1956) classic model abstracts the field of play in the sprawling fragmented twentieth-century metropolis, characterized by a fairly undesirable central city (i.e., a place undergoing an "urban crisis" to some extent) and many nearby, relatively small managerial

[4] Brookings/Urban Tax Policy Center: www.taxpolicycenter.org/briefing-book/what-breakdown-revenues-among-federal-state-and-local-governments.

[5] Author's analysis of Pierson, Hand, and Thompson (2015) and data from the Government Finance Database.

democracies. But if the productive or consumption benefits of physical proximity are high, as they were in the nineteenth century and may be again today as the agglomeration patterns of the KE clarify, they may swamp the marginal costs and benefits of local policies. This can help explain the New York tales described previously: though costly, locating in Manhattan appears to provide a competitive advantage for Amazon.

COMPETITION AND THE MONOCENTRIC MODEL

The relative place-parity assumed in some models of interjurisdictional competition is in tension with the workhorse model of urban land values – the monocentric model – which posits that land values (and economic and social activity in general), will be higher in central locations than in peripheral locations, principally because of proximity to markets and other actors (Muth 1969; von Thünen 1921).[6] Though never a perfect predictor of actual urban form, the monocentric model has a clear theoretical prediction about the "natural" condition of city value: a negative association between distance from the core and land values. When this gradient is strong, it suggests that the advantages of central location are so strong that the marginal incentives on offer from peripheral communities may be less relevant to location choice, and weaken the exit threat of mobile actors.

The mid-twentieth-century moment in which models of interjurisdictional competition were developed was a distinctively decentralized time in the United States, when land gradients were likely to be weak. Transport and manufacturing innovations allowed for a much greater dispersion of production and residence (Jackson 1985).[7] Public policies, including highway development and the "redlining" home financing regime, privileged new construction in homogeneous white neighborhoods located at the metropolitan fringe and dramatically devalued older, central areas (Massey and Denton 1993; Rae 2003; Thurston, this volume).[8] The result was a drained tax base, fiscal crisis, and diminished public spending in central cities.

Since the nadir of the American city in the 1970s and 1980s, two centripetal forces have shifted to contribute to a *re*-centralizing regime

[6] See Lichtenberger (2015) for a summary of alternative models.

[7] See Rodden (2019) for an account of this shift.

[8] Like many of our racist policies, the spatial pattern of redlining seems distinctively American. Major cities abroad often have regulations that concentrate, displace, and disadvantage the poor, but I am aware of none that designed or implemented a regulatory regime that so powerfully hollowed out the center of the metropolis.

in intrametropolitan marketplaces of places. The broadest is the sectoral shift to the service and knowledge economy. Perhaps somewhat surprisingly, this shift seems to make place *more* important, not less. As emphasized by Soskice (this volume), physical proximity to highly educated workers, competing and complementary firms, and investors are all advantages for KE firms (Moretti 2012). The corporate headquarters and high-end professional services (so-called FIRE industries – finance, insurance, and real estate – along with legal services) that are hallmarks of "global cities" are similarly clustered (Sassen 2001). Auxiliary and lower-paid services also cluster there and are non-exportable. There are large differences across metropolitan areas, but proximity *within* metros is important as well – as shown in the following, the reemergence of monocentric value is particularly strong in leading KE cities.

The agglomeration effects of both corporate services and KE work shift the parameters of interjurisdictional competition. In a terrain in which places are interchangeable, individual firms can more credibly exit into a more remote location, and municipalities may be caught in a prisoner's dilemma, bidding themselves to the floor (McGuire 1991; Wolkoff 1992). When firm success is more dependent on proximity, exit would be more costly for an individual firm and it is the *firms* who are caught in a prisoner's dilemma: while they might each prefer to pay less rent, individual defectors lose out on the agglomeration effects that drive success. This inverted dynamic suggests that central locations in the knowledge and global economies may have gained leverage (relative to their metropolitan neighbors, and to their own past).

The second dynamic reshaping place markets is the end of the redlining regime. After the Community Reinvestment Act of 1977 (as well as subsequent regulations), large areas that had previously been excluded from real estate credit markets were now available. Redevelopment areas near city centers (for instance, western Brooklyn and the West Loop of Chicago) have made many of these areas magnets for residential and commercial development, especially in KE cities. Racial discrimination in real estate has not ended (even in these very places), but older *areas* are far less disadvantaged in the marketplace of places.

Land gradients have evolved over the last century, and today both centripetal and centrifugal forces operate. Even as suburbanization continues, many American cities have experienced a "renaissance" in rebounding from the structural changes associated with deindustrialization. Today in these places, gentrification and high housing costs are a more severe problem than white flight or disinvestment. A core element of cities' recovery is the revalorization of central city real estate, a phenomenon that provides greater fiscal capacity for polities that often rely on property taxes for revenue. These *re*valorizations suggest a reinvigoration of the monocentric model, and a shift in the bargaining power of central cities *vis* potentially mobile businesses (Schragger 2009). In the next section, I take a descriptive look at how city value gradients have changed in recent decades.

US URBAN LAND VALUE GRADIENTS, 1980–2010

In deindustrialized cities, real estate values in central cities were *lower* than in surrounding areas, but they tend to be higher today. As a concrete example, consider the maps of (part of) New York's metropolitan area in Figure 6.1.

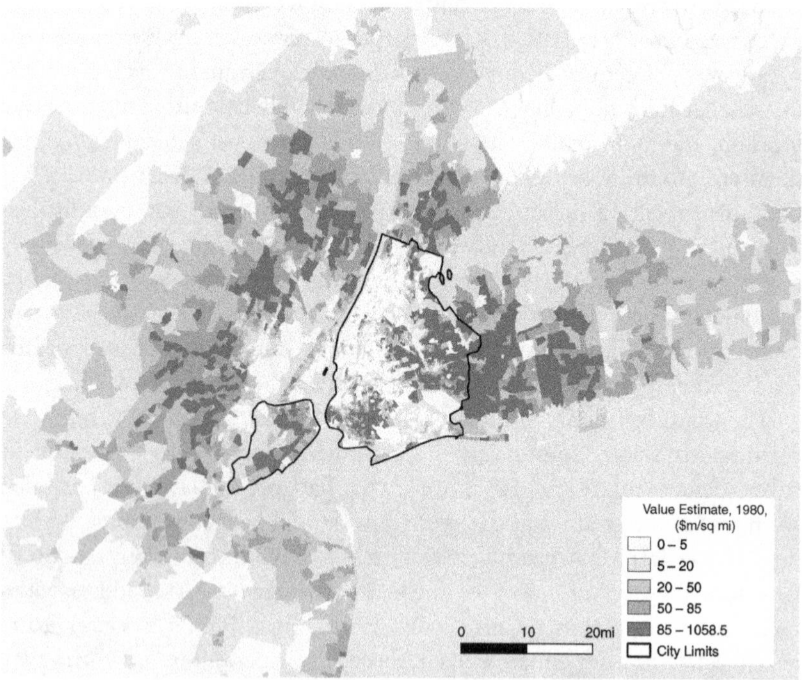

FIGURE 6.1 An example of re-centering: Relative value shifts in New York City
Note: Tract-level estimated aggregate residential real estate value per square mile in New York City Inner Metro Area: 1980 at left, and 2010 at right. Values in current dollars. *Source*: NHGIS.[9]

[9] Steven Manson, Jonathan Schroeder, David Van Riper, and Steven Ruggles. *IPUMS National Historical Geographic Information System*: Version 14.0 [Database]. Minneapolis, MN: IPUMS. 2019.

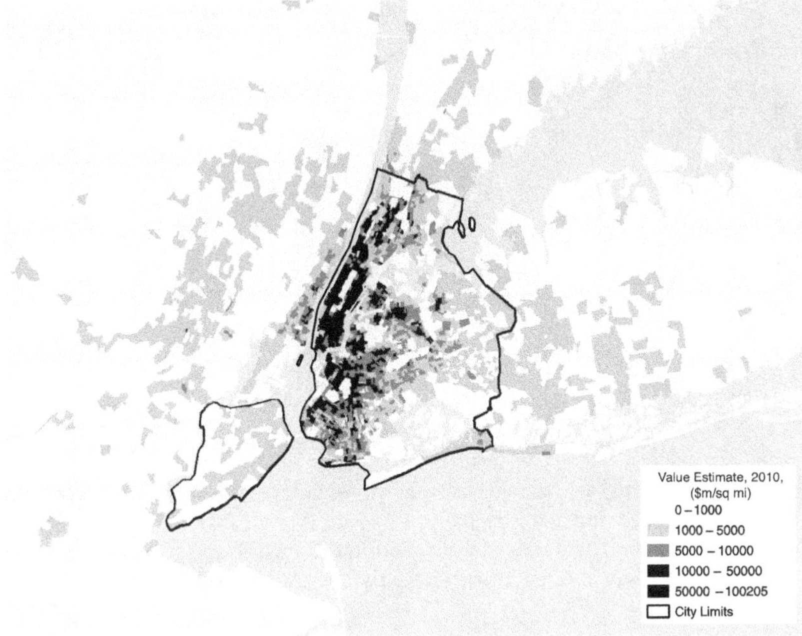

FIGURE 6.1 (cont.)

This figure maps a measure of the aggregate residential real estate values per square mile in 1980 (first figure) and 2010 (bottom figure). To estimate this value, I added the total value of all occupied homes in each census tract, then divided that sum by the area of the tract in square miles.[10] In each map, darker shades represent higher real estate values. The change over time is striking at a glance. Values were lower in the central city and higher in the periphery in 1980. The pattern is basically inverted in 2010, with the highest values in Manhattan and brownstone Brooklyn, and relatively low values further out.

Figure 6.2 simplifies the maps by plotting curves representing the tracts' values against distance from the center in 1980 and 2010. In each subfigure, the lines indicate the average tract values at each distance from the City Hall. The black line represents tracts within the city and the grey line tracts in the suburbs. In 1980, the gradient is basically increasing *from* the center – the opposite relationship of what the monocentric model

[10] The value of rental homes is estimated as equal to the monthly rent times an equalizing factor to adjust for the fact that the census reports owner-occupied homes in terms of overall values and rental homes in terms of monthly rents. For more details on the measure, see tomogorzalek.com/s/OnlineAppendixCRC.pdf.

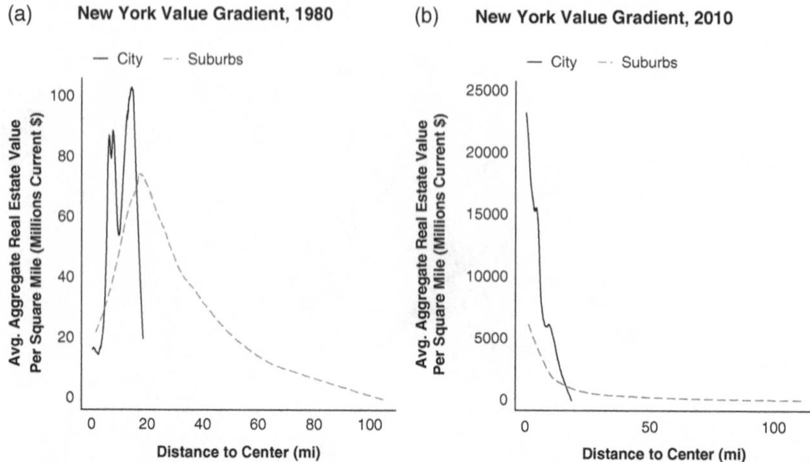

FIGURE 6.2 Locally fit averages of real estate values for all NY metropolitan tracts in 1980 (left) and 2010 (right)
Note: In each figure, averages of tracts within the central city are noted with the solid line, and tracts in other cities within the metropolitan area with the dashed line.

predicts – until it peaks at about $80–100 m per square mile (current values) about twenty miles out and then declines into the hinterland beyond. In 2010, by contrast, values are far higher (about $10b/sq. mi, on average) in the center, and diminish monotonically and exponentially with distance, very consistent with the monocentric model.

While we might expect this shift in a "superstar" city like New York, the changed pattern holds across many large US metros as well. Figure 6.3 plots real estate gradients for twenty-four large cities in 1980 (first matrix) and 2010 (second matrix). In these plots, I have standardized the land values and distance measures within each metro area so that the figures are comparable for visualization. The *y*-axis is therefore interpreted as standard deviations above or below the metro's average. Note that this allows us to see the patterns within metros, but masks large differences in values across metro areas.

While the curves vary across cities, two patterns are of note. First, the shift observed in New York is not exceptional. In 1980, values typically *rose* from the center, peaked at a ring near the central city limits, and then gradually fell again approaching the fringe. In 2010, in most cities and overall, value declines monotonically from the center, often very dramatically. Each curve is different, but we can estimate their average

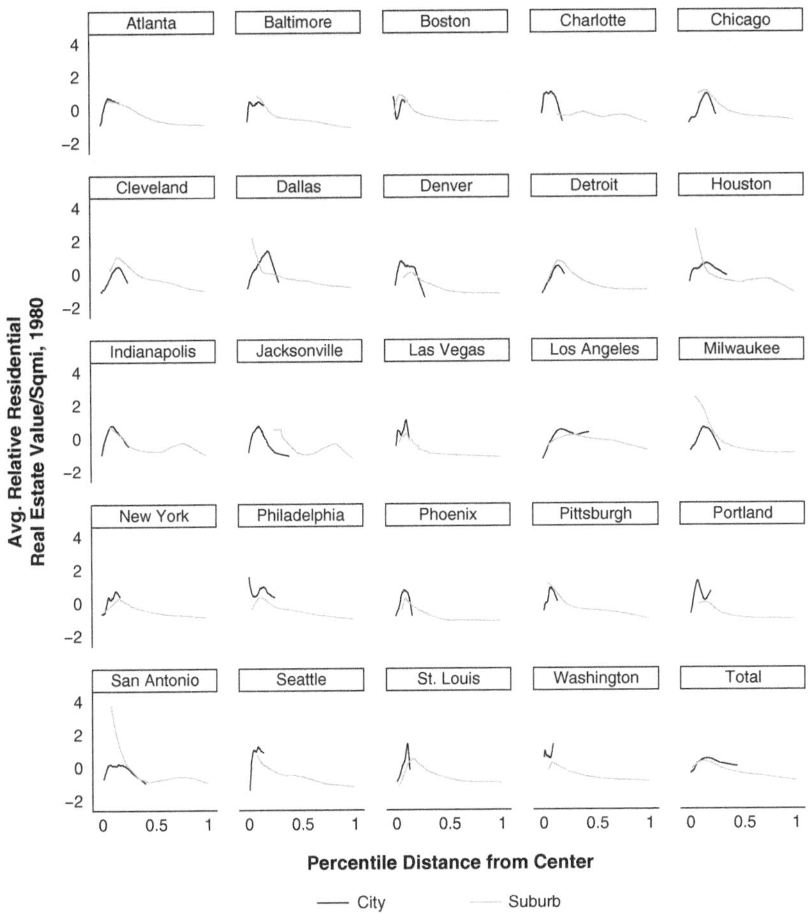

FIGURE 6.3 Average tract-level estimated aggregate residential real estate value by distance from city center across 24 US metropolitan areas
Source: NHGIS
Note: Patterns from 1980 at left, 2010 at right. Black lines represent tracts in central city, grey lines for suburban tracts. Estimates standardized within metro. *X*-axis calibrated to percentile-distance from center to equalize across metros. Tracts < 1 mile from city hall and with no residential real estate excluded. Lower-right subplot in each group represents averages of pooled tracts.

trends to make some basic comparisons. Figure 6.4 plots the overall gradient, using nonparametric estimates of the relationship between value and distance for forty-two large metros (those selected above, plus eighteen more) in 1980 (*x*-axis) and 2010 (*y*-axis). The more negative the gradient, the steeper the decline in value from the center; positive

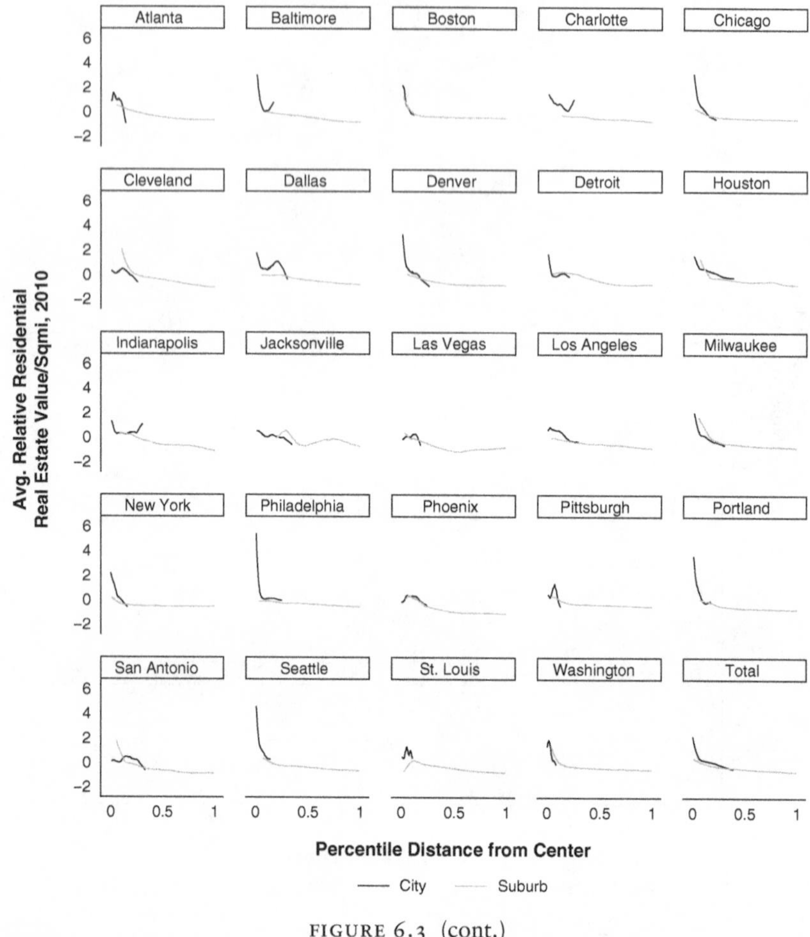

FIGURE 6.3 (cont.)

value gradients suggest an *increase* in value from the center, the opposite of the monocentric model.[11] The diagonal line indicates $y = x$, so a point on that line would show no change over 1980–2010. A point on the dashed vertical and horizontal lines would have a flat gradient for 1980 or 2010, respectively. For instance, New York had the patterns illustrated in Figures 6.1 and 6.2; that means it is located in the lower-right

[11] These gradients are bivariate nonparametric kernel-based regularized least squares regression coefficients of the tract-level (non-CBD tracts) relationship between value and (log) distance. The measure is essentially the average estimated slope along the curves in Figure 6.3. Details at www.tomogorzalek.com/s/OnlineAppendixCRC.pdf.

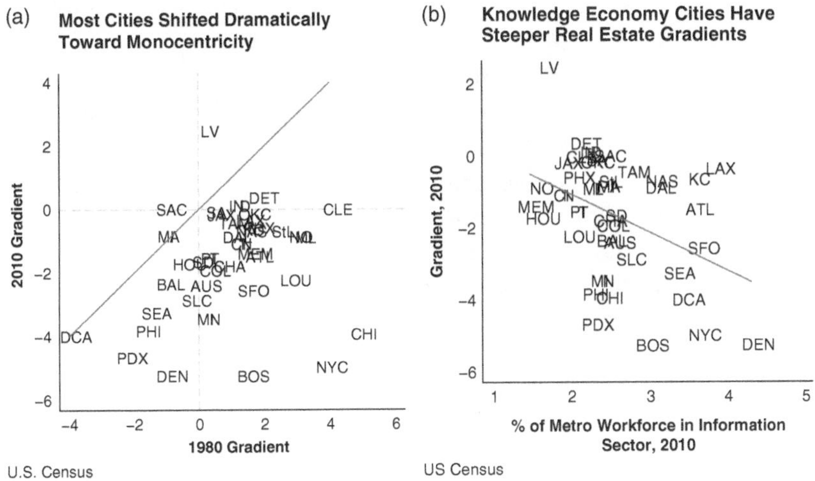

FIGURE 6.4 Metropolitan gradient changes and the knowledge economy
Note: At left, metropolitan land value gradient estimates by city in 1980 and 2010. Estimates are coefficents of nonparametric regression of tract level land values on distance from the center. More negative values mean steeper value declines with distance from the center. Diagonal line indicates no change. At right, Metro-level information sector employment by metro with land gradients in 2010. Line indicates linear best-fit.

hand corner of the figure, with a positive gradient from the center in 1980 and a negative gradient in 2010.

The large vertical distance between the diagonal line and the point for New York (and Boston, and Chicago) indicates that these cities saw particularly big changes, but they are not unique. Consistent with the curves in Figure 6.4, most cities lie in the lower-right quadrant, suggesting that their value patterns inverted from devalued to highly valued centers. Thirty-nine cities lie below the diagonal line, indicating that the gradient moved *closer* to the monocentric model's prediction of a monotonic negative relationship between value and distance in almost every city. This describes a common phenomenon of relative central revalorization across these very different cities.

The second note is that while almost all cities saw their gradients steepen over the three decades, there are clear differences in 2010. Centrality appears strongest in older cities like New York and San Francisco; it is weaker (though still present) in newer, sprawled Sunbelt places like Los Angeles and Dallas. Some Rust Belt cities, like Detroit, have seen very little change at all. Most relevant for this volume, gradients are stronger among metropolitan areas with more high-end KE workers. The right-hand panel in Figure 6.4 shows the relationship between information sector employment and gradients in 2010. The relationship is noisy, but the cities at the bottom right are the expected ones: New York, Boston, San Francisco, Seattle, Washington, DC. Other factors associated with steeper gradients include central place income, the number and percentage of rich households in the center city, region of the country, and overall metro size. The main observation is that rather than central areas being the least valuable land, as was the case in 1980, it is now in many cases by far the most valuable.

LAND GRADIENTS AND POLICY

The recentralization of value in the American metropolis may represent an opportunity for central cities long faced with existential fiscal crises. Urbanists have long theorized that "local governments that hold powerful economic positions ... will be in a better position to deal with private investment markets [and] should be able to use a greater proportion of their resources to achieve ambitious social agendas" (Savitch and Kantor 2002: 150). These ambitious agendas may be driven by big-city publics and leaders who are more inclined toward redistribution than their peers elsewhere in the country, and made more achievable by this market power.[12] Before the urban crisis, American cities (most notably New York) had a range of policies built around a "robust public sector aimed at supporting the working classes" but white flight, deindustrialization, and debt crises created a conventional wisdom that such policies were ill-advised (Phillips-Fein 2017: 8). The reversal of value gradients described in the previous section both increases the available tax base and serves as an indicator of potential leverage these central places might have against mobile actors (Schragger 2009). If the urban theorists are correct, we should expect to see larger public budgets and decommodifying policies in cities where the gradients are steeper. In this section, I test this theory by examining the associations between land gradients and decommodifying policies in big American cities using four policy data sources: the Berkeley Labor Center's Inventory of US City and County Minimum Wage Ordinances[13]; the

[12] The Democratic lean of big-city electorates is well-documented; see, e.g., Rodden (2019). On leaders, see Einstein and Glick (2017).

[13] http://laborcenter.berkeley.edu/minimum-wage-living-wage-resources/inventory-of-us-city-and-county-minimum-wage-ordinances/.

Lincoln Institute of Land Policy's database of provides real-per capita revenue and spending in large cities from 1977–2016[14]; the Government Finance Database (Pierson, Hand, and Thompson 2015), which includes municipal spending data from hundreds of cities over recent decades[15]; and the "cityhealth" (*sic*) project by the Kaiser Family Foundation that rates implementation of a range of recommended "best practice" local health and human development policies.[16]

These policies represent a range of policies that might be part of local decommodification agenda. Some are direct measures of the local fisc: locally generated revenue, revenue from property taxes, and overall spending from local programs (i.e., not including intergovernmental pass-throughs from higher levels).[17] Increases in these figures suggest an easing of fiscal crisis. For instance, if cities are still in a very weak bargaining position, per-capita property tax revenues may remain the same even with property value growth if cities were focused on limiting spending and passing potential revenues on to residents. These spending figures also include local government employment, a category that often decreases city workers' exposure to market vicissitudes through collective bargaining, defined-benefit retirement plans, and in some cases less racial discrimination. I also include the estimates of cities' own spending on health and human services (HHS), the category of spending in which most welfare relief and redistributive healthcare programs are included. More discrete policies in the analysis include local laws raising the minimum wage, inclusive zoning affordable housing policies, mandatory paid sick leave, and universal pre-K school programs. These policies are less directly comparable across cities because they are not budget line items; they are evaluated by the cityhealth program's policy experts according to "best practices" criteria.[18]

[14] See www.lincolninst.edu/research-data/data-toolkits/fiscally-standardized-cities/explanation-fiscally-standardized-cities for more details on the Lincoln Institute dataset, which is ultimately based on data for individual local governments provided by the US Census Bureau in the quinquennial Census of Government Finance and the Annual Surveys of State and Local Government Finance.

[15] See Pierson, Hand, and Thompson (2015).

[16] See cityhealth.org for details. The cities evaluated by cityhealth are a subset of those presented previously.

[17] The Lincoln Institute database reports these figures as standardized real per-capita figures, allowing meaningful comparisons across cities and time.

[18] Cityhealth rates each city's program on a zero-to-three scale (signified by gold, silver, and bronze "medals") in each area. Their foundation focus is on health policy, but takes an evidently holistic approach.

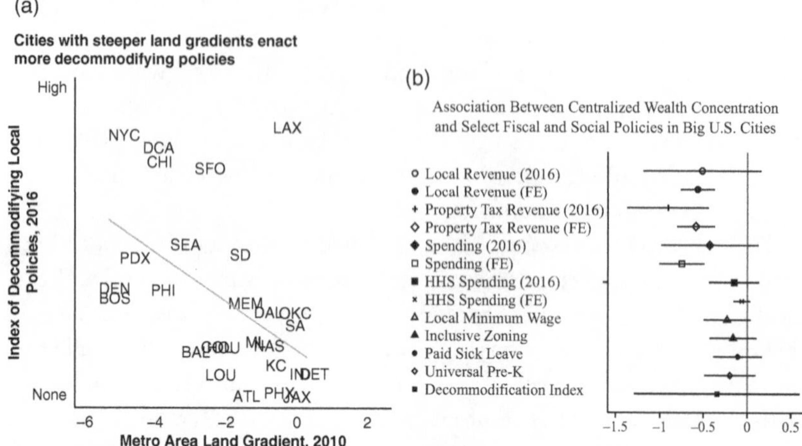

FIGURE 6.5 Land gradients and decommodifying policies in big American cities
Note: At left, the relationship between land gradients in 2010 and a decommodifying policy index in 2016. Points indicated by city abbreviation, and the line is a linear best fit. At right, standardized multivariate regression coefficient estimates with 90% confidence intervals of the relationship between value gradients and the policy outcomes listed at left.

In all of these policy areas (except paid sick leave), cities with steep gradients are more likely to enact the policy or collect/spend more: the bivariate relationships between each of these outcomes is statistically significant. When we consider the redistributive policies together as an index, the relationship is noisy but highly suggestive. The left panel of Figure 6.5 shows the relationship between metro-area gradients and an index of overall redistributive effort by the cities evaluated by cityhealth.[19] The downward slope of the line shows that, on average, there is a relationship between gradients and policy adoption in general.

To take a closer look at whether this relationship holds up when considered alongside other factors shaping local policy, I estimated regression models for each of the policy measures. For each fiscal category (total locally generated revenue, property taxes, local net spending, and spending on HHS), I estimated a cross-sectional multivariate model using 2016

[19] This is a simple additive index of the cityhealth scores for inclusive zoning, universal pre-K, local minimum wage, and overall local-program HHS spending (standardized to a mean of 0 and cap of 2 to limit the impact of outliers). All variables scale to (0,1)

data to assess the cross-city relationship and a fixed-effects model to assess changes over time (from 1980 to 2016) within cities. For each discrete policy (minimum wage, inclusive zoning, paid sick leave, and universal pre-K), I estimate a cross-sectional OLS model with the assessment of the policy's enactment as the dependent variable. Most of these policies were enacted quite recently and are not appropriate for testing by comparing to 1980. All ratio-level variables (i.e., the gradients and budget items) are standardized to a mean of 0 and standard deviation of 1 for visibility in the figure.[20]

Also included in the models (but not shown here for clarity) are covariates theoretically linked to local fiscal capacity and policy decisions: the sectoral makeup of the local economy, metropolitan fractionalization and popular support for a minimum wage (for 2016 cross-sectional models only).[21] If value gradients are related to policy decisions, the coefficient of gradient should be negative. Each model of fiscal measures and minimum wage ordinances includes forty-three cities (with two observations each, from 1980 and 2010, for the fixed effects models), and each policy measure from cityhealth includes the twenty-seven cities they evaluated. The right-hand panel of Figure 6.5 shows the regression coefficient estimates for the relationship between value gradients and spending or enactment in the different policy areas.

The association between gradients and policy is all in the predicted direction, though for most we cannot be confident the relationships are statistically significant from zero. Cities with steep gradients – namely 1 standard deviation steeper than the mean – would be expected to raise about an extra \$650–750 per capita in 2016, including about \$300–450 per capita in increased property taxes. Cities with steep gradients appear to engage in more overall spending as well. In general, gradients are associated with an increased local fisc, though it is not clear that this extends much to redistributive spending *per se*: there is no significant increase in HHS spending with a steeper gradient, either within or across cities.

[20] The decommodifying index is scaled (0,5) and can be roughly interpreted as a "count" of such policies, with each policy naïvely given equal weight. These analyses are meant to be illustrative rather than definitive. For technical details of the analysis and full results, see www.tomogorzalek.com/s/OnlineAppendixCRC.pdf.

[21] In nearly all models, none of these covariates were statistically significant. In some instances, support for minimum wage was positively associated with policy passage. In the model of decommodifying index, an index measuring the proclivity for pre-emption by a city's state government was also associated with less policy enactment.

For the other policies, the evidence is also weak but suggestive. The relationships are estimated in the expected direction, but none of them are statistically significant. This may be due in part to the smaller number of measured observations on these policies, but also to other major factors that influence local policy enactment. Even among cities well positioned to act on inequality-ameliorating impulses and with strong information economies, not all enact or implement such policies. Conversely, a steep gradient is not required for enactment of these policies: for instance, Los Angeles scores very high on the index despite its famously decentralized development patterns. While monocentricity is associated with local decommodification policy adoption, it is neither necessary nor sufficient for such changes; other factors matter powerfully as well.

Chief among these are state-level preemption laws. While shifts in factors like gradients and public opinion can provide incremental leverage that makes policy change marginally more or less likely, cities' place in their state constitutional order can make these kinds of discrete local policies *impossible.* For instance, according to data from the 2016 Cooperative Congressional Election Study, voters in every city in this dataset overwhelmingly support an increased minimum wage.[22] Some cities have made that policy change, but twenty-eight are barred by their state from doing so. Similarly, seventeen of the cities face specific preemptions on local paid sick leave requirements, and ten are preempted from passing inclusionary zoning laws.[23] As Alexander Hertel-Fernandez details in this volume, state politicians have recently been passing these preemption laws specifically to block big-city attempts at these kinds of policies, another powerful reminder that even as economic obstacles to local policy are easing in some places, the other barriers remain and are sufficient to stymie local decommodification. In my analysis of the index, the only coefficient that *was* significant was an index of state preemption activity.

DISCUSSION: CLEARING ALL THE HURDLES

While far from conclusive, these relationships are suggestive of the intuition behind theorists who argue that places with stronger leverage may

[22] Author's analysis. The mean support for an increased minimum wage among subsets of that sample from the cities in this analysis was 79 percent (Ansolabehere and Schaffner 2008).

[23] Preemption data collected from the Temple University Law School Policy Surveillance Program, http://lawatlas.org/datasets/preemption-project.

use it to gain some fiscal breathing room. However, in complex policy arenas like this, the enactment and successful implementation of more specific decommodification policies may depend on the confluence of multiple necessary conditions and sustained campaigns. Space constraints limit fine-grained discussion of many cases, but we can draw some lessons from notable successes in some of the places that score higher on the decommodification index.

First, as noted in the previous section, the political and institutional context in which these policies are pursued matters. For decades, big-city leaders have mostly embraced a market-oriented neoliberal consensus that "government should give way to governance" (Gross and Hambleton 2007), often at the expense of other community or democratic values, and often eroding the public sector in the name of efficiency. These mayors often faced very low levels of electoral competition. Over the last decade or so, as the local negative externalities of this model (especially inequality, rising housing costs, and an increasingly punitive surveillance regime) clarified, opposition coalitions have become more organized and successful in contesting that neoliberal paradigm, in both specific policy campaigns and elections. It has taken a long time, but something like oppositional parties have arisen in several cities, often from factions within the local ruling coalition. In Chicago and New York, for instance, coalitions led by labor unions and operating under "working families" banners have organized at the sub-city level and built legislative coalitions that have substantially changed the policy agenda in their cities, even as their overall coalitions continue to substantially overlap with national and local Democratic Parties. In places such as Seattle and San Francisco, where some notable "firsts" in local minimum wage and health-care programs were passed, similar coalitions each employed a sophisticated two-step institutional approach, backing direct-democracy campaigns to change the representational structure of their city council, from at-large to ward-based representation. This kind of council representation has long been associated with more class- and race-based descriptive representation and a larger local fisc (Bridges 1997; Welch and Bledsoe 1998). Shortly after the institutional changes, the new Board of Supervisors in San Francisco enacted the 2007 Healthy SF program, and the Seattle City Council enacted the first big-city $15 local minimum wage (Grumbach 2020).

In Illinois, Washington, and California, the most assertive recent local measures have passed shortly after Democrats gained control in the statehouse or governor's seat, and many of the most progressive policies on the subnational agenda are happening statewide *instead* of at the local level (though driven by city delegations) because of the states' overwhelming

Democratic majorities. Statewide measures mute the intrametropolitan competition dynamics described previously, so winning as a statewide coalition is also a win for the city. Blue cities in Red states face major hurdles, but such laws are not given: state policies are the result of state politics, in which major cities can play an important role, particularly if they can convince other interests that local policies are truly local, will effectively solve urban challenges, and help generate positive externalities for the state. Thus while we might think of local leverage as a probabilistically associated cause of local passage, an insurgent progressive coalition to mobilize public sentiment against neoliberal received wisdom and at least tacit state approval appear to be necessary factors in pursuing this kind of agenda.

While we might conceive of these policies as part of a shared agenda, and in general their adoption is mostly correlated across cities, some of them target different constituencies with different effects and tradeoffs. These will create divergent interests and potentially complex coalitional dynamics. Minimum wage policies help "pre-distribute" income to workers, who may or may not be residents of the city in which the ordinance is enacted. The distribution of work-residence combinations (live and work in the center, live in the suburbs and work in the city, etc.) varies mostly by region rather than KE presence, so it is unclear what effects this would have. Universal pre-K benefits parents, firms, and (ideally) children, but only residents of the city. As working families and new Americans are displaced to the periphery, this policy becomes less effective as a tool to mitigate educational inequalities.

The most controversial and perennial policy challenge in many of these KE capitals is housing. Making real, coordinated efforts to address the growing housing affordability crisis in particular is absolutely crucial to produce decommodified life or even the "escalator" effect of connecting people to the KE. Because access to the KE is in part a function of physical proximity to it, the very land gradients that provide cities with leverage also make housing highly unaffordable for many current and potential city-zens. There is a universal housing crisis for working-class people across metropolitan America: in every one of the metropolitan areas and central cities included in this chapter's analyses, more than half of all households earning less than $50,000 per year spend more than 30 percent of their income on housing.[24] This is taken to extremes in KE hubs: in San Francisco, San Diego, Los Angeles, New York, Boston, and Seattle, more

[24] The national standard for housing affordability is 30 percent.

that 75 percent of such working-class households pay that much, and more than half of households with incomes $50,000–75,000 do as well. When coupled with (or causing) low savings rates, this is a recipe for dire insecurity and disappearance from the economy through homelessness and involuntary mobility. Despite this clear area for improvement, housing programs and particular projects often meet extreme resistance from existing residents and public officials alike. The United States has never done well to provide housing support, and today the nation's housing agenda (and the national urban agenda broadly) relies almost entirely on incentives for private action that are insufficient to meet this challenge. Inclusionary zoning regulations to produce and protect affordable homes in these KE hubs are a step in the right direction, but are clearly insufficient – all six of those cities score high on the cityhealth assessment of affordable housing policy, but their policies are little more than window dressing in practice, insufficient to address the scale of the challenge. Le Galès and Pierson (2019) show that this problem is not unique to America's "superstar" cities, but they also observe that American cities do less to address the problem. Robust metropolitan-level authorities like in London and more aggressive housing production plans like in Paris still do not fully solve the problem, but they might alleviate it significantly (Le Galès and Pierson 2019; cf. Enright 2016). There is a serious political tension here, because the reason for the gradient shift and relative fiscal cushion is the successful commodification of land, measured by its skyrocketing exchange vales. But what is good for the city is not always good for the city-zen. Without such effort, other elements of the decommodification agenda, such as an increased wages for workers, will simply be transferred in directly to landlords. After all, even if a New Yorker gets paid leave and free health care, a $15 minimum wage does not even pay the rent on the city's average one-bedroom apartment, which goes for $2,800 per month. Given that even current residents struggle to afford living there, it appears unlikely many more can be drawn in from elsewhere to experience these benefits. This was the core of the national urban agenda for decades, and even with a greater commitment of resources it is not obvious what the right approach would be.

Finally, the policies mentioned here are in line with traditional welfare-state policies, and focused on material security or provision for households. Decommodification can also be undertaken creatively in other areas as well, by treating the community rather than the household. If the KE is as big a shift as the industrial revolution, it may entail a durable change in our vision of the good life as well. Such community foundations of life are easier in places built for public interaction, and center cities' public policy can be adjusted to actually create such places. Often this can be accomplished without exorbitant expense or the kinds of visible actions that state legislatures may be tempted to preempt. Three examples are (1) subsidized cultural production by local residents, drawing on local and international traditions, which can provide diversion, meaning, professional development, access to KE niches, and employment while contributing directly to both gentrifiers' taste for variety and KE firms' appetite for creative content; (2) enhanced public goods such as libraries, which can provide educational services, bridge stubborn digital divides, and serve as community-oriented "palaces for the people" (Klinenberg 2018); and (3) heavily subsidized, high-quality mobility alternatives, including encouraging cycling and public transit, and which might mitigate some of the inequalities generated by residential segregation, promote dense affordable development, improve health outcomes related to sedentary car-based lifestyles, and ease environmental degradation. This is a shortcoming in most North American cities, but a push for transportation reform is long overdue.

CONCLUSION AND NOTES FROM 2020

The theories and new patterns discussed in this chapter are based on observations from before 2020; the COVID-19 pandemic illustrates the limits of localist hopes that city leaders can "run the world." First, the scale of the epidemic quickly overwhelmed local governments' material capacity to respond to significant challenges alone, and their biggest strengths in normal times – openness, connectedness, and density of activity – were devastating vulnerabilities for this kind of threat. Second, the inequalities of the KE were laid bare and exacerbated by the epidemic itself: while many white-collar workers could transition online, persons who perform the embodied work of the digital economy and its attendant lifestyle amenities, especially in big cities, were much more exposed to both the disease and the pursuant economic downturn. The ultimate effects of this will not be understood until well after this book is in print. One question that was asked early in the pandemic was whether cities are "done" due to concerns about density and disease. This is likely an overreaction, but the forced test-run of remote work, especially for KE jobs, may indeed have significant effects, decreasing some agglomeration economies and reducing demand for central city office space.

Another shift has been made more obvious and urgent by the uprisings and protests in response to police violence in many cities across the country. Because race and class are deeply entwined in most American cities and the nation as a whole, it is impossible to actually pursue a decommodification agenda at the local level without making it a racial equity agenda (Flynn, Holmberg et al. 2017). The artificially flattened cities of 1980 were the result of explicitly racist policies, and the mass incarceration of the subsequent decades separates many, especially Black Americans, from real participation in economic and civic life. In this area, the egalitarian policy requires a long overdue scaling back of carceral state activity, which remains particularly intense even in many otherwise progressive cities.

Finally, even as some central cities recover and enact decommodifying policies, spatial inequalities are sure to persist or grow at several scales. Nationally, even if gradients tended to steepen in all kinds of cities, the differences in value across city-regions are large and growing, and aggressive decommodication may be a luxury good (Moretti 2012). Development and decommodification strategies may need to vary widely across cities. While New York can reject a major project like Amazon HQ2 and offset the loss by taxing nine-figure penthouses, Detroit's political agenda includes neither option.

At a metropolitan scale, the "urban renaissance" is not the only change afoot. While some suburbs remain exclusive and homogeneous, suburbia as a whole is rapidly diversifying. Central-city policies would do little for suburban communities where traditionally "urban" concerns with expensive solutions like poverty, aging populations, decaying infrastructure, and even immigrant incorporation measures are becoming more salient features of the governing agenda. Many older-inner-ring suburbs may now have more in common with their central cities than with favored-quarter enclaves, but are even less equipped to compete. Their fiscal scarcity is liable to be even more severe (Jimenez 2014). Along with a recent leftward shift in inner-suburban national partisan affiliation, these circumstances may help reconnect some cities and suburbs and help to develop some of the regional institutions common in cities abroad. Though this is not particularly *likely*, such steps would enhance the efficacy of using local policy to promote equitable social outcomes.

Finally, at a city and neighborhood scale, as Jessica Trounstine notes, affluent property holders have frequently – perhaps always – sought to insulate themselves from redistribution through territorial regulations including zoning and government formations of various types; they have been adaptive, creative, and resilient in doing so (Nightingale 2012; Trounstine 2018). Those returning to contemporary cities may be no different. Today, similar institutions such as opportunity zones, business improvement districts, and tax-increment-financing districts concentrate the benefits of revalorization rather than sharing them citywide. Study of this policy area is highly technical and varies by place and even individual project. Without capture of this value for general purposes, increased value in these cities will exacerbate inequality – even those with access to spillover benefits of the KE will struggle to remain within their own communities. Single policies will not do the trick; sophisticated, adaptive problem-solving to a range of challenges will be required to meet the democratic demands of the twenty-first-century metropolis.

7

The Political Economies of Red States

Jacob M. Grumbach, Jacob S. Hacker, and Paul Pierson

A striking feature of the American political economy is its fragmentation. The constitutionally protected role of the states and the localized quality of many crucial policies foster a political economy that is at once national – the rich world's most extensive nation-spanning market – and sectional, with states or groups of states constituting distinct political economies that often have enormous scope of their own.

Historically, this decentralization has promoted and protected a high level of regional diversity. Whether the subject is the "peculiar institution" of slavery in the South, the extractive economies of the West, or the industrial economies of the Midwest, American economic history is often told as the story of distinct geographic sectors that exist in tension – and, at times, conflict – with each other. In his *Sectionalism and American Political Development, 1880–1980*, for example, Richard Bensel traces the persistent struggle between an industrial "core" and nonindustrial "periphery," in which each "carve[d] up the national political economy into sectors which the sectional poles could then control" (Bensel 1984: 53).

A generation on from Bensel's classic, regional diversity remains a fundamental feature of the American political economy. Indeed, Bensel's analysis concludes almost exactly when a pivotal turn began – the end of a long era of *convergence*. The industrial economy featured declining differences across states and regions. The knowledge economy has reversed that trend. States that were once catching up are now holding steady or even falling behind. Within states, large metro areas are pulling further and further ahead of less populated nonurban areas.

These trends might have been expected to internally fracture America's two major parties, as sectional divides often have in the past. But while economic diversity is rising, the two parties are becoming more distinct from each other, more internally homogenous, and more similar from place to place – in a nutshell, more polarized and more nationalized (Pierson and Schickler 2020). In contrast to James Madison's vision of a far-flung nation with scores of competing interests that produce shifting coalitions from issue to issue, an encompassing partisan divide runs from the heights of national politics all the way down.

This hardening partisan divide has gone hand in hand with more intense and stable geographic splits. Compared with even the relatively recent past, the American political map looks remarkably fixed from election to election (Hopkins 2017). Red states cast their lot with Republicans in both presidential and Senate elections (and, increasingly, they elect Republican "trifectas," too, with the governor's mansion, state house, and state senate all held by the GOP). Blue states cast their lot with Democrats. There are not just fewer swing voters; there are fewer swing places.

These three developments – growing economic diversity, nationalized partisan polarization, and a hardening electoral map – cry out for a renewed focus on the interplay of subnational political economies and the national political order. Yet when we look at this interplay, what we find is puzzling. At the national level, the Republican Party's ongoing shift from the center has produced a highly conservative party that is closely allied with business elites and the biggest winners from rising inequality (Hacker and Pierson 2016). Yet as inequality has grown across places as well as across people, the regions on the losing side of this spatial transformation have generally sided with Republicans, not Democrats.

Blue America is increasingly buoyed by the knowledge economy, where urbanization and intangible investment are rewarded (albeit very unevenly across workers and locales). By contrast, red America is struggling to find a viable growth model for the twenty-first century. Outside the small number of states with abundant energy reserves, red America's economic performance is falling behind blue America's. In the 2020 election, Democratic presidential candidate Joe Biden captured roughly 51 percent of the national popular vote; yet he won counties representing 71 percent of US GDP (Muro et al. 2020).

Red America is not only ceasing to converge with blue America, it lacks anything like the successful (if highly exclusionary and unequal) strategies for rapid growth associated with the economic periphery in the past. Neither state-level GOP policies nor national-level GOP priorities currently offer realistic hope for most of these regions to overcome their economic disadvantages. To the contrary, as we will show, Republican-backed policies often compound those disadvantages.

If distinct regional economies are the basis for national coalitions, how can we understand this disconnect? Why do policy approaches in struggling red states seem so out of step with new economic realities? Why do national parties' stances – and, in particular, the Republican Party's stance – seem so at odds with their "home" region's dominant model? And how can both state and national Republicans sustain policy agendas that provide so little of economic benefit to the denizens of red America?

In this chapter, we offer an initial set of answers to these questions. First, we seek to chart the diverse but generally checkered response of red America to the new realities of the knowledge economy. More specifically, as the title of our chapter suggests, we look at the diverse experience of red *states*. Though geographic divides occur within as well across states, states have a privileged place in the American constitutional design, both as sites of governance and as bastions of electoral power. States have long been entryways for groups and movements seeking to create regionally distinctive policy agendas, even when their corresponding national party might prefer otherwise (Sanders 1999; Schickler 2016). As federal governance has gridlocked over the past generation, states' policies have become more important in shaping the lives of their residents (Grumbach 2018), while major interest groups have focused more on shaping those policies (Hertel-Fernandez 2019). Meanwhile, as noted, the national parties have become more reliant on specific states for electoral power, and, with regard to the Republican Party in particular, more reliant on state-level gerrymandering and state-level laws that discourage the participation of voters of the other party.

We define red states as those where voters have consistently sided with the Republican Party in presidential elections since 2000 – a simple definition that overlaps considerably with other possible ones. We show that this electoral definition coincides with an economic divide. Compared with blue states, red states are generally struggling economically, especially when judged against the rapid catch-up of prior decades. A very small group of red states that we call the "energy trio" (Alaska, North Dakota, and Wyoming) has prospered through fossil-fuel production. Most red states, however, have not enjoyed this advantage. We call this much larger group "low-road states," because of their common reliance on a low-wage, low-tax model that offers less advantage in the knowledge economy than it did in the past. In addition, we identify a third group of states in the declining industrial heartland that may be moving into the red state column, which we call "left-behind states."

We then turn from description to explanation: What explains the difficulties faced by red America in transitioning to the knowledge economy? Much of the problem reflects path dependence: states that once competed *within* the American political economy now must compete within a global economy in which low wages, weak unions, or prior manufacturing experience offer limited advantage. Instead, as David Soskice argues in his contribution to this volume, the big rewards come from shifting toward sectors that depend heavily on urban and educational strength. Such a shift poses enormous challenges for any state specializing in low-wage labor or manufacturing. It has posed special challenges for red states, which, we show, have often pursued policies that have compounded their difficulties.[1]

Finally, we focus on the national Republican Party, and the seeming disconnect between its priorities and the challenges facing red America. Here, it becomes clear that the poor experiences of red states reflect, in part, the lack of federal investments that once promoted convergence. Jonathan Rodden (2018; 2019), among others, has offered strong arguments for why as the parties have polarized geographically their agendas should align with their new territorial bases of support. Rodden's account illuminates the increasing partisan divide over social issues along urban/rural lines. Yet it falters when we turn to the parties' *economic* agendas. The GOP should have electoral reasons to shift its economic priorities toward the heavily Republican states where much manufacturing and fossil-fuel extraction is now located. The embrace of climate-change denialism and lax environmental laws fit this pattern, as, perhaps, does a belated (and perhaps only Trump-centered) turn to protectionism and massive farm-state subsidies. Yet the larger thrust of GOP economic policy mostly does not cater to red-state economic interests, despite the electoral incentives that Rodden identifies. Why?

The answer, we argue, is rooted in the character of Republicans' organized coalition. The influential role of national business groups and organized wealthy backers within the contemporary GOP encourages national Republicans to pursue highly inegalitarian policies that are responsive to

[1] We do not want to over-emphasize the autonomy of state economic policies. State governments face well-known constraints, including fiscal federalism, low legislative capacity, and federal law. Nonetheless, studies suggest that state policies in areas such as health care, labor relations, criminal justice, and the environment can have important social and economic consequences (e.g., Bastian and Michelmore 2018; Borgschulte and Vogler 2020; Cengiz et al 2019; Lindo and Pineda-Torres 2019).

concentrated economic interests. These policies are not particularly attentive to locally based businesses within Republican regions, and they have limited appeal to the poorer nonurban voters on which the party increasingly relies. Indeed, they undercut the prospects for robust intergovernmental transfers, both to spur local economic development and to finance the social programs on which these constituents depend more and more. But the need for responsiveness to these voters' economic concerns has been diminished by their social, geographic, and informational isolation; by the capacity of GOP elites to mobilize them through identity appeals rooted in racial and cultural backlash; and by the (partially GOP-engineered) overweighting of nonurban areas in the American electoral system. The ability of Republicans to mobilize white working-class voters on the basis of racial resentment and anti-immigrant backlash has proven particularly important in the South and industrial heartland, and it provides yet another example of the centrality of race to the structure of the American political economy.

All these conclusions are offered in the spirit of field-building. Sectionalism remains a powerful feature of the American political economy. Yet we lack even a basic body of observations about how it works today. Trans-state political actors (particularly business groups) have focused enormous attention on states as sites of governance and sources of national party strength. Political analysts, for the most part, have not. We make no pretense that we offer the last word on this large topic and, indeed, welcome debate over how best to map a vast territory. But we hope to show that many puzzling features of the American political economy cannot be navigated without recognizing the profound ways in which the relationship between local and national politics has changed in an era of divergent places and nationalized parties.

AMERICAN SECTIONALISM, PAST AND PRESENT

Sectionalism describes political conflict between regions to control important public decisions – particularly, in the study of the American case, decisions that shape the national political economy and the interregional distribution of costs and benefits within it (Bensel 1984). The analysis of sectionalism in the United States has focused primarily on the North-South divide, and for good reason. Even after the abolition of slavery, the political economies of Southern states were highly distinct, and those who represented Southern states in national politics constituted an identifiable and powerful coalition. We briefly trace out this familiar story to set up our key questions about contemporary red states and the Republican Party.

For much of the twentieth century, the national representatives of former slave states were Southern Democrats. Facing no partisan competition, they rose to powerful positions in the congressional hierarchy and provided the decisive votes for a "conservative coalition" that crosscut the two parties (Katznelson 2013). These legislators backed policies that served the interests of dominant regional groups, who hoped to maintain segregation and foster industrialization based on low-wage competition. Decentralized wage-setting and industrial relations were critical to this vision, and Southern politicians were tenacious in protecting them. Their success was far from complete. During the early New Deal, policies effectively set a national wage floor in key sectors, transforming the South as its living standards rapidly rose toward the North's (Wright 1987). New Deal farm policies also had the effect of accelerating the exodus of rural Blacks from the South, sparking convergence as many of the region's poorest workers migrated to growing industrial centers in search of economic opportunity.

Yet as Ira Katznelson and his collaborators have argued, Southern representatives broke with the New Deal on critical dimensions, especially after 1935. They utilized their pivotal position in Congress to protect the interests of regional economic elites and encourage inward private investment (Bateman et al. 2018; Farhang and Katznelson 2005; Katznelson et al. 1993). Most important, they worked effectively to prevent the coalescence of a truly national system of collective bargaining, which might have allowed unions to organize the South and reduced the region's appeal to firms seeking a nonunion workforce (see the chapter by Alex Hertel-Fernandez and, in particular, his discussion of the pivotal Taft–Hartley Act of 1947).

These political actors also worked to influence federal spending to support their vision of sectional economic development. Fearing that new social welfare programs might undercut an important competitive advantage as well as Jim Crow, they forced revisions to limit the emerging welfare state's impact on reservation wages, especially for Black workers. However, they also supported the construction of a better-funded federal state, the spending of which (especially defense spending) could foster economic development. Increasing intergovernmental transfers – financed overwhelmingly by richer states – was a good way to foster economic development without threatening the South and Sunbelt's status as a comparatively low-wage, nonunion target for private investment.

During this critical period, in short, sectional interests based in the nation's poorer states actively advanced a reasonably coherent economic agenda both at the state level and in Congress. More often than not, they succeeded. The role of the federal government in the economy would grow, but it would do so mostly on terms consistent with the development strategies of Southern and Sunbelt elites. These development strategies were surely not growth-maximizing – they sought to boost growth while preserving white supremacy – and they produced high levels of inequality, locking out of the region's emerging prosperity not just African Americans but also many poor whites. Still, there was a basic logic to the Southern growth model that was defended by national politicians allied with the region: the South could undercut the North with anemic wages, low taxes, and limited regulations, while extracting federal dollars that did not come with unwanted strings attached.

To what extent is something similar happening today? The motive for the question is conveyed in Figure 7.1 (based on Ganong and Shoag 2017), which shows the relationship between growth rates and initial income per capita (logged) across the states for two thirty-year periods: 1940–1960 and 1990–2010. As Figure 7.1 makes clear, there is a near-perfect relationship between prior economic standing and long-term growth in the immediate post-World War II period, with poorer states rapidly catching up. Since 1990, there is little relationship. Take out North Dakota and Wyoming, the two big energy producers in this set (which does not include Alaska, because it was not a state in the first period), and the regression line would be flat. The great economic convergence of the mid-twentieth century has ended.

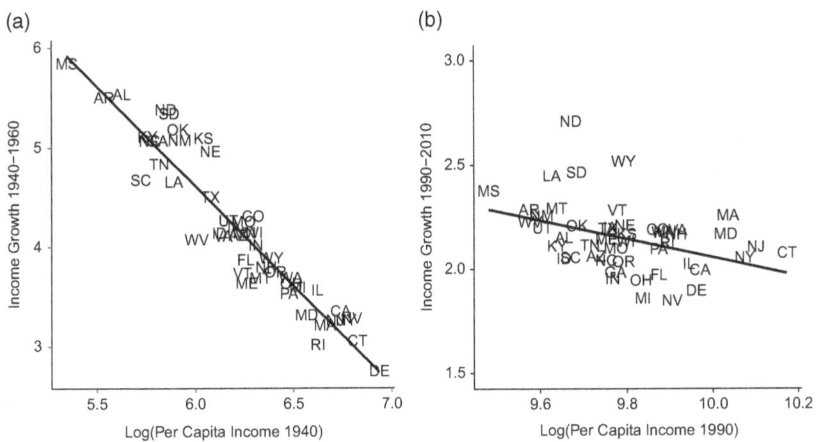

FIGURE 7.1 State growth rates versus per capita income, 1940–1970 and 1990–2020

A glance at Figure 7.1 also suggests that it is red states that have mostly lost out. While there is no agreed-upon definition of red and blue states, the original designation comes from a famous 2000 electoral map published in the *New York Times*, which showed the states won by Bush and Gore in the Electoral College (the graphics designer said he chose red for Republicans because both words start with the letter R). Since 2000, the lineup of states behind the two party's presidential nominees has proved remarkably stubborn. Twenty-two states have sided with the Republican candidate in all five presidential elections from 2000 through 2016; fifteen have consistently sided with Democratic candidates (because the former states are more sparsely populated on average, the distribution of votes is close to parity).

Given this stability and the ease of interpreting presidential election results, we define states as "red" when Republican presidential candidates have won at least three of the five presidential elections over the 2000–16 period; and "blue" when Democratic presidential candidates have won at least three of five. This division correlates highly with other possible definitions – for example, state election results or party control of state governments – and results in twenty-six red states and twenty-four blue states (we exclude the District of Columbia). Ranked in order of Trump's share of the two-party vote in 2016, the red states are Wyoming (WY), West Virginia (WV), North Dakota (ND), Oklahoma (OK), Idaho (ID), South Dakota (SD), Kentucky (KY), Alabama (AL), Arkansas (AR), Tennessee (TN), Nebraska (NE), Utah (UT), Kansas (KS), Louisiana (LA), Indiana (IN), Missouri (MO), Montana (MT), Mississippi (MS), Alaska (AK), South Carolina (SC), Texas (TX), Ohio (OH), Georgia (GA), North Carolina (NC), Arizona (AZ), and Florida (FL).

It will not go without notice that these states include only two of the industrial heartland states that we associate with Donald Trump's rise to the presidency: Indiana and Ohio. These states – the aforementioned two plus Michigan, Wisconsin, and Pennsylvania – have received enormous focus in recent years, not just because they are critical battleground states, but because they are seen to foretell a transformed GOP coalition that rests heavily on disaffected white working-class voters. At the state level, this transformation involves the shift of once-progressive industrial bastions toward more conservative and anti-union economic policies. These are the potentially red-shifting states that we term left-behind states, and we use them to clarify the specific state economic transformations that seem to be associated with the hardening red-blue divide. Similarly, we make brief reference to once-solidly red states that are trending blue, such as Georgia, Arizona, and North Carolina, which highlight the opposite developmental trajectory.

Three Red-State Types

We adopt an inductive approach to classifying states. As noted, prior scholarship has generally started by associating economic sectionalism with Southern exceptionalism: a distinctive regional economy backed by a defined faction within the national Democratic party (but see Bensel 1984, who bases his sectional classification on centers of trade within the United States, inductively dividing them between "core" and "periphery" regions). But we are interested in understanding both how distinctive the South – now a Republican bastion – still is, and what characteristics it shares with other states. For that purpose, we collected a wide range of data on prominent indicators of economic and policy outcomes over time for both red and blue states. We then reduced these indicators to five measures (ranging from 0 to 1) using Bayesian factor analysis (Quinn 2004): (1) dependence on extraction and energy production, (2) wage and income levels, (3) economic policy conservatism, (4) levels of urbanization, and (5) social and economic performance. Table 7.1 summarizes our approach.[2]

TABLE 7.1 *Measuring state characteristics*

Measure	Indicators
Energy and Extraction	Percent of Gross State Product (GSP) in energy production; percent of employment in natural resources and mining; percent of GSP in natural resources and mining
Wage and Income	Median household income; poverty rate
Economic Policy Conservatism	30 policies (welfare state, labor relations, education spending, taxation)
Urbanization	Urban population as share of total population; urban land mass as share of total land mass; density of urban areas.
Socioeconomic Performance	Labor force participation; prime-age mortality

[2] Tables 7.A2 and 7.A3 in the Appendix describe the relationships between these measures, as well as how well they predict wages.

To keep our presentations simple and maintain our focus on red states, we plot these five measures for our core group of twenty-six red states and present only averages of these measures for the blue states. We should stress, however, that our economic data closely align with our electoral definition across the full sample. We use the presidential vote to define red states because our interest is in understanding the relationship between state and national parties within America's durable red/blue map. But looking at our economic measures, we find that there is indeed a distinct red-state economic profile that is more or less shared by the red states in which energy is not a major part of the state economic mix. (To survey our results for the entire set of states, see the Appendix.)

Figure 7.2 plots our measure of energy and extraction in standard deviations from the mean state (on the x-axis) against state median hourly wage (on the y-axis). The shading of a state's initials represents its two-party Trump vote share, with darker shading representing a greater electoral victory for Trump. As Figure 7.2 makes clear, red states with higher

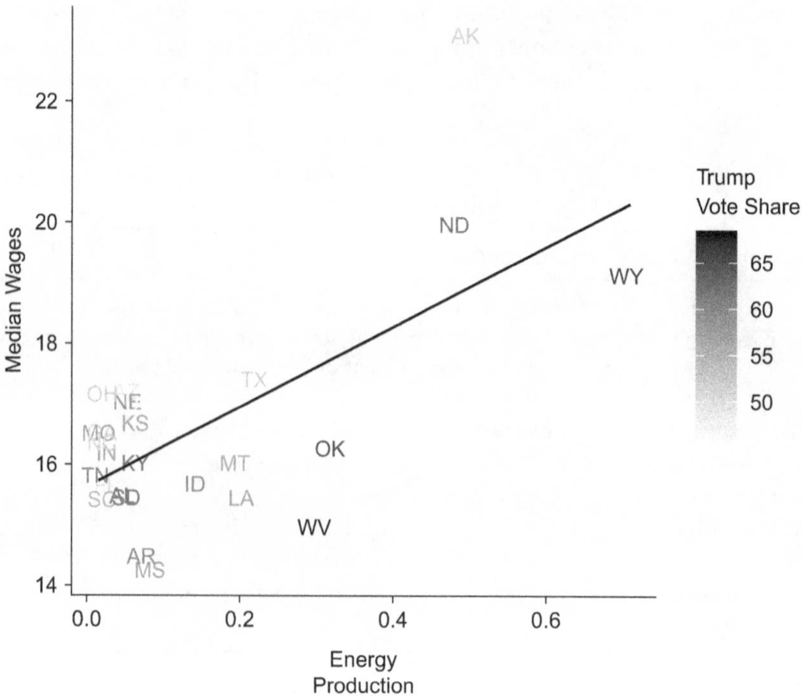

FIGURE 7.2 Energy production, wages, and Trump vote

wages tend to have higher concentrations of energy production. However, energy extraction is highly concentrated. Only five states stand out as highly reliant on energy, and only three look to be thriving as a result: Alaska, North Dakota, and Wyoming. We call these three states the "energy trio," our first (small) grouping of states.

Figure 7.3 offers a different perspective on red state performance, looking at the relationship between economic policy conservatism and median wages. We include all fifty states in this figure to show how red states compare with other states on our measure of economic policy conservatism. In general, red states are on the higher end of our policy conservatism scale (the measure is bounded from 0 to 1). Yet there is a considerable amount of variation even among the red states.

In Figure 7.3, the shading of the states reflects how urbanized they are according to our index, with the most urban in black. The more urbanized red states generally come closer to the median wage levels of the blue states. By contrast, the lightly shaded states cluster at the bottom of the figure; the notable exception is the rural but relatively high-wage energy

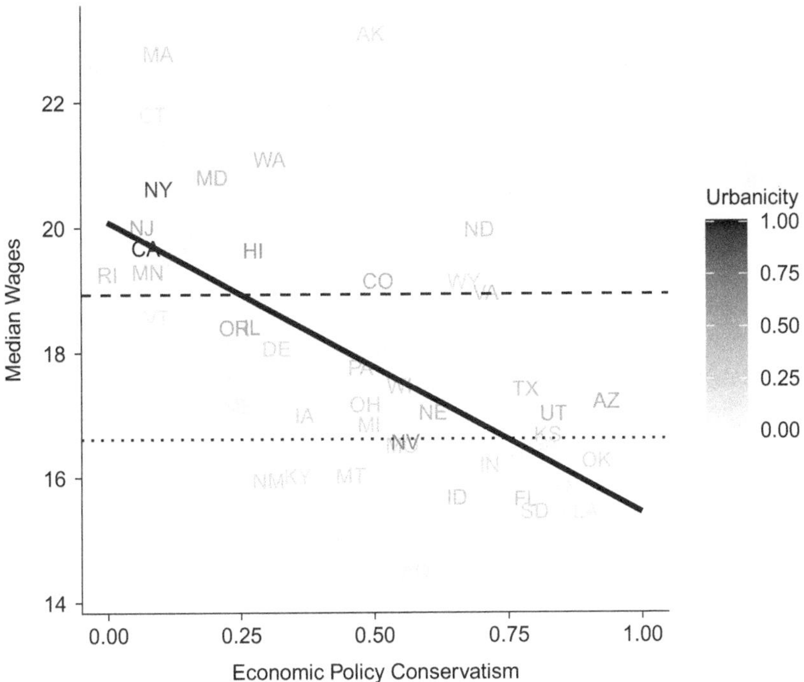

FIGURE 7.3 State economic policy, wages, and urbanization

trio (Alaska, North Dakota, and Wyoming). The top dashed line shows the unweighted average of median wages for all the blue states. The lower dotted line shows the unweighted average of median wages for all the red states.

Looking at Figure 7.3, we can identify a second and much larger group of red states, which we will call low-road states. Figure 7.3 makes clear that the states with the lowest wages are those with smaller governments that lack dense urban centers (that is, those with the lightest initials in the figure's bottom right). Most of these states are located in the South. This familiar regional set long competed within the United States on the basis of anemic unions and low wages. Yet this "low road" has become much rockier because of the globalization of production and rise of China.

Figure 7.3 also makes clear that there is diversity among red states and, indeed, even among red states in the South. Although the red states all cluster below the average wage level of blue states, some come closer to the blue-state level than others. The four most conspicuous examples are Arizona, Utah, Texas, and Nebraska. As the darker shading of their initials suggests, they look to have higher wages in part because they are more urbanized. (Texas also benefits from energy extraction.) All four of these states have thriving urban centers in which a substantial share of state residents live. Healthy inflows to these red state's cities reflect a mix of factors, including warmer weather, Hispanic immigration, and relatively low-cost housing. Crucially, however, these dense metro areas were well established before the shift from convergence to divergence began.

The third group of states that we examine is mostly absent from Figure 7.2: the industrial heartland states identified earlier. Centered in the Midwest, this group includes two states that meet our definition of red states – Ohio and Indiana – along with Michigan, Pennsylvania, and Wisconsin. All these states have trended Republican, and Trump carried all of them in 2016 (though Biden won back all three of the less solidly red ones). Within this cluster of states, we find the places that have lost the most ground from the transition to the knowledge economy: thriving industrial regions now struggling with low labor-force participation, high poverty, and alarmingly subpar health.

We call this third group left-behind states. They share in common with their Southern cousins a relative shortage of vibrant non-extractive production that can prosper in the global knowledge economy. Unlike the South, however, they also carry the legacies of once-progressive policies governing unions, education, and other public goods – and the ongoing partisan struggle over these policies is a major part of their distinctive developmental trajectory. We now turn to explaining these dynamics.

RED STATES CONFRONT THE KNOWLEDGE ECONOMY

What explains the divergent trajectories of low-road states, left-behind states, and the energy trio – both compared with each other and, far more consequential, compared with blue states? We start with the largest group, low-road states, and then consider the energy trio and left-behind states in turn.

Low-Road States: From Internal to External Competition

Most red states have been poor and conservatively governed for a long time. The main thing that has changed in recent decades is their context: the simultaneous rise of the knowledge economy, the globalization of low-wage manufacturing, and the decline of federal investment. Because of this contextual change, once-narrowing gaps have become wider and wider.

The shift toward the knowledge economy has disadvantaged low-road states for at least two reasons. First, in a new kind of economy that provides significant first-mover advantages, they started way behind: they were already the states with the lowest education levels, and many entered the 2000s lacking dense urban centers. Second, for those not reliant on energy, their economic strategy rested on their ability to undercut Northern wages within a national "single market" that allowed labor and capital mobility along with local control over important economic policies. This advantage, however, became less important as the global economy shifted. Rather than competing with high-union, high-tax states, red states had to compete with huge pools of cheap labor in foreign countries. Rather than stealing manufacturing from the North, they increasingly needed to create indigenous sources of innovation and foster human capital.

At the same time, the decline of federal investments has particularly disadvantaged these states. The economic convergence of the mid-twentieth century owed much to the workings of a single integrated market. Yet it was also propelled by huge national investments in the South. Federal income transfers to poorer states grew, military bases and weapons production were deliberately located in the South, and a host of other policies were specifically designed to shower disproportionate benefits on laggard states. As already discussed, many of these policies can be traced to the leverage the South and Sunbelt gained from their pivotal position as a distinctive coalition in national politics (Katznelson 2013).

Starting in the late 1970s, however, the shift of national politics to the right and increasing federal gridlock undermined many of these policies. Declining national regulation – and, in particular, antitrust, labor, and financial regulation – furthered a shift of economic activity toward a more oligopolistic corporate world and a smaller number of high-growth urban areas, weakening the rural areas and mid-sized economic centers that were characteristic of many red-state political economies (as flagged by Suresh Naidu in his chapter).

Meanwhile, the end of the Cold War sharply reduced defense spending, and defense spending also became less capable of fostering regional convergence, as a focus on basic transport and weaponry for a conscript military centered in the South gave way to a focus on using public-private partnerships to give a smaller voluntary service a technological edge (Weiss 2014). As Soskice's chapter shows, both defense and nondefense federal R&D spending also plummeted as share of total R&D spending.

The fall in federal investment can be seen in Figure 7.4, which shows federal spending on grants for states and localities as a share of GDP. State aid is provided through both "discretionary" spending, which must be

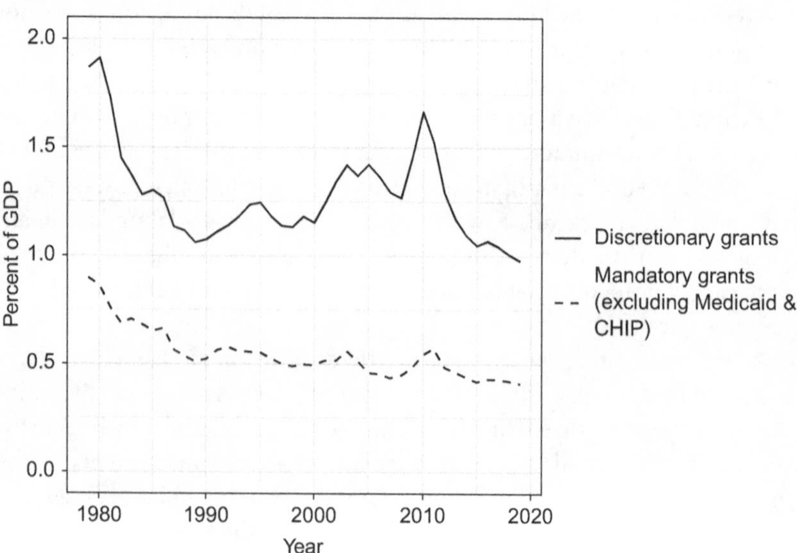

FIGURE 7.4 Federal grants for states and localities, 1980–2020

appropriated, and "mandatory" spending, which is provided automatically by formula. Figure 7.4 excludes federal outlays for Medicaid, because their rise over time is so driven by health spending. (They also require state-matching payments, making them a strain on state budgets even as they provide vital health protections to an increasing share of state residents.) As can be seen, mandatory and discretionary outlays as a percentage of GDP each fell by almost half by 2019. Over the same period, the federal government shifted the policymaking responsibilities of taxation and public investment down to state governments.

These changes have contributed to a stark economic divergence of outcomes, policies, and partisan governance. Poorer regions have stopped catching up. Wealthier areas are pulling ahead. This divergence can be seen within red America as well as between red America and blue America. In general, red states have not fared well in this new context. But those that have fared better (besides the big energy producers) generally host dense urban hubs and the institutions that are associated with them: colleges, universities, innovative firms, and more educated workforces.

It is important to note that the progress of such urban hubs seems to have occurred mostly *despite* the influence of GOP politicians within these states. The traditional red-state package of low taxes and wages, no unions, and limited zoning restrictions and other regulations does offer a few advantages in the knowledge economy. In particular, these policies generate a lower overall cost of living, particularly more affordable housing, which has encouraged in-migration (while highlighting the challenges of urban agglomerations in blue states discussed in Ansell and Gingrich's contribution to this volume). Yet Republican state leaders have shown themselves to be mostly hostile to the needs of thriving urban centers, especially as they have become more and more reliably blue. For example, state GOP parties have thwarted local innovation through "preemption" rules that have made it harder for local leaders to adopt higher labor standards (minimum wages, mandatory benefits) and invest in public goods to create livable and productive cities. Equally important, they have underfunded education, infrastructure, and other public goods at the state level – anti-urban policies that clearly come at the expense of state prosperity (see, e.g., Dar and Lee 2014).

Energy States: Few and Fragile

The energy trio stands out because these three states have managed to achieve relatively high wages with a sector-specific economic strategy.

Most red states, however, have lacked the luxury of abundant energy reserves. Moreover, outside of the energy trio, even those with significant reserves do not consistently show good outcomes. In a modern knowledge economy, the model is Silicon Valley, not Saudi Arabia. Extraction-oriented states will struggle to move into a low-carbon future.

States dependent on energy are also famously subject to boom-bust cycles. Although wise policies could reduce the impact of these swings on state finances, resource-dependent states have generally failed to use good times to prepare for bad. During booms, higher state revenues have often been translated into tax cuts; and during busts, these states have cut spending, especially on education – further hindering their chances of building a more diversified economic base (Dadayan and Boyd 2016).

In this respect, energy states look similar to red states that are highly dependent on agriculture, which also face boom-bust swings due to global price fluctuations. Indeed, we considered breaking out agriculture-dependent states from our larger category of low-road states. Ultimately, however, farm states do not look much like the energy trio. Even the red states most dependent on agricultural production – South Dakota, Nebraska, North Dakota, and Idaho – have strikingly little employment in the sector (no more than 5 percent of state jobs), and the share of their state income that comes from farming is only 7 to 11 percent (Y Analytics 2020). (Another farming-oriented state, Iowa, is not a red state by our definition.) Moreover, a growing share of net farm income – nearly 40 percent in 2020 – actually comes from the federal government, as we shall discuss later in this chapter (USDA 2020). As an indigenous source of prosperity, as opposed to a route to federal assistance, agriculture seems scarcely more promising as a long-term growth strategy than energy.

Left-Behind States: Heading for the Low Road?

Our third group – what we have called left-behind states – face their own challenges. Disproportionately white and working class, with a relatively limited share of workers possessing a college degree, these states are part of what Austin, Glaeser, and Summers (2018) term the "Eastern Heartland" – a region that exhibits much poorer health outcomes and labor market performance than the "Western Heartland" of the interior West. The Eastern Heartland is where we see the biggest fall in the labor-force attachment of working-age adults; it is also the epicenter of the opioid epidemic.

When commentators talk about the parts of American left behind, they generally mean the Eastern Heartland.

Again, the majority of these states fall outside our definition of "red" states. Large and closely divided, they remain contested by – and pivotal to the electoral prospects of – both parties (Hopkins 2017). Still, they appear to be drifting toward the GOP. Not only are they coming to look more like the red states just described (the "Southernization" process mentioned earlier), but many have also experienced unified Republican governance that has severely weakened once-powerful unions, slashed taxes, and cut back state investments in education, as well as put in place highly GOP-friendly state and federal electoral maps (Hertel-Fernandez 2019). Within these states, as in national politics overall, areas experiencing economic decline have become the core of a powerful backlash coalition that has supported conservative Republicans and contributed to polarized economic governance. The paradoxical relationships between economic hardship, voter backlash, and GOP policies are our next subject.

THE ECONOMIC GOVERNANCE OF RED STATES

The persistent under-performance of red states presents a puzzle. Parties that consistently fail to produce prosperity should pay an electoral price. Moreover, the classic arguments about sectionalism made by scholars like Bensel and Katznelson suggest that parties within distinctive regional bases should use national politics to advance sectional interests. If red states have distinctive growth needs, those should impose constraints on state leaders. More important, because American political institutions provide powerful transmission belts for the advancement of territorially grounded interests, it should also encourage their partisan allies in national government to at least try to cater to those needs.

In the next two sections, we consider why these expectations seem not to be met. In this section, we show that most red states have adopted economic policies that hew to the national party's conservative approach, and that these policies have been associated with poor outcomes, controlling for prior economic characteristics. We then turn to the role of partisan forces at the national level, where we show that national Republicans, too, have not much catered to red states' economic interests. In each case, we ask why there is a disconnect between what produces prosperity in red states and what Republicans seek to do, and why the party nonetheless maintains a strong hold on governing power.

What Should Red States Want?

In the classic accounts of Bensel, Katznelson, and others, sectional political coalitions can be expected to pursue sectional economic interests. What would such interests look like today? The answer is not immediately obvious. First, there is considerable heterogeneity among the red states. Second, it is no easy task to identify attractive development strategies for many of these states in a fundamentally new economic context. A strategy of exploiting lower wages and hostility to unions within an integrated market had much to recommend it in the mid-1950s industrial economy. It has far fewer advantages when low-wage manufacturers must compete with China rather than Chicago.

For clues, we can turn to the recent pathbreaking work of Rodden (2019) mentioned earlier. In his recent book, *Why Cities Lose* and related writings, Rodden makes two key analytic moves. First, he emphasizes that majoritarian electoral systems like the United States demand that parties be broad coalitions based on the bundling of disparate policy stances. Second, he argues that the American system of territorially based, winner-take-all elections advantages the less-urban political coalition. Republicans have benefited from the growing rural-urban cleavages, winning sparsely populated states and areas in both national and state contests, and they have used their geographically grounded electoral advantages to magnify their edge through partisan gerrymandering and efforts to suppress Democratic votes. The upshot of these twin factors in Rodden's account is that the GOP, while necessarily a broad coalition, should be expected to gravitate toward an economic agenda that reflects their electoral dependence on low-road and left-behind states and the energy trio.

For the trio of energy states this description fits well. For them and for national GOP politicians catering to fossil-fuel producers, a strategy of intensifying extractive efforts and backing supportive national deregulatory and land use policies makes some sense – at least if your time horizons are short.

Most red states, however, lack abundant energy reserves. Most, too, were never fully incorporated in the industrial economy (much of the South) or were heavily invested in now-declining manufacturing (the industrial heartland). For these states, good policy options are harder to identify (Austin et al. 2018). Struggling red states that lack existing knowledge hubs will likely find it impossible to create the critical mass needed to build such arrangements now. Moreover, taking steps in that direction by increasing investments in human capital is vulnerable to poaching. States, like firms, may find that the reward for greater investments in human capital is to watch these young skilled workers move to regions offering greater opportunities.

States also face inherent limits in their capacity to use public policy to respond to the dramatic economic changes we have discussed. Not only do they have to work with the preexisting endowments they have; they have to do so with limited tools. Unlike the national government, states have no levers of monetary policy. And while states can use taxes and other fiscal policies, they face greater constraints on doing so. Virtually all have balanced budget rules, and firms and wealthy residents can move across state boundaries far more easily than across national boundaries. These realities create significant bias against policies that impose large costs on mobile economic actors.

What we should expect, though, is that these states would seek increased economic help from the federal government. Ideally, the federal government would transfer resources from richer states – as they did during and after the New Deal – in ways that allow wages and unionization to remain relatively low, preserving local competitive advantages. Among the plausible policy options would be expansions of unrestricted intergovernmental transfers, targeting of military spending to red states, the expansion of (targeted) agricultural subsidies; protection or expansion of critical forms of social insurance for aging workers, as well as other social programs that do not raise reservation wages; targeted investments in higher education that foster and strengthen the localized benefits of research institutions where they exist; and place-based federal investments in distressed areas. More generally, since red states are considerable net winners from federal expenditures (Krimmel and Rader 2017), we might expect support for federal policies that would expand such transfers.

What Do Red States Do?

With few exceptions, this is not what we see. Instead, red state politicians have increasingly embraced a uniform nationalized agenda that is focused on tax cuts and aggressive deregulation and is hostile to federal transfers. This agenda seems to reflect the preferences of national actors and party priorities rather than local conditions, voter demands, or (in some cases) even major local economic interests (Hertel-Fernandez 2019). Moreover, it is broadly associated with generally subpar economic outcomes.

One can see this result in both the policies that red states enact and the ones they support at the federal level. With the federal government often gridlocked, state economic policies have become more important and distinctive between red and blue states, and national political actors have focused more on influencing those policies. With federal investment declining, the states as a whole have become an increasingly prominent part of the national fiscal picture. These trends have affected red and blue states in different ways. Generally professionalized and often building on decades of state policy activism, blue states have implemented major policies in such crucial areas as health care and environmental regulation. Increased state tax rates, especially on high earners, have partly offset the decline in federal transfers.

But while blue states have attempted to fill in where the federal government has pulled back, most red states have reduced their tax capacity and public investment, especially following the Republican sweep of state governments in 2010. With partisanship more nationalized, red states appear less guided by the particular characteristics of their economies. Instead, they have pursued low-road strategies almost regardless of context. Under GOP control, for example, Wisconsin implemented a conservative agenda diametrically opposed to the approach of its broadly similar neighbor, Minnesota, where Democrats retained a greater degree of power.

The widening disparities across states can be seen in many domains (Caughey, Xu, and Warshaw 2017; Grumbach 2018). In health care, for example, party control of state government increasingly predicts rates of insurance coverage. Public health scholars find growing effects of state-level policies on life expectancy, infant mortality, and other health outcomes (Borgschulte and Vogler 2020). Levels of state public employment, a major route into the middle class, have polarized as well. The financial crisis hurt public employment everywhere, but blue states were more likely to increase taxes to keep workers in their school systems, universities, and other public institutions. Tax policy, too, has seen a growing divide, as shown (alongside labor and health/welfare) in Figure 7.5.

Indeed, labor relations are the area of policy that has most dramatically polarized in recent years. Upon taking control of state legislatures and governorships in 2011, Republicans in Indiana, Michigan, and Wisconsin restricted the bargaining power of public sector unions and implemented laws that greatly restricted both public and private unions' capacity to require dues from workers. Rather than reflecting the demands of local

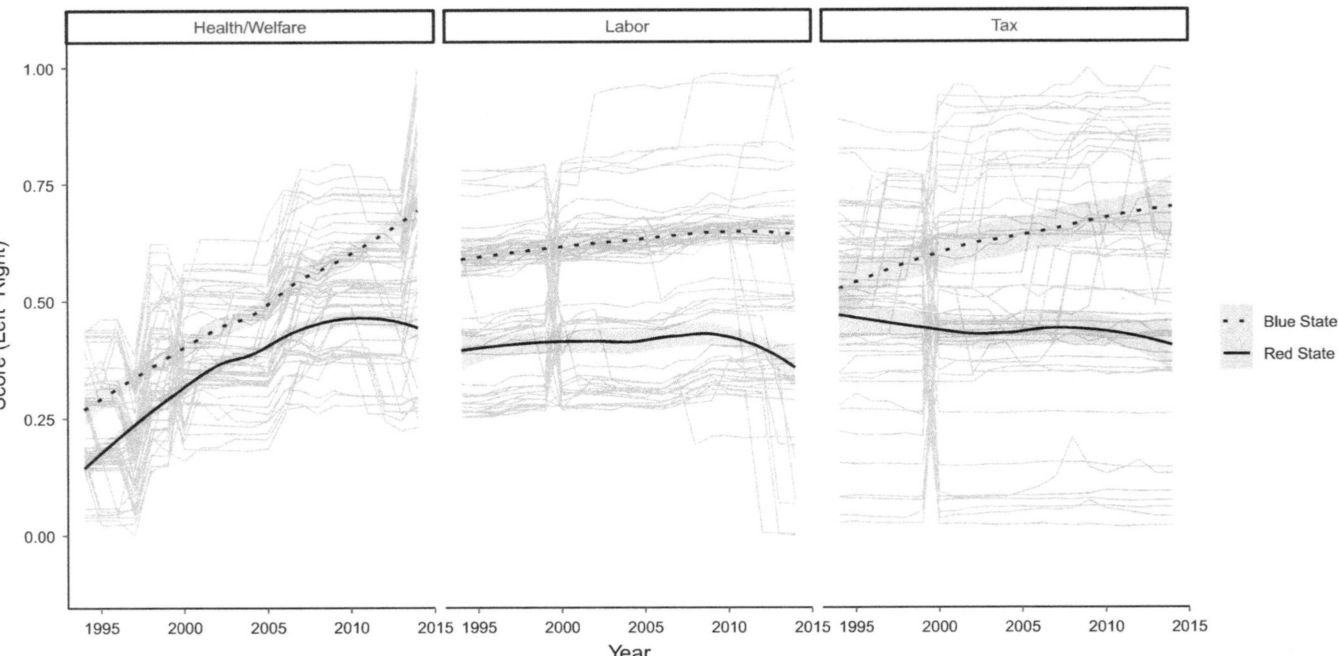

FIGURE 7.5 Expanding variation in state economic policy
Note: State labor, tax, and health/welfare policies have become increasingly varied, and this variation is increasingly predicted by party control. Plots show issue-specific state policy liberalism (grey lines) from 1994–2014. The bold lines represent our 24 blue states (dotted line) and 26 red states (solid line). State policy liberalism measures are from Grumbach (2018).

voters, there is compelling evidence that national interest group networks pushed heavily for this agenda (Hertel-Fernandez 2019). As mentioned, such policies have reflected and furthered the (potentially decisive) shift of these states into the Republican column, as well as contributing directly to declining wages among middle-skill workers.

Nor have red state leaders shown themselves to be aggressive seekers of federal funds, despite the highly advantageous structure of intergovernmental transfers for poorer states. Nowhere is this clearer than in the case of the Medicaid expansion authorized by the 2010 Affordable Care Act. Although a Republican-led Supreme Court unexpectedly gave states the option of rejecting the expansion, it still should have been highly attractive to red states. With the national government paying virtually all the costs and local residents disproportionately likely to benefit, ACA expansion promised not just improved health care but infusions of many billions of dollars into red state economies. Recognizing these benefits, state economic elites – including both the health care industry and local chambers of commerce – generally supported expansion. So did many Republican governors, the state elected officials with the largest stake in supporting the economic health of their states (Skocpol and Hertel-Fernandez 2016). Yet feeding off the hostility of Republican-controlled legislatures, most red states initially balked. The majority (twelve at last count) are still holding out, while not a single blue state has refused the expansion.

Partisan Approaches, Poor Outcomes

Assessing how these policies have affected red state outcomes is not a simple task. As emphasized, states' preexisting characteristics strongly predict their present-day outcomes, and red states started in a poor position. For example, Austin, Glaeser, and Summers (2018) find that 2010 outcomes can be fairly well predicted by 1980 structural differences.

But policies at the state level matter, too. In Table 7.2, we reproduce Austin, Glaeser, and Summers' results, focusing on the authors' two main outcomes (labor force participation and median household income) as well as median wages. Following their reduced-form models, we include as independent variables the 1980 percentages of adult residents who are college graduates and who do not have high school diploma, and the 1980 percentages of employment in manufacturing industries. However, we also include our main policy variable, "economic policy conservatism." We then compare the relative impact on

TABLE 7.2 *Comparing structural and policy explanations*

	Dependent Variable:					
	LFP (2009–2014)		Median Hourly Wage (2009–2014)		Median HH Income (2009–2014)	
	(1)	(2)	(3)	(4)	(5)	(6)
Economic Policy Conservatism	−5.215***	−3.720***	−4.234***	−4.786***	−12.144***	−12.824***
	(0.951)	(1.043)	(0.347)	(0.381)	(1.560)	(1.739)
% College Grad 1980	−2.971***	−2.523***	0.697***	0.532***	1.650***	1.447**
	(0.332)	(0.355)	(0.121)	(0.129)	(0.545)	(0.591)
% Below HS 1980	−4.810***	−4.200***	−0.558***	−0.783***	−4.019***	−4.296***
	(0.353)	(0.395)	(0.129)	(0.144)	(0.580)	(0.659)
% Manufacturing 1980	0.067***	0.085***	0.011	0.005	0.101**	0.093**
	(0.024)	(0.025)	(0.009)	(0.009)	(0.040)	(0.041)
% Black		−0.087***		0.032***		0.039
		(0.027)		(0.010)		(0.045)
Constant	61.481***	62.636***	14.781***	14.354***	43.743***	43.218***
	(0.859)	(0.917)	(0.314)	(0.335)	(1.408)	(1.528)
Year FEs	Yes	Yes	Yes	Yes	Yes	Yes
Observations	300	300	300	300	300	300
R^2	0.463	0.482	0.661	0.673	0.607	0.608
Adjusted R^2	0.447	0.465	0.651	0.662	0.594	0.594

Note: We measure participation in percentage points, household income in thousands of dollars, and median hourly wages in dollars.
$^{*}p < 0.1$; $^{**}p < 0.05$; $^{***}p < 0.01$

current economic outcomes of both 1980 economic variables and our index of state policy choices.

The results are striking. Like Austin, Glaeser, and Summers, we find a strong relationship between 1980 characteristics and contemporary outcomes. Yet, even with all these historical variables included in the model, we also find that state policy is strongly related to contemporary outcomes. Compared to the smallest state government (with an index of 0), the model predicts that the largest state government (an index of 1) has considerably higher labor force participation (LFP), wages, and median incomes. To illustrate the magnitude of these effects, our results imply that a state with policies like Kentucky's (0.64 on our index) will have a median hourly wage about $2 higher than a state with policies like Oklahoma's (0.09). The model also predicts a nearly $5,000 difference in median income between these states – roughly the difference between West Virginia and Texas.

We would not want to overinterpret these results; state policies and state outcomes are clearly mutually dependent on each other. Our point is that states do appear to have some scope to disrupt the vicious cycle of economic decline. But this raises an obvious question: If Republican leaders are pursuing policies that are not conducive to prosperity, why do voters in these states elect them? More puzzling still, why does the national Republican Party – increasingly dependent on these states in an era of razor-thin electoral margins – seem so tied to national business and economic elites, despite electorally grounded arguments that they should be pulled toward a distinctive red-state-centered model of economic development (Rodden 2019)? Because these questions are so closely interconnected, we consider them together in the next section.

SECTIONALISM AND THE GOP'S NATIONAL ECONOMIC AGENDA

When we look at the Republican Party's national economic agenda, it is even more difficult to discern much of a connection to red state interests. To be sure, there is one point of strong affinity: support for extraction, reflected in aggressive stances with respect to both deregulation and use of federal lands. As we have emphasized, even this area of reasonable affinity is not a viable long-term economic strategy. Indeed, the evidence is that the economic impact of climate change is likely to be particularly negative for red states, because of their warmer climates, greater exposure to storms, and weaker infrastructure, including water systems (Hsaing et al. 2017).

Elsewhere, the fit between sectional interests and national party priorities is far less evident. Consider high-end tax cuts, which have become the cornerstone of GOP policy. Ironically, given the spatial distribution of affluence in the United States, direct beneficiaries of these tax cuts disproportionately reside in blue states. Moreover, the losers from a diminished national fiscal capacity are more likely to reside in red states. Over the medium-run, this reduced federal capacity is almost certain to diminish the flow of resources from blue to red states. Compared to other federal systems in rich nations, the United States has always produced considerably more limited subsidies to poorer regions. Grants and subsidies from the central government make up a much smaller share of subnational government revenues, and the United States lacks federal tax sharing with either states or local governments – a common approach abroad. Most important, it is an extreme outlier when it comes to so-called fiscal equalization, with no unconditional federal funding to either local or state governments (OECD 2016b). Although some grants to states automatically provide a larger "match" to states with lower incomes, the United States stands out for its weak efforts to reduce inequalities in fiscal capacity among states.

The priorities of the national GOP seem likely to intensify this distinctiveness. For instance, having just pushed through almost $2 trillion in mostly high-end and corporate tax cuts, the GOP resisted adequate new federal spending to deal with the opioid epidemic – a core dimension of the "deaths of despair" dynamic that Anne Case and Angus Deaton have shown is disproportionately ravaging areas of GOP electoral strength (Case and Deaton 2019). Nor has it moved forward on infrastructure or prescription drug proposals that might create jobs or lower the cost of living for less affluent workers. In 2009 (when Democrats had the White House) and even amid the COVID-19 pandemic in 2020 (when Republicans did), national Republicans also resisted aid to hard-hit states and localities suffering because of a nationwide economic downturn.

Over the long run, the GOP priority on high-end tax cuts poses a clear threat to the GOP electorate. It is likely to generate acute fiscal pressure on major social spending programs on which aging red-state residents disproportionately rely, including Social Security, Medicare, Medicaid, and disability insurance. For the population of most red states – and more specifically the electoral base of the GOP in those states – this constitutes a huge risk.

As noted, a version of this dynamic has played out on health care. While state Republican leaders refused to expand Medicaid, national Republicans voted again and again for repeal of the Affordable Care Act (without success, due to President Obama's veto power), despite the law's disproportionate benefits in areas where Republicans had strong electoral support.

When Republicans gained a "trifecta" in Washington in 2016, their actions on health care once again signaled the economic priorities of the national party and its indifference to sectional economic interests (Hacker and Pierson 2020). Republican policies to repeal the ACA and squeeze Medicaid would have had a devastating impact on the availability and affordability of health care in red states. Although Republican proposals polled catastrophically, almost all national Republicans supported repeal. They did so not just because they wanted to reverse the sharp increase in coverage under "Obamacare," but because repealing the law would have allowed a rollback of the high-end taxes that provided the program's extremely progressive financing. Moreover, the additional Medicaid cuts could be leveraged into even deeper tax cuts in the tax law that would follow. Only the defection of a handful of Republicans in the Senate saved the ACA.

Identity over Interests

Given these patterns of governance, it might be supposed that the conservative economic policies Republicans support at the state and national level have a deep well of support within the Republican electoral base. Yet this is not the case. Indeed, as the party has relied more and more heavily on white voters without a college degree to win elections, it has also brought into its coalitions many more voters who are quite skeptical of high-end tax cuts and highly supportive of federal transfers, so long as they are focused on older white voters. Although we cannot review the entire body of evidence here, both opinion polls and salient policy fights show a substantial disconnect between elite GOP priorities on health care, taxes, and Social Security and the stances of most rank-and-file GOP voters. The major fiscal proposals of national Republicans have combined high-end tax cuts with sharp proposed spending cuts. This was the formula embodied, for example, in Paul Ryan's high-profile budget plan developed to counter President Obama. According to national polling, the Ryan plan lacked majority support not only among Democrats but also among Republicans – and, indeed, even among Republican donors as a whole. Only among GOP donors with incomes greater than $250,000 a year did support outweigh opposition (Hacker and Pierson 2020).

It is difficult to make a case that the core of the GOP's national economic policy agenda has emerged, a la Rodden, from core economic interests of the regions on which the party heavily relies. Instead, the evidence is more consistent with an agenda driven by a nationalized interest group coalition. But this raises an obvious question: How have Republicans proved able to maintain these policy stances while deepening their support among non-affluent white voters in struggling areas of the country? A big part of the answer is that the party has successfully used issues of social identity as a powerful second dimension of conflict. Their policy bundling, in other words, has combined ethnonationalist appeals associated with fringe right-wing parties abroad with economic policies highly favorable to elite interests – from wealthy donors like Charles Koch and his network of well-resourced groups and givers to corporate lobbies like the US Chamber of Commerce to particular rent-seeking sectors like the fossil-fuel industry.

It is now widely recognized that the exploitation of racial backlash has been critical to Republicans' electoral success both inside and outside the South. Particularly in states with large white non-college educated voting blocs facing economic duress, Republicans have capitalized on racial and anti-immigrant resentment to maintain power even as their economic policies largely reflect national partisan priorities. These efforts are bolstered by key activist groups like the NRA and Christian Right, as well as right-wing media. These "surrogate groups" are skilled at making identity appeals based on the perceived threat of demographic and cultural change. Meanwhile, they do not challenge the party's inegalitarian economic priorities, and indeed side with them in key domains, such as Supreme Court nominations, where intraparty logrolls between the activist and elite wings of the party are possible (Hacker and Pierson 2020).

In this respect, the politics of the GOP coalition reflects a structural logic that has been identified in both historical (Ziblatt 2017) and more contemporary (Tavits and Potter 2014) cross-national studies. In a context of high and rising inequality, conservative parties with close ties to corporate and economic elites face growing incentives to shift the electorate's focus to "second dimension" social issues. Rapidly changing demographics only add to the incentive, creating a salient threat to future Republican electoral success while making it easier to radicalize white voters' with regard to immigration and racial and ethnic cleavages.

In these developments, we can also see clearly how the combination of nationalized partisan polarization, state policies that undercut unions, and the growing reliance of the GOP on rural states and regions has undercut electoral accountability. Even as the geographic isolation of GOP voters increases the incentive and capacity for Republican elites to push cultural issues that tilt in their direction locally (Hopkins 2017), the decline of organized labor reduces the chance that these voters will receive contrary signals. Among the white working class, unionized workers are far more likely to vote for Democrats (Frymer and Grumbach 2020). Indeed, core GOP voters are much more likely than other voters to rely exclusively on national partisan media, in part because nonurban areas have seen the steepest decline in local news. These trends help explain why recent research has suggested there is almost no electoral penalty for state legislators who vote for policies "out of step" with the opinions of their districts (Rogers 2017).

On top of this, there is the sharp tilt of the American electoral system toward nonurban areas. A large (and growing) rural bias is baked into Senate apportionment, of course, and this partly carries over to the Electoral College. Moreover, because population density is increasingly associated with liberalism, Democratic voters are naturally clustered in a small number of (urban) districts. In House and state legislative elections, Republicans have accentuated the effect of this natural clustering through extreme partisan gerrymandering and through voter restrictions focused on core Democratic voters. These advantages are worth a lot, especially in the Senate. Republicans have held the Senate for just over half of the past two decades. During that period, however, they have represented states with a majority of the nation's population for only two years (Brownstein 2020). The upshot is that the same rural bias that Rodden argues should reorient the GOP toward nonurban interests makes it easier for the GOP to ignore those interests.

In short, red state politicians at both the state and national levels have been able to win despite limited responsiveness to the economic concerns of their voters. Even when they have emphasized economically populist themes, they have mostly governed as hard-right economic conservatives, exploiting racial backlash to maintain support even when their policies do not provide much economic benefit or even cause economic harm.

The Trump Presidency: Signs of Change?

No modern president has been as sectional in his rhetoric as Donald Trump. Styling himself as the president of a forgotten red America, Trump routinely denigrated blue states and made almost no effort to appeal to their voters. More than any prior GOP candidate, Trump in 2016 also combined racial and cultural appeals with anti-elite, pro-worker populism, at one point suggesting he wanted to make the Republican Party "a worker's party" (Gass 2016).

How much did this rhetoric lead to economic policies beneficial to red state voters? The evidence for a major realignment is weak. Trump's anti-immigration policies, while squarely pitched to red state voters, were rarely framed as relating to jobs or economic growth. In general, these policies were less about making an economic appeal to the GOP base than about substituting a focus on ethnic threat for a concern with economic issues.

Trade was the clearest instance of Trump actually pursuing, rather than just promising, a real departure from the established agenda of GOP elites. And there is evidence that Trump's base found his posture appealing (Ruffini 2018). By 2019, however, it was clear that trade wars were not so "easy to win," as Trump had tweeted in 2018. Rather, the short-term costs were substantial, and fell largely on US consumers and producers. Economists suggested that just the Chinese tariffs would cost Americans $1,000 per year per household (Telford 2019). The hit from foreign retaliation to Trump's tariffs was greatest in rural areas and small towns, precisely where Trump's support was strongest (Parilla and Bouchet 2018). Trump's main effort to deal with this economic battering was a massive increase in farm subsidies that may well constitute the single clearest example of a "red state" economic gambit during his presidency. As noted earlier, direct government aid to US farmers spiked in 2020, accounting for nearly four in ten dollars of net farm income. Courtesy of the federal treasury, American agriculture had its third most profitable year in the past half-century (USDA 2020).

Elsewhere, however, the Trump record is one of continuity – even intensification – of policies geared to the GOP's national elite coalition rather than its regional electoral base. Trump's pledge to "drain the swamp" may have suggested a departure from past GOP policies catering to the narrow interests of big donors and specific business sectors. Yet, as president, he nominated executive appointees and federal judges more business-friendly than any of his recent GOP predecessors had. Those in the executive branch embarked on an aggressive campaign of environmental, labor, health care, and consumer deregulation that thrilled establishment Republicans even as it weakened protections for everyday Americans. Looking back on the first year of the Trump presidency, Senate Majority Leader Mitch McConnell pronounced it to be "the best year for conservatives – on all fronts – in thirty years" (quoted in Hacker and Pierson 2020, which contains additional evidence of executive actions tilted toward corporate interests).

Equally revealing was what Trump pledged during the campaign but did not push for once in office. His call for massive investments in infrastructure was both popular with his base and could have been used to generate development in struggling regions. Republican members of Congress showed zero interest, however, and it never got off the drawing board. Serious spending on this (or the opioid crisis, to take another telling example) would have conflicted with the top congressional priority: cutting taxes on the wealthy and corporations as much as they could manage. Another of Trump's popular promises was to do something about pharmaceutical costs. Yet with the powerful industry strongly aligned with the GOP, serious action on drug costs remained parked in a holding area somewhere behind the always-just-around-the-corner "infrastructure week."

Here, as in many areas, Trump simply continued or intensified the GOP pattern: a focus on benefits for corporations and the rich, coupled with neglect for the party's own voters. Certainly, he did not usher in anything resembling the historical dynamics Katznelson and Bensel highlighted or reflecting the contemporary alliances Rodden anticipates – that is, of distinctively *sectional* interests playing a decisive role in shaping *national* economic policy.

CONCLUSION

The era of economic convergence has ended. A new sectional divide cleaves a high-productivity core linked to the knowledge economy from a lower-productivity periphery struggling to find a viable model of economic growth. As in the past, we would expect this profound cleavage to have profound consequences for American politics, and it has. Yet these consequences do not fit many of our expectations, and in this chapter we have sought to understand why. In particular, we have sought to understand why, as the parties have polarized and nationalized, the regions of the United States falling behind have become closely allied with a party that does not seem to be pursuing sectional economic interests in ways that either historical precedents or political science theorizing suggest it should.

Our most basic claim is that red states constitute a distinctive part of the American political economy, and that this distinctive set of states mostly stands in contrast to urbanized blue regions that have flourished in recent decades. We know a fair amount about states that are doing well in the knowledge economy. We know much less about states that are not. Our inductive typology of red states (which we see as only a first step that we hope will spark further research) identifies three basic models. In addition to the energy trio that has taken the extractive route to (at least near-term) prosperity, we have identified two other groups – one solidly red, the other increasingly so. The first, mostly in the South, has struggled in the new economic order, hit by cheap foreign production on one side and lacking many of the prerequisites for postindustrial prosperity on the other. A second group of states in the industrial heartland – once characterized by vibrant manufacturing economies and progressive policies – has faced similar challenges and provided fertile ground for the politics of resentment that has increasingly characterized Republican campaigning nationwide. In the bargain, these left-behind states have experienced worsening social outcomes and the rapid regression of policies that at one time defined the progressive frontier of American politics and policy.

Yet if red states are struggling economically, the national coalition they are part of is politically formidable – buoyed by the advantages our territorial electoral system confers on sparsely populated states and regions. With the GOP's economic policies mostly divorced from its sectional economic foundations, national Republican leaders have hewed to an agenda much more consistent with the demands of their wealthiest organized supporters than the economic imperatives of the states that side with them. Rather than push back, state GOP leaders have climbed aboard. The electoral overweighting of the GOP's voting base has made this a viable strategy; the ability of GOP elites to mobilize this base using racial and cultural backlash has made it a successful one. The consequence is the great paradox of American politics: a political economy in which the losers from the knowledge economy, radicalized and resentful, bolster the political strength of a governing coalition that has done little ease their plight.

APPENDIX

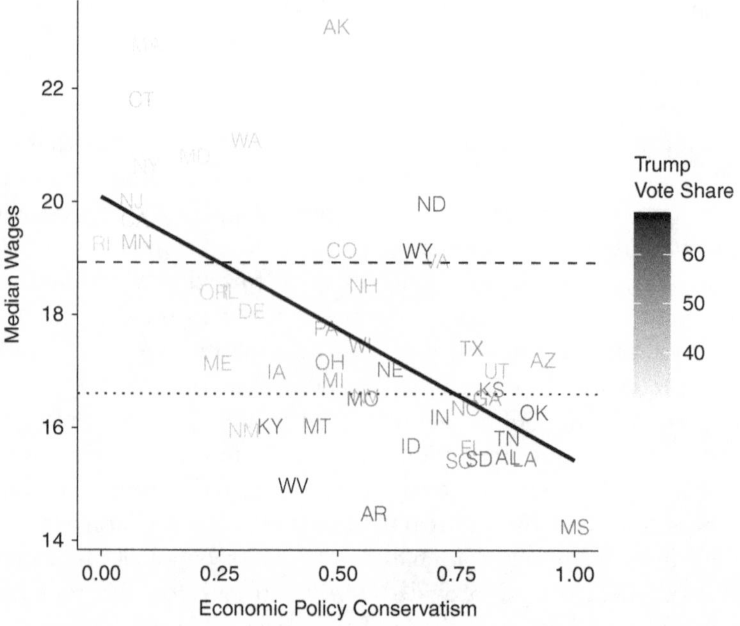

FIGURE 7.A1 Economic policy conservativism, wages, and Trump vote

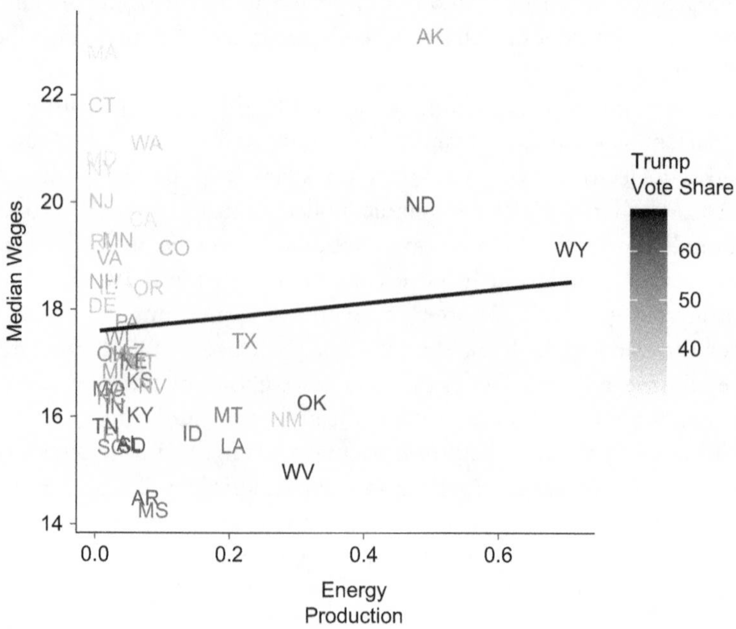

FIGURE 7.A2 Energy, wages, and Trump vote

TABLE 7.A1 *Comparing structural and policy explanations (including energy production and Trump vote)*

	Dependent Variable:					
	LFP (2009–2014)		Median Hourly Wage (2009–2014)		Median HH Income (2009–2014)	
	(1)	(2)	(3)	(4)	(5)	(6)
Economic Policy Conservatism	−5.054***	−7.247***	−4.361***	−3.755***	−11.968***	−9.937***
	(0.953)	(1.386)	(0.342)	(0.497)	(1.568)	(2.383)
% College Grad 1980	−3.041***	−2.229***	0.752***	0.453***	1.574***	1.178*
	(0.334)	(0.353)	(0.120)	(0.127)	(0.549)	(0.608)
% Below HS 1980	−4.837***	−4.635***	−0.537***	−0.648***	−4.049***	−3.970***
	(0.353)	(0.398)	(0.127)	(0.143)	(0.580)	(0.684)
% Manufacturing 1980	0.043	0.029	0.030***	0.034***	0.074	0.087*
	(0.028)	(0.028)	(0.010)	(0.010)	(0.047)	(0.048)
Energy Ideal Point	−0.404*	−1.230***	0.317***	0.596***	−0.442	0.078
	(0.240)	(0.288)	(0.086)	(0.103)	(0.395)	(0.496)
% Black		−0.064**		0.028***		0.012
		(0.027)		(0.010)		(0.047)
% Trump Vote		0.159***		−0.052***		−0.108
		(0.039)		(0.014)		(0.066)

(continued)

TABLE 7.A1 *(continued)*

	Dependent Variable:					
	LFP (2009–2014)		Median Hourly Wage (2009–2014)		Median HH Income (2009–2014)	
	(1)	(2)	(3)	(4)	(5)	(6)
Constant	62.183***	54.271***	14.230***	16.729***	44.511***	50.340***
	(0.952)	(2.478)	(0.342)	(0.889)	(1.566)	(4.262)
Observations	300	300	300	300	300	300
R^2	0.469	0.519	0.676	0.708	0.608	0.613
Adjusted R^2	0.450	0.499	0.665	0.695	0.595	0.596

Note: $^{*}p < 0.1$; $^{**}p < 0.05$; $^{***}p < 0.01$

TABLE 7.A2 *Correlations between measures*

	Urban	Wages	Economic Performance	Energy and Extraction	Economic Policy Conservatism
Urban	1	0.36	−0.13	−0.14	−0.3
Wages	0.36	1	−0.6	−0.16	−0.5
Economic Performance	−0.13	−0.6	1	0.06	0.17
Energy and Extraction	−0.14	−0.16	0.06	1	0.21
Economic Policy Conservatism	−0.3	−0.5	0.17	0.21	1

TABLE 7.A3 *Explaining variation in state wages*

Relationship to Wages:	**Mean Squared Error**	**Adj. R^2**
Urban	0.028	0.172
Economic Performance	0.025	0.266
Energy and Extraction	0.033	0.024
Economic Policy Conservatism	0.022	0.358

III

CORPORATE POWER AND CONCENTRATION

8

Mo' Patents, Mo' Problems: Corporate Strategy, Structure, and Profitability in America's Political Economy

Herman Mark Schwartz

> John Spartan (i.e., Sylvester Stallone): "Taco Bell, I thought we were going to a great restaurant. Is this a mistake?"
>
> Lenina Huxley (i.e., Sandra Bullock): "Not at all. Since the great franchise wars, all restaurants are now Taco Bell."
>
> *Demolition Man*, 1993

How has America's political economy changed from the long post-war "Fordist" era to the contemporary post-Fordist or knowledge economy? How has this shift affected economic growth and inequality of income and regions? Most analyses focus on specific aspects, like aggregate income inequality, or the rise of a shareholder-value model for corporate governance, or increased trade competition (aka globalization), or the financial sector's disproportionate power and profitability (aka financialization).

These explanations are important, and mostly correct. That said, they are also largely incomplete and causally weak because they ignore the sources of profit, even when they discuss the rising share of profits relative to wages or of "financial sector" profits relative to "manufacturing sector" profits. Yet the origin of – and distributional conflict over – profits is as important as the distributional conflict between profits and wages for understanding a capitalist political economy. A unified explanation based on firms' profit strategies and the organizational structures they construct to pursue those strategies better explains the dynamics and malaise of the current US political economy. To steal a phrase, it's like the more patents (copyrights, brands, etc.) we come across, the more problems we see.

Put extremely simply, changes in corporate strategy and structure from the Fordist to the current era changed the distribution of profits among and within firms, in turn generating our current economic problems. While the distribution of profits across firms was highly unequal in both eras, changes in corporate strategy and structure have concentrated profits in firms with small labor headcounts, a low marginal propensity to invest, and the ability to avoid taxation. Reduced investment and worsening income inequality in turn slow GDP growth and aggravate social and regional tensions. These changes have gone furthest in the United States but are generic to the rich countries. Per William Gibson, "The future is already here – it's just not evenly distributed."

Broadly, Fordist-era firms sought oligopoly profits by controlling asset-specific physical capital. Yet profitability, let alone profit maximization, using asset-specific physical capital required uninterrupted production at near full capacity. In turn, this required embedding physical capital in large, vertically integrated firms and pacifying direct employees by sharing oligopoly profits. Vertical integration insured continuous and stable flows of inputs (Chandler 1990; Davis 2016; Piore and Sabel 1984). Shared rents bought labor peace. Both generated positive macroeconomic outcomes. Firms' high labor headcounts combined with unionization to flatten the income distribution, boosting aggregate demand. The strategic emphasis on using large fixed investments in physical capital as a barrier to entry generated continuous investment with strong multiplier effects, again bolstering aggregate demand. Firms' desire for stable inputs and demand in largely national markets oriented their political behavior toward seeking macroeconomic stability (Aglietta 1979; Fligstein 2002; Shonfield 1965; Swenson 2002).

Yet not all firms succeeded in creating an oligopoly or inserting themselves into government or corporate planning routines. Fordist-era economies thus tended to polarize into larger, more highly profitable firms with stable markets and smaller, less profitable firms in unstable or marginal markets (Galbraith 1967; Piore and Sabel 1984). Markets and employers also sorted workers into two groups: largely male, white workers with stable, higher wage employment; and largely minority, immigrant, and female workers with unstable, lower wage employment.

Equally simply, today's firms seek monopoly profit via control over intellectual property (IP), that is, via intellectual property rights (IPRs) like patents, brands, copyrights, and trademarks. These convey an exclusive right to extract value from a given production chain. For example, Qualcomm's patents on the technologies linking cell phones to cell towers and Wi-Fi enable it to levy a 2–5 percent royalty on the average selling price of almost all cell phones. Likewise, winners in many nontech sectors have pursued an IPR-based strategy. The salience of "tech" today suggests that IP is something new. But integrated firms pursued formal IP even before the Fordist era (Fisk 2009). The key difference is that IPR-based profit strategies combined with pressure from capital markets influenced by the shareholder-value model to drive vertical *disintegration* of commodity chains. Firms try to shed the risks inherent in fixed investments and a large labor force while using robust IPRs to extract large shares of the value created in their commodity chain. Thus vertical disintegration has concentrated and segregated IP ownership into a small number of legally distinct and highly profitable firms.

As in the Fordist era, not all firms can succeed in capturing oligopoly or monopoly profits. Strategic interaction among firms has produced three different *ideal typical* firms out of the Fordist-era ideal-typical dual structure: human capital-intensive, low headcount firms whose high profitability stems from robust IPRs; physical capital-intensive firms whose moderate profitability stems from investment barriers to entry or tacit production knowledge; and labor-intensive, high headcount firms producing undifferentiated services and commodities with low volumes of profit. Naturally, some firms blend characteristics of two of the levels, with Intel or Siemens, for example, blending the top two levels (IP and physical capital, as with Intel's semiconductor fabs), and Hon Hai Precision (aka Foxconn) attempting to blend the lower two (labor intensive assembly plus a big physical capital investment in robotics).

This tripartite structure affects the distribution of income, the level of investment, and the state's fiscal base. Firms still redistribute some of their excess profits inside the firm as wages (Card et al. 2018: 1–3), but the concentration of profit into a small number of firms with low headcounts limits internal redistribution to a smaller slice of the population. Consequently, *inter*-firm rather than *intra*-firm disparities largely drive wage inequality (Barth et al. 2014; Song et al. 2019). The concentration of profit into human-capital-intensive firms limits the volume of and multipliers from investment – investment for IP firms generally means hiring more well-paid people with a lower marginal propensity to consume (Schwartz 2016). Meanwhile physical-capital-intensive firms with reasonable fears of excess capacity have both limited resources and appetite for new net investment. Finally, IPR-rich firms can easily shift the legal domicile of IP offshore to tax havens, limiting government taxation of corporate profits.

Top-tier firms emerge from an *offensive concentration* of IPRs through internal R&D and acquisition of potential rival firms. This creates and enforces an entry barrier to their markets (Hall et al. 2015; Shapiro 2001). Second-tier firms emerge from a *defensive horizontal* integration through mergers to concentrate control over asset-specific and very expensive physical capital investments. Alternately, significant tacit knowledge can protect a firm from commoditization of its products, as with many German *mittelstand* firms and some US small- and medium-sized enterprises. The many more numerous firms without legal, investment, or tacit knowledge barriers sink to the bottom layer. Many firms are called to the IPR faith, but few are chosen, given the exclusivity IPRs convey.

The competitive struggle among firms and between capital and labor also generates different varieties of labor expulsion designed to shore up profitability without losing effective control over the production process. The *ideal typical* form of expulsion is franchising, in which a firm holding IPRs licenses use of that IP to a franchisee who directly controls labor in the production process, but does so in conformity with substantial direction from the IP owner. Franchisees for fast food restaurants or hotels, for example, are legally bound to follow highly detailed instructions from the franchisor that de facto amount to managerial control. But the expulsion of labor has also occurred via outsourcing, off-shoring, and domestic geographic dispersion.

Manufacturing firms with weaker barriers to entry shifted work to low-wage zones overseas through off-shoring, out-sourcing, and dispersing production to rural areas in the United States. This reversed the gradual convergence of US regional and personal incomes characteristic of the Fordist era, aggravating the "red-state economy" pattern Grumbach et al. detail (this volume). A large swath of new service-sector firms emerged with a conscious strategy of avoiding direct legal responsibilities via the franchise model and contracting. Finally, many of today's "superstar" tech (usually software) firms were born and persisted with relatively narrow headcounts. Firms engaged in political and legal struggles to enable these transformations, which were neither purely internal organizational matters nor the exogenous effects of new technologies.

The economic transformation described here is a global phenomenon. This chapter concentrates on the United States for four reasons. First, these processes are most advanced in the United States. Second, the US state and corporate actors have deeply integrated the US economy with the global economy and structured that economy in ways that comport with their interests, reproducing the US tripartite structure globally. This partially explains the relative concentration of physical capital-intensive production in Germany, Japan, and Korea and the corresponding *relative* absence of dominant IPR firms. Third, the United States still possesses a disproportionate global economic weight, comprising about 40 percent and 24 percent of OECD and world GDP, respectively, at 2019 market exchange rates.

Section 8.1 of the chapter briefly elaborates and contrasts the two different eras with respect to corporate strategy and structure. Section 8.2 provides empirical data on the distribution of profits to sustain immediate claims about the two concentrations and later claims that the tripartite distribution of firms affects the income distribution and investment. Section 8.3 discusses labor control strategies and their consequences for wage, income and regional inequality. Section 8.4 investigates the political and economic implications of the shift toward an "IPR-economy," including contrasts with other rich economies.

8.1 FROM FORDISM TO FRANCHISE

Touring an automobile factory in the 1960s or 1970s you would have seen many different people engaged in direct and indirect production tasks. Semi-skilled workers on the assembly line would loom large, both in real life and in the academic imagination. But around them were specialist toolmakers, engineers, designers, janitorial staff, and logistics workers. Further out – caterers, guards, groundskeepers, accountants, white-collar management, and a second set of logistics workers unloading parts coming from components factories. All these workers were typically legally inside the firm as employees and, white-collar workers aside, union members.

Touring in the 2000s reveals a more racially and gender diverse workforce still doing similar jobs. Automation would have replaced many semi-skilled workers, but the logistics personnel, caterers, security, accountants, designers, engineers, etc. remain. The critical differences are largely legal and organizational: where everyone used to be an employee of the core firm, workers doing logistics now might be legally employees of XPO Logistics, DHL, or UPS; security guards legally employees of Securitas or G4S; caterers employees of Aramark or perhaps small local firms. Astoundingly, between 20 and 30 percent of line workers are typically contracted-in or temporary employees who are technically not employees of the factory owner. The proportion of unionized workers has also shrunk, though much less so in Europe. Where firms once did much component production in-house, they now buy in many parts, some design work, and a considerable volume of the software and electronics that now constitute about 20 percent of a vehicle's total cost. From a production point of view, these essentially legal changes have not impeded increased productivity. But from a macroeconomic point of view, or with an eye toward income inequality, the shift in the legal boundaries around workers is enormously consequential. What explains the shift and why does it matter?

Changes in corporate strategy and structure have fragmented formerly integrated production structures into legally distinct firms. In the Fordist era, firms sought stable oligopolies by concentrating control over physical production, and using trusts and patent pools to limit competition (Chandler 1990; Peinert 2020; Veblen 1904). Investment in large-scale, dedicated production equipment yielded huge productivity increases (Chandler 1990; Lazonick 1990). But profitability rested on the ability to run factories continuously. Continuous production in turn required stable sources of inputs and tractable labor. Vertical integration obtained the first.

But workers unionized in the face of increased assembly line speeds and decreased dignity, interrupting production. State-enforced compromises regulating conflict and enabling unions to claim part of firms' oligopoly profits emerged everywhere after two decades of turmoil and contestation. High and stably growing wages both increased and stabilized demand; stably increasing demand encouraged more investment in productivity enhancing physical capital and provided the profits to do so; more productivity generated fiscal room for expanding the income-stabilizing parts of the welfare state; security of life-cycle income encouraged workers to spend more now, generating new demand that supplemented high multiplier-effect investment (Aglietta 1979).

A wave of strikes in the late 1960s and 1970s shattered this compromise, lifting the wage share of GDP to unprecedented post-war levels and threatening management's control over the factory floor. The wage share of value added per manufacturing employee in the USA increased by 5.9 percentage points, from 1964 to 1974, in Germany 5.3 pp, in France, 7.1 pp, and in Japan, 12.2 pp.[1] Firms responded with public and private political strategies to reduce the wage share and regain control. Privately, consistent with Hertel-Fernandez's (this volume) rebooting of Claus Offe's argument about dual logics of collective action, firms

[1] European Commission, DG ECFIN, Ameco database Series ALCD0 at https://ec.europa.eu/economy_finance/ameco/user/serie/SelectSerie.cfm.

deconcentrated production and shed legal responsibility for their workers by de-merging, moving production offshore, contracting out (both on- and off-shore), dispersing production geographically, and adopting variants of the franchise format. European firms similarly dispersed production, especially to post-1989 Eastern Europe.

In the iconic Fordist automobile industry, employment moved steadily "south" to non-union "right-to-work" states in the US, then to Mexico, and finally to low-wage Asia (Murray and Schwartz 2019). This new spatial division of labor tended to leave more IP-intensive design and engineering activity behind in the old corporate locations. Foreign firms largely opened greenfield plants in US rural areas distant from the highly unionized upper Midwest. GM and Ford de-merged parts production into the independent firms Delphi and Visteon in 1999 and 2000. By 2008, both Delphi and Visteon had more Mexican than American employees (Klier and Rubenstein 2008: 51–52). Where the old GM had generated 70 percent of final value in-house, and Ford 50 percent, almost all automobile firms were down to 20 percent by the 2000s (Klier and Rubenstein 2008: 47). The major auto assemblers expelled lower-skill, labor-intensive activity into the newly emerging bottom layer of firms, while retaining the top two layers – IP-intensive design and capital-intensive assembly. In Naidu's (this volume) terms, firms retained the workers most responsive to labor discipline or efficiency wages while expelling those who could be exploited via various forms of labor market monopsony.

Finally, franchise firms, initially centered in the restaurant and hospitality sectors, organized a twenty-year legal campaign to remove antitrust laws banning vertical restraints and to establish that franchisees, not franchisors, were the legal employer of the growing pool of low-wage labor. The International Franchise Association won court, Federal Trade Commission, and National Labor Relations Board decisions that enabled franchisors to license brands and trademarks to their franchisees, to tightly control the nature of their operations, and to supply critical inputs while avoiding legal responsibility for their workforce (Callaci 2018). The contradictory combination of tight control and zero responsibility created incentives to expand the franchise model from the restaurant and hotel sectors to encompass the whole gamut of service sector industries. By 2017, roughly 3,400 franchisors licensed to 800,000 franchised establishments who directly employed 9 million people and accounted for about 5 percent of private sector US GDP. On a narrow definition of franchise (which, for example, excludes the hotel industry), 6 percent of US employees work in a franchised business: Weil (2014) estimates a much higher third of the labor force. For franchisors, the franchise model combines the profitability and administrative benefits of vertical integration without any of the related costs.

US politicians and the US state abetted these shifts by creating new legal forms and protections for IPRs and the new franchise model, while attacking unions. Ostensibly well-intentioned legal changes like the Employee Retirement Income Security Act 1974 forced firms to move their underfunded pension liabilities onto their books while also reining in union discretion over pension funds. By mandating equivalent benefits for all workers in a firm, ERISA reinforced firms' motivation to massively reduce direct employment of low-wage, low-skill workers in the face of rising health insurance and pension benefit costs. Health insurance for professional employees might amount to 10 percent of their total cost of employment, but for a $9 per-hour janitor it could easily double their total cost to the employer. Far better to fire the janitor and pay a cleaning service $10 per hour to bring that employee back in at $9 per hour without health insurance coverage. With respect to unionization, the 1947 Taft–Hartley Act had already effectively capped the unionized share of the private workforce. But administrations after 1980 made collective action increasingly difficult and often legally impossible. Combined with geographic dispersion, this gradually decreased union coverage. In the extreme case, antitrust law actually bans workers for "gig" economy firms like ride share or delivery services from unionizing because it construes workers as independent firms.

The US state also undertook a concerted, forty-year campaign to create and extend US IPR law globally in order to secure revenue streams for the US firms concentrating on production of information-rich goods while offshoring production (Drahos and Braithwaite 2002; Hurt 2010; Sell 2003). As early as the 1973–9 Tokyo GATT Round, the United States tried to export stronger IPR law to the rest of the world. This matured into the Trade-Related Aspects of Intellectual Property Rights (TRIPs) annex to the World Trade Organization agreement. The proposed, now defunct, Trans-Pacific Partnership (TPP) and Transatlantic Trade and Investment Partnership (TTIP) trade deals would also have strengthened patents and other IPRs. These agreements increased firms' desire to pare themselves down into pure IP holders in pursuit of IP-based monopoly profits.

Changes to US domestic antitrust and IP law also abetted increased concentration and monopoly power (Ansell and Gingrich, this volume; Christophers 2016; Peinert 2020). During the Fordist era, the reality or threat of antitrust litigation motivated "hi-tech" firms like ATT or IBM to restrain their IP licensing fees. Chicago school "law and economics" arguments blessing monopoly if consumer surplus increased influenced the Justice Department, the Federal Trade Commission, and some judges to wave through mergers that would have been banned in earlier decades (Christophers 2016; Rahman and Thelen, this volume). Legislation enabled the copyrighting or patenting of software in 1968, 1976, and 1980; strengthened trademark protection in 1988; and extended copyright on works for hire to 105 years in 1998. The Supreme Court expanded the scope of IP protection in novel ways, such as the 1980 *Diamond v. Chakrabarty* decision permitting patenting of genetically modified organisms and the 1998 affirmation of business process patents (important in finance) in *State Street Bank v. Signature Financial Services*.

Weaker antitrust enforcement also opened the door to *defensive*, largely horizontal concentration by second-layer firms seeking to preserve their profit streams. Product market concentration has grown markedly in the United States and elsewhere since the 1980s, increasing firms' mark-up power. This has four aspects: first, fewer firms overall; second, fewer firms for any given product market; third, among those firms, market power decisively shifted to those controlling a bottleneck in any given commodity chain or to those with robust IPRs, and finally, though the evidence here is more ambiguous, larger firms in any given sector tended to have larger profits (Autor et al. 2017; Manyika et al. 2018).

De Loecker and Eeckhout (2017, 2018; see also Benmelech et al. 2018; Grullon et al. 2019; Manyika et al. 2018; but Traina 2018 dissents) report that the average markup rose from 18 percent to 67 percent for publicly listed firms from 1980 to 2014. The largest increases occurred for the top 10 percent of firms by profit, and most of these increases occurred after the 2000 and 2008 recessions. Among them, IPR-based firms loomed largest, with tech firms obtaining margins twice the average level. Nine IPR-rich firms accounted for 47 percent of the expansion in margins among the S&P500 firms through 2018 (Kostin 2018: 14).

Thus, by the 2000s, Fordist-era vertically integrated firms had given way to an ideal typical tripartite structure, with significant concentration and skew-ness in profits and wages. Davis (2016) has labeled this process "Nikefication," arguing that firms were disappearing into a nexus of contracts, while employees in parallel were being "Uberized," that is turned into independent, on-demand contractors. Davis – for good reasons – concentrates on only one slice of what we should instead envision as a three-layer structure in order to understand macroeconomic dynamics. Nike-fied firms with high human capital, low employee headcount, and low physical capital certainly comprise the highly profitable top layer. But physical capital-intensive firms comprise the less profitable middle layer; high employee headcount, low physical and human capital-intensive firms comprise the bottom layer. And in the messy world of the real, many firms still blend two or even three layers, depending on the precise nature of the production process and lingering legal responsibilities. Where automobile firms and line workers emerged as the iconic firms and labor model of the Fordist era in people's imagination, tech firms and "gig work" constitute the imaginary iconic firms and labor model today. And indeed, the tech world does exhibit precisely this structure: consider the relations in the iPhone value chain among software firms Apple and Qualcomm in layer 1, manufacturing firms Intel and Corning in layer 2, and assembly firms like Hon Hai and Pegatron, in layer 3. The first group does nothing but design products, the second group produces parts for those products, and the last group assembles those parts.

But it is wrong to think that this ideal typical three-layer structure is limited to or only characterizes tech, and that these changes are caused by technological change exogenous to public and private policy choices. Rather, the three-layer structure pervades almost all parts of the US economy, and most people work for firms that simply do not provide benefits or good pay. Consider the very low-tech world of hotels (on-line booking is hardly high-tech, aside from web analytics). The major hotel brands neither own physical buildings nor directly employ most of the workers. Hilton (Hilton Worldwide Holdings), for example, has 15 carefully gradated and curated brands and 5,900 registered trademarks, but directly owned or leased only 71 of the 5,685 properties carrying those brands as of December 2018.[2] In short, it is an IP-rich firm whose major asset is its brands. Europe's largest hotel group, Accor, directly owned only 1.5 percent of the hotels carrying its brands, leased another 50 percent, and franchised out the remaining 48.5 percent in 2019. Globally, only about 20 percent of hotel buildings by value are owned by the brand adorning their façade.

The hotel buildings themselves are a large physical asset, variously owned by private equity firms, family trusts, and real estate investment trusts, and they constitute the middle layer in the new industrial structure. For example,

[2] Hilton Worldwide 2019 US Securities and Exchange Commission Form 10k filing, https://otp.tools.investis.com/clients/us/hilton_worldwide2/SEC/sec-show.aspx?FilingId=13217616&Cik=0001585689&Type=PDF&hasPdf=1. Hilton also managed 689 buildings on a contractual basis.

a different "Apple" – Apple Hospitality Real Estate Investment Trust – owns 242 hotels in the United States, largely under various and nominally competing Hilton and Marriott brands.[3] Apple Hospitality REIT's buildings are managed under contract by hotel management firms. These management firms either directly employ or contract in labor from third-layer firms like Hospitality Services Group or the GHJC Group. These jobs can be gig-like but are more often standard employment relations. Thus, even a low-tech sector like hotels has a tripartite division combining firms specializing in IP production, firms holding physical capital, and firms supplying low-skill labor power, with coordination verging on de facto managerial control coming from the top layer.

Table 8.1 shows the evolution of Hilton Hotels/Hilton Worldwide from an owner-operator of hotel rooms whose revenues largely derived from rooms it directly owned or leased to a brand owner whose revenues derived largely from franchising. The changing balance between intangible assets and fixed assets in the form of property, plant, and equipment – that is, buildings – shows a sharp rise as of the 1990s (unfortunately there are no data for the 1980s). Similarly, the 1966 annual report does not have data on the relative shares of owned versus franchised rooms. But the report for that year gives the impression that Hilton directly owned or leased the majority of rooms carrying its sole brand at that time. Franchising began in 1966 under the Statler-Hilton label, with nine hotels in operation or under construction, as compared to the thirty hotels Hilton owned outright. The data do show a steady decline in the share of owned as opposed to franchised rooms. That said, franchise revenues were trivial until the end of the 1990s, and the decisive turn toward an "asset-light" model did not occur until after the Blackstone group took a controlling stake in Hilton when it shifted from private to public ownership. If this is a general phenomenon, it signals a significant consequence of financialization.

Why does this tripartite structure distribute profits across firms in ways that inhibit investment and aggravate income inequality?

8.2 WHO GETS WHAT? PROFITS IN TWO ERAS

The macroeconomic and political significance of this tripartite structure flows from the *kind of firms* capturing the bulk of profit more so than the

[3] Apple Hospitality REIT 2019 US Securities and Exchange Commission Form 10k filing, https://ir.applehospitalityreit.com/SEC_Filings. Apple Hospitality REIT has no relationship to Apple Computer.

TABLE 8.1 *Owned, managed and franchised shares of rooms and revenues for all Hilton Hotel brands, and ratio of all intangible assets to property, plant and equipment, various dates*[*]

		1966	1978	1988	1999	2006	2013	2018
Rooms	Owned[**]	–	45.3%	28.5%	21.7%	18.7%	9.1%	2.4%
	Managed	–	11.6%	14.0%	17.3%	19.4%	22.2%	23.6%
	Franchised	–	43.1%	57.5%	61.0%	61.2%	68.8%	74.0%
Revenues	Owned[**]	99.1%	97.1%	95.4%	85.5%	59.6%	23.7%	16.7%
	Managed	0.8%	1.7%	2.3%	5.6%^	8.4%^	81.8%^	83.0%^
	Franchised	0.1%	1.2%	2.3%				
		1966	1973	1996	1999	2006	2013	2018
Ratio of intangibles to PPE		1.0%	1.4%	22.7%	48.2%	100%	124%	1,334%

[*] May not sum to 100 because of minor omitted revenue sources
[**] Includes leased buildings and joint ventures
^ Disaggregated data unavailable after 1995
Source: Author calculations from Hilton Hotels/Hilton Worldwide SEC 10 k reports and annual reports and from WRDS Compustat data

concentration of profit itself. Profits were highly unequally distributed across publicly listed American firms in both broad eras. The gini index for cumulative gross profits for the 7,982 publicly listed US firms existing from 1950 to 1980 was 0.876; the gini for cumulative gross profits for the 19,678 publicly listed firms existing from 1992 to 2017 was 0.922.[4] By contrast, the gini index for US household pretax income inequality in 2017 was 0.48. The slight increase in the corporate profit gini in the transition from Fordism matters less than the changing nature of the firms capturing those profits. Top-layer, IPR-rich firms with relatively smaller physical capital and employee headcounts capture high profit volumes. Their low marginal propensity to invest and the smaller number of workers to whom they redistribute part of their profits depresses both aggregate investment and wage income (Christophers 2016; Haskel and Westlake 2017; Schwartz 2016). The next paragraphs present data to support the analysis of investment and consumption in subsequent sections.

The following figures highlight three major changes from the Fordist to the current era: profits have dramatically shifted toward sectors characterized by robust IPRs, as well as toward finance, which itself is increasingly an IP sector (Figure 8.1) (Schwartz 2017). Second, even in the context of a general decline in capex as a percent of gross profit, current high-profit sectors tend to transform much less of their gross profit into capital expenditure (capex; Figures 8.2 and 8.3). Third, the concentration of profits into IPR firms means profit is now concentrated into firms that do relatively little capex in relation to their share of profits (Figure 8.4).

Figures 8.1–8.4 show only the top 100 firms among all firms listed in Compustat from 1961 to 1965 and 2013 to 2017. These arguably are the peak of the Fordist and knowledge economy eras.[5] The top 100 matter macroeconomically because they capture the bulk of profits – over 40 percent in each era – and do a significant but diverging share of capex – 40.5 percent and 34 percent, respectively. Most of the remaining 99 percent have little in the way of excess profit to invest and thus contribute

[4] All data on profits, employee headcount, and capital expenditure are from WRDS *Compustat*, unless otherwise noted. Ginis calculated only for firms with positive net profits. Profitable N = 7,756 out of 7,982 firms, 1950–80; N = 11,038 out of 19,678 firms, 1992–2017. While Compustat only has data on listed firms, Manyika et al. (2018) suggest similar levels of concentration including privately held firms.

[5] Firms are characterized into sectors by their main activity, with one exception. Integrated manufacturing refers to firms that were "hi-tech" in the 1950 to 1980 era, like Boeing, Sperry, and RCA. They were and largely remain relatively vertically integrated firms with large physical capital footprints and high head counts. Their "hi-tech" status in the earlier period reflects connections to the defense establishment.

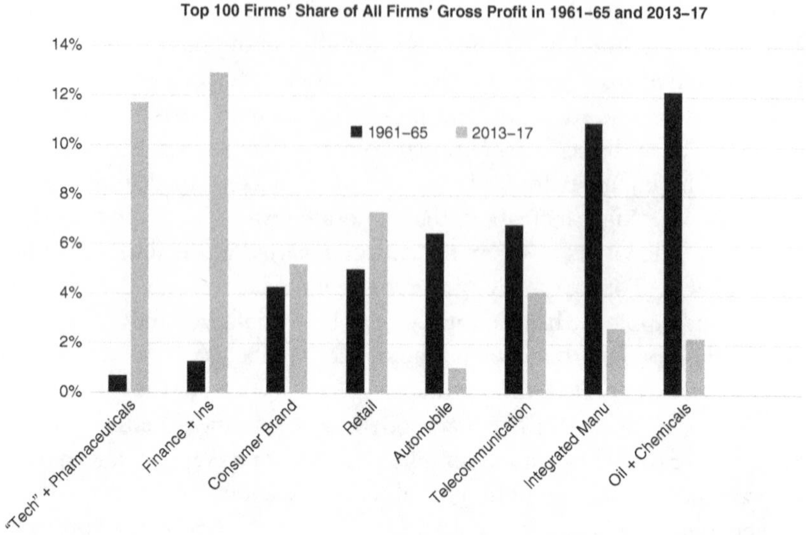

Top 100 Firms' Share of All Firms' Gross Profit in 1961–65 and 2013–17
14%
12%
10%
8%
6%
4%
2%
0%
1961–65
2013–17
"Tech" + Pharmaceuticals
Finance + Ins
Consumer Brand
Retail
Automobile
Telecommunication
Integrated Manu
Oil + Chemicals

FIGURE 8.1 Top 100 firms' share of all firms' gross profit in 1961–1965 and 2013–2017
Note: By sector, (%). Ranked by 1961–65 Profit Share. "Tech" = hardware and software.
Source: Author calculation from Compustat

Top 100 Firms' Share of All Firms' Gross Profit and Capital Expenditure, 1961–65
18%
16%
14%
12%
10%
8%
6%
4%
2%
0%
1961–65 Gross profit
1961–65 Capex
"Tech" + Pharmaceuticals
Finance + Ins
Consumer Brand
Retail
Automobile
Telecommunications
Integrated Manu
Oil + Chemicals

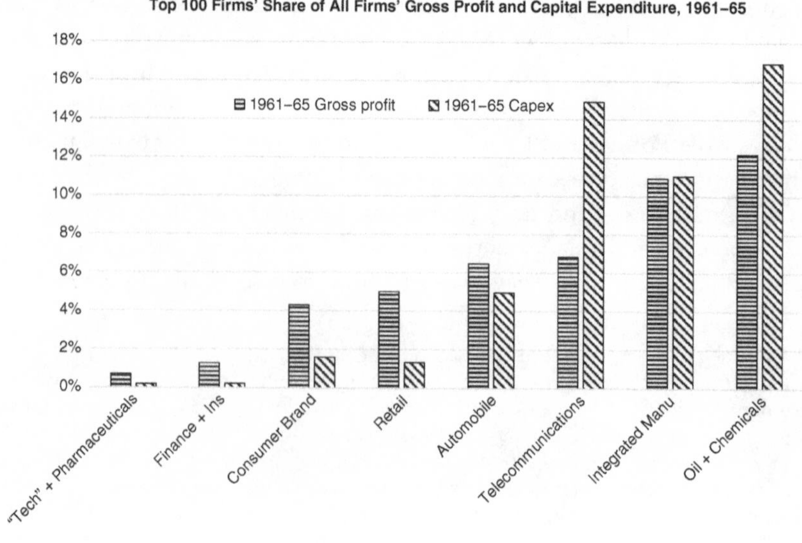

FIGURE 8.2 Top 100 firms' share of all firms' gross profit and capital expenditure, 1961–1965
Note: By sector (%). "Tech" = hardware and software.
Source: Author calculation from Compustat

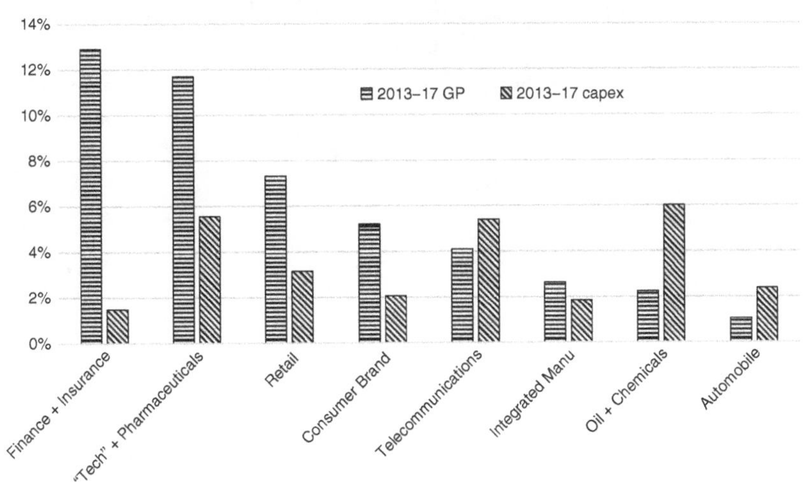

FIGURE 8.3 Top 100 firms' share of all firms' gross profit and capital expenditure, 2013–2017
Note: "Tech" = hardware and software.
Source: Author calculation from Compustat

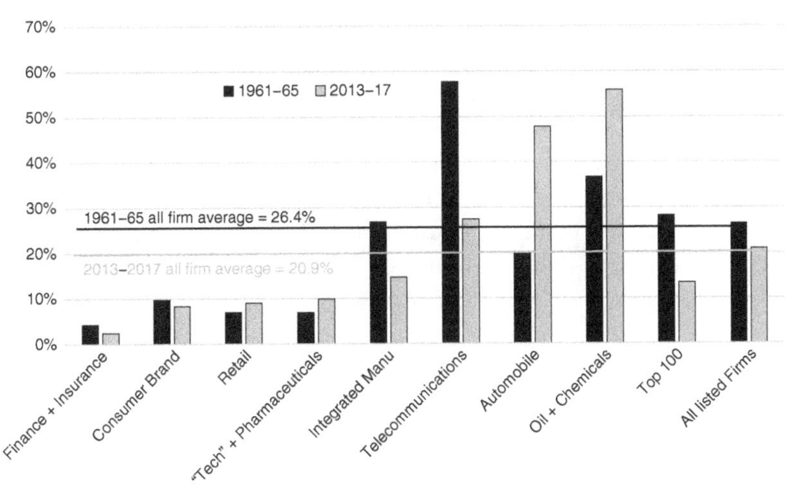

FIGURE 8.4 Top 100 firms' capital expenditure as a percentage of gross profit by sector, 1961–1965 versus 2013–2017 (%)
Note: Ranked by 2013–17 ratio. "Tech" = hardware and software.
Source: Author calculation from Compustat

relatively little to net investment. As Bessembinder (2018) shows, from 1926 to 2016, out of the remaining 99 percent of listed US firms, half did not cover their cost of capital, defined generously as the return on the one-month Treasury bill, while the other half generated only minimal returns over the Treasury bill. By contrast, the top 1.3 percent of firms accounted for half of all returns in excess of the one-month Treasury bill.

Figure 8.1, of course, shows the shift in the location of gross profit from the old Fordist oil-plus-manufacturing complex toward the new IPR-plus-finance complex. Figures 8.2 and 8.3 show that while the profit share of tech, pharmaceuticals, and finance has risen sharply, their propensity to reinvest those profits as capital expenditures remains low. By contrast, the integrated manufacturing firms surviving to 2013–17 invest a relatively large share of their reduced profits. Figure 8.4 shows that overall, capex as a share of gross profit by the top 100 firms has fallen by roughly half. What is more significant though, is that in the earlier era both the top 100 firms in aggregate and the firms capturing the most profit tended to reinvest that profit as capex at rates above the average listed firm (black line), while today the top 100 and the firms capturing the most profit do capex at rates below the average firm (grey line). Consequently, the average age of US private fixed capital has gradually risen from nineteen to twenty-three years, between 1981 and 2018, despite huge investments in information and communication technology (*Wall Street Journal*, 2019). Why?

While tech firms accounted for 28 percent of business capex in 2018 (Kostin 2018: 28, 54, 56–57), firms whose profits derive from IPR-based monopolies face less pressure to invest or innovate because competitors are effectively locked out of their markets. Moreover, investment in the form of R&D by these firms largely means hiring more humans. Tech and financial firms – and within that group a very few firms – simultaneously accounted for 40 percent of 2018 share buybacks, which absolutely exceeded capex; combined, buybacks and dividends exceeded capex plus R&D. Lazonick (2017), and more generally the financialization literature, has criticized firms in the aggregate for prioritizing buybacks over investment, but the problem is actually limited to a narrow slice of firms. Firms without significant profits cannot do significant buybacks.

Meanwhile, profit and demand realities hobble physical capital-based firms that might do investment with high Keynesian multipliers. They are relatively starved of profits and fear creating excess capacity in a slow-growth environment. Consider the world from their point of view: most developed-country markets in the 2000s were growing at about the rate of population growth, roughly 1 percent per year, and even formerly dynamic sectors like smartphones slowed markedly after 2016. The big manufacturing firms in the top 100 or 200 firms can generate about 2 to 3 percent productivity growth each year simply through process engineering. This lowers the incentive to invest in new capacity. Replace depreciated capital? Yes. Create even greater excess capacity? No. Indeed, in North America, the automobile industry shed about 15 percent of capacity after 2010 in order to bring supply and demand into rough balance. By contrast, Europe's automobile sector still had roughly 15 percent excess capacity and China's roughly 25 percent in 2018. Similarly, major semiconductor firms – one of the most capital-intensive production processes in the world – moderated investment after 2010 to avoid excess capacity.

Figure 8.1 also shows the massive shift toward finance, which is generally not considered an IPR sector.[6] Space constraints prohibit full exposition of the voluminous financialization literature and why finance should be considered as an IPR sector (but see Schwartz 2017). The more general trends described here subsume "financialization" for three reasons. First, the sector exhibits the same three-layer structure as other IPR sectors, with profits highly concentrated at the top; the gini for cumulative profits in the financial sector is 0.95 for both gross and net income, 1992 to 2017. Those top firms capture the bulk of profits by selling bespoke derivatives and managing IPOs and investment funds (Braun, this volume). Small teams with high human capital and an ICT and software heavy production process generate those derivatives, much as in software and biotech (Bernstein 2008). Second, generic, easily copied derivatives make little money. But subsequent to a 1998 federal court decision permitting patenting of mathematical and business algorithms, investment banks increasingly rely on Class 705 business process patents to protect new derivatives and processes. In 2014, for example, Bank of America filed roughly the same number of successful US patents as Novartis, Rolls Royce, or MIT, and JP Morgan as many as Genentech or Siemens.[7]

Third, finance and the tech world are organically connected. Tech IPOs have been among the largest IPOs in the past two decades. Investment

[6] Readers might ask why Figure 8.1 shows a 12.9% cumulative gross profit share for finance when the figure most commonly cited is 40%. First, this is only firms in the top 100. Second, the 40% data point is *net domestic* income as defined in the national accounting statistics. The 12.9% data point is top 100 financial firms' share of *gross global* profits for US firms in the Compustat database. Gross global profits are the relevant metric in relation to investment behavior affecting the global economy.

[7] US Patent and Trademark Organization, "Patenting by organization, 2014," www.uspto.gov/web/offices/ac/ido/oeip/taf/topo_14.htm.

banks typically charge a 7 to 8 percent commission for IPOs, making tech IPOs a major revenue source (Ghosh 2017). These IPOs, of course, are also how the venture capital slice of finance captures profit and exits its positions. High-profit financial firms are also are a conduit for other actors' money. The outsized profits that IPR firms capture need to be recycled in some form if they are not committed to productive investment. These funds account for a significant share of the funds translated into rising indebtedness for governments and households, given the inversion of the old pattern where households lent to firms. But even if we separate finance from the IPR sectors, which would be the weaker case, the core macroeconomic problem remains: finance underinvests relative to its profit share. The IPR sectors' total gross profit somewhat exceeds that of finance, so if the financial share of profit is a problem, then *pari passu* so is the IPR sectors' share because of their common low marginal propensity for capex.

The overall point here is not that investment has seen a Great Depression–style collapse, but rather that the shift of profits toward firms with a lower propensity to invest drives the secular decline in gross and net fixed capital formation. Gross fixed capital formation in the United States fell from 23.2 percent to 20.6 percent of GDP, between 1980 and 2017. Net investment drives new growth, but private sector *net* domestic investment fell from 29.8 percent to 15.6 percent of gross private domestic investment.[8] Similar trends held in most other advanced economies. These profits have to go somewhere, and the counterpart to this lower propensity to invest is rising corporate cash hoards disproportionately held by IPR-rich firms (Chen et al. 2017). Microsoft, for example, would be the eighth largest holder of US Treasury bonds if it were a country; Apple has been described by the *Economist* magazine as an investment bank that also makes phones.

8.3 RISING WAGE INEQUALITY

The concentration of profits into low-headcount, IPR-rich firms also directly and indirectly affects income distribution, and through that growth and politics. The top 100 firms by cumulative profit 1961 to 1965 accounted for 49.8 percent of profits and 42.1 percent of employment for listed firms, a ratio of 1.18, but in 2013 to 2017 they accounted

[8] Department of Commerce, Bureau of Economic Analysis, www.bea.gov/data/investment-fixed-assets.

for 49.4 percent of profits and at most 32.1 percent of employment, a ratio of 1.54. IPR firms and finance accounted for 29.8 percent of total profits but only 11.9 percent of all employees, a ratio of 2.50.

This matters because firms with bigger profits pay higher wages. Wages increasingly depend on who you work for in the three-layer economy, not what you do. Barth et al. (2014; see also Song et al. 2019 and Autor 2019), show that wage dispersion across firms rather than within firms accounts for much of rising income inequality in the United States. The higher profitability of IPR-rich firms flows over into high wages, with workers capturing between thirty and forty-two cents of every dollar of patent-generated surplus as higher earnings, and with longer-serving workers (who are likely to be higher paid) disproportionately benefiting (Berger et al. 2019: 3; Kline et al. 2019: 1346–7). In the past, unionization, sociological factors, and the need for continuous production dispersed oligopoly profits across a wider range of employees. The legal trifurcation of employment instead concentrates profit redistribution onto a much smaller employee footprint.

Firms with weak IPRs and weak profits held down wage costs by dispersing production into rural, nonunion US labor markets where they could exercise monopsony power, and by moving production to Asia (see Moretti 2012; Naidu, this volume; Tijdens and van Klaveren 2011). Going from a very competitive to a highly concentrated job market is associated with a 15 to 25 percent decline in wages overall (Azar et al. 2020), while increased concentration in the service sector accounts for roughly a third of the decline of the labor share of revenue after 1982 (Autor et al. 2017). Both geographic shifts blocked part of the old manufacturing path to a stable middle-class life (Autor 2019).

Franchising also truncates the old pathways into the lower levels of the bourgeoisie, inhibiting new firm formation (Akcigit and Ates 2019b; Hathaway and Litan 2014). While franchising lowers the probability of failure in starting a business, it also removes much of the "residual claim" that owners used to exercise. The franchise phenomenon now encompasses traditional upwardly mobile blue-collar occupations like home repair, plumbing, and electrical work. Franchising effectively turns owners into de facto managers with no stock options.

The franchise phenomenon is both iconic and generic of the new economy. It encompasses the separation of IP from production, the fissuring of legal responsibility, and the decapitation of the small-business class. This decapitation turns the old small, local business class into ferocious advocates for a politics of labor repression and limited welfare, because the only production input they control in a franchise is labor costs. Franchising also abets a fine-grained segmentation of consumer identities that limits collective action. Finally, many franchised brands are at least partially owned by private equity firms. This also limits investment, as private equity is loath to make fixed investments and has a propensity for loading up the firms they own with debt.

The concentration of profits into IPR firms with small headcounts thus helps depress the labor share of GDP. As with investment, this does not cause a complete collapse of consumption. But it dampens growth in consumption. Meanwhile increased precarity and the truncation of upward mobility options for non-college educated and/or entrepreneurial males undoubtedly creates a political opening for antiestablishment politics based on racial and migration-related resentments.

8.4 AMERICAN EXCEPTIONALISM?

Is this a uniquely American story reflecting, among other things, its highly racialized politics (Thurston, this volume), the sheer size of its economy, and the weakness of its labor movement (Hertel-Fernandez, this volume)? The United States is simultaneously exceptional and not. Comparative political economy typically sins by studying national political economies as if they existed in isolation aside from homogenous trade or financial flows. The US economy is part of a global division of labor in which the three-layer production structure is replicated both internal to national economies and globally. A global division of labor implies heterogeneity across national and regional economies in terms of what kinds of goods are produced, and how they are produced (Schwartz 2007).

The concentration of physical capital-intensive export production in Germany, Japan, and Korea, and of labor-intensive export production in China and South Asia is the global version of the US internal tripartite production structure, complete with the uneven distribution of profits and exploitation of labor found in the United States. Table 8.2 shows the internal share of profits by sector for the US, German, and Japanese firms that have ever appeared on the Forbes Global 2000 list from 2006 to 2020 (N = 4039), and highlights the salience of automobile and related heavy industrial production in Germany and Japan versus the salience of the IPR and finance sectors in the United States. America is exceptional in this global division of labor because it provides the dominant international currency, and thus necessarily runs a current account deficit. In turn, other countries tolerate this deficit precisely because the extreme

TABLE 8.2 *Eight largest sectors in Forbes Global 2000 by share of cumulative profits in Germany, Japan, and the USA, 2005 to 2019 (%)*

USA		Germany		Japan	
Tech-hardware	14.0%	Autos-heavy	31.4%	Autos-heavy	23.0%
Financials	13.2%	Chemicals	14.3%	Financials	12.1%
Consumer Branded	8.7%	Insurance	11.9%	Retail	9.8%
Oil Sector	8.6%	*Tech-hardware**	8.5%	Telecoms	8.0%
Tech-software	7.8%	Utilities	6.1%	Transport	5.4%
Pharma & biotech	7.4%	*Tech-software***	4.2%	Financials-misc.	4.9%
Retail	6.7%	Transport	4.0%	*Consumer Branded*	4.7%
Telecoms	5.0%	*Consumer Branded*	3.8%	*Tech-hardware*	4.2%
IPR share of all US firms in the FG2k	37.9	... German ...	16.4	... Japanese ...	8.9

Note: IPR sectors in *italics*.
* Mostly (78%) Siemens ** Entirely SAP
Sector names are aggregated from FG2k industry labels:
Tech-hardware = semiconductors, electronics, computer storage devices, technology hardware and equipment, computer hardware (includes Apple)
Finance = banks-major, banks-regional, investment services
Tech-software = software & programming, software & services, computer services
Autos-heavy = auto and truck manufacturers and parts producers, and heavy equipment producers
Source: Author's calculation from Forbes Global 2000 data, various years

concentration of highly profitable IPR-rich firms in the US economy both validates their accumulation of dollar-denominated assets and enables them to export (Schwartz 2019).

The United States also is exceptional in the weakness of its labor movement and stratification of its welfare state. But employment precarity has increased across the rich OECD, with similar political consequences, as firms all try to pursue the same profit strategies. "Fissuring" has happened in Europe via the proliferation of temporary or Hartz IV–type jobs, and through outsourcing to Eastern Europe (Goldschmidt and Schmieder 2017). Many of these jobs are what Autor (2019) calls "last mile" jobs – low wage service sector work like delivery, catering, or personal services in urban areas. Immigrants often bring lower wage norms into this sector. The OECD (2015: 144–46) estimates that the share of nonstandard jobs in total employment increased from 21 to 34 percent in France, 25 to 39 percent in Germany, and 29 to 40 percent in Italy from 1985 to 2013; Gordon (2017) estimates that nonstandard employment rose from 15 to 38 percent in Japan, between 1982 and 2014. Women, youth, and minorities are typically in nonstandard employment in all these countries.

All these countries still have broader social protection for nonstandard workers though, easing but not eliminating the harshness of precarity. The contrast is sharply visible in the US health-care sector, which is rife with monopoly, has double the per capita cost of other rich countries' systems, and still does not manage to cover everyone or prevent financial hardship. In short, the US economy looks different because relatively speaking it has a larger proportion of "apex" firms, a harsher labor-relations system, and a stratified welfare state. But it is not unique in terms of general trends.

CONCLUSION

The US political economy today exhibits slow growth and rising income inequality. These do not directly cause the racial and gender status anxiety that drives much antiestablishment political fervor; they do contribute to and magnify that fervor. Had incomes risen across the entire US population, and had traditional routes to upward mobility persisted, the share of the population willing to engage in nihilistic politics would likely be smaller. The shift in corporate strategy and thus structure from pursuit of oligopoly profits via control over physical capital embedded in large, vertically integrated firms to the pursuit of monopoly profit through control over IPRs embedded in a vertically disintegrated production chain is the main cause for decreased investment, which contributes to slower growth, and for a concentration of excess profits over a smaller employee footprint, which contributes to rising income inequality. Finally, the profits from IPRs are easily transferred to tax havens, limiting fiscal responses to slow growth and stagnant incomes in the bottom 60 percent of the population. All these features depress aggregate demand. While the peculiar nature of IPRs as intangible assets matters (Haskel and Westlake 2017), so does industrial organization in the deployment of those assets.

Piore and Sabel's 1984 classic argued that rich countries facing a second industrial divide might find both stability and equality by disintegrating production. But Piore and Sable assumed some equality among firms in those chains. Instead, disintegration in the context of the franchise model has generated a less pleasant world of slower growth, rising inequality, and recurrent financial crisis. Rising inequality – Piore and Sabel's pessimistic "Victorian" scenario of a one-third, one-third, one-third society – has emerged from the concentration of profits into low-headcount, IPR-rich firms. Financial crises themselves reflect the effects of concentrated profit. Profits arriving as cash need to be transformed into assets, fueling speculation and asset bubbles. Moreover, as all financial assets necessarily have corresponding liabilities, the increased debt accrued by income-short consumers trying to maintain a given lifestyle, or accrued by states attempting to sustain spending in the face of weak revenue growth creates additional barriers to growth (Streeck 2014). A tsunami of profit flowing into a limited number of passive investment channels necessarily produces a backwash of unsustainable debt and overpriced positional goods.

These problems are not intractable, but implementing solutions requires the kind of sustained political movement that might only just be emerging, though only a fool would venture predictions during the COVID-19 pandemic and after the 2020 US election produced a closely divided government. Administratively simple but politically difficult solutions like higher minimum wages, stronger antitrust enforcement, more stringent criteria for granting IPRs with shorter terms, universal access to health care, and recognition that lead firms in commodity chains have some responsibility for workers in the bottom tier would go a long way toward fixing the problems limned here. In the 1930s, some firms seem to have grasped the connection between broader prosperity and their own profitability (Piore and Sabel 1984; Swenson 2002; van der Pijl 1984). The subsequent wartime experience necessitated and validated a massive expansion of state control over the economy and provision of social policy. Today, lead firms' reliance on global rather than national markets and their use of commoditized inputs orients their political behavior toward litigation and lobbying to reinforce their IPRs (Bessen 2016). In short, the major economic problem the United States faces today is not just concentration of profits – which characterizes both the Fordist and current era – but concentration into specific kinds of politically powerful firms subsequent to a legal fissuring of production activities and labor forces. It remains to be seen if a COVID-enforced deglobalization reorients their political preferences.

9

Asset Manager Capitalism as a Corporate Governance Regime

Benjamin Braun

INTRODUCTION

For too long, students of the political economy of corporate governance have been enthralled by the language of ownership and control. This language stems from Berle and Means (1932), who observed that trust-busting policies and the diversification of robber-baron fortunes had dispersed stock ownership in the United States, while concentrating corporate control in the hands of a small class of managers.[1] Jensen and Meckling's (1976) agency theory, while reiterating the notions of shareholder dispersion and weakness, conceptualized shareholders as principals – the only actors with a strong material interest in the economic performance of the corporation. Offering a simple solution to what Berle and Means had considered a complex political problem, agency theory reduced corporate governance to the problem of protecting outside minority shareholders against "expropriation" by insiders, namely corporate managers and workers (La Porta et al. 2000: 4). Notwithstanding

Work on this paper began in 2015 and I have since accumulated many debts. Earlier drafts were presented at the Max Planck Institute for the Study of Societies, the Watson Institute at Brown University, the Center for European Studies at Harvard University, and at the Institute for Advanced Study in Princeton. For helpful comments, I am indebted to Ruth Aguilera, Lucio Baccaro, Jens Beckert, Gordon Clark, Sahil Dutta, Jan Fichtner, Peter Hall, Lena Lavinas, Perry Mehrling, Suresh Naidu, Herman Mark Schwartz, David Soskice, Cornelia Woll, Nick Ziegler and, especially, the conveners of the American Political Economy project, Jacob Hacker, Alexander Hertel-Fernandez, Paul Pierson, and Kathy Thelen.

[1] Among others, Marx (1981 [1894]), Hilferding (1985 [1910]), and Veblen (1923) had already written extensively about the relationship between finance capital and corporate ownership and control.

the political chasm between these two pairs of authors – New Deal liberals versus pro-market libertarians – the field of corporate governance melded these ideas into a single Berle-Means-Jensen-Meckling (BM-JM) ontology – the United States as a society in which shareholders, while dispersed and weak, are the owners and principals of the corporation. This ontology underpins "shareholder primacy" (or "shareholder value"), which in the late twentieth century emerged as the dominant corporate governance regime. This regime was geared toward three goals: ensuring a market for corporate control, allowing shareholders to monitor managerial performance, and aligning the material interests of managers with those of shareholders (Fourcade and Khurana 2017: 355). So complete was its victory that two prominent legal scholars announced the "[t]he triumph of the shareholder-oriented model of the corporation" and the "end of history for corporate law" (Hansmann and Kraakman 2001: 468).

When history resumed its course, it wrong-footed many students of corporate governance. Comparative political economy (CPE) scholars, while adding important institutional detail, have largely taken the BM-JM ontology for granted, assuming dispersed, weak (and impatient) shareholder-principals (Aguilera and Jackson 2003; Gourevitch and Shinn 2005; Hall and Soskice 2001; Roe 1994).[2] Since Hansmann and Kraakman's (and Hall and Soskice's) writing, however, the reconcentration of US stock ownership has dramatically accelerated (Fichtner et al. 2017). Today, three asset managers – Vanguard, BlackRock, and State Street Global Advisors – together hold more than 20 percent of the shares of the average S&P 500 company (Backus et al. 2020: 19). Today, the investment chain is dominated by for-profit asset management firms rather than by the pension funds that shaped the CPE literature's perception of the shareholder primacy regime (see Figure 9.1). While "asset manager" comprises "alternative" asset managers – namely, hedge, private equity, and venture capital funds – the bulk of capital is invested via mutual funds and exchange-traded traded funds, which are the focus of this chapter.[3] My central argument is that this new "asset manager capitalism" constitutes a distinct corporate governance regime.

Four hallmarks characterize this new corporate governance regime. First, US stock ownership is *concentrated* in the hands of giant asset managers. Second, due to the size of their stakes, asset managers are, in

[2] For a notable exception, see Davis (2008).

[3] Private equity and venture capital funds are excluded by this chapter's focus on holdings in *listed* companies.

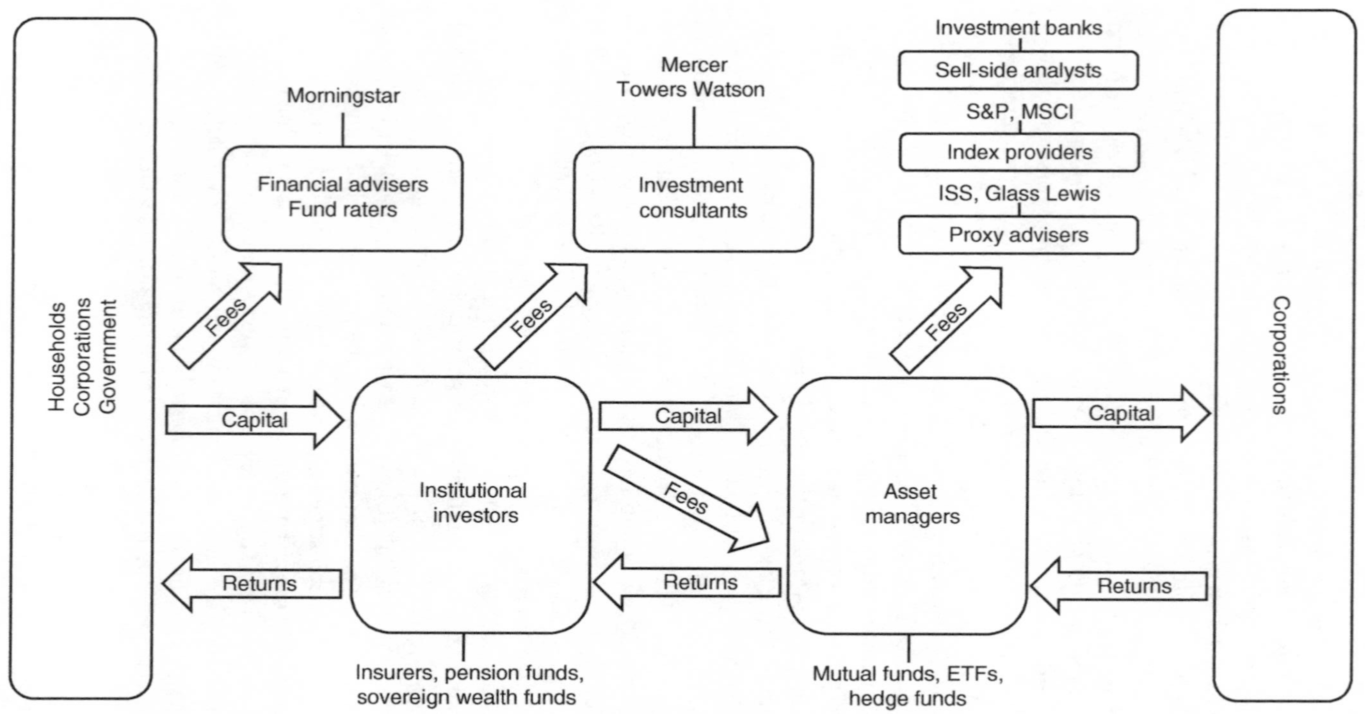

FIGURE 9.1 The equity investment chain

principle, *strong* shareholders with considerable control over corporate management. While this divergence from "dispersed and weak" alone would require corporate governance scholars to rekindle their conceptual toolkit, two additional features distinguish asset manager capitalism from previous corporate governance regimes. The third hallmark is that large asset managers are "universal owners" that hold fully *diversified* portfolios (Hawley and Williams 2000). Finally, as for-profit intermediaries with a fee-based business model, asset managers hold *no direct economic interest* in their portfolio companies. Whereas under the shareholder primacy regime the dominant shareholders sought to maximize the stock market value of specific firms, under asset manager capitalism the dominant shareholders are incentivized to maximize their assets under management. Clearly, the BM-JM ontology does not map onto this new landscape (Gilson and Gordon 2013).

The chapter is organized as follows. The next section gives a big-picture overview of the evolution of US stock ownership and corporate governance regimes. The third section traces the policies and economic developments behind the growth of the asset management sector since the Revenue Act of 1936. The next section takes a critical look at the promise of universal ownership and at assets managers' economic interests. The fifth section zooms in on the economic and political power of asset managers at the firm, sectoral, and macroeconomic levels, with a focus on the relationship between asset manager capitalism and inequality. The conclusion highlights broader implications for corporate governance studies and comparative political economy.

CORPORATE GOVERNANCE REGIMES IN HISTORICAL PERSPECTIVE

The comparative political economy and corporate finance literatures used to consider it "one of the best established stylized facts" that "ownership of large listed companies is dispersed ... in the U.S. and concentrated in most other countries" (Franks et al. 2008: 4009). This stylized fact does not hold anymore. Charting the historical development of US stock ownership concentration no longer yields an L-shaped curve, but a U-shaped one. A period of high-concentration in the late nineteenth century gave way to a period of highly dispersed share ownership in the mid-twentieth century, which has been followed by a long (and ongoing) period of reconcentration. The condensed overview presented in this section and summarized in Table 9.1 compares four successive corporate governance

TABLE 9.1 *Stock ownership, corporate governance regimes, and macro regimes*

Main Shareholders	Robber Barons	Households	Pension Funds	Asset Managers
Concentration of **ownership**	High	Low	Medium	High
Control of shareholders	Strong	Weak: exit	Medium: exit or voice	Potentially strong: voice, no exit
Portfolio **diversification**	Low	Low	Medium	High (indexed)
Interest in firms	High	High	Medium	Low
Corp Gov Regime	Finance capitalism	Managerialism	Shareholder primacy	Asset manager capitalism
Macro Regime	Monopoly capitalism	Fordism	Privatized Keynesianism	Asset manager capitalism

regimes across four shareholder-related dimensions. Preparing the ground for the discussion of macro-level implications, the periodization also relates corporate governance regimes to each period's growth regime.[4]

By the end of the nineteenth century, corporate America was largely owned and controlled by a handful of corporations and banks, in turn owned and controlled by the "blockholder oligarchy" formed by figures such as J. P. Morgan, Andrew Carnegie, and John D. Rockefeller (Gourevitch and Shinn 2005: 244). Best captured by Hilferding's (1985 [1910]) concept of "finance capitalism," this corporate governance regime was characterized by concentrated stock ownership and strong control, exercised directly by owner-managers or indirectly via financial conglomerates. The latter's portfolios were undiversified, giving them a strong stake in the fortunes of their corporate empires.[5] The investment-led growth regime of the period around 1900 is best captured by the concept of "monopoly capitalism" (Baran and Sweezy 1966).

Several factors contributed to the dissolution of the concentrated ownership structure of the Gilded Age, including Progressive Era antitrust laws, war-related federal taxes forcing robber barons to sell shares for cash, and the stock market boom of the 1920s, which turned millions into stockholders (Ott 2011). By 1945, households held 94 percent of US corporate equity (Figure 9.2).[6] The weakness of these dispersed shareholders concentrated power in the hands of the managers of increasingly large corporations, giving rise to the corporate governance regime of "managerialism" (Chandler 1977). At the macro level, managerialism, strong trade unions, Keynesian macroeconomic management, and the Bretton Woods system coalesced into the growth regime of "Fordism" (Aglietta 1979).

Whereas stock ownership concentration in the late nineteenth century was propelled by industrial monopolization, the main drivers of concentration in the twentieth and twenty-first centuries were developments within the investment chain. The first development was the emergence and growth of capital-pooling institutional investors, notably pension

[4] "Growth regime" is used here in the tradition of "modes of regulation" (Aglietta 1979) and "regimes of accumulation" (Kotz et al. 1994), both of which comprise more than corporate governance arrangements.

[5] Gourevitch and Shinn (2005: 243) note that this "blockholder trust model ... made the United States look rather like Germany at the turn of the last century." What Morgan and Carnegie were to the former, Deutsche Bank and Allianz were to the latter (Windolf and Beyer 1996).

[6] This dispersion was never even across the wealth distribution. US share ownership was, and is, concentrated at the top (Figure 9.5).

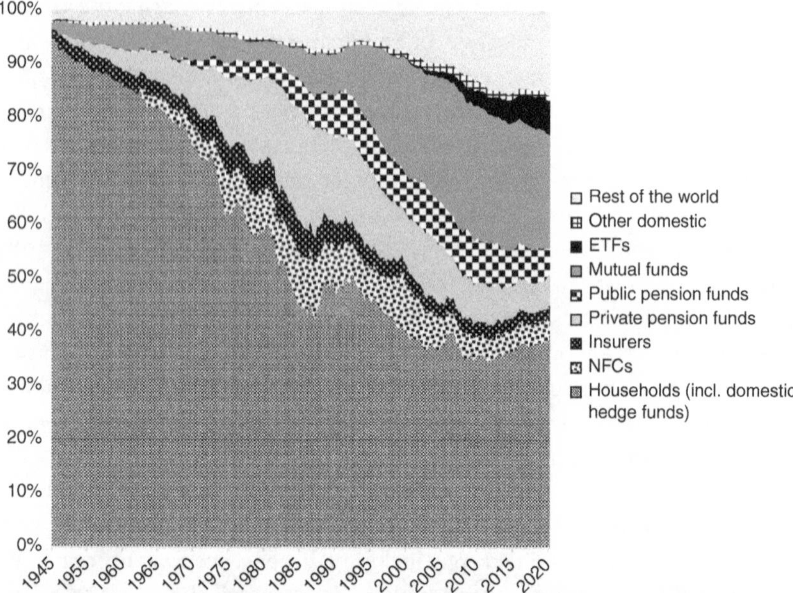

FIGURE 9.2 The structure of US corporate equity ownership, 1945–2020
Note on types of equity: The data comprises equity issued by US-listed foreign corporations (21 percent of the total) and closely held equity (15 percent of the remaining *domestic* equity). The total dollar value of US corporate equity by year-end 2019 was USD 55 trillion.
Note on holders of equity: The recent expansion of the categories "rest of the world" and "households" hides the growth of private equity funds and hedge funds. (1) Closely held equity has increasingly become dominated by private equity funds, subsumed here under "households." By a rough estimate, private equity funds hold 2–3 percent of US corporate equity. (2) Hedge fund holdings (roughly 10 percent of the total) are displayed as assets of households (for domestic hedge funds) or of the rest of the world (for foreign hedge funds, including US funds registered in offshore jurisdictions, see www.federalreserve.gov/releases/Z1/z1_technical_qa.htm).
Source: Financial accounts of the United States (Z.1).

funds, whose direct equity holdings reached an all-time high of 27 percent in 1985 (Figure 9.2). While the investor configuration was dubbed "investor capitalism" (Useem 1996) or "pension fund capitalism" (Clark 2000), the corporate governance regime it gave rise to was shareholder primacy (Lazonick and O'Sullivan 2000).[7] Its hallmarks were

[7] For the argument that financial logics had penetrated managerial corporate governance already in the 1960s, see Knafo and Dutta (2020).

moderately dispersed stock ownership; institutional investors large enough to be heard (voice) yet small enough for their ownership stakes to be liquid (exit); and moderately diversified not-for-profit institutional investors, who retained enough "skin in the game" to take a strong interest in their portfolio companies. At the macro level, shareholder primacy coevolved with the debt-led growth regime of "privatized Keynesianism" (Boyer 2000; Crouch 2009).

The investment chain lengthened a second time when, starting in the 1980s, institutional investors began to delegate to for-profit asset managers.[8] Along the four dimensions that define the corporate governance regime, asset manager capitalism diverges starkly from shareholder primacy: stock ownership is concentrated in the hands of a few giant asset managers; the latter hold large minority stakes despite being fully diversified; and their interest in the economic performance of individual portfolio firms is weak.

At the macro level, the parallel increase in market concentration, which is particularly pronounced in the United States (Philippon 2019), makes it tempting to diagnose a twenty-first-century version of the finance capitalism–monopoly capitalism configuration. While it is too early to define macro-level correlates, it is worth noting that no separate term may be needed to describe the current growth regime. The core feature of this regime would be "asset dominance" – the idea that asset prices, rather than wages, drive investment and consumption, and therefore become the chief targets of macroeconomic policy (Adkins et al. 2020; Ansell 2012: 533; Christophers 2020; Chwieroth and Walter 2019). I will return to the macro implications of asset manager capitalism in a later section.

THE GREAT RE-CONCENTRATION

Mark Roe (1994) has explained the policies sustaining dispersed ownership as the result of Americans' deep-seated opposition to concentrated economic or political power. From this perspective, asset manager capitalism constitutes a puzzle. By contrast, Hilferding (1985 [1910]) and Marxist scholars in the regulationist and social-structures-of-accumulation traditions have long argued that capitalist accumulation has a built-in tendency

[8] "Asset manager" here refers to pure asset management firms such as BlackRock (publicly listed) and Vanguard (mutually owned by the shareholders of its funds), as well as to the asset management arms of insurers (such as Allianz) and of banks (such as J.P. Morgan Chase).

toward greater concentration, and that mature capitalist accumulation exerts a strong pressure on finance capital to concentrate over time (Aglietta 1979; Kotz et al. 1994). From this perspective, the Berle and Means world was the anomaly and the "Great Re-Concentration" – a seven-decade period during which shareholdings shifted from households to pension funds and, more recently, to asset management companies (see Figure 9.2) – was overdetermined. Even if that were the case, however, we would still need to identify the specific policies and developments that enabled the Great Re-Concentration, which I will attempt in the remainder of this section. During a first phase (1936–2000), tax rules for mutual funds, retirement legislation, and financial regulation fed the *growth* of the asset management sector. Since 2000, the dominant dynamic has been *concentration* within the asset management sector.

Feeding the Growth of Asset Management, 1936–2000

Between the end of World War II and the turn of the twentieth century, the share of corporate equity held directly by households declined steadily, falling below 40 percent after the bursting of the dotcom bubble in 2000. This decline was the flipside of the pooling of savings via collective investment vehicles, which increased their share of equity holdings from virtually zero in 1945 to 42 percent in 2000.

The big picture can be read in Figure 9.3. Total mutual fund assets (solid black line) have grown in lockstep with retirement assets since 1984. That growth accelerated when defined contribution (DC) plan and individual retirement account (IRA) assets took off in the mid-1990s. The share of retirement assets in total mutual fund assets doubled over the course of the 1990s, from 20 to 40 percent (dotted line). This share has recently plateaued at 45 percent, whereas mutual fund assets have continued to rise, indicating the growing importance of (non-retirement) household savings as well as foreign investment in US mutual fund shares.

The explosive growth of mutual fund assets was not preordained. Mutual funds are legal constructs built, over a long period, on regulatory statutes and on various pieces of tax and retirement legislation. The first such piece was the Revenue Act of 1936, which allowed mutual funds to pass dividends on to investors untaxed, thus ensuring that fund shareholders were not disadvantaged vis-à-vis direct stock investors (Fink 2008: 28). Congress made this tax privilege conditional on mutual funds owning no more than 10 percent of the voting stock of any corporation, with the explicit goal of preventing them from acquiring controlling stakes

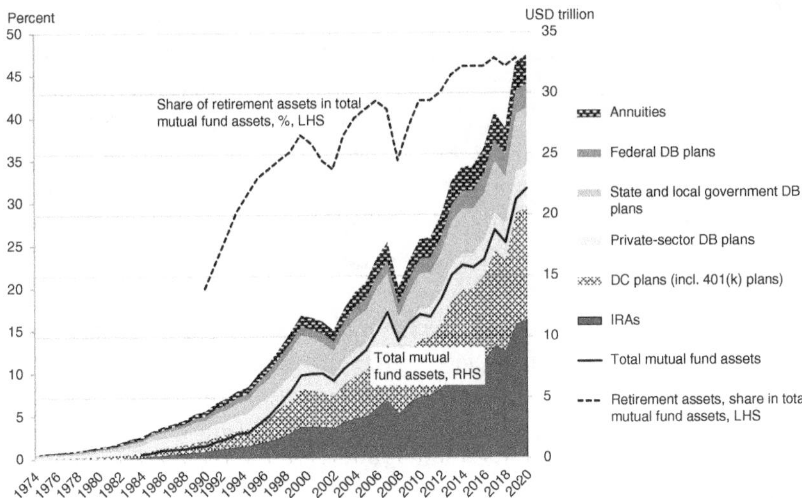

FIGURE 9.3 Retirement assets and their share of mutual fund assets, 1974–2020Q3
Source: Investment Company Institute.

(Fink 2008: 28). Today, the tax exemption lives on in the Internal Revenue Code (Coates 2009: 596).[9]

Fund size continued to be key issue in the run-up to the Investment Company Act of 1940. While mutual funds supported the idea of legislation, they opposed certain provisions in the original bill drafted by the Securities and Exchange Commission (SEC). Arguing that investment companies selling securities into a falling market had been one of the sources of the 1929 crash and seeking to avoid such "runs" on mutual funds in the future, the SEC was proposing to limit their size to USD 150 million. The mutual fund lobby strongly opposed the size limitation and, rejecting the bank-run analogy, succeeded in keeping it out the final version of the bill (Fink 2008: 39). Section 14(b) of the Investment Company Act, which authorized the SEC to reexamine future increases in fund size, was never activated.

The Revenue Act and the Investment Company Act established the legal foundation for the existence of mutual funds without, however, doing

[9] This rule applies at the level of the *individual* fund. Breaches of this threshold by fund *families* – an imminent scenario for BlackRock or Vanguard – thus fall within the letter of the 1936 law but may conflict with its spirit.

much to feed their business.[10] The tide of retirement assets that eventually flooded the asset management sector was the cumulative effect of four subsequent pieces of retirement legislation: Taft–Hartley (1947), ERISA (1974), the 401(k) provision (1978), and universal IRAs (1981). Long before Peter Drucker warned of "pension fund socialism" coming to America (Drucker 1976), the anti-labor Taft–Hartley Act of 1947 prohibited employers from contributing to union-controlled pension funds (McCarthy 2017: 95–100). The Employment Retirement Income Security Act (ERISA) of 1974, which brought the riskiness of private pension promises – hitherto negotiated between employers, unions, and employees – under federal government regulation (Wooten 2004: 3), further weakened labor control over the investment of retirement assets. It did so by tightening a fiduciary requirement originally introduced by Taft–Hartley. In 1979, the Department of Labor specified that prudence was a matter not of individual securities but of portfolio construction, thus tying fiduciary duty to the prescriptions of modern portfolio theory (Montagne 2013: 53). By narrowing the prudent person rule down to best practice as it prevailed in the financial sector, ERISA created a strong incentive for retirement plan managers to share fiduciary responsibility with professional, external asset managers (Clark et al. 2017; van der Zwan 2017).

For all of the mutual fund industry's legislative victories, its growth had stalled amidst the 1970s bear market (Clowes 2000: 192). Growth resumed in a big way with the addition of section 401(k) to the Internal Revenue Code in 1978 and the Economic Recovery Tax Act of 1981. Although the mutual fund industry had not lobbied for the 401(k) provision – the DC-plan implications of which were "discovered" only in 1980 by Ted Benna, and confirmed by the IRS in 1981 (Hacker 2019: 110) – it proved a godsend for the industry. In contrast to the "mostly inadvertent" birth of the 401(k) provision (Hacker 2019: 110), the "universal IRA" – which allowed annual tax-deductible IRA contributions of up to USD 2000 – had been invented by, and lobbied for, the Investment Company Institute (Fink 2008: 125). In the 1980s, IRA and DC assets became the fastest-growing segments of the retirement market, and today account for two thirds of all retirement assets, and for an even larger share of retirement assets invested in mutual fund and ETF shares.

[10] Defined benefit plans, which then did not invest in mutual funds, prevailed in the corporate retirement market, while the small market for defined contribution plans was dominated by banks and insurers (Fink 2008: 113).

By the year 2000, a series of tax rules, retirement laws, and financial regulations had helped create a USD 7 trillion mutual fund sector that managed USD 2.6 trillion of retirement assets (Figure 9.3). The *dominant shareholders*, however, were still the public pension funds, which campaigned aggressively for the corporate governance reforms that institutionalized the shareholder primacy regime, including independent directors, destaggered boards, and proxy voting (Davis et al. 1994; Webber 2018: 45–78). However, even the largest holdings of the largest public pension funds barely reached 1 percent of a corporation's market capitalization in the 1990s. Dispersed share ownership thus remained a hallmark of pension fund capitalism.

Consolidation within the Asset Management Sector, 2000–Present

The aggregate stock ownership data in Figure 9.2 suggests that little has changed over the last twenty years, bar a modest expansion of foreign ownership, continued growth of mutual funds, and the emergence and growth of exchange-traded funds. This continued growth of the *overall* asset management sector cannot, however, explain the jump in the largest asset managers' average ownership stakes from 1 percent in the 1990s to almost 10 percent today. Indeed, in contrast to the slow growth of the underlying asset pool in the late twentieth century, the crucial dynamic in the twenty-first century has been *concentration within* the asset management sector.

At present, this concentration is uneven. The overall asset management sector remains relatively fragmented, and observers expect mergers and acquisitions to further accelerate and bring higher future concentration (Flood 2020). Already, following a decade of increasing consolidation, the largest 1 percent of asset managers today control 61 percent of the assets managed by the sector (Riding 2020). At the very top, the dominance of the Big Three is the result of their cornering the now highly concentrated ETF market – BlackRock (39 percent), Vanguard (25 percent) and SSGA (16 percent) control a combined market share of 80 percent (Kim 2019).

While the contingency of the 2008 financial crisis played an important role, concentration in the financial sector has been driven by some of the same forces as concentration in labor and product markets (Ansell and Gingrich this volume; Naidu this volume; Rahman and Thelen this volume; Schwartz this volume). Although asset managers compete on performance and cost, the cost of investing via for-profit asset managers is high. Between 1980 and 2007, asset management revenues (mutual, money market, and exchange-traded funds) quintupled from about 0.2 percent to just under 1 percent of GDP (Greenwood and Scharfstein 2013: 9). Casting a bright light on remuneration in the financial sector generally, the financial crisis of 2008 accelerated the shift from expensive active funds into low-cost index funds, which had been underway since the early 1990s (Figure 9.4) (Braun 2016; Petry et al. 2019). The cost difference between active equity funds and index equity funds (traditional and ETFs) is significant, and has increased over time. The expense ratio of active funds was four times higher than that of index funds in 2000 and is nearly ten times higher today (Figure 9.4). In the United States, this cost advantage has been reinforced by a tax loophole for ETFs (Poterba and Shoven 2002). In addition, the financial crisis dealt a heavy blow to the banking sector. While asset managers generally benefitted from distrustful investors moving money out of the banking sector, BlackRock in particular gained from its June 2009 acquisition of the asset management arm of Barclays, which included iShares, then the world's leading ETF brand (Mooney and Smith 2019).

If the contingency of the financial crisis made investors more cost-sensitive, structural forces have helped translate that focus on cost into accelerated concentration. While intellectual property rights have become

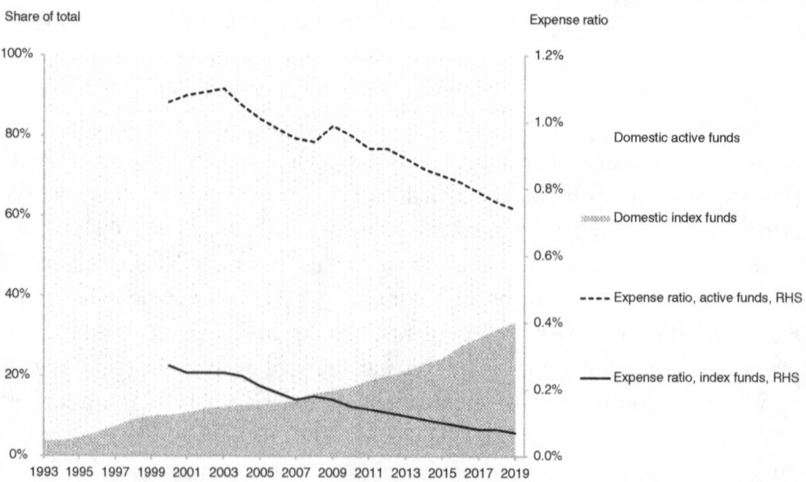

FIGURE 9.4 Domestic active equity funds versus domestic index equity funds (incl. ETFs), relative market share (1993–2019) and expense ratios (2000–19)
Note: Expense ratios are asset-weighted averages.
Source: Investment Company Institute.

more important for financial sector firms in general (Schwartz 2017), asset management in particular resembles digital platform industries, where network effects and scale economies drive monopolization (Rahman and Thelen 2019; Srnicek 2017).[11] Three elements underpin the "almost unlimited scale economies" of these "digital asset management platforms" (Haberly et al. 2019: 169). First, the fixed cost structure of ETFs – an expensive infrastructure on the back end, combined with constant marginal costs – creates conventional scale economies.[12] Second, unlike active mutual funds, whose transaction costs tend to increase beyond a certain size threshold, ETFs benefit from network effects – more investors make the shares of an ETF more liquid. Third, asset management companies have increasingly benefitted from data-based returns to scale. This trend is epitomized by BlackRock's Aladdin, a risk-management system so widely used in the asset management industry that BlackRock's CEO has described it as "the Android of finance" (Haberly et al. 2019: 172). Even BlackRock's immediate rivals use Aladdin (Zetzsche et al. 2020: 290). In sum, capturing the ETF market and exploiting economies of scale has made the Big Three the largest asset managers in the world. (How) do these firms wield their new power?

DIVERSIFIED AND DISINTERESTED

Besides stock ownership dispersion, asset manager capitalism also undercuts two further tenets of the BM-JM ontology, namely that institutional investors are speculators making targeted bets and that their primary economic interest is in the performance of their portfolio firms.

Diversified: The Promise of Universal Ownership

Political economists have long equated LME-type institutional investors (a catch-all category comprising both pension funds and mutual funds) with "impatient" capital, in contrast to the "patient" capital provided by banks and other strategic blockholders in coordinated market economies

[11] Exchanges and index providers – key components of the infrastructure of asset management – display similar dynamics, and even higher concentration (Petry 2020; Petry et al. 2019).

[12] The SEC recently changed the rules governing the share creation and redemption mechanism at the heart of ETFs in an explicit attempt to lower barriers to entry and enhance competition (SEC 2019: 197–98).

(Culpepper 2005; Goyer 2011; Hall and Soskice 2001; Höpner 2003).[13] Concentration and the rise of indexing, however, have effectively eliminated "exit" as an option for the largest asset managers (Jahnke 2019). This scenario was not anticipated. In a clear-eyed survey of the changing US shareholder landscape, Davis still highlighted a "surprising combination of concentration *and liquidity* [my emphasis]" as the core features of what he termed – referencing Hilferding – the "new finance capitalism" (Davis 2008: 20). Analyzing data up to 2005, in which index fund providers such as Vanguard did not yet appear as blockholders with multiple stakes above 5 percent, Davis noted that index funds "typically end up with smaller ownership positions in a larger number of companies" (Davis 2008: 15). By the time Davis' article was published, BlackRock's *average* S&P 500 shareholding had already surpassed the 5 percent threshold. Vanguard followed in 2012 and today holds an average stake of 9 percent (Backus et al. 2020: 19). This was a watershed moment: full diversification and large blockholdings ceased to be mutually exclusive.

Today, large asset management companies are quintessential "universal owners" (Hawley and Williams 2000; Monks and Minow 1995). The promise associated with this concept is enormous. As holders of the market portfolio, universal owners should, in principle, internalize all externalities arising from the conduct of individual portfolio companies (Condon 2020). The concept of the universal owner conjures the image of a utilitarian social planner curbing economic activities – above all: carbon emissions – whose aggregate monetary cost exceeds their aggregate monetary value (Azar et al. 2020). While the concept is not new, it has become more compelling in that the growth of index funds and ETFs has deprived the largest universal owners of the option of exit (reinforcing the internalization of externalities), while the size of their blockholdings affords them considerable power through voice (Fichtner and Heemskerk 2020; Jahnke 2019).[14] Besides carbon emissions, asset managers calling on pharma companies to set competition aside and cooperate in the search for a COVID-19 vaccine offers a striking example of universal ownership in action (Mooney and Mancini 2020). The example also illustrates the close link – and slippery conceptual slope – between externality-reducing universal ownership and competition-reducing common ownership (as will be discussed later).

[13] For notable exceptions, see Dixon (2012) and Deeg and Hardie (2016).

[14] Capital invested via index funds is "steered" not by individual fund managers but by index providers such as MSCI or S&P, which often exercise considerable discretionary power (Petry et al. 2019).

The Big Three have been quick to harness the promise of universal ownership to shape their public image as long-term shareholders whose interests are fundamentally aligned with environmental, social, and governance (ESG) sustainability. BlackRock CEO Larry Fink's annual letters to CEOs and to investors exemplify this rhetoric (Condon 2020: 54), which seeks to replace shareholder value as the dominant corporate governance ideology with a "stewardship" model. Whereas the shareholder value regime made good corporate governance a matter of corporate accountability to shareholders, in recent years the latter (i.e., asset managers), have themselves faced demands for accountability from *their* principals. The global spread of stewardship codes illustrates this ideological and regulatory shift (Hill 2017). Investors increasingly expect asset managers to act as stewards of their capital in ways that go beyond maximizing short-term returns, above all in the context of global warming (Christophers 2019). In theory, the logic of universal ownership is compelling. In practice, it is counteracted by the causes of diversification – indexing and size – and by the economic incentives faced by asset managers.

Disinterested: The Separation of Legal and Economic Ownership

Perhaps the most destructive effect of the BM-JM ontology has been the notion that shareholders "own" the corporation. In large part due to the work of Lynn Stout (2012), it is increasingly recognized that US corporate law does not actually assign ownership rights to shareholders (see also, Ciepley 2013).[15] Asset manager capitalism has added an important twist to this: the separation of the legal ownership of a stock from the economic interest in the return from that stock.

Berle and Means' (1932: 119) defined ownership as "having interests in an enterprise" and control as "having power over it." The separation of the two, they noted, reduced "the position of the owner ... to that of having a set of legal and factual interests in the enterprise." Agency theorists sought to reunite ownership and control by strengthening shareholder protection and by aligning the incentives of managers with those of shareholders (Jensen and Meckling 1976). Indeed, giving managers "interests in the enterprise" via stock options and other forms of incentive pay during the 1990s merged the interests – and, by implication, the class

[15] Hence the use of "stock ownership" rather than "corporate ownership" in the present chapter.

position – of the two groups, strengthening shareholder control at the expense of labor (Boyer 2005; Goldstein 2012). Since Jensen and Meckling, the concentration of stock ownership has further increased shareholder power, thus seemingly perfecting the reunification of ownership and control. The rise of asset management companies, however, has perfected a different separation – that between the "legal interest" and the "factual interest" in the enterprise. Indeed, the separation of ownership and control has been joined by the "separation of ownership from ownership" (Strine Jr. 2007: 7; cf. Gilson and Gordon 2013).

Agency theory rests on the assumption that shareholders have more skin in the game than managers or workers (Fama and Jensen 1983: 301). While that was always questionable, what agency theorists ignored entirely is the shareholder without any skin in the game at all – one that holds the legal title (shares and the attached voting rights) but not the economic interest. Today, the dominant shareholders are "disinterested" in this way. While mutual funds and ETFs legally own stocks, they pass on any returns to the fund's investors, the ultimate "asset owners" (retail or institutional investors).[16] For revenue, asset managers rely on fees. Unlike alternative investment vehicles such as hedge funds, whose fee structure usually includes a large performance-based component, mutual funds and ETFs typically charge their investors fees that amount to a fixed percentage of the assets invested (this "expense ratio" is displayed in Figure 9.4).

The economic interests of asset managers thus are different from the economic interests ascribed to shareholders in the BM-JM ontology. Simply put, asset managers are incentivized to maximize assets under management. For actively managed funds, adequate relative returns matter, but only to the extent that they cause clients to switch to competitors. For indexed funds, the return equals the benchmark return (minus a "tracking error" that index funds seek to minimize), which eliminates even the indirect nexus between returns and revenue.

From an agency theory perspective, the implications of this "double-agency society" – a phrase coined by the late founder of Vanguard (Bogle 2012: 29) – are analogous to the separation of ownership and control.[17]

[16] On hedge fund strategies to disentangle legal ownership from the risk of the underlying asset, see Ringe (2016).

[17] See also Gilson and Gordon (2013) on "agency capitalism." The spread of outsourcing and franchising (Schwartz this volume; Weil 2014) points to the proliferation of agency relationships also on the production side. In the platform economy especially, economic activity is coordinated via arms-length, market-based relationships rather than direct control.

Asset owners (the principal) hiring asset managers (the agent) must fear that the latter's incentives are not aligned with their interests. In the standard investment chain configuration, this agency problem repeats itself at least once, between the asset owner (a pension fund) and the ultimate beneficiaries (the plan members). Thus, the supposed principals in the shareholder-manager relationship are themselves agents to a chain of principals, namely asset owners and ultimate beneficiaries (Arjaliès et al. 2017; Bebchuk et al. 2017; Clark and Monk 2017; Kay 2012). The result of this proliferation of agency relationships is a proliferation of conflicts of interest.

THE POLITICAL ECONOMY OF ASSET MANAGER CAPITALISM

Shareholder primacy refers to a corporate governance regime under which the interests of institutional investors – in close alliance with corporate managers – dominated over those of workers and society at large. While this power imbalance may well persist, the most powerful actors in the equity investment chain are no longer institutional asset owners but their agents, the asset managers. From a Hilferdingian perspective, the concentration of finance capital should strengthen the structural power of asset owners, by facilitating coordination among fewer and more homogenous agents.[18] At the same time, however, the interests of asset owners are not necessarily aligned with those of asset managers. This section discusses the political economy of asset manager capitalism at the firm, sectoral, and macroeconomic levels.

Firm Level: The Cost of Engagement

In the BM-JM ontology, shareholders as principals have a vital interest in the performance of their portfolio companies, which they therefore monitor closely. US securities and corporate law, however, has always sought to limit the role of large shareholders in corporate governance (Roe 1994: 102), as illustrated by the ongoing conflict between the SEC and business groups over proxy access rules (Rahman and Thelen this volume). By contrast, under asset manager capitalism, the issue has shifted from too much engagement to too little engagement.

[18] Note that asset managers are merely the most visible actors in a sprawling "wealth defense industry" (Ajdacic et al. 2020; Winters 2017).

Monitoring and engaging with portfolio companies is costly, and asset managers do not directly benefit from the returns to such stewardship activities (Coffee 1991). Some argue that competition solves this problem – investors increasingly demand stewardship services from their asset managers, and failure to monitor and engage with firms diminishes returns, driving investors away (Fisch et al. 2019; Jahnke 2019). For index funds, this is doubtful from a purely theoretical perspective: any performance gains they achieve by engaging with a specific company are reaped disproportionately by active funds with bets on that specific company (Lund 2017). Empirically, studies of voting and other stewardship-related activities shows that index funds are less likely than other funds to engage with portfolio firms (Heath et al. 2021), even on negative externalities that universal owners should, in theory, seek to curb (Briere et al. 2019).[19]

The problem of the direct cost of engagement is exacerbated by the indirect cost of alienating corporate managers – portfolio firms are often also *clients* of asset managers. As a consequence, the asset management arms of large banks, for instance, tilt their equity investments toward the clients of their parent banks (Ferreira et al. 2018). For pure asset managers, 401(k) plan assets are an important source of revenue that provides a strong incentive to not alienate corporate management. For the Big Three, the proportion of US client assets coming from 401(k) plans in 2017 ranged from 14 to 20 percent (Bebchuk and Hirst 2019: 2062). Proxy voting data shows that the largest asset managers overwhelmingly vote with management, especially on controversial issues (Heath et al. 2021). Out of almost 4,000 shareholder proposals submitted to companies in the Russell 3000 index between 2008 and 2017, not a single one came from one of the Big Three (Bebchuk et al. 2017: 48).

As the Big Three have grown in size and (potential) power, regulators across the world have become increasingly concerned by their lack of monitoring and engagement. The global diffusion of so-called stewardship codes (Hill 2017) should be seen in that light – as an attempt to ward off more heavy-handed forms of regulatory intervention. By signing on to stewardship codes, asset managers commit, for instance, to voting their shares and to making (aggregate) disclosures about their engagements

[19] This is reflected by their stewardship teams, which remain far too small to monitor thousands of portfolio companies: the ratios of stewardship personnel to portfolio companies worldwide are 45/11,246 for BlackRock, 21/13,225 for Vanguard, and 12/12,191 for SSGA (Bebchuk and Hirst 2019: 2077).

with individual portfolio firms. Whereas stewardship codes aim at getting asset managers more involved in corporate governance, other policy proposals focus on "disintermediating" voting by giving asset owners (such as pension funds), or even ultimate beneficiaries (individual savers), the right to decide how their shares should be voted (Griffin 2020).

Sector Level: Common Ownership

The concentration of corporate ownership among a small number of very large asset managers gives rise to the phenomenon of "common ownership" (Azar et al. 2018; Backus et al. 2020; Elhauge 2016). If all major firms in a given sector have the same (large) shareholders, the theory goes, shareholder returns are maximized if these firms engage in monopolistic pricing. The agenda-setting study on the anticompetitive effects of common ownership in the airline industry highlighted four potential causal mechanisms: "voice, incentives, and vote – as well as doing nothing, that is, simply not pushing for more aggressive competition" (Azar et al. 2018: 1557). The potential implications are grave. From an "antitrust as allocator of coordination rights" perspective, by allowing common ownership, antitrust rules grant the largest asset managers coordination power unavailable to any other actors in the economy (Paul 2020). In the extreme case of all shareholders being fully diversified, shareholder value maximization implies "an economy-wide monopoly" (Azar 2020: 275).

The theory that common ownership has anticompetitive effects has rapidly gained traction among national (Federal Trade Commission 2018) and international (OECD 2017) policymakers. The stakes are high for the asset management sector, which has contested the underlying research, while opposing regulatory initiatives (Fox 2019). Policy proposals are necessarily radical. One group of authors has suggested enforcing section 7 of the 1914 Clayton Act, which would prohibit asset managers from owning more than 1 percent in more than a single firm in oligopolistic industries (Posner et al. 2017).

Macro Level I: Capital-Labor Split

At the macro level, the key question from a political economy perspective concerns the distributive consequences of asset manager capitalism. The shareholder primacy regime relentlessly pursued an agenda of strengthening the protection of (minority) shareholder rights while weakening the

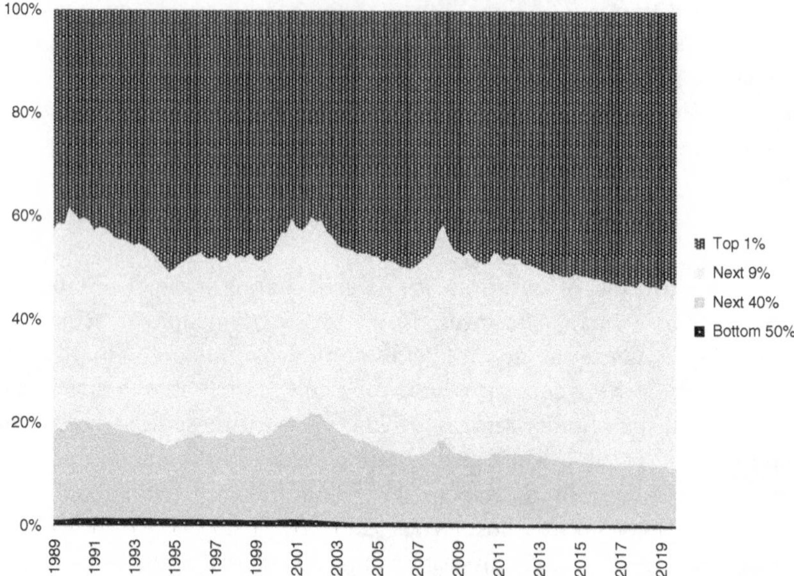

FIGURE 9.5 Distribution of equity and mutual fund holdings by wealth group, 1989–2020Q3, share of total
Source: Federal Reserve, US distributional financial accounts.

power of labor and pushing down wages (Hertel-Fernandez this volume; Steinbaum 2021). The negative externalities – for example, for public health or social cohesion – were not priced in by institutional investors with shareholdings in individual companies. Do universal owners price the social and economic costs of inequality differently?

Here, we encounter a fundamental problem with the promise of universal ownership. While asset managers are universal shareholders, the distribution of share ownership in society is extremely unequal. Figure 9.5 shows that the top 1 percent of the wealth distribution own 50 percent of the corporate equity and mutual fund shares (versus 35 percent of total wealth), while the top 10 percent own 86 percent. This concentration of share ownership at the top counteracts the benign logic of universal ownership – shareholders may be fully diversified, but only half of the population own any shares at all.[20] The test case for this argument are

[20] Note that Figure 9.5 does not include retirement assets, which in 2018 stood at just over USD 25 trillion, equivalent to roughly 50 percent the market value of US corporate equity. A large share of that capital is invested in stocks, via pension funds. Compared to direct equity and mutual fund holdings, the distribution of retirement assets is less skewed

corporate strategies whose profits are outweighed by negative externalities that are, however, borne primarily by those who own few or no shares. Consider the example of worker pay. Wage stagnation for the bottom 50 percent of the wealth distribution (those without shares) certainly has some negative externalities for the economy as a whole, notably in the form of lower aggregate demand. For shareholders, however, these externalities may be outweighed by higher corporate profits and thus higher returns. In other words, a negative externality for the poor can be a positive externality for the rich. Given the highly unequal distribution of shareholdings, even truly universal owners – such as the Big Three asset managers – should be expected to push the economy toward the lowest sustainable labor share.

Proposals to counter concentrated and coordinated shareholder power aim at re-empowering workers. One way to achieve this is by wielding "labor's last best weapon," namely its pension funds (Webber 2018). However, pension fund activism has been fighting an uphill battle against existing rules and investment norms, which push them into the arms of asset managers (McCarthy et al. 2016). A different set of proposals aim at strengthening the power of workers in the boardroom, either through a German-style system of "codetermination" (Palladino 2019) or through full-blown "economic bicamerialism" (Ferreras 2017).

Macro Level II: The Politics of Asset Price Inflation

The business model of BlackRock is geared toward maximizing (the value of) assets under management. While competition for existing savings is zero sum, government policy in general, and retirement policy in particular, determine how and how much people save. With retirement assets accounting for the biggest chunk of the asset management pie – 46 percent of US mutual fund assets; see Figure 9.3 – asset managers have a strong vested interest in retirement policy (Naczyk 2013; 2018). The scope of this interest is global. When the Group of Thirty published a report on "Fixing the Pension Crisis," the six-member working group included representatives of BlackRock and UBS (Group of Thirty 2019). When protests erupted in France against President Macron's planned pension reforms,

toward the top 1 percent but still almost entirely passes by the bottom 50 percent. Compared to other countries, US households' financial assets account for a particularly large contribution to wealth inequality, relative to housing assets and non-housing real assets (Pfeffer and Waitkus 2020: 26–28).

protesters targeted BlackRock, which had published a white paper in favor of pension privatization, and whose CEO had been photographed at the Élysée Palace (Alderman 2020; BlackRock 2019).

Whereas social policy can mobilize more of the base ingredient (savings), macroeconomic policy has the power to inflate the pie (asset prices).[21] Since asset management fees are charged as a percentage of the current value of a client's assets, asset price inflation is a substitute for fund inflows. And other things equal, a fall of the interest rate increases asset prices. The implications for the political economy of monetary policy are substantial. The financial sector has long been treated as the most powerful "hard money" constituency because inflation devalues banks' nominal claims against borrowers (Posen 1993). Asset managers, by contrast, fear a devaluation of their asset base more than inflation, making them a powerful "easy money" constituency. BlackRock's deep ties with central banks across the world illustrate the point. The Federal Reserve has hired BlackRock to manage distressed asset portfolios and conduct corporate bond purchases, and BlackRock has performed similar services for the central banks of Canada, the euro area, and Sweden. This role as conduit for unconventional monetary policy implementation affords BlackRock considerable "infrastructural power" vis-à-vis state policymakers (Braun 2020). In order to wield that power effectively, BlackRock has hired former senior central bankers, including Philipp Hildebrand (former chairman of the Swiss National Bank, hired in 2012), Jean Boivin (deputy governor of the Bank of Canada, 2014), and Stanley Fischer (vice-chairman of the Fed, 2019). In August 2019, this trio presented a paper titled "Dealing with the Next Ddownturn" at the Fed's annual Jackson Hole symposium that called for audacious monetary easing in the next crisis. The paper urged central banks to "go direct" by getting "central bank money directly in the hands of public and private sector spenders" while seeking explicit coordination with fiscal policy in order to prevent interest rates from rising (BlackRock 2019: 2). "Going direct" was indeed what the Fed did in response to the COVID-19 crisis, illustrating BlackRock's transition from being a monetary policy taker to acting as a monetary policy maker.[22]

[21] Aggregate stock market valuations can also be increased through the corporate governance process. Diversified asset managers calling on pharma companies to adopt a cooperative approach to developing a COVID-19 vaccine – instead of maximizing profits from individual patents – can be understood in this manner (Levine 2020).

[22] Another policy area in which asset managers exercise outsize influence is development finance (Gabor 2021).

CONCLUSION

At first blush, the new shareholder structure resembles that of the late nineteenth century: the equity of a concentrated corporate sector is concentrated in the hands of only a handful of financial firms. Two features, however, distinguish the new asset manager capitalism from finance capitalism. First, unlike their robber baron predecessors, today's dominant owners are fully diversified across the entire stock market. In the case of the largest asset managers, which overwhelmingly are invested in corporate equity via index-tracking funds, this increasingly holds for the global stock market. Second, asset managers are economically disinterested intermediaries – they lack skin in the corporate game. Unlike robber barons, their business model is to compete for capital and management fees from investors. The returns from their shareholdings matter in this competition, but the largest asset managers in particular only own the legal title, not the economic interest in the corporations whose stock they hold. At closer inspection, therefore, asset manager capitalism is without historical precedent.

Moving beyond the BM-JM ontology opens up promising avenues for research on the political economy of asset manager capitalism and corporate governance. The first relates to the stakeholder coalition perspective that has dominated the CPE literature on corporate governance (Aguilera and Jackson 2003; Gourevitch and Shinn 2005; Höpner 2003). This literature has interpreted the shareholder primacy regime in LMEs as an alliance of shareholders and workers – embodied in powerful public pension funds – against corporate managers. Like other aspects of the CPE literature, this interpretation reflected early-1990s pension fund capitalism but was largely obsolete by the early 2000s, when shareholders had closed ranks with managers, in terms of both ideology and class (Boyer 2005; Duménil et al. 2011; Goldstein 2012). However, these accounts still conceptualize shareholders as owners. As the discussion of the incentives of today's asset management conglomerates shows, what has come to pass is an alliance between managers and asset managers. Unprecedented shareholder power coexists with a corporate governance world of "managers all the way down." One potential consequence of the disinterested nature of large diversified asset managers is the empowerment of corporate managers, at the expense of shareholders. Equally plausible, however, is the argument that power shifts to other types of shareholders (Deeg and Hardie 2016). For instance, the initiative for engagements with individual companies now often comes from activist hedge funds that then seek the support of the Big Three (Aguilera et al. 2019). Another empowered shareholder category is sovereign wealth funds, the largest of which are also universal owners but without some of the business-model related conflicts of interest (Babic et al. 2020). Mapping the new distribution of power between these various actors calls for close examination of increasingly complex investment chain dynamics.

Secondly, my analysis challenges the view, widespread in CPE, that stock ownership patterns and corporate governance regimes are stable, rooted in national institutional and ideological legacies. As one proponent of this view has noted, corporate governance "is partly just the tail to the larger kite of the organization of savings" – that is, of the investment chain (Roe 1994: xv). However, whereas in Roe's theory the investment chain is shaped by policies conditioned by history and political ideology – in the US case: mistrust of concentrated financial power – this chapter shows that the investment chain is *also* the tail to the larger kites of capitalist accumulation, wealth inequality, and financialization. Fostering private wealth accumulation – a US policy priority for the last seven decades – and restricting concentrated financial power in the asset management sector are likely two inconsistent policy goals. The ease with which the latter goal has recently been abandoned supports the view that the investment chain is, in fact, prone to dramatic regime shifts. Moreover, in a globalized financial system, the investment chain in any individual country – and thus its corporate governance regime – is also a function of the organization and regulation of savings in the rest of the world (Oatley and Petrova 2020). This holds both ways – 40 percent of BlackRock's assets are managed for clients outside of the United States (BlackRock 2019: 1), while BlackRock is also a shareholder in thousands of non-US firms across the globe. Asset manager capitalism is a global regime.

10

Labor Market Power in the American Political Economy

Suresh Naidu

The importance of labor market dynamics to the study of American political development has never been in question. The labor market is, at one and the same time, a point of distribution of economic production, an arena for political interest articulation, and – perhaps most interesting – an allocation of private political power. Of course, there are other markets with these properties (in particular housing and credit), but labor income still predominates the budgets of most of the population, time at work dominates the activity of most working-age adults, and political emotions such as status and dignity clearly owe a great deal to the distribution of power and autonomy at the gates of and inside the "hidden abode of production" (Marx 1981 [1867]; see also Anderson 2019; Bowles and Gintis 1993; Dahl 1957; Gaventa 1980).

In this chapter, I provide economic microfoundations for labor market politics based on recent research on the important role of firms in setting wages in labor markets. Rather than thinking of the labor market as a primordial institution, we can unpeel the concept of the "market" into its constituent parts. On one side are businesses, who (still) need human skills and talents to make goods and services that customers value, but are constrained in the wage policies they can offer due to internal administrative limits as well as considerations of equity and shop-floor relationships. On the other side are workers, who have to trade off wages and work with all of the other dimensions of their lives – from providing care to family

This paper draws on material from my book, *Terms of Service* under contract with Harvard University Press. I thank Jacob Hacker, Alex Hertel-Fernandez, Tom Ogorzalek, and Kathleen Thelen for comments.

members to civic activities – while handling the bumps and shocks of a society where all types of social insurance and public goods are only weakly provided.

The result of these two sets of frictions is what economists call "monopsony." Monopsony is both the absence of immediate substitute jobs in the labor market for workers, as well as the internal constraints on employer wage policies that keep them from differentiating wages too much across workers with similar productivities. The number summarizing this relationship is labor supply elasticity to the firm – which can be intuitively understood as the responsiveness of worker turnover to changes in their wages. In a frictionless labor market, this number should be very high, say 10 or higher, implying that a 5 percent cut in wages leads to at least a 50 percent increase in turnover. As discussed more in the following, the availability of linked worker–firm data from administrative sources has allowed for precise estimates of labor supply elasticity across multiple types of labor markets, with estimates in the United States lying in the 2–5 range even for low-wage workers. What these estimates show in the US context is that labor markets are far from frictionless and employers have substantial labor market power, allowing them to set wages well below what would be implied by perfect competition. From the point of view of employers, the market wage is more of a suggestion than an imperative; from the point of view of employees, jobs as good as the one you have are few and far between.

While monopsony is experiencing an intellectual moment in the sun, there is another core labor market model that suggests a different notion of power. This is the classic "labor discipline" model (which I will also call "efficiency wages"),[1] in which the problem for firms is effectively monitoring workers. If workers can shirk/steal/damage equipment on the job and can only be detected some of the time, then incentives must be provided to keep workers supplying the care, attention, and exertion that is required for production. The labor discipline model suggests that firms solve this problem by paying wages *higher* than a worker's next-best alternative, so that getting fired is costly, and the fear of getting fired is what keeps workers working. If the unemployment rate gets too low, then worker insubordination to manager authority rises, making the politics of the workplace depend on aggregate macroeconomic outcomes (Kalecki 1943).

[1] Technically, labor discipline is just one variant of efficiency wages. For an introductory economics textbook treatment of the labor discipline model see Unit 6 of *The Economy*, https://core-econ.org/the-economy/book/text/06.html.

Labor discipline and monopsony interact in counterintuitive ways, as the former increases wages but decreases employment, blunting the latter's effect on wages but exacerbating the overall effect on employment. However, I argue that efficiency wages have *decreased* in importance in recent decades, due to improvements in designing incentives and monitoring workers. These improvements in monitoring, from video cameras at work to GPS sensors in warehouse worker badges to the ubiquitous "This call may be monitored for quality purposes," reduce the incentive rents captured by workers, facilitate outsourcing, and raise the relative wages of work that remains hard to monitor. It is well known that performance pay has increased in incidence over the past decades (Lemieux et al. 2009), and partly this is due to improvements in tracking worker performance as well as organizational changes. As efficiency wages become a less important force in low-wage labor markets, monopsony winds up taking center stage, and so we get a world where (nonunion) employers are more worried about labor shortages than shirking or poor performance. This decline of incentive rents may account for some of the decline in the firm-size premium as well as the constancy of the share of wages explained by firms even as the covariance of worker and firm components have increased (Song et al. 2019): low-wage workers once captured more revenue because employers needed to provide incentives, blunting the effects of latent monopsony.

As we shall see, labor market power is by itself a form of unchecked private power whose exercise ought to be analyzed (Anderson 2019; Hertel-Fernandez 2019), but it also has implications for the political coalitions that will form over labor market policy. Imagine a polity split into large, "granular" employers like Walmart or Amazon and smaller, less productive employers like local small retailers. Granular employers are large, economy-wide players whose human-resource policies can set wages and standards throughout the economy, while smaller employers are much more local and are able to thrive due to the fact that neither the labor market nor product markets are perfectly competitive. Under perfectly competitive labor markets these two groups of employers would pay the same wage, and could have quite similar labor market policy interests. But in monopsonistic labor markets, their preferences diverge: minimum wages and sectoral standards are much more threatening to the smaller employers than to the bigger, while enterprise unions and antitrust, where large high-revenue employers are ripe targets for union organizers and government enforcers, are much more threatening to the bigger employers than to the smaller. Put differently, when low-wage and high-wage employers coexist in the same labor market, policies that set floors will be borne by the former, while policies that employ third-party actors (like unions or regulators) to exercise discretion to go after firm-specific rents will likely be borne by the latter.

These wedges, in turn, create the space for otherwise-unexpected coalitions between workers (either high-skill or low-skill) and different groups of employers, as well as giving rise to novel dimensions of employer interest. For example, monopsony implies that even low-wage employers are "labor-hungry" and thus will demand policies that increase the supply of labor and skill – for example, by reducing unemployment insurance benefits and expanding the Earned Income Tax Credit (EITC), or by relentlessly pressuring politicians to address a purely imaginary "skills gap." During the COVID-19 crisis, this labor-hunger is manifesting as widespread employer demands for states to kick workers off Pandemic Unemployment Assistance. What an economic model focused on monopsony can hope to add is some analytic heft about over which policies business coalitions and groups of workers form coalitions and where they conflict.

Such a model also shifts our eyes away from the cooperative politics of human capital formation toward the highly conflictual arena of labor market interventions. If the focus of the Varieties of Capitalism literature was institutions for skill building, perhaps the focus of APE should be the institutions regulating wage-setting, workplace governance, employee retention, and recruitment by firms – practices that are traditionally under the jurisdiction of private employers, but are still shot through with economic and political power differentials. Above all, this analysis ought to remind scholars of American politics of the centrality of individual firms as both economic and political actors.

LABOR MARKET POWER: ANALYTICS

In this section, I use some simple Marshallian diagrams to illustrate the analytics of labor market power. I begin with a graphic illustration of monopsony, and the resulting transfer of surplus from workers to employers. I then illustrate the labor discipline model in the same framework, as later on this will be used to illustrate employer "arbitrary whim" in the labor market. The next section turns to the evidence.

Labor markets are naturally monopsonistic, and thus labor market power is pervasive, not just the result of rural concentration of industries nor of legal artifices such as non-compete and no-poaching agreements (all of which exacerbate labor market power, but do not exhaust it). Monopsony can shed light on how gender norms within the household (who has to move for whose job) explain gender gaps in the labor market, how racist employers and managers cannot just survive but lower wages for Black and brown workers throughout the economy, and why rural labor markets may suffer more from industrial consolidation than previously thought. Labor discipline can shed light on employer surveillance, capital-skill complementarity, outsourcing, and the credible threat of firing induced by at-will employment. However, labor market power is also variable across space and time, and there is good reason to think it is particularly marked (and particularly tilted in favor of employers) in the United States as a result of welfare state and labor market policies.

Sources of Monopsony: Concentration, Search Frictions, and Differentiated Jobs

Why might laissez-faire in the labor market be characterized by pervasive wage-setting power? In modern labor economics, there are three widely considered sources of employer power. The first is the basic "few employers and high barriers to entry" version of monopsony that characterizes rural, highly concentrated labor markets or affects workers with occupationally specific skills. In these types of labor markets, employers are simply few and far between, and any one employer's demand for labor raises wages at other firms. A narrow number of employers further facilitates collusion and cartelization. This is the form of monopsony identified by recent papers that regress wages on measures of labor market concentration. While many labor markets are concentrated, however, most workers are not in these labor markets. There is also only mixed evidence that concentration in labor markets has increased (Rinz 2018), although the boundaries of labor market definition are unlikely to be stable over long periods. Moreover, concentration is highly correlated with labor demand (industries experiencing high demand will also be getting new entrants and thus become less concentrated), making the establishment of causation difficult.

Still, it is certainly the case that there are important labor markets where concentration and collusion matter. As other chapters in this volume have shown, regional divergence has featured urban growth and rural decline. At the same time, rural labor markets in tradable products are increasingly consolidated. These markets raise few concerns under current antitrust doctrines, because the prevailing focus on product market power implies little cause for concern in industries participating in national and global trade. But the labor-market effects of a town going from two mine owners to one, or a merger of two factories, may be considerable even as the product-market effects are not. Even in non-tradable sectors, like healthcare/hospitals, the labor market may be even narrower (for example, due to skill specificity) than the product market even if they are geographically similar. Further, the relative absence of geographic mobility for jobs, particularly among workers without a college degree, means that the normal force arbitraging wage differences across labor markets – migration – is attenuated, so employers have more scope to exercise their market power.

The second source of monopsony animating current research is "search frictions," where workers do not see all offers available at the same time, but must instead wait until they encounter a sufficiently attractive offer. In a seminal 1946 discussion, Lloyd Reynolds, explained:

> The assumption that workers are fully informed and completely responsive to wage differences may be altered in three main ways. It may be assumed that workers are ignorant of the wages paid by other employers, or that they are perfectly informed concerning wages but are deterred from changing jobs by considerations of security, or that they are perfectly informed concerning wages but differ in their evaluation of the non-base-rate components of the wage. (Reynolds 1946: 393)

This second focus fits nicely with the first: the concentration approach successfully predicts a robust negative correlation between employer consolidation and wages; the search-frictions view has successfully shown that flows between firms are not terribly responsive to wage differences, even in putatively thick labor markets, while explaining the widespread concern employers express with respect to turnover. The turnover margin has been especially important for accounting for the effects of the minimum wage on employment. While it is difficult to detect an effect of minimum wages on employment, Dube et al. (2016) show that there are very strong effects on flows: firms affected by the minimum wage reduce recruitment, but also see separations fall, so the net employment effect is zero.

The third area of focus is, in my view, the most intuitive explanation of monopsonistic competition: the gap between the value of a job to a worker and the wage. Jobs are highly differentiated bundles of characteristics, and nonwage characteristics are extremely important in this bundle. Jobs are differentiated both spatially (for example, location of employer and hence commute times) and along bundles of amenities, both tangible (benefits, job safety, and so on) and less tangible (relationships with managers and coworkers). As Joan Robinson put it in a classic 1969 account, "[T]here may be workers attached to the firm by preference or custom and to attract others it may be necessary to pay a higher wage." In particular, workers may value jobs because of *where* they are as well as *what* they are, and employers may have "to pay a wage equal to what they can earn near home plus their fares to and fro" (Robinson 1969: 269).

Such nonwage features are a substantial reason why workers select and stay with a particular job. Indeed, Maestas et al. (2018) use a survey experiment to document that, when workers value jobs, nonwage elements can account for up to one-third of the value. Not only do these elements vary across many dimensions, but workers also value these dimensions differently. In models of random utility, workers have idiosyncratic, unobservable utility over different jobs. Crucially, firms may not be able to observe this taste heterogeneity, and internal constraints on wage discrimination (for example, internal equity) may force firms to post only one wage per job.

The unobservability is what makes labor market power inefficient: if firms could perfectly tailor the wage to each worker's taste for working at that firm, there could still be market power, but it would be efficient. In short, firms know there are some workers who would work for the firm at a lower wage, but do not know which workers those are.[2] So the profit-maximizing strategy is to pay below marginal product, accepting the loss of the workers who prefer working somewhere else in exchange for the profits made off those workers who stay.

Labor Market Power, Wages, Efficiency, and Profits

The other crucial ingredient in these models is the level and slope of underlying labor demand function of the firm. The demand for labor of a given business will depend on its product market, its management practices, and the technology and capital that it has access to. An extremely elastic labor demand will be the result of marginal revenue not diminishing too strongly as more workers are hired, while an extremely inelastic labor demand will suggest that additional workers are much less valuable than the initial workers.

We can see how monopsony works by examining a company like Convergys, the call-center company discussed in the 2019 book *On the*

[2] Indeed, recent advances in HR analytics are exactly about predicting individual recruitment, retention, and responsiveness to pay and promotions.

Clock by Emily Guendelsberger (2019).[3] In this company, let us say there are two potential workers, Emily and Kolbi, and both would generate $20 an hour for Convergys. Emily is educated and single and knows people who work in other companies that are growing, and so she has a pretty good outside option – say, a job that pays $18 an hour. Kolbi knows of a few other jobs but they would require her to move. Kolbi's daughter really likes their daycare, her husband is insistent that they stay for his job, and she likes the easy commute to Convergys from her house, so her outside option is $12.

We show Kolbi's and Emily's outside options, together with their chance of working for Convergys, on two axes in Figure 10.1. We can think of these as being two individuals out of many, many potential workers Convergys could hire, whose outside options are given by the line called "outside options." The lowest outside option is unemployment, with some combination of unemployment insurance, food stamps, and family support, which, let us suppose, pays everyone an income equivalent to $6 an hour.

What's the outcome that generates the most total value? The profit per worker is measured in Figure 10.1 by the vertical distance from the revenue-per-worker line and the wage paid: revenues minus costs. If Convergys employed both Emily and Kolbi at anything between $18 and $20, it would make $40 in revenue, and Emily and Kolbi would make between $18 and $20 each. But Convergys would make at most $4 in profit.

What is the wage that Convergys chooses? Convergys doesn't know Emily and Kolbi's outside offers, so it has to pick a wage guessing at who would stay and who would take their outside offer. If Convergys pays less than $12, it will lose both Emily and Kolbi. If it paid between 12 and 18, it would lose Emily but keep Kolbi. At $17, Convergys would only get $3 in profits from Kolbi alone, lower than if the firm had tried to keep both workers at $18. But if Convergys lowered its wage to $15 it would now be able to keep Kolbi and make $5 in profits off $20 in revenue, clearly a higher profit choice.

The choice to keep Kolbi at a lower wage and lose Emily is the logic of monopsony: firms trade off profits per worker against the number of workers who want to work at the firm to maximize overall profit. This trade-off means that firms will employ fewer workers than the value-maximizing choice. Indeed, Guendelsberger reports that Convergys has incredibly high turnover, with a business model that takes this into account. The hunt for profits doesn't necessarily lead to more jobs, let alone higher-paying ones.

[3] N. B. Guendelsberger and I are related by law, further evidence for homophily in interests.

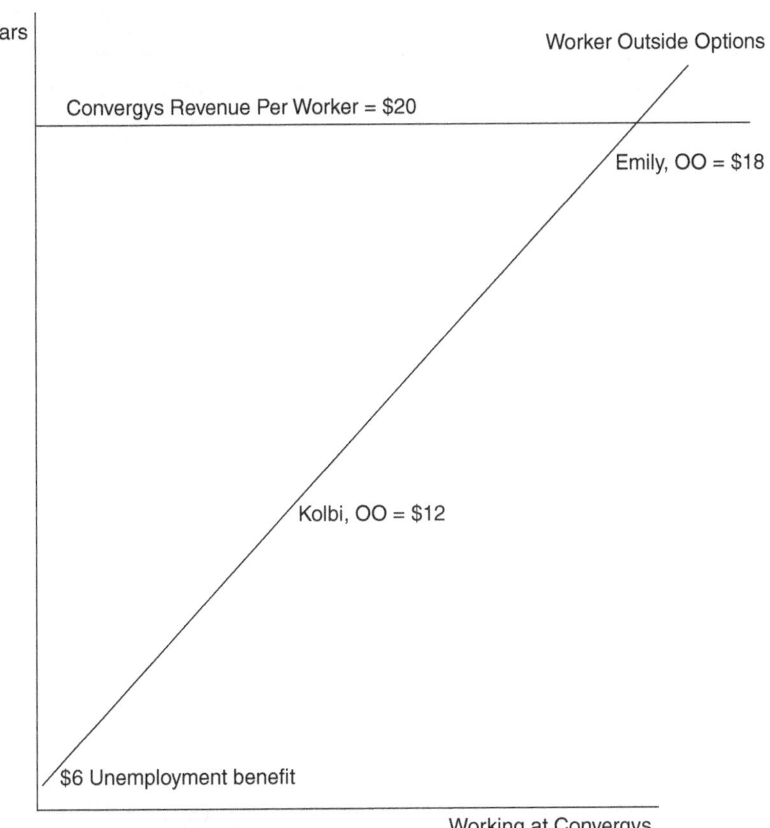

FIGURE 10.1 Monopsony at Convergys
Note: The *x*-axis is the probability that a worker (say Emily or Kolbi) stays at Convergys. The vertical axis measures the wage paid to workers and the revenue generated. The "OO" line gives the wage it would take to induce a worker to stay, and thus gives the outside option (hence OO) each worker has. Convergys could pay up to $20 an hour and still break even from hiring both Emily and Kolbi, but would make even higher profit by paying a lower wage, say $12, and losing Emily (who has an outside option worth $18) but keeping Kolbi and still making a profit of $8.

Monopsony and Inequality

If even a moderate amount of monopsony is pervasive, this matters for the distribution of wealth and income. Naidu et al. (2018) calibrate a simple macroeconomic model (with a public good financed out of labor taxes) to observed degrees of monopsony. They find that a moderate amount of monopsony reduces the labor share of income by up to 20 percent in an otherwise standard macroeconomic setup. While quite high, this follows from the fact that even a small amount of monopsony (e.g., an elasticity of roughly 4) already implies that wages are considerably below marginal product (e.g., 20 percent) *if* labor supply is the only major constraint facing employers, which is unlikely. Berger et al. (2019) show a more sophisticated model and find that the labor share is also considerably depressed. Wealth to income is, mechanically, 1 minus the labor share of income divided by the rate of return on capital (Naidu 2018).[4] The increasing wealth to income ratios documented by Piketty (Piketty 2014) don't just reflect high productivity of capital, they also reflect the profits (and expected future profits) accruing to market power. This includes both product market power (e.g., patents and brands) as well as labor market power, some of which might be capitalized into the value of commercial and residential real estate. The implication, then, is that the increase in the importance of monopsony power in the American labor market may be one force driving increasing wealth accumulation, and the disjuncture between market and book values of capital.[5]

The Other Face of Labor Market Power: Labor Discipline and Efficiency Wages

The other model I want to quickly review is the labor discipline model, which emphasizes the supply of hard-to-monitor effort (these are also dubbed efficiency wages models). Both efficiency wages and monopsony are instances of incomplete contracts, reflecting the technological and legal constraints on writing labor contracts promising that you (a prospective employee) will work hard (i.e., you won't shirk) and stay with the firm even when you get an outside offer. The lack of enforceable indentured labor contracts makes retention a problem to be solved with the wage, and the lack of costless monitoring of effort makes labor discipline

[4] Piketty writes wealth to income as $W/Y = B$, so the labor share of income is $a=1-rB$; since labor and capital shares sum to 1, we get wealth-to-income ratio $W/Y= 1-a/r$. So the increase in wealth-to-income ratios documented by Piketty correspond to falls in the labor share of income, holding the rate of return constant. Interestingly, recent work by Gutierrez and Piton (2020) shows that only the United States has experienced an increase in capital shares once housing is accounted for.

[5] One particular piece of evidence for the monopsony channel is the unusually high ratio of market capitalization to value of capital stock (generally greater than 1 and often greater than 2) for the staffing services industry (where profits are almost pure monopsony arbitrage). For example, in June 2020, market capitalization of, for example, Manpower Inc. is around $60–100 a share, but book value is only $45 a share.

a problem, also to be addressed with the wage. The multiple objectives of recruitment, retention, workplace relationships, and incentives managed by a small set of prices is part of what makes the labor market fail to reliably live up to the Hayekian ideal, creating spaces for supra-market and intra-workplace governance.

Among the crucial features that make the labor market different from most other markets is that workers need to exert effort on the job and to take care, pay attention, and experience physical discomfort while working. Employers need to give workers a reason to expend all this energy. Returning to our Convergys example above, one might wonder why the HR department might not drive the wage even lower? One answer is provided by the need to attract qualified workers (for example, because of adverse selection), but a more "political economy" answer is provided by labor discipline. So if Kolbi is only getting paid barely above $12, nothing stops Kolbi from slacking off at Convergys. If a manager catches her playing Candy Crush on her phone instead of answering calls, she could get fired, but the next job she gets will be pretty similar to this one, so no big deal. Candy Crush it is!

Convergys, or at least their HR department, understands this, so it needs to make Kolbi's video game consumption at work costly. But in a free labor market the worst thing a company can do to Kolbi is fire her. How to get her to work? One strategy is to pay Kolbi more than $15, say $17, so that Kolbi loses $5 if she's fired. This extra component to the wage (also called a rent) would make Kolbi worried about getting fired and thus curbs Candy Crush at work, raising whatever revenue Convergys makes from Kolbi answering phones. The "labor discipline" model is so named because the fear of unemployment works to discipline workers into exerting effort.

Convergys would like to keep this rent low, so it might instead choose to prohibit cell phones at work, record call transcripts, and put cameras in each cubicle to make sure it can detect slacking off. But it cannot eliminate these sorts of behaviors entirely (at least not yet): Convergys has to pay each of its workers more than their outside option in order to get them to work. We can represent this "rent" on the same graph, shown in Figure 10.2, as a level shift upwards of the outside options line for each worker, which we call the "no-slacking line."

The no-slacking line in Figure 10.2 illustrates the core of the labor discipline model. The idea is that the Kolbi's wage needs to be higher than Kolbi's outside option, otherwise Kolbi will not care enough about getting fired and will stare at her phone instead of paying attention to customers,

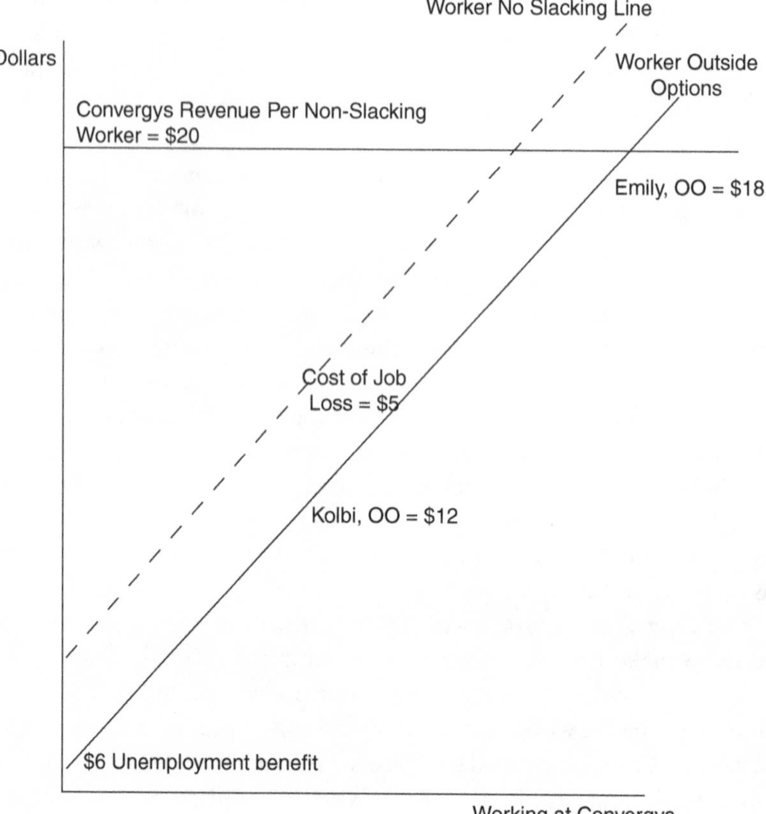

FIGURE 10.2 Labor discipline at Convergys
Note: The x-axis is the probability that a worker (say Emily or Kolbi) stays at Convergys. The vertical axis measures the wage paid to workers and the revenue generated. The "OO" line gives the wage it would take to induce a worker to stay, and thus gives the outside option (hence OO) each worker has. Convergys must pay at least $5 more than each worker's outside option to get them to exert effort, hence the "no-slacking" constraint, and this makes firing a worker a credible threat.

what HR managers call "time theft" in their pursuit of every last drop of attention from their workforce. Most workers have many ways to exercise discretion on the job, ranging from just being careless to deliberately sabotaging or stealing from their employers. Employers can choose to either police their workers, by hiring many supervisors or installing expensive monitoring equipment, or they can choose to give their workers generous wages and steep wage-tenure profiles, hoping that the fear of losing those wages acts as a sufficient incentive to get workers to exert effort.

As noted, the labor discipline model predicts involuntary unemployment. Convergys pays Kolbi a wage that is higher than her outside option. And Convergys will not hire Emily at any wage, because it would have to pay Emily $23 to get her to both show up and exert effort, and that is more than the value that Emily generates. If Emily has no other employer that values her at more than $23, she will be unemployed despite being willing to work at $18, because she can't promise to work and not play Candy Crush for anything less than $23. In the labor discipline model, then, involuntary unemployment occurs because workers are willing to work at wages below what employers are offering but employers don't want to hire them.

These two forces, monopsony and labor discipline, show the two faces of power in the labor market. They are at the heart of why the labor market is much more complicated than just supply and demand, as might be the case in the market for chairs. Pervasive monopsony means that employers can exploit their workers, and pervasive labor discipline means that workers work under the fear of losing their jobs and joining the ranks of the involuntarily unemployed.

LABOR MARKET POWER: NEW EVIDENCE FOR AN OLD CONCEPT

What is the evidence for monopsonistic competition in the labor market? Direct estimates of monopsony power that are obtained in thick labor markets are the most compelling evidence, but there are a variety of relevant findings.

Experimental Results

The most credible evidence is provided by the few randomized controlled experiments where wages are randomized for identical jobs in markets with many wage-setters and little in the way of barriers to mobility. Sydnee Caldwell and Emily Oehlsen (2018) randomize wages for Uber drivers, including those that also drive for Lyft. They examine the rate at which drivers switch, and find a surprisingly low elasticity of between 4 and 5 (so that a 5 percent decrease in earnings on Uber results in only a 25 percent chance of logging onto Lyft), given that workers literally just have to switch apps on their phone.

Similarly, Arin Dube and coauthors (Dube et al. 2020) experimentally vary wages for an identical task and find substantial monopsony power even on (putatively thick) Amazon Mechanical Turk, and Dube et al. (2019) show that a large national retailer implemented a national wage increase policy pretty much independently of any local labor market condition, using a policy that has cutoffs that depend on workers' initial wages. They find that workers' sensitivity of quits to wage changes is pretty low, implying a labor supply elasticity of 4.6. If labor markets were super competitive, it would be pretty hard for a national retailer to have such uniform wage policies, as completely ignoring local labor market conditions would make it very difficult to profitably hire workers in a given labor market. Bassier, Dube, and Naidu (2019) use administrative data from Oregon and estimate firm-specific labor supply elasticities of around 4, even in thick labor markets. Dube, Manning, and Naidu (2018) combine administrative data from Oregon, MTurk experiments, and conjoint experiments with Walmart workers and conclude that residual labor supply elasticities lie in the 3–5 range for low-wage workers in the United States.

A separate literature looks at direct shocks to firm labor demand, generated by sudden co-worker deaths, changes in incumbent worker mobility, firm-specific patents, exporting contracts, and so on (Cho 2019; Garin 2018; Jäger and Hening 2019; Kline et al. 2019; Kroft et al. 2020; Naidu et al. 2016). This "rent-sharing" literature revolves around the hypothesis that if the market was perfectly competitive, then firm wages wouldn't respond to that company facing a particular demand shock, because wages would be set by the market, not the particular firm, which this literature thoroughly rejects. While this literature often interprets rent-sharing as evidence for monopsony (also with labor supply elasticities in the 3–5 range), it is important to note that labor discipline could also account for both wage and employment increases in response to productivity shocks (Rebitzer and Taylor 1993).

The upshot of this literature is that wages are up to 25 percent below marginal product, suggesting that there is considerable latitude for firm discretion in wage-setting. Moreover, this discretion rises with higher labor market concentration. According to a spate of recent studies, roughly 10 percent higher concentration (using the common Herfindahl Index) implies as much as 1 percent lower wages. There are also direct negative effects of mergers on wages (Arnold 2020; Benmelech et al. 2018; Marinescu and Hovenkamp 2019; Prager and Schmitt 2019), and this evidence has spurred a movement to broaden antitrust regulation to include labor market effects.

A Brief Historical Foray

The importance of monopsony has arguably risen in recent decades, but it is not a recent development. Often, scholars speak of the period between 1870 and 1914 as the closest to laissez-faire capitalism that the American North experienced, as relatively unregulated national markets came together with a steady inflow of migrant labor. But as I hope the theoretical discussion has made clear, unregulated does not necessarily imply perfect competition in the labor market. For example, when Henry Ford raised wages from $2.30 to $5 in 1914, quits of autoworkers fell considerably, but were still nowhere close to 0 even after the increase. In fact, quits fell by between 56 percent and 87 percent (Raff and Summers 1987), but given that the wage was doubled, the implied labor supply elasticity is still less than 2, suggesting plenty of scope for market power. Indeed, Naidu and Yuchtman (2018) put forward evidence that labor markets during the Gilded Age were no less frictional than our present labor markets, and present estimates of the firm labor supply elasticity of around 2, using local product market prices as instruments for firm value-added within city-industry-year cells. Perhaps this should not be surprising given that this period was also marked by stark imbalances of power between labor and capital and by the reign of concentrated industry leaders known as "trusts."

That even archetypically laissez-faire labor markets exhibited symptoms of labor market power gives us some suggestion that the default state of the labor market is not wage-taking firms, but instead firms with some wage-setting power – which helps explain why, prior to the New Deal, historians argue that turnover and quits were endemic problems (Jacoby 1983; Ross 1958). Turnover is an outcome of firms exercising their monopsony power: a labor market that might exhibit low turnover when competitive can exhibit high turnover when monopsonistic.

Evidence on Efficiency Wages

The evidence on efficiency wages is much less developed than the evidence on monopsony. This is unsurprising: being able to measure effort well would eliminate the labor discipline problem! Lazear, Shaw, and Stanton (2016) document how productivity of workers on an identical job increased with local unemployment, suggesting that workers were afraid of losing their jobs. Another paper by Pierce, Snow, and McAfee (2015) looks at the effect of "Restaurant Guard," which flags various forms of employee theft (which can be thought as another form of effort) of servers in restaurants. They found that Restaurant Guard induced workers to work harder, increasing customer satisfaction with service (revealed by higher tips), but also that turnover increased for workers who had benefitted from low monitoring before the adoption of the technology, consistent with the theory.

A recent paper, by Coviello, Deserrano, and Persico (2018) that provides compelling evidence on efficiency wages looks at the effects of minimum wage increases on individual worker productivity in a large multi-state retail firm. They show that a $1 increase in the minimum wage raises within-worker sales by 4.5 percent, and that this effect is (a) concentrated among low-productivity workers who would have had their take-home pay affected by the minimum wage, and (b) higher during periods of high unemployment. The latter result, in particular, suggests that it is the additional rents, above and beyond their outside option, that workers are getting as a result of the minimum wage that is resulting in higher effort: when unemployment is high, having a higher-wage job is more valuable, and thus worth keeping by exerting higher effort.

Many experimental papers document a positive effect of wages on output, consistent with the labor discipline model. For example, Hedblom et al. (2019) randomized wages within an image tagging job and found that worker accuracy responded to the wage increase (though note that Dube et al. 2020 also randomized wages for image tagging on Mturk and found no increase in accuracy). But the labor discipline model has a very specific mechanism, where the reason wages have a positive effect on effort is because the threat of firing becomes scarier. No experimental paper has isolated this mechanism.

As suggested in the introduction to this chapter, organizational technological changes may have made efficiency wages less of a concern than before. In the United States, there has been a marked increase in performance pay over time, including commissions and tips as well as bonuses. Performance pay, where worker productivity can be easily observed and directly rewarded, makes the need to pay rents in order to secure effort less necessary for the firm. This pushes wages down and employment up, but also makes the outside option curve central to the monopsony model more binding than the no-shirking line central to the labor discipline model. Perhaps, then, the increased surveillance and measurement of workers is a contributor to the rise of monopsony; the offsetting constraint of efficiency wages has become less important.

A recent paper by Stansbury and Summers (2020) is consistent with the view that worker rents have fallen over the past forty years. Unfortunately, the authors conflate rents that are due to institutional forces such as unions and within-firm pay norms and rents that are due to the need to provide incentives in the face of monitoring (and screening) problems. They confusingly label these both as "worker power," but who controls the rents is very different in each case! The authors claim that much of the fall of the labor share can be accounted for by falling worker rents, which has the additional benefit of accounting for a falling natural rate of unemployment. But they interpret this as evidence that changes in labor market monopsony can't account for the change in labor share, where I would interpret it as a decline in forces that countered latent monopsony power while lowering the marginal cost of labor (like improved surveillance, deunionization, etc.).

POLITICAL IMPLICATIONS OF LABOR MARKET POWER

American political scientists have traditionally studied the distribution of public power. Yet the models we have discussed here suggest that the distribution of private power in the workplace should be a central concern as well. There is of course a distinguished tradition in political science of mapping the class positions of citizens in the private economy into relative public power (e.g., Dahl 1957; Gaventa 1980), but the empirical study of power inside the workplace has largely been studied by sociologists (e.g., Burawoy 1982) and the rare comparative politics scholar or rarer radical economist (Edwards 1979).[6]

Political Theory and Labor Market Power

While empirical work has been rare, political theorists have begun to theorize the presence of private power in the economy. In Elizabeth Anderson's 2019 book *Private Government*, for example, she implicitly endorses a view of monopsony plus labor discipline in the labor market. Key for her argument that voice is required to limit the authority of employers is that exit is not so easy. She variously mentions monopsony, and efficiency wages (albeit without that terminology) as mechanisms by which exit may be insufficient to guarantee freedom at work.

[6] An important exception is *Every 12 Seconds*, which is an outstanding ethnography of meat processing by a political scientist (Pachirat 2011).

Similarly, the concept of domination has been extensively theorized by neo-Republican theorists. Pettit (2014) defines domination as being "subject to the arbitrary whim" of another. Republican freedom is thus "non-domination," and it is different from either of Isaiah Berlin's (2002) distinctions of negative and positive liberties. Emphasizing the connection to work, Alex Gourevitch (2014) shows the emergence of a labor republican theory, critical of wealth inequality, low wages, and authority in the workplace, expressed in the writings of the nineteenth-century American labor movement. Dominated transactions can be mutually improving and mutually consensual, but still be an affront to a democratic private sphere.[7] And the labor market is exactly the place where most people give up their republican freedom in exchange for a wage.

The neo-Republican tradition is somewhat split about the role markets play in securing freedom. For example, Robert Taylor (2017) is optimistic about the positive role that competitive markets play in delivering republican freedom, arguing that competition is an important countervailing power to dominating relationships, giving agents freedom via exit. Tellingly, Taylor uses labor markets to illustrate his argument. He concedes that company towns, such as Butte, Montana, violate republican liberty, but argues that such "pure" labor market monopsony is rare, and largely a historical phenomenon.

In the terminology just described, Taylor believes the elasticity of labor supply facing the firm, which measures the degree of monopsony power, is also a measure of the extent of domination.[8] Figure 10.3 shows this intuition for private power semiformally via the envelope theorem: small deviations around the wage (due to "arbitrary" whim, for example) have only negligible effects on profits, but significant effects on workers. Starting at the profit-maximizing wage, Convergys choosing to cut wages a bit only costs them a little bit of profit, because their lost effective labor is made up for by lower payroll costs. But it has big effects on workers, both by inducing a few workers (e.g., Kolbi in the figure) to shirk and get fired (or simply be unable to credibly commit to not shirking) to significantly worse options (the labor discipline channel) and by reducing the wages of those workers who stay (the monopsony channel).

[7] Vrousalis (2013) argues that this "domination" characteristic is definitive of exploitation: a transaction is exploitative if A instrumentalizes their domination of B in order to enrich themselves.

[8] Theoretically, he also neglects the case that if every employer requires subordination as a condition of employment (e.g., the labor discipline case), then there is no non-dominating option.

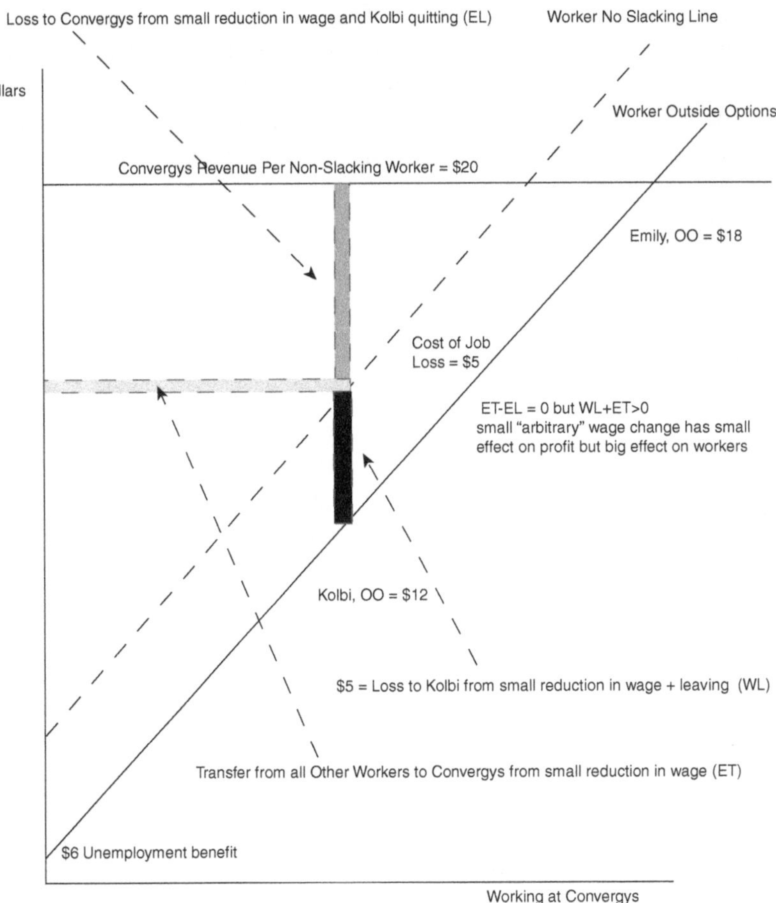

FIGURE 10.3 Envelope theorem and "arbitrary wage cut" at Convergys
Note: The setup is the same as the previous graphs. Starting at a wage of $17, suppose that Convergys cuts its wage by a small amount. Kolbi will quit (or will shirk and get fired), and this will cost the firm 20 – 17 = 3 dollars. But it is now paying all the workers that are staying a bit less, and they are still exerting effort. If $17 maximized profits, the additional savings in payroll will also equal close to $3. So the net cost to Convergys is close to 0. On the other hand, Kolbi has lost the $5 in rent she was were getting from her job at Convergys relative to her next-best job, and those workers who remain are also now taking home less in pay. So the effects on workers are **not** close to 0. An arbitrary and small wage cut (or similar small change in benefits/amenities/working conditions), conducted perhaps by a flinty manager, will not cost employers much under conditions of labor market power, but will still cost workers. The property of second-order costs to employers with market power and first-order costs to workers from small wage changes captures some intuitions about domination in the labor market.

A similar implication would follow from Convergys choosing to lay off Kolbi: wages could be lowered for everyone else to offset the lower revenue, while Kolbi would have to take her next, much worse, option. Taylor's identification of labor market power with republican domination has the virtue of being an empirically verifiable claim about the world – rare for a normative theory, but unfortunately rejected by the evidence presented here.

Business, Labor, and Coalition-Building

A literature in public choice economics has considered the political economy of endogenous market power, making the important observation that employers would be willing to spend up to their excess profits in order to defend their privileges from reformers. Because excess profit "rectangles" are in general larger than social deadweight loss "triangles," it would be exceedingly hard for general interest reformers to overcome the opposition of employers with market power (Tollison and Wagner 1991).

One reason monopsonistic employers may be particularly interested in demanding policies from the government is because there is less concern about new entrants capturing the additional employer surplus induced by policy. This makes the returns to policy particularly high for incumbent employers, relative to other, more competitive markets. If entry is easy, even a small, concentrated industry might find itself unable to capture the additional profits from a policy action. High barriers to entry into the labor market ensure that policies benefit the current set of employers.

The countervailing political group would thus have to be led by "factional" reformers, who favor groups specifically harmed by the exercise of market power. These would be the political agents with sufficient economic or ideological incentives to overcome the defensive expenditures of incumbent employers. In the labor market context these would be unions and organizations of workers themselves.

The public choice view is a bit too reduced-form and mechanical to go much further this simple account of the free-rider problem, and doesn't consider the organizational variation for solving collective action problems of workers and employers. But we can readily build on the theory to consider different configurations of political coalitions that may form over labor market policy, and the logic of imperfect labor markets allows for within-business and within-labor splits to be theorized.

In the case of business, we could consider at least two groups: large businesses, with high productivity of labor, willing to pay a high wage; and small businesses, with low productivity of labor, but able to retain workers because of labor market frictions. Employment and wages are thus higher in the high labor productivity firm, contrary to "the law of one price."

The Minimum Wage. The minimum wage (and similar policies like sectoral wage boards) is a policy that creates a clear split of interests among employers. In perfectly competitive labor markets, all employers face the same wage, and so all are negatively impacted by the minimum wage. But with monopsonistic labor markets, small, low-productivity, and low-wage firms are impacted much more than larger, more productive firms. This is because the minimum wage drives low-wage employers out of business, but at least some of those displaced workers are now employed by the higher productivity firm.

This heterogeneity of impact is one reason that minimum wage effects on employment are so hard to detect, despite a small army of labor economists working on the question. Small employers that are driven out of business cost jobs, but this is offset by expansion of businesses that survive. So the net effect of the minimum wage on employment depends on the relative weight of these two effects. In some labor markets, the effect on firm closure will dominate; in others, the expansion of employment at high-productivity firms will dominate.

The cleanest empirical evidence on this can be find in Dustmann et al. (2019), which shows these two effects at work in Germany. But indirect evidence exists in the United States: Cengiz et al. (2019) find that minimum wage increases do in fact eliminate jobs below the new minimum wage, but all those jobs reappear just above the new minimum. Similarly, Dube et al. (2016) find that while new hires fall after a minimum wage increase, so do separations, so that the net effect on employment is 0. When employers lose the ability to lower wages by bearing extra turnover, turnover falls, at the expense of profits. The minimum wage thus acts primarily as a transfer from employers to workers, rather than to workers at the expense of increased unemployment. These findings have two broad political-behavioral implications: larger employers will be more supportive of the minimum wage than smaller employers, and workers who work at or above the minimum wage will generally favor the minimum wage.

The evidence for the former is overwhelming. Politically, low-wage employer organizations have historically waged the most aggressive anti-minimum-wage efforts. Many large employers, by contrast, have not opposed state minimum wages in the United States – for example, McDonalds has dropped its opposition to minimum wage increases. Further, some large low-wage employers, like Walmart, Amazon, and Target, have voluntarily adopted national minimum wages quite above the federal minimum. Some of this is due to the tightening of the labor market, but the suspiciously round numbers they have used ($11, $15, and so on) make it seem that this was also a response to political pressure. It could also be a reflection of market power: In monopsonistic labor markets, big firms might drive up wages in order to hurt the competition (similar to predatory price-cuts in the product market), and small firms will find hiring labor quite hard when Walmart is paying $11 an hour.

What about workers? Some suggestive evidence can be found in survey evidence. For example, in the General Social Survey and CCES, even unemployed and part-time workers support the minimum wage at high levels, although this may not reflect self-interest. Furthermore, low-wage worker organizations, and unions with members well above the minimum wage, both strongly support minimum wage efforts. There is some evidence that this pays off for unions; Clemens and Strain (2020) present evidence that union membership among unaffected workers increases following minimum wage increases. If we take these actions and attitudes as reflecting economic interests, they suggest that workers want minimum wages, which is not consistent with the notion that they have strong negative effects and is consistent with the notion that they result in transfers to workers.

Demand for Publicly Subsidized Skills. One of the signatures of monopsony is that employers persistently ask for more workers. Because they make positive profits on every additional worker, from the point of view of a monopsonistic employer labor (and skill and effort) are always in short supply. Thus employers, both big and small, should be expected to lobby and demand for policies to raise the supply of qualified labor at taxpayer expense. Employers with market power will also demand additional skill and conscientiousness, even in the absence of true shortages, without being willing to raise the wage to the marginal product of said skilled and conscientious worker.

Importantly, employers constrained by their labor-supply curve will always hunger for more labor, while simultaneously being unwilling to raise the wage. This is in contrast to the labor discipline model, where workers are readily sacked, as they are necessarily replaceable in order to retain their effort. If we have seen technological improvements in monitoring that have eliminated the no-shirking constraint, then monopsony becomes more important than labor discipline, and employers will be more "labor-hungry" than they were before, and unemployment will be lower.

All this may help explain why a business discourse around the "skills gap" has emerged in the past twenty years, with a number of commentators asserting that American workers do not have the skills that employers want. A multi-billion-dollar philanthropy effort has focused on funding increases in training programs. But almost never are employers asked to raise the wage, provide stable jobs with career ladders, and see what skills and behaviors the resulting workers wind up displaying.

Perpetual labor and skill scarcity may also go some distance in explaining why large employers, in particular, generate advocacy organizations with outside interest in school reform. The classic argument in *Schooling in Capitalist America* (Bowles and Gintis 2011) was that schooling instilled characteristics that were more in demand by employers than by the requirements of a democracy's citizenry. If the "bourgeois behaviors" so in demand by employers are not being fostered by the schooling system, then business may see educational philanthropy and policy mobilization as a natural extension of its interests.

Employment Incentives (and Unemployment Disincentives). A similar example is employer demands for EITC expansion. The EITC is a subsidy to low-earnings workers designed to encourage workers to participate in the labor market. Labor market power goes a long way toward explaining why even employers of low-wage workers are generally enthusiastic about the EITC. Work subsidies increase labor supply, some of which appears as lower wages for the already employed, but also an increase in profits of monopsonistic firms. The existing research is in flux, but Leigh (2010) suggests a 10 percent increase in the EITC results in a 5 percent decrease in the wages of high school dropouts. Thus, a portion of each dollar of EITC money actually paid to low-skill single mothers is captured by employers.

Similarly, hostility to unemployment insurance expansions, which have reached a fever pitch in the wake of the Pandemic Unemployment Assistance package passed in March 2020, is evidence of employer demands for increases in both labor supply and effort. States worried about labor shortages due to the $600 a week expanded UI went as so far as to set up snitching websites for employers to report their workers. Notably the calls to reduce unemployment benefits come from both the National Federation of Independent Business as well as big business organizations. The expiration of pandemic benefits on July 31, 2020, however, has not resulted in a surge of employment.

Varieties of Collective Bargaining in the Shadow of Monopsony

We can also use monopsony to illuminate diverging interests across workers and additional difficulties in resolving collective action problems.

Mitchell and Erickson (2005) argue that the alternative to unionized labor markets is nothing like market-clearing supply and demand, but rather closer to monopsonistic labor markets. If the switch from deunionized to unionized labor markets is seen as a switch from monopsony to union wages, rather than a transition from the efficient benchmark to the union outcome, many empirical facts become natural. For example, deunionization did not come with increased employment as well as lower wages, an outcome that would be predicted by the neoclassical model. An increase in union density would be associated with an increase in the labor share, and its decrease would reduce labor share as well. Unionization, particularly at the firm level, becomes a pure distributional fight over rents, with little in the way of employment consequences.

Enterprise-based unions (and labor law enforcers) might naturally target their efforts to high-rent and large firms, which will have relatively high-wage workers, like Amazon. On one hand, organizing the relatively high-wage workers would mute the resulting effects on inequality. On the other hand, the labor market spillovers from organizing the "commanding heights" of a sector could be quite large, raising wages throughout the labor market (see Farber et al. 2020 for some evidence that twentieth-century unionization had a large spillover effect onto nonunion workers). Just as monopsony suggests heterogeneity across employers, it also illuminates new divisions between workers and obstacles facing worker organizations. Over some policies there will be a division between high-outside-option workers (with low firm-specific rents) and low-outside-option workers (with high firm-specific rents). Both of these kinds of workers will be in many firms, exacerbating the difficulties in worker collective action noted by Offe and Wiesenthal (1980), Olson (1965), and Michels (1911).

Monopsony adds yet another obstacle: high turnover of the low-rent workers. When employers choose a low-wage, high-turnover pay policy, fewer workers have an interest in improving conditions in their current job, because there are many jobs that are better and expected duration of the current job is low. Further, there is little time for a collective identity to form. Coupled with even moderate employer resistance to unionization, it becomes well-nigh impossible to build an organizing effort. But this leaves the high-rent workers alone to contest employers, and these are the workers for whom this job is particularly scarce and valuable.

These obstacles are driven home by Reich and Bearman's 2018 work on Walmart organizing: they find there are two groups of Walmart workers, one which has no intention of staying for an extended period, and another for whom the Walmart job is the best option they, or anybody they know, could hope to have; neither of these groups of workers have any particular interest in unionizing Walmart.

The Limits of City Limits

Monopsony in any given labor market wouldn't be a problem if workers were readily mobile across markets. The view that Americans are a mobile population of job shoppers remains fixed in the national imagination, and makes some skeptical of the importance of labor market power. In economics, spatial equilibrium implies that workers are indifferent across locations in the long run (Roback 1982; Rosen 1974), and even single-employer labor markets cannot pay workers below marginal productivity for very long. The political economy version of this argument, the Tiebout model, puts hard constraints on what subnational governments can do: migration of people and resources eventually discipline local governments into a narrower range of policy options than most reformers would like.

But evidence has been building that spatial mobility isn't as fluid as we thought. Yagan (2019) uses the huge variation in unemployment across commuting zones generated by the Great Recession to look at the extent to which migration allowed workers to mitigate their exposure to unemployment shocks. The answer: not much. Alex Bartik (2018) similarly looks at migration responses to both the China import shock studied by Autor et al. (2013) as well as the labor demand shock induced by fracking. In both cases migration does not lead to anything close to full adjustment. There is good evidence of falling internal migration rates (Molloy et al. 2011) and some evidence that the responsiveness of migration to spatial economic differences has also fallen (Ganong and Shoag 2017), resulting in stalled economic convergence across regions.

One implication of all this is that workers stand to capture more of the returns (relative to landlords) from "place-based policies," which may widen geographic or other forms of inequality. Another is that federal or state government policies that target particular geographies can effect considerable redistribution. Perhaps the most important implication, as discussed in other chapters in this volume, is that subnational governments have more leeway than the Tiebout model implies: dampened migration means that exodus is less of a constraint on local government.

But not all citizens are equally inelastic. The lack of spatial mobility for some workers implies that Tiebout competition services only the mobile workers, so that policies chosen by most local jurisdictions will be disproportionately accountable to their most elastic workers, who can afford to move elsewhere. Taxes, schools, zoning, and (crucially in 2020) policing will serve the interests of the mobile residents of a jurisdiction at the expense of those unable to readily relocate.

CONCLUSION

From the economics perspective, the combination of monopsony and labor discipline resolves many issues that plague each separately. The result is a model that has a laissez-faire equilibrium where employers have private power over the terms of the labor contract and the conduct of workers in the workplace. This private economic power is a form of governance, I and others would argue, as worthy of the attention of American political scientists as the more commonly studied levers of public power.

A number of political economy observations likewise follow. First, not only is there is plenty of scope for state- and local-level interventions in the labor market, but also "granular" employers, who are the largest employers in their markets, become important objects of policy and political pressure. The granular employer in each state lines up surprisingly well with other features of a state's policy environment: many low-wage red states have Walmart as their largest employer; many high-wage blue states have state university systems as their largest employer. Second, monopsony generates the phenomenon of the "labor-hungry employer" who demands more workers, with more skills and conscientiousness, but is unwilling to raise wages or provide costly on-the-job training. These employers then demand skills programs and employment subsidies from the government, but oppose minimum wages and expanded unemployment benefits. Above all, however, this perspective urges US-focused scholars of political economy to take the political and economic preferences and power of individual firms seriously.

IV

THE AMERICAN KNOWLEDGE ECONOMY

11

The United States as Radical Innovation Driver: The Politics of Declining Dominance?

David Soskice*

Perhaps the most extraordinary contribution of the United States since the late nineteenth century has been as driver of the three great successive waves of radical technological and techno-organizational innovation through the subsequent 120 or so years. Economic historians often refer to these three waves respectively as the Scientific Revolution (late nineteenth and early twentieth century);[1] the Fordist Revolution (1920s to the 1970s); and the ICT Revolution (1980s on).[2] (They were preceded by the first wave, the so-called Industrial Revolution, based on iron, steam, coal and textiles, and centered on the UK, which had taken place from the late eighteenth through the mid nineteenth century.) By driver of radical innovation is meant the carrier-through of these innovation waves across

* Very many thanks indeed to Paul Pierson and Kathy Thelen for their comments and encouragement over several years and in writing this paper. My main debts are to Torben Iversen, from whom many of the ideas here came from our joint work; also to Niki Lacey for discussion from related work on crime and punishment in the USA; to Michael Storper and Neil Lee for persuading me of the importance of economic geography, and to Catherine Boone, Peter Trubowitz, Andrew McNeil, and Frieder Mitsch for discussion. I should acknowledge help from Norface DIAL PII.

[1] Germany also played a main role in the Scientific Revolution, including in its scientific leadership, but it was increasingly dominated by the USA.

[2] Some innovation theorists have suggested a fourth wave of technological change, referred to as the 4th Industrial Revolution or the AI Revolution; here again the driving forces are American (even if China is now a competitor). This paper treats these as constituting together the ICT Revolution and the technological basis of the Knowledge Economy. There is no simple way to distinguish them, and there are in any case a whole range of partially associated radical innovations (e.g., cloud and edge computing, quantum computing, 5G, blockchains) taking place in parallel; in addition, the breakthroughs in life sciences, such as CRISPR, and the advances in immunology do not easily fit in.

society, typically from research to the rapid scaling-up of giant companies. The USA has also been central to scientific inventions.[3] As driver of the radical innovation waves of the twentieth century, it led to massive rises in living standards in America and then through the advanced world.

But each prolonged wave has also been massively destabilizing – socially, geographically, financially, economically, and politically; and we are currently living through the political instability of the ICT revolution. Schumpeter described the destabilizing nature of these prolonged waves as "creative destruction" (Schumpeter 1942). Carlota Perez entitled her magnum opus *Technological Revolutions and Financial Capital: Financial Bubbles and Golden Ages* (Perez 2010). Tylecote's sweeping book is called *The Long Wave in the World Economy: The Current Crisis in Historical Perspective* (Tylecote 2013). And Clayton Christensen, leading theorist of US innovation in recent decades, refers to it as "disruptive" (Christensen 2013). Orthodox political science has largely ignored both this Schumpeterian view of advanced capitalism and the key disruptive role of the American political economy. Understanding why the USA has driven radical innovation is therefore of importance in theorizing the American political economy, and the tentative explanation put forward in this chapter is congruent with the intellectual drive of this volume.

In the first section of the chapter, America as driver of radical innovation is argued to reflect two self-reinforcing institutional complexes, both decentralized and relatively weakly regulated. The first complex is research/finance/market-governed research, professional/technological labor markets, and finance; the other is legal/political-governed courts, politics, and lobbying. I show how advanced companies have made use of these two complexes. While these institutions have evolved, they are historically embedded and go back to at least the strategic political choices of the Republican Ascendency in the gilded age. The important point is that the American system, decentralized, money-porous and weakly regulated, is quite different from the other Liberal Market Economies and notably different from the UK. Perhaps most interestingly, China is the only other nation which has emerged recently as capable of radical innovation, though not necessarily (at least yet) the inventions behind it (Economy 2018); China is evidently very different from the USA, but the section closes by pointing out the functional equivalence of the American

[3] As, on a much smaller scale, has the UK (DNA, radar, etc.); the innovative capacity of the UK has, however, been weak since the mid to late nineteenth century, when UK institutions were much less centralized than they became.

framework to the Chinese, especially with respect to the courts-politics-lobbying complex.

The second section shows how the ICT revolution has led to radical geographic change in the USA with the economic upsurge of key graduate-intensive and innovation-oriented cities – Storper's "Great Inversion" – in an increasingly mass-educated graduate population among the younger generations.

The third section asks why radical innovation has slowed in the twenty-first century, with the USA lead over China remaining but declining. This is seen, in terms of the American courts-politics-lobbying complex, as a consequence of the growing polarization of party politics stemming from the alignment of the Democrats with the big successful cities, and Republicans abjuring public spending and focusing on tax cuts. The fourth section concludes.

There is a large literature on national systems of innovation, including the US system, on which I draw. Atkinson (2020) has a very useful recent discussion. I approach the question in a slightly different way, in particular to draw out the role of politics and political economy and to locate the argument in the framework provided by Hacker, Hertel-Fernandez, Pierson, and Thelen (Introduction, this volume).

While there is no agreed definition of radical innovation, I take the most notable aspect of the major waves of technological-organizational breakthroughs as the rapid growth (scaling-up, also mergers) of small companies or hostile spin-offs or start-ups into giant companies. I will loosely refer to this as radical innovation capacity (in contemporary discussion this is the capacity to create unicorns). See also Block (2010), Hughes (1987), and Mazzucato (2015) for a wider discussion of the role in this of the federal government.

Explaining radical innovation capacity, I focus on two core institutional complexes: a research/market/finance complex governing the relations between research and research universities, professional and technological labor markets, and business finance; and a legal/political/lobbying complex governing the relations between courts, party politics, and lobbying. Critically, these complexes operate in a decentralized and weakly regulated way in the USA, quite in contrast to the UK and the other LMEs (with the partial exception of Israel), as well as in contrast to more statist advanced Asian economies and CMEs. As noted previously, the only country which currently parallels the USA in radical innovation capacity is China; and we will suggest below that China has functionally equivalent complexes (Ang 2016, 2020).

The chapter argues that the two aforementioned institutional complexes are responsible for the radical innovation capacity of the USA. Both complexes go back at least to the late nineteenth century in the USA and the institutional components of each are *decentralized* and *weakly regulated* as well as strongly complementary to each other. In the case of the research-professionals-finance complex they are (1) the system of higher education and research, (2) fluid and deep professional and technological labor markets, and (3) business finance, respectively.

This complex reflects a particular institutional heritage going back to the (re)foundational period of advanced capitalism by the Republican Ascendancy presidents in the 1880s after the failure of Reconstruction. (This history is discussed later.) The institutions that took shape were unique among the emerging advanced economies, and unusually propitious to radical innovation:

(1) Highly flexible, decentralized, and competitive systems of research and higher education, largely at the university level and in the research diaspora of universities, and/or in the research laboratories of large corporations. Leading universities were set up privately and/or with close connections to wealthy communities.

(2) A high-level (professional and technical) labor market that allows easy movement across professions (via professional schools), enables talented individuals to form spin-offs from existing (advanced) companies, and allows individuals to recover status after unsuccessful innovative projects. Flexibility in the high-end labor market has facilitated spin-offs, which boosted American capacity for radical innovation over the last century (Klepper 2001, 2007, 2009, 2010; Klepper and Sleeper 2005; Klepper and Thompson 2010). And companies could scale-up rapidly with access to such a low risk-averse market. (Morris (1994) provides a contrast with the UK.)

(3) Equally flexible and decentralized systems of finance, widely geographically distributed and with a wide variety of institutions, relatively little regulation, and substantial capacity for investment in high risk ventures as well as ones potentially disruptive to existing corporations (Davis and Neal 2007).

(4) As more rapidly growing start-ups, typically founded near big research universities, demanded professionals (managers, media, lawyers, etc.), and technologists (especially software engineers), so large residential areas built up, attracting high-risk specialist finance (especially VC), specialist lawyers, headhunters, patent scientists,

and other constituents of relevant ecosystems. This greatly facilitated start-ups and their subsequent growth, as well as critically reducing the risk of failure.

Complementing this decentralized and deregulated research-professionals-finance agglomerated market complex was the courts-politics-lobbying complex. This is at the heart of the Hacker, Hertel-Fernandez, Pierson, and Thelen (HHPT) understanding of the American Political Economy. It is equally decentralized and deregulated; more accurately it is perhaps an environment of regulations highly open to reregulation. The HHPT insight is to see the courts-politics-lobbying complex as decentralized, "multi-venue," and business porous. Those multiple venues include counties, cities, states, as well as the federal level, the Presidency, and Congress, with courts, elections, parties, boards, and agencies at each level. What is absent at all these venues – in comparison to other advanced national systems – are stable and established bureaucracies. The vacuum is filled by lobbying, lawyers, and investment in politicians.

But this has a positive side in radical innovation, both in terms of the public resources and (often radically different) rulemaking needed as a new technology is developed and introduced. And in terms of rapidly growing and radically innovating companies, what is needed is protection from politicians, and perhaps from voters, and the ability to access those shaping regulations and resources. For while the American complex has multiplied vetoes, and opened multiple opportunities for engaging in (conservative) state lawmaking (Hertel-Fernandez 2019), presidents, governors, and mayors of big cities, but also lawyers, lobbyists, and aspiring politicians have had space to intervene. (The role of the state in the ICT revolution is set out in the second section.)

Finally, two key unifying conditions constrain the decentralization of these two complexes of institutions. The first is the Interstate Commerce clause of the Constitution, which in effect requires free trade within the United States and prevents individual states adopting protectionist policies in relation to the other states. The second is the requirement of market competition under the federal Sherman and the Clayton Acts (albeit with varying interpretations).

Call these two systems (the research-relevant markets and courts-politics and lobbying systems), and these two overarching legal conditions (anti-protectionist and pro-competitive) the "American framework." The contention of the chapter is that the American framework promoted radical innovation.

Rethinking Varieties of Capitalism: USA as Sui Generis Rather than Paradigmatic Case

One implication which we want to emphasize is that we should put the USA in a category of its own in terms of varieties of capitalism; or at least as a different category of LME, and certainly instead of treating it as the paradigmatic LME. In any case, understanding the radical difference of the USA underlines the case for studying the American political economy as sui generis.

It is worth underlining the far greater degree of centralization of the relevant UK institutions, starting from the focus of power on the prime minister with a majority in the House of Commons and the strength of the national government vis-à-vis localities. Large differences are also apparent in the other contributors to radical innovation just highlighted. The Bank of England (private or nationalized) has had a high degree of de facto control of financial institutions going back to the nineteenth century. The university system (even Oxford and Cambridge) has de facto long been influenced and standardized, as well as partially financed and increasingly regulated, by the government. And in relation to the construction of giant companies, when competition legislation was initially enacted in the UK in 1948, its concern was the market share of leading corporations – there was no goal of rolling out "good" giant companies, in part because for a long period governments were nervous of imposing "the right to manage" on the shop floor. This does not (remotely) equate the UK to Coordinated Market Economies such as Germany; brilliant breakthroughs have come in the UK (largely from Cambridge), such as the structure of DNA, but the transformation of basic science into large-scale production systems is American.[4]

China as the Other Radical Innovation Driver

With the sole (possible) serious comparison of China very recently, the USA is the only large advanced capitalist system with these institutional characteristics. We take (very loosely) the transformation of start-ups (or spin-offs) into giant companies in a short period as a measure of radical innovation capacity, and hence use data on the number of unicorns. As noted previously, China has a level of unicorns to rival the US level, with

[4] The only other LME that has been successful given its size in creating unicorns is Israel, which also has institutional parallels to the USA, but our work is not sufficiently advanced yet to draw strong conclusions.

the USA and China much higher than any other country. And, while the BAT companies (Baidu, Alibaba, Tencent) plus Huawei, Bytedance, Lenovo, and Xiaomi are tech giants to rival FAANG plus Microsoft, Intel, and IBM, the USA and China far outdistance any other country.[5]

Our argument for the radical innovation capacity of the USA gains plausibility if some parallel institutional argument could be made for China. Of course, China is organized along very different lines than the USA institutionally. And apart from a number of AI areas, Chinese science and technology is not yet at the same level as that in the USA. Still, we suggest that the relevant institutions in the two countries may be functionally equivalent.

If we take the research-professionals-finance complex, an editorial in *Finextra* commented (20/1/2020):

> China's FinTech industry is incomparable to the rest of the world. It is home to eight of the world's leading FinTech unicorns, with an average value of $26.8BN – eight times greater than the average value of North American FinTech unicorns. But, behind China's rapid FinTech development lies a country with unique circumstances, consisting of a large, tech-savvy population, and an open regulatory environment. The unique landscape is only reinforced by China's dedication to its tech giants – Baidu, Alibaba, and Tencent, who have never had restrictions imposed on their growth. Currently, there is no single regulatory body responsible for the regulation of FinTech products and services. Instead, different FinTech services and products are regulated by different regulatory bodies and there is a requirement to bring order to the rapidly expanding industry.

China also has the largest banking system in the world, with City and County Banks, as well as four huge state banks, and a large shadow-banking sector. In the second quarter of 2018, Chinese start-ups accounted for 47 percent of world venture capital funding surpassing the USA (KrAsia, May 14, 2020). And there is widespread informal lending through Guanxi networks. Business finance is thus equally decentralized and weakly regulated as in the USA.

Next there is a large and deep pool of professionals, technologists, engineers, and computer programmers. In the Shanghai ranking of world universities by subjects, 29 of the top 100 university departments in engineering and programming were in Chinese universities and 27 in American. It is harder to get data directly linking start-ups to university research.

In sum, this suggests that the research-professionals-finance complex is powerful, as well as being decentralized and relatively unregulated. A

[5] Tse (2015) and Fannin (2019) have interesting accounts of these Chinese tech giants.

compelling overall picture of the degree of intense market competition in the research and innovation arena is set out in Breznitz and Murphree's (2011)*Run of the Red Queen: Government, Innovation, Globalization and Economic Growth in China.*

This is reinforced by Ang's marvelous and provocative work on the decentralization of the political system in China (Ang 2016, 2020). This is almost perfectly the functional equivalent of the American courts-politics-lobbying complex discussed earlier. In the Chinese version of this that Ang sets out, provincial and city party leaders are judged by Beijing for subsequent promotions based on economic growth and avoidance of unrest; and incentives for good economic performance are reinforced by (good) corruption: helping dynamic companies with finance or regulations, resolving legal problems, or facilitating permissions and the right introductions higher up in the party or government, in exchange for shares in the company or other benefits. Clearly start-ups need to meet the market test! But if they can, this "Chinese framework" can explain its success in producing unicorns.

US Dominance in Radical Innovation

There is no agreed way of measuring a country's performance in radical innovation. Winning Nobel prizes is not equivalent to radical innovation, but it gives a (lagged) measure of breakthrough science. A rough idea of the USA in the leading innovative edge of science over the past century or so is shown in table 1.2 of Urquiola (2020), which tracks national affiliations of Nobel prizewinners. There are various ways of showing this to be the case, taking account of the implicit lags. Urquiola uses biographical details of Nobel Prize winners to show the institutions to which they had affiliations (Urquiola 2020). (The winners may have been in more than one country, and thus the table is without reference to their nationalities. In addition, although the first Nobel Prize was only in 1901, the list includes the prior history of the prize winner's affiliations.) For each academic Nobel Laureate, Urquiola (2020, table 1.2) shows the number of institutional (generally university) affiliations by nation in each period, including the affiliation when the prize was won but not subsequent affiliations (see Figure 11.1). It does not measure number of prizes: In the interwar period the USA, Germany, and the UK were roughly even in the number of Nobel prizes. In Physics, Chemistry, and Medicine/Physiology each won six. After World War II, the USA had significantly more prize winners, with most of those having American institutional affiliations before the War. China is late in this game.

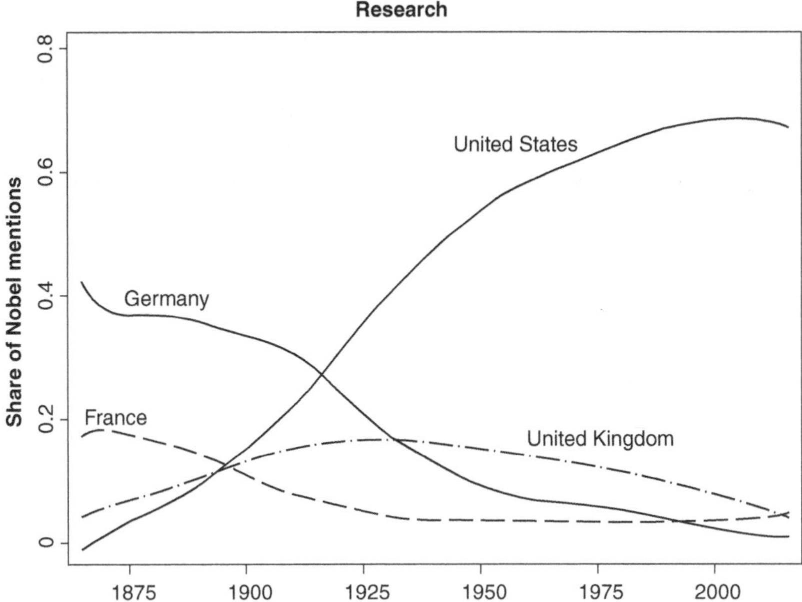

FIGURE 11.1 Nobel institutional mentions over time
Source: Urquiola (2020, table 1.2)

Another measure (with its own imperfections) of recent innovation dominance is the number of unicorns. CB Insights shows the USA as the leading country, by far, in the number of unicorns – privately held start-ups with valuations of over $1 billion – in 2015 (CB Insights 2020). It has roughly double the number in China, with China having roughly four times the number in the UK, the next highest total. More recent data, using different sources, has China as close to or overtaking the USA, thus further posing the possibility of developing US weakness. But most commentators believe that the USA is currently still significantly ahead of China in most areas of science, even if the relative standing of the USA may be declining.

A Brief History

Some elements of this institutional system go back to the original colonization of America. But following Bensel (also Gerstle), the key elements of the institutional strategy of industrialization were developed during the last third of the nineteenth century under a string of Republican presidents following the failure of Reconstruction (Bensel 2000, Gerstle 2017).

Indeed, the clues to understanding the multi-venue complexity of the contemporary American political economy, and the power therein of big business and finance today to access political systems, lie in this (re-) foundational period. That period was in turn based on the rich pre-foundational tapestry of more strongly and more loosely regulated municipalities and counties, as well as the states in which they were embedded (Novak 1996).

The Republican Ascendency presidents from 1877 on were confronted with the failure of Reconstruction on the one hand and the success of European industrialization on the other. Close both to Northern industrialists and to financial capital, they saw forced industrialization as a central goal given the evident strength of European industrialization and military power (notably in England and Germany). But as Germany and England in the late nineteenth century show in different ways, a great range of centralized framework institutions is needed for advanced industrialization. Little of that then existed in Washington, and the Federal government had minimal administrative capacity. This was not a "weak American state" (Novak 2008). But it was not a strong centralized state. Administrative capacity instead lay in the big and rapidly growing cities of this period, mainly in the Northeast and Midwest, and in a limited number of state capitols. It lay too in the railroad companies, as well as in northern manufacturing companies (partly as a result of the Civil War). The South – where the states were more organized and powerful – was hostile to industrialization for fear it would give employment and education to the black population. Thus Republican presidents excluded the former Confederacy – in any event a stronghold of the Democratic Party after the collapse of Reconstruction – from their industrialization strategy. As a model of successful corporate growth, they had the example of the well-organized and highly scaled transcontinental railroad companies (Chandler 1965).

Confirming the argument of Rahman and Thelen in this volume, the distinctive foundations of radical innovation in the United States relied as well on contributions from the courts. The strategy rested on permissive Supreme Court decisions, while elected officials "stuffed" the court with lawyers who had been directors of the railroad companies (Bensel 2000). Although the reality was far more complex, there were two key elements:

(1) An American (and latterly Borkian) "rule of reason" interpretation of competition policy encouraged giant companies along the lines of the major railroad companies by allowing trusts and mergers and encouraging rather than regulating the uncoordinated

finance sector in the process. Eventually, presidents could use threats of the Sherman Antitrust Act (1890) to distinguish between Theodore Roosevelt's "good" and "bad" trusts. This meant that giant corporations had a powerful incentive to use economies of scale and scope to keep costs and unit profitability low, to be able to invoke the "rule of reason," and show that consumers benefitted from market dominance.

(2) Prevention of protection at the level of cities or states encouraged the transcontinental "rollout" of the highly scaled giant corporations. This was enforced through Supreme Court interpretations of the Interstate Commerce clause, which also encouraged cities to make conditions attractive to these corporations (bringing employment and rising property values to the city), in part by preventing or limiting unionization of their semi-skilled workforces. These legal constraints had the consequence of reinforcing the organization and control of production in large-scale industry to engineers and foremen rather than to skilled workers and their unions. AFL unions thus organized skilled services and smaller manufacturing companies.

Important though parties were (Aldrich 2011), Congressional politicians were rooted in city and state politics rather than in centralized and disciplined parties. Both corporations and cities engaged in congressional politics to safeguard their specific interests. Given the decentralization of the parties and the power of individual members of Congress, local economic interests had the incentives and capacity to "invest" in those members. Those investments served in turn to maintain the legislature's porousness. And the more laws Congress passed and the greater the role of Federal agencies became over time, the greater the incentive to invest in politicians. Given the continuing role of state politics as well as those of the big cities, parties remained relatively undisciplined as individual politicians retained independent sources of power – a quite different environment than the UK, where parties were centralizing over this period (Cox 1987).

One might have expected that financial institutions would have developed in similar ways to the giant industrial corporations. Large-scale commercial banks, however, would have required branch banking, and the distribution of political power across municipalities and states blocked branch banking in many environments. The McFadden Act (1927) formally prohibited interstate branch banking. The Interstate Commerce clause was deemed not to apply. More widely and despite many attempts, there was relatively little general regulation of financial institutions until Glass-Steagall in 1933 (which prohibited commercial banks from investing in companies). Even then, American financial institutions remained relatively unregulated, thus permitting very large investment banks to develop, often institutionalized as trusts. A myriad of deposit banks sent reserves to financial institutions in New York for short-term lending. In turn, investment banks used these resources, as well as the value of their investments in large manufacturing companies, to finance the merger wave of the early twentieth century. The New York Stock Exchange could adopt rules to cover the companies quoted on it but not on the riskier Curb Market in New York (O'Sullivan 2006).

More basically, a large amount of money was available for investments, and outside the formal commercial banking system and (to a lesser extent) the NYSE and the SEC there was relatively little in the way of centralized regulation. Thus the constraints on the financial system were those which municipalities and/or states imposed. This favored risky finance (outside commercial banks, where residents' money was at risk) when the risk finance came from outside (or from the wealthy) while the successful developments benefited in part the residents.

Universities developed in a decentralized fashion for broadly similar reasons. The Federal government had only limited administrative capacity. Frameworks for higher education were largely provided at the state level through state university systems. The 1862 Morrill Act provided endowments for colleges in the form of grants of land (30,000 acres per state member of Congress) to be used to teach agriculture and engineering (mechanics). This in fact favored the more industrialized Northeastern and Midwest states; they could be and were run in ways tailored to benefit local industry. Apart from Cornell and MIT, they have remained public institutions, and they played a major role in producing more engineers annually than Germany by the end of the nineteenth century. The trustees who ran the older universities (inter alia Harvard, Princeton, Yale, Columbia) pushed those universities in a more industrial/scientific/engineering direction. So did the philanthropic founders of the period, mainly from the newly successful companies (inter alia Carnegie, Mellon, Duke, Stanford, MIT, Caltech).

For similar reasons, trustees and philanthropists, state governments and city elites, and the growing corporations themselves, were concerned to develop flexible professional schools at the universities (in law, engineering, and management) to staff corporations. But the concern was to use them in building organizations rather than consolidate formalized professions. So these professional schools developed high intellectual standards, but where general argument was prized. Above all they enabled mobility, geographical as well as professional, capable of working across disciplines and of management (in the broadest sense).

The strength of the university system combined with the flexibility of professional training and its deployment have been important drivers of radical innovation. A key empirical industry study (by an ex-engineer) comparing the very different development of the American and British microelectronics industry is illustrative (Morris 1994):

> A further advantage held by American microelectronics industry over that of Britain has been that because of its large-scale industrial development, there were many more sophisticated firms operating within the electronic industry, with a much larger potential pool of skilled personnel. Unlike the situation in Britain, skilled labour mobility within the United States has tended to be high. Because of this culture of high labour mobility, a sizable reservoir of highly skilled scientists, engineers and technicians has constantly been available for recruitment into any new rapidly developing technical field. This factor is of particular importance within such an industry as semiconductor manufacture, which, because of its multidisciplinary nature, involves bringing together numbers of chemists, physicists, metallurgists and engineers in order to form balanced teams. The relative strength of these teams, whether operating at the research or development-production level, must largely determine the rate of technical progress and production efficiency. A specific case where labour mobility greatly assisted the early growth of semiconductor manufacture in America, is the well-known example of the diffusion of technical expertise from Bell Laboratories to an extremely large number of firms. In this respect, Bell was unique in providing a technical stimulus. In general, movement between academia and industry has been much more frequent within the United States, and a higher proportion of goal-oriented work carried out within the universities. (Morris 1994: 247)

The Earlier Technological Revolutions

It is worth noting briefly that many of the distinctive institutional features that helped advance the ICT revolution were in evidence during the two other main periods of radical innovation in which America acted as technology driver. Central to both cases were revolutionary breakthroughs in techniques to operate at mass scale. Standardization and scalability characterized these innovatory episodes as they have the ICT revolution. First, in the late nineteenth and early twentieth centuries, across a whole range of industries, Chandlerian corporations built integrated operations from basic research through to marketing, sales, and distribution. Economic historians often refer to this period as the Second Industrial Revolution. These corporations used the transcontinental railroad systems built (with extensive federal land-grants) since the Civil War. They also copied the sophisticated logistical systems the railroad companies had developed. They did this, Hamiltonian-style, behind a tariff wall, making use of European technology where necessary. More important, they also developed a range of sophisticated but relatively standardized goods produced at great scale, with machinery and equipment designed by their engineers (electro-mechanical and electro-chemical) and scientists. These goods were mainly produced by process-manufacturing (steel, nonferrous metals, sugar, rubber, pharmaceuticals, cement, chemicals, petroleum). These developments were flanked by a quite astonishing range of new products and technologies:

> Concentrated in this short time span were inventions of electric generators, dynamite, photographic film, light bulbs, electric motors, internal combustion engines, steam turbines, aluminum, and pre-stressed concrete and all this even before the turn of the century. The pre-World World War I surge of invention culminated with airplanes, tractors, radio, plastics, neon lights, and synthetic fertilizers in the first decade of the twentieth century. (Davis and Neal 2007: 129–130)

Industrial monopolies were formed across many industries with the use of trusts, in the so-called Great Merger movement of the late 1890s and early 1900s (Lamoreaux 1988). What is significant (albeit disputed) in facilitating this process was Teddy Roosevelt's use of the "rule of reason" in deploying the Sherman Act to distinguish between "good" and "bad" trusts. A similarly disruptive period in the 1920s ushered in the Fordist revolution, with spin-offs and heightened competition as Ford put together his company. These developments were facilitated by both a highly flexible financial system and the federal government's beneficent attitude toward the rapid scaling up of giant companies.

THE ICT REVOLUTION

The centrality of the United States to the ICT revolution developed in part from many of the same favorable institutional conditions. The ICT revolution emerged in the United States far earlier than elsewhere. The Federal government (and principally the Department of Defense) both funded basic university research across a wide range of areas and subsidized technology companies. The extensive but loose and flexible networks described earlier played a central role in translating this initial research and funding into dynamic and scalable companies. One can trace a sequence of firms and scientists (with much movement early on from Cambridge, Massachusetts, to Silicon Valley), with the Engineering department at Stanford and Terman, its entrepreneurial Dean, playing an important mediating function. Following the move of Shockley (who broke with Bell Labs and then Raytheon on the East Coast), a cascade of spin-offs took place. The "traitorous 8" left Shockley to found Fairchild, from which Noyce and Moore then broke off to set up Intel. All of these firms were close to Stanford, where Hewlett-Packard was already established.

In this brief summary, it is important to stress that as the revolution developed it fostered the build-up of a number of hugely powerful cities and their metropolitan areas in which the breakthroughs in radical innovation were located. These early Silicon Valley entrants became part of a sprawling agglomeration, supported by massive public funding and increasing private capital. The rapidly expanding network included Berkeley and UCSF, as well as a growing ecology of venture capitalists, investment banks, technology, and patent lawyers, many based in San Jose, then San Francisco, and later still Oakland. Similar, if smaller, agglomerations developed later in the Boston area, because the advanced companies there were initially more established and internally hierarchical, and less porous to external interchanges (Gertler et al. 1995; Saxenian 1994). More would follow in New York, Seattle, and other major cities. As is well-known, these science-based agglomerations have subsequently developed in the NC Research Triangle, in Austin, Texas, in San Diego, Boulder, Madison, Pittsburgh, etc. (But it will be an important part of the later argument that they did not develop in a large number of "red" states, stacking up the political polarization underlying the ICT revolution in the USA.)

The ICT Revolution and Returns to Analytic and Social (but Not Physical) Skills and Horizontal Organizations

The big cities in which many have benefited from the ICT revolution have become complex and shifting constellations that create considerable challenges for urban politicians striving to maintain unity despite divisions (Ogorzalek 2018). The cities themselves are divided between very poor ethnic areas and the rest; and the rest is divided between the highly educated areas (such as in Manhattan and parts of Brooklyn in

New York) and other, less educated but far from poor areas. The surrounding suburbs are divided both ethnically and on educational and economic grounds.

These new cleavages reflect the dynamics of agglomeration, where one part of the population invested heavily in university education, and this dramatically transformed the high skill and innovative economies of key large cities. To understand how this has worked itself out, we have to analyze the way IT has transformed company structures and management practices. There is in fact huge variation in company performance in the United States, even within narrowly defined sectors and within different establishments of the same company. In this section we discuss the high value-added establishments of companies, largely employing graduates. Knowledge-based establishments of companies, with much oversimplification, are organized on a project group basis (for example, developing a new product line), with relatively short lines of communication with top management. We refer to this type of organization as having a "horizontal" or "relational" structure in what follows.

Returns to Skills

The ICT revolution occurred over a long period of time, so in describing its effects on skills temporal compression is necessary. But there is some agreement that there have been three main effects on the return to skills:

(1) As a result of massive technical change in the workplace, the demand for physical skills has greatly declined. Although manufacturing output remains high, this has gone with a sharp decline in the manufacturing workforce, reflecting high productivity in production facilities located in the USA. Outsourcing and the transfer of much production to China and South East Asia and the Subcontinent, via global value chains, or through direct import competition, has reinforced this employment decline. Moreover, the demand for significant physical strength in the service sectors, in which most employment is now created in the USA, is quite limited.

(2) For what can be called knowledge-based sectors, the ability to access information and software via a computer console, and the payoff from being able to use that information, increases the return to analytic skills. These skills are especially in demand in service or technology/research sectors, which account for perhaps 50 percent of employment of the workforce under 40. In nearly all these

sectors, this work requires a college education or at least associate degree level in a community college. Currently around 40 percent of the labor force over twenty-five are college graduates or above; and in addition 28 percent have some college or an associate degree (BLS data for 2016, see Brundage 2017).

(3) In moving from a Fordist world of relatively hierarchical companies with well-defined ranges of tasks and instructions to one of project groups in knowledge-based establishments, social skills have become increasingly important. The ability to interact with others requires more than analytic abilities. Now employers seek a wide range of competences: the ability to communicate easily, negotiate, provide leadership, to possess e-skills and the ability to "read" others, be empathetic, reliable, imaginative, likeable, capable of developing good and durable working relations, be tolerant of diversity, and so on. These all become desirable assets, as does the ability to exercise them in relation to those of a broadly similar educational level. Acquisition of some or all of these skills is most commonly learnt in higher education, not in lectures but through living, discussing, and organizing life with fellow students.

All of this has increased the demand by knowledge-based companies for graduates with both analytic and social skills. As a result, the return to college has increased relative to high school graduation over several decades. There have been two consequences for investment in education. The first is that university participation has increased. In this BLS data, the percentage of college graduates in the labor force rose 13 percent from 1992 to 2016. NCES data show that 36 percent of those aged between eighteen and twenty-four were in college, implying a rate of college participation over a four-year period of around 55 percent, against 39 percent in 1991. (A point we will come back to is that participation stabilized between 2010 and 2016.) The second implication was that there was a bigger payoff for women than for men, since physical skills were no longer so valuable. The participation rate for women in higher education in the USA was about 8 to 9 percent above that for men in 2017 (OECD 2018).

The Growing Incentives for Colocation

The United States is undergoing a "great inversion," where high-skilled workers return in large numbers to large cities (Storper 2013). Why has the "flat earth" which Thomas Friedman (2005) predicted as a result of the ICT revolution not happened? Why have smart people increasingly located close together? Knowledge-based companies generally require their workers to work in the same physical location, to "co-locate." There is no agreed theory of why this is the case; but it is central (at least at the moment) to the way knowledge economies work in all advanced economies. In our view, it is linked to the need in project groups for people to work together over a period of time to develop projects; this is a world of (at best) incomplete contracts, tying a number of people together over uncertain lengths of time during which ideally they need to build relations of implicit obligation toward each other. This is very difficult to do if they live and work in different places, perhaps in different countries. It is almost impossible for other members of a project group to monitor how someone in a different geographical place is spending their time (they might be working for someone else or not working). Moreover, in most joint working systems, individual effort is important but difficult to factor into rewards, so interpersonal ties and implicit obligations become important – and interpersonal relationships develop (if they were not there beforehand) through personal interaction over time. If strong interpersonal relations within a group are important for the group to function cohesively and deal with the myriad of conflicts and opportunities which arise within it, then that seems closely linked to physical proximity. A family, or a group of close friends, is an analogy; it would be difficult to evolve close relations if people lived apart.

Skill Clusters

Overlapping skill clusters are evident in large successful urban agglomerations. The most obvious sectors are:

- High value-added services, including finance, law, accounting and management consultancies, and advertising
- Culture, media, entertainment and high-end retail
- Knowledge intensive business services (KIBS) and software
- Medical, research universities and professional schools, research facilities and think tanks

Urban agglomerations in the knowledge economy provide a wide range of complex high-skill-intensive products largely in the form of services from their skill clusters. These are sold within the metro area, in other urban agglomerations within North America, or in other advanced economies. These skill clusters also induce two sorts of major companies to locate in the urban agglomeration:

- Subsidiaries of knowledge-based multinationals, buying into (often technological research-based) relevant skill clusters
- Headquarters of advanced companies, able to access easily the multiple high-level specialized business services available (which in the Fordist era they would likely have produced in-house)

Graduate Social Networks

Skill clusters constitute one way of looking at the relations among graduates across the successful big city. But these relationships are held together by the even more powerful glue of social networks. Interwoven social networks linking friends and partners (discussed later) are critical to urban agglomeration.

Urban areas, even New York, are far from homogeneous. The overall proportion of graduates in New York, 36 percent (in the twenty-five to sixty-four age group in 2009–13), compares with the US average of 30 percent. But this ranges from 59 percent in Manhattan to 18 percent in the Bronx. (These figures would be higher if I took the twenty-five to thirty-four age group.) Manhattan south of Harlem has an extraordinarily high rate of college graduates, with seventeen of its neighborhoods having above 70 percent rates; large chunks of both Queens and Brooklyn also have high rates. But contrast this with other parts of Brooklyn, Queens, and the Bronx. (The Centre for an Urban Future uses data from the 2011–15 American Community five-year estimates from American Bureau of the Census to derive data on the New York Boroughs and Precincts.)

Assortative Mating

One of the most marked social phenomena of recent decades is that of *assortative mating*. Young people tend to find their future partners among people of the same educational background. This is particularly true of graduates. Permanent relationships tend to start much later than was the case in earlier decades. But frequently this happens through the social networks formed during higher education, or through people met subsequently via a member of the network. Assortative mating significantly increases the attractiveness of agglomerations. If both partners are pursuing careers in different high-level occupations, they can only live in a city that has enough skill clusters to accommodate both of them. In that case, cities of residential choice will likely be large cities with wide ranges of skill clusters. The absence of a wide range of clusters has handicapped highly specialized manufacturing cities, such as Detroit or Cincinnati.

The incentive of preserving graduate social networks reinforces this bias toward the large (or very large city). This is an area on which more work needs to be done, but the likelihood that the best companies in a particular sector will be in a very large city, and that there will be many sectoral clusters in such a city, makes it sensible to stay in, or move to, a large city if your social network is already there. The combination of these considerations with assortative mating gives a strong upward twist to successful agglomerating cities.

Agglomerations and Property Prices

This is accompanied by a further dynamic. The more intense the desired geographical interactions, the more costly the price of property since there will be high demand for property close to the "right sort of people" (as Henry James might have said). Assortative mating only intensifies this dynamic; it provides extra financial resources for such property, and hence plays a major role in raising prices.

A large part of the increase in wealth inequality to which Piketty has pointed, results not from increased investment in business capital, but from rising house prices in the large urban agglomerations (Bonnet et al. 2014). Piketty pays little attention to technological change and the ICT revolution, but much of the increase in wealth he describes can be attributed to it in this indirect way (Piketty 2014).

To summarize: the ICT revolution has dramatically altered economic geography. It has encouraged the development of skill clusters in urban agglomerations, and this process has fed on itself as graduates face incentives to move into these agglomerations to work in these clusters, preserve social networks, and facilitate assortative mating. This whole process concentrates human capital, as well as wealth through rising urban house prices.

SEGREGATION AND SLOWDOWN: EMERGING OBSTACLES TO RADICAL INNOVATION

There is growing agreement that radical innovation in the USA has slowed down in the twenty-first century, especially during and after the Great

Recession. It would certainly be wrong to suggest that the USA has become incapable of radical innovation. A lot of evidence, however, including that of the steady decline of productivity growth, points to a slowdown. While few observers see China as close to being competitive with the USA currently, it has clearly been catching up. In a decade it is likely to be a challenger in a number of key areas, notably AI.

The general argument of the chapter is that two broad sets of factors explain American dominance in radical innovation. First, a unique set of institutions – highly competitive research systems; relatively unregulated financial systems; scalable companies; and professional and technologically oriented labor markets that facilitate spin-offs and career switching. These institutions have not significantly changed.

The other reason for the success of American dominance of radical innovation over the long term has been – in many different ways – a supportive federal government. This support took somewhat different forms in different periods of technological change. For the ICT revolution several elements stand out. As we saw in the last section, developing the new ICT technology required increasingly expensive research. The Federal government provided massive support for the initial substantial investment in the necessary basic and applied science.

Political Geography and the Decline of the Military-Industrial Complex

Large investments in basic science (in a whole range of different disciplines including new interstitial disciplines) appear key to the maintenance of radical innovation. Yet this support has gradually declined. A major argument in this section is that such support has increasingly posed a dilemma in a context where the immediate benefits of these investments seem highly geographically concentrated. Given the way political incentives are structured in the USA it is difficult to deliver such benefits, and the increasingly spatial character of partisan polarization has only increased the difficulty.

Within the American constitutional design, presidents have the clearest incentives to think about the broad preconditions for economic prosperity. Yet to carry Congress, which is based on territorial representation, presidents need to demonstrate that the benefit of major spending programs will be geographically widespread. Members of Congress must be convinced that their constituents will benefit from the spending or approve of it. This can happen in two ways: the spending may offer direct (geographically specific) benefits to their constituents; or it may be seen as benefitting the nation (or a class therein) as a whole.

Much of the federal government's foundational spending on R&D came from the Department of Defense. Defense spending may directly benefit constituencies via companies (defense contractors) or via the service sector supplying military institutions or research establishments located there. Indirectly, during the Cold War, specialized defense expenditures in research laboratories were seen as protecting the nation as a whole against the Soviet threat. Eisenhower explained it thus, in leaving office in 1961 early in the build-up (Farewell Address 1961):

> A vital element in keeping the peace is our military establishment. Our arms must be mighty, ready for instant action, so that no potential aggressor may be tempted to risk his own destruction ... This conjunction of an immense military establishment and a large arms industry is new in the American experience. The total influence – economic, political, even spiritual – is felt in every city, every Statehouse, every office of the Federal government ... We recognize the imperative need for this development. Yet we must not fail to comprehend its grave implications. ... In the councils of government, we must guard against the acquisition of unwarranted influence, whether sought or unsought, by the military-industrial complex. .... Akin to, and largely responsible for the sweeping changes in our industrial-military posture, has been the technological revolution during recent decades. In this revolution, research has become central; it also becomes more formalized, complex, and costly.

Just as earlier presidencies had idealized "growth" models – the railroad companies in the later nineteenth century, and Ford and GM in the early Fordist era, Eisenhower signals the broad benefits – and also potential dangers – of the military-industrial complex. This brief passage (subtly) first explains the "national" benefit then the localized benefits, and (somewhat hidden) the acceptance that research is key and it will only take place in particular places.

By the mid-1980s, however, the Cold War threat began to lose its sharpness. Federal funding's share of national R&D spending declined from the mid-late 1980s on from over 50 percent to one-third in the mid 1990s and then less than a quarter by 2015 (NSF 2020). As Barnes shows in her contribution to this volume, US public investments in R&D have also declined in comparison with other rich democracies (see also OECD 2019b). While the *scientific* case for spending on basic research in IT and a range of associated sciences was increasing, the end of the Cold War

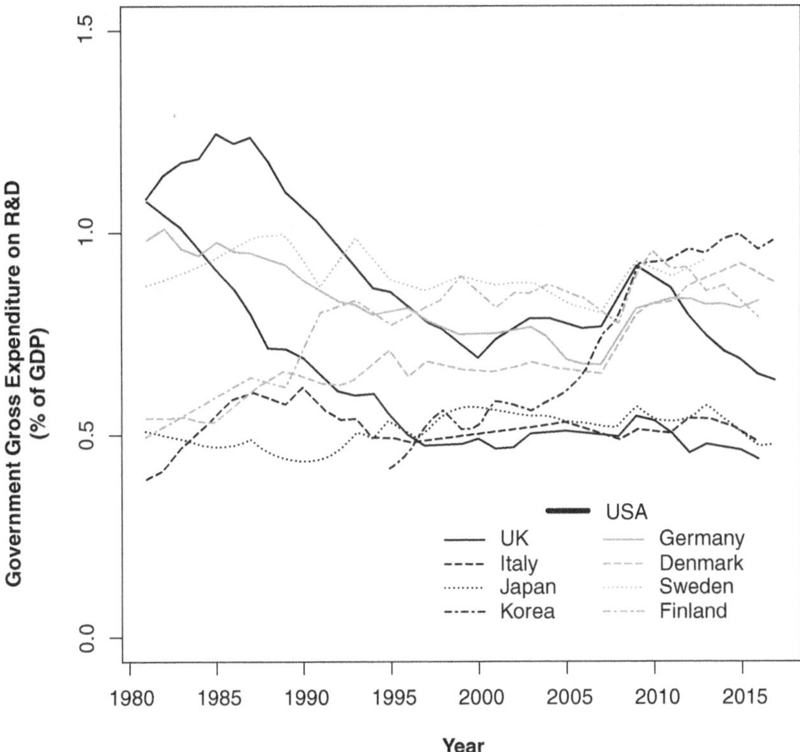

FIGURE 11.2 Comparative government expenditure on R&D (GERD)
Source: OECD, Main Science and Technology Indicators. Vol. 1 (2019)

and collapse of the USSR made the Federal case for support harder (see Figure 11.2).

Political Geography, Research Agglomerations, and Left-Behind Areas

In the second section we showed the centrality of the Great Inversion to the ICT revolution (Storper 2013). From the 1980s on, the driving areas of research (and as a result, radical innovation) have largely been located in a relatively small number of hugely successful cities. Most notable are San Francisco (with San Jose and the Bay Area), Boston (and Cambridge), New York, DC (with Baltimore and parts of Maryland and Virginia), as well as Austin, Pittsburgh, Seattle, Denver/Boulder, Chicago, San Diego, and the Research Triangle. These wealthy areas are in turn linked to a small number of mainly private universities. In turn a small number of states are the key beneficiaries (New York, California, Massachusetts, Washington, Colorado).

This narrow geographic concentration of activity has collided with an American federal system that systematically underrepresents these urban centers. Not only are rural and exurban areas overrepresented, especially in the Senate, but this has become much more consequential given the increasing spatial polarization of the parties (see Grumbach, Hacker, and Pierson's contribution to this volume). The geography of electoral districts, combined with the demography of groups with different interests, creates a truly massive anti-Democratic bias within the American federal system. The result of this geographically distributed demography effectively rules out political support in Congress for Federal funding of basic research, even given the lobbying efforts of "Cities on the Hill" (Ogorzalek 2018).

Nor are there major lobbies for basic research, at least outside the life sciences. First, the major companies who benefit in principle from basic research in universities (mainly the FAANG+M companies) have very large R&D budgets of their own. It pays them to target much of their own – some relatively basic – research collaborations with universities or research institutions close to their own long-term development requirements. An additional formidable obstacle, as will be discussed in the context of fiscal policy, is a pervasive preoccupation among many business leaders (outside advanced research-driven sectors) with tax reductions, which fuels hostility to public expenditure. Thus the public sector has declined steadily over time from its leading position in financing basic research. We see this as playing a major role in the relative decline of the United States as the driver of radical innovation.

Decline of Basic Research in the Private Sector

Nor has an increase in basic research in the private sector compensated for the decline of basic research in public sector funding. Instead, the decline in the public sector knocked on directly to the private, because of the decline in public sector training of scientists working in the relevant areas, the complementarity between research in the two sectors, and the loss of federal funding that partially covered private sector activity.

Moreover, and of greater concern, public corporations have positively retreated from science research. A detailed paper by Arora et al. (2018) makes this point at length:

> We document a shift away from science by large corporations between 1980 and 2006. We find that publications by company scientists have declined over time in a range of industries. ... Large firms still value the golden eggs of science (as reflected in patents) but seem to be increasingly unwilling to invest in the golden goose itself (the internal scientific capabilities). (p. 3)

In other words, these large (quoted) American companies are engaged in knowledge-intensive markets. They value technical knowledge. But they have moved away from science. Arora et al. (2015) show basic research in non-Federal R&D to have dropped by around 50 percent since the later 1980s (NSF 2007).

As recently as the 1980s, many of the Chandlerian conglomerate corporations had major research laboratories. "Reconfigured" by the junk bond–financed managed buy-outs, investment decisions were de facto moved from the investment committees of these companies to Wall Street. Many of these firms were downsized (or even profitably broken up) into individually profitable units. The consequence was that most large public corporations closed their research laboratories and moved away from research into basic (and even much applied) science.

The FAANG+M companies are partially exempt from this line of argument. Indeed, radical innovation in the twenty-first century has been largely focused on these companies, which have become the dominant drivers of US R&D in recent decades. Because their founders retained some form of ownership control as they grew rapidly, the issue of management buyouts in FAANG+M did not arise. GM and Ford and Big Pharma (Johnson & Johnson, Pfizer, Merck, Lilly) come some way behind. Moreover, Amazon and Alphabet have at least in part acted as giant venture capitalists, prepared to take very major risks in developing new areas, especially in AI and the associated technologies. Even here, they have been concerned with resources; and – depending on the definition of basic science (in relation to AI) – basic science has been left to universities. Thus again the absence of the Federal government is likely to be a major cause of the relative decline in radical innovation.

A Reconfigured Party System and Declining Support for Radical Innovation

The Republican Party has gradually withdrawn support for the broad policies of state underpinning needed to deepen American leadership in the ICT revolution in the twenty-first century. The end of the Cold War weakened its perception that these public investments provided general benefits. The concentrated benefits attached to these expenditures fell in the successful big city agglomerations, where fewer and fewer Republican voters were to be found.

At a deeper level, the Republican Party's withdrawal sat very comfortably with a fundamental (unifying) shift away from public expenditure and toward low taxation. This shift reflected the basic cleavage opened up by the development of the American knowledge economy – a cleavage that can be seen in raw form in the Trumpian coalition. The major part of this coalition – increasingly at the heart of the Republican party – is declining middle-class and working-class white America, primarily the non-college educated and those segregated or "sorted" into less-well-to-do suburbs, small towns, and more rural exurbs. The other part – increasingly financing the Republican Party – are the wealth holders of capitalist America. Both groups want low taxes, and both groups are hostile to public expenditure. Critically, *neither* of these groups has an interest in public infrastructure in general. The party's electoral base (however deprived it may feel itself) is hostile to any form of potentially redistributive state expenditure, seen as potentially benefitting ethnic minorities (the "underserving poor"). Moreover, living outside dense cities, where social investment in transport, housing, and the environment is necessary, their main concern is either local public goods whose benefits they can keep to themselves (K to 12 education, for example) or low taxes. And here they share the ostensible interest of lower-productivity businesses, as well as those wealthy families who live from their capital. Hence the Republican Party has come, in the knowledge economy, to stand (united) against public expenditure and (united) in favor of low taxation.

The Democrats have also been pushed by the knowledge economy, but in the opposite direction. For the Democrats, the alliance is a metropolitan one, between the winners of the knowledge economy (younger, college-educated, residents of successful big city agglomerations, in which women have more power if not more resources), FAANGM+ capitalism and related high value-added service sectors, together with middle-class ethnic groups. These groups share a common concern in supporting the public infrastructures needed for dense urban environments to work.

CONCLUSION

Why has the USA been the global driver of radical innovation since the early twentieth century? Why, very recently, is this dominant role being partially challenged by China (with the USA still remaining the driver in most areas, and dominant in invention)? And why was the UK, the initiator of the first Industrial Revolution in the eighteenth and early nineteenth centuries, subsequently unsuccessful?

The first part of the answer lies in the way the "research-market-finance" complex works in America: a highly competitive research system, starting in the research universities and their diaspora; a relatively unregulated multiply differentiated financial system, promoting creation and destruction; and a flexible high-level labor market for professionals and technologists, allowing spin-offs from established companies, career and professional switches, and multiple de facto safety nets. The second complementary part of the answer lies in a supportive court-politics-lobbying complex at *both federal (providing heavy investments in basic science) and regional/city level.* Rapidly scalable companies, if successful, are protected from antitrust rules and from unions.

Our claim is that China has formally different but functionally equivalent "market" institutions and that its political system at both the national and regional levels – despite corruption – is broadly supportive of radical innovation. The UK is – like the USA – an LME, but its two "complexes" function quite differently. This reflects – over a long period and with many qualifications – the tight political control of the central government over the university system and the financial system (via the tacit power of the Bank of England); strong contract law and antitrust legislation focused on market share not the "rule of reason"; an independent centralized judiciary, with strong control over local government; and centralized parties. Thus we distinguish centralized/regulated LMEs from decentralized/weakly regulated LMEs, the USA. The only other decentralized money-porous LME is Israel, also for its size a leader in unicorn generation, and ahead of the UK and all the other centralized LMEs.

These US complexes remain very much in place. But to flourish, they have needed and need massive (thus far in practice Federal) public sector resources. And Federal support for the ICT revolution has declined dramatically in recent decades. This we attribute to the end of the Cold War, the reduction in "national" electoral support for Federal resources, the beneficiaries of ongoing support being increasingly located in urban agglomerations that are also increasingly Democratic; and the broader anti-state shift of the Republican coalition – against public expenditure and pro lower taxation.

That shift reflected the geographical divergence (Storper's Great Inversion) of the knowledge economy, which opened up the whole range of less successful states to the Republican Party. The latter has been hostile to fiscal expansion via public expenditure (both redistribution seen as favoring the ethnic poor, and social investment seen as favoring the cities), but open to tax cuts. It has been tacitly financed by the anti-statist pro-business ideologues rewriting the rules in state legislatures and courts (Hertel-Fernandez 2019).

This chapter seeks to situate contemporary developments in the context of the great waves of radical innovation since the late nineteenth century. This deliberately emphasizes both the extraordinary advances in living standards which they have each and cumulatively led to over that long period and at the same time the deep Schumpeterian instability, pain, and conflict necessarily gone through in these periodic waves of creative destruction, and from the latest of which we are hopefully emerging.

This chapter shares in part the dysfunctional interpretation of the courts-politics-lobbying complex of the Hacker, Hertel-Fernandez, Pierson, and Thelen approach to the American system. But at the same time it suggests the need to look at how coalitions emerge to produce improvement over time (Iversen and Soskice 2019). First, "blocking" parties cannot easily remain in power without policies that benefit the "left behind" constituencies of the United States. It seems clear that that requires an activist fiscal policy. Second, there is a structural dynamism in the US system: we suggest that the more evident the gridlock in DC, the greater the shift of political action to those states (including California, Massachusetts, New York, and Washington) with a clear return to activist policies in the knowledge economy arena, notably in higher education and research, together with K–12 education and the whole area of health and the life sciences, as well as the environment. Even within conservative states, knowledge economy cities are developing where there is electoral pressure for change. And finally (paralleling previous innovation waves), as developing technologies raise the return to increased education, straightforward demographic forces are raising the proportion of the better educated in the electorate, with important consequences for the evolution of party coalitions in the United States and the prospects for policies more supportive of radical innovation. That is what my recent work with Torben Iversen suggests (Iversen and Soskice 2019).

12

Public Investment in the Knowledge Economy

Lucy Barnes

In the spring of 2020, the world was faced with a new, highly contagious and deadly disease, and at the time of writing, it is not clear what the long-term consequences of the Coronavirus pandemic will be. Epidemiological, medical and public health expertise rapidly became salient due to the potential life-and-death consequences of scientific technology and expertise. From its outset, the importance of knowledge and scientific expertise in government responses and national well-being provided a stark example of a more general underlying trend in the political economies of advanced industrialized capitalist democracies. Though without the same universal life-and-death stakes, changing technologies of production have been increasing the importance of knowledge as an input to economic progress and prosperity for the past forty years.

But ensuring adequate investment in knowledge is difficult, whether through market mechanisms or democratic political processes. In the United States, proposals for the federal budget made by the president before the outbreak of the pandemic included reductions in federal research spending for the fourth year running, including deep cuts to the budgets of the National Institutes of Health and the National Science Foundation (Mervis 2020). Meanwhile, public support for American higher education has also been in long-run decline, as direct state support has declined, and federal aid to students (such as Pell grants) covers only a diminishing share of the cost of pursuing tertiary education (Mettler 2014).

Viewed in isolation, it is possible to see these outcomes as the apotheosis of a particular, but long-running, Republican aversion to science (Mooney 2005) and to (generally liberal) institutions of higher education

(Fingerhut 2017). But these explanations (and typically, criticisms) neglect broader challenges to public investment that are exacerbated by two features of knowledge generation. Both the public goods characteristics of knowledge and the long-run character of its payoffs complicate the creation of knowledge. A well-developed literature in political economy highlights potential political-institutional and socioeconomic features that better allow public goods investment for the long run. Thus, this chapter aims to illuminate the dynamics of public investment in these two inputs to the knowledge economy – tertiary education and research and development (R&D) – situating the contemporary United States in both comparative and historical perspective, and to consider the determinants of these public knowledge investments.

This is an important gap to fill in the comparative literature as well as in understanding the American political economy, because most analyses of the knowledge economy transition have focused on its highly visible distributive consequences – rising inequality (see Introduction, Kelly and Morgan, and Ansell and Gingrich, all in this volume) and government interventions to address inequality through fiscal redistribution, welfare-state policy, and supply-side regulation. In contrast, while public goods provision will have distributive consequences, it stands in principle to have positive direct effects on long-run aggregate economic performance. Thus the political economy of knowledge production harks back to older challenges for government intervention in the provision of basic public goods – public health and primary and secondary education, for example (Lindert 2004).

What explains public investment in knowledge economy inputs, taking this comparative perspective? Political institutions matter. In particular, veto and access points to political decision-making tend to undermine both public goods investments, and political decisions for the long run. Thus the fragmentation of the American political system may not only undermine pro-poor policy (Kelly and Morgan, this volume), but also investments with widespread aggregate benefit. At the societal level, diversity and conflict – both economic inequality and ethnic fractionalization – may prevent the social compromise necessary for effective knowledge investment. The balance of this internal conflict with external threats which serve to mobilize perceptions of the shared payoffs of making sacrifices for long-run public goods is central to the comparative politics of innovation overall (Taylor 2016).

In considering public spending on R&D, on the one hand, and higher education, on the other, I find that these political institutions – single-member electoral districts and federalism, in particular – do indeed matter for public knowledge investment: fragmented majoritarian institutions are associated with lower levels of provision. Equally, economic inequality tends to reduce public knowledge investment. External threats act as a countervailing force on R&D spending, but not public support for tertiary education, while ethnic diversity undermines the latter but not the former.

This particular difficulty with securing public support for higher education spending in heterogeneous populations is readily comprehensible given the framing of higher education as a private, distributive benefit rather than a public good (Newfield 2008) and racial and ethnic political divisions over this kind of welfare support (Thurston, this volume).

THE COMPARATIVE POLITICAL ECONOMY OF KNOWLEDGE ECONOMIES

Comparative political economy scholarship at the turn of the millennium was strongly influenced by attention to broad differences between American and western European political economies. Accounts focused on differences in outcomes other than economic growth – such as inequality and poverty (Alesina and Glaeser 2004) – and highlighted different "varieties" of advanced capitalism that, counter to the expectations and strict prescriptions of neoliberal economic theory, were delivering economic prosperity in different ways, even when faced with similar pressures from increasing international economic openness. These models also highlighted different outcomes in terms of employment and economic structure. The wage compression associated with the coordinated model inhibited the growth of low-wage service employment (Iversen and Wren 1998). In terms of knowledge investments, one of the central distinctions between the liberal model (as exemplified by the United States), and the coordinated model (exemplified by Germany) was in the propensity for the former to generate general skills and radical innovation, while the latter made progress through specific (and often highly technical) skills, and incremental improvements to products and processes.

The expectation that the liberal model would be better at delivering both service sector expansion, radical innovation, and general (especially, general university level) skills is easy to translate, informally, to the expectation that the liberal model might also better provide for knowledge economy expansion. Combined with variations in systems of university education, which also show some clustering across types of political economy, the liberal market, US-style political economy was marked as superior in creating high-skill service employment in the private sector (Ansell and Gingrich 2013). However, while this pattern seems to have held in the early years of the new century, American leadership in the creation of knowledge intensive service employment has since been eclipsed. Figure 12.1 highlights that while Germany continues to lag behind, many other western European countries now employ a larger share of their workforce in high-skill service jobs. Moreover, the trajectory of this kind of employment in the United States has flattened since

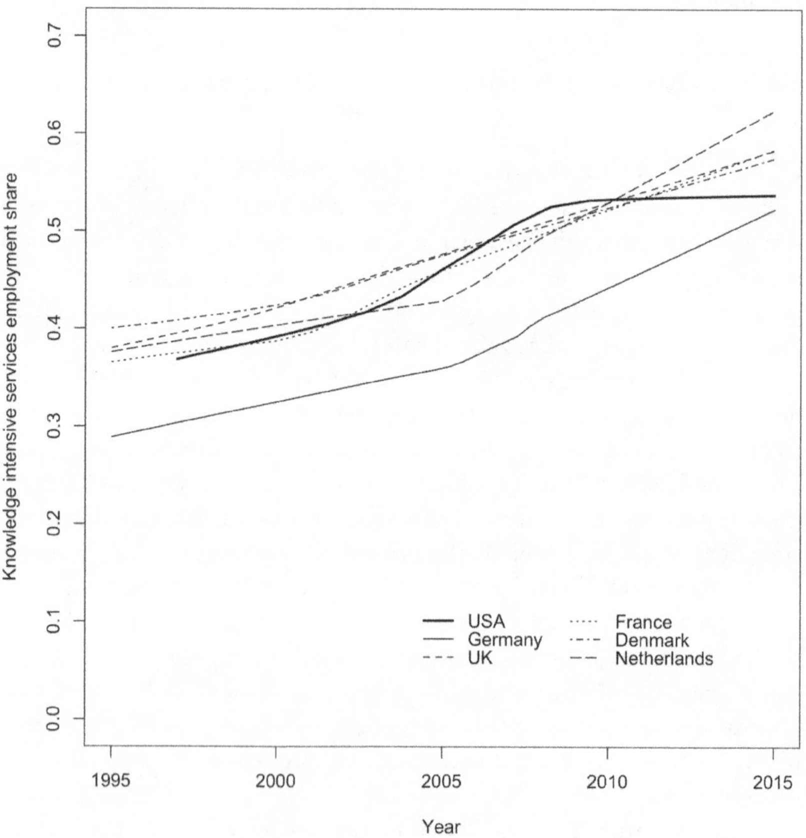

FIGURE 12.1 The expansion of knowledge employment: Share of persons engaged in work in knowledge-intensive services
Source: Brady et al. 2020; EUKLEMS 2018

2010, while other countries continue to increase their skilled service share.[1]

This trend of declining American leadership in knowledge economy development echoes concerns evident in recent scholarship on American politics which highlights declining American leadership in the public provision of investment in two of the central inputs of the knowledge economy: higher education and R&D (Hacker and Pierson 2016; Mettler 2014). Public investment in these knowledge economy inputs provides an important case study through which to link these specific challenges for the American political economy to the broader comparative literature – including what we know about how political institutions affect public goods provision as well as the more visibly distributive politics of inequality highlighted by Kelly and Morgan (this volume).

INVESTMENT IN KNOWLEDGE: EXTERNALITIES AND PUBLIC INTERVENTION

I focus on the determinants of public investment in higher education and R&D for three reasons. First, the transition to the knowledge economy makes investment in these two types of knowledge increasingly important. Second, the inherent characteristics of knowledge investment imply important public goods characteristics, which drives my focus on public provision. Moreover, public spending in these areas is a relatively uncomplicated policy lever. Finally, knowledge investment can be made to fit into existing accounts of policy variation only with some difficulty. As such, understanding what explains variation in public knowledge investments is an outstanding question within the comparative political economy literature.

The increasing importance of these inputs to the economy stems from changing technologies of production. Driven at base by the technological change of information and communications technology, filtered and developed by government policy, economic change led, by the end of the twentieth century, to a situation where knowledge investment is one of the essential "public goods of advanced capitalism" (Iversen and Soskice 2019: 157). My focus on R&D and higher education as public goods

[1] Figures 12.1 to 12.3 show the American case in comparison to Germany, the UK, France, Denmark, and the Netherlands, to illustrate the comparative context. The full analyses also include Finland, Ireland, Italy, Japan, Portugal, Sweden, and Spain, which are omitted from the figures here to maintain their legibility.

inputs to the knowledge economy is distinct from questions of labor regulation, distribution and redistribution, where inequality acts primarily as an outcome of public action (or rather, inaction) (Huber et al. 2017). While public investment in knowledge goods (and the way that it is financed) clearly has important distributive effects, I follow a distinct literature on the provision of public goods which centers on distributive conflict as an important explanation of variation across space and time.

Scholarship on government intervention in the economy, in the specific context of the knowledge transition, has primarily focused on three policy areas. The first two – labor market regulation and redistribution (efforts to reduce income inequality) – fall squarely into traditional comparative political economy concerns with inequality and the welfare state. Government intervention in the economy in the knowledge economy is thus argued to be increasingly important for distributive outcomes as the industrial relations regimes which underpinned egalitarian outcomes under Fordism have eroded (Iversen and Soskice 2015). Similarly, formal regulation of the labor market remains an important political lever to reduce wage inequalities (Hope and Martelli 2019).

The third area of scholarship on the political economy of the knowledge economy focuses more directly on knowledge production, as I do here. There is a large literature on the comparative political economy of education and skill formation. In this, education is usually taken quite broadly, and focused on compulsory school systems or on the entirety of education spending (Busemeyer 2007). Many of these studies also echo the distributive focus of the welfare state literature (Busemeyer 2014), and others stress the interaction between systems of education and training and labor market institutions as part of overall varieties of capitalism with different distributive outcomes, different outcomes in innovation terms, and with different institutional underpinnings (Estevez-Abe et al. 2001). Relatedly, the politics of higher education policy have been brought into the mainstream of comparative political economy in accounts that focus on the partisan politics of university expansion and financing (Ansell 2008; Garritzmann 2015). These treatments again tend to focus on the distributive interests of different socioeconomic groups, and the implications of different education policy choices for them, to create explanations of policy variation that run through differences in partisan control, as different parties channel the interests of these different groups.

There has been much less attention in comparative politics to the question of variation in research and innovation policy. This is readily comprehensible in light of the much smaller levels of public funds spent on

R&D. R&D spending is also typically a low-salience area of government activity, either for its supporters or its opponents (Williamson 2017). It has less obvious distributive consequences than other forms of government spending.

Nevertheless, I take investment in R&D and in higher education together as both are critical inputs to the knowledge economy. The two types of spending on knowledge inputs have three critical commonalities that we might expect to govern their place and dynamics within the advanced capitalist political economies. First, and as discussed in more detail in the following, both have important public goods characteristics. Second, both R&D spending and higher education spending represent a particular commitment to the funding of innovation: continued technological and economic innovation require both good projects and highly skilled people to work on them. Finally, the returns to both higher education spending and R&D spending are likely to be relatively slow to emerge. In part, this is an inherent feature of investment of any kind. But the uncertain, cumulative, and complementary nature of intangible investments in knowledge exacerbates this dynamic. For both types of knowledge investment, the long-run payoffs must nevertheless be paid for by immediate financial commitment. The democratic political provision of this kind of good raises a specific set of considerations (Jacobs 2011).

KNOWLEDGE INVESTMENTS AS PUBLIC GOODS

Finally, public investment in knowledge investment has important public goods characteristics. That is, knowledge investment in general has public goods features that lead us to expect its systematic under-provision by private actors, and thus the need for public subsidy or other intervention. The general arguments for government spending on public goods are well known, and I will not rehearse them here. However, the characterization of investments in R&D and in higher education as public goods is more contentious, and thus merits some discussion.

The public goods features of knowledge investment stem largely from the nature of the investment and the surrounding context. Knowledge as generated by investments both in R&D and higher education is a highly intangible output, not a tangible physical asset (Haskel and Westlake 2017). Haskel and Westlake document the increasing importance of intangible investments and summarize four distinctive features: intangible investments are scalable (non-rival); they are subject to both spillovers (non-excludability) and synergies; and finally, they are highly specific in the precise sense that separating the investment from the original investor is often extremely difficult.[2] The first two of these properties are classic components of the definition of public goods, and apply particularly to advanced R&D. The last, the specificity of investment, is particularly salient for human capital investments. That is, the specificity of a knowledge investment, such as a degree, makes the investment hard to separate from the firm (or student) who makes the initial investment. The knowledge gained working on a particular research project, or through a university degree, cannot easily be sold on, separated from the initial investor. This has the important consequence of making borrowing to finance the initial investment more difficult, as the underlying asset – the knowledge developed – provides no collateral.

Higher education has typically been seen as a less public good than primary and secondary education, on the grounds that the lion's share of the benefits to higher education are captured by the individual decision-makers involved. That is, the extent of spillovers to higher education, that increase social benefits above the private benefits, has generally been assumed to be relatively limited (Barr 2001). However, more recent evidence indicates that higher education investment may have important external spillover effects. First, in line with the importance of "synergies" in intangible investments, higher education increases the wages not only of the educated individual, but also of other workers (Moretti 2004; Valero and Van Reenen 2019). Taking into account both the effects on wages and the possibility of endogenous changes in the accumulation of new ideas and technologies makes estimating the effect of externalities to higher education on GDP in the longer run more difficult, but existing estimates are large (if varied).[3]

Importantly, though empirical estimates of the social returns to higher education investments are harder to quantify than the private returns (McMahon 2018), the idea that the balance between private and social returns would remain constant over time and across contexts – and particularly as technologies of production and the share of other workers and jobs with tertiary level skills or requirements change – seems hard to maintain theoretically. The expansion of information and communication technology, the rise of knowledge as an input to production, and changes

[2] Haskel and Westlake (2017) use the term "sunkenness" but specificity captures the dynamics relevant here more clearly.

[3] Hermannsson et al. (2017) estimate forty-year effects of around 12 percent for Scotland; McMahon (2002) estimates an effect of 37 percent globally.

of work organization of the knowledge economy all point to increasing externalities to higher education through its impact on others' productivity as well as the generation of new ideas.

This shift in the "publicness" of a specific good – in this case, higher education – has historical precedent in the late nineteenth century. As externalities to primary and secondary education became more important within industrial production processes, these levels of education came to have the "public" quality we associate with them today (Lizzeri and Persico 2004). Similarly, public health and sanitation measures became critical public goods only as industrial technologies concentrated populations within cities. The externalities associated with individual decision-making, and thus what public goods provision entails, depend on the prevailing technologies in the political economy.

Research and development investment has a similarly variable ratio of private to social return, depending on the context of production technologies as well as other legal and institutional features. For example, the prevailing intellectual property regime will shape the extent to which private investors in R&D can protect their knowledge from spillover externalities. If spillovers can be minimized, then, perhaps private incentives to invest in new R&D can secure high levels of scientific progress and innovation.[4] Under these conditions, and on this account, maintaining strong material rewards for successful innovation is more important than public funding for research. Moreover, reducing the private returns to innovative success through higher income tax rates (needed to finance public funding) leads innovators to shift their activities across international and US state boundaries, as well as reduce innovative effort (Akcigit, Baslandze, and Stantcheva 2016; Akcigit et al. 2018). Strong material incentives, in the form of high levels of inequality, have been argued to support high rates of US innovation that outpace other advanced economies (Acemoglu et al. 2017).

A similar incentives logic is articulated in the "varieties of capitalism" account of innovation, whereby high private material rewards (and the privatization and licensed-distribution model of returns to innovation) drive more radical innovation in liberal market economies; their absence (as well as other positive institutional supports to process improvements

[4] However, this kind of proprietary protection may have offsetting costs to the extent that it encourages rent seeking rather than, or alongside, innovation (see Mark Schwartz, this volume).

throughout the production chain) lead to more incremental innovation in coordinated market economies (Hall and Soskice 2001).

There are two central problems with these narratives. First, the "stylized fact" of higher levels of innovation in the United States that material inequality is seen to incentivize, while apparent in data on American patents, does not appear in the international (triadic) patent data more appropriate for international comparison (Maliranta et al. 2012). Second, the characterization of the American system of innovation that emphasizes private financial incentives radically understates the importance of less "liberal market" features in twentieth century US R&D, especially in the most radical innovations. Government support for small business innovation (especially through the SBIR program), and public support linking academic, corporate, and government labs in dense collaborative networks, and the government as a guaranteed buyer for novel technologies, for example, speak to a much more "coordinated" system of scientific and technological development (Keller and Block 2011; Weiss 2014).

AMERICAN KNOWLEDGE ECONOMY INVESTMENT IN COMPARATIVE PERSPECTIVE

In the mid-1990s, public spending on our two knowledge economy inputs together made up 2.3 percent of GDP, putting America in a group of high-spending countries alongside New Zealand and just behind Denmark. Only the three other Nordic countries, Sweden, Finland, and Norway, spent more public money on higher education and R&D. By 2013, however, the last year for which comparable data are available, US spending had fallen by 12 percent to just over 2 percent of GDP, while most of the other high-investment countries increased their spending (Brady et al. 2020). America's ranking in terms of this combined investment measure dropped from fifth to eleventh, of the twenty countries for which we have data (Brady et al. 2020). That is, despite the rise of the knowledge economy, American public investment in these two central inputs declined in both absolute terms, and compared to other advanced industrialized countries.

For R&D spending, American decline is even more apparent over a longer time span. Figure 12.2 shows data from the OECD (2020b) from 1980 to 2017, comparing the United States to the same five other advanced industrial economies as Figure 12.1. Both the United States and France show a similar pattern here of large declines in public research

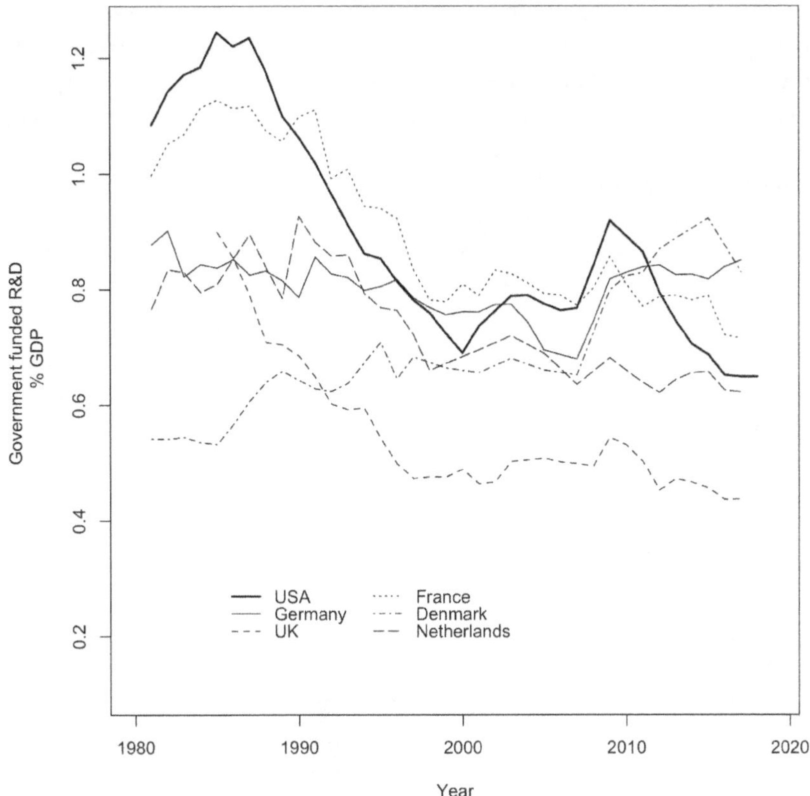

FIGURE 12.2 Government-funded research and development as a percentage of GDP
Note: Total funding from government sources (2015 dollars, constant prices, and PPPs) divided by GDP. Selected countries.
Source: OECD 2020b; OECD 2020c.

funding over the late 1980s and 1990s. In part, this reflects the declining incentive to fund scientific investment occasioned by the waning of the Cold War, but the material imperatives of military and economic competition had been reinforced by a more ideational commitment to R&D as a public good. From the Bush (1945) report onward, US science policy was underpinned by the idea that "the proper concern of the federal government should be the provision of a rich fund of fundamental knowledge" (Elzinga 2012). In short, mid-century American R&D policy was one of high levels of public spending in consequence of the public good characteristics of basic science.

This did not imply a blank-check commitment to scientific public goods; rapid wartime and postwar expansion of scientific research funding was met, by the late 1960s, with increasing calls for accountability and budget consciousness (Elzinga 2012). Even stabilization (rather than growth) of overall resources devoted to R&D required shifts to the internal culture of scientific work, including greater competition for resources and changes to the structure of careers. It also brought a greater emphasis on the external, and usually economic, benefits of scientific research, to be quantified and evaluated (Ziman 1994).

But in the more recent years shown in Figure 12.2, after some recovery in the 2000s, American R&D funded by the government is in steady decline. This more recent decline is not strongly mirrored in any other national series. While there are still a number of countries who commit less public finding to science, recent political developments in these countries have emphasized the importance of increasing R&D capacity, and of the role of expanding government funding to that end. The United Kingdom, for example, a laggard as shown in Figure 12.2, has recently seen multi-year commitments to increasing government spending on science and research (Royal Society 2019).

American public funding of higher education has not recently been such a positive outlier in comparative perspective. Nevertheless, the available comparative data show a decline in public funding in America, even from its lower relative position. Figure 12.3 again shows the same six countries. While the data are somewhat patchy, American public investment in tertiary education, as a share of GDP, is lower than any of the other countries here except the United Kingdom. From the peak (in this series) in 1997, the most recent levels of spending represent (again) around a 13 percent decline.

The radical decline in measured UK spending levels shown in Figure 12.3 highlights that the level of public funding for higher education does depend on the funding model, and public spending is not the only way to fund higher education. However, as noted previously, the maintained argument here is that assuming that higher education does indeed have considerable public good spillovers, we should be interested in the direct public component of spending. Moreover, though the increasing importance of private sources of funding has played an important part in the funding model of the American system over the long run (Garritzmann 2014), an important change occurred around the turn of the millennium when private resources shifted from bringing in additional resources to the funding of higher education, to substituting for public funds (Carpentier 2018).

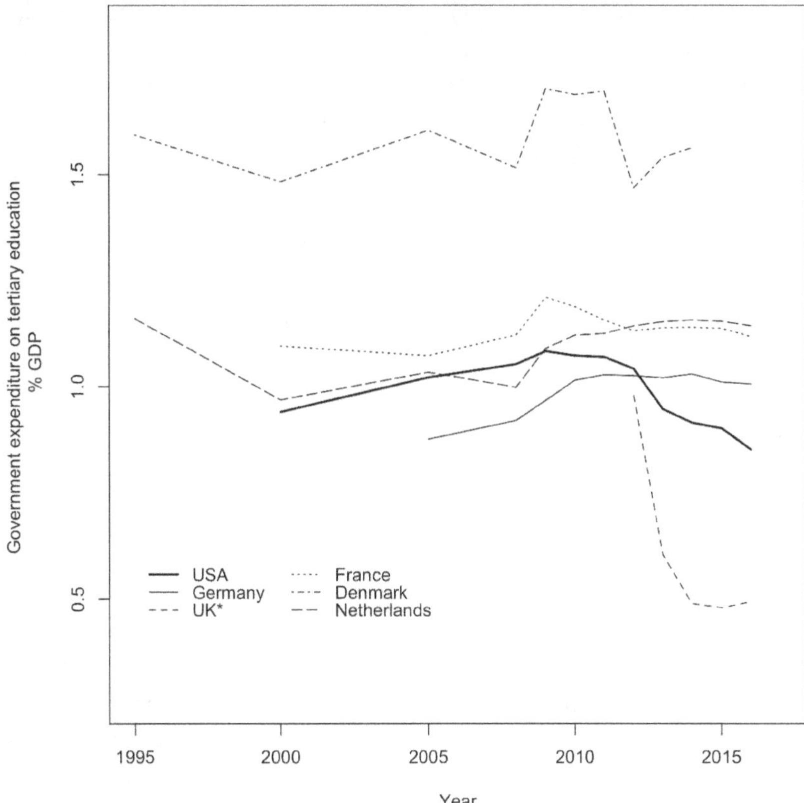

FIGURE 12.3 General government spending on tertiary education as a percentage of GDP
Note: Direct spending on ISCED levels 5–8, all educational institutions. Selected countries. UK data reflect the transition to a tuition fee funding model in 2012/13 when most ongoing direct public funding for teaching in England was cut.
Source: OECD 2020a.

The decline in American public funding for higher education in comparative context is also echoed in more detailed data considering the United States alone. Suzanne Mettler (2014) calculates that between 1990–1 and 2009–10, American states' per capita funding of higher education fell 26 percent.

With the shift of emphasis in scientific research from basic public knowledge toward a more accountable and economically functional vision of research work, perceptions of higher education and its public funding base shifted. Where mid-century ideas emphasized the public good value of higher education, stressing collective benefits and widespread spillovers, by the late twentieth century higher education was viewed almost exclusively as an individual investment choice and cost-benefit analysis (Newfield 2008). This ideational change justified a shift toward tuition-based, private funding and the decline of public support.

WHAT EXPLAINS PUBLIC INVESTMENT IN KNOWLEDGE ECONOMY INPUTS?

The comparative political economy treatments of public goods provision, investment in long-run goods, and innovation policy provide a clear set of expectations for explaining variation in public investment in knowledge economy inputs across countries and over time.

First, an extensive literature on the economic effects of constitutional provisions has taken the provision of public goods – both overall, and as compared to targeted public spending on transfers, with more particularistic benefits – as a central puzzle (Persson and Tabellini 2000). Lizzeri and Persico (2001) argue that the majoritarian, single-member district systems suffer from the under-provision of public goods compared to proportional systems, because of the greater electoral payoffs to more particularistic spending under majoritarian institutions in general. Similarly, presidential systems provide lower levels of public goods than parliamentary regimes as a consequence of the smaller incentives for legislative cohesion, but greater separation of powers, in the former (Persson et al. 2000). This emphasis on the separation of powers in presidential systems echoes the idea that blocking expansions of public spending is easier for (minority) groups in systems with a higher number of veto points that has been emphasized (Immergut 1992), and their importance in preventing policy adaptations to new economic conditions in the United States has been highlighted in this volume with reference to inequality (Kelly and Morgan, this volume).

The importance of veto players – and their negative effect on public investment – is also highlighted in explanations of variation in investments that are politically difficult because of the long time frame associated with their benefits (Jacobs 2011). In considering pension reforms, Jacobs highlights the importance of government insulation from interest groups that are likely to bear, and be aware of, the short-term costs of long-term investments, and thus seek to block them. Lower levels of openness to external influence, in terms of both the veto points and the access points highlighted by Kelly and Morgan in considering hurdles to egalitarian economic policies, also insulate governments to enable worthwhile long-run investments. Similarly, the access that the courts, and strong systems of judicial review, can provide to organized interests (Rahman and Thelen, this volume) is likely to dampen knowledge investment as long-run public good provision. On the other hand, the strength of organized interests in areas which are obscure, rather than electorally salient, does not necessarily impede the sacrifices necessary for knowledge investments. Jacobs (2011) highlights the potential for obscurity surrounding the short-run cost of investments, and clarity and high salience of the long-run benefits, to provide better political cover for would-be public investors. In short, the median voter may not prefer the necessary sacrifice either.

Federalism and decentralization provide a particular kind of veto point, particularly important in the American case (see Introduction, as well as Kelly and Morgan, this volume). Here, however, expectations for public goods investment are mixed. Federalism increases the number of points at which present-oriented interests can gain access to political decision-making and block investment for the long run. Similarly, transferring provision of knowledge goods to the subnational level replicates the public goods problem that individual actors face: any given state will be better off free-riding on knowledge investment pursued elsewhere, rather than making the initial sacrifice of current consumption themselves. On the other hand, federalism may allow decentralized decision-makers to externalize (some of) the present-day costs of financing the public goods (Besley and Coate 2003). To the extent that this sacrifice of current consumption can be moved to other states, while benefits accrue more locally, the distributive (rather than public goods) characteristics of knowledge investment spending may lead to greater provision under federal systems.

When the spillover benefits of knowledge investment are geographically concentrated, as documented by Ansell and Gingrich (this volume) – federalism may have particularly limiting effects on investment, as pivotal decision-makers are less able to benefit from social spillovers. The question of the geographic and economic concentration of knowledge spillovers is a complicated one, which requires reconsideration of the pure public goods characterization of knowledge investment (and as such is beyond the scope of this chapter). However, it is worth highlighting as it indicates that federal political systems may operate differently, in terms of their impact on investment in the inputs to knowledge, in contexts with different levels of inequality.

How do these institutional characteristics differentiate the American political economy from comparator countries? The United States is not unique in having any of the specific features of strong federalism, single-member majority electoral districts, or strong processes of judicial review. Among the countries considered in the analysis here, Germany shares strong federalism with the United States; the UK shares a system of uniquely single-member majoritarian electoral representation; and only the UK, Netherlands, and Finland lack judicial review (according to the Comparative Welfare States data). However, as this makes clear, the American system is unique in combining all three of these institutional features.

The salience and national benefits of long-run knowledge investment, in particular, are also highlighted in Taylor (2016) in considering the politics of innovation. Specifically, Taylor argues that external threats – both economic and military – increase countries' willingness to sacrifice current consumption to invest in innovation. Both reliance on foreign imports for strategic goods like food and energy and military threats from abroad increase the salience of technical progress, highlighting the benefits that will accrue to the necessary investments. Taylor also notes that the willingness of countries to incur the short-run costs that innovation requires depends on the level of internal conflict. High levels of internal distributive conflict will lead to lower levels of innovation. Taylor highlights economic inequality as an important element of this domestic conflict, but the logic also echoes a broader literature on the negative impact of racial and ethnic heterogeneity on public goods provision cross-nationally (Alesina and Glaeser 2004) as well as within the United States (Trounstine 2013). In essence, the argument highlights that innovation requires shared sacrifice in the short term; internal division based on economic or identity grounds will make societies less able to agree on who should bear the burdens of that sacrifice, and less willing to share it.

On these characteristics, too, the United States is somewhat distinctive. As highlighted by much of the rest of this volume, the income share of the top 10 percent is high in America, in comparative perspective: the average value in the United States for the years providing observations for analysis here (1997–2011) is 0.44, where the overall sample average is 0.34. The United States is also more fractionalized in ethnic terms, although the highest value of fractionalization (which includes religious and linguistic, as well as racial differences) is found in Spain. The American sample average indicates about a fifty-fifty chance of two randomly selected

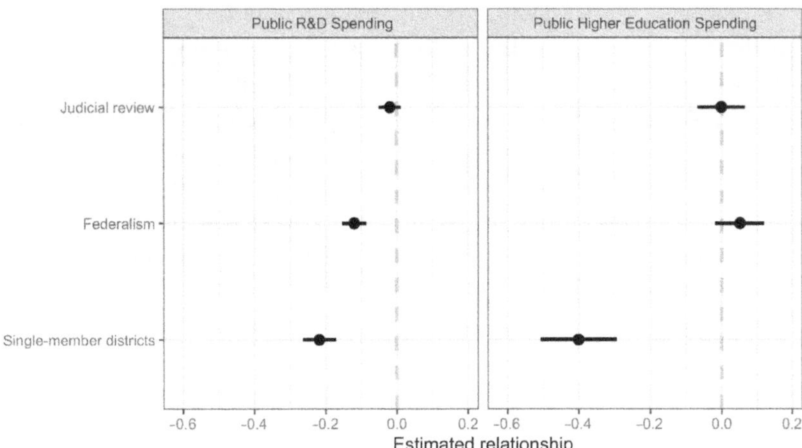

FIGURE 12.4 The relationships between political institutions and public knowledge investment spending
Note: Coefficient estimates from linear models as described in the main text.
Source: Brady et al. 2020.

people coming from different ethnic groups (0.47) where the sample average is about a one in four chance. Finally, the United States is much more involved in foreign conflict in the period under analysis than almost all other countries. In just over two-thirds of the years observed, the United States is involved in foreign conflict – mainly to do with the war on terror. The UK is similarly involved 41 percent of the time, while all the remaining countries in the sample are not involved in external conflict.[5]

We can get a sense of the relationships between these institutional and political-economic characteristics and knowledge input investment by comparing both characteristics and outcomes across countries and through time. Figure 12.4 shows the estimated relationships between the presence of the three institutional characteristics highlighted previously. Single-member districts are expected to be associated with lower levels of public goods provision as a consequence of the electoral incentives they create, while judicial review and federalism both provide present-day actors liable for shouldering the costs of long-run investment opportunities to block it. This would also reduce public spending on knowledge inputs.

[5] I use the threshold of "war" (1,000 or more battle-related deaths in a given year) to code external conflict.

In the case of R&D investment, these theoretical expectations are largely confirmed, although there is no real directional relationship between judicial review and spending.[6] Jurisdictions with single-member-district-only electoral systems are estimated to commit 0.22 percent less of GDP to R&D spending – since the full range of that outcome runs only from 0.1 to 1.3, this is a substantively large change. It represents one standard deviation's difference, or the gap between Austria (the top spender) and France (the 7th highest) in 2015. The impact of federalism is an also important 0.12 percentage points.

Single-member district electoral systems are also associated with lower levels of spending on higher education. Again the substantive size of the estimated association is large – around one standard deviation: the variable ranges up to 2.6 percent of GDP. The 0.4 percent difference associated with single-member districts is the difference between the high-spending Nordics and Australia in 2015. Though neither federalism nor judicial review are significantly associated with higher education spending, on the whole the results are striking: the features of institutional fragmentation known to reduce public goods expenditure in general seem to translate to lower public commitment to investments in the necessary inputs to the knowledge economy.

Table 12.1 extends the analysis to consider the faster-changing features of the political economy cited in explanations of public goods provision in addition to the institutional features. I use the income share of the top 10 percent to measure income inequality, and an index of ethnic fractionalization (Drazanova 2019) to capture ethnic diversity. To indicate the level of external threat, I use an indicator variable equal to 1 when a country is involved in an external armed conflict (Pettersson et al. 2019; Gleditsch et al. 2002). To capture the capacity of policymakers to obfuscate the short-term costs required for long-run payoffs, I use the size of the government's budget deficit under the assumption that higher deficits make all current spending more salient and contested, while periods of surplus allow for the present-day sacrifices involved in knowledge investments to be more readily obscured.

The results in Table 12.1 are quite striking. Economic inequality and external threat affect public research funding exactly as expected, though

[6] These estimates come from models that include all three institutional variables together, as well as controls for per capita GDP, population, and the share of employment in the knowledge economy, and a linear time trend, to account for straightforward structural differences across place and time. The data for the analyses come from Brady et al. (2020).

TABLE 12.1 *Explanations of public knowledge investment*

	Research spending			Higher Ed. spending		
	Model 1	Model 2	Model 3	Model 4	Model 5	Model 6
Income inequality	−1.513***	−1.970***	−1.990***	−5.939***	−5.181***	−0.174
	(0.370)	(0.530)	(0.490)	(0.752)	(1.364)	(0.976)
Ethnic fractionalization	0.019	−0.049	−0.536	−0.565***	−0.544***	−0.078
	(0.083)	(0.072)	(0.367)	(0.174)	(0.165)	(0.638)
External threat	0.137***	0.133***	0.094***	0.131	0.193*	−0.003
	(0.045)	(0.041)	(0.028)	(0.117)	(0.113)	(0.060)
Budget deficit	−0.354	0.247	0.760***	−2.309***	−2.133***	−0.015
	(0.247)	(0.218)	(0.176)	(0.511)	(0.505)	(0.331)
Single-member districts		−0.115*			−0.070	
		(0.068)			(0.180)	
Federalism		0.233***			0.363***	
		(0.046)			(0.105)	
Judicial review		−0.244***			0.044	
		(0.031)			(0.065)	
Time trend	Linear	Linear	Year FEs	Linear	Linear	Year FEs
Country fixed effects	N	N	Y	N	N	Y
N	172	172	172	153	153	153
R-squared	0.453	0.632	0.925	0.720	0.756	0.966
Adj. R-squared	0.422	0.604	0.895	0.702	0.735	0.955

$^{***}p < 0.01$; $^{**}p < 0.05$; $^{*}p < 0.1$

Note: All models include controls for GDP per capita, population, knowledge employment, and economic growth.

there is no obvious negative association with ethnic fractionalization. In contrast, ethnic fractionalization is significantly negatively associated with higher education outlays. Economic inequality also dampens public higher education spending, but external threat is of little consequence. Higher budget deficits do appear to reduce higher education spending, but the results for R&D investment are inconsistent across specifications, and wrongly signed where statistically significant. The negative association with higher education spending is consistent with the logic of electoral insulation being required for long-run investment, and the difference between the two types of investment makes sense given the higher visibility and higher levels of expenditure on higher education compared to R&D. However, budget deficits are also likely to put downward pressure on spending via mechanisms other than electoral insulation (such as constitutional budget rules or economic pressures). As such this result should be taken as only indicative of the plausibility of this logic.

Models 2 and 4 add the institutional variables to the analyses with little substantive change to the conclusions about inequality, fractionalization and external threat, and cost-obscuring. Models 3 and 6 add country fixed effects to the analyses to capture the effects of any unobserved, time-invariant characteristics across countries. The patterns of spending on R&D are robust to the inclusion of these variables, but the higher education investment results are not. The latter time series is of shorter duration, and we see relatively less variation within countries, so this is not a surprising finding. While our interest in the differences across countries point to the value of leverage derived from the cross-country variation (in models 4 and 5), this does counsel against strong causal interpretations of the higher education associations, since there may well be unobserved country characteristics which drive inequality, fractionalization, and public higher education investment.

Nevertheless, the finding that ethnic fractionalization is associated negatively with higher education provision resonates not only with the comparative political economy literature on public goods provision, but also with explanations of increasing American underinvestment in higher education over time. As noted by Thurston (this volume), American willingness to support public spending on higher education has been undermined by the perception of an increasingly nonwhite student population and resistance – especially among (white) Republicans – to expanding spending seen as a private benefit to a racial or ethnic out-group (Taylor et al. 2020).

Figure 12.5 shows the conditional relationships between knowledge investment and inequality as estimated in models 2 and 4, which show the negative relationship, in both cases, quite clearly. In both cases we also note that the United States is not providing particularly high-leverage observations: conditional on the other covariates in the model, its values for inequality are relatively near the cross-national average. Second, for R&D spending, the US observations lie close to the overall regression line, indicating that the relationship between inequality and R&D spending in the United States is quite similar to the overall cross-national association. For higher education investment, the US observations are not dissimilar to the overall pattern, but they do show greater variation. Significantly, though, it is the UK (in 2000 and 2001), Spain, the Netherlands, and Germany (in 2008) which provide the high-leverage, high-inequality, low public investment observations in the bottom right corner of Figure 12.5, rather than the United States.

While we would not want to overinterpret these results, the negative associations between inequality and public investment in knowledge in the form of R&D and higher education spending are particularly important in the context of other known dynamics about the knowledge economy. That is, we know that the knowledge economy transition increases inegalitarian pressures on incomes, if not redressed by government intervention in the form of redistribution and regulation (Iversen and Soskice 2019). But it arguably makes public investment in knowledge increasingly important (Haskel and Westlake 2017). If increases in inequality are an endogenous consequence of increasing knowledge economy production, but also undermine the conditions for effective investment in continued economic success in a high-knowledge context, the long-run prospects for adequate public goods provision without deliberate redistribution are dim. Indeed, those countries which have maintained or increased public knowledge investment are also those that feature high levels of this kind of egalitarian intervention – Denmark (as in Figures 12.2 and 12.3) and (to a lesser degree) the other Scandinavian countries.

CONCLUSION

A comprehensive account of all the details of American investment in knowledge, placed into broad comparative and historical context, would require a more extensive treatment than a single essay can allow. Nevertheless, this chapter describes the contemporary challenge facing American public support for research and for higher education, documenting its recent decline in

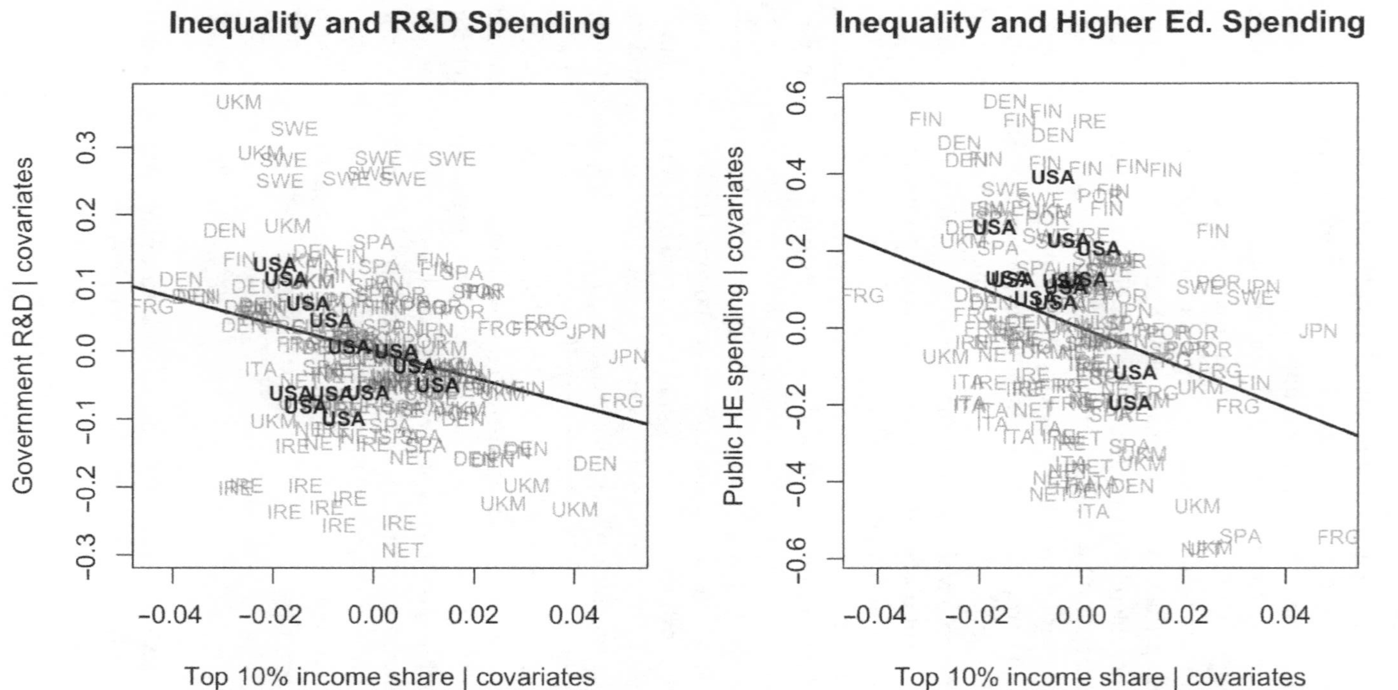

FIGURE 12.5 Conditional relationships between economic inequality and public investment in knowledge economy inputs
Note: Added-variable plots from models 2 and 4, Table 12.1.

both absolute and comparative terms. I argue that this is a particular problem due to the increasing importance, and increasing "publicness" of knowledge in modern economies, and with this motivation try to explain variation in this public support on the basis of canonical political economy approaches.

Overall, the implications for understanding the American political economy are threefold. First, economic production in twenty-first-century advanced industrialized countries – knowledge economies – requires us to reconsider the nature of various government interventions in the economy. The importance of different inputs to production (among other things) changes with technological change, and the characteristics of these inputs also change. High-skill knowledge is increasingly required for inclusion in the productive economy (Carnevale et al. 2013), and new ideas at the technological frontier increasingly necessary for economic progress. Both exemplify intangible capital investments, with important public goods characteristics (Haskel and Westlake 2017). As such, we should see government intervention in these areas not – or not only – as distributive and redistributive social policy, but also through the lens of public goods provision. This requires broadening any comparative political economy focus away from the questions of inequality and redistribution that have dominated treatments of the knowledge economy transition so far.

Second, this broader literature in political economy, and studies of the comparative politics of long-run investment and of innovation, provide useful candidate explanations for variation across time and across countries in this kind of public goods provision. While the broad comparative lens derived from this kind of general theory necessarily requires some abstraction of the details of the political economy of any given state, it does allow us to place particular cases – such as the United States – in the context of these general explanations. Not only does this help us understand the challenges to American public knowledge funding, it also considers some of the important features of the American political economy (as highlighted elsewhere in this volume) through the question of their impact on knowledge investment provision.

The marriage of the quantitative CPE approach to the study of American knowledge investment pursued in this chapter also imports another feature of this comparative political economy tradition, namely the focus on national-level aggregates, institutions, and explanations. In this specific context, this leads to two important caveats to the analysis. First, the scope of the spillovers to knowledge investment may not be truly national. This implies that while individual decision-making would still lead to the under-provision of investment, national-level subsidies will have important geographic distributive consequences. In the cases of higher education and R&D funding, these could well look like redistribution toward the most prosperous areas within national economies (see Ansell and Gingrich, this volume). This raises important questions as to the economic desirability, political feasibility, and normative justice of public funding which are side-stepped here. Second, these dynamics will obviously play out differently across countries with varying levels of political and fiscal decentralization. Given the importance of federalism in the American political economy, this feature of empirical reality is a question of substantive importance (see also Grumbach, Hacker, and Pierson, this volume).

Finally, the prognosis for continued growth in knowledge production and economic well-being may be less optimistic than other treatments allow, both generally and for the United States in particular (Iversen and Soskice 2019). My analyses of the correlates of public investment in higher education and R&D indicate that the fragmentation of American political institutions, and its majoritarian single-member districts in particular, undermine the provision of these valuable knowledge inputs. Similarly, while external threats may increase the capacity of the political system to find compromises facilitating valuable long-run public goods investment, internal divisions undermine it. To the extent that increasing economic inequality and social division are a consequence of other trends in the knowledge economy, the endogenous dynamics of change in public investment may mean that ensuring good (innovation) challenges can be paired with the good (well-educated) workers to solve them is increasingly difficult.

13

Concentration and Commodification: The Political Economy of Postindustrialism in America and Beyond

Ben Ansell and Jane Gingrich

INTRODUCTION

In the past decades, two features of the American political economy have been at the heart of policy and political debates – growing income inequality and growing regional inequality. The period since the 1980s witnessed a dramatic reversal in the postwar fall in inequality, with a rising of share of income earned by the wealthiest Americans (Piketty and Saez 2003). Before taxes and transfers, the incomes of the top 1 percent of Americans now constitute over 20 percent of total income, with close to half of all income earned by the top 10 percent of earners.[1] Inequalities in income mirror inequalities in other domains: education, health, and happiness (Case and Deaton 2019).

At the same time, growth, especially in the most innovative industries, has been increasingly concentrated in urban areas (Moretti 2012). The century-long trend of regional income convergence across US states and labor mobility among them, has weakened since the 1980s (Ganong and Shoag 2017). Geographic inequalities between superstar cities and older industrial regions have intensified, in turn, creating gaps in housing prices (and wealth) between those in the most desirable cities, towns and even neighborhoods and the rest (Ogorzalek, this volume). Figure 13.1 shows the increasing concentration of innovation in a few key areas. Using data on usage patents from the United States Patents and Trademarks Office, we can see that one metro-region – the San Jose-Santa Clara area, home of

Jane Gingrich gratefully acknowledges funding support from the ERC project SCHOOLPOL 759188.

[1] https://wid.world

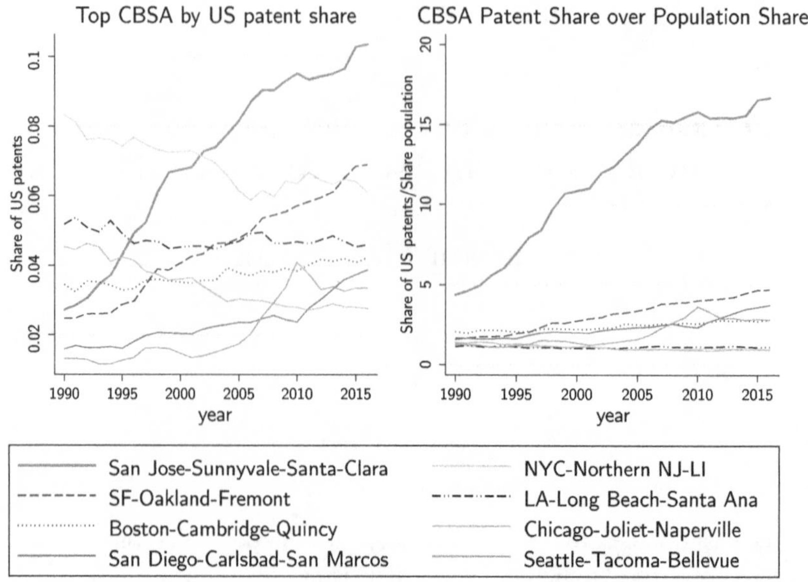

FIGURE 13.1 Patent shares by US core-based statistical area

Silicon Valley – dominates.[2] While the dominance of Silicon Valley in US innovation is no surprise, its magnitude is staggering. In 2016 the Santa Clara area was home to only 6 out of every 1,000 Americans, but filed 100 out of every 1,000 patents, with a corresponding to 450 percent increase in house prices since 1995 – more than double the national average.[3]

While countless observers have described – and often bemoaned – the surge in income and geographic inequality in the United States, the causes of these shifts are a matter of debate. Some argue that rising inequality is the dark side of technological development, a necessary counterpart of the turn toward a knowledge economy (Kwon 2016). In particular, the rise of industrial sectors with heavy investments in so-called intangible assets intensifies rising inequalities among people, firms, and regions (Haskel and Westlake 2017).

We argue that the varied experiences of other industrialized nations suggest that public policies remain important. The knowledge economy, without policy intervention, has a tendency to accentuate regional and

[2] The eight regional areas shown in Figure 13.1 are the top "core based statistical areas" by patenting over the 1990–2016 time period.

[3] https://fred.stlouisfed.org/series/ATNHPIUS41940Q.

income inequality, by *concentrating* the gains of growth in particular firms located in particular places. At the same time, as access to this "economic tournament" is dependent on expensive education or housing, the well-being of citizens in multiple spheres is increasingly *commodified*. Policies can lean into, or against, these inequality-producing economic trends.

A first set of policies can reduce – or enhance – the *commodification* of education, health, and housing, shaping how far the inequalities produced by the growing knowledge economy affect citizen well-being in the labor market. Spending on services like universal (higher) education and affordable housing detaches access to the best jobs from family income, whereas labor protection, universal healthcare, and support for childcare can fundamentally reshape the nature of the economic tournament, potentially giving workers more collective power in the labor market. More generally, a larger fiscal presence tempers inequality. But governments can also lean toward commodification – privatizing education and health markets or subsidizing (typically regressively) credit markets in housing.

A second set of policies look to shape the structure of the market itself. Policymakers can choose to intensify *concentration* of the gains of economic growth among a few groups of people, firms, and places, by channeling further resources to booming areas and away from those "left-behind"; by keeping a light touch on competition laws; and by loosening labor laws. Or they can push away from these concentrations of gains by subsidizing and investing in declining regions, actively reallocating productivity gains across firms, and strongly enforcing competition law and labor regulations.

American governments have largely made the choice to sail with the winds of the knowledge economy, amplifying concentration and commodification. Governments across the industrialized world have made different choices. Why have American policymakers adopted fewer policies of decommodification or deconcentration?

There is much work on American social policy, law, economic regulation, structural racism, and urban governance, including representation in this volume, which looks to explain the structure and limits of the American state. In this chapter, we focus on just one facet: the way the formal electoral institutions and the constitutional structure shape outcomes (Hacker and Pierson 2010; Iversen and Soskice 2019; Rodden 2019).

We argue that in both Europe and the United States political parties face distinct challenges in addressing the new forms of inequality created by the knowledge economy. The geographic basis of the US electoral system places limits on the viability of coalitions of voters seeking to both decommodify and deconcentrate policies. While new left voters in nearly all countries include high-skilled urban voters, the extent to which voters in new innovative sectors both support redistribution and vote for the left varies. Ironically, in contrast to many European countries, a decommodifying knowledge economy coalition, which includes knowledge economy workers, *does* exist in the United States. Both high- and low-income voters in knowledge-intensive sectors are supportive of decommodifying policies, whereas in Europe these groups are more divided. In both cases, these voters are more tepid toward deconcentration.

However, both the electoral system, and structural racism (see Thurston, this volume) that frames many decommodifying policies as supporting the urban minority poor, mean that the increasing reliance of US Democrats on cross-class urban coalition – and the Republicans on the cross-class exurban and rural coalition – has led to both greater partisan polarization around decommodification and less extensive investment in deconcentrating policies. When combined with institutional fragmentation that allows mobilized actors to block many nationally decommodifying policies (see Kelly and Morgan, and Thelen and Rahman, both this volume) the result is more varied local pockets of decommodification and weaker overall regulation, industrial policy, and place-based policies than elsewhere.

The next section examines the structural economic and social transformations of the knowledge economy and their heightening of individual and regional inequality. We show that, at the aggregate level, these choices have played out differently in the United States and Europe, in part due to the structure of political coalitions and their ability to enact policy. We then argue that governments can respond either by changing the degree of commodification or concentration produced by these shifts. We then turn to the politics of these shifts.

STRUCTURAL SHIFTS IN THE KNOWLEDGE ECONOMY: THE RISE OF INTANGIBLES

Scholars working on comparative political economy have provided deep accounts of how postindustrial transformations have put pressure on traditional labor market institutions. Early work examined how slowing productivity growth in the emerging service sector (Iversen and Wren 1998), growing complementarity of technology and high-skilled work

(Boix 1998; Goldin and Katz 2008), and a more limited revenue-raising capacity of the state (Beramendi and Rueda 2007) collectively produced greater wage inequality and new constraints on policymakers.

By the turn of the twenty-first century, however, instead of a uniform increase in the returns to skills, employment growth in many labor markets was most pronounced at the top and bottom end of the service sector. Eckert, Ganapati, and Walsh (2019) argue that workers in "skilled tradeable services" (lawyers, financiers, programmers) found new information technologies allowed them to serve a far larger market. Next to a boom in these high-skilled service jobs lay growing demand for lower-paid personal services. A new wave of scholarship looked to explain these trends, arguing that changes in technology and trade dramatically reshaped occupational task structures and the demand for particular skills; the result being a general "hollowing out" of demand for mid-skilled manufacturing and service jobs (Autor et al. 2003; Goos et al. 2009). These shifts created new political dynamics, with electoral and producer group divides not just across the service and manufacturing sectors but within them (Huber and Stephens 2014; Kitschelt and Rehm 2014; Thelen 2014).

The rapid increase in earnings at the top end of the labor market, and the concomitant rise of superstar firms and cities, has raised new questions for scholars of postindustrialism. Understanding both income and regional inequality requires understanding growing variation in productivity growth across firms *within* the same sectors and across individuals with *similar* levels of skills (Andrews et al. 2016; Song et al. 2019). Indeed, the booming innovative sectors in the United States have been accompanied by growing market concentration, gaps between leader and laggard firms, rising firm markups, declining worker mobility and a weakening of labor power (Akcigit and Ates 2019a). Political scientists have moved away from a singular emphasis on skills and occupational task structures to argue that the intersection of political institutions and technological developments underpin market power and corresponding distributive outcomes (Hacker and Pierson 2010).

To understand these shifts, we argue that it is useful to conceptualize the knowledge economy in terms of the outputs of production as well as in terms of skills as inputs to production. These outputs increasingly involve commodified intangible assets – managerial processes, branding, and intellectual property – which are coproduced through the skills of employees and a legal and policy framework (Haskel and Westlake 2017). The way that the gains of the knowledge economy are distributed then, is a function of both technological shifts and how the institutional environment allows actors to capture its gains: for example, by exercising monopsony power over employees (Naidu, this volume), capturing rents or limiting competition (Schwartz, this volume) or outsourcing production (Weil 2014).

We develop these claims in the following section to argue that (a) the shift toward intangibles is central to understanding the contemporary dynamics of growth in the knowledge economy but that (b) because the rise of intangibles creates new trade-offs, public policies remain crucial for shaping inequality outcomes.

Intangibles and Inequality

As the name "intangibles" suggests, these are investments made by firms into assets that cannot be easily measured or even directly observed. Tangible assets are forms of physical capital: plants (the buildings and machinery that make up production factories), commercial land holdings, materials from production inputs, and held inventory of final outputs.

Intangible capital refers to value that firms hold that cannot be reduced to these types of physical investments. Corrado et al. (2016) argue that it embodies three particular qualities: computerized information, innovative property, and economic competencies. Computerized information includes software purchases and in-house development along with the value of firm-held databases. Innovative property includes research and development, design, mineral exploration, financial innovation, and artistic originals. Economic competencies include advertising, market research, owned and purchased organizational capital, and training. As Corrado et al. note, what these all have in common is that they "enable knowledge to be commercialised" (2016: 78).

Many of these forms of intangible capital seem rather ethereal. A brand is largely based on reputation, which can be fragile. Regulatory arbitrage is generally time-limited in well-functioning democracies. Even research and development is only profitable when protected through intellectual property law. But intangibles have many advantages. Once a firm has invested in the fixed cost of developing a brand, a patent, or a form of management, it can scale it up almost for free – there are minimal variable costs. This situation in turn permits intangible-intensive firms to dominate markets rapidly, acquiring near-monopoly status, oftentimes on a global level.

Figure 13.2 draws on the INTAN-INVEST dataset to illustrate gross investment in intangibles as a proportion of overall gross value added for

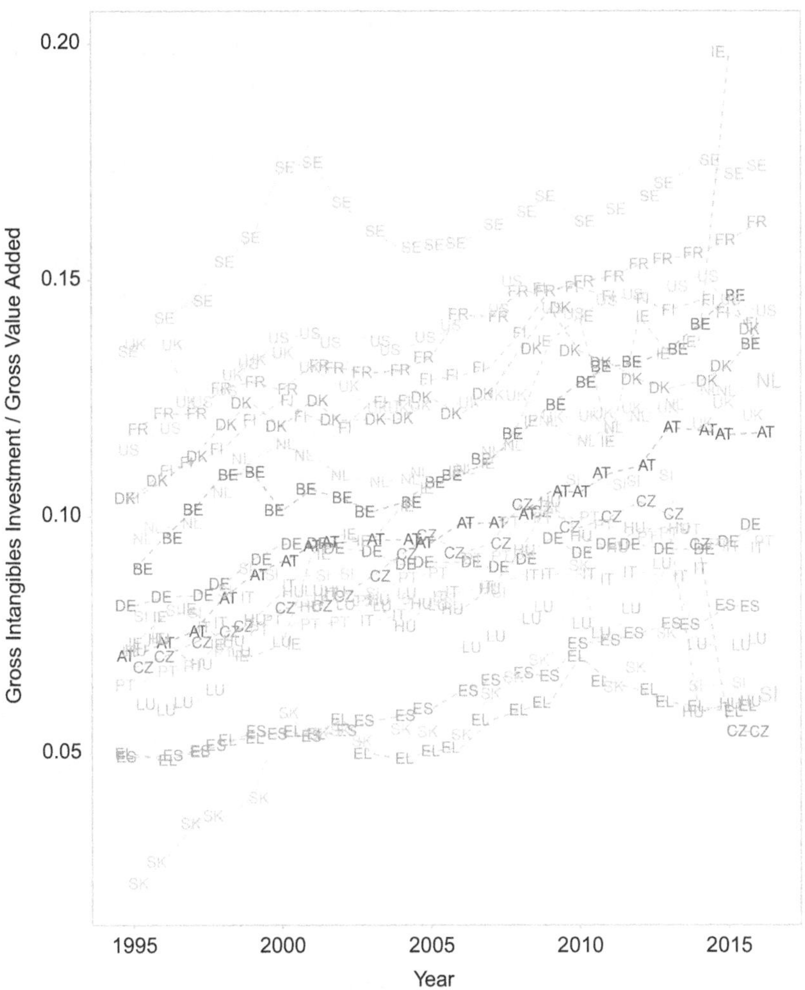

FIGURE 13.2 Gross investment in intangibles, 1995–2016

the United States and nineteen European countries between 1995 and 2016 (Corrado et al. 2016). It shows that the United States is a relative leader in intangible investments, hovering at around 15 percent of GVA. It is joined, and indeed led by, a number of other countries, including Sweden, Finland, France, Denmark, Ireland, and the UK. By contrast, both the major exporters of Continental Europe, Austria, and Germany, and the Southern and Eastern European countries, have substantially lower levels of intangibles investment.

What are the consequences of these shifts? We examine in turn (a) within-country geographical inequality, (b) inequality among firms even in the same sector, and (c) inequality in the labor market more generally.

The rise of intangibles has the potential to produce a surge in *geographical inequality*, as particular city-regions reap the lion's share of the spoils of high-end service and technology sector growth. The value of intangibles-intensive firms comes from their stock of human capital and internal processes. The high-skilled workers and firms that employ them, tend to congregate in a select group of city-regions: New York, the Bay Area, London. They do so in part because the value of intangibles depends on human relationships – legal, governmental, marketing, entertainment, and so on – creating some advantage to agglomeration. However, they also do so for sociological reasons. Rising high-skilled female labor force participation has made the issue of "co-location" for dual-earner couples (and the need for manageable commute times) an increasingly important component of residential choices (Costa and Kahn 2000; Iversen and Soskice 2019). Thus, ironically, the rise of intangibles, in pushing up house prices in favored urban areas, has a striking impact on the distribution of the very tangible asset of housing.

The rise of intangibles contributes to another key shift in the postindustrial economy: the growth of between-firm differences in productivity, profitability, and compensation. Recent work by in the United States (Song et al. 2019), in Germany (Card et al. 2013), and the OECD (Tomaskovic-Devey et al. 2020) has found increasing differences among firms in the same sector in terms of productivity, pay, and performance. Song et al. (2019) argue that two-thirds of the rise of variance in earnings in the United States occurred due to rising differences between firms in earnings, as opposed to those in management or other positions within a firm being paid more. OECD work shows that the gap between highly productive "frontier" firms (those in the top 5 or 10 percent) and all others is growing globally, as is the survival of "zombie firms" with low productivity (and often correspondingly low wages) (Andrews et al. 2016). These trends are not exclusive to intangible-heavy sectors, but slower rates of diffusion of technology and practices across firms and the rise of dominant superstar firms, often follows from both the commodification of particular forms of know-how and limits on its diffusion.

Finally, intangibles affect labor market inequality more generally. The geographic and firm concentration discussed previously have consequences for individual-level inequality, creating gaps between labor market insiders and outsiders enhanced by extensive "fissuring" of production

(Weil 2014). Labor market fissuring refers to the consequences of almost-complete outsourcing of the supply chain. Information technology has made it possible to automate human resources functions, allowing the outsourcing of commodifiable low-skill tasks such as cleaning, security, and data entry. At the other end of the labor market, firms reliant on intangibles require few workers, but the human capital of those highly paid workers – in combination with ICT – is crucial for the creation and maintenance of their value.

How extensive have these potential dis-equalizing effects been? Figure 13.3 shows the trends in income and regional inequality for both the US states and a range of European countries. The *y*-axis shows on each graph shows a measure of the Gini coefficient of household income before taxes and transfers at the US state level (top figure) or European country level (bottom figure).[4] The *x*-axis of each figure shows a measure of regional dispersion.

The top figure examines regional dispersion *within* US states. For each US state, we rank order its counties by average county-level income and compare the average income of the county that contains the 10th percentile to the average income of the county containing the 90th percentile. To measure regional dispersion within European countries we use a similar method for NUTS 3 regions. These regions are much larger than most US counties but are the smallest consistent unit across Europe. Here we use GDP per capita, rather than average income, as the latter is not available.[5]

Figure 13.3 suggests two things. First, there has both been a nearly universal increase in the pretax and transfer Gini coefficient across US states and European countries from 1990 to 2016, but a more varied path in terms of regional inequality. Second, substantial cross-national and cross-state variation in the level of both types of inequality remains.

How do these patterns connect to intangibles? The American states demonstrate a general rise in regional inequality along with a uniform rise in income inequality. The states seeing large increases in regional inequality are some of the states most associated with expansion of investment in intangibles and the rise of mega-cities: New York, Washington, California, and Virginia. These states that were already more unequal in

[4] For the United States, these data come from the US census and and current population survey, www.census.gov/topics/income-poverty/income-inequality.html. For Europe, they come from Solt's Standardized World Income Inequality Database https://fsolt.org/swiid/.

[5] The US data come the US census for 1990 and 2000, and the American Community Survey five-year estimates for 2016. The European data come from the Cambridge Econometrics Regional Economic Database.

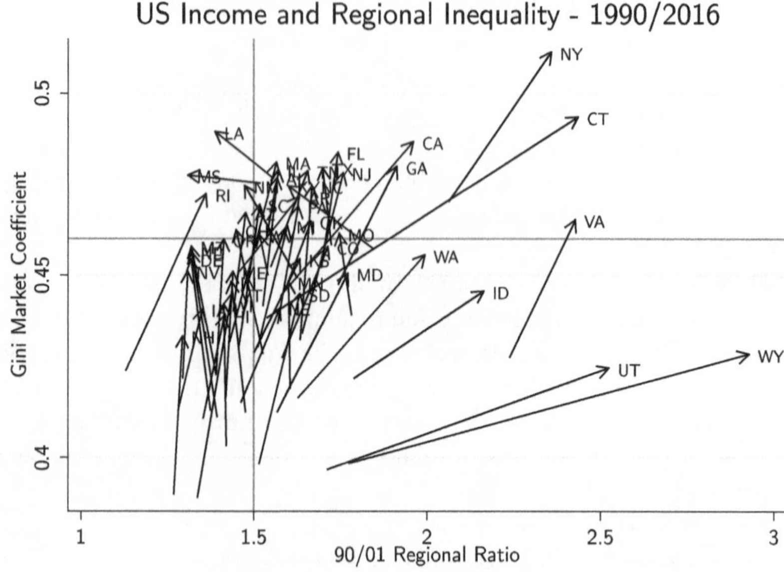

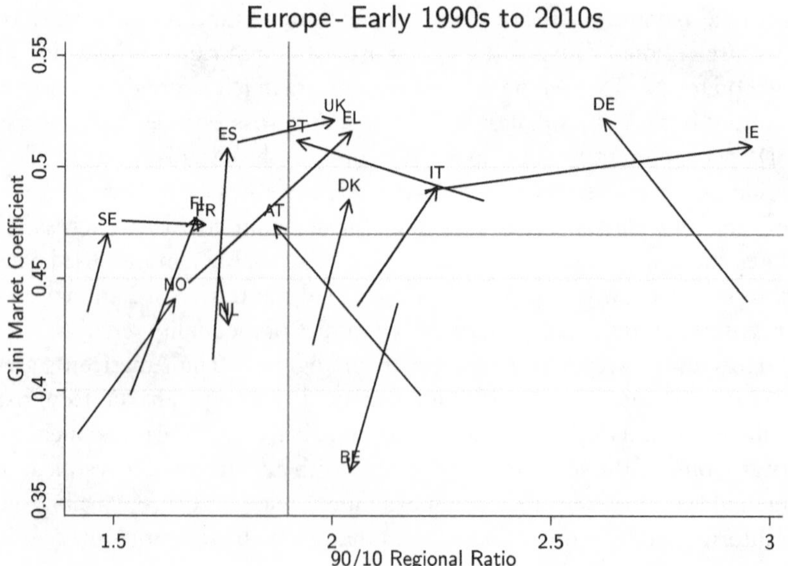

FIGURE 13.3 Income inequality and regional inequality by state (USA) and country (Europe)

the 1990s and have tended to become more so over time. Relatively few states have seen a decline in regional inequality; those that have tend to be states with less knowledge economy growth rather than an obvious strategy of dispersing growth: Mississippi, Louisiana, New Mexico, and Kentucky (see Grumbach, Hacker, and Pierson, this volume).

Among European countries, we see rather different trends. Once again, there is a relatively uniform increase in income inequality. Despite these common increases, among the intangible intensive countries – the United States, United Kingdom, Sweden, Denmark, France, and Ireland – we see wide variation in outcomes. Regional dispersion in incomes appears related to the highly market-driven rise of high-skill service cities such as Paris, Dublin, and London. Stockholm, Copenhagen, and Helsinki are as dominant in their national contexts, but the structure of their national welfare states redistributes more growth outward (discussed in the following) and also reduces the translation of the growing pre-fiscal inequality shown here into extensive post-tax and transfer inequality.

The less intangible-intensive economies also exhibit variation. The decline in regional concentration in Germany and Austria is striking, and related to diffuse overall economic strategy emphasizing manufacturing as opposed to concentrated high-skill services. However, longstanding regional differences remain strong in the economies of Greece and Italy, which have faced economic stagnation in recent years.

To more directly look at these relationships, Figure 13.4 demonstrates the average country-level relationship since 1995 between intangible investment and these two forms of inequality. Each country's average is denoted by its three-letter country code and these country codes in turn are shaded according to their average level of spending on social policies during the same period, with darker shades denoting higher spending.

In aggregate, there does not appear to be any cross-sectional pattern between investment in intangibles and either form of inequality. Yet when we subdivide countries into those with lower or higher levels of social spending than 20 percent of GDP (roughly the median level), we see that whereas for low spenders, higher investment in intangibles appears associated with higher pretax and transfer income inequality for the country as a whole and higher inequality across regions, the reverse is true for the group of higher spenders.

Although inequality is rising everywhere, there is no determinative relationship between the rise of the knowledge economy and inequality outcomes. In aggregate, social spending appears to moderate the relationship between investment in intangibles and higher income and regional

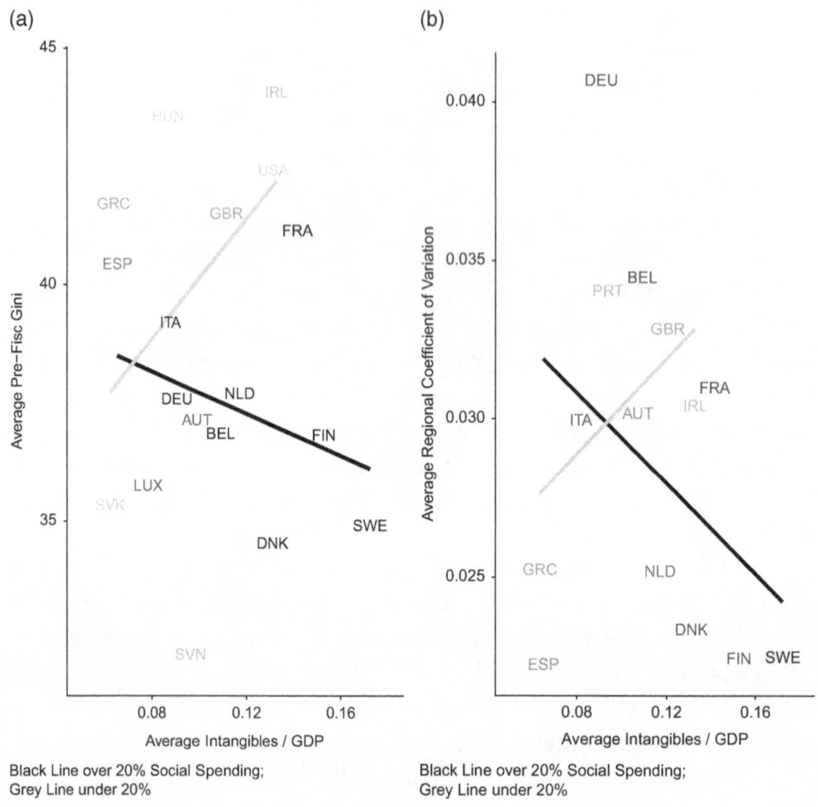

FIGURE 13.4 Intangibles and national/regional inequality

inequality. In order to understand why this is the case, we turn to theorizing these policy choices.

Policy Choices

The rise of intangibles tends to generate inequality. However, this process does not follow mechanically from technology. Policies matter to the way skills, and the value of intangibles, are commodified, the collective power of labor, and the way growth is dispersed across place.

In this section, we argue that the inequality-producing aspects of intangible production in a knowledge economy can be moderated or accentuated in three ways. First, by *limiting* the development of the knowledge economy. While supporting intangibles may bring greater inequality and new policy challenges, limiting them can threaten economic stagnation. Where the knowledge economy develops, countries therefore face the question of whether to try and curb such inequalities by altering the access and functioning of the labor market through *decommodifying* policies, or reshaping production itself through *deconcentrating* policies. Both decommodifying and deconcentrating policies involve substantial financial or regulatory outlays.

Limiting

The knowledge economy is not destiny. Even if most countries consume the products of the knowledge economy, that does not imply they will produce them. Indeed, if the structure of intangible investment means that only a few firms dominate international markets, it may not even be possible for all countries to have a meaningful presence in such production.

Other forms of production still generate revenues and growth. As we showed previously, many Continental European economies continue to maintain successful high-end manufacturing sectors. However, outside of these high-skilled export-oriented economies, abandoning the knowledge economy risks long-run economic stagnation.

Despite these risks, many countries lack the basic investment and regulatory structures needed for the development of high-skilled services. And that choice may be partially deliberate. Where professional services are extremely strongly regulated – indeed captured by domestic insiders – it will be difficult to develop new providers serving a global market. Services are often more regulated than manufacturing production – from German retail laws to the proliferation of well-paid and protected public notaries across France and Italy.

There is no single necessary nor sufficient set of reforms that will produce a surge in investment in intangible capital. However, typically, to produce high-skilled globally traded services, countries must deregulate aspects of their financial and professional service sector, and adopt a mass higher-education system that facilitates the emergence of "global universities."

Commodification

Presuming governments facilitate the rise of a knowledge economy, they may do so in ways that lean into or push against the *commodification* of well-being: the degree to which citizens' income and well-being is dependent on access to high quality employment.

The question of how labor market and welfare institutions shape the commodification of labor, and the connection between these institutions and labor's collective power, has long been at the heart of scholarship on welfare institutions. Esping-Andersen (1990) popularized the concept of "decommodification" – the ability of workers to secure a standard of living outside of dependence on the labor market. Knowledge economy production tends to both magnify the commodification of skills and commodify previously non-commodified (or less commodified) factors. Intangible assets involve, in part, the commodification of "ways of interacting" – managerial competences and government relations and the protection of property rights over objects that previously lacked any status as property – for example, information on consumer behavior, or friendship networks. Put differently, they pull more and more forms of well-being into dependence on the market. What policies and institutions can affect this trend?

First, citizens' ability to acquire the skills and cultural capital that determine success in the knowledge economy is increasingly important. Where access to education is related to one's own existing income – or family income – the educational structure magnifies these inequalities. This combines with an ever-greater commodification of place. Since high-end service jobs have tended to concentrate in major cities, the skyrocketing value of property in those cities can limit access to these booming markets (Hsieh and Moretti 2019).

Where the market fully decides access to education or housing, then access to the best jobs is itself commodified. Governments can decommodify this access, through both transfers and in-kind benefits that support education and housing. For example, where the government controls the provision of higher education or subsidizes (often fully) tuition, a greater number of citizens will find themselves able to access the paths to the elite jobs associated with the knowledge economy. Governments can also provide public housing or subsided public transit, that make it possible for a wider range of citizens to live in the booming cities. These "pre-distribution" policies decommodify aspects of the acquisition of skills and regional mobility needed to take part in the market.

Second, decommodifying policies can shape the nature of the labor market, not just access to it. Union organization, collective wage bargaining, and other labor rights and protections produce wage compression – at least across unionized workers. Hope and Martelli (2019) show that the inequality-increasing impact of knowledge economy production is lower where labor organization is stronger. Not least, these institutions enable workers to bargain more effectively for a higher labor share of earnings, limiting monopsonistic practices (Naidu, this volume).

Finally, more traditional decommodifying policies look to remove some domains of well-being from market forces. Where the welfare of citizens is more market-dependent, increasingly unequal market incomes will refract into other forms of inequalities. Where good quality health insurance is dependent on one's job and earnings, differences in job quality translate into differences in access to health, further limiting workers.

These three domains of decommodification are often reinforcing. Overall levels of redistribution will reduce the dependency of citizens on their precise position in the knowledge economy, and since they compress the posttax wage distributions. They may further reduce the ability of the wealthy to bid up the prices of positional goods, including housing and education (Ahlquist and Ansell 2017).

As is well known, the US welfare state is particularly commodifying on all three dimensions – housing and education are largely market based, with even public universities charging high tuition; private sector unions are relatively weak and limited (see Hertel-Fernandez, this volume), and unemployment and work-based benefits (with the exception of social security) are limited and variable in many states; and finally, the United States has neither fully universal affordable health insurance nor subsidized childcare, an exception among advanced industrial countries. Access to the market, performance in it, and the determinacy of the market for individual well-being are all more commodified in the United States; and with the important exception of some recent legislation – like the Affordable Care Act – much of the direction of policy at the state and national level has been toward enhancing all three forms of commodification.

Concentration

While policies of commodification shape the connection between the labor market and individual well-being, government policies can also affect the structure of the market itself. Intangibles can contribute to concentration in market structures: the growing tendency for a few firms, regions, and indeed individuals, to disproportionately benefit from production in the knowledge economy.

Governments have a variety of policy and institutional tools that can alter the concentration of production in the knowledge economy. We examine in turn (i) industrial and competition policy and (ii) regional development policies.

Industrial and competition policy refers to the ways in which governments shape, regulate, or actively interfere in product markets. As Schwartz (in this volume) argues, the legal infrastructure underpinning intangibles, particularly the system of patenting, has been crucial in shaping their evolution (see also Pistor 2019). Gutiérrez and Philippon (2018) further point to the structure of competition policy, arguing that a key difference in firm concentration between the United States and Europe is a more aggressive pro-competition policy under the aegis of the European Union. They further argue that where regulatory institutions do exist in the United States, firms have mobilized to capture many areas in order to bolster their market position. As Thelen and Rahman (in this volume) argue, business has often used the American court system to achieve both collectively and individually favorable outcomes.

Another broad strategy for changing concentration is more active government industrial policy. Here governments support, subsidize, or protect particular industries. Industrial policy does not necessarily reduce concentration – as traditional funding of "national champions" in some European countries demonstrates. Moreover, the subsidization of weaker firms in order to reduce concentration can allow capture by larger firms. Industrial policy can, though, channel resources to industries that invest in tangible capital, indirectly reducing concentration by diversifying production. The subsidization of intangibles-intensive areas could also deconcentrate, if support is targeted to smaller firms in new sectors (e.g., green energy).

The second set of policies affecting the concentration of production are regional policies. Policies that directly transfer resources from the wealthier to poorer regions deconcentrate the gains of growth. Many governments passively enact such policies through national taxation and redistribution (i.e., the decommodifying policies discussed previously). Even federal states such as the United States create de facto interregional transfers through programs such as social security. With that said, there is substantial variation. Federal political institutions are likely to increase concentration if poorer regions are unable to access tax revenues collected and dispensed at the subnational level (Beramendi 2012). More direct regional funding, through specific infrastructure policies (constructing roads, railways, and ports), regional development grants, or siting key public services in less-wealthy areas, can be used to channel investment outside of core cities. For instance, the European Union spends around one-third of its revenues on interregional transfers for the development of poorer regions (albeit from a limited budget). But governments may also end up favoring core regions – particularly if they coincide with the capital city – thereby accentuating concentration.

THE POLITICS OF CONCENTRATION AND COMMODIFICATION

Why do some countries end up responding to the challenges of the knowledge economy with decommodifying or deconcentrating policies while others let the forces of commodification and concentration rip? In this section, we turn to the demand side of politics, examining how the knowledge economy affects the type of political coalitions that can emerge. We argue that the electoral institutions in the United States have tended to limit a dually redistributive decommodifying and deconcentrating electoral coalition. When combined with a number of veto points (Kelly and Morgan, this volume) and strong judiciary (Thelen and Rahman, this volume) that empower interest groups as "repeat players," the result is uneven and locally set decommodifying policies and limited deconcentration.

A range of recent scholarship conceptualizes how structural changes in knowledge economy labor markets have reshaped the coalitions that underpin them. Iversen and Soskice (2019) (see also Soskice, this volume) argue that the urbanized nature of production in the knowledge economy limits capital mobility and means that governments retain substantial tools to redistribute wealth. However, whether these materialize, depends on the preferences of middle-income voters. "Inclusionary" coalitions between high- and low-skilled workers become more challenging as these groups increasingly meet different economic fates. In majoritarian electoral systems, or in countries like Germany, where centrist parties can govern without the left, the low skilled are often excluded. While this work explains the persistence of a long-standing outcome – a weaker welfare state in the United States – it leaves a puzzle. Middle-class urban voters are often heavily supportive (in surveys) of redistribution, rather than pushing against it. Why, given this potential base of support, does more extensive decommodifying policy not emerge?

A second answer, also emphasizing the intersection of the electoral system with knowledge economy growth, comes from Jonathan Rodden (2019), who argues that cities "lose" precisely because of the concentration of left voters in them, meaning that progressive voters are unable to form broader alliances with centrist voters in suburbs and rural areas for spending. The result is an underrepresentation of left policies nationally, and an underinvestment in urban infrastructure. However, given cities, and the booming sectors in them, have largely been winners in a range of areas – from competition policy to trade policy through to their relative autonomy on zoning – why do they lose on economic redistribution?

We build on this work to argue that the combination of structural economic changes and electoral systems is central shaping redistributive coalitions in the electorate. We argue that economic policy preferences are multidimensional, involving preferences over both decommodification and deconcentration, meaning that voters can support one without supporting the other. Decommodifying policies and deconcentrating policies affect both income and regional inequality; however, decommodification is more visibly linked to the former and deconcentration to the latter.

As Rodden (2019) argues, a key feature of electoral systems lies in how they structure the geographical nature of coalition-building. In majoritarian systems, like the United States, wealthy individuals, who are a numeric minority, are split across different geographic areas. This situation means that it is more difficult to band together as a class in electoral politics (they can through interest groups). Instead, they must cut deals with other groups in the same geographic areas in order to win particular seats.

As regional economic fates diverge, the relative importance of coordinating by region can change. In majoritarian countries, where new groups of higher-skilled voters are concentrated in cities, they may prefer to coalesce with lower-income voters in supporting decommodifying policies rather than with other high- and middle-income voters outside the urban core demanding deconcentrating policies. In other words, they prefer intraregional redistribution to interregional distribution (Beramendi 2012). High-income groups' support for decommodifying policies such as minimum wages, investment in education, and other services, may be built on "conditional altruism" (Rueda and Stegmueller 2020) or on cultural liberalism and the link between "first" and "second" dimension issues. In rural areas, the reverse pattern may occur, where poorer citizens may be mobilized on cultural or nationalist dimensions to oppose redistribution to the cosmopolitan cities and their ethnically diverse inhabitants.

Since urban elites in intangibles-intensive sectors have been the core beneficiaries of the rise of the knowledge economy, their choice between alliances dependent on decommodification versus those dependent on deconcentration is important. In majoritarian systems such as the United States, they need to ally with other residents of major cities in order to secure representation – this means a center-left alliance in the cities. This alliance is likely to produce a coalition for decommodification but only within knowledge-economy-intensive states. Moreover, no such coalition across states for deconcentration will emerge. By contrast, in countries with proportional representation, both relatively wealthy and relatively poorer citizens can ally with others in their class across different regions, without having to cut a deal to win a particular region as they might in a majoritarian system. This means that there are coherent coalitions for *both* decommodification *and* deconcentration in proportional countries.

We expect that in majoritarian systems, wealthy voters in intangibles-intensive sectors and locations will be more interested in decommodifying policies based on an urban coalition with poorer voters than in deconcentrating policies that lead to interregional distribution. In proportional systems, a cross-regional alliance of the well-to-do means these same intangibles-employed urban rich will be much less supportive of decommodification. This pattern helps explain why the majoritarian United States lacks national consensus on policies that push for decommodification or deconcentration in the face of rising inequality produced by the knowledge economy. By contrast, proportional European countries find it easier to maintain such coalitions and to temper the edges of the knowledge economy. It also helps us understand why wealthy knowledge workers in the United States are willing to ally with the urban poor on quite redistributive but locally focused policies, whereas their counterparts in Europe are less supportive of redistribution.

While our argument hitherto has been about policy preferences, these attitudes are also likely to affect voting behavior. In majoritarian countries, such as the United States (and the United Kingdom), the urban intangibles-employed rich will coalesce with poorer urban voters and vote for the center-left. By contrast, in the proportional countries of Europe, an interregional alliance of the rich is possible, and these same voters will be attracted to the center-right.

An example of the way that the regional divides play out in United States can be seen clearly in Figures 13.5a and 13.5b, comparing voting by type of area in the United States and a composite of the proportional systems in Europe.[6] These figures show disaggregated voting for left-wing

[6] The data come from a number of national sources, drawn together with support from the ERC project SCHOOLPOL 759188. This dataset measures national-level election results at the level of local area units (LAU), the base unit for European geographic hierarchies, with the exception of Greece (NUTS 3) and Portugal (Concelho). In the United States, data is gathered at the county level using the County Presidential Election Returns 2000–16 from the MIT election data, and David Liep's election database for the earlier years.

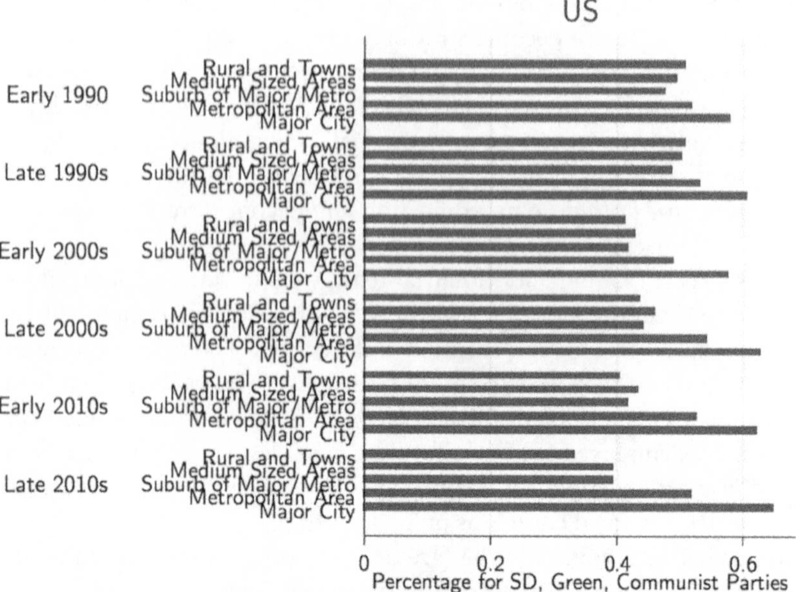

FIGURE 13.5A Voting for the Democratic party and urban-rural divides

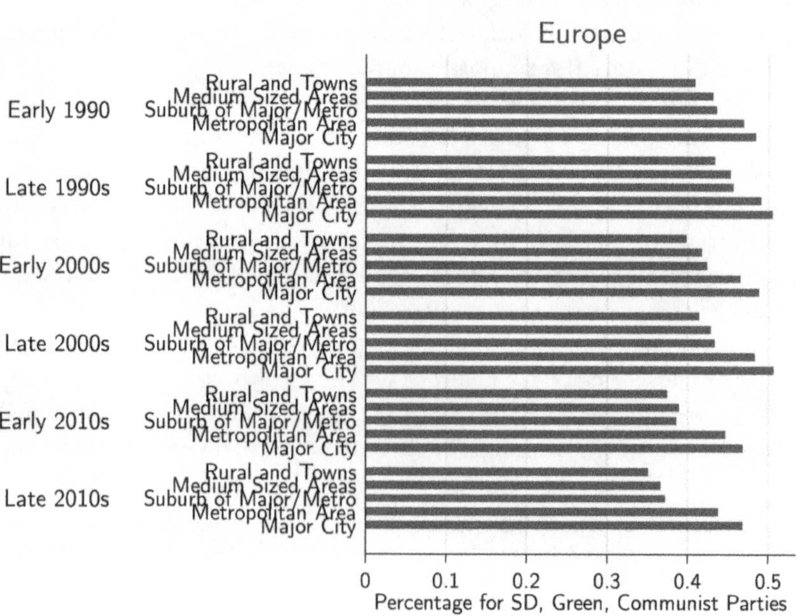

FIGURE 13.5B Voting for left parties and the urban-rural divide in Europe

parties (coding the Democrats as left-wing) in the United States and the proportional systems of the EU-15 (excluding the UK, Ireland, and Luxembourg and including Norway and Switzerland) since the early 1990s. The figures break localities (US counties; municipalities in Europe) into five geographic types: rural, medium-sized areas, metropolitan areas, suburbs of major cities, and major cities.[7]

In both cases, left support is becoming more urbanized, but the gaps are much larger in the United States. As the knowledge economy has developed, the political preferences of major cities have diverged rapidly away from other areas – moving strongly to the left, such that Democrats win two-thirds of votes in counties based in major cities but just a third in rural areas. That gap was less than 10 percentage points in the early 1990s.

Within European countries, the gradients vary, with some remaining relatively nonexistent (the Southern European countries), others looking more "American" in the growth of an urban-rural gradient (e.g., Switzerland). In most, there is an intermediate position, where traditional social democrats continue to mobilize voters in towns and in some cases rural areas, but surging support for Green parties in urban areas mean that left voting is becoming more urban (e.g., Austria, Germany, the Netherlands). Take one well-known example of left dominance, Sweden. In the early 1990s, in the countryside, the Social Democrats (SAP) polled 46 percent and other left parties an additional 9 percent, with the SAP polling 34 percent in major cities and other left parties 12 percent. In the late 2010s, the SAP fell to 31 percent in the countryside and 24 percent in major cities, with other left parties continuing to poll 9 percent of the countryside but rising to 17 percent of the urban vote. The Swedish pattern demonstrates a more general phenomenon that places with larger welfare states had leftist parties with a greater depth of support outside of urban areas and that these differences continue to matter today (Rodden 2019).

Individual Attitudes and Voting Behavior

In order to test these claims more systematically, we turn to the individual level. We hypothesize that high-income individuals who work in

[7] This draws on the OECD functional urban area classification. Major cities are defined as the core areas – city and inner suburbs – of major cities, suburbs are the outer areas of the same unit, metropolitan areas – both core and suburb – are included as cities, medium-sized areas are combined with towns not classified by the OECD.

intangibles-intensive sectors and live in urban areas should behave differently across countries with different electoral systems. In majoritarian countries they should ally with the urban/intangibles poor and be more supportive of decommodifying policies, less supportive of deconcentrating policies, and more likely to vote for the left. By contrast, in proportional systems, we expect the alliance of urban/intangibles rich and urban/intangibles poor to be much weaker. Instead we expect more alignment across class groups regardless of industry or region.

We test these claims first with the 2016 Cooperative Congressional Election Study conducted in the United States and several waves of the European Social Survey conducted between 2002 and 2016 with fifteen Western European countries included. In both cases, we focus our analysis on the preferences of groups defined first by their income and by the industry they work in, specifically how intangibles intensive it is. Our interest in particular is in whether high-income groups behave differently when they work in high or low intangibles industries, and in the gap between high- and low-income individuals working in the same sector, across sectors defined by their intangible-intensiveness.

CCES 2016

We begin with the Cooperative Congressional Election Survey taken before the 2016 presidential election, which provides excellent data on household income and on the industrial sector of employment. It also has a number of questions that help us measure attitudes toward decommodification and (less precisely) deconcentration.

The intangible measure is similar to that used earlier at the national level but now captures investment in intangibles as the percent of value added in each industry, measured by one-digit NACE (Rev-2) codes taken from the INTAN-INVEST dataset. The CCES uses a twenty-three-point scale that corresponds closely to NAICS (North American Industry Classification System): we match this to the INTAN-INVEST coding. We have data on intangibles-intensiveness for sixteen sectors, however, we have to drop those for which there is no data largely due to measurement issues for the intangibles variable: these are real estate, public administration, education, and health/social work. Thus, our analysis is limited largely to the private sector and excludes individuals employed in private education or health companies, as well as real estate. We also limit our analysis to individuals who are currently employed.

We use a measure of household income that is a sixteen-point index from under $10,000 to over $500,000. In a number of models, we interact this variable with the intangible-intensiveness of an individual's industrial sector. We include dummies (not shown) for education level (below high school, high school, some college, two-year degree, four-year degree, postgraduate), gender, and children living at home, and we also include an age variable. In all our analyses, we include dummies for the state in which the individual lives and we cluster standard errors at the state level.

Table 13.1 has six models, each examining a different dependent variable. Models 1 and 2 examine an item asking people how they would wish to balance the federal budget – through raising taxes, cutting defense spending, or cutting domestic spending. Our interest is in where they rank the third option, since this option most directly connects to decommodification preferences. We recode this variable such that 0 means ranking domestic spending cuts lowest as a priority and 2 means ranking domestic spending cuts as the highest priority. Models 3 and 4 examine the probability of supporting the repeal of Obamacare – another decommodifying policy (albeit with important regionally redistributive effects). Models 5 and 6 examine the probability of supporting greater spending on highways and infrastructure – a potentially deconcentrating policy since much of this spending would connect regions. Finally, Models 7 and 8 examine vote intention – specifically whether the respondent intended to vote for Donald Trump in the 2016 election. Odd-numbered models enter the intangible-intensiveness of the respondent's sector directly, whereas even-numbered models also include the interaction of intangible-intensiveness with household income.

Our interest is in whether high-income people in intangibles-intensive sectors behave differently from those in tangible-intensive sectors and whether a potential decommodifying "coalition" between rich and poor is more likely in intangibles-intensive sectors.

We begin by examining Models 1 and 2 with preferences over cutting domestic spending. Model 1 shows that while higher-income households prefer cutting spending compared to lower-income households, people working in intangibles-intensive sectors are less supportive of making domestic spending cuts. Model 2 shows that this effect is largely driven by high-income households. This can be seen in Figure 13.6a. The intangible-intensiveness of a respondent's industry is negatively associated with supporting for cutting domestic spending among high-income households (those with household incomes between $150,000 and $200,000), whereas for low-income households ($20,000 to $30,000) there is no relationship

TABLE 13.1 *Cooperative Congressional Election Study 2016*

	Cut Spending Model 1	Cut Spending Model 2	Repeal OC Model 3	Repeal OC Model 4	Infrastructure Model 5	Infrastructure Model 6	Vote Trump Model 7	Vote Trump Model 8
Intangible Share	−0.371	0.409	−1.107	0.415	−0.047	0.666	−0.780	0.254
	(0.138)	(0.263)	(0.189)	(0.507)	(0.267)	(0.623)	(0.322)	(0.532)
Family Income	0.013	0.027	0.015	0.043	0.011	0.024	0.031	0.049
	(0.002)	(0.004)	(0.005)	(0.011)	(0.006)	(0.012)	(0.004)	(0.010)
Inc*Intangibles		−0.101		−0.197		−0.096		−0.132
		(0.026)		(0.065)		(0.083)		(0.067)
Age	0.002	0.002	0.008	0.008	0.016	0.016	0.031	0.031
	(0.000)	(0.000)	(0.001)	(0.001)	(0.001)	(0.001)	(0.001)	(0.001)
Female	−0.062	−0.062	−0.180	−0.181	−0.365	−0.365	−0.393	−0.394
	(0.011)	(0.011)	(0.026)	(0.026)	(0.032)	(0.032)	(0.034)	(0.033)
Children	−0.098	−0.097	−0.351	−0.350	0.200	0.201	−0.146	−0.146
	(0.013)	(0.013)	(0.038)	(0.038)	(0.036)	(0.036)	(0.052)	(0.052)
Constant	1.283	1.183	0.991	0.794	0.689	0.598	−0.765	−0.898
	(0.041)	(0.043)	(0.095)	(0.113)	(0.158)	(0.194)	(0.131)	(0.137)
Observations	23,385	23,385	23,648	23,648	23,610	23,610	19,847	19,847

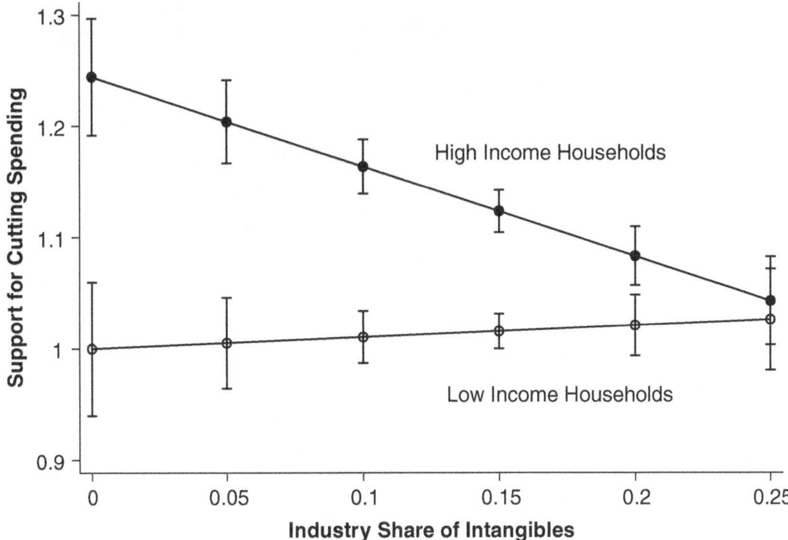

FIGURE 13.6A Intangibles, income, and preferences about cutting domestic spending

evident. Among those employed in the sectors most dominated by intangible investment, the spending preferences of high- and low-income individuals is indistinguishable. In other words, in such sectors – and the places where these individuals live – a decommodifying coalition is viable.

Models 3 and 4 show a similar story in terms of support for repealing Obamacare. Once again, it is high-income people who are most affected by the intangible-intensiveness of their industry of work. And again we see a potential coalition for decommodification (relatively lower support for repealing Obamacare) between high- and low-income people in intangibles-intensive sectors in Figure 13.6b.

Models 5 and 6 examine support for highways and infrastructure spending – a policy that is more deconcentrating than decommodifying. Here we see a different pattern – high-income people become marginally *less* supportive of this deconcentrating policy when they work in intangibles-intensive sectors, though their preferences remain similar to low-income people in those sectors. This pattern can be seen in Figure 13.6c.[8]

Finally, Models 7 and 8 look at Trump vote intention. Here we see that high-income people in intangibles-intensive sectors are much less supportive

[8] The effect is even stronger if we use log intangibles as opposed to the non-logged figure.

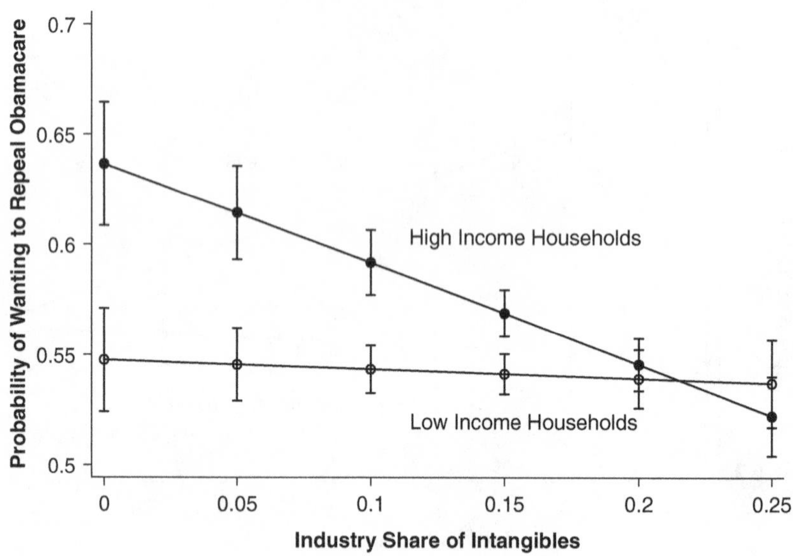

FIGURE 13.6B Intangibles, income, and preferences about repealing Obamacare

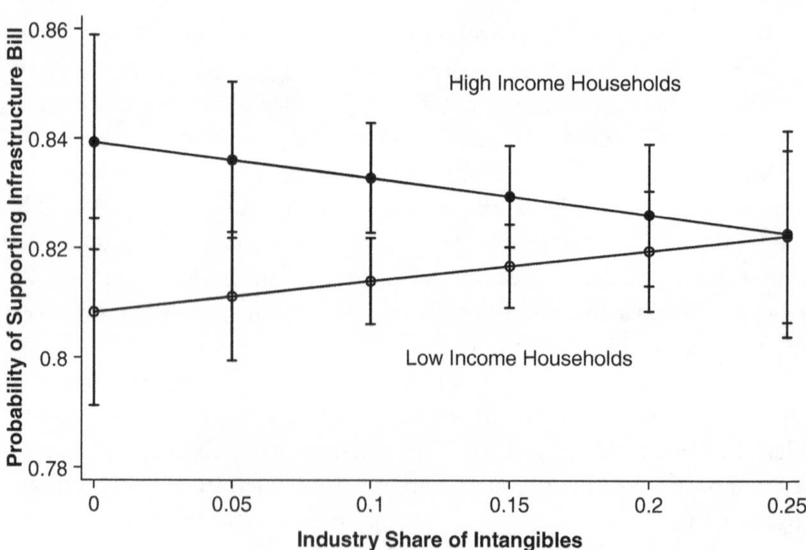

FIGURE 13.6C Intangibles, income, and preferences about increasing infrastructure spending

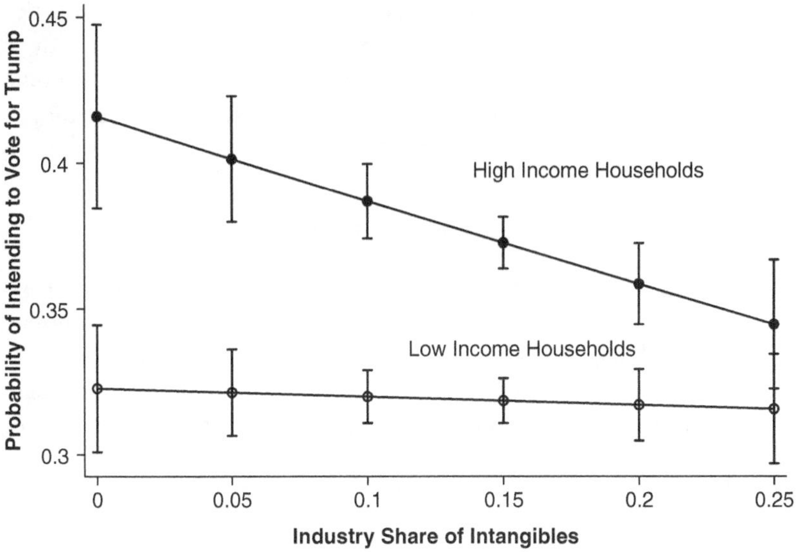

FIGURE 13.6D Intangibles, income, and voting intention

of Donald Trump – indeed, their preferences are similar to those with low incomes, regardless of sector. Figure 13.6d demonstrates this pattern.

In separate analyses (not shown), we find a similar pattern in terms of attitudes to redistribution and healthcare spending with the urban-rural cleavage structuring how household income shapes attitudes. We find that high-income workers in urban areas are much closer to their urban counterparts with low incomes than they are to their rural high-income counterparts. Since geographical divides and employment in intangibles sectors are so highly correlated in America we view these as different sides of the same underlying dynamic. To summarize, our analysis of the CCES provides some support for the claim that high-skilled workers in the intangibles sector are more likely to favor decommodifying policies that benefit low-paid workers in their own industries/regions than they are deconcentrating policies that have wider geographical spread. Arguably this has shaped the new coalition of support that the Democrats rely on in elections, though its concentration in urban areas may be politically inefficient (Rodden 2019).

Beyond these divides based around geography and production, decommodifying policies are further undermined by other features of American politics. First, the racialized nature of American politics makes decommodification difficult: low-income white rural voters have often baulked at redistribution perceived to benefit urban minorities (Thurston, this volume). Second, the status quo bias of the US political system, with its myriad legislative and judicial veto points, means that even should a decommodifying coalition emerge, it may struggle to convert political demand into supply (Kelly and Morgan, this volume).

European Social Survey

We now turn to the European Social Survey (ESS), one of the only cross-national surveys with detailed industry and occupational data. Although we lack enough national variation to talk meaningfully about how existing policies of deconcentration and decommodification might offset these structural forces, we are in these analyses able to identify how the rise of intangibles and global labor markets shape the attitudes of citizens to such policies and to different political parties.

When examining the ESS we find very different patterns to the United States. In Europe, by and large, the winners of the rising knowledge economy – those in intangible-intensive sectors or those more driven by international labor markets for skilled human capital – are actually the least supportive of redistribution (decommodifying policies) and are inclined to vote for the right. In the United States, by contrast, this group were relatively supportive of decommodifying policies and unsupportive of the political right.

Instead, in Europe, this group's political preferences are much more similar to other wealthy people in different sectors and regions than they are to low-income workers in their industry or region. We argue that this is in part a consequence of different electoral systems. Since proportional systems allow the rich to pool their votes across districts, wealthy workers in intangibles-intensive sectors and regions have no need to develop an urban support coalition with poorer voters. Hence, they will be less supportive of decommodifying policies and more supportive of right-wing parties than in the American context.

The intangibles measure is the same as for the CCES (intangible share of sector in a given country in a given year) but we log it because it is right-skewed across countries and time. Results are very similar with the non-logged version. Thus, the first core variable is the log of intangibles as a share of value added in industry i in country j for year t. Again, because data on intangibles-intensiveness is limited to the private sector, we exclude public sector workers and those in education, health, and real estate.

We start in Table 13.2 by estimating linear probability models for support for redistribution – a measure of base support for less commodifying policies

TABLE 13.2 *European Social Survey: Support for redistribution*

	Redist Model 1	Redist Model 2	Redist Model 3	Vote CR Model 4	Vote CR Model 5	Vote CR Model 6
Age	0.001**	0.001	0.001**	−0.136***	−0.192***	−0.153***
	(0.000)	(0.001)	(0.000)	(0.044)	(0.071)	(0.044)
Female	0.055***	0.055***	0.059***	0.004	0.007**	0.004
	(0.008)	(0.009)	(0.008)	(0.003)	(0.003)	(0.003)
Degree	−0.091***	−0.086***	−0.088***	0.181**	0.140*	0.177**
	(0.012)	(0.012)	(0.012)	(0.081)	(0.073)	(0.074)
No Secondary	0.021	0.031	0.019	−0.373***	−0.306**	−0.400***
	(0.014)	(0.020)	(0.014)	(0.097)	(0.137)	(0.084)
Partner Works	0.016		0.015	−0.002		−0.007
	(0.010)		(0.010)	(0.030)		(0.028)
Children	−0.005	−0.006	−0.006	0.055	0.029	0.047
	(0.006)	(0.010)	(0.006)	(0.050)	(0.061)	(0.050)
Income	−0.085**	−0.069*	−0.097**	−0.214	0.065	0.165
	(0.034)	(0.034)	(0.036)	(0.229)	(0.295)	(0.197)
Intangibles	0.038***	0.031**	0.035***	−0.564***	−0.479***	−0.310***
	(0.007)	(0.011)	(0.011)	(0.097)	(0.078)	(0.113)
Inc* Intangibles	−0.067***	−0.062***	−0.058***	0.465***	0.393***	0.286**
	(0.012)	(0.019)	(0.012)	(0.126)	(0.138)	(0.112)
Constant	−0.091***	−0.086***	−0.088***	0.404	0.201	0.680**
	(0.012)	(0.012)	(0.012)	(0.295)	(0.284)	(0.302)
Industry Dummies	N	N	Y	N	N	Y
Observations	54,032	25,883	54,032	51,124	24,328	51,124

for EU-15 countries. For each model we include controls for age, education (a dummy for no secondary and a dummy for a college degree), gender, having children, and having a working spouse. All models are restricted only to those in the labor force. Income is measured as the in-sample percentile of the income distribution. As income is measured as net family income, to measure individual income, Model 2 is estimated using only those with no working spouse (single respondents and core breadwinners). Model 3 is estimated with fixed effects for industry. Our main interest is in the interaction of income with the intangibles variable.

Model 1 in Table 13.2 shows that exposure to intangibles has a positive direct effect on support for redistribution, but a negative interactive effect with income. This latter effect holds up when limited to primary earners only (Model 2) and when industry dummies are included (Model 3). Substantively, this effect is large. Figure 13.7a shows the predicted probability of supporting redistribution, drawn from Model 1. High-income people in high-intangibles industries are much more likely to be skeptical of redistribution than are high-income in low-intangible industries and indeed than low-income people in high-intangible industries. In other

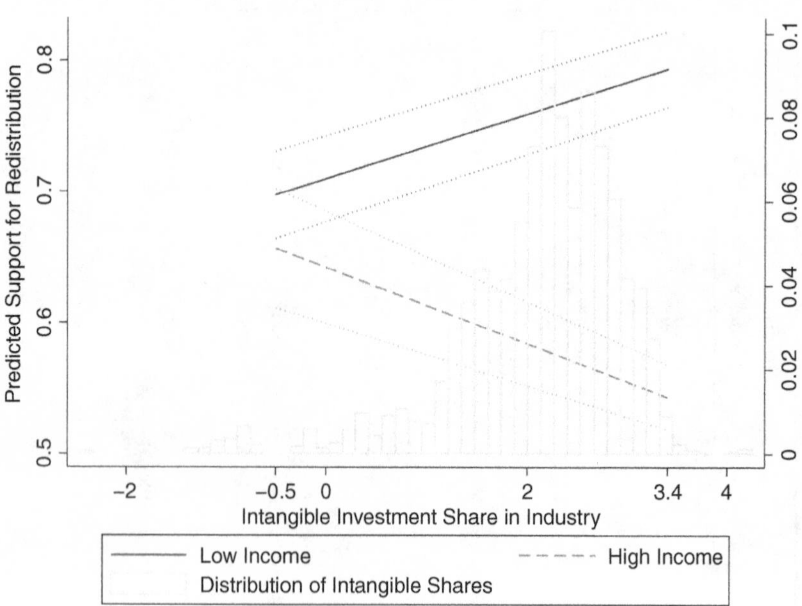

FIGURE 13.7A Predicted redistribution support by income and industry-level investment in intangibles

words, whereas in traditional sectors that had low levels of intangibles, the redistributive preferences of high- and low-income individuals are remarkably similar, in industries characterized by high levels of investment in intangibles, there is a huge redistributive preference divide between workers with different incomes. The winners of the rise of intangibles are particularly opposed to redistribution.

The implication is that where individuals are in industries with higher levels of investment in intangibles, their preferences over redistribution are much more greatly shaped by their income than individuals in relatively "unexposed" industries or occupations. Since the knowledge economy drives both widespread investment in intangibles and appears to be widening intra-occupational wage gaps in America (and indeed elsewhere), we should expect, on aggregate, for there to growing divides over redistribution in these booming sectors. The knowledge economy may be underpinning polarization in attitudes to redistribution, despite the more optimistic forecasts in, for example Iversen and Soskice (2019).

We see a somewhat similar pattern as regards voting for center-right parties. Again, using the European Social Survey, we ran a multinomial analysis of vote choice across fifteen countries between 2002 and 2016. While the multinomial model incorporates vote choice across five party families, we present here the results for voting for center-right parties (Liberals, Christian Democrats, and Conservatives), with the baseline being voting for parties of the left. In sectors with high levels of investment in intangibles, there are large differences between those with high and low income in terms of their propensity to vote for a center-right party. These are especially apparent in the predicted probabilities displayed in Figure 13.7b. Low-income people in sectors with high levels of investment in intangibles are particularly unlikely to vote for the center-right (although those in intangible-light industries are). By contrast, high-income people in intangible-heavy sectors are not that different from other high-income voters.

CONCLUSION

In sum, the knowledge economy is almost certainly shaping potential coalitions around policies of decommodification and deconcentration but is doing so differently in America and Europe, in part for reasons related to the different incentives produced by electoral systems. In Europe, because economically disadvantaged groups can make common cause across regions, there is still a clear coalition for policies that are both

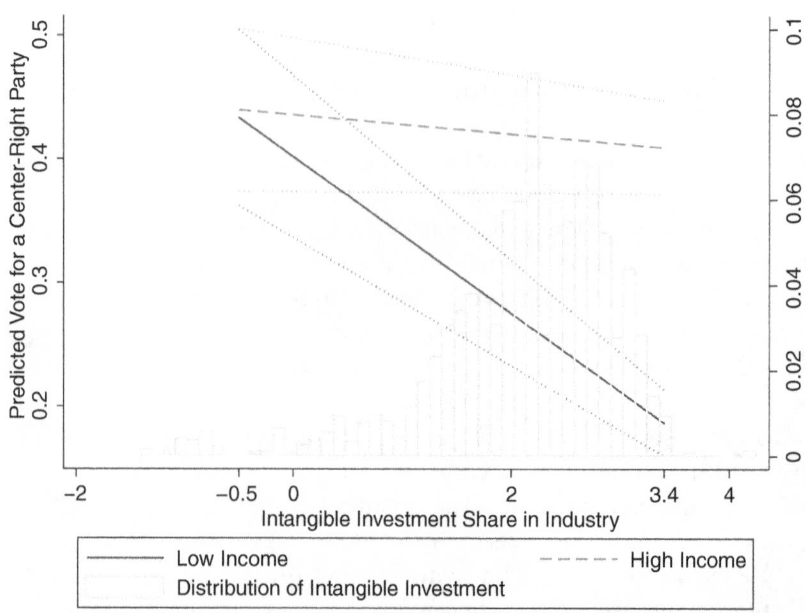

FIGURE 13.7B Probability of voting center right by industry intangible investment and income

deconcentrating and decommodifying and which can command majority support. The winners of the knowledge economy may be the "odd men out" of this array of preferences.

In the United States (and also the UK) the geographical nature of the electoral system means groups must ally *within* regions and because the knowledge economy is geographically asymmetrically distributed this means cross-class alliances in areas that specialize in intangible production. The winners of the knowledge economy will ally with low-paid workers in urban areas over decommodifying policies and support center-left parties but will be less keen on deconcentrating policies. The recent experience of the Democrats and the UK Labour Party speak to the proprieties of such an alliance. By contrast, the right may end up moving toward deconcentrating policies, such as Boris Johnson's talk of "leveling up" or Trump's focus on aid to farmers and trade protection.

EPILOGUE

The American Political Economy Confronts COVID-19

Jacob S. Hacker, Alexander Hertel-Fernandez, Paul Pierson, and Kathleen Thelen

As this group met in Cambridge in late February 2020 to discuss revised chapters for this project, we did not know that a COVID-19 super-spreader event was unfolding less than three miles away – ironically, at the conference of a major bio-technology firm. By October, estimates suggested that the strains unleashed at that single event might have infected 300,000 Americans (Wines and Harmon 2020). Well before then, of course, it was clear that a world-historical calamity was unfolding before us.

Crises fundamentally challenge existing institutions and practices. For this reason, they can be deeply illuminating for social scientists. Like stress tests of financial entities, they reveal structural sources of resilience and weakness that are less evident during normal periods (e.g., Gourevitch 1986). COVID-19 has tested the capacities of all rich democracies, and none will emerge from the pandemic without serious losses. As we put the finishing touches on this book in early 2021, the situation remains deeply unsettled. In the United States and United Kingdom, vaccines are being rolled out at an accelerating pace, even as new strains of the virus are spreading globally. But already it is clear that some countries have weathered their stress tests better than others, and that the American experience stands out in both profoundly positive and negative ways.

The most positive development to date has been the extremely rapid development and deployment of effective vaccines. In addition, despite intense partisan polarization, Congress responded to the emergency with large relief packages that have softened the economic impact of the crisis. On other fundamental dimensions, however, the American experience has looked much less positive. In the pandemic's first year, job losses, infections, and deaths were all tragically high. By the time the death toll reached 500,000 Americans in late February 2021, the United States, with around 1 in 200 of the world's people, accounted for around 1 in 5 known COVID-19-related deaths (Tompkins et al. 2021). Moreover, all the negative effects of the pandemic have been distributed dramatically unequally across lines of class, race, and ethnicity.

In this epilogue, we examine these contrasting features of the American experience over the first year of the crisis, stretching from the initial lockdowns of 2020 to the ongoing vaccine deployment of early 2021. Our goal is to explore how key elements of the US response – the examples of innovation and leadership as well as the instances of policy failure and their large and disparate costs – are linked to the distinctive characteristics of the American political economy discussed in this volume.

EVALUATING THE AMERICAN EXPERIENCE

At this point, a definitive assessment of the US response is impossible. Even for the period we are looking at, we lack the full data and distance necessary for a comprehensive comparative analysis. More important, the pandemic is far from over, and the situation is changing rapidly. Over the course of this project alone, the United States has careened from recording the worst health and employment outcomes among rich democracies to outperforming most of its peers with regard to the reported pace of vaccine administration and the projected pace of economic growth. In light of these information gaps and uncertainties, it would be unwise for us to attempt an overall assessment of the United States' relative ability to deal with this unprecedented crisis, much less to identify all the reasons why the US response succeeded or fell short.

What we *can* do, however, is to identify those aspects of the American experience to date that appear to reflect the more enduring *structural* features of the American political economy explored in the chapters to this volume. We start by considering one of the APE's longstanding comparative advantages: the strength of its scientific community and the role the APE plays in generating what the Varieties of Capitalism literature calls "radical" innovation. We then turn to the three core features of the APE explored in the Introduction, which, we show, served the country less well overall.

THE US KNOWLEDGE ECONOMY COMES THROUGH

In its response to the COVID-19 crisis, the United States has clearly stood out among affluent democracies in one critical respect: it was at the leading edge in developing the remarkable vaccines that have offered the best news since the onset of the pandemic. There is good reason to see this success as linked to distinctive features of the American political economy. Comparative scholars have long noted the comparative advantage of liberal market economies (the US and UK in particular) in fostering radical innovation (Hall and Soskice 2001). As Soskice emphasizes in his chapter, critical features of the American path of economic development – strength in scientific research; bountiful, flexible, and risk-accepting finance; and a continental scale that facilitated the emergence of companies with the necessary mix of capacities – provided the foundation for a cutting-edge pharmaceutical sector. It is probably no coincidence that three of the successful initial vaccines were developed by American firms Johnson & Johnson, Moderna, and Pfizer (which partnered with a German company in developing its vaccine).

Yet it would be highly misleading to ascribe this achievement to the triumph of "private" initiative or ingenuity unleashed by free market forces. As both Soskice and Barnes emphasize, the American economic model of radical innovation has always relied heavily on a combination of public and private efforts. The federal government has long played a critical role in encouraging and financing basic scientific research. The foundation for the most effective vaccines – the mRNA technology – came from the labs of bench scientists whose work was funded decades ago by the National Institutes of Health and the Defense Department. Likewise, many of the more recent innovations that led to the final vaccine breakthroughs benefited from generous public support and public-private collaborations (Allen 2020).

Contemporary federal action also facilitated rapid vaccine development. The Food and Drug Administration (FDA) has a long and distinguished history of independence and power that sets it apart from many other government agencies (see especially Carpenter 2010). In this respect, it bears similarity to the Federal Reserve, which is in fact independent from the elected branches of government. Despite the Trump administration's attempts to politicize testing, treatments, and vaccine development, the FDA was able to leverage its considerable administrative capacity, strong reputation, and long experience with the country's massive drug companies to promote rapid scientific advances while sustaining sufficient autonomy from political interference to retain public confidence (Peterson 2020). In this critical area, the Trump administration and Congress also provided abundant support, pouring $10.5 billion into vaccine development and creating a structure that essentially guaranteed against downside risk for firms making the necessary research and production commitments. The United States also imposed strict rules for US-based companies limiting their capacity to export their products (which has simultaneously increased American supplies and reduced European and Canadian ones) (Keating 2021).

The United States has also moved comparatively quickly to distribute and administer vaccines – critical measures given the race against the spread of more contagious and deadly variants. It is too soon to determine the extent to which federal and state governments deserve credit for the brisk rollout, or whether it simply reflects the large supplies US firms were able to generate quickly and the aggressive government efforts to procure vast stockpiles. What seems undeniable is that the distinctive strengths of the American knowledge economy played an essential role in advancing this vital response to the pandemic.

Another notable area of US action was one that (unlike vaccine development) cut against expectations: a series of generous relief packages passed by Congress between March 2020 and April 2021. Under normal circumstances, partisan polarization and Republicans' longstanding aversion to spending might well have thwarted such measures. The fragmentation of American political institutions discussed throughout this volume certainly would have provided ample blocking opportunities. That these packages nonetheless went through reflects, we think, more contingent factors. In the case of the first relief package, a raging pandemic and a looming election likely combined to soften Republican resistance to spending. (Leaders facing reelection in other countries spent even more freely.) Likewise, despite Trump's loss in the general election, the remaining special elections – with the Senate majority on the line – likely facilitated the second relief bill's passage. And when those elections delivered a Democratic majority in the Senate to go along with a freshly elected Democratic president, the way was clear for the third package. That the successful passage of these three bills turned on more contingent factors does not diminish their importance to the American response to the crisis. Following enactment of the American Rescue Plan, the US economy looked poised to rebound more rapidly, at least with respect to GDP growth, than the economies of most rich democracies.

In other respects, however, America's fragmented democracy produced outcomes that were far less positive. The next sections briefly explore several of the specific challenges that appear to be linked to core features of the American political economy highlighted in the introduction: (1) the fragmentation and decentralization of American political institutions; (2) the particular nature of US interest organization; and (3) the deep racial divisions embedded in the American political economy.

INSTITUTIONAL FRAGMENTATION AND UNEVEN GOVERNMENT CAPACITY

The institutional fragmentation of the APE was clearly an obstacle in the early stages of the COVID-19 crisis. Without strong federal leadership, the United States' distinctive version of federalism descended into a chaotic set of conflicting responses. Within weeks of the outbreak, the states were competing with one another for necessary medical equipment, setting in motion bidding wars over crucial supplies that not only raised the prices that revenue-strapped state governments had to pay, but also hindered any coordinated effort to ensure these supplies flowed to the areas of greatest need (Ranney et al. 2020).

Coordination at the federal level was further complicated by the stark partisan differences across "red" and "blue" states, which often took wildly different approaches to rules governing masks, lock-downs, and social distancing. (This cross-state partisan divergence continues to this day.) Not only were some states and cities slow to respond, but some actively resisted efforts at limiting commercial activity or imposing public health safeguards. Indeed, prominent GOP-controlled states used "preemption" against cities and counties that sought to implement more proactive measures (Davidson and Haddow 2020; Rainwater 2020). Thus, the pandemic highlighted an increasingly striking feature of the American political economy: the growing frequency of policy stand-offs between red states and blue cities.

To be sure, President Donald Trump exacerbated these tensions with his own particular brand of right-wing populism. For example, he feuded prominently with blue state governors over the appropriateness and enforcement of pandemic restrictions. But the president was hardly the only cause of the explosive partisan conflict. The different approaches taken by leaders in red and blue states and cities also reflected the broader stance and composition of the Republican Party. As several chapters in the volume have argued, the GOP coalition has become an uneasy alliance of business-friendly economic conservatives (though "conservative" understates how radically anti-government many of them are) and ethnonationalist populists with strong ties to right-wing media and grassroots conservative groups.

These two sides of the alliance were reflected in Republican attitudes and activities amid the pandemic, both within the activist mass public and among politicians in office. Right-wing groups and voters quickly mobilized against a more ambitious COVID-19 response. While vaccine hesitancy and conspiracy theorizing is hardly distinct to the United States, in no other rich democracy did opinion and behavior around common-sense public health measures like mask-wearing and social distancing become so politically polarized. Standoffs with armed demonstrators in state capitols – foreshadowing the assault on the US Capitol in January by backers of President Trump seeking to overturn the election – were a reminder of the distinct governance challenges created by a two-party system in which one party is closer to fringe right-wing parties than to the conventional center-right parties common elsewhere.

The role of economic conservatives was more evident in Washington, as Republicans held up the first relief package throughout the summer of 2020 to demand cuts in the aid it offered to state and local governments – provisions that Senate Majority Leader Mitch McConnell argued amounted to a "blue state bailout" (Kilgore 2020). In fact, red states were at least as fiscally damaged as blue states. But on this economic issue, as on many others, national Republicans simply did not place much priority on helping them (Grumbach, Hacker, and Pierson, this volume). As will be discussed shortly, Republicans did put a high priority on the demands of business groups for corporate immunity from COVID-related lawsuits, further complicating congressional bargaining.

Finally, the weakness and politicization of the federal bureaucracy examined in this volume was also a chronic problem. Not all government agencies enjoyed (or practiced) the political independence of the FDA. A striking counter-example that was arguably more representative overall involves the Occupational Safety and Health Administration (OSHA), the federal agency charged with setting and enforcing workplace health and safety standards. Even under the most favorable conditions, OSHA lacks sufficient resources and authority to realize its mandate. Upon entering office in 2017, the Trump administration further weakened and politicized the agency. COVID-19 thus hit when OSHA's already-insufficient enforcement staff had fallen to the lowest level in decades and its agency leadership was in turmoil (Berkowitz 2020). With OSHA largely absent from the scene, workplaces became an important source of transmission of the virus. Tragically, it was often already-disadvantaged workers who bore the brunt of the virus's spread across weakly regulated workplaces (e.g., Kindy 2020). In short, the combination of decentralized federalism, uneven federal capacity, and stark polarization undercut public health and economic recovery in 2020.

THE HIGH COST OF DISORGANIZED INTERESTS

The organization of major economic interests in the United States also had significant implications during the initial COVID crisis. In many European countries, labor representatives were included alongside business leaders and health experts in peak-level discussions over the COVID response (ILO 2020). At the same time, and arguably more important to the lived experience of ordinary workers, stronger employment protections and a more pervasive union presence in most of Europe allowed workers to call out unsafe conditions with less fear of retribution. In the United States, the lack of peak-level coordination and the weakness of organized labor meant that most of the economy was marked by a free-for -all of voluntary standards and weak testing – and widespread sickness (Hertel-Fernandez et al. 2020).

Unemployment also soared in the United States to levels not seen in other rich democracies. Whereas in Europe, so-called short-time work policies allowed workers to earn subsidized wages and keep their jobs, the American response focused on direct aid to unemployed workers. Although the level of benefits made available was generous, any analysis must bear in mind that a large share of these funds was required to compensate for pre-pandemic social policies that offered far less protection than those in other rich democracies – including employment-based health benefits that vanished when workers most needed them.

However generous, the unemployment insurance extension was also nightmarishly difficult to administer. Unemployment insurance is run under relatively loose federal rules by each of the fifty states. In many of these states, eligible workers had difficulty accessing benefits because decades of "starving the beast" had emaciated administrative capacities in the unemployment bureaus. Studies showed that at the height of the unemployment crisis, millions of unemployed workers were unable to submit a claim as a result of antiquated systems (Zipperer and Gould 2020; also Cohn 2020).

Those federal policies that sought specifically to preserve employment also bore a distinctive US imprint. The main such policy was the Paycheck

Protection Plan (PPP), which targeted small and medium sized firms. This policy provided forgivable loans to small businesses to cover ongoing operating costs (including, centrally, payroll) if they avoided layoffs. Whatever its ultimate impact on employment, the PPP program serves as a classic example of the United States' longstanding reliance on the private sector to deliver government benefits.[1] Any firm wishing to tap into PPP funding was directed not to a government agency but to one of a number of designated banks that would then vet the application and disburse the funds. This arrangement not only proved lucrative for the banks (Covert 2020; Fischer and Gould-Werth 2020); it also allowed them to insert additional conditions and hurdles for companies seeking assistance. Unsurprisingly, funding went first (and in some cases only) to companies that already had accounts with these banks, especially to those with the biggest accounts (Cowley and Flitter 2020). In effect, private lenders in the United States were in a position to pick winners and losers, while collecting a fee on each loan.

Another crucial aspect of the US relief effort was the aggressive response of the Federal Reserve. The Fed, perhaps the strongest independent policy institution within a generally weak administrative state, took extraordinary measures to keep interest rates low and asset prices high. Necessarily, these efforts were mostly beneficial to businesses and investors who continued to profit amid the crisis. By contrast, the Fed could not do much for those whose enterprises and jobs were unable to continue. This was a task for Congress and the President. Yet the relief package that Congress crafted for large firms carried none of the same conditions that had been attached to relief for small- or medium-sized businesses. Financial support for big business was not contingent on avoiding layoffs; indeed, it did not even include measures to force companies to limit dividends, reduce executive pay, or forgo stock buybacks (Stein and Whoriskey 2020).

Meanwhile, the organized representatives of the American business community – notably the US Chamber of Commerce – initially circled the wagons around a remarkably narrow agenda, centering largely on the demand for legal immunity for businesses if front-line workers became ill with or died from COVID on the job, a position that, as noted, complicated relief negotiations in Congress in 2020 (Kopp 2020). The Chamber did not have much trouble getting the GOP on board. Indeed, in the wake

[1] At least some preliminary studies suggest that, while the program provided needed liquidity to small businesses, it was not particularly effective in sustaining employment (Chetty et al. 2020).

of the initial relief bills, McConnell made corporate liability limits a top priority in any future relief legislation (Bolton 2020). Meanwhile, at least sixteen states – nearly all under Republican control – enacted COVID-related liability shields for businesses through legislation or executive action at the behest of business demands (Hishamunda and Young 2020).

RACE AND THE UNEQUAL CONSEQUENCES OF COVID

COVID-19 was like tracer injected into the American political economy, illuminating people and places disproportionately vulnerable because of systemic discrimination and unequal power. And what became clear almost immediately was that those most vulnerable were mostly nonwhite (Parker et al. 2020).

Low-income communities of color disproportionately faced sickness and death, reflecting their greater likelihood of employment in frontline occupations, their more limited access to health care, and their heightened exposure to social and personal risks (due to crowded housing, lack of affordable childcare, high rates of asthma, and other systemically grounded inequities). Shockingly, life expectancy among Latinos fell by more than three years in 2020, compared with a roughly eight-month drop for white Americans. Among Black Americans, it fell by more than 2 years (Andrasfay and Goldman 2021).

The disparities in economic outcomes across income, racial, and ethnic groups were also stark. One obvious reason was differential exposure to economic losses. Less obvious, but also fundamental to the American political economy, was differential access to vital benefits in America's racially divided public-private system of social protection (see Thurston, this volume). Sick pay and health coverage provide two telling examples. Particularly important during a pandemic, sick pay was mandatory across the European Union well before the virus hit, and many European governments further expanded it in response to the crisis. By contrast, less than a third of American workers in the lowest income decile had access to even a single day of paid leave when the crisis came (BLS 2017). At the height of the pandemic, only 34 percent of "essential workers" were certain they would receive paid time off if they had a fever (Hertel-Fernandez et al. 2020). As a result, disadvantaged racial and socioeconomic groups were much more likely to get sick or sicken others at work (e.g., Chang et al. 2020).

In March 2020, Congress did pass an emergency federal leave program as part of its omnibus response to the crisis. But the program was limited:

workers were ineligible if they worked at a company with more than 500 employees, and businesses with fewer than 50 people were allowed to opt out. With those broad restrictions and its clunky tax-credit–based design, potentially as few as a quarter of workers qualified for the temporary leave benefit (Miller and Tankersley 2020).

The pandemic also exposed another critical way in which race pervades the American political economy. The legacies of slavery, Jim Crow, and racialized zoning live on in stark geographic segregation and a huge wealth gap between Black and white families. The two are intimately related: housing is the biggest component of both personal wealth and local revenue bases. At the household and community levels, lack of wealth increases the need for public protections. Yet in our decentralized federal system, the same geographically grounded inequalities undercut the generosity and reach of those protections. Many important safety net programs are run through the states, with varying levels of generosity, coverage, and administrative capacity. For reasons that have much to do with the political consequences of racial division, the adequacy and effectiveness of these programs is closely related to the share of state residents who are nonwhite, with larger minority populations associated with poorer programs (e.g., Hero 2000). Moreover, Black workers are overrepresented in state and local jobs, which have faced devastating cuts. Here, too, the lack of a stronger federal role amid the crisis inflicted disproportionate harm on nonwhite Americans.

In a word, the insecurities faced by low-income communities of color were *compounding* – the result of multiple intersecting inequalities in the job and housing markets and in America's decentralized framework of provision. In few areas was this more apparent than with regard to public schooling – essential not just to the education of the young, but also to the ability of their parents to work. But with schools going remote due to COVID-19, this prerequisite of both child opportunity and parental employment was thrown into disarray. The (still-spotty) evidence suggests that remote K–12 education was most prevalent precisely in the most disadvantaged communities (Smith and Reeves 2020). Early results suggest that these disruptions will permanently disadvantage poor and nonwhite students living in low-income communities (Agostinelli et al. 2020). These are, of course, the students already most poorly served by America's highly stratified educational system. The effects on these students' parents are likely to be just as disproportionate. Thus, the pandemic has cast in sharp relief the ways in which deep inequities are built into America's decentralized governance.

Among those inequities is one we have not focused on in this volume, but which future work must grapple with: the stark gender disparities seen in many elements of the COVID crisis. Most notably, the employment effects of the crisis disproportionately fell on women, and in particular working mothers. The United States has long been seen as an exemplar of the "liberal market" approach to female employment, in which high levels of female labor force participation coexist with weak public supports for working parents (e.g., Iversen and Rosenbluth 2011). Yet female workforce participation has been falling behind the levels seen in other rich democracies for some time, and for many families the COVID-19 crisis detonated the fragile private arrangements they had cobbled together, with devastating consequences for those with limited resources. It was not just that women were more likely to be in affected occupations. It was also that they were uniquely vulnerable to the lack of a strong set of social protections for families with children in the United States (Djankov and Zhang 2020). Just as an approach focused on political economy highlights how racial and ethnic division are built into economic and policy structures, so too it will have to understand how gender divisions are embedded in such arrangements as well.

A CLARIFYING CRISIS

It is too soon to issue a final verdict on the US response to COVID-19. That has not been our goal in this chapter. Rather, we have aimed to show how America's pandemic year cast in sharp relief many of the core structural features of the American political economy. The strengths of the US knowledge economy were on display in the rapid development of new treatments and vaccines. The pockets of administrative leadership at the FDA and Federal Reserve proved crucial to both public health and economic stability. These positive outcomes, along with the unexpected (and we think contingent) willingness of Congress to pass large relief bills, left the United States in a stronger place in early 2021 than many other rich democracies. Yet the toll of that terrible year – in lost jobs and lost lives, shattered dreams and social discord – looms large in cross-national relief. These outcomes too, we have argued, showcase distinctive features of the American political economy.

Crises lay bare societies' fault lines. They can also lay bare their strength and resilience. As we write in March 2021, state and federal governments are rapidly deploying the biotechnology that the American political economy encouraged to address the destructive effects of COVID-19 that the

American political economy exacerbated. An emotion that has recently been in short supply is spreading through America: hope. Still, the Biden administration and the fragile Democratic majority in Congress will face daunting obstacles as they seek to refashion American governance to meet the nation's current challenges. If the analyses offered in this book carry any single message, it is that the structure of the American political economy will heavily shape and constrain politics and policy going forward.

Bibliography

Abdul-Razzak, N., Prato, C. & Wolton, S. (2019). After Citizens United: How Outside Spending Shapes American Democracy. https://ssrn.com/abstract=2823778.

Abrams, C. (1955). *Forbidden Neighbors: A Study in Housing Prejudice*, New York: Harper and Brothers.

Acemoglu, D., Robinson, J. A. & Verdier, T. (2017). Asymmetric Growth and Institutions in an Interdependent World. *Journal of Political Economy*, 125(5), 1245–305.

Achen, C. H. & Bartels, L. M. (2016). *Democracy for Realists: Why Elections Do Not Produce Responsive Government*, Princeton, NJ: Princeton University Press.

Addo, F. R., Houle, J. N. & Simon, D. (2016). Young, Black, and (Still) in the Red: Parental Wealth, Race, and Student Loan Debt. *Race and Social Problems*, 8(1), 64–76.

Adkins, L., Cooper, M. & Konings, M. (2020). *The Asset Economy*, Cambridge, UK: Polity.

Adler, J. (2016). *Business and the Roberts Court*, Oxford, UK: Oxford University Press.

Aglietta, M. (1979). *A Theory of Capitalist Regulation: The US Experience*, London: Verso.

Agostinelli, F., Doepke, M., Sorrenti, G. & Zilibotti, F. (2020). When the Great Equalizer Shuts Down: Schools, Peers, and Parents in Pandemic Times. *IZA* Discussion Paper No. 13965.

Aguilera, R. V. & Jackson, G. (2003). The Cross-National Diversity of Corporate Governance: Dimensions and Determinants. *The Academy of Management Review*, 28(3), 447–65.

Aguilera, R. V., Federo, R. & Ponomareva, Y. (2019). Gone Global: The International Diffusion of Hedge Fund Activism Outside the United States. https://ssrn.com/abstract=3402966.

Ahlquist, J. S. (2012). Public Sector Unions Need the Private Sector or Why the Wisconsin Protests Were Not Labor's Lazarus Moment. *The Forum*, 10(1).

Ahlquist, J. S. & Ansell, B. (2017). Taking Credit: Redistribution and Borrowing in an Age of Economic Polarization. *World Politics*, 69(4), 640–75.

Ajdacic, L., Heemskerk, E. M. & Garcia-Bernardo, J. (2020). The Wealth Defence Industry: A Large-scale Study on Accountancy Firms as Profit Shifting Facilitators. *New Political Economy*, 1–17.

Akcigit, U. & Ates, S. T. (2019a). Ten Facts on Declining Business Dynamism and Lessons from Endogenous Growth Theory. *NBER* Working Paper 25755.

Akcigit, U. & Ates, S. T. (2019b). What Happened to US Business Dynamism? *NBER* Working Paper 25756.

Akcigit, U., Baslandze, S. & Stantcheva, S. (2016). Taxation and the International Mobility of Inventors. *American Economic Review*, 106(10), 2930–81.

Akcigit, U., Grigsby, J., Nicholas, T. & Stantcheva, S. (2018). Taxation and Innovation in the 20th Century. *NBER* Working Paper 24982.

Alderman, L. (2020). BlackRock Becomes a Symbol for Anticapitalist Fervor in France. *New York Times*, www.nytimes.com/2020/02/14/business/france-blackrock-protests.html (accessed 15 May 2020).

Alderson, A. S. & Nielsen, F. (2002). Globalization and the Great U-Turn: Income Inequality Trends in 16 OECD Countries. *American Journal of Sociology*, 107 (5), 1244–99.

Aldrich, J. H. (2011). *Why Parties? A Second Look*, Chicago: University of Chicago Press.

Aldrich, J. H. & Rohde, D. W. (2000). The Republican Revolution and the House Appropriations Committee. *Journal of Politics*, 62(1), 1–33.

Alesina, A. & Glaeser, E. (2004). *Fighting Poverty in the U.S. and Europe: A World of Difference*, New York: Oxford University Press.

Allen, A. (2020). For Billion-Dollar Covid Vaccines, Basic Government-Funded Science Laid the Groundwork. *Scientific American*, November 18, 2020, www.scientificamerican.com/article/for-billion-dollar-covid-vaccines-basic-government-funded-science-laid-the-groundwork/.

Anderson, E. (2019). *Private Government: How Employers Rule Our Lives (and Why We Don't Talk about It)*, Princeton, NJ: Princeton University Press.

Anderson, J., Bergamini, E., Brekelmans, S., et al. (2020). The Fiscal Response to the Economic Fallout from the Coronavirus, Bruegel Datasets. www.bruegel.org/publications/datasets/covid-national-dataset/.

Anderson, J., Brees, A. & Reninger, E. (2008). A Study of American Zoning Board Composition and Public Attitudes toward Zoning Issues. *The Urban Lawyer*, 40(4), 689–745.

Andrasfay, T. & Goldman, N. (2021). Reductions in 2020 US life expectancy due to COVID-19 and the disproportionate impact on the Black and Latino populations. Proceedings of the National Academy of Sciences Feb 2021, 118 (5) e2014746118, http://doi.org/10.1073/pnas.2014746118.

Andrews, D., Criscuolo, C. & Gal, P. (2016). *The Global Productivity Slowdown, Technology Divergence and Public Policy: A Firm Level Perspective*, Global Forum on Productivity.

Andrias, K. (2016). The New Labor Law. *Yale Law Journal*, 126(1).

Andrias, K. & Rogers, B. (2018). *Rebuilding Worker Voice in Today's Economy*, The Roosevelt Institute.

Ang, Y. Y. (2016). *How China Escaped The Poverty Trap*, Ithaca, NY: Cornell University Press.

Ang, Y. Y. (2020). *China's Gilded Age: The Paradox of Economic Boom and Vast Corruption*, Cambridge, UK: Cambridge University Press.

Ansell, B. (2012). Assets in Crisis: Housing, Preferences and Policy in the Credit Crisis. *Swiss Political Science Review*, 18(4), 531–37.

Ansell, B. (2014). The Political Economy of Ownership: Housing Markets and the Welfare State. *American Political Science Review*, 108(2), 383–402.

Ansell, B. W. (2008). University Challenges: Explaining Institutional Change in Higher Education. *World Politics*, 60(2), 189–230.

Ansell, B. W. & Gingrich, J. (2013). A Tale of Two Trilemmas: Varieties of Higher Education and the Service Economy. In Wren, A., ed., *The Political Economy of the Service Transition*, Oxford: Oxford University Press, pp. 195–224.

Ansolabehere, S. & Schaffner, B. F. (2008). *CCES Common Content*, Harvard Dataverse.

Ansolabehere, S., de Figueiredo, J. M. & Snyder, J. M. (2003). Why Is There So Little Money in U.S. Politics? *Journal of Economic Perspectives*, 17(1), 105–30.

Anzia, S. (forthcoming). *Local Interests: Interest Groups and Public Policy in U.S. City Government*. University of Chicago Press, Unpublished manuscript.

Anzia, S. F. (2019). Looking for Influence in All the Wrong Places: How Studying Subnational Policy Can Revive Research on Interest Groups. *The Journal of Politics*, 81(1), 343–51.

Anzia, S. F. & Moe, T. M. (2016). Do Politicians Use Policy to Make Politics? The Case of Public-Sector Labor Laws. *American Political Science Review*, 110(4), 763–77.

Arjaliès, D.-L., Grant, P., Hardie, I., MacKenzie, D. & Svetlova, E. (2017). *Chains of Finance: How Investment Management Is Shaped*, Oxford: Oxford University Press.

Arnold, D. (2020). Mergers and Acquisitions, Local Labor Market Concentration and Worker Outcomes, Princeton University, Working Paper.

Arnold, R. D. (1990). *The Logic of Congressional Action*, New Haven, CT: Yale University Press.

Arora, A., Belenzon, S. & Patacconi, A. (2015). Killing the Golden Goose? The Decline of Science in Corporate R&D. *NBER* Working Paper 20902.

Arora, A., Belenzon, S. & Patacconi, A. (2018). The Decline of Science in Corporate R&D. *Strategic Management Journal*, 39(1), 3–32.

Arria, M. (2018). Arizona Rank-and-File Teachers Plan Day of Action in "Ground Zero" for Koch Brothers' Agenda, *Shadowproof*.

Ash, E., Chen, D. L. & Naidu, S. (2020). Ideas Have Consequences: The Impact of Law and Economics on American Justice. Columbia University Working Paper.

Ashby, S. (2017). Assessing the Fight for Fifteen Movement from Chicago. *Labor Studies Journal*, 42(4), 366–86.

Atkinson, R. D. (2020). *Understanding the US System of Innovation*, Information Technology & Innovation Foundation.

Austin, B., Glaeser, E. & Summers, L. H. (2018). Saving the Heartland: Place-Based Policies in 21st Century America, Brookings Papers on Economic Activity Conference Drafts.

Autor, D. (2019). Work of the Past, Work of the Future. *NBER* Working Paper 25588.

Autor, D. & Reynolds, E. (2020). *The Nature of Work after the COVID Crisis: Too Few Low-Wage Jobs*, Washington, DC: Brookings Institution/The Hamilton Project.

Autor, D., Dorn, D., Katz, L. F., Patterson, C. & Van Reenen, J. (2017). Concentrating on the Fall of the Labor Share. *American Economic Review* 107 (5), 180–85.

Autor, D. H., Dorn, D. & Hanson, G. H. (2013). The China Syndrome: Local Labor Market Effects of Import Competition in the United States. *American Economic Review*, 103(6), 2121–68.

Autor, D. H., Levy, F. & Murnane, R. J. (2003). The Skill Content of Recent Technological Change: An Empirical Exploration. *The Quarterly Journal of Economics*, 118(4), 1279–1333.

Awrey, D. (2012). Complexity, Innovation, and the Regulation of Modern Financial Markets. *Harvard Business Law Review*, 2(2), 235–294.

Azar, J. (2020). The Common Ownership Trilemma. *The University of Chicago Law Review*, 87(2), 263–96.

Azar, J., Marinescu, I. & Steinbaum, M. I. (2017). Labor Market Concentration. Working Paper No. w24147. Chicago: National Bureau of Economic Research.

Azar, J., Marinescu, I. & Steinbaum, M. I. (2020). Labor Market Concentration. *Journal of Human Resources*.

Azar, J., Schmalz, M. C. & Tecu, I. (2018). Anticompetitive Effects of Common Ownership. *The Journal of Finance*, 73(4), 1513–65.

Babic, M., Garcia-Bernardo, J. & Heemskerk, E. M. (2020). The Rise of Transnational State Capital: State-Led Foreign Investment in the 21st Century. *Review of International Political Economy*, 27(3), 433–75.

Baccaro, L. & Pontusson, J. (2016). Rethinking Comparative Political Economy: The Growth Model Perspective. *Politics & Society*, 44(2), 175–207.

Backus, M., Conlon, C. & Sinkinson, M. (2019). Common Ownership in America: 1980–2017. *NBER* Working Paper 25454.

Backus, M., Conlon, C. & Sinkinson, M. (2020). Common Ownership in America: 1980–2017. *American Economic Journal: Microeconomics*. Advance Online Publication.

Balkin, J. (2012). From Off the Wall to On the Wall: How the Mandate Challenge Went Mainstream. *The Atlantic*, www.theatlantic.com/national/archive/2012/06/from-off-the-wall-to-on-the-wall-how-the-mandate-challenge-went-mainstream/258040/ (accessed 11 December 2020).

Baradaran, M. (2019). *The Color of Money: Black Banks and the Racial Wealth Gap*, Cambridge, MA: Harvard University Press.

Baran, P. A. & Sweezy, P. M. (1966). *Monopoly Capital*, New York: New York University Press.

Barber, B. (2013). *If Mayors Ruled the World: Dysfunctional Nations, Rising Cities*, New Haven, CT: Yale University Press.

Barnes, J. & Burke, T. F. (2015). *How Policy Shapes Politics: Rights, Courts, Litigation and the Battle Over Injury Compensation*, New York: Oxford University Press.

Barnes, R. & Mufson, S. (2018). White House Counts on Kavanaugh in Battle against "Administrative State". *Washington Post*, www.washingtonpost.com/politics/courts_law/brett-kavanaugh-and-the-end-of-the-regulatory-state-as-we-know-it/2018/08/12/22649a04-9bdc-11e8-8d5e-c6c594024954_story.html (accessed 11 December 2020).

Barr, N. (2001). *The Welfare State as Piggy Bank: Information, Risk, Uncertainty, and the Role of the State*, Oxford: Oxford University Press.

Bartels, L. M. (2005). Homer Gets a Tax Cut: Inequality and Public Policy in the American Mind. *Perspectives on Politics*, 3(1), 15–31.

Bartels, L. M. (2008). *Unequal Democracy: The Political Economy of a New Gilded Age*, Princeton, NJ: Princeton University Press.

Bartels, L. M. (2016). Elections in America. *ANNALS of the American Academy of Political and Social Science*, 667(1), 36–49.

Barth, E., Bryson, A., Davis, J. & Freeman, R. (2014). It's Where You Work: Increases in Earnings Dispersion across Establishments and Individuals in the US. *NBER* Working Paper 20447.

Bartik, A. W. (2018). Moving Costs and Worker Adjustment to Changes in Labor Demand: Evidence from Longitudinal Census Data. Manuscript, University of Illinois at Urbana-Champaign.

Bassier, I., Arindrajit D. & Naidu, S. (2019). Monopsony in Movers: The Elasticity of Labor Supply to Firm Wage Policies. *NBER* Working Paper 27755. www.nber.org/system/files/Working_Papers/w27755/w27755.pdf.

Bastian, J. & Michelmore, K. (2018). The Long-Term Impact of the Earned Income Tax Credit on Children's Education and Employment Outcomes. *Journal of Labor Economics*, 36(4), 1127–1163.

Bateman, D. A., Katznelson, I. & Lapinski, J. S. (2018). *Southern Nation: Congress and White Supremacy after Reconstruction*, Princeton, NJ: Princeton University Press.

Batstrand, S. (2015). More than Markets: A Comparative Study of Nine Conservative Parties on Climate Change. *Politics and Policy*, 43(4), 538–61.

Bawn, K., Cohen, M., Karol, D., Masket, S., Noel, H. & Zaller, J. (2012). A Theory of Political Parties: Groups, Policy Demands and Nominations in American Politics. *Perspectives on Politics*, 10(3), 571–97.

Baxter, L. (2011). Capture in Financial Regulation: Can We Channel It toward the Common Good? *Cornell Journal of Law and Public Policy*, 21(1), 175–200.

Bayer, P., Ferreira, F. & McMillan, R. (2007). A Unified Framework for Measuring Preferences for Schools and Neighborhoods. *Journal of Political Economy*, 115(4), 588–638.

Bebchuk, L. A. & Hirst, S. (2019). Index Funds and the Future of Corporate Governance: Theory, Evidence, and Policy. *Columbia Law Review*, 119(8), 2029–145.

Bebchuk, L. A., Cohen, A. & Hirst, S. (2017). The Agency Problems of Institutional Investors. *Journal of Economic Perspectives*, 31(3), 89–102.

Been, V. (2018). City NIMBYS. *Journal of Land Use*, 33(3), 217–50.

Beland, D. (2007). Ideas and Institutional Change in Social Security: Conversion, Layering, and Policy Drift. *Social Science Quarterly*, 88(1), 20–38.

Bell, S. (2012). The Power of Ideas: The Ideational Shaping of the Structural Power of Business. *International Studies Quarterly*, 56(4), 661–73.

Benmelech, E., Bergman, N. & Kim, H. (2018). Strong Employers and Weak Employees: How Does Employer Concentration Affect Wages? US Census Working Paper, number CES-18-15.

Bennett, J. (2018). *Why State Attorneys General Races Are the Next Frontier for Out-of-State Influence*, Center for Public Integrity.

Bensel, R. F. (1984). *Sectionalism and American Political Development, 1880–1980*, Madison: University of Wisconsin Press.

Bensel, R. F. (2000). *The Political Economy of American Industrialization, 1877–1900*, New York: Cambridge University Press.

Beramendi, P. (2012). *The Political Geography of Inequality: Regions and Redistribution*, New York: Cambridge University Press.

Beramendi, P. & Rueda, D. (2007). Social Democracy Constrained: Indirect Taxation in Industrialized Democracies. *British Journal of Political Science*, 37(4), 619–41.

Berger, D., Herkenhoff, K. & Mongey, S. (2019). Labor Market Power. *NBER* Working Paper 25719.

Berkowitz, D. (2020). *Workplace Safety & Health Enforcement Falls to Lowest Levels in Decades*, New York: National Employment Law Project.

Berle, A. A. & Means, G. C. (1932). *The Modern Corporation and Private Property*, New York: Macmillan.

Berlin, I. (2002). Two Concepts of Liberty. In Hardy, H., ed., *Liberty: Incorporating Four Essays on Liberty*. Oxford: Oxford University Press, pp. 166–217.

Berman, E., Bound, J. & Machin, S. (1998). Implications of Skill Biased Technological Change: International Evidence. *Quarterly Journal of Economics*, 113(4), 1245–79.

Bernauer, T. (2013). Climate Change Politics. *Annual Review of Political Science*, 16, 421–48.

Bernstein, J. (2008). *Physicists on Wall Street and Other Essays on Science and Society*, New York: Springer Science & Business Media.

Berry, J. M., Portney, K. E. & Thomson, K. (1993). *The Rebirth of Urban Democracy*, Washington, DC: Brookings Institution Press.

Besley, T. & Coate, S. (2003). Centralized versus Decentralized Provision of Local Public Goods: A Political Economy Approach. *Journal of Public Economics*, 87 (12), 2611–37.

Bessembinder, H. (2018). Do Stocks Outperform Treasury Bills? *Journal of Financial Economics*, 129(3), 440–57.

Bessen, J. (2016). Accounting for Rising Corporate Profits: Intangibles or Regulatory Rents? Boston University School of Law, Law and Economics Research Paper, 16–18.

Bidgood, J. (2018). West Virginia Teachers' Strike Ends with a Promise to Raise Pay. *The New York Times*, www.nytimes.com/2018/02/27/us/west-virginia-teachers-strike-ends.html (accessed 11 December 2020).

Biggs, M. (2005). Strikes as Forest Fires: Chicago and Paris in the Late Nineteenth Century. *American Journal of Sociology*, 110(6), 1684–714.

Binder, S. A. (2003). *Stalemate: Causes and Consequences of Legislative Gridlock.* Washington, DC: The Bookings Institution Press.

Birchfield, V. & Crepaz, M. (1998). The Impact of Constitutional Structures and Collective and Competitive Veto Points on Income Inequality in Industrialized Democracies. *European Journal of Political Research*, 34(2), 175–200.

Bivens, J., Mishel, L. & Schmitt, J. (2018). *It's Not Just Monopoly and Monopsony: How Market Power Has Affected American Wages*, Washington, DC: Economic Policy Institute.

BLS (2017). *Table 32: Leave Benefits: Access, Civilian Workers, March 2017*, Bureau of Labor Statistics.

BlackRock. (2019). *Loi Pacte: Le bon plan Retraite.* www.blackrock.com/corporate/literature/whitePaper/viewpoint-loi-pacte-le-bon-plan-retraite-juin-2019.pdf.

Block, F. (1977). The Ruling Class Does Not Rule. *Socialist Revolution*, 33, 6–28.

Block, F. (2010). *Revising State Theory: Essays in Politics and Postindustrialism*, Philadelphia, PA: Temple University Press.

Board of Governors of the Federal Reserve System (2019). *Report on the Economic Well-Being of U.S. Households in 2018.*

Bobo, L. (2001). Racial attitudes and relations at the close of the twentieth century. In Smelser, N. J., Wilson, W. J. & Mitchell, F., eds., *America Becoming: Racial Trends and Their Consequences*, Vol. 1. Washington, DC: National Academy Press, pp. 264–301.

Bobo, L. & Zubrinsky, C. L. (1996). Attitudes on Residential Integration: Perceived Status Differences, Mere In-Group Preference, or Racial Prejudice. *Social Forces*, 74(3), 883–909.

Bobo, L., Kluegel, J. R. & Smith, R. A. (1997). Laissez-Faire Racism: The Crystallization of a Kinder, Gentler, Antiblack Ideology. In Tuch, S. A. and Martin, J. K., eds., *Racial Attitudes in the 1990s: Continuity and Change*, Boston: Greenwood Publishing Group, pp. 15–42.

Bogle, J. C. (2012). *The Clash of the Cultures: Investment vs. Speculation*, Hoboken, NJ: John Wiley & Sons.

Boix, C. (1998). *Political Parties, Growth and Equality: Conservative and Social Democratic Economic Strategies in the World Economy*, Cambridge, UK: Cambridge University Press.

Boix, C. (2019). *Democratic Capitalism at the Crossroads: Technological Change and the Future of Politics*, Princeton, NJ: Princeton University Press.

Bolton, A. (2020). McConnell proposes keeping liability protection and state, local funding out of coronavirus relief bill. *The Hill*, https://thehill.com/homenews/senate/529295-mcconnell-proposes-keeping-liability-protection-and-state-local-funding-out (accessed 10 January 2021).

Bonica, A. & Sen, M. (2017). The Politics of Selecting the Bench from the Bar: The Legal Profession and Partisan Incentives to Introduce Ideology into Judicial Selection. *Journal of Law and Economics*, 60(4), 559–95.

Bonica, A. & Sen, M. (2021). *The Judicial Tug of War: How Lawyers, Politicians, and Ideological Incentives Shape the American Judiciary*, New York: Cambridge University Press.

Bonnet, O., Bono, P.-H., Chapelle, G. C. & Wasmer, E. (2014). *Capital Is Not Back: A Comment on Thomas Piketty's* Capital in the 21st Century, London: VOX CEPR's Policy Portal.

Booysen, S. (2016). *Fees Must Fall: Student Revolt, Decolonisation and Governance in South Africa*, Johannesburg: Wits University Press.

Borgschulte, M. & Vogler, J. (2020). Did the ACA Medicaid Expansion Save Lives? *Journal of Health Economics*, 72, 102333.

Borick, C. P., Rabe, B. G. & Mills, S. (2015). Acceptance of Global Warming among Americans Moderately Increases in Late 2014. *Issues in Energy and Environmental Policy*, 19.

Borodovsky, L. (2019). U.S. Fixed Assets Continue to Get Older. *Wall Street Journal*, www.wsj.com/articles/the-daily-shot-the-nations-fixed-assets-continue-to-get-older-01576489627 (accessed 8 January 2021).

Bottari, M. & Fischer, B. (2013). Efforts to Deliver "Kill Shot" to Paid Sick Leave Tied to ALEC. *PR Watch*, www.prwatch.org/news/2013/04/12037/efforts-deliver-kill-shot-paid-sick-leave-tied-alec (accessed 13 December 2020).

Bound, J. & Johnson, G. (1992). Changes in the Structure of Wages in the 1980s: An Evaluation of Alternative Explanations. *American Economic Review*, 82(3), 371–92.

Boustan, L. P. (2010). Was Postwar Suburbanization "White Flight"? Evidence from the Black Migration. *The Quarterly Journal of Economics*, 125(1), 417–43.

Bowles, S. & Gintis, H. (1993). The Revenge of Homo Economicus: Contested Exchange and the Revival of Political Economy. *Journal of Economic Perspectives*, 7(1), 83–102.

Bowles, S. & Gintis, H., (2011). *Schooling in Capitalist America: Educational Reform and the Contradictions of Economic Life*, Chicago: Haymarket Books.

Boyer, R. (2000). Is a Finance-Led Growth Regime a Viable Alternative to Fordism? A Preliminary Analysis. *Economy and Society*, 29(1), 111–45.

Boyer, R. (2005). From Shareholder Value to CEO Power: The Paradox of the 1990s. *Competition & Change*, 9(1), 7–47.

Brady, D. & Volden, C. (2005). *Revolving Gridlock: Policy and Politics from Jimmy Carter to George W. Bush*, New York: Routledge, Taylor & Francis.

Brady, D., Huber, E. & Stephens, J. D. (2020). *Comparative Welfare States Data Set*, University of North Carolina and WZB Berlin Social Science Center.

Braun, B (2016). From Performativity to Political Economy: Index Investing, ETFs and Asset Manager Capitalism. *New Political Economy*, 21(3), 257–73.

Braun, B. (2020). Central Banking and the Infrastructural Power of Finance: The Case of ECB Support for Repo and Securitization Markets. *Socio-Economic Review*, 18(2), 395–418.

Breznitz, D. & Murphree, M. (2011). *Run of the Red Queen: Government, Innovation, Globalization, and Economic Growth in China*, New Haven, CT: Yale University Press.

Bridges, A. (1997). *Morning Glories: Municipal Reform in the Southwest*, Princeton, NJ: Princeton University Press.

Briere, M., Pouget, S. & Ureche, L. (2019). Do Universal Owners Vote to Curb Negative Corporate Externalities? An Empirical Analysis of Shareholder Meetings, https://ssrn.com/abstract=3403465.

Briffault, R. (1990). Our Localism: Part II–Localism and Legal Theory. *Columbia Law Review*, 90(1), 1–115.

Brody, B. (2020). U.S. Chamber Lobbies against Rules, Liability as States Reopen. *Bloomberg*, www.bloomberg.com/news/articles/2020-04-28/u-s-chamber-pushes-back-on-new-business-rules-in-reopening (accessed 10 January 2021).

Browning, R., Marshall, D. R. & Tabb, D. (1984). *Protest Is Not Enough: The Struggle for Blacks and Hispanics for Equality in Urban Politics*, Berkeley: The University of California Press.

Brownstein, R. (2020). Democrats' Real Liability in the House. *The Atlantic*, www.theatlantic.com/politics/archive/2020/11/bidens-popular-vote-win-didnt-help-house-democrats/617211/ (accessed 5 January 2020).

Brueckner, J. K. (1998). Testing for Strategic Interaction among Local Governments: The Case of Growth Controls. *Journal of Urban Economics*, 44(3), 438–67.

Brundage, Jr., V. (2017). *BLS Spotlight on Statistics: Profile of the Labor Force by Educational Attainment*. Washington, DC: US Department of Labor, Bureau of Labor Statistics.

Bucci, L. C. (2018). Organized Labor's Check on Rising Economic Inequality in the US States. *State Politics & Policy Quarterly*, 18(2), 148–73.

Budryk, Z. (2020). Fauci: Differing State Responses a "Major Weakness" in Fighting Coronavirus. *The Hill*, https://thehill.com/policy/healthcare/531787-fauci-states-differing-responses-a-major-weakness-in-fighting-coronavirus (accessed 10 January 2021).

Buenker, J. D. (1973). *Urban Liberalism and Progressive Reform*, New York: Norton.

Burawoy, M. (1982). *Manufacturing Consent: Changes in the Labor Process under Monopoly Capitalism*. Chicago: University of Chicago Press.

Burbank, S. & Farhang, S. (2017). *Rights and Retrenchment: The Counterrevolution against Federal Litigation*, New York: Cambridge University Press.

Burns, J. (2014). *Strike Back: Using the Militant Tactics of Labor's Past to Reignite Public Sector Unionism Today*, New York: Ig Publishing.

Burns, N. (1994). *The Formation of American Local Governments: Private Values in Public Institutions*, New York: Oxford University.

Busemeyer, M. R. (2007). Determinants of Public Education Spending in 21 Oecd Democracies, 1980–2001. *Journal of European Public Policy*, 14(4), 582–610.

Busemeyer, M. R. (2014). *Skills and Inequality: Partisan Politics and the Political Economy of Education Reforms in Western Welfare States*, Cambridge, UK: Cambridge University Press.

Busemeyer, M. & Thelen, K. (2020). Institutional Source of Business Power. *World Politics*, 74(3), 448–80.

Bush, V. (1945). *Science, the Endless Frontier. A Report to the President*, United States Government Printing Office.

Cairns, K. (2016). *The Case of Rose Bird: Gender, Politics, and the California Courts*, Lincoln: University of Nebraska Press.

Caldwell, S. & Oehlsen, E. (2018). Monopsony and the Gender Wage Gap: Experimental Evidence from the Gig Economy. Working Paper. https://sydneec.github.io/Website/Caldwell_Oehlsen.pdf.

Callaci, B. (2018). *Control without Responsibility: The Legal Creation of Franchising 1960–1980*, Washington Center for Equitable Growth.

Cameron, C. M., Gray, C., Kastellac, J. P. & Park, J.-K. (2018). From Textbook Pluralism to Modern Hyper-Pluralism: Interest Groups and Supreme Court Nominations 1930–2017. *Journal of Law and Courts*, 8(2), 301–32.

Campbell, J. E. (2011). The Economic Records of the Presidents: Party Differences and Inherited Economic Conditions. *Forum: A Journal of Applied Research in Contemporary Politics*, 9(1), Article 7.

Caraley, D. (1992). Washington Abandons the Cities. *Political Science Quarterly*, 107(1), 1–30.

Card, D., Cardoso, A. R., Heining, J. & Kline, P. (2018). Firm and Labor Market Inequality: Evidence and Some Theory. *Journal of Labor Economics*, 36(S1), S13–S70.

Card, D., Heining, J. &, Kline, P. (2013). Workplace Heterogeneity and the Rise of West German Wage Inequality. *The Quarterly Journal of Economics*, 128(3), 967–1015.

Card, D., Mas, A. & Rothstein, J. (2008). Tipping and Dynamics of Segregation. *The Quarterly Journal of Economics*, 123(1), 177–218.

Carnes, N. (2013). *White-Collar Government: The Hidden Role of Class in Economic Policy Making*, Chicago: University of Chicago Press.

Carnevale, A. P., Smith, N. & Strohl, J. (2013). *Recovery: Job Growth and Education Requirements Through 2020*, Washington, DC: Georgetown University Center on Education and the Workforce.

Carpenter, D. (2001). *The Forging of Bureaucratic Autonomy: Reputations, Networks, and Policy Innovation in Executive Agencies, 1862–1928*, Princeton, NJ: Princeton University Press.

Carpenter, D. (2010). *Reputation and Power: Organizational Image and Pharmaceutical Regulation at the FDA*. Princeton, NJ: Princeton University Press.

Carpenter, D. & Moss, D. (2013). *Preventing Regulatory Capture: Special Interest Influence and How to Limit It*, New York: Cambridge University Press.

Carpentier, V. (2018). Expansion and differentiation in higher education: the historical trajectories of the UK, the USA and France. Centre for Global Higher Education Working Paper Series No. 33.

Carré, F. (2015). *(In)dependent Contractor Misclassification*, Washington, DC: Economic Policy Institute.

Carter, T. (2002). Boosting the Bench. *ABA Journal*, 29–33.

Case, A. & Deaton, A. (2019). *Deaths of Despair and the Future of Capitalism*, Princeton, NJ: Princeton University Press.

Caughey, D., Xu, Y. & Warshaw, C. (2017). Incremental Democracy: The Policy Effects of Partisan Control of State Government. *The Journal of Politics*, 79(4), 1342–58.

CB Insights (2020). *The Complete List of Unicorn Companies*. New York: CB Insights.

CBPP (2020). *Tracking the COVID-19 Recession's Effects on Food, Housing, and Employment Hardships*, Center on Budget and Policy Priorities: COVID Hardship Watch.

Cellini, S. R. & Turner, N. (2019). Gainfully Employed? Assessing the Employment and Earnings of For-Profit College Students Using Administrative Data. *Journal of Human Resources*, 54(2), 342–70.

Cengiz, D., Dube, A., Lindner, A. & Zipperer, B. (2019). The Effect of Minimum Wages on Low-Wage Jobs. *The Quarterly Journal of Economics*, 134(3), 1405–54.

CFPB (2015). *CFPB Study Finds that Arbitration Agreements Limit Relief for Consumers*, Washington, DC: Consumer Financial Protection Bureau.

Chandler, A. D. (1965). *The Railroads: The Nation's First Big Business; Sources and Readings*, San Diego, CA: Harcourt, Brace & World.

Chandler, A. D. (1977). *The Visible Hand: The Managerial Revolution in American Business*, Cambridge, MA: Harvard University Press.

Chandler, A. (1990). *Strategy and Structure: Chapters in the History of the Industrial Enterprise*, Cambridge, MA: MIT Press.

Chang, S., Pierson, E., Koh, P. W., Geradin, J., Redbird, B., Grusky, D. & Leskovec, J. (2020). Mobility Network Models of COVID-19 Explain Inequities and Inform Opening. *Nature*, 589, 82–87.

Charles, C. Z. (2003). "The Dynamics of Racial Residential Segregation." *Annual Review of Sociology*, 29(1), 167–207. http://doi.org10.1146/annurev.soc.29.010202.100002. www.annualreviews.org/doi/abs/10.1146/annurev.soc.29.010202.100002.

Charron-Chénier, R. (2020). Predatory Inclusion in Consumer Credit: Explaining Black and White Disparities in Payday Loan Use. *Sociological Forum*, 35(2), 370–92.

Chen, P., Karabarbounis, L. & Neiman, B. (2017). The Global Rise of Corporate Saving. *Journal of Monetary Economics*, *89*, 1–19.

Chetty, R., Friedman, J. N., Hendren, N., Stepner, M. & the Opportunity Insights Team (2020). The Economic Impacts of COVID-19: Evidence from a New Public Database Built Using Private Sector Data. *NBER* Working Paper 27341.

Chikane, R. (2018). *Breaking a Rainbow, Building a Nation: The Politics Behind #MustFall Movements*, Johannesburg: Picador Africa.

Cho, D. (2019). Essays on the Determination of Employment and Wages. Doctoral dissertation, Princeton University, Economics Department.

Christensen, C. M. (2013). *The Innovator's Dilemma: When New Technologies Cause Great Firms to Fail*, Brighton, MA: Harvard Business Review Press.

Christophers, B. (2016). *The Great Leveler: Capitalism and Competition in the Court of Law*, Cambridge, MA: Harvard University Press.

Christophers, B. (2019). Environmental Beta or How Institutional Investors Think about Climate Change and Fossil Fuel Risk. *Annals of the American Association of Geographers*, 109(3), 754–74.

Christophers, B. (2020). *Rentier Capitalism: Who Owns the Economy, and Who Pays for It?* London: Verso.

Chwieroth, J. M. & Walter, A. (2019). *The Wealth Effect: How the Great Expectations of the Middle Class Have Changed the Politics of Banking Crises*, Cambridge, UK: Cambridge University Press.

Ciepley, D. (2013). Beyond Public and Private: Toward a Political Theory of the Corporation. *American Political Science Review*, 107(01), 139–58.

Clark, G. (2000). *Pension Fund Capitalism*, Oxford: Oxford University Press.

Clark, G. L. & Monk, A. H. B. (2017). *Institutional Investors in Global Markets*, Oxford, UK: Oxford University Press.

Clemens, E. (2006). Lineages of the Rube Goldberg State: Building and Blurring Public Programs, 1900–1940. In Shapiro, I., Skowronek, S. & Galvin, D., eds., *The Art of the State: Rethinking Political Institutions*. New York: New York University Press, pp. 380–443.

Clemens, J. & Strain, M. R. (2020). Public Policy and Participation in Political Interest Groups: An Analysis of Minimum Wages, Labor Unions, and Effective Advocacy. *NBER* Working Paper 27902.

Clinton, J. D. (2012). Congress, Lawmaking, and the Fair Labor Standards Act, 1971–2000. *American Journal of Political Science*, 56(2), 355–72.

Clowes, M. J. (2000). *The Money Flood: How Pension Funds Revolutionized Investing*, Hoboken, NJ: Wiley.

Coates, J. C. (2009). Reforming the Taxation and Regulation of Mutual Funds: A Comparative Legal and Economic Analysis. *Journal of Legal Analysis*, 1(2), 591–689.

Coffee, J. C. Jr. (1991). Liquidity versus Control: The Institutional Investor as Corporate Monitor. *Columbia Law Review*, 91(6), 1277–368.

Cohen, A. (2021). *Supreme Inequality: The Supreme Court's Fifty-Year Battle for a More Unjust America*, London: Penguin Random House.

Cohn, J. (2020). How COVID-19 Overwhelmed the American State. *The Huffington Post*, www.huffpost.com/entry/us-unemployment-health-care-coronavirus-europe_n_5ebef6f1c5b678dd13cc04bb (accessed 10 January 2021).

Colvin, A. J. S. (2018). *The Growing Use of Mandatory Arbitration: Access to the Courts Is Now Barred for More Than 60 Million American Workers*, Washington, DC: Economic Policy Institute.

Colvin, A. J. S. & Shierholz, H. (2019). *Noncompete Agreements: Ubiquitous, Harmful to Wages and to Competition, and Part of a Growing Trend of Employers Requiring Workers to Sign Away Their Rights*, Washington, DC: Economic Policy Institute.

Condon, M. (2020). Externalities and the Common Owner. *Washington Law Review*, 95, 1–81.

Conley, D. (2010). *Being Black, Living in the Red: Race, Wealth, and Social Policy in America*, Berkeley: University of California Press.

Connolly, N. D. B. (2014). *A World More Concrete: Real Estate and the Remaking of Jim Crow South Florida*, Chicago: University of Chicago Press.

Converse, P. (1964). The Nature of Belief Systems in Mass Publics. *Critical Review*, 18(1–3), 1–74.

Corkery, M. (2017). Betty Dukes, Greeter Whose Walmart Lawsuit Went to Supreme Court, Dies at 67. *New York Times*, nytimes.com/2017/07/18/business/betty-dukes-dead-walmart-worker-led-landmark-class-action-sex-bias-case.html (accessed 17 December 2020).

Cornell, H. W. (1958). Collective Bargaining by Public Employee Groups. *University of Pennsylvania Law Review*, 107, 43–64.

Corrado, C., Haskel, J., Jona-Lasinio, C. & Iommi, M. (2016). Intangible Investment in the EU and US Before and Since the Great Recession and Its Contribution to Productivity Growth. *EIB* Working Paper.

Costa, D. L. & Kahn, M. E. (2000). Power Couples: Changes in the Locational Choice of the College Educated, 1940–1990. *The Quarterly Journal of Economics*, 115(4), 1287–315.

Cottom, T. M. (2017). *Lower Ed: The Troubling Rise of For-Profit Colleges in the New Economy*, New York: The New Press.

Cover, J., Spring, A. F. & Kleit, R, G. (2011). Minorities on the Margins? The Spatial Organization of Fringe Banking Services. *Journal of Urban Affairs*, 33(3), 317–44.

Covert, B. (2020). Banks Stand to Make $18 Billion in PPP Processing Fees from Cares Act. *The Intercept*, https://theintercept.com/2020/07/14/banks-cares-act-ppp/ (accessed 10 January 2021).

Coviello, D., Deserranno, E. & Persico, N. (2018). Minimum Wage and Individual Worker Productivity: Evidence from a Large US Retailer. *Northwestern University*, Working Paper.

Cowley, S., Flitter, E. & Enrich, D. (2020). Some Small Businesses That Got Aid Fear the Rules Too Much to Spend It. *New York Times*, www.nytimes.com/2020/05/02/business/economy/loans-coronavirus-small-business.html (accessed 10 January 2021).

Cox, G. W. (1987). *The Efficient Secret: The Cabinet and the Development of Parties in Victorian England*, New York: Cambridge University Press.

Cox, G. W. & Magar, E., (1999). How Much is Majority Status in the US Congress Worth? *American Political Science Review*, 93(2), 299–309.

Cox, G. W. & McCubbins, M. D. (2005). *Setting the Agenda: Responsible Party Government in the U.S. House of Representatives*, New York: Cambridge University Press.

Cramer, K. J. (2014). Political Understanding of Economic Crises: The Shape of Resentment toward Public Employees. In L. Bartels and N. Bermeo, eds., *Mass Politics in Tough Times: Opinions, Votes and Protest in the Great Recession*, New York: Oxford University Press, pp. 72–104.

Cramer, K. J. (2016). *The Politics of Resentment*, Chicago: University of Chicago Press.

Cremers, K. J. M. & Sepe, S. M. (2018). Institutional Investors, Corporate Governance, and Firm Value. *Seattle University Law Review*, 41(2), 387–418.

Crepaz, M. & Moser, A. W. (2004). The Impact of Collective and Competitive Veto Points on Public Expenditures in the Global Age, *Comparative Political Studies*, 37(3), 259–85.

Crouch, C. (2009). Privatised Keynesianism: An Unacknowledged Policy Regime. *British Journal of Politics & International Relations*, 11(3), 382–99.

Culpepper, P. D. (2005). Institutional Change in Contemporary Capitalism: Coordinated Financial Systems since 1990. *World Politics*, 57(2), 173–99.

Culpepper, P. D. (2010). *Quiet Politics and Business Power: Corporate Control in Europe and Japan*, New York: Cambridge University Press.

Culpepper, P. D. (2015). Structural Power and Political Science in the Post-Crisis Era. *Business and Politics*, 17, 391–409.

Culpepper, P. D. & Reinke, R. (2014). Structural Power and Bank Bailouts in the United Kingdom and the United States. *Politics and Society*, 42(4), 427–54.

Curry, J. M. & Lee, F. E. (2019). Non-Party Government: Bipartisan Lawmaking and Party Power in Congress. *Perspectives on Politics*, 17(1), 47–65.

Cutler, D. M., Glaeser, E. L. & Vigdor, J. L. (1999). The Rise and Decline of the American Ghetto. *Journal of Political Economy*, 107(3), 455–506.

Dadayan, L. & Boyd, D. (2016). *Double, Double, Oil and Trouble*, Albany, NY: Rockefeller Institute of Government.

Dahl, R. A. (1957). The Concept of Power. *Behavioral Science*, 2(3), 201–15.

Dahl, R. A. (1961). *Who Governs? Democracy and Power in an American City*, New Haven, CT: Yale University Press.

Dalton, M., Handwerker, E. W. & Loewenstein, M. A. (2020). *Employment Changes by Employer Size during the COVID-19 Pandemic: A Look at the Current Employment Statistics Survey Microdata*, Washington, DC: Bureau of Labor Statistics Monthly Labor Review.

Danielson, M. (1976). *The Politics of Exclusion*, New York: Columbia University Press.

Danziger, S. & Gottschalk, P. (1995). *America Unequal*, New York: Russell Sage Foundation.

Dar, L. & Lee, D.-W. (2014). Partisanship, Political Polarization, and State Higher Education Budget Outcomes. *Journal of Higher Education*, 85(4), 469–98.

Darity, W. A. & Mullen, A. K. (2020). *From Here to Equality: Reparations for Black Americans in the Twenty-First Century*, Chapel Hill: University of North Carolina Press.

Darity, W. A., Hamilton, D. & Stewart, J. B. (2015). A Tour de Force in Understanding Intergroup Inequality: An Introduction to Stratification Economics. *Review of Black Political Economy*, 42(1–2), 1–6.

Davidson, N. & Haddow, K. (2020). State Preemption and Local Responses in the Pandemic, Washington, DC: American Constitution Society: Expert Forum. www.acslaw.org/expertforum/state-preemption-and-local-responses-in-the-pandemic/.

Davies, R., Haldane, A., Nielsen, M. & Pezzini, S. (2014). Measuring the Costs of Short-Termism. *Journal of Financial Stability*, 12, 16–25.

Davis, B. & Haddon, H. (2020). Big Restaurant, Hotel Chains Won Exemption to Get Small Business Loans. *Wall Street Journal*, www.wsj.com/articles/big-restaurant-hotel-chains-won-exemption-to-get-small-business-loans-11586167200 (accessed 10 January 2021).

Davis, G. (2009). *Managed by the Markets: How Finance Re-Shaped America*, New York: Oxford University Press.

Davis, G. F. (2008). A New Finance Capitalism? Mutual Funds and Ownership Re-concentration in the United States. *European Management Review*, 5(1), 11–21.

Davis, G. F. (2015). Corporate Power in the Twenty-First Century. In Rangan, S., ed., *Performance and Progress: Essays on Capitalism, Business, and Society*, Oxford: Oxford University Press, pp. 395–414.

Davis, G. (2016). *The Vanishing American Corporation: Navigating the Hazards of a New Economy*, Oakland, CA: Berrett-Koehler Publishers.

Davis, G. F. & Thompson, T. A. (1994). A Social Movement Perspective on Corporate Control. *Administrative Science Quarterly*, 39(1), 141–73.

Davis, L. E. & Neal, L. (2007). Why did finance capitalism and the second industrial revolution arise in the 1890s? In Lamoreaux, N. R. & Sokoloff, K. L., *Financing Innovation in the United States, 1870 to the Present*, Cambridge, MA: MIT Press, pp. 129–61.

Dawson, M. C. & Ming Francis, M. (2016). Black Politics and the Neoliberal Racial Order. *Public Culture*, 28(1), 23–62.

De Loecker, J. & Eeckhout, J. (2017). The rise of market power and the macroeconomic implications. *NBER* Working Paper 23687.

De Loecker, J. & Eeckhout, J. (2018). Global market power. *NBER* Working Paper 24768.

Decker, J. (2016). *The Other Rights Revolution: Conservative Lawyers and the Remaking of American Government*, New York: Oxford University Press.

Deeg, R. & Hardie, I. (2016). What Is Patient Capital and Who Supplies It? *Socio-Economic Review*, 14(4), 627–45.

Delli Carpini, M. X. & Keeter, S. (1997). *What Americans Know About Politics and Why It Matters*, New Haven, CT: Yale University Press.

Dettling, L. J., Hsu, J. W., Jacobs, L., Moore, K. B. & Thompson, J. P. (2017). *Recent Trends in Wealth-Holding by Race and Ethnicity: Evidence from the Survey of Consumer Finance*, Washington, DC: Board of Governors of the Federal Reserve System.

Diermeier, D., Keane, M. & Merlo, A. (2005). A Political Economy Model of Congressional Careers. *American Economic Review*, 95(1), 347–73.

Dimick, M. (2014). Productive Unionism. *UC Irvine Law Review*, 4(2), 679–724.

Dixon, A. D. (2012). Function before Form: Macro-Institutional Comparison and the Geography of Finance. *Journal of Economic Geography*, 12(3), 579–600.

Djankov, S. & Zhang, E. (2020). *COVID-19 Widens Gender Gap in Labor Force Participation in Some but Not Other Advanced Economies*, Washington, DC: Peterson Institute for International Economics.

Drahos, P. & Braithwaite, J. (2002). *Information Feudalism: Who Owns the Knowledge Economy?* New York: The New Press.

Drazanova, L. (2019). *Historical Index of Ethnic Fractionalization Dataset (HIEF) Version V1*, Cambridge, MA: Harvard Dataverse.

Dreier, P., Mollenkopf, J. & Swanstrom, T. (2004). *Place Matters: Metropolitics for the Twenty-First Century*, Lawrence: Kansas University Press.

Drucker, P. F. (1976). *The Unseen Revolution: How Pension Fund Socialism Came to America*, New York: Harper & Row.

Drutman, L. (2010). Congressional Fellowship Program: The Complexities of Lobbying: Toward a Deeper Understanding of the Profession. *PS: Political Science and Politics*, 43(4), 834–37.

Dube, A., Giuliano, L. & Leonard, J. (2019). Fairness and Frictions: The Impact of Unequal Raises on Quit Behavior. *American Economic Review*, 109(2), 620–63.

Dube, A., Jacobs, J., Naidu, S. & Suri, S. (2020). Monopsony in Online Labor Markets. *American Economic Review: Insights*, 2(1), 33–46.

Dube, A., Lester, T. W., & Reich, M. (2016). Minimum Wage Shocks, Employment Flows, and Labor Market Frictions. *Journal of Labor Economics*, 34(3), 663–704.

Dube, A., Manning, A. & Naidu, S. (2018). Monopsony and Employer Misoptimization Explain Why Wages Bunch at Round Numbers. *NBER* Working Paper 24991.

Duménil, G. & Lévy, D. (2011). *The Crisis of Neoliberalism*, Cambridge, MA: Harvard University Press.

Dustmann, C., Lindner, A., Schonberg, U., Umkehrer, M. & Vom Berge, P. (2019). *Reallocation Effects of the Minimum Wage: Evidence from Germany*, London: Centre for Research and Analysis of Migration, University College London.

Eckert, F., Ganapati, S. & Walsh, C. (2019). Skilled Tradable Services: The Transformation of US High-Skill Labor Markets, Opportunity and Inclusive Growth Institute Working Paper.

Economy, E. (2018). *The Third Revolution: Xi Jinping and the New Chinese State*, Oxford, UK: Oxford University Press.

Edwards, R. (1979). *Contested Terrain: The Transformation of the Workplace in the Twentieth Century*. New York: Basic Books.

Egede, L. & Walker, R. J. (2020). Structural Racism, Social Risk Factors, and Covid-19 – A Dangerous Convergence for Black Americans. *New England Journal of Medicine*, 383, e77.

Ehrenhalt, A. (2013). *The Great Inversion and the Future of the American City*, New York: Vintage Books.

Eidelson, J. (2018). Koch Brothers-Linked Group Declares New War on Unions. *Bloomberg*, www.bloomberg.com/news/articles/2018-06-27/koch-brothers-linked-group-declares-new-war-on-unions (accessed 24 December 2020).

Einhorn, R. (2006). *American Taxation, American Slavery*, Chicago: University of Chicago Press.

Einstein, K. L. & Glick, D. M. (2017). Cities in American Federalism: Evidence on State–Local Government Conflict from a Survey of Mayors. *Publius: The Journal of Federalism*, 47(4), 599–621.

Einstein, K. L., Glick, D. M. & Palmer, M. (2019). *Neighborhood Defenders: Participatory Politics and America's Housing Crisis*, New York: Cambridge University Press.

Elhauge, E. (2016). Horizontal Shareholding. *Harvard Law Review*, 129, 1267–317.

Ellen, I. G. (2000). *Sharing America's Neighborhoods: The Prospects for Stable Racial Integration*, Cambridge, MA: Harvard University Press.

Elmendorf, C. (2019). Beyond the Double Veto: Land use Plans as Preemptive Intergovernmental Compacts. *71 Hastings Law Journal*, 79.

Elzinga, A. (2012). Features of the Current Science Policy Regime: Viewed in Historical Perspective. *Science and Public Policy*, 39(4), 416–28.

Emerson, M. O., Chai, K. J. & Yancey, G. (2001). Does Race Matter in Residential Segregation? Exploring the Preferences of White Americans. *American Sociological Review*, 66(6), 922–35.

Enns, P. K. (2015). Relative Policy Support and Coincidental Representation. *Perspectives on Politics*, 13(4), 1053–64.

Enns, P. K., Kelly, N. J., Morgan, J., Volscho, T. & Witko, C. (2014). Conditional Status Quo Bias and Top Income Shares: How US Political Institutions Have Benefited the Rich. *The Journal of Politics*, 76(2), 289–303.

Enright, T. (2016). *The Making of Grand Paris: Metropolitan Urbanism in the Twenty-First Century*, Cambridge, MA: MIT Press.

Epic Systems (2018). *Epic Systems Corp. v. Lewis*, Oyez.

Epstein, L., Landes, W. M. & Posner, R. A. (2013). *The Behavior of Federal Judges: A Theoretical and Empirical Study of Rational Choice*, Cambridge, MA: Harvard University Press.

Epp, C. R. (1998). *The Rights Revolution: Lawyers, Activists and Supreme Courts in Comparative Perspective*, Chicago: University of Chicago Press.

Epp, C. R. (2009). *Making Rights Real: Activists, Bureaucrats and the Creation of the Legalistic State*, Chicago: University of Chicago Press.

Erikson, R., MacKuen, M. & Stimson, J. (2003). *The Macro Polity*, New York: Cambridge University Press.

Esping-Andersen, G. (1990). *The Three Worlds of Welfare Capitalism*, Princeton, NJ: Princeton University Press.

Estevez-Abe, M., Iversen, T. & Soskice, D. (2001). Social Protection and the Formation of Skills: A Reinterpretation of the Welfare State. In Hall, P. and Soskice, D., eds., *Varieties of Capitalism: The Institutional Foundations of Comparative Advantage*. Oxford, UK: Oxford University Press, pp. 145–83.

EU KLEMS (2018). *Growth and Productivity Accounts September 2017*, EU KLEMS.

Fairfield, T. (2015). *Private Wealth and Public Revenue*, New York: Cambridge University Press.

Fama, E. F. & Jensen, M. C. (1983). Separation of Ownership and Control. *The Journal of Law and Economics*, 26(2), 301–25.

Fannin, R. (2019). *Tech Titans of China: How China's Tech Sector Is Challenging the World by Innovating Faster, Working Harder, and Going Global*, London: Nicholas Brealey.

Farber, H. S. & Western, B. (2001). Accounting for the Decline of Unions in the Private Sector, 1973–1998. *Journal of Labor Research*, XXII(3), 459–85.

Farber, H. S., Herbst, D., Kuziemko, I. & Naidu, S. (2020). Unions and Inequality Over the Twentieth Century: New Evidence from Survey Data. NBER Working Paper 24587.

Farewell Address (1961). *Reading copy of the speech*. Abeline, KS: Dwight D. Eisenhower Presidential Library.

Farhang, S. & Katznelson, I. (2005). The Southern Imposition: Congress and Labor in the New Deal and Fair Deal. *Studies in American Political Development*, 19(1), 1–30.

Faricy, C. G. (2015). *Welfare for the Wealthy: Parties, Social Spending, and Inequality*, New York: Cambridge University Press.

Farley, R., Steeh, C., Krysan, M., Jackson, T. & Reeves, K. (1994). Stereotypes and Segregation: Neighborhoods in the Detroit Area. *American Journal of Sociology*, 100(3), 750–80.

Farrell, J. (2016). Corporate Funding and Ideological Polarization about Climate Change. *PNAS*, 113(1), 92–97.

Federal Trade Commission (2018). *FTC Hearing #8: Common Ownership*.

Feigenbaum, J., Hertel-Fernandez, A. & Williamson, V. (2019). From the Bargaining Table to the Ballot Box: Political Effects of Right to Work Laws. *NBER* Working Paper 24259.

Fergus, D. (2013). The Ghetto Tax: Auto Insurance, Postal Code Profiling, and the Hidden History of Wealth Transfer. In Harris, F. C. and Lieberman, R. C., eds., *Beyond Discrimination: Racial Inequality in a Postracist Era*. New York: Russell Sage Foundation, pp. 277–316.

Ferreira, M. A., Matos, P. & Pires, P. (2018). Asset Management within Commercial Banking Groups: International Evidence. *The Journal of Finance*, 73(5), 2181–227.

Ferreras, I. (2017). *Firms as Political Entities: Saving Democracy through Economic Bicameralism*, Cambridge, UK: Cambridge University Press.

Fichtner, J. & Heemskerk, E. M. (2020). The New Permanent Universal Owners: Index Funds, Patient Capital, and the Distinction between Feeble and Forceful Stewardship. *Economy and Society* Advance Online Publication.

Fichtner, J., Heemskerk, E. M. & Garcia-Bernardo, J. (2017). Hidden Power of the Big Three? Passive Index Funds, Re-concentration of Corporate Ownership, and New Financial Risk. *Business and Politics*, 19(2), 298–326.

Filindra, A. & Kaplan, N. (2020). Beyond Performance: Racial Resentment and Whites' Negativity toward Government, https://ssrn.com/abstract=3574804.

Fingerhut, H. (2017). *Republicans Skeptical of Colleges' Impact on U.S., but Most See Benefits for Workforce Preparation*, Washington, DC: Pew Research Center.

Fink, M. P. (2008). *The Rise of Mutual Funds: An Insider's View*, New York: Oxford University Press.

Finocchiaro, C. J. & Rohde, D. W. (2008). War for the Floor: Partisan Theory and Agenda Control in the U.S. House of Representatives. *Legislative Studies Quarterly*, 33(1), 35–61.

Fisch, J. E., Hamdani, A. & Solomon, S. D. (2019). The New Titans of Wall Street: A Theoretical Framework for Passive Investors. *University of Pennsylvania Law Review* 17.

Fischel, W. A. (2001). *The Homevoter Hypothesis: How Home Values Influence Local Government Taxation, School Finance, and Land-Use Policies*, Cambridge, MA: Harvard University Press.

Fischer, A. & Gould-Werth, A. (2020). *Broken Plumbing: How Systems for Delivering Economic Relief in Response to the Coronavirus Recession Failed the US Economy*, Washington Center for Equitable Growth.

Fischer, C. S., Stockmayer, G., Stiles, J. & Hout, M. (2004). Distinguishing the Geographic Levels and Social Dimensions of U.S. Metropolitan Segregation, 1960–2000. *Demography*, 41(1), 37–59.

Fisk, C. (2009). *Working Knowledge: Employee Innovation and the Rise of Corporate Intellectual Property, 1800–1930*, Chapel Hill: University of North Carolina Press.

Flavin, P. & Hartney, M. T. (2015). When Government Subsidizes Its Own: Collective Bargaining Laws as Agents of Political Mobilization. *American Journal of Political Science*, 59(4), 896–911.

Fligstein, N. (2002). *The Architecture of Markets: An Economic Sociology of Twenty-First Century Capitalist Societies*, Princeton, NJ: Princeton University Press.

Flood, C. (2020). The $5tn club: Merger mania sweeps asset management industry. *Financial Times*, www.ft.com/content/d8e07916-a5ea-451f-acf2-35cd1be6639d (accessed 7 January 2021).

Flynn, A., Holmberg, S. R., Warren, D. T. & Wong, F. J. (2017). *The Hidden Rules of Race: Barriers to an Inclusive Economy*, New York: Cambridge University Press.

Foglesong, R. (2001). *Married to the Mouse: Walt Disney World and Orlando*, New Haven, CT: Yale University Press.

Foohey, P. & Martin, N. (2021). Reducing the Wealth Gap Through Fintech "Advances" in Consumer Banking and Lending. *University of Illinois Law Review*.

Forbath, W. E. (1991). *Law and the Shaping of the American Labor Movement*. Cambridge, MA: Harvard University Press.

Forman, J. (2017). *Locking Up Our Own: Crime and Punishment in Black America*, New York: Farrar, Straus and Giroux.

Foster, D. & Summers, A. (2005). Current State Legislative and Judicial Profiles on Land-Use Regulations in the United States. *Zell/Lurie Real Estate Center* Working Paper.

Fourcade, M. & Healy, K. (2017). Seeing Like a Market. *Socio-Economic Review*, 15(1), 9–29.

Fourcade, M. & Khurana, R. (2017). The Social Trajectory of a Finance Professor and the Common Sense of Capital. *History of Political Economy*, 49(2), 347–81.

Fowler, A., Garro, H. & Spenkuch, J. L. (2020). Quid Pro Quo? Corporate Returns to Campaign Contributions. *Journal of Politics*, 82(3), 844–58.

Fox, B. (2019). Asset managers fight to prevent limits on company ownership. *Financial Times*, www.ft.com/content/af19e6ca-2f02-11e9-ba00-0251022932c8?shareType=nongift (accessed 04/ 20/2019).

Francia, P. (2013). Onward Union Soldiers? Organized Labor's Future in American Elections. In Herrnson, P., Deering, C. & Wilcox, C., eds., *Interest Groups Unleashed*, Washington, DC: CQ Press, pp. 138–39.

Francis, M. M. (2019). The Price of Civil Rights: Black Lives, White Funding, and Movement Capture. *Law and Society Review*, 53(1), 275–309.

Franko, W. & Witko, C. (2017). *The New Economic Populism: How States Respond to Economic Inequality*, New York: Oxford University Press.

Franko, W. W., Tolbert, C. & Witko, C. (2013). Inequality, Self-Interest and Public Support for "Robin Hood" Tax Policies. *Political Research Quarterly*, 66(4), 923–37.

Franks, J., Mayer, C. & Rossi, S. (2008). Ownership: Evolution and regulation. *The Review of Financial Studies*, 22(10), 4009–56.

Frasure-Yokley, L. (2015). *Racial and Ethnic Politics in American Suburbs*, New York: Cambridge University Press.

Frazelle, B. R. (2019). *Corporations and the Supreme Court*, Washington, DC: Constitutional Accountability Center.

Freemark, Y., Steil, J. & Thelen, K. (2020). Varieties of Urbanism: A Comparative View of Inequality and the Dual Dimensions of Metropolitan Fragmentation. *Politics & Society*, 48(2), 235–74.

Freund, D. M. P. (2010). *Colored Property: State Policy & White Racial Politics in Suburban America*, Chicago: University of Chicago Press.

Friedman, T. L. (2005). *The World Is Flat: A Brief History of the Twenty-First Century*, New York: Macmillan.

Frisch, J. (2016). The New Governance and the Challenge of Litigation Bylaws. *Brooklyn Law Review* 81.

Frymer, P. & Grumbach, J. M. (2020). Labor Unions and White Racial Politics. *American Journal of Political Science*, 0(0), 1–16.

Funk, R. J. & Hirschman, D. (2014). Derivatives and Deregulation: Financial Innovation and the Demise of Glass-Steagall. *Administrative Science Quarterly*, 59, 669–704.

Gabor, D. (2021). The Wall Street Consensus. *Development & Change*, Advance Online Publication.

Galanter, M. (1974). Why the "Haves" Come out Ahead: Speculations on the Limits of Legal Change. *Law and Society Review*, 9(1), 95–160.

Galbraith, J. (1967). *The New Industrial State*, Boston: Houghton, Mifflin.

Galster, G. & Godfrey, E. (2005).By Words and Deeds: Racial Steering by Real Estate Agents in the U.S. in 2000. *Journal of the American Planning Association*, 71(3), 251–68.

Galston, W. (2015). Against Short-Termism. *Democracy: A Journal of Ideas*, 38.

Galvin, D. J. (2016). Deterring Wage Theft: Alt-Labor, State Politics, and the Policy Determinants of Minimum Wage Compliance. *Perspectives on Politics*, 14, 324–50.

Galvin, D. J. & Hacker, J. S. (2020). The Political Effects of Policy Drift: Policy Stalemate and American Political Development. *Northwestern Institute for Policy Research* Working Paper Series WP-19-12.

Ganong, P. & Shoag, D. (2017). Why Has Regional Income Convergence in the US Declined? *Journal of Urban Economics*, 102, 76–90.

Garin, A. (2018). Essays on the Economics of Labor Demand and Policy Incidence. Doctoral dissertation, Harvard University, Graduate School of Arts & Sciences.

Garritzmann, J. L. (2014). *The Political Economy of Higher Education Finance: The Politics of Tuition Fees and Subsidies in OECD Countries, 1945–2015*, London, UK: Palgrave.

Garritzmann, J. L. (2015). Attitudes towards Student Support: How Positive Feedback-Effects Prevent Change in the Four Worlds of Student Finance. *Journal of European Social Policy*, 25(2), 139–58.

Gass, N. (2016). Trump: GOP Will Become "Worker's Party" under Me. *Politico*, www.politico.com/story/2016/05/trump-gop-workers-party-223598 (accessed 5 January 2020).

Gaventa, J. (1980). *Power and Powerlessness: Quiescence and Rebellion in an Appalachian Valley*, Champaign: University of Illinois Press.

Geithner, T. F. (2014). *Stress Test: Reflections on Financial Crises*, New York: Crown Publishers.

Gerstle, G. (2017). *Liberty and Coercion: The Paradox of American Government from the Founding to the Present*, Princeton, NJ: Princeton University Press.

Gertler, M. S., Oinas, P., Storper, M. & Scranton, P. (1995). Discussion of *Regional Advantage: Culture and Competition in Silicon Valley and Route 128* by Annalee Saxenian. *Economic Geography*, 71(2), 199–207.

Ghosh, A. (2017). *Pricing and Performance of Initial Public Offerings in the United States*, London: Routledge.

Gibson, E. L. (2013). *Boundary Control: Subnational Authoritarianism in Federal Democracies*, New York: Cambridge University Press.

Gidron, N. & Hall, P. A. (2019). Populism as a Problem of Social Integration. *Comparative Political Studies*, 53(7), 1027–59.

Gingrich, J. (2011). *Marking Markets in the Welfare State: The Politics of Varying Market Reforms*, Cambridge, UK: Cambridge University Press.

Gilens, M. (1999). *Why Americans Hate Welfare: Race, Media, and the Politics of Antipoverty Policy*, Chicago: University of Chicago Press.

Gilens, M. (2012). *Affluence and Influence: Economic Inequality and Political Power in America*, Princeton, NJ: Princeton University.

Gilens, M. & Page, B. I. (2014). Testing Theories of American Politics: Elites, Interest Groups, and Average Citizens. *Perspectives on Politics*, 12(03), 564–81.

Gilman, H. (1993). *The Constitution Besieged*, Durham, NC: Duke University Press.

Gilson, R. J. & Gordon, J. N. (2013). The Agency Costs of Agency Capitalism: Activist Investors and the Revaluation of Governance Rights. *Columbia Law Review*, 113(4), 863–927.

Glaeser, E. & Gyourko, J. (2018). The Economic Implications of Housing Supply. *Journal of Economic Perspectives*, 32(1), 3–30.

Glaeser, E. & Ward, B. A. (2009). The Causes and Consequences of Land Use Regulation: Evidence from Greater Boston. *Journal of Urban Economics*, 65, 265–78.

Glaeser, E., Gyourko, J. & Saks, R. E. (2005). Why Have Housing Prices Gone Up? *American Economic Review*, 95(2), 329–33.

Gleditsch, N. P., Wallensteen, P., Eriksson, M., Sollenberg, M. & Strand, H. (2002). Armed Conflict 1946-2001: A New Dataset. *Journal of Peace Research*, 39(5), 615–37.

Glickfield, M. & Levine, N. (1992). *Regional Growth and Local Reaction: The Enactment and Effects of Local Growth Control and Management Measures in California*, Cambridge, MA: Lincoln Institute of Land Policy.

Goldin, C. D. & Katz, L. F. (2008). *The Race between Education and Technology*, Cambridge, MA: Harvard University Press.

Goldschmidt, D. & Schmieder, J. (2017). The Rise of Domestic Outsourcing and the Evolution of the German Wage Structure. *The Quarterly Journal of Economics*, 132(3), 1165–217.

Goldstein, A. (2012). Revenge of the Managers: Labor Cost-Cutting and the Paradoxical Resurgence of Managerialism in the Shareholder Value Era, 1984 to 2001. *American Sociological Review*, 77(2), 268–94.

Goldstein, M. (2018). Brett Kavanaugh Likely to Bring Pro-Business Views to Supreme Court. *New York Times*, www.nytimes.com/2018/07/10/business/kavanaugh-supreme-court-business-regulation.html (accessed 25 December 2020).

Goodman, D. J. (2019a). Amazon Pulls Out of Planned New York City Headquarters. *New York Times*, www.nytimes.com/2019/02/14/nyregion/amazon-hq2-queens.html (accessed 25 December 2020).

Goodman, D. J. (2019b). De Blasio Unveils Health Plan for Undocumented and Low-Income New Yorkers. *New York Times*, www.nytimes.com/2019/01/08/nyregion/de-blasio-health-care-plan.html (accessed 25 December 2020).

Goos, M., Manning, A. & Salomons, A. (2009). Job Polarization in Europe. *American Economic Review*, 99(2), 58–63.

Gordon, A. (2017). New and Enduring Dual Structures of Employment in Japan: The Rise of Non Regular Labor, 1980s–2010s. *Social Science Japan Journal*, 20(1), 9–36.

Gosnell, H. (1935). *Negro Politicians: The Rise of Negro Politics in Chicago*, Chicago: University of Chicago Press.

Gottschalk, M. (2006). *The Prison and the Gallows: The Politics of Mass Incarceration in America*, New York: Cambridge University Press.

Gourevitch, A. (2014). *From Slavery to the Cooperative Commonwealth: Labor and Republican Liberty in the Nineteenth Century*, New York: Cambridge University Press.

Gourevitch, P. (1986). *Politics in Hard Times: Comparative Responses to International Crises*, Ithaca, NY: Cornell University Press.

Gourevitch, P. A. & Shinn, J. (2005). *Political Power and Corporate Control: The New Global Politics of Corporate Governance*, Princeton, NJ: Princeton University Press.

Goyer, M. (2011). *Contingent Capital: Short-Term Investors and The Evolution of Corporate Governance in France and Germany*, Oxford, UK: Oxford University Press.

Grant, J. T. & Kelly, N. J. (2008). Legislative Productivity of the U.S. Congress, 1789–2004. *Political Analysis*, 16(3), 303–23.

Greenhouse, S. (2016). How the $15 Minimum Wage Went from Laughable to Viable. *New York Times*, www.nytimes.com/2016/04/03/sunday-review/how-the-15-minimum-wage-went-from-laughable-to-viable.html (accessed 25 December 2020).

Greenwood, R. & Scharfstein, D. (2013). The Growth of Finance. *The Journal of Economic Perspectives*, 27(2), 3–28.

Griffin, C. N. (2020). We Three Kings: Disintermediating Voting at the Index Fund Giants. *Maryland Law Review*.

Grimm, D. (2015). The Democratic Costs of Constitutionalisation: The European Case. *European Law Journal*, 21(4), 460–73.

Gross, J. S. & Hambleton, R. (2007). Global Trends, Diversity, and Democracy. In Gross, J. S. & Hambleton, R, *Governing Cities in a Global Era: Urban Innovation, Competition, and Democratic Reform*. New York: Palgrave Macmillan, pp. 1–12.

Grossman, M. & Hopkins, D. A. (2016). *Asymmetric Politics: Ideological Republicans and Group Interest Democrats*, New York: Oxford University Press.

Group of Thirty (2019). *Fixing the Pension Crisis: Ensuring Lifetime Financial Security*.

Grullon, G., Larkin, Y. & Michaely, R. (2019). Are US Industries Becoming More Concentrated? *Review of Finance*, 23(4), 697–743.

Grumbach, J. (2018). From Backwaters to Major Policymakers: Policy Polarization in the States, 1970–2014. *Perspectives on Politics*, 16(2), 416–35.

Grumbach, J. (2020). Testing City Limits: Local Redistribution and the Rise of Healthy San Francisco. Working Paper.

Grusky, D. B., Hall, P. A. & Markus, H. R. (2019). The Rise of Opportunity Markets: How Did It Happen & What Can We Do? *Daedalus*.

Guendelsberger, E. (2019). *On the Clock: What Low-Wage Work Did to Me and How It Drives America Insane*, New York: Little, Brown and Company.

Gutiérrez, G. & Philippon, T. (2018). How EU Markets Became More Competitive Than US Markets: A Study of Institutional Drift. *NBER* Working Paper 24700.

Gutiérrez, G. & Piton, S. (2020). Revisiting the Global Decline of the (Non-Housing) Labor Share. *American Economic Review: Insights*, 2(3), 321–38.

Gyourko, J., Saiz, A. & Summers, A. (2008). A New Measure of the Local Regulatory Environment for Housing Markets: The Wharton Residential Land Use Regulatory Index. *Urban Studies*, 45(3), 693–729.

Haberly, D., MacDonald-Korth, D., Urban, M. & Wójcik, D. (2019). Asset Management as a Digital Platform Industry: A Global Financial Network Perspective. *Geoforum*, 106, 167–81.

Hacker, J. S. (2002). *The Divided Welfare State: The Battle over Public and Private Social Benefits in the United States*, New York: Cambridge University Press.

Hacker, J. S. (2004). Privatizing Risk without Privatizing the Welfare State: The Hidden Politics of Social Policy Retrenchment in the United States. *American Political Science Review*, 98(2), 243–60.

Hacker, J. S. (2005). Policy Drift: The Hidden Politics of US Welfare State Retrenchment. In Streeck, W. & Thelen, K., *Beyond Continuity: Institutional Change in Advanced Political Economies*. Oxford, UK: Oxford University Press, pp. 40–82.

Hacker, J. S. (2019). *The Great Risk Shift: The New Economic Insecurity and the Decline of the American Dream*, 2nd ed., New York: Oxford University Press.

Hacker, J. S. & Pierson, P. (2002). Business Power and Social Policy: Employers and the Formation of the American Welfare State. *Politics and Society*, 30(2), 277–325.

Hacker, J. S. & Pierson, P. (2010). Winner-Take-All Politics: Public Policy, Political Organization, and the Precipitous Rise of Top Incomes in the United States. *Politics & Society*, 38(2), 152–204.

Hacker, J. S. & Pierson, P. (2016). *American Amnesia: How the War on Government Led Us to Forget What Made America Prosper*, New York: Simon & Schuster.

Hacker, J. S. & Pierson, P. (2020). *Let Them Eat Tweets: How the Right Rules in an Age of Extreme Inequality*, New York: Liveright.

Hacker, J. S., Pierson, P. & Thelen, K. (2015). Drift and Conversion: Hidden Faces of Institutional Change. In Mahoney, J. & Thelen, K., eds., *Advances in Comparative-Historical Analysis*. New York: Cambridge University Press, pp. 180–208.

Hackworth, J. (2007). *The Neoliberal City: Governance, Ideology, and Development in American Urbanism*, Ithaca, NY: Cornell University Press.

Hajnal, Z. (2010). *America's Uneven Democracy: Race, Turnout, and Representation in City Politics*, New York: Cambridge University Press.

Hajnal, Z. L. & Trounstine, J. (2014). What Underlies Urban Politics? Race, Class, Ideology, Partisanship, and the Urban VBote. *Urban Affairs Review*, 50(1), 63–99.

Hall, A. & Yoder, J. (2019). Does Homeownership Influence Political Behavior? Evidence from Administrative Data. Working Paper.

Hall, B., Helmers, C. & von Graevenitz, G. (2015). Technology Entry in the Presence of Patent Thickets. *NBER* Working Paper 21455.

Hall, P. A. & Soskice, D. (2001). Introduction. In Hall, P. A. & Soskice, D., eds., *Varieties of Capitalism: The Institutional Foundations of Comparative Advantage*. New York: Oxford University Press, pp. 1–68.

Hamaji, K., Deutsch, R., Nicolas, E. et al. (2019). *Unchecked Corporate Power: Forced Arbitration, The Enforcement Crisis, and How Workers Are Fighting Back*, Washington, DC: The Center for Popular Democracy, Economic Policy Institute.

Hamilton, D., Austin, A. & Darity Jr., W. A. (2011). *Whiter Jobs, Higher Wages: Occupational Segregation and the Lower Wages of Black Men*, Washington, DC: Economic Policy Institute.

Hamilton, D. & Darity, W. (2010). Can "Baby Bonds" Eliminate the Racial Wealth Gap in Putative Post-Racial America? *Review of Black Political Economy*, 37(3), 207–16.

Hampson, R. (2019). "Any Talks of Striking?": How a West Virginia Teacher's Facebook Post Started a National Movement. *USA Today*, www.usatoday.com/story/news/education/2019/02/20/teacher-strike-west-virginia-school-closings-education-bill/2848476002/ (accessed 25 December 2020).

Hamilton Project (2014). *Incarceration Rates in OECD Countries*, Washington, DC: The Hamilton Project.

Hanks, A., Solomon, D. & Weller, C. E. (2018). *Systematic Inequality: How America's Structural Racism Helped Create the Black-White Wealth Gap*, Washington, DC: Center for American Progress.

Hansmann, H. & Kraakman, R. (2001). The End of History for Corporate Law. *Georgetown Law Journal*, 89, 439–68.

Hanson, A. (2013). *When Education and Legislation Meet: Teacher Collective Bargaining in Canada*, Belleville, ON: Canadian Teachers' Federation.

Harell, A., Soroka, S. & Iyengar, S. (2016). Race, Prejudice and Attitudes toward Redistribution: A Comparative Experimental Approach. *European Journal of Political Research*, 55(4), 723–44.

Harris, F. C. & Lieberman, R. C. (2013). Introduction. In Harris, F. C. & Lieberman, R. C., eds., *Beyond Discrimination: Racial Inequality in a Postracist Era*. New York: Russell Sage Foundation, pp. 1–36.

Hartney, M. T. (2014). Turning Out Teachers: The Causes and Consequences of Teacher Political Activism in the Postwar United States. University of Notre Dame Doctoral Dissertation in Political Science.

Hartocollis, A. (2018). Revelations over Koch Gifts Prompt Inquiry at George Mason University. *New York Times*, www.nytimes.com/2018/05/01/us/koch-george-mason-university.html (accessed 25 December 2020).

Harvey, A. & Mattia, T. (2019). Does Money Have a Conservative Bias? *Public Choice* online version.

Haselswerdt, J. & Bartels, B. L. (2015). Public Opinion, Policy Tools, and the Status Quo: Evidence from a Survey Experiment. *Political Research Quarterly*, 68(3), 607–21.

Hasen, R. L. (2013). End of the Dialogue: Political Polarization, the Supreme Court, and Congress. *Southern California Law Review*, 86(2), 205–62.

Haskel, J. & Westlake, S. (2017). *Capitalism without Capital: The Rise of the Intangible Economy*, Princeton, NJ: Princeton University Press.

Hassel, A. & Thelen, K. (2020). Europe Has Kept Down Pandemic Unemployment – and the US Hasn't. Here's Why. *Washington Post*, www.washingtonpost.com/politics/2020/04/24/europe-has-kept-down-pandemic-unemployment-us-hasnt-heres-why/ (accessed 10 January 2021).

Hatch, M. E. & Rigby, E. (2014). Laboratories of (In)equality? Redistributive Policy and Income Inequality in the American States. *Policy Studies Journal*, 43 (2), 163–87.

Hathaway, I. & Litan, R. (2014). *Declining Business Dynamism in the United States: A Look at States and Metros*, Washington, DC: Brookings Institution Press.

Hattam, V. C. (1993). *Labor Visions and State Power: The Origins of Business Unionism in the United States*, Princeton, NJ: Princeton University Press.

Hauser, C. (2018). West Virginia Teachers, Protesting Low Pay, Walk Out. *New York Times*, www.nytimes.com/2018/02/23/us/west-virginia-teachers-strike.html (accessed 25 December 2020).

Hawley, J. P. & Williams, A. T. (2000). *The Rise of Fiduciary Capitalism: How Institutional Investors Can Make Corporate America More Democratic*, Philadelphia: University of Pennsylvania Press.

Hayward, C. (2013). *Americans Make Race: Stories, Institutions, Spaces.* New York: Cambridge University Press.

Hayward, C. R. (2009). Urban Space and American Political Development: Identity, Interest, Action. In Dilworth, R., ed., *The City in American Political Development.* New York: Routledge, pp. 141–53.

Heath, D., Macciocchi, R. M., & Ringgenberg, M. (2021). Do Index Funds Monitor? *Review of Financial Studies.* Advance Online Publication.

Hedblom, D., Hickman, B. R. & List, J. A. (2019). Toward an Understanding of Corporate Social Responsibility: Theory and Field Experimental Evidence. *NBER* Working Paper 26222.

Helper, R. (1969). *Racial Policies and Practices of Real Estate Brokers*, Minneapolis: University of Minnesota Press.

Hermannsson, K., Lisenkova, K., Lecca, P., McGregor, P. G. & J. Swales, K. (2017). The external benefits of higher education. *Regional Studies*, 51(7), 1077–88.

Hero, R. (2000). *Faces of Inequality: Social Diversity in American Politics*, New York: Oxford University Press.

Hertel-Fernandez, A. (2019a). Power and Politics in America's Private Governments. *The Journal of Politics*, 82(1), e13–e20.

Hertel-Fernandez, A. (2019b). *State Capture: How Conservative Activists, Big Businesses, and Wealthy Donors Reshaped the American States – and the Nation*, Oxford, UK: Oxford University Press.

Hertel-Fernandez, A., Naidu, S. & Reich, R. (2021). Schooled by Strikes? The Effects of Large-Scale Labor Unrest on Mass Attitudes towards the Labor Movement. *Perspectives on Politics*, 19(1), 73–91.

Hertel-Fernandez, A., Naidu, S. & Youngblood, P. (2020). *Understanding the COVID-19 Workplace: Evidence from a Survey of Essential Workers*, New York: Roosevelt Institute.

Highsmith, B. (2019). Partisan Constitutionalism. *Wisconsin Law Review*, 101, 913–96.

Hilferding, R. (1985) [1910]. *Finance Capital: A Study of the Latest Phase of Capitalist Development*. Philadelphia, PA: Routledge.

Hill, J. G. (2017). Good Activist/Bad Activist: The Rise of International Stewardship Codes. *Seattle University Law Review*, 41, 497–524.

Hill, S. (2017). *Report: Blacks in Boston Have a Median Net Worth of $8, Whites Have $247 K*, Black Enterprise.

Hinton, E. (2016). *From the War on Poverty to the War on Crime: The Making of Mass Incarceration in America*, Cambridge, MA: Harvard University Press.

Hinton, E., Henderson, L. & Reed, C. (2018). An Unjust Burden: The Disparate Treatment of Black Americans in the Criminal Justice System, *Vera Institute of Justice*.

Hirsch, F. (1976). *Social Limits to Growth*, Cambridge, MA: Harvard University Press.

Hirsch, A. (1983). *Making the Second Ghetto: Race and Housing in Chicago 1940–1960*, Chicago: University of Chicago Press.

Hishamunda, H. & Young, K. (2020). *COVID-19 Liability Shields: Today's Legislative Trend, Tomorrow's Legal Defense*, Seyfarth Legal Update.

Holland, M. M. & DeLuca, S. (2016). "Why Wait Years to Become Something?" Low-Income African American Youth and the Costly Career Search in For-Profit Trade Schools. *Sociology of Education*, 89(4), 261–78.

Holman, M. (forthcoming). The Hidden Face of Power: Local Appointed Boards in the United States.

Hope, D. & Martelli, A. (2019). The Transition to the Knowledge Economy, Labor Market Institutions, and Income Inequality in Advanced Democracies. *World Politics*, 71(2), 236–88.

Hopkins, D. A. (2017). *Red Fighting Blue: How Geography and Electoral Rules Polarize American Politics*, Cambridge, UK: Cambridge University Press.

Höpner, M. (2003). *Wer beherrscht die Unternehmen? Shareholder Value, Managerherrschaft und Mitbestimmung in Deutschland*, Frankfurt: Campus Verlag.

Höpner, M. (2015). Der integrationistische Fehlschluss. *Leviathan*, 43(1), 29–42.

HoSang, D. & Lowndes, J. E. (2019). *Producers, Parasites, Patriots: Race and the New Right-Wing Politics of Precarity*, Minneapolis: University of Minnesota Press.

Howard, C. (1993). The Hidden Side of the American Welfare State. *Political Science Quarterly*, 108(3), 403–36.

Howard, C. (1997). *The Hidden Welfare State: Tax Expenditures and Social Policies in the United States*, Princeton, NJ: Princeton University Press.

Howard, C. (2007). *The Welfare State Nobody Knows: Debunking Myths about U.S. Social Policy*. Princeton, NJ: Princeton University Press.

Howe, F. C. (1905). *The City, The Hope of Democracy*, New York: C. Scribner.

Hoxby, C. (2003). *The Economics of School Choice*. ed. Caroline Hoxby, Chicago: University of Chicago Press.

Hsaing, S., Kopp, R., Jina, A. et al. (2017). Estimating Economic Damage from Climate Change in the United States. *Science*, 356, 1362–69.

Hsieh, C.-T. & Moretti, E. (2019). Housing Constraints and Spatial Misallocation. *American Economic Journal: Macroeconomics*, 11(2), 1–39.

Huber, E. & Stephens, J. D (2001). *Development and Crisis of the Welfare State: Parties and Policies in Global Markets*, Chicago: University of Chicago Press.

Huber, E. & Stephens, J. D. (2014). Income Inequality and Redistribution in Post-Industrial Democracies: Demographic, Economic and Political Determinants. *Socio-Economic Review*, 12(2), 245–67.

Huber, E., Huo, J. & Stephens, J. D. (2017). Power, Policy, and Top Income Shares. *Socio-Economic Review*, 17(2), 231–53.

Huelsman, M. (2015). Betrayers of the Dream: How Sleazy For-Profit Colleges Disproportionately Targeted Black Students. *The American Prospect*, https://prospect.org/labor/betrayers-dream/ (accessed 6 January 2021).

Hughes, T. P. (1987). The Evolution of Large Technological Systems. In *The Social Construction of Technological Systems: New Directions in the Sociology and History of Technology*, Bijker, W. E., Hughes T. P. &. Pinch T. eds., Cambridge, MA, & London: MIT Press, 51–82.

Huntington, S. P. (1968). *Political Order in Changing Societies*, New Haven, CT: Yale University Press.

Hurd, R. W. & Lee, T. L. (2014). Public Sector Unions under Siege: Solidarity in the Fight Back. *Labor Studies Journal*, 39(1), 9–24.

Hurt, S. (2010). Science, Power and the State: U.S. Foreign Policy, Intellectual Property Law, and the Origins of Agricultural Biotechnology, 1969–1994. *New School for Social Research* unpublished dissertation.

ILO (2020). *Covid-19 and the World of Work: Country Policy Responses*, Geneva: International Labour Organization.

Immergut, E. (1992). *Health Politics: Interests and Institutions in Western Europe*, New York: Cambridge University Press.

Iversen, T. & Rosenbluth, F. (2011). *Women, Work, and Politics: The Political Economy of Gender Inequality*, New Haven, CT: Yale University Press.

Iversen, T. & Soskice, D. (2015). Democratic Limits to Redistribution: Inclusionary versus Exclusionary Coalitions in the Knowledge Economy. *World Politics*, 67(2), 185–225.

Iversen, T. & Soskice, D. (2019). *Democracy and Prosperity: Reinventing Capitalism in a Turbulent Century*, Princeton, NJ: Princeton University Press.

Iversen, T. & Wren, A. (1998). Equality, Employment, and Budgetary Restraint: The Trilemma of the Service Economy. *World Politics*, 50(04), 507–46.

Jackson, K. (1985). *Crabgrass Frontier: The Suburbanization of the United States*, New York: Oxford University Press.

Jacobs, A. M. (2011). *Governing for the Long Term: Democracy and the Politics of Investment*, Cambridge, UK: Cambridge University Press.

Jacobs, L. & King, D. (2016). *Fed Power: How Finance Wins*, New York: Oxford University Press.

Jacoby, S. M. (1983). Industrial Labor Mobility in Historical Perspective. *Industrial Relations*, 22(2), 261–82.

Jäger, S. & Heining, J. (2019). How substitutable are workers? evidence from worker deaths. *Evidence from Worker Deaths*. http://economics.mit.edu/files/16635.

Jahnke, P. (2019). Ownership Concentration and Institutional Investors' Governance through Voice and Exit. *Business and Politics* online version.

Jamieson, D. (2018). Labor Critic Claims Union Behind the "Fight for $15" Cut Funding for Fast-Food Campaigns. *The Huffington Post*, www.huffpost.com/entry/union-behind-the-fight-for-15-cuts-funding-for-fast-food-campaign_n_5abfe925e4b055e50ace1a2d (accessed 26 December 2020).

Jardina, A. (2019). *White Identity Politics*, New York: Cambridge University Press.

Jargowsky, P. (2014). Segregation, Neighborhoods, and Schools. In Lareau, A. & Goyette, K., eds., *Choosing Homes, Choosing Schools*. New York: Russell Sage Foundation, pp. 97–136.

Jensen, M. C. & Meckling, W. H. (1976). Theory of the Firm: Managerial Behavior, Agency Costs and Ownership Structure. *Journal of Financial Economics*, 3(4), 305–60.

Jimenez, B. S. (2014). Separate, Unequal, and Ignored? Interjurisdictional Competition and the Budgetary Choices of Poor and Affluent Municipalities. *Public Administration Review*, 74(2), 246–57.

Johnson, A. (2017). That Was No Typo: The Median Net Worth of Black Bostonians Really Is $8. *Boston Globe*, www.bostonglobe.com/metro/2017/12/11/that-was-typo-the-median-net-worth-black-bostonians-really/ze5kxC1jJelx24M3pugFFN/story.html (accessed 26 December 2020).

Jones-Correa, M. (1998). *Between Two Nations: The Political Predicament of Latinos in New York City*, Ithaca, NY: Cornell University Press.

Kagan, R. A. (2001). *Adversarial Legalism: The American Way of Law*, Cambridge, MA: Harvard University Press.

Kagan, R. A. (2019). *Adversarial Legalism: The American Way of Law*, 2nd ed., Cambridge, MA: Harvard University Press.

Kalecki, M. (1943). Political Aspects of Full Employment 1. *The Political Quarterly*, 14(4), 322–30.

Kane, J. V. & Newman, B. (2019). Organized Labor as the New Undeserving Rich? Mass Media, Class-Based Anti-Union Rhetoric and Public Support for Unions in the United States. *British Journal of Political Science*, 49(3), 997–1026.

Kantor, P. (2011). *Struggling Giants: City-Region Governance in London, New York, Paris, and Tokyo*, Minneapolis: University of Minnesota Press.

Kapczynski, A. (2018). The Lochnerized First Amendment and the FDA: Toward a More Democratic Political Economy. *Columbia Law Review*, 118(7), 179–206.

Katz, A. (2015). *The Influence Machine: The US Chamber of Commerce and the Corporate Capture of American Life*, New York: Spiegel & Grau.

Katz, A. (2018). The Chamber in the Chambers: The Making of a Big-Business Judicial Money Machine. *DePaul Law Review*, 67(2), 319–31.

Katz, B. & Nowak, J. (2018). *The New Localism: How Cities Can Thrive in the Age of Populism*, Washington, DC: Brookings Institution Press.

Katznelson, I. (2005). *When Affirmative Action Was White: An Untold History of Racial Inequality in Twentieth-Century America*, New York: W.W. Norton & Co.

Katznelson, I. (2013). *Fear Itself: The New Deal and the Origins of Our Time*, New York: W. W. Norton & Company.

Katznelson, I., Geiger, K. & Kryder, D. (1993). Limiting Liberalism: The Southern Veto in Congress, 1933–1950. *Political Science Quarterly*, 108(2), 283–306.

Kau, J. B., Keenan, D. & Rubin, P. H. (1982). A General Equilibrium Model of Congressional Voting. *The Quarterly Journal of Economics*, 97(2), 271–93.

Kaufman, D. (2018). *The Fall of Wisconsin*, New York: W. W. Norton.

Kaufmann, K. (2004). *The Urban Voter: Group Conflict and Mayoral Voting Behavior in American Cities*, Ann Arbor: University of Michigan Press.

Kay, J. (2012). The Kay Review of UK Equity Markets and Long-Term Decision Making, Review commissioned by the Secretary of State for Business, Innovation and Skills.

Keating, D. (2021). How the EU's Naivety Led to Its Vaccine Debacle, *New Statesman,* March 24, 2021. www.newstatesman.com/world/europe/2021/03/how-eu-s-naivety-led-its-vaccine-debacle.

Keith, D., Berry, P. & Velasco, E. (2019). *The Politics of Judicial Elections, 2017–18*, Brennan Center for Justice.

Kelemen, R. D. (2011). *Eurolegalism: The Transformation of Law and Regulation in the European Union*, Cambridge, MA: Harvard University Press.

Keller, E. & Kelly, N. J. (2015). Partisan Politics, Financial Deregulation, and the New Gilded Age. *Political Research Quarterly*, 68(3), 428–42.

Keller, M. R. & Block, F. L. (2011). *State of Innovation: The U.S. Government's Role in Technology Development*, Philadelphia, PA: Routledge.

Kelly, N. J. (2009). *The Politics of Income Inequality in the United States*, New York: Cambridge University Press.

Kelly, N. J. (2020). *America's Inequality Trap*, Chicago: University of Chicago Press.

Kelly, N. J. & Enns, P. K. (2010). Inequality and the Dynamics of Public Opinion: The Self-Reinforcing Link between Economic Inequality and Mass Preferences. *American Journal of Political Science*, 54(5), 855–70.

Kelly, N. J. & Witko, C. (2012). Federalism and American Inequality. *The Journal of Politics*, 74(2), 414–26.

Kenney, M. & Zysman, J. (2019). Unicorns, Cheshire Cats, and the New Dilemmas of Entrepreneurial Finance. *Venture Capital*, 21(1), 1–16.

Kenworthy, L. (2004). *Egalitarian Capitalism: Jobs, Income, and Growth in Affluent Countries*, New York: Russell Sage Foundation.

Kenworthy, L. (2010). How Much Do Presidents Influence Income Inequality? *Challenge*, 53(2), 90–112.

Kenworthy, L. & Pontusson, J. (2005). Rising Inequality and the Politics of Redistribution in Affluent Countries. *Perspectives on Politics*, 3(3), 449–71.

Kersten, J. (2018). Baurecht. In Schoch, F., ed., *Besonderes Verwaltungsrecht*. München: C. H. Beck, pp. 428–625.

Kessler, J. K. (2016). The Early Years of First Amendment Lochnerism. *Columbia Law Review*, 116(8), 1915–2004.

Kijakazi, K. (2016). Closing the Racial Wealth Gap: Establishing and Sustaining an Initiative. *Race and Social Problems*, 8(1), 136–45.

Kilgore, E. (2020). McConnell Calls General Relief for States "Blue-State Bailouts." *New York Magazine: Intelligencer*, https://nymag.com/intelligencer/2020/04/

mcconnell-calls-general-state-relief-blue-state-bailouts.html (accessed 10 January 2021).

Kim, C. (2019). The ETF Business Is Dominated by the Big Three. The SEC Is Suddenly Concerned. *Barron's*, www.barrons.com/articles/etfs-are-dominated-by-blackrock-vanguard-and-state-street-the-sec-is-concerned-51554512133 (accessed 15 April 2019).

Kim, S. E., Urpelainen, J. & Yang, J. (2016). Electric Utilities and American Climate Policy: Lobbying by Expected Winners and Losers. *Journal of Public Policy*, 36(2), 251–75.

Kinane, C. & Mickey, R. (2018). The Benefits of Concentrated Power: Public Sector Unions and Lawmaking in American Legislatures. Unpublished Working Paper.

Kindy, K. (2020). More than 200 Meat Plant Workers in the U.S. Have Died of Covid-19. Federal Regulators Just Issued Two Modest Fines. *Washington Post*, www.washingtonpost.com/national/osha-covid-meat-plant-fines/2020/09/13/1dca3e14-f395-11ea-bc45-e5d48ab44b9f_story.html (accessed 10 January 2021).

King, D. (2015). America's Segregated State: How the Federal Government Shaped America's Racial and Welfare Orders. In Kettunen, P., Michel, S. & Petersen, K., eds., *Race, Ethnicity and Welfare States: An American Dilemma?* Northhampton MA: Edward Elgar, pp. 47–71.

King, D. & Lieberman, R. C. (2009). Review: Ironies of State Building: A Comparative Perspective on the American State. *World Politics*, 61(3), 547–88.

King, D. S. (2017). Forceful Federalism against American Racial Inequality. *Government and Opposition*, 52(2), 356–82.

King, D. S. & Smith, R. M. (2005). Racial Orders in American Political Development. *American Political Science Review*, 99(1), 75–92.

Kitschelt, H. & Rehm, P. (2014). Occupations as a Site of Political Preference Formation. *Comparative Political Studies*, 47(12), 1670–706.

Kitschelt, H. & Rehm, P. (2015). Party Alignments: Change and Continuity. In Beramendi, P., Häusermann, S., Kitschelt, H. & Kriesi, H., *The Politics of Advanced Capitalism*. New York: Cambridge University Press, pp. 179–201.

Klein, J. (2006). *For All These Rights: Business, Labor, and the Shaping of America's Public-Private Welfare State*, Princeton, NJ: Princeton University Press.

Kline, P., Petkova, N., Williams, H., & Zidar, O. (2019). Who Profits from Patents? Rent-Sharing at Innovative Firms. *The Quarterly Journal of Economics*, 134(3), 1343–04.

Klepper, S. (2001). Employee Startups in High-Tech Industries. *Industrial and Corporate Change*, 10(3), 639–74.

Klepper, S. (2007). Disagreements, Spinoffs, and the Evolution of Detroit as the Capital of the US Automobile Industry. *Management Science*, 53(4), 616–31.

Klepper, S. (2009). Spinoffs: A Review and Synthesis. *European Management Review*, 6(3), 159–71.

Klepper, S. (2010). The Origin and Growth of Industry Clusters: The Making of Silicon Valley and Detroit. *Journal of Urban Economics*, 67(1), 15–32.

Klepper, S. & Sleeper, S. (2005). Entry by Spinoffs. *Management Science*, 51(8), 1291–306.

Klepper, S. & Thompson, P. (2010). Disagreements and Intra-industry Spinoffs. *International Journal of Industrial Organization*, 28(5), 526–38.

Klier, T. & Rubenstein, J. (2008). *Who Really Made Your Car? Restructuring and Geographic Change in the Auto Industry*, Kalamazoo, MI: W.E. Upjohn Institute.

Kline, P., Petkova, N., Williams, H., & Zidar, O. (2019). Who Profits from Patents? Rent-Sharing at Innovative Firms. *The Quarterly Journal of Economics*, 134(3), 1343–404.

Klinenberg, E. (2018). *Palaces for the People: How Social Infrastructure Can Help Fight Inequality, Polarization, and the Decline of Civic Life*, 1st ed., New York: Crown.

Knafo, S. & Dutta, S. J. (2020). The Myth of the Shareholder Revolution and the Financialization of the Firm. *Review of International Political Economy*, 27(3), 476–99.

Kocherlakota, N. (2020). The Fed Should Never Lend to Anyone Other Than Banks. *Bloomberg Opinion*, www.bloomberg.com/opinion/articles/2020-03-23/coronavirus-crisis-fed-should-never-lend-outside-banking-system (accessed 10 January 2021).

Kogan, V., Lavertu, S. & Peskowitz, Z. (2018). Election Timing, Electorate Composition, and Policy Outcomes: Evidence from School Districts. *American Journal of Political Science*, 62(3), 637–51.

Koger, G. (2010). *Filibustering: A Political History of Obstruction in the House and Senate*, Chicago: University of Chicago Press.

Koger, G. & Lebo, M. J. (2017). *Strategic Party Government: Why Winning Trumps Ideology*, Chicago: University of Chicago Press.

Kopp, E. (2020). As Workers Face Virus Risks, Employers Seek Liability Limits. *Roll Call*, www.rollcall.com/2020/04/17/as-workers-face-virus-risks-employers-seek-liability-limits/ (accessed 10 January 2021).

Korpi, W. (1983). *The Democratic Class Struggle*, London: Routledge Press.

Korver-Glenn, E. (2018). Compounding Inequalities: How Racial Stereotypes and Discrimination Accumulate across the Stages of Housing Exchange. *American Sociological Review*, 83(4), 627–56.

Kostin, D. (2018). *Where to Invest Now: 2019 US Equity Outlook*, New York: Goldman Sachs.

Kotz, D. M., McDonough, T. & Reich, M. (1994). *Social Structures of Accumulation: The Political Economy of Growth and Crisis*, Cambridge, UK: Cambridge University Press.

Kraus, M. W., Rucker, J. M. & Richeson, J. A. (2017). Americans Misperceive Racial Economic Equality. *Proceedings of the National Academy of Sciences of the United States of America*, 114(39), 10324–31.

Krehbiel, K. (1998). *Pivotal Politics: A Theory of U.S. Lawmaking*, Chicago: University of Chicago Press.

Krimmel, K. & Rader, K. (2017). Behind the Federal Spending Paradox: Economic Self-Interest and Symbolic Racism in Contemporary Fiscal Politics. *American Politics Research*, 45(5), 727–54.

Krippner, G. R. (2012). *Capitalizing on Crisis: The Political Origins of the Rise of Finance*, Cambridge, MA: Harvard University Press.

Kroft, K., Luo, Y., Mogstad, M. & Setzler, B. (2020). *Imperfect Competition and Rents in Labor and Product Markets: The Case of the Construction Industry*. No. w27325. National Bureau of Economic Research.

Krolikowski, P. & Weixel, A. (2020). *Short-Time Compensation: An Alternative to Layoffs during COVID-19*, Federal Reserve Bank of Cleveland.

Kruse, K. (2005). *White Flight: Atlanta and the Making of Modern Conservatism*, Princeton, NJ: Princeton University Press.

Krysan, M. (2002). Whites Who Say They'd Flee: Who Are They, and Why Would They Leave? *Demography*, 39(4), 675–96.

Krysan, M., Farley, R. & Couper, M. P. (2008). In the Eye of the Beholder: Racial Beliefs and Residential Segregation. *Du Bois Review*, 5(1), 5–26.

Kübler, D. & Rochat, P. E. (2019). Fragmented Governance and Spatial Equity in Metropolitan Areas: The Role of Intergovernmental Cooperation and Revenue-Sharing. *Urban Affairs Review*, 55(5), 1247–79.

Kwak, J. (2014). Cultural Capture and the Financial Crisis. In Carpenter, D. & Moss, D. A., eds., *Preventing Regulatory Capture: Special Interest Influence and How to Limit It*. New York: Cambridge University Press, pp. 71–98.

Kwon, R. (2016). A New Kuznetsian Dynamic: The Knowledge Economy and Income Inequality in the United States, 1917–2008. *The Sociological Quarterly*, 57(1), 174–204.

La Porta, R., Lopez-de-Silanes, F., Shleifer, A. & Vishny, R. (2000). Investor Protection and Corporate Governance. *Journal of Financial Economics*, 58 (1), 3–27.

Lacey, N. & Soskice, D. (2015). Crime, Punishment and Segregation in the United States: The Paradox of Local Democracy. *Punishment & Society*, 17(4), 454–81.

Lamoreaux, N. R. (1988). *The Great Merger Movement in American Business, 1895–1904*, Cambridge, UK: Cambridge University Press.

Lazear, E. P., Shaw, K. L. & Stanton, C. (2016). Making Do with Less: Working Harder During Recessions. *Journal of Labor Economics*, 34(S1), S333–S360.

Lazonick, W. (1990). *Competitive Advantage on the Shop Floor*, Cambridge, MA: Harvard University Press.

Lazonick, W. (2017). The New Normal Is "Maximizing Shareholder Value": Predatory Value Extraction, Slowing Productivity, and the Vanishing American Middle Class. *International Journal of Political Economy*, 46, 217–26.

Lazonick, W. & Mazzucato, M. (2013). The Risk-Reward Nexus in the Innovation-Inequality Relationship: Who Takes the Risks? Who Gets the Rewards? *Industrial and Corporate Change*, 22(4), 1093–128.

Lazonick, W. & O'Sullivan, M. (2000). Maximizing Shareholder Value: A New Ideology for Corporate Governance. *Economy and Society*, 29(1), 13–35.

Lazonick, W., Hopkins, M., Jacobson, K., Sakinc, M. E. & Tulum, O. (2017). US Pharma's Financialized Business Model. *Institute for New Economic Thinking* Working Paper.

Le Galès, P. & Pierson, P. (2019). "Superstar Cities" and the Generation of Durable Inequality. *Daedalus*, 148(3), 46–72.

Leachman, M. & McNichol, E. (2020). *Pandemic's Impact on State Revenues Less Than Earlier Expected but Still Severe*, Washington, DC: Center on Budget and Policy Priorities.

Leigh, A. (2010). Who Benefits from the Earned Income Tax Credit? Incidence among Recipients, Coworkers and Firms. *The BE Journal of Economic Analysis & Policy*, 10(1), 1–41.

Lemieux, T., MacLeod, W. B. & Parent, D. (2009). Performance Pay and Wage Inequality. *The Quarterly Journal of Economics*, 124(1), 1–49.

Leonhardt, D. (2018). The Monopolization of America. *New York Times*, www.nytimes.com/2018/11/25/opinion/monopolies-in-the-us.html (accessed 26 December 2020).

Levine, M. (2020). Investors Want a Cure, Not a Winner. *Bloomberg*, www.bloomberg.com/opinion/articles/2020-04-24/investors-want-a-cure-not-a-winner?sref=1kJVNqnU (accessed 1 June 2020).

Lichtenberger, E. (2015). Cities: Internal Structure. In Smelser, N. & Baltes, P., eds., *International Encyclopedia of the Social & Behavioral Sciences*. New York: Elsevier, pp. 593–604.

Lichtenstein, N. (1989). *The Rise and Fall of the New Deal Order, 1930–1980*, Princeton, NJ: Princeton University Press.

Lichtenstein, N. (1998). Taft-Hartley: A Slave-Labor Law? *Catholic University Law Review*, 47(3), 763–89.

Lichtenstein, N. (2002). *State of the Union: A Century of American Labor*, Princeton, NJ: Princeton University Press.

Lieberman, R. C. (1998). *Shifting the Color Line: Race and the American Welfare State*, Cambridge, MA: Harvard University Press.

Lieberman, R. C. (2006). *Shaping Race Policy: The United States in Comparative Perspective*, Princeton, NJ: Princeton University Press.

Lieberman, R. C. (2011). Why the Rich Are Getting Richer: American Politics and the Second Gilded Age. *Foreign Affairs*, 90(1), 154–58.

Lijphart, A. (2012). *Patterns of Democracy*, 2nd ed., New Haven, CT: Yale University Press.

Lin, C. (2020). COVID-19 Unemployment Fail: State Labor Departments Hobbled by 1970s Tech. *Fast Company*, www.fastcompany.com/90486794/covid-19-unemployment-fail-state-labor-departments-hobbled-by-1970s-tech (accessed 10 January 2021).

Lindblom, C. (1977). *Politics and Markets*, New York: Basic Books.

Lindblom, C. (1982). The Market as Prison. *Journal of Politics*, 44(2), 324–36.

Lindert, P. (2004). *Growing Public*, Cambridge, UK: Cambridge University Press.

Lindo, J. M. & Pineda-Torres, M. (2019). New Evidence on the Effects of Mandatory Waiting Periods for Abortion, *NBER* Working Paper 26228.

Linneman, P., Summers, A., Brooks, N. & Buist, H. (1990). *The State of Local Growth Management*, Philadelphia: The Wharton School, University of Pennsylvania.

Liptak, A. (2018). Supreme Court Upholds Workplace Arbitration Contracts Barring Class Actions. *New York Times*, www.nytimes.com/2018/05/21/business/supreme-court-upholds-workplace-arbitration-contracts.html (accessed 26 December 2020).

Liptak, A. (2019). Split 5 to 4, Supreme Court Deals a Blow to Class Arbitrations. *New York Times*, www.nytimes.com/2019/04/24/us/politics/supreme-court-class-arbitrations.html (accessed 26 December 2020).

Livni, E. (2020). Senators Demand Records Illuminating Dark Money Ties to Supreme Court Appointments. *Quartz*, https://qz.com/1816542/senators-demand-records-on-dark-money-ties-to-court-appointments/ (accessed 26 December 2020).

Lizzeri, A. & Persico, N. (2001). The Provision of Public Goods under Alternative Electoral Incentives. *American Economic Review*, 91(1), 225–39.

Lizzeri, A. & Persico, N. (2004). Why Did the Elites Extend the Suffrage? Democracy and the Scope of Government, with an Application to Britain's "Age of Reform." *The Quarterly Journal of Economics*, 119(2), 707–65.

Logan, J. (2006). The Union Avoidance Industry in the United States. *British Journal of Industrial Relations*, 44(4), 651–75.

Logan, J. & Molotch, H. (1986). *Urban Fortunes: The Political Economy of Place*, Berkeley: University of California Press.

Logan, J. R. & Rabrenovic, G. (1990). Neighborhood Associations: Their issues, Their Allies, and Their Opponents. *Urban Affairs Review*, 26(1), 68–94.

Lowery, A. (2013). Wealth Gap among Races Has Widened Since Recession. *New York Times*, www.nytimes.com/2013/04/29/business/racial-wealth-gap-widened-during-recession.html (accessed 26 December 2020).

Lund, D. S. (2017). The Case against Passive Shareholder Voting. *Journal of Corporation Law*, 43, 493–536.

Luttig, M. (2013). The Structure of Inequality and Americans' Attitudes toward Redistribution. *Public Opinion Quarterly*, 77(3), 811–21.

MacLean, N. (2017). *Democracy in Chains*, New York: Penguin.

Maestas, N., Mullen, K. J., Powell, D., von Wachter, T. & Wenger, J. B. (2018). The Value of Working Conditions in the United States and Implications for the Structure of Wages. *NBER* Working Paper 25204.

Maliranta, M., Määttänen, N. & Vihriälä, V. (2012). *Are the Nordic Countries Really Less Innovative than the US?* CEPR Policy Portal.

Manduca, R. (2019). Antitrust Enforcement as Federal Policy to Reduce Regional Economic Disparities. *Annals of the American Academy of Political and Social Sciences*, 685(1), 156–71.

Manyika, J., Ramaswamy, S., Bughin, J., Woetzel, J., Birshan, M. & Nagpal, Z. (2018). "Superstars": The Dynamics of Firms, Sectors, and Cities Leading the Global Economy, McKinsey Global Institute (MGI) Discussion Paper.

Marble, W. & Nall, C. (2018). Where Interests Trump Ideology: The Persistent Influence of Homeownership in Local Development Politics. Working Paper. https://williammarble.co/docs/MarbleNallJOP.pdf.

Marinescu, I. & Hovenkamp, H. J. (2019). Anticompetitive Mergers in Labor Markets. *Indiana Law Journal*, 94(3), 1031–63.

Martin, C. J. (1991). *Shifting the Burden: The Struggle over Growth and Corporate Taxation*, Chicago: University of Chicago Press.

Martin, C. J. (2000). *Stuck in Neutral: Business and the Politics of Human Capital Investment Policy*, Princeton, NJ: Princeton University Press.

Martin, C. J. & Swank, D. (2012). *The Political Construction of Business Interests: Coordination, Growth, and Equality*, New York: Cambridge University Press.

Marx, K. (1981) [1867]. *Capital*, Vol. 1, London: Penguin.
Marx, K. (1981) [1894]. *Capital*, Vol. 3, London: Penguin.
Marx, A. (1998). *Making Race and Nation: A Comparison of the United States, South Africa, and Brazil*, New York: Cambridge University Press.
Massey, D. S. (2007). *Categorically Unequal: The American Stratification System*, New York: Russell Sage Foundation.
Massey, D. S. & Denton, N. A. (1993). *American Apartheid: Segregation and the Making of the Underclass*, Cambridge, MA: Harvard University Press.
Massey, D. S., Rugh, J. S., Steil, J. P. & Albright, L. (2016). Riding the Stagecoach to Hell: A Qualitative Analysis of Racial Discrimination in Mortgage Lending. *City and Community*, 15(2), 118–36.
Massoglia, A. (2020). *Trump's Judicial Adviser's "Dark Money" Network Hides Supreme Court Spending*, Center for Responsive Politics.
Mayhew, D. (2005). *Divided We Govern: Party Control, Lawmaking, and Investigations, 1946–2002*, 2nd ed., New Haven, CT: Yale University Press.
Mayhew, D. R. (1974). *Congress: The Electoral Connection*, New Haven, CT: Yale University Press.
Mazzucato, M. (2015). *The Entrepreneurial State: Debunking Public vs. Private Sector Myths*, London, UK: Anthem Press.
McCarthy, M. A. (2017). *Dismantling Solidarity: Capitalist Politics and American Pensions Since the New Deal*, Ithaca, NY: Cornell University Press.
McCarthy, M. A., Sorsa, V.-P. & van der Zwan, N. (2016). Investment Preferences and Patient Capital: Financing, Governance, and Regulation in Pension Fund Capitalism. *Socio-Economic Review*, 14(4), 751–69.
McCartin, J. A. (2008). "A Wagner Act for Public Employees": Labor's Deferred Dream and the Rise of Conservatism, 1970–1976. *Journal of American History*, 95(1), 123–48.
McCarty, N., Poole, K. & Rosenthal, H. (2006). *Polarized America*, Cambridge, MA: MIT Press.
McGuire, T. J. (1991). Federal Aid to States and Localities and the Appropriate Competitive Framework. In Kenyon, D. & Kincaid, J., *Competition among States and Local Governments: Efficiency and Equity in American Federalism*. Washington, DC: Urban Institute Press, pp. 153–166.
McIntosh, K., Moss, E., Nunn, R. & Shaumbaugh, J. (2020). *Examining the Black-White Wealth Gap*, Washington, DC: Brookings Institution Press.
McMahon, W. W. (2002). *Education and Development: Measuring the Social Benefits*, Oxford, UK: Oxford University Press.
McMahon, W. W. (2018). The Total Return to Higher Education: Is There Underinvestment for Economic Growth and Development? *The Quarterly Review of Economics and Finance*, 70, 90–111.
McMichael, S. & Bingham, R. (1923). *City Growth and Values*, Cleveland, OH: The Stanley McMichael Publishing Organization.
McNicholas, C. & Jones, J. (2018). *Black Women Will Be Most Affected by Janus*, Economic Policy Institute.
McCubbins, M. D., Noll, R. G., Weingast, B. R. (1995). Politics and Courts: A Positive Theory of Judicial Doctrine and the Rule of Law. *Southern California Law Review*, 68, 1631–83.

McWilliams, C. (1964). *Brothers under the Skin*, Boston: Little, Brown.

Melnick, R. S. (1983). *Regulation and the Courts: The Case of the Clean Air Act*, Washington, DC: Brookings Institution Press.

Melnick, R. S. (1994). *Between the Lines: Interpreting Welfare Rights*, Washington, DC: Brookings Institution Press.

Mervis, J. (2020). Trump's New Budget Cuts All But a Favored Few Science Programs. *Science Magazine*, www.sciencemag.org/news/2020/02/trump-s-new-budget-cuts-all-favored-few-science-programs (accessed 26 December 2020).

Mettler, S. (2005). *Soldiers to Citizens: The GI Bill and the Making of the Greatest Generation*, New York: Oxford University Press.

Mettler, S. (2010). Reconstituting the Submerged State: The Challenges of Social Policy Reform in the Obama Era. *Perspectives on Politics*, 8(03), 803–24.

Mettler, S. (2011). *The Submerged State: How Invisible Government Policies Undermine American Democracy*, Chicago: University of Chicago Press.

Mettler, S. (2014). *Degrees of Inequality: How the Politics of Higher Education Sabotaged the American Dream*, New York: Basic books.

Mettler, S. (2016). The Policyscape and the Challenges of Contemporary Politics to Policy Maintenance. *Perspectives on Politics*, 14(2), 369–90.

Mettler, S. (2018). *The Government-Citizen Disconnect*, New York: Russell Sage Foundation.

Mettler, S. & SoRelle, M. (2014). Policy Feedback Theory. In Sabatier, P. A. & Weible, C. M., *Theories of the Policy Process*, 3rd ed., New York: Westview Press, pp. 151–181.

Metzger, G. (2017). 1930s Redux: The Administrative State under Siege. *Harvard Law Review*, 131, 1–95.

Meyer, S. G. (2000). *As Long As They Don't Move Next Door: Segregation and Racial Conflict in American Neighborhoods*, Lanham, MD: Rowman & Littlefield.

Michels, R. (1915). *Political Parties: A Sociological Study of the Oligarchical Tendencies of Modern Democracy*. New York: Hearst's International Library Co.

Michener, J. (2019). Policy Feedback in a Racialized Polity. *Policy Studies Journal*, 47(2), 423–50.

Michener, J., SoRelle, M. & Thurston, C. (2020). From Margins to Center: A Bottom-up Approach to Welfare State Scholarship. *Perspectives on Politics*, online version, 1–16.

Mickey, R. (2015). *Paths out of Dixie: The Democratization of Authoritarian Enclaves in America's Deep South, 1944–1972*, Princeton, NJ: Princeton University Press.

Mildenberger, M. (2020). *Carbon Captured: How Business and Labor Control Climate Politics*, Cambridge, MA: MIT Press.

Miller, C. C. & Tankersley, J. (2020). Paid Leave Law Tries to Help Millions in Crisis. Many Haven't Heard of It. *New York Times*, www.nytimes.com/2020/05/08/upshot/virus-paid-leave-pandemic.html (accessed 10 January 2021).

Miller, G. J. (1981). *Cities by Contract: The Politics of Municipal Incorporation*, Cambridge, MA: MIT Press.

Mitchell, D. J. B. & Erickson, C. L. (2005). Not Yet Dead at the Fed: Unions, Worker Bargaining, and Economy-Wide Wage Determination. *Industrial Relations: A Journal of Economy and Society*, 44(4), 565–606.

Molloy, R., Smith, C. L. & Wozniak, A. (2011). Internal Migration in the United States. *Journal of Economic Perspectives*, 25(3), 173–96.

Monkkonen, E. H. (2018). America Becomes Urban: The Development of U.S. Cities and Towns, 1780–1980. *The Annals of Iowa*, 50(4), 428–30.

Monks, R. A. G. & Minow, N. (1995). *Corporate Governance*, Malden, MA: Basil Blackwell.

Montagne, S. (2013). Investing Prudently: How Financialization Puts a Legal Standard to Use. *Sociologie du Travail*, 55(Supplement 1), 48–66.

Mooney, A. & Mancini, D. P. (2020). Drugmakers Urged to Collaborate on Coronavirus Vaccine. *Financial Times*, www.ft.com/content/b452ceb9-765a-4c25-9876-fb73d736f92a (accessed 1 June 2020).

Mooney, A. & Smith, P. (2019). Larry Fink, Barclays and the Deal of the Decade. *Financial Times*, www.ft.com/content/48e703d8-6d87-11e9-80c7-60ee53e6681d (accessed 5 February 2020).

Mooney, C. (2005). *The Republican War on Science*, New York: Basic Books.

Moretti, E. (2004). Estimating the Social Return to Higher Education: Evidence from Longitudinal and Repeated Cross-Sectional Data. *Journal of Econometrics*, 121(1), 175–212.

Moretti, E. (2012). *The New Geography of Jobs*, New York: Houghton Mifflin Harcourt.

Morgan, J. (2011). *Bankrupt Representation and Party System Collapse*, University Park: Penn State University Press.

Morgan, K. J. & Campbell, A. L. (2011). *The Delegated Welfare State: Medicare, Markets, and the Governance of Social Policy*, New York: Oxford University Press.

Morris, P. R. (1994). *The Growth and Decline of the Semiconductor Industry within the U.K. 1950–1985*. The Open University PhD thesis.

Muñoz, A. P., Kim, M., Chang, M. et al. (2015). *The Color of Wealth in Boston*, Federal Reserve Bank of Boston.

Muro, M., Duke, E. B., You, Y. & Maxim, R. (2020). *Biden-Voting Counties Equal 70% of America's Economy. What Does This Mean for the Nation's Political Divide?* Washington, DC: Brookings Institution Press.

Murray, J. & Schwartz, M. (2019). *Wrecked: How the American Automobile Industry Destroyed Its Capacity to Compete*, New York: Russell Sage Foundation.

Muth, R. F. (1969). *Cities and Housing: the Spatial Pattern of Urban Residential Land Use*, Chicago: University of Chicago Press.

Mutz, D. C. (2018). Status Threat, Not Economic Hardship, Explains the 2016 Presidential Vote. *Proceedings of the National Academy of Sciences of the United States*, 115(19), E4330–E9.

Myrdal, G. (1944). *An American Dilemma: The Negro Problem and Modern Democracy*, New York: Harper and Brothers Publishers.

Naczyk, M. (2013). Agents of Privatization? Business Groups and the Rise of Pension Funds in Continental Europe. *Socio-Economic Review*, 11(3), 441–69.

Naczyk, M. (2018). When Finance Captures Labor's Capital: Dominant Personal Pensions, Resurgent Occupational Provision in Central and Eastern Europe. *Social Policy & Administration*, 52(2), 549–62.

Naidu, S. (2018). A Political Economy Take on W/Y. In Boushey, H., DeLong, J. B. & Steinbaum, M., eds., *After Piketty*. Cambridge, MA: Harvard University Press, 99–125.

Naidu, S. & Yuchtman, N. (2018). Labor Market Institutions in the Gilded Age of American Economic History. In Cain, L. P., Fishback, P. V. & Rhode, P. W., eds., *The Oxford Handbook of American Economic History*, Vol. I. Oxford, UK: Oxford University Press, pp. 329–54.

Naidu, S., Posner, E. A. & Weyl, E. G. (2018). Antitrust Remedies for Labor Market Power. *Harvard Law Review*, 132, 536–601.

Naidu, S., Nyarko, Y. & Wang, S-Y. (2016). Monopsony power in migrant labor markets: evidence from the United Arab Emirates. *Journal of Political Economy*, 124(6), 1735–92.

Nall, C. (2018). *The Road to Inequality: How the Federal Highway Program Created Suburbs, Undermined Cities, and Polarized America*, New York: Cambridge University Press.

Nall, C. & Marble, W. (2020). Where Self-Interest Trumps Ideology: Liberal Homeowners and Local Opposition to Housing Development. *Journal of Politics*. https://doi.org/10.1086/711717.

Newfield, C. (2008). *Unmaking the Public University: The Forty-Year Assault on the Middle Class*, Cambridge, MA: Harvard University Press.

Nichols, J. B., Oliner, S. & Mulhall, M. (2013). Swings in Commercial and Residential Land Prices in the United States. *Journal of Urban Economics*, 73 (1), 57–76.

Nightingale, C. (2006). The Transnational Contexts of Early Twentieth-Century American Urban Segregation. *Journal of Social History*, 39(3), 667–702.

Nightingale, C. H. (2012). *Segregation: A Global History of Divided Cities*, Chicago: The University of Chicago Press.

Novak, W. J. (1996). *The People's Welfare: Law and Regulation in Nineteenth-Century America*, Chapel Hill: University of North Carolina Press.

Novak, W. J. (2008). The Myth of the "Weak" American State. *The American Historical Review*, 113(3), 752–72.

NRA (2020). *Association Statement on Centers for Disease Control Study*, Washington, DC: National Restaurant Association Statement.

NSF (2007). *Survey of Industrial Research and Development*. Alexandria, VA: National Science Foundation.

NSF (2020). *Federal Funds for R&D*. Alexandria, VA: National Science Foundation.

Nunn, R., Parsons, J. & Schambaugh, J. (2018). *The Geography of Prosperity*. Washington, DC: Hamilton Project.

Oatley, T. & Petrova, B. (2020). The Global Deregulation Hypothesis. *Socio-Economic Review*, OnlineFirst.

O'Connell, J., Van Dam, A., Gregg, A. & Fowers, A. (2020). More than Half of Emergency Small-Business Funds Went to Larger Businesses, New Data Shows. *Washington Post*, www.washingtonpost.com/business/2020/12/01/ppp-sba-data/ (accessed 10 January 2021).

OECD (1994). *Collective Bargaining: Levels and Coverage*, Paris: OECD Employment Outlook.

OECD. (2007). Political Advisors and Civil Servants in European Countries. *SIGMA Papers*, No. 38.

OECD (2015). *In It Together: Why Less Inequality Benefits All*, Paris: OECD.

OECD (2016a). *Fiscal Federalism 2016: Making Decentralisation Work*, Paris: OECD.

OECD (2016b). *Subnational Governments around the World Country Profiles: The United States*, Paris: OECD.

OECD (2017). *Hearing on Common Ownership by Institutional Investors and Its Impact on Competition: Summaries of Contributions*, Paris: OECD.

OECD (2018). *Education at a Glance 2018*, Paris: OECD.

OECD (2019a). *Decentralisation in the Health Sector and Responsibilities across Levels of Government*, Paris: OECD.

OECD (2019b). *Main Science and Technology Indicators*, Paris: OECD.

OECD (2020a). *Educational Finance Indicators – EAG 2020*, Paris: OECD.

OECD (2020b). *Gross Domestic Expenditure on R&D by Sector of Performance and Source of Funds*, Paris: OECD.

OECD (2020c). *Gross Domestic Product (GDP)*, Paris: OECD.

Offe, C. & Wiesenthal, H. (1980). Two Logics of Collective Action: Theoretical Notes on Social Class and Organizational Form. *Political Power and Social Theory*, 1(1), 67–115.

Ogorzalek, T. (2018). *The Cities on the Hill: How Urban Institutions Transformed National Politics*, New York: Oxford University Press.

Oliver, J. E. & Ha, S. (2007). Vote Choice in Suburban Elections. *American Political Science Review*, 101(3), 393–408

Oliver, M. L. &. Shapiro, T. M. (1995). *Black Wealth/White Wealth: A New Perspective on Racial Inequality*, New York: Routledge.

Olson, M. (1965). *The Logic of Collective Action: Public Goods and the Theory of Groups*, Cambridge, MA: Harvard University Press.

Orren, K. (1991). *Belated Feudalism: The Workplace in America*, New York: Cambridge University Press.

OSHA (n.d.). *Infectious Diseases Rulemaking*, Occupational Safety and Health Administration.

O'Sullivan, M. (2006). Funding New Industries: A Historical Perspective on the Financing Role of the U.S. Stock Market in the Twentieth Century. In Lamoreaux, N. R. & Sokoloff, K. L., eds., *Financing Innovation in the United States, 1871 to the Present*. Cambridge, MA: MIT Press, pp. 163–216.

Ott, J. C. (2011). *When Wall Street Met Main Street*, Cambridge, MA: Harvard University Press.

Owens, M. L. (2007). *God and Government in the Ghetto: The Politics of Church-State Collaboration in Black America*, Chicago: University of Chicago Press.

Pachirat, T. (2011). *Every Twelve Seconds: Industrialized Slaughter and The Politics of Sight*, New Haven, CT: Yale University Press.

Page, B. I., Seawright, J. & Lacombe, M. J. (2018). *Billionaires and Stealth Politics*, Chicago: University of Chicago Press.

Pager, D. (2003). The Mark of a Criminal Record. *American Journal of Sociology*, 108(5), 937–75.

Pager, D. & Shepherd, H. (2008). The Sociology of Discrimination: Racial Discrimination in Employment, Housing, Credit, and Consumer Markets. *Annual Review of Sociology*, 34(1), 181–209.

Paglayan, A. (2019). Public-Sector Unions and the Size of Government. *American Journal of Political Science*, 63(1), 21–36.

Paik, A., Heinz, J. P. & Southworth, A. (2011). Political Lawyers: The Structure of a National Network. *Law & Social Inquiry*, 36(4), 892–918.

Palladino, L. (2019). Worker Representation on U.S. Corporate Boards, https://ssrn.com/abstract=3476669.

Parilla, J. & Bouchet, M. (2018). *Which US Communities Are Most Affected by Chinese, EU, and NAFTA Retaliatory Tariffs?* Washington, DC: Brookings Institution Press.

Parker, K., Minkin, R. & Bennet, J. (2020). *Economic Fallout from COVID-19 Continues to Hit Lower-Income Americans the Hardest*, Washington, DC: Pew Research Center.

Paul, S. (2020). Antitrust as Allocator of Coordination Rights. *UCLA Law Review*, 67(2), 1–64.

Peinert, E. (2020). Cartels, Competition, and Coalitions: The Domestic Drivers of International Orders. *Review of International Political Economy*, 1–25.

Pendall, R., Puentes, R. & Martin, J. (2006). *From Traditional to Reformed: A Review of the Land Use Regulations in the Nation's 50 Largest Metropolitan Areas*, Washington, DC: Brookings Institution Press.

Percheski, C. & Gibson-Davis, C. (2020). A Penny on the Dollar: Racial Inequalities in Wealth among Households with Children. *Socius: Sociological Research for a Dynamic World*, 6, 1–17.

Perez, C. (2010). Technological Revolutions and Techno-Economic Paradigms. *Cambridge Journal of Economics*, 34(1), 185–202.

Perry, A. M. (2020). *Know Your Price: Valuing Black Lives and Property in America's Black Cities*, Washington, DC: Brookings Institution Press.

Perry, A., Rothwell, J. & Harshbarger, D. (2018). *The Devaluation of Assets in Black Neighborhoods: The Case of Residential Property*, Washington, DC: Brookings Institution Press.

Persson, T. & Tabellini, G. (2000). *Political Economics*, Cambridge MA: MIT Press.

Persson, T., Roland, G. & Tabellini, G. (2000). Comparative Politics and Public Finance. *Journal of Political Economy*, 108(6), 1121–61.

Peterson, M. (2020). What the FDA and Pfizer Need from Each Other. *Barrons*. December 10, 2020. www.barrons.com/articles/what-the-fda-and-pfizer-need-from-each-other-51607607804.

Peterson, P. E. (1981). *City Limits*, Chicago: University of Chicago Press.

Peterson, P. E. (1995). *The Price of Federalism*, Washington, DC: Brookings Institution Press.

Petry, J. (2020). From National Marketplaces to Global Providers of Financial Infrastructures: Exchanges, Infrastructures and Structural Power in Global Finance. *New Political Economy*, 1–24.

Petry, J., Fichtner, J. & Heemskerk, E. (2019). Steering Capital: The Growing Private Authority of Index Providers in the Age of Passive Asset Management. *Review of International Political Economy*, 1–25.

Pettersson, T., Högbladh, S. & Öberg, M. (2019). Organized Violence, 1989–2018 and Peace Agreements. *Journal of Peace Research*, 56(4), 589–603.

Pettit, P. (2014). *Just Freedom: A Moral Compass for a Complex World*, New York: WW Norton & Company.

Pfaff, J. (2017). *Locked In: The True Causes of Mass Incarceration – and How to Achieve Real Reform*, New York: Basic Books.

Pfeffer, F. & Waitkus, N. (2020). Wealth Inequality of Nations. *LWS* Working Paper 33.

Philippon, T. (2019). *The Great Reversal: How America Gave Up on Free Markets*, Cambridge, MA: Harvard University Press.

Phillips, M. (2020). Investors Bet Giant Companies Will Dominate After Crisis. *New York Times*, www.nytimes.com/2020/04/28/business/coronavirus-stocks.html?referringSource=articleShare (accessed 10 January 2021).

Phillips-Fein, K. (2017). *Fear City: New York's Fiscal Crisis and the Rise of Austerity Politics*, 1st ed., New York: Metropolitan Books.

Piaker, Z. (2016). *Help Wanted: 4,000 Presidential Appointees*, Washington, DC: Partnership for Public Service Center for Presidential Transition.

Pierce, L., Snow, D. C. & McAfee, A. (2015). Cleaning House: The Impact of Information Technology Monitoring on Employee Theft and Productivity. *Management Science*, 61(10), 2299–320.

Pierson, P. & Schickler, E. (2020). Madison's Constitution under Stress: A Developmental Analysis of Political Polarization. *Annual Review of Political Science*, 23, 37–58.

Pierson, K., Hand, M. & Thompson, F. (2015). The Government Financial Database: A Common Resource for Quantitative Research in Public Financial Analysis. *PLoS ONE*, 10(6), 1–22.

Piketty, T. (2014). *Capital in the Twenty-First Century*, Cambridge, MA: Harvard University Press.

Piketty, T. & Saez, E. (2003). Income Inequality in the United States, 1913–1998. *The Quarterly Journal of Economics*, 118(1), 1–41.

Pinderhughes, D. (1987). *Race and Ethnicity in Chicago Politics: A Reexamination of Pluralist Theory*, Champaign: University of Illinois Press.

Piore, M. & Sabel, C. (1984). *The Second Industrial Divide: Possibilities for Prosperity*, New York: Basic Books.

Pistor, K. (2019). *The Code of Capital: How the Law Creates Wealth and Inequality*, Princeton, NJ: Princeton University Press.

Pollman, E. & Barry, J. M. (2017). Regulatory Entrepreneurship. *Southern Carolina Law Review*, 90, 383–448.

Pontusson, J. (2005). *Inequality and Prosperity: Social Europe vs. Liberal America*. Ithaca, NY: Cornell University Press.

Pope, J. G. (2004). How American Workers Lost the Right to Strike, and Other Tales. *University of Michigan Law Review*, 10(3), 518–53.

Posen, A. S. (1993). Why Central Bank Independence Does Not Cause Low Inflation: There Is No Institutional Fix for Politics. In O'Brien, R., ed., *Finance and the International Economy: 7, The AMEX Bank Review Prize Essays*. Oxford, UK: Oxford University Press, pp. 41–65.

Posey, P. (2019). Refinancing the American Dream: The Consequences of Targeted Financial Policy for Political and Racial Inequality in the United States, University of Pennsylvania, PhD dissertation.

Posner, E. A., Scott Morton, F. M. & Weyl, E. G. (2017). A Proposal to Limit the Anti-Competitive Power of Institutional Investors. *Antitrust Law Journal*, 81 (3), 669–728.

Poterba, J. M. & Shoven, J. B. (2002). Exchange-Traded Funds: A New Investment Option for Taxable Investors. *American Economic Review*, 92(2), 422–27.

Powell, R. J., Clark, J. T. & Dube, M. P. (2020). Partisan Gerrymandering, Clustering, or Both? A New Approach to a Persistent Question. *Election Law Journal*, 19(1), 79–100.

Prager, E. & Schmitt, M. (2021). Employer Consolidation and Wages: Evidence from Hospitals. *American Economic Review*, 111(2), 397–427.

Prasad, M. (2006). *The Politics of Free Markets: The Rise of Neoliberal Economic Policies in Britain, France, Germany, and the United States*, Chicago: University of Chicago Press.

Prasad, M. (2012). *The Land of Too Much: American Abundance and the Paradox of Poverty*, Cambridge, MA: Harvard University Press.

Press, E. (2020). Trump's Labor Secretary is a Wrecking Ball Aimed at Workers. *New Yorker*, www.newyorker.com/magazine/2020/10/26/trumps-labor-secretary-is-a-wrecking-ball-aimed-at-workers (accessed 10 January 2021).

Prison Policy Initiative (n.d.). *Data toolbox*.

Public Citizen (2008). *US Chamber of Commerce Attacks Arbitration Fairness Act, Surprised?* Public Citizen. www.citizen.org/news/u-s-chamber-of/.

Purdy, J. (2014). Neoliberal Constitutionalism: Lochnerism for a New Economy. *Law and Contemporary Problems*, 77, 195–213.

Purdy, J. (2018). Beyond the Boss' Constitution: The First Amendment and Class Entrenchment. *Columbia Law Review*, 118(7), 2161–86.

Pusser, B. & Wolcott, D. A. (2006). A Crowded Lobby: Nonprofit and For-Profit Universities and the Emerging Politics of Higher Education. In Breneman, D. W., Pusser, B. & Turner, S. E., *Earnings from Learning: The Rise of For-Profit Universities*. Albany: State University of New York Press, pp. 167–94.

Quick, K. & Kahlenberg, R. (2019). *Attacking the Black-White Opportunity Gap That Comes from Residential Segregation*, New York: The Century Foundation.

Quinn, K. M. (2004). Bayesian Factor Analysis for Mixed Ordinal and Continuous Responses. *Political Analysis*, 12(4), 338–53.

Quinn, S. L. (2019). *American Bonds: How Credit Markets Shaped a Nation*, Princeton, NJ: Princeton University Press.

Rabe, B. G. (1999). Federalism and Entrepreneurship: Explaining American and Canadian Innovation in Pollution Prevention and Regulatory Integration. *Policy Studies Journal*, 27(20), 288–306.

Rae, D. W. (2003). *City: Urbanism and Its End*, New Haven, CT: Yale University Press.

Raff, D. M. G. & Summers, L. H. (1987). Did Henry Ford Pay Efficiency Wages? *Journal of Labor Economics*, 5(4), S57–S86.

Rahman, K. S. & Thelen, K. (2019). The Rise of the Platform Business Model and the Transformation of Twenty-First-Century Capitalism. *Politics and Society*, 47(2), 177–204.

Rainwater, B. (2020). States Are Abusing Preemption Powers in the Midst of a Pandemic. *Bloomberg CityLab*, www.bloomberg.com/news/articles/2020-07-01/how-states-co-opted-local-power-during-coronavirus (accessed 10 January 2021).

Ranney, M., Griffeth, V. & Jha, A. (2020). Critical Supply Shortages: The Need for Ventilators and Personal Protective Equipment during the Covid-19 Pandemic. *New England Journal of Medicine*, 382, e41.

Rappaport, J. (2005). *The Shared Fortunes of Cities and Suburbs*, Federal Reserve Bank of Kansas City.

Ratliff, K. A., Redford, L., Conway, J. & Smith, C. T. (2019). Engendering Support: Hostile Sexism Predicts Voting for Donald Trump over Hillary Clinton in the 2016 U.S. Presidential Election. *Group Processes & Intergroup Relations*, 22(4), 578–93.

Reardon, S. F. & Firebaugh, G. (2002). Measures of Multigroup Segregation. *Sociological Methodology*, 32(1), 33–67.

Rebitzer, J. B. & Taylor, L. J. (1993). Incentive Structures and Market Outcomes: The Case of Law Firms, *Proceedings of the Forty-Fifth Annual Meeting of the Industrial Relations Research Association Series*, 32–41.

Reich, A. & Bearman, P. (2018). *Working for Respect: Community and Conflict at Walmart*, New York: Columbia University Press.

Reich, A. & Prins, S. (2020). The Disciplining Effect of Mass Incarceration on Labor Organization. *American Journal of Sociology*, 125(5), 1303–44.

Reisenbichler, A. & Morgan, K. J. (2012). From "Sick Man" to "Miracle": Explaining the Robustness of the German Labor Market during and after the Financial Crisis 2008–09. *Politics & Society*, 40(4), 549–79.

Reynolds, L. G. (1946). The Supply of Labor to the Firm. *The Quarterly Journal of Economics*, 60(3), 390–411.

Rhee, N. (2013). *Race and Retirement Insecurity in the United States*, Washington, DC: National Institute on Retirement Security.

Rhode, P. W. & Strumpf, K. S. (2003). Assessing the Importance of Tiebout Sorting: Local Heterogeneity from 1850 to 1990. *American Economic Review*, 93(5), 1648–77.

Riding, S. (2020). Trillion-Dollar Club Tightens Grip on Fund Market during Crisis. *Financial Times*, www.ft.com/content/a6aa1010-3dff-4521-af52-fbadb496c89d (accessed 14 May 2020).

Ringe, W.-G. (2016). *The Deconstruction of Equity: Activist Shareholders, Decoupled Risk, and Corporate Governance*, Oxford, UK: Oxford University Press.

Rinz, K. (2018). Labor Market Concentration, Earnings Inequality, and Earnings Mobility, United States Census Bureau Working Paper.

Roback, J. (1982). Wages, Rents, and the Quality of Life. *Journal of Political Economy*, 90(6), 1257–78.

Robertson, D. B. (2018). *Federalism and the Making of America*, New York: Routledge Press.

Robinson, J. (1969). *The Economics of Imperfect Competition*, New York: Springer.

Rocco, P. (2017). Informal Caregiving and the Politics of Policy Drift. *Journal of Aging and Social Policy*, 29(5), 413–32.

Rodden, J. (2018). *Keeping Your Enemies Close: Electoral Rules and Partisan Polarization*, Cambridge, MA: Harvard Center for European Studies.

Rodden, J. (2019). *Why Cities Lose: Political Geography and the Representation of the Left*, New York: Basic Books.

Roe, M. J. (1994). *Strong Managers, Weak Owners: The Political Roots of American Corporate Finance*, Princeton, NJ: Princeton University Press.

Rogers, S. (2017). Electoral Accountability for State Legislative Roll Calls and Ideological Representation. *American Political Science Review*, 111(3), 555–71.

Rolf, D. (2016). *The Fight for Fifteen: The Right Wage for a Working America*, New York: The New Press.

Rosen, S. (1974). Hedonic prices and implicit markets: product differentiation in pure competition. *Journal of Political Economy*, 82(1), 34–55.

Rosenberg, N. (1991). Young Mr. Lincoln: The Lawyer as Super-Hero. *Legal Studies Forum*, 15(3), 215–32.

Rosenblum, J. (2017). Fight for $15: Good Wins, but Where Did the Focus on Organizing Go? *Labor Studies Journal*, 42(4), 387–93.

Rosenfeld, J. (2014). *What Unions No Longer Do*, Cambridge, MA: Harvard University Press.

Rosenthal, A. (2020a). Investment and Invisibility. *Du Bois Review*, 16(2), 511–33.

Rosenthal, A. (2020b). Submerged for Some? Government Visibility, Race, and American Political Trust. *Perspectives on Politics*, First View, 1–17.

Ross, A. M. (1958). Do We Have a New Industrial Feudalism? *The American Economic Review*, 48(5), 903–20.

Rothstein, R. (2017). *The Color of Law: A Forgotten History of How our Government Segregated America*, New York: Norton.

Royal Society (2019). *Investing in UK R&D*.

Rozell, M. J. & Wilcox, C. (2020). Federalism in a Time of Plague: How Federal Systems Cope with Pandemic. *American Review of Public Administration*, 50 (6–7), 519–25.

Rueda, D. & Stegmueller, D. (2020). *Who Wants What? Redistributive Preferences in Comparative Perspectives*. Cambridge, UK: Cambridge University Press.

Ruffini, P. (2018). Far from Settled: Varied and Changing Attitudes on Immigration in America, Voter Study Group.

Rugh, J. S. (2020). Why Black and Latino Home Ownership Matter to the Color Line and Multiracial Democracy. *Race and Social Problems*, 12(1), 57–76.

Ruiz, R., Gebeloff, R., Eder, S. & Protess, B. (2020). A Conservative Agenda Unleashed on the Federal Courts. *New York Times*, www.nytimes.com/2020/03/14/us/trump-appeals-court-judges.html (accessed 27 December 2020).

Salter, M. (2012). How Short-Termism Invites Corruption … and What to Do about It. *Harvard Business School* Research Paper No. 12-094.

Sampson, R. J. (2011). *Great American City: Chicago and the Enduring Neighborhood Effect*, Chicago: The University of Chicago Press.

Sampson, R. J., Morenoff, J. D. & Gannon-Rowley, T. (2002). Assessing "Neighborhood Effects": Social Processes and New Directions in Research. *Annual Review of Sociology*, 28(1), 443–78.

Sanders, E. (1999). *Roots of Reform: Farmers, Workers, and the American State, 1877–1917*, Chicago: University of Chicago Press.

Sassen, S. (2001). *The Global City*, Princeton, NJ: Princeton University Press.

Savit, E. (2017). The New Front in the Clean Air Wars: Fossil-Fuel Influence over State Attorneys General – and How It Might be Checked. *Michigan Law Review*, 115(6), 839–64.

Savitch, H. V. & Kantor, P. (2002). *Cities in the International Marketplace: The Political Economy of Urban Development in North America and Western Europe*, Princeton, NJ: Princeton University Press.

Sawyer, W. & Wagner, P. (2020). *Mass Incarceration: The Whole Pie 2020*, Easthampton, MA: Prison Policy Institute.

Saxenian, A. (1996). Inside-Out: Regional Networks and Industrial Adaptation in Silicon Valley and Route 128. *Cityscape*, 2(2), 41–46.

Scharpf, F. W. (1999). *Governing in Europe: Effective and Democratic?* Oxford, UK: Oxford University Press.

Scharpf, F. W. (2010). *Community and Autonomy: Institutions, Policies and Legitimacy in Multilevel Europe*, Chicago: University of Chicago Press.

Scharpf, F. W. (2017). De-constituitonalization and Majority Rule: A Democratic Vision for Europe. *European Law Journal*, 23(5), 315–34.

Schattschneider, E. E. (1960). *The Semi-Sovereign People: A Realist's View of Democracy in America*, New York: Holt, Rinehart and Winston.

Schickler, E. (2016). *Racial Realignment: The Transformation of American Liberalism, 1932–1965*, Princeton, NJ: Princeton University Press.

Schickler, E. & Caughey, D. (2011). Public Opinion, Organized Labor, and the Limits of New Deal Liberalism, 1936–1945. *Studies in American Political Development*, 25(2), 162–89.

Schlozman, D. S. (2015). *When Movements Anchor Parties: Electoral Alignments in American History*, Princeton, NJ: Princeton University Press.

Schlozman, K. L., Verba, S. & Brady, H. E. (2012). *The Unheavenly Chorus*, Princeton, NJ: Princeton University Press.

Schmidt, S. (2018). *The European Court of Justice and the Policy Process*, Oxford, UK: Oxford University Press.

Schoch, F. (2018). Polizei- und Ordnungsrecht. In Schoch, F., ed., *Besonderes Verwaltungsrecht*. München: C. H. Beck, pp. 127–300.

Schragger, R. (2009). Mobile Capital, Local Economic Regulation, and the Democratic City. *Harvard Law Review*, 123(2), 482–540.

Schragger, R. (2016). *City Power: Urban Governance in a Global Age*, New York: Oxford University Press.

Schuman, H., Steeh, C. & Bobo, L. 1985. *Racial attitudes in America: Trends and interpretations*, Cambridge, MA: Harvard University Press.

Schumpeter, J. A. (1942). *Capitalism, Socialism and Democracy*, New York: Harper.

Schwartz, H. (2007). Dependency or Institutions? Economic Geography, Causal Mechanisms, and Logic in the Understanding of Development. *Studies in Comparative International Development*, 42(1–2), 115–35.

Schwartz, H. (2016). Wealth and Secular Stagnation: The Role of Industrial Organization and Intellectual Property Rights. *Russell Sage Foundation Journal*, 2(6), 226–49.

Schwartz, H. (2017). Club Goods, Intellectual Property Rights, and Profitability in the Information Economy. *Business and Politics*, 19(2), 191–214.

Schwartz, H. (2019). American Hegemony: Intellectual Property Rights, Dollar Centrality, and Infrastructural Power. *Review of International Political Economy*, 26(3), 490–519.

Seamster, L. & Charron-Chénier, R. (2017). Predatory Inclusion and Education Debt: Rethinking the Racial Wealth Gap. *Social Currents*, 4(3), 199–207.

SEC (2019). *Release No. 33-10695 on Exchange-Traded Funds*, New York: Securities and Exchange Commission.

Seibel, W. (2017). *Verwaltung verstehen. Eine theoriegeschichtliche Einführung*, 3rd ed., Berlin: Suhrkamp.

Self, R. O. (2003). *American Babylon: Race and the Struggle for Postwar Oakland*, Princeton, NJ: Princeton University Press.

Sell, S. (2003). *Private Power, Public Law: The Globalization of Intellectual Property Rights*, Cambridge, UK: Cambridge University Press.

Sessa-Hawkins, M. & Perez, A. (2017). White House Relied upon Dark Money Lobbyist to "Quarterback" Gorsuch Confirmation. *Dark Money Watch*, www.darkmoneywatch.org/tag/supreme-court/ (accessed 7 January 2021).

Servon, L. (2017). *The Unbanking of America: How the New Middle Class Survives*, New York: Mariner Books.

Shah, N. (2001). *Contagious Divides: Epidemics and Race in San Francisco's Chinatown*, Berkeley: University of California Press.

Shapiro, C. (2001). Navigating The Patent Thicket: Cross Licenses, Patent Pools, and Standard Setting. In Jaffe, A., Lerner, J. & Stern, S., eds., *Innovation Policy and the Economy*. Cambridge, MA: MIT Press, pp. 119–50.

Shapiro, T. (2017). *Toxic Inequality: How America's Wealth Gap Destroys Mobility, Deepens the Racial Divide, and Threatens Our Future*, New York: Basic Books.

Shapiro, T., Meschede, T. & Osoro, S. (2013). *The Roots of the Widening Racial Wealth Gap: Explaining the Black-White Economic Divide*, Waltham, MA: Institute on Assets and Social Policy.

Shelton, J. (2017). *Teacher Strike!: Public Education and the Making of a New American Political Order*, Champaign: University of Illinois Press.

Shertzer, A., Twinam, T. & Walsh, R. (2016). Race, Ethnicity, and Discriminatory Zoning. *American Economic Journal: Applied Economics*, 8(3), 217–46.

Shertzer, A., Twinam, T. & Walsh, R. (2018). Zoning and the Economic Geography of Cities. *Journal of Urban Economics*, 105, 20–39.

Shonfield, A. (1965). *Modern Capitalism: The Changing Balance of Public and Private Power*, New York: Oxford University Press.

Shugerman, J. H. (2012). *The People's Courts: Pursuing Judicial Independence in America*, Cambridge, MA: Harvard University Press.

Sides, J., Tesler, M. & Vavrick, L. (2018). *Identity Crisis: The 2016 Presidential Campaign and the Battle for the Meaning of America*, Princeton, NJ: Princeton University Press.

Skocpol, T. (2013). *Naming the Problem: What It Will Take to Counter Extremism and Engage Americans in the Fight against Global Warming*, Prepared for the Symposium on The Politics of America's Fight against

Global Warming, Columbia School of Journalism and the Scholars Strategy Network.

Skocpol, T. & Hertel-Fernandez, A. (2016). The Koch Network and Republican Party Extremism. *Perspectives on Politics*, 14(3), 681–99.

Skocpol, T. & Williamson, V. (2012). *The Tea Party and the Remaking of Republican Conservatism*, New York: Oxford University Press.

Skocpol, T., Ganz, M. & Munson, Z. (2000). A Nation of Organizers: The Institutional Origins of Civic Voluntarism in the United States. *American Political Science Review*, 94(3), 527–46.

Skowronek, S. (1982). *Building a New American State*, New York: Cambridge University Press.

Smith, C. (2013). *City Water, City Life: Water and the Infrastructure of Ideas in Urbanizing Philadelphia, Boston, and Chicago*, Chicago: University of Chicago Press.

Smith, E. & Reeves, R. V. (2020). *Students of Color Most Likely to Be Learning Online: Districts Must Work Even Harder on Race Equity*, Washington, DC: Brookings Institution Press.

Smith, M. (2000). *American Business and Political Power: Public Opinion, Elections, and Democracy*, Chicago: University of Chicago Press.

Song, J., Price, D. J., Guvenen, F., Bloom, N. & Von Wachter, T. (2019). Firming up Inequality. *The Quarterly Journal of Economics*, 134(1), 1–50.

SoRelle, M. (2020). *Democracy Declined: The Failed Politics of Consumer Financial Protection*, Chicago: University of Chicago Press.

Soroka, S., Wright, M., Johnston, R. et al. (2017). Ethnoreligious Identity, Immigration, and Redistribution. *Journal of Experimental Political Science*, 4 (3), 173–82.

Soroka, S. N. & Wlezien, C. (2008). On the Limits of Inequality in Representation. *PS: Political Science and Politics*, 41(2), 319–327.

Soskice, D. (2010). American Exceptionalism and Comparative Political Economy. In Brown, C., Eichengreen, B. J. & Reich, M., eds., *Labor in the Era of Globalization*. New York: Cambridge University Press, pp. 51–93.

Soss, J. & Weaver, V. (2017). Police Are Our Government: Politics, Political Science, and the Policing of Race–Class Subjugated Communities. *Annual Review of Political Science*, 20(1), 565–91.

Soule, S. A. (1997). The Student Divestment Movement in the United States and Tactical Diffusion: The Shantytown Protest. *Social Forces*, 75(3), 855–82.

South, S. J. & Crowder, K. D. (1997). Escaping Distressed Neighborhoods: Individual, Community, and Metropolitan Influences. *American Journal of Sociology*, 102(4), 1040–84.

Spence, L. (2015). *Knocking the Hustle: Against the Neoliberal Turn in Black Politics*, New York: Punctum Books.

Srnicek, Nick. (2017). *Platform Capitalism*, Cambridge, UK: Polity.

Stansbury, A. & Summers, L. H. (2020). Declining Worker Power and American Economic Performance, Brookings Papers on Economic Activity.

Staszak, S. (2015). *No Day in Court: Access to Justice and The Politics of Judicial Retrenchment*, New York: Oxford University Press.

Stein, J. & Whoriskey, P. (2020). The U.S. Plans to Lend $500 Billion to Large Companies. It Won't Require Them to Preserve Jobs or Limit Executive pay. *Washington Post*, www.washingtonpost.com/business/2020/04/28/federal-reserve-bond-corporations/ (accessed 10 January 2021).

Steinbaum, M. (2021). Common Ownership and the Corporate Governance Channel for Employer Power in Labor Markets. The *Antitrust Bulletin*. 66(1), 123–39. doi: https://doi.org/10.1177/0003603X20985801.

Stepan, A. & Linz, J. J. (2011). Review: Comparative Perspectives on Inequality and the Quality of Democracy in the United States. *Perspectives on Politics*, 9 (4), 841–56.

Stewart, N. & Gelles, D. (2019). The $238 Million Penthouse, and the Hedge Fund Billionaire Who May Rarely Live There. *New York Times*, www.nytimes.com/2019/01/24/nyregion/238-million-penthouse-sale.html (accessed 27 December 2020).

Stokes, L. (2020). *Short Circuiting Policy: Interest Groups and the Battle Over Clean Energy and Climate Policy in the American States*, New York: Oxford University Press.

Stone, C. (1989). *Regime Politics: Governing Atlanta, 1946–1988*, Lawrence: University Press of Kansas.

Storper, M. (2013). *Keys to the City: How Economics, Institutions, Social Interaction, and Politics Shape Development*, Princeton, NJ: Princeton University Press.

Stout, L. A. (2012). *The Shareholder Value Myth: How Putting Shareholders First Harms Investors, Corporations, and The Public*, San Francisco: Berrett-Koehler Publishers.

Streeck, W. (1997). Beneficial Constraints: On the Economic Limits of Rational Voluntarism. In J. Hollingsworth, & Boyer, R., eds., *Contemporary Capitalism: The Embeddedness of Institutions*. New York: Cambridge University Press, pp. 197–219.

Streeck, W. (2014). *Buying Time: The Delayed Crisis of Democratic Capitalism*, London: Verso Books.

Strine Jr.,L. E. (2007). Toward Common Sense and Common GroundRreflections on the Shared Interests of Managers and Labor in a More Rational System of Corporate Governance. *The Journal of Corporation Law*, 33(1), 1–20.

Strolovitch, D. Z. (2007). *Affirmative Advocacy: Race, Class, and Gender in Interest Group Politics*, Princeton, NJ: Princeton University Press.

Suárez, S. & Kolodny, R. (2011). Paving the Road to "Too Big to Fail": Business Interests and the Politics of Financial Deregulation in the United States. *Politics & Society*, 39, 74–102.

Sugrue, T. (1996). *The Origins of the Urban Crisis: Race and Inequality in Postwar Detroit*, Princeton, NJ: Princeton University Press.

Sullivan, L., Meschede, T., Dietrich, L. & Shapiro, T. (2015). *The Racial Wealth Gap: Why Policy Matters*, Demos.

Surgey, N. (2020). New Filing Shows Massive Dark Money Support from Judicial Crisis Network to Republican Attorneys General Association, Documented.

Swank, D. (1992). Politics and the Structural Dependence of the State in Democratic Capitalist Nations. *American Political Science Review*, 86, 38–54.

Swank, D. (2002). *Global Capital, Political Institutions, and Policy Change in Developed Welfare States*, New York: Cambridge University Press.

Swenson, P. (2002). *Capitalists against Markets: The Making of Labor Markets and Welfare States in the United States and Sweden*, New York: Oxford University Press.

Tavits, M. & Potter, J. (2014). The Effect of Inequality and Social Identity on Party Strategy. *American Journal of Political Science*, 59(3), 744–58.

Tax Policy Center (2020). *Briefing Book*. Washington, DC: Tax Policy Center, Urban Institute and Brookings Institution Press.

Taylor, B. J., Cantwell, B., Watts, K. & Wood, O. (2020). Partisanship, White Racial Resentment, and State Support for Higher Education. *The Journal of Higher Education*, 91(6), 858–887.

Taylor, K.-Y. (2019). *Race for Profit: How Banks and the Real Estate Industry Undermined Black Homeownership*, Chapel Hill: University of North Carolina Press.

Taylor, M. Z. (2016). *The Politics of Innovation: Why Some Countries Are Better than Others at Science and Technology*, Oxford, UK: Oxford University Press.

Taylor, R. S. (2017). *Exit Left: Markets and Mobility in Republican Thought*, Oxford, UK: Oxford University Press.

Taylor, S. (2019). EU Moves Closer to Legalizing Class Action. *Law.com*, www.law.com/2019/12/02/eu-takes-steps-toward-legalizing-class-actions-405-49431/ (accessed 27 December 2020).

Teaford, J. C. (1979). *City and Suburb: The Political Fragmentation of Metropolitan America, 1850–1970*, Baltimore, MD: Johns Hopkins University Press.

Teles, S. M. (2008). *The Rise of the Conservative Legal Movement*. Princeton, NJ: Princeton University Press.

Telford, T. (2019). Trump's Trade War Comes for Consumers: Tariffs Could Cost U.S. Families Up to $1,000 a Year, JPMorgan Forecasts. *Washington Post*, www.washingtonpost.com/business/2019/08/20/trumps-trade-war-comes-consumers-tariffs-will-cost-us-families-year-jp-morgan-forecasts/ (accessed 27 December 2020).

Tesler, M. (2012). The Spillover of Racialization into Health Care: How President Obama Polarized Public Opinion by Racial Attitudes and Race. *American Journal of Political Science*, 56(3), 690–704.

Tesler, M. (2016). *Post-Racial or Most-Racial? Race and Politics in the Obama Era*, Chicago: University of Chicago Press.

Tett, G. (2020). Why the US Federal Reserve Turned Again to BlackRock for Help. *Financial Times*, www.ft.com/content/f3ea07b0-6f5e-11ea-89df-41bea055720b (accessed 4 January 2020).

The Economist (2019). New Research Confirms Old Suspicions about Judicial Sentencing. *The Economist*, www.economist.com/united-states/2019/04/27/new-research-confirms-old-suspicions-about-judicial-sentencing (accessed 27 December 2020).

Thelen, K. (2014). *Varieties of Liberalization and the New Politics of Social Solidarity*, Cambridge, UK: Cambridge University Press.

Thelen, K. (2018). Regulating Uber: The Politics of the Platform Economy in Europe and the United States. *Perspectives on Politics*, 16(4), 938–53.

Thelen, K. (2019). The American Precariat: U.S. Capitalism in Comparative Perspective. *Perspectives on Politics*, 17(1), 5–27.

Thompson, D. (2016). *The Schematic State: Race, Transnationalism, and the Politics of the Census*, New York: Cambridge University Press.

Thompson, J. P. & Suarez, G. A. (2019). *Accounting for Racial Wealth Disparities in the United States*, Federal Reserve Bank of Boston.

Thurston, C. (2015). Policy Feedback in the Public-Private Welfare State: Advocacy Groups and Access to Government Homeownership Programs. *Studies in American Political Development*, 29(2), 250–67.

Thurston, C. (2018). *At the Boundaries of Home Ownership: Credit, Discrimination, and the American State*, New York: Cambridge University Press.

Tiebout, C. M. (1956). A Pure Theory of Local Expenditures. *The Journal of Political Economy*, 64(5), 416–24.

Tijdens, K. & van Kleveren, M. (2011). *Domestic Workers: Their Wages and Work in 12 Countries*, The Hague: Data Archiving and Networked Services.

Tollison, R. D. & Wagner, R. E. (1991). Romance, Realism, and Economic Reform. *Kyklos*, 44(1), 57–70.

Tomaskovic-Devey, D., Rainey, A., Avent-Holt, D. et al. (2020). Rising Between-Workplace Inequalities in High-Income Countries. *PNAS*, 117(17), 9277–83.

Tomkins, L., Smith, M., Bosman, J. & Pietsch, B. "Entering Uncharted Territory, the US Counts 500,000 Covid-Related Deaths," New York Times, February 22, 2021, www.nytimes.com/live/2021/02/22/world/covid-19-coronavirus%23us-covid-deaths-half-a-million

Torres-Rouff, D. (2013). *Before L.A.: Race, Space, and Municipal Power in Los Angeles, 1781–1894*, New Haven, CT: Yale University Press.

Traina, J. (2018). Is Aggregate Market Power Increasing? Production Trends using Financial Statements, https://ssrn.com/abstract=3120849.

Trounstine, J. (2013). One for You, Two for Me: Support for Public Goods Investment in Diverse Communities. University of California–Merced Working Paper.

Trounstine, J. (2018). *Segregation by Design: Local Politics and Inequality in American Cities*, New York: Cambridge University Press.

Trounstine, J. (2020). The Geography of Inequality: How Land Use Regulation Produces Segregation. *American Political Science Review*, 114(2), 443–55.

Tse, E. (2015). *China's Disruptors: How Alibaba, Xiaomi, Tencent, and Other Companies Are Changing the Rules of Business*, London: Penguin.

Tsebelis, G. (1999). Veto Players and Law Production in Parliamentary Democracies: An Empirical Analysis. *American Political Science Review*, 93 (3), 591–608.

Tushnet, M. (2011). Administrative Law in the 1930s: The Supreme Court's Accommodation of Progressive Legal Theory. *Duke Law Journal*, 60, 1565–637.

Tushnet, M. (2013). *In the Balance: Law and Politics on the Roberts Court*, New York: Norton.

Tylecote, A. (2013). *The Long Wave in the World Economy: The Current Crisis in Historical Perspective*, Philadelphia, PA: Routledge.

Uetricht, M. & Eidlin, B. (2019). U.S. Union Revitalization and the Missing "Militant Minority." *Labor Studies Journal*, 44(1), 36–59.

Urquiola, M. (2020). *Markets, Minds, and Money: Why America Leads the World in University Research*, Cambridge, MA: Harvard University Press.

US Chamber Litigation Center (2007). *Chamber Appoints Robin Conrad Executive Vice President of National Chamber Litigation Center.*

USDA (2020). *Data Files: U.S. and State-Level Farm Income and Wealth Statistics*, United States Department of Agriculture Economic Research Service.

Useem, M. (1996). *Investor Capitalism: How Money Managers Are Changing The Face of Corporate America*, New York: Basic Books.

Valero, A. & Van Reenen, J. (2019). The Economic Impact of Universities: Evidence from across the Globe. *Economics of Education Review*, 68, 53–67.

van der Pijl, K. (1984). *The Making of an Atlantic Ruling Class*, London: Verso.

van der Zwan, N. (2017). Financialisation and the Pension System: Lessons from the United States and the Netherlands. *Journal of Modern European History*, 15 (4), 554–84.

Van Horn, R. (2011). Chicago's Shifting Attitude toward Concentrations of Business Power (1934–1962). *Seattle University Law Review*, 34(4), 1527–44.

Van Horn, R. (2018). Corporations and the Rise of Chicago Law and Economics. *Economy and Society*, 47(3), 477–99.

Veblen, T. (1904). *The Theory of Business Enterprise*, New York: Scribner.

Veblen, T. (1923). *Absentee Ownership: Business Enterprise in Recent Times – The Case of America*, New York: B.W. Huebsch.

Visser, J. (2019). ICTWSS: Database on Institutional Characteristics of Trade Unions, Wage Setting, State Intervention and Social Pacts in 55 countries between 1960 and 2018, Princeton University Library.

Vogel, D. (1989). *Fluctuating Fortunes: The Political Power of Business in America*, New York: Basic Books.

Vogel, S. K. (2018). *Marketcraft: How Governments Make Markets Work*, New York: Oxford University Press.

Volscho, T. W. & Kelly, N. J. (2012). The Rise of the Super-rich: Power Resources, Taxes, Financial Markets, and the Dynamics of the Top 1 Percent, 1949–2008. *American Sociological Review*, 77(5), 679–99.

von Thünen, J. H. (1921). *Der Isolierte Staat in Beziehung Auf Landwirtschaft Und Nationalökonomie*. 2. Aufl. Neudruck nach der Ausg. letzter hand (2. bzw. 1. aufl., 1842 bzw. 1850) eingeleitet von ... Heinrich Waentig .... Jena: Fischer.

Vrousalis, N. (2013). Exploitation, Vulnerability, and Social Domination. *Philosophy & Public Affairs*, 41(2), 131–57.

Wagner, W. (2010). Administrative Law, Filter Failure, and Information Capture. *Duke Law Journal*, 59(7), 1321–432.

Walker, A. N. (2014). Labor's Enduring Divide: The Distinct Path of Public Sector Unions in the United States. *Studies in American Political Development*, 28(2), 175–200.

Wang, D. J. & Soule, S. A. (2012). Social Movement Organizational Collaboration: Networks of Learning and the Diffusion of Protest Tactics, 1960–1995. *American Journal of Sociology*, 117(6), 1674–722.

Warren, D. T. (2013). Racial Inequality in Employment in Postracial America. In Harris, F. C. & Lieberman, R. C., eds., *Beyond Discrimination: Racial Inequality in a Postracist Era*. New York: Russell Sage Foundation, pp. 135–54.

Webber, D. (2018). *The Rise of the Working-Class Shareholder: Labor's Last Best Weapon*, Cambridge, MA: Harvard University Press.

Weeden, K. A. (2019). *State of the Union 2019: Occupational Segregation*, Stanford: Stanford Center on Poverty and Inequality.

Weil, D. (2014). *The Fissured Workplace*, Cambridge, MA: Harvard University Press.

Weir, M. (2005). States, Race, and the Decline of New Deal Liberalism. *Studies in American Political Development*, 19, 157–72.

Weir, M. (2009). *"Beyond the Plant Gates": Postwar Labor and the Organizational Substructure of Liberalism*, Los Angeles: Institute for Research on Labor and Employment.

Weir, M., Wolman, H. & Swanstrom, T. (2005). The Calculus of Coalitions: Cities, Suburbs, and the Metropolitan Agenda. *Urban Affairs Review*, 40(6), 730–60.

Weiss, L. (2014). *America Inc.? Innovation and Enterprise in the National Security State*, Ithaca, NY: Cornell University Press.

Welch, S. & Bledsoe, T. (1998). *Urban Reform and Its Consequences: A Study in Representation*, Chicago: University of Chicago Press.

Western, B. & Beckett, K. (1999). How Unregulated Is the U.S. Labor Market? The Penal System as a Labor Market Institution. *American Journal of Sociology*, 104(4), 1030–60.

Western, B. & Pettit, B. (2010). *Incarceration & Social Inequality*, Cambridge, MA: Daedalus.

Wiedemann, A. (2021). *Indebted Societies: Credit and Welfare in Rich Democracies*, Cambridge, UK: Cambridge University Press.

Williamson, V. S. (2017). *Read My Lips: Why Americans Are Proud to Pay Taxes*, Princeton, NJ: Princeton University Press.

Wilson, W. J. (1987). *The Truly Disadvantaged: The Inner City, the Underclass, and Public Policy*, Chicago: University of Chicago Press.

Wilson, W. J. (1996). *When Work Disappears: The World of the New Urban Poor*, New York: Vintage.

Windham, L. (2017). *Knocking on Labor's Door: Union Organizing in the 1970s and the Roots of a New Economic Divide*, Chapel Hill: University of North Carolina Press.

Windolf, P. & Beyer, J. (1996). Co-Operative Capitalism: Corporate Networks in Germany and Britain. *British Journal of Sociology*, 47(2), 205–31.

Wines, M. & Harmon, A. (2020). What Happens When a Superspreader Event Keeps Spreading. *New York Times*, www.nytimes.com/2020/12/11/us/biogen-conference-covid-spread.html (accessed 10 January 2021).

Winkler, A. (2018). *We the Corporations*, New York: Norton.

Winters, J. A. (2017). Wealth Defense and The Complicity of Liberal Democracy. *Nomos*, 58, 158–225.

Witko, C., Morgan, J., Kelly, N. J. & Enns, P. K. (2021). *Hijacking the Agenda: Economic Power and Political Influence*, New York: Russell Sage Foundation.

Wolfe, J. & Schmitt, J. (2018). *A profile of union workers in state and local government*, Washington, DC: Economic Policy Institute.

Wolkoff, M. J. (1992). Is Economic Development Decision Making Rational? *Urban Affairs Quarterly*, 27(3), 340–55.

Wolman, H., McManmon, R., Bell, M. & Brunori, D. (2008). Washington, DC: Brookings Institution Press

Wooten, J. (2004). *The Employee Retirement Income Security Act of 1974: A Political History*, Vol. 11, Berkeley: University of California Press.

Wright, G. (1987). The Economic Revolution in the American South. *Journal of Economic Perspective*, 1(1), 161–78.

Wright, M. & Reeskens, T. (2013). of What Cloth Are the Ties That Bind? National Identity and Support for the Welfare State across 29 European Countries. *Journal of European Public Policy*, (10), 1443–63.

Y Analytics (2020). *Sectoral Analysis of COVID-19's Economic Impact and the Effects of Reopening*, Y Analytics.

Yagan, D. (2019). Employment Hysteresis from the Great Recession. *Journal of Political Economy*, 127(5), 2505–58.

Zaller, J. (1992). *The Nature and Origins of Mass Opinion*, Cambridge, UK: Cambridge University Press.

Zetzsche, Dirk A., William A. Birdthistle, Douglas W. Arner, and Ross P. Buckley. 2020. Digital Finance Platforms: Toward a New Regulatory Paradigm. *University of Pennsylvania Journal of Business Law* 23(1), 273–339.

Ziblatt, D. (2017). *Conservative Parties and the Birth of Democracy*, New York: Cambridge University Press.

Ziegler, J. N. & Woolley, J. T. (2016). After Dodd-Frank: Ideas and the Post-enactment Politics of Financial Reform in the United States. *Politics & Society*, 44, 249–80.

Ziman, J. M. (1994). *Prometheus Bound*, Cambridge, UK: Cambridge University Press.

Zipperer, B. & Gould, E. (2020). *Unemployment Filing Failures*, Economic Policy Institute.

CPSIA information can be obtained
at www.ICGtesting.com
Printed in the USA
BVHW031556011121
620464BV00001B/1